To Secure the Blessings of Liberty

Selected Writings of Gouverneur Morris

Gouverneur Morris

To Secure the Blessings of Liberty

Selected Writings of Gouverneur Morris

EDITED AND WITH AN
INTRODUCTION BY

J. Jackson Barlow

LIBERTY FUND | *Indianapolis*

Introduction, editorial additions, and index © 2012 by Liberty Fund, Inc.

Cover and frontispiece: Portrait of Gouverneur Morris, 1810, by James Sharples, the Elder, from the National Portrait Gallery, Smithsonian Institution/Art Resource, New York. Gift of Miss Ethel Turnbull in memory of her brothers, John Turnbull and Gouverneur Morris Wilkins Turnbull.

C 10 9 8 7 6 5 4 3 2 1
P 10 9 8 7 6 5 4 3 2 1

Library of Congress Cataloging-in-Publication Data
Morris, Gouverneur, 1752–1816.
To secure the blessings of liberty: selected writings of Gouverneur Morris
Edited and with an introduction by J. Jackson Barlow.
p. cm.
Includes bibliographical references and index.
ISBN 978-0-86597-834-8 (hc: alk. paper) —
ISBN 978-0-86597-835-5 (pbk.: alk. paper)
1. United States—History—Colonial period, ca. 1600-1775—Sources.
2. United States—History—Revolution, 1775-1783—Sources.
3. United States—History—1783-1815—Sources.
4. United States—Politics and government—1775-1783—Sources.
5. United States—Politics and government—1783-1865—Sources.
6. Morris, Gouverneur, 1752-1816. I. Barlow, J. Jackson. II. Title.
E302.6.M7A4 2012   973.2—dc23

LIBERTY FUND, INC.
8335 Allison Pointe Trail, Suite 300
Indianapolis, Indiana 46250-1684

Contents

Introduction

IT SEEMS TO BE customary to begin any discussion of the life and legacy of Gouverneur Morris by lamenting his neglect by later generations, as all four of his recent biographers have done. But however shameful posterity's treatment of Morris may be, it is about what he expected. This was not because he despaired of America's future or thought that the mob rule of the Jeffersonians would ruin the country, nor was it because he worried that Americans would be somehow deficient in reverence for their Founding Fathers. It was rather because he expected them to be forever looking forward. He was optimistic about the American future because he thought the spirit of the people would triumph over all difficulties, even the self-imposed ones: their own political follies and ignorance of the past.

Morris was born into a political family in 1752, the son of Lewis Morris, an Admiralty judge in New York, and his second wife Sarah Gouverneur. Three generations of the Morris family had held important positions in colonial government, while the Gouverneurs were merchants and landowners of Huguenot origin. It was as aristocratic a pedigree as anyone in the new world could claim.

Young Gouverneur was a good student, first at the Reverend Tetard's school in New Rochelle and then at the Philadelphia Academy. At the age of twelve, he enrolled in King's College (now Columbia University) and received his B.A. in 1768, at the age of sixteen, and a master of arts in 1771. Although a gifted student, Morris was hardly the ponderous academic. In his undergraduate years we have the first evidence of his irreverent streak coming to the surface, with his involvement in circulating a scandalous attack on one of the professors. For his oration at the commencement, he chose to speak on "Wit and Beauty."[1]

Since his older half brothers had inherited the bulk of his father's estate, Gouverneur needed a profession. Thus, upon completing his B.A. he began

---

1. The oration is in the Gouverneur Morris Papers, Rare Book and Manuscript Library, Columbia University, item 794.

reading law in the office of William Smith, then one of the leaders of the New York bar. There he formed lifelong friendships with two of Smith's other young protégés, Robert R. Livingston and John Jay. Smith's busy practice brought Gouverneur into the center of New York's governmental and commercial life. While still a seventeen-year-old clerk, Morris wrote and published his first commentary on a public matter, a letter opposing a new issue of bills of credit by the New York colony. The letter earned favorable notice and gained the young lawyer a reputation for expertise in public finance.

Although Morris took the colonists' side in the constitutional dispute with Britain, he was a late convert to the cause of independence, giving him a reputation as a closet Tory that dogged him later. But once he became an advocate of separation, Morris never looked back. By early 1776 he was taking a prominent part in revolutionary committees and had become a strong advocate of setting up an effective machinery of government. Elected from Westchester County as a delegate to the first and third provincial congresses, his knowledge of law and public finance, together with his skills as a writer and debater, earned him a place on many of the important committees.

Morris and his fellow law clerks, Livingston and Jay, were largely responsible for drafting the New York Constitution of 1777. Later that year, Morris was elected a New York delegate to the Continental Congress, and he assumed his post early in 1778. He arrived in York, Pennsylvania, Congress's temporary home, to find American fortunes and morale at perhaps their lowest ebb. The British had occupied Philadelphia, forcing Congress to scurry to safety across the Susquehanna; the army—what was left of it— was encamped in dangerously inadequate conditions at Valley Forge.

Morris took on his duties energetically. No sooner had he arrived in York than he was appointed to a committee charged with inspecting the conditions of the army. During his visit to Valley Forge, Morris consulted closely with George Washington on the needs of the army and the reforms needed to make it more effective. Morris came away with a report for Congress, and also with a lifelong admiration for the general. Returning to York, Morris immersed himself in Congress's work, and over the next two years he served on many committees, often as chair, and drafted scores of resolutions and reports.

Morris's visit to Valley Forge convinced him that the organization of government under the Continental Congress was seriously flawed. By mid-1778 he was putting substantial energy into proposals for reform. The root of the problem, in his view, was the absence of an effective executive power. Congress, however, was not ready to accept this conclusion, and his proposals were largely ignored. So were his suggestions for reforming the nation's finances, even though the depreciation of Congress's paper currency was beginning to create widespread economic distress.

In the spring of 1778 Congress, recognizing that American morale had declined sharply and apprehensive that the Carlisle Commission would bring proposals from England that would undermine it further, Morris began a public relations offensive. He was prominent in these efforts, not only penning Congress's public response to the Carlisle Commissioners' proposals, but publishing several letters of his own. In these essays Morris first used the pseudonym "An American," which he would use for the rest of his life.

Back home, Morris's enemies in the New York legislature accused him of neglecting the state's interests in Congress, and he was not reelected in 1779. Since New York City was still occupied by the British, he settled in Philadelphia, practicing law and engaging in business. While he was working to establish himself, he also found the time to solidify his reputation as a somewhat reckless young man-about-town. On May 15, 1780, as he leaped into his carriage, the horses started and Morris caught his foot in a wheel, badly breaking his ankle.[2] The doctors recommended amputation, and Morris submitted to the operation gamely. He seems to have adapted well to the wooden leg. Even late in his life he rode, hiked, and danced— "hobbled," he said—with few complaints and only minor mishaps.

One of Morris's business partners was the Philadelphia merchant Robert Morris (to whom he was not related). Robert Morris's financial genius was already legendary, and Gouverneur seems to have been an eager student. When "The Financier" became superintendent of finance for the Confederation Congress in 1781, he brought Gouverneur back into government as his assistant. Together they shaped American fiscal policy until the war ended. Many of Gouverneur's ideas for reforming public finance were adopted in Robert's "Report on the Public Credit" of 1782, which in turn influenced Alexander Hamilton's report of the same name a decade later. While he was in the finance office, Gouverneur also made the first proposal

2. There have been recurring suspicions that the carriage story is merely a cover and that Morris in fact broke the ankle jumping from a window to escape an inconveniently timed husband. At this distance in time, it is impossible to determine which is true.

to create a decimal currency in the United States. In 1787 Robert persuaded the Pennsylvania legislature to appoint Gouverneur a delegate to the Constitutional Convention.

In James Madison's words, Morris was "an able, an eloquent, and an active member" of the convention from the beginning of July on. Before that he had mostly been absent, called away to deal with his mother's estate and the harbingers of collapse for Robert Morris's business empire. Even so, he has the distinction of speaking more often than any other member. Although the final document differs substantially from the proposals Morris advocated in the convention, he supported it without reservation. What is more, he wrote the final draft, giving the Constitution its organization and its distinctive style. Madison said:

> The *finish* given to the style and arrangement of the Constitution fairly belongs to the pen of Mr. Morris; the task having, probably, been handed over to him by the chairman of the Committee [William Samuel Johnson], himself a highly respectable member, and with the ready concurrence of the others. A better choice could not have been made, as the performance of the task proved. It is true, that the state of the materials . . . was a good preparation for the symmetry and phraseology of the instrument, but there was sufficient room for the talents and taste stamped by the author on the face of it.[3]

After the convention, Morris turned down Hamilton's invitation to help write *The Federalist Papers* and returned to business and his law practice. But his long-awaited opportunity to go to Europe came in 1788, as Robert Morris's European business interests soured further. Robert needed someone he trusted completely to oversee his European operations, and who better than his bright, energetic assistant? Gouverneur arrived in Paris early in 1789, and for the next three years was a private citizen, based in Paris but frequently traveling to London or elsewhere on business.

Because the United States did not yet have a minister in London, George Washington asked Morris to make some confidential soundings of the British government. Although Morris did not achieve his or Washington's aims in London (his enemies claimed, with some justification, that he compromised the mission by confiding it to the French ambassador), this did

---

3. Both quotations are from James Madison to Jared Sparks, April 8, 1831, in *The Records of the Federal Convention of 1787*, ed. Max Farrand, rev. ed. (New Haven: Yale University Press, 1911–87), 4:498–99.

not prevent Washington from submitting his name in late 1791 as U.S. minister to France. The appointment was controversial. He was known to be pessimistic about the course of the French Revolution, and to some, including Secretary of State Thomas Jefferson, pessimism was identical with hostility. Worse, he had been known to have helped—and, it was rumored, advised—Louis XVI. Beyond that, his lack of reserve in expressing his opinions, his indiscretion in London, and his taste for fast living had given Morris a reputation as anything but diplomatic. Washington knew all this. Yet Morris was his candidate in spite of others' reservations:

> I will place the ideas of your political adversaries, in the light which their arguments have presented them to me, vizt. That the promptitude, with which your lively and brilliant imagination is displayed, allows too little time for deliberation and correction; and is the primary cause of those sallies, which too often offend, and of that ridicule of characters, which begets enmity not easy to be forgotten, but which might easily be avoided, if it was under the control of more caution and prudence. In a word, that it is indispensably necessary, that more circumspection should be observed by our representatives abroad, than they conceive you are inclined to adopt.[4]

Over the next two years, Morris tried to live up to Washington's admonitions, even as he faced as challenging an assignment as any American diplomat has ever had. The Revolution entered its most turbulent phase in 1792, and often it was difficult even to know who was in charge. Each succeeding faction tried to destroy the members of the one that preceded it; any diplomat who had good relations with one government was likely to be persona non grata to the next. As long as he remained minister, Morris did what he could to protect Americans and French citizens alike from the worst ravages of the Reign of Terror. For a time he was the only foreign diplomat remaining in Paris; the others had all decided it was too dangerous. Of course, as one who was known to have advised the king, and whose lack of "caution and prudence" before his appointment made his opinions public knowledge, Morris was an obvious target, and in mid-1794 he was replaced by James Monroe.

Relieved to be a private citizen again, Morris left France in the fall of

---

4. George Washington to Gouverneur Morris, January 28, 1792, in *The Writings of George Washington*, ed. John Fitzpatrick (Washington, D.C.: U.S. Government Printing Office, 1939), 31:469.

1794 and spent the next four years in Europe, traveling, visiting French exiles, and conducting his business. Wherever he went, he circulated among the social and political elite, and he freely passed on intelligence and gossip as he made the rounds. Politics intruded frequently. In Vienna he lobbied the Austrian government, all the way to the emperor, to release Lafayette from prison. In Britain, he found time to write a pamphlet opposing the radical reform proposals of the London Corresponding Society. But finally in 1798 he came back to the United States and settled in at Morrisania, the family home in what is now the Bronx.

Morris filled one more public office, elected to an unexpired term in the U.S. Senate in 1800 but not reelected in 1802. After that, he continued to speak and write on public affairs and to perform public service when called upon. In 1807 he served on the commission that laid out the street grid for New York City. Despite their political differences, the Federalist Morris and the Democratic-Republican DeWitt Clinton (nephew of his old colleague and mentor, Governor George Clinton) would work together on many public projects. Their most enduring achievement came from their membership on New York's Commission on Internal Navigation, better known as the Erie Canal Commission.

Morris was deeply skeptical of innovations in politics and was persuaded that human nature dictated a powerful role for self-interest in any governmental scheme. He was thus distrustful of the elite and the mob equally, although at different times he saw each as the more immediate threat. After the Jeffersonians' victory in 1800, he was convinced that the mob had come to power. But this mob was not ruling in its own interest; it was being manipulated by a Southern slaveholding elite bent on using government to protect its privileges. The three-fifths clause, which Morris had opposed at the Constitutional Convention, gave the slaveholding power an edge in the House of Representatives and the Electoral College, but to secure its rule this faction needed to curb the power of Northern commercial interests. It proceeded to pick a series of unnecessary fights with England, and from 1806 forward, the Jeffersonians' trade policies seriously damaged the economies of New York and other trading states.

The Jeffersonian ascendancy left Morris gloomy about American politics in his last years. Nevertheless, he remained optimistic about the American future. His own last years featured a domestic contentment that he had never known before. In 1809 the fifty-seven-year-old bachelor finally married. His wife, Anne Cary Randolph, was a Virginia Randolph and younger sister of John Randolph of Roanoke. In spite of or because of her own scandalous past, they were a good match. Their son, also named Gouverneur, was born in 1813. By this time Morris was an elder statesman, sought for Fourth of July speeches and civic committees, and he retained the optimism and the serene temperament that had always been part of his makeup. On his deathbed in November 1816 he expressed no regrets: "Sixty-four years ago, it pleased the Almighty to call me into existence—here on this spot, in this very room; and now shall I complain that he is pleased to call me hence?"[5]

5. *The Diary and Letters of Gouverneur Morris,* ed. Anne Cary Morris (New York: C. Scribner's Sons, 1888; repr., n.p.: Dodo Press, n.d.), 2:495.

Acknowledgments

THIS PROJECT HAS benefited from the help of many people. Foremost among them have been the staffs of the many libraries that I have consulted. Bernard Crystal, and later Jennifer Lee, of the Rare Book and Manuscript Library at Columbia University facilitated my access to the Morris manuscripts deposited there, as did Patrick Kerwin and Emily Howie of the Library of Congress. The staff of Houghton Library, Harvard University, guided me to the Jared Sparks papers, and Roy Goodman of the American Philosophical Society gave helpful encouragement and advice. The staffs of the Boston Athenaeum, Beinecke Library of Yale University, Pattee Library of Penn State University, and Firestone Library of Princeton University also provided helpful and timely assistance. This project would never have been completed, however, if it had not been for the staff of L. A. Beeghly Library at Juniata College. Lynn Jones was persistent in prying materials from reluctant lenders through interlibrary loan. Julie Woodling put me onto the Charles Brockden Brown Archive and Scholarly Edition and alerted me to the archivists' skepticism about Brown's authorship of "The British Treaty." Andy Dudash—Old Faithful—came through time and again with information and sources, and introduced me to the Juniata pamphlet collection. I am very grateful to all of them.

The James Madison Program at Princeton University provided me an incomparable place to work during my sabbatical in 2007–8. I am grateful to the program's founder and director, Robert P. George, and to Executive Director Brad Wilson, for being such generous hosts, and to the Garwood family for their support of my fellowship. Duanyi Wang is a magician with computer files; without her help this project would never have been done on time. Juniata College provided the sabbatical leave, and the Provost's Office—Jim Lakso and Joanne Krugh—has supported this project in many ways large and small since the very beginning.

A number of Juniata students have worked on this project over the seven years from its first conception until its completion: Nicole Watson, Rebecca Zajdel, Amber Laird, Emily Hauser, Sarah Weick, Mariel

Little, Jacob Gordon, Manal Daher-Mansour, Jordan Yeagley, and Madeline Rathey have all contributed in helpful ways.

Many colleagues have offered encouragement and support for the project as well, prominent among them Michael Zuckert, William B. Allen, John Kaminski, Art Kaufman, Melanie Miller, James Kirschke, and Barbara Oberg. My class of fellows at the James Madison Program—Robert L. Clinton, David Ericson, Paul Kerry, Daryl Charles, and Sebastien Viguier—provided help and good conversation. My Juniata colleagues Jim Tuten, David Sowell, David Hsiung, Emil Nagengast, and Dennis Plane have also been very supportive; Belle Tuten advised me on many of the Latin translations. Laura Goetz of Liberty Fund has been consistently helpful and patient throughout the project. I am also grateful for the very helpful and careful editing by the Liberty Fund staff.

Most of all I am grateful for the support of my family—my wife, Kathleen, and our children, Susan, David, and Julia—who have suffered through this project in many ways. My son David was the only one who actually had a hand in it, however, and I appreciate his careful editing of many of the headnotes and the introduction.

The errors are mine.

A Note on the Texts

IN THINKING ABOUT the selections for this collection, I considered what writings of Morris were already available, and what would be most useful. His diaries have been published twice, first in a heavily edited form by his granddaughter in 1888, and in a somewhat less censored form by his great-granddaughter in 1939. Many of his more interesting letters are quoted, sometimes (but not always) in their entirety, in Sparks's biography or in the 1888 edition of the *Diary and Letters*. His public writings—speeches, newspaper articles, and reports—were often difficult to find, however. In these writings, Morris develops his arguments more fully than is often the case in his letters, and so they help us attain a more complete view of his political and economic thinking. This selection includes published writings as well as several unpublished essays and speeches. They are presented chronologically for the sake of simplicity and to provide a minimum of editorial intrusion.

In the 1830s Morris's widow, Anne, turned over the full collection of his manuscripts to Jared Sparks, but since that time they have been scattered. Some have disappeared. Those published in Morris's lifetime were available in various newspapers or pamphlets but sometimes not identified or misidentified. Many are available in the American Antiquarian Society's useful collections of Early American Imprints and American Historical Newspapers. Even so, only someone with access to both the manuscript collection and printed sources could identify, with any confidence, writings that had been published anonymously or under pseudonyms.

Even with the restriction to writings for the public, I have had to be selective. Not included in this collection are his two graduation orations from 1768 and 1771, "Wit and Beauty" and "Love," respectively. Both of these are available in the manuscript collection at Columbia University, together with an 1805 "Oration on Music," also not included here. Among printed documents, I have omitted the "Observations on the American Revolution," written for Congress in 1778, because it is primarily composed of quotations from other documents. It, along with Morris's speech in the

Senate on the Ross Resolutions, his eulogy of George Clinton, and the joint Morris/Robert Fulton pamphlet "Advantages of the Proposed [Erie] Canal," are available in microform or electronically through the American Antiquarian Society's Early American Imprints series.

Several newspaper essays have also been omitted, most of them published in the *New-York Evening Post* under Morris's pseudonym "An American."[1]

All manuscript material is from the Rare Book and Manuscript Library, Columbia University. The material published in Morris's lifetime has long since become part of the public domain, but it is scattered widely, and I am grateful to the libraries and institutions that have allowed me access to their collections. I have included information on the holding institution with the documents. Where no holding institution is indicated, the material is from the microform collection in Pattee Library of Penn State University.

I have tried to track down all of Morris's quotations, as well as key references in the documents, although a few left me stumped. In several places I have silently corrected typographical errors in the published material. The transcriptions and all of the shorter translations are mine. I have used Sparks's translation of the French portions of the "Observations on the New Constitution of France," however, which seems to have relatively few errors and would scarcely be improved by adding new errors of my own.

---

1. Although these essays use Morris's pseudonyms, in some cases I am not entirely certain that they are his, although the probability is high. The essays in the *Evening Post* are: three essays on the naval operations in the Mediterranean, October 25 and November 21 and 28, 1804; three on American-British relations, February 13, 15, and 22, 1812; two on the Jeffersonians' public policies, January 7 and 8, 1813; one on the War of 1812, September 22, 1814. There are also several essays signed "An American" in the (Philadelphia) *U.S. Gazette:* three essays on the "Dispute with Spain," October 5, 8, and 11, 1804; and three very short pieces, October 20, 1804; August 23, 1806; and August 22, 1807.

Two essays signed "An Observer" in the *Evening Post,* February 11, 1815, and August 13, 1816, also may be Morris's.

Finally, Allan Nevins (in *The Evening Post: A Century of Journalism,* [New York: Boni and Liveright, 1922]) and Howard Swiggett have attributed three anonymous essays on the Peace of Amiens to Morris. They were published in the *Evening Post* November 30 and December 2 and 7, 1801.

Selected Bibliography

Primary Sources

Morris, Gouverneur. *The Diaries of Gouverneur Morris: European Travels, 1794–1798.* Edited by Melanie Randolph Miller. Charlottesville: University of Virginia Press, 2011.

————. *The Diary and Letters of Gouverneur Morris.* Edited by Anne Cary Morris. 2 vols. New York: C. Scribner's Sons, 1888; reprint, n.p.: Dodo Press, n.d.

————. *A Diary of the French Revolution.* Edited by Beatrix Cary Davenport. 2 vols. Boston: Houghton Mifflin, 1939; reprint Westport, Conn.: Greenwood Press, 1972.

————. Papers. Manuscript Division, Library of Congress.

————. Papers. Rare Book and Manuscript Library, Columbia University.

Sparks, Jared. *The Life of Gouverneur Morris, with Selections from his Correspondence and Miscellaneous Papers.* 3 vols. Boston: Gray & Bowen, 1832.

Biographies

Adams, William Howard. *Gouverneur Morris: An Independent Life.* New Haven: Yale University Press, 2003.

Brookhiser, Richard. *Gentleman Revolutionary: Gouverneur Morris — The Rake Who Wrote the Constitution.* New York: Free Press, 2003.

Crawford, Alan Pell. *Unwise Passions: A True Story of a Remarkable Woman — and the First Great Scandal of Eighteenth-Century America.* New York: Simon & Schuster, 2000.

Kirschke, James J. *Gouverneur Morris: Author, Statesman, and Man of the World.* New York: St. Martin's Press, 2005.

Kline, Mary-Jo. *Gouverneur Morris and the New Nation, 1775–1788.* Dissertations in American Economic History Series. New York: Arno Press, 1978.

Miller, Melanie Randolph. *Envoy to the Terror: Gouverneur Morris and the French Revolution.* Dulles, Va.: Potomac Books, 2005.

————. *An Incautious Man: The Life of Gouverneur Morris.* Wilmington, Del.: ISI Books, 2008.

Mintz, Max M. *Gouverneur Morris and the American Revolution.* Norman: University of Oklahoma Press, 1970.

Roosevelt, Theodore. *Gouverneur Morris.* New York: Houghton Mifflin, 1898.

Swigett, Howard. *The Extraordinary Mr. Morris.* Garden City, N.Y.: Doubleday, 1952.

Articles, Chapters, and Dissertations

Adams, Willi Paul. "'The Spirit of Commerce Requires That Property Be Sacred': Gouverneur Morris and the American Revolution." *Amerikastudien* 21 (1976): 327–31.

Fassiotto, Marie-José. "Gouverneur Morris, peintre oublié de la Révolution française." *French Review* 62 (1989): 997-1007.

Kaufman, Arthur P. "The Constitutional Views of Gouverneur Morris." PhD diss., Georgetown University, 1992.

Mintz, Max M. "Gouverneur Morris, George Washington's War Hawk." *Virginia Quarterly Review* 79 (2003): 651–61.

Nedelsky, Jennifer. "Aristocratic Capitalism: The Federalist Alternative of Gouverneur Morris." Chapter 3 in *Private Property and the Limits of American Constitutionalism.* Chicago: University of Chicago Press, 1990.

Robinson, Donald L. "Gouverneur Morris and the Design of the American Presidency." *Presidential Studies Quarterly* 17 (1987): 319–28.

Ziesche, Philipp. "Exporting American Revolutions: Gouverneur Morris, Thomas Jefferson, and the National Struggle for Universal Rights in Revolutionary France." *Journal of the Early Republic* 26 (2006): 419-47.

To Secure the Blessings of Liberty
Selected Writings of Gouverneur Morris

1 ❀ To the Inhabitants of the Colony of New-York (1769)

The first of Morris's works that has come down to us is his oration on "Wit and Beauty" for the King's College commencement exercises upon completing his B.A. in 1768. Three years later, receiving his M.A., he delivered an address on "Love."[1] His biographers have not failed to note that in these addresses, Morris sounded academic themes well suited to his unique blend of the intellectual and the romantic.

Meanwhile, on completing his B.A. he had embarked on a more prosaic career as a lawyer. But it, too, seemed to fit him well. His apprenticeship in the law office of William Smith immersed Morris in the commercial and political life of colonial New York; and there he formed lifelong friendships with his fellow law clerk John Jay and a young lawyer in Smith's office, Robert R. (Chancellor) Livingston.

In 1769, the New York Assembly decided to finance the colony's debts through an issue of bills of credit. This was a frequent expedient in the colonies, where a shortage of hard currency restricted commerce and left governments perpetually short of revenue.[2] But paper money brought its own problems, and even though New York's was better managed than some, the commercial and creditor interests stood opposed. In this letter Morris, just shy of his 18th birthday, displays the ability to understand and explain the intricacies of public finance that would mark him as a young man on the rise.

The *New York Chronicle*, December 25, 1769, p. 1. Courtesy American Antiquarian Society. Excerpts from the letter are printed in Sparks, *Life*, 1:14.

1. Both orations are in the Gouverneur Morris Papers, Rare Book and Manuscript Library, Columbia University.

2. E. James Ferguson, *The Power of the Purse: A History of American Public Finance, 1776–1790* (Chapel Hill: University of North Carolina Press, 1961), 3–24; Margaret G. Myers, *A Financial History of the United States* (New York: Columbia University Press, 1970), 6–12.

Gentlemen,

There is a report, that our assembly have been promised the royal assent to the issuing a paper currency. Many in this province declaim against it as pernicious, many extol it as productive of the most solid advantages.

Unpracticed in civil policy, wholly ignorant of exchequer business, and almost a stranger to this currency, I lay before you, the unprejudiced sentiments of a private citizen. Sentiments which reason impresses upon his mind, which a love of his country, and a tender solicitude for its welfare, compels him to make known. Bear with me then a little, whilst I endeavour to trace the effects attendant upon public bills of credit. To evolve which, let us suppose

The money in a country		£.1000
The yearly exported produce		1000
Foreign goods imported yearly	equal	600
And the sum struct be to cancelled	to	
in twenty years by an equable tax		2000
during that term		

Let us suppose farther that such a country is indebted to a foreign state 4000*l.* at *5 per cent. per annum.*

Hence it is apparent, that if no money is struck, the foreign debt will, in twenty years, with interest, amount to   £.8000.

The ballance of trade in their favour of 400*l. per ann.* will in twenty years amount to   £.8000

Remains due   £.0000

The interest at *5 per cent* upon that ballance, from the time it arises to the end of that term of twenty years is.................................... £.3800 which would remain and circulate among the inhabitants let this money be struck.

Now since it is an invariable true maxim, that the prices of all commodities rise and fall, according to the relative scarceness or plenty of money; since it is as true, that the value both of home produce exported, and foreign goods imported, must be estimated by that price for which they sell, at the place where they are sold; and since by stricking the above supposed sum, the quantity of current money would be encreased two thirds, therefore foreign goods imported will thereupon rise to the value of £1000, and this equals their exported produce, so that no ballance will (as before) remain to pay their debt. But further, as this debt would continually demand payments, because continually increased by the importation of foreign goods; as these payments will always (for convenience of those in trade, and for other reasons too tedious to mention) be made by bills of exchange; and as these for the reason above mentioned will rise two thirds; consequently every year's remittance will be lessened in that proportion, but to obviate objections which may be made, let us suppose barely one fifth which they most certainly would; then instead of £1000 they would remit £800 and the account would stand thus,

Original debt ....£.4000
Interest for twenty years, at *5 per cent*..........................£.4000
Yearly increase of debt by £200 through
default of remittances for twenty years   £.4000
Interest upon that increase from time of default to the
end of the term ....£.1900
£.13,900

These therefore would be the consequences of a paper currency under such circumstances. Instead of having a debt of £4000 paid, and their current gold and silver increased by £3800, they would find them in the same situation as before, and their debt increased to £13,900. Their loss therefore upon the whole would be £17,700, a sum so large that the above supposed ballance of trade in their favour, would not pay the interest at 2½ *per cent*. I shudder with horror when I would apply this calculation to the province.

It is said that the foreign manufactures imported into this colony exceed in value, the home produce which we export, if so, what will be our situation twenty years hence if this paper currency takes place? A question will naturally arise here; Why are the inhabitants of the colony so fond of this currency, if it be so pernicious in its consequences? It is because they do not know those consequences, because they will not know them; because they are in debt one to another, and because, from a selfishness they ought to be ashamed of, they would pay those debts at the expence of the province: The farmer owes money to the merchant, and will be able to pay it by taking up money at interest, two *per cent* cheaper than he can now; the merchant if the farmer is enabled to pay him two *per cent* cheaper, thinks he will pay him; and if he does, he can buy bills at an exorbitant price to pay part of his debts in Great-Britain, and gain credit to run himself farther in debt: as to his loss on sterling bills, that may at any time be compensated, by raising the price of his sterling manufactures. And thus that the debtors in the province, and who compose but a part of the province, may clear two *per cent* on the monies they owe; the province itself is to be ruined, and that some men may be relieved of a present burden, which extravagance has laid upon their shoulders; posterity is to be involved beyond a possibility of re-demption.

I am sorry; that to this argument, the advocates for a paper currency reply in such manner as is really shocking to humanity. For when the abyss into which they are endeavouring to plunge the province, opens itself be-fore them, and discovers all its horrors; when convinced that such a mea-sure will inevitably ruin their children, if on that account some members of the community less infatuated than the rest, prays them to desist, and be-seeches them if they will not help themselves, not to entail ruin upon pos-terity: The answer is, "Let posterity be ruined. What mighty obligations have our children conferred upon us, that to free them from a burden, we should bear it ourselves? Will they thank us for so doing?" Partial reason-ers! To relieve yourselves of a small weight, you strive to crush them with a great one; and for a little present ease to yourselves, you are accumulating a load of ills which in a little time will bear them down, under the weight of which, they must sink. Surely for such conduct, they will have reason to curse such parents. But even if you have no regard for them, at least take care of yourselves, it is putting the evil day off for a very little while. Many of us may live above twenty years, and feel the bad effects of our miscon-duct, and if we do not live so long these effects are not the produce of a moment, they will grow up with an equal increase during the whole of that term, and we shall certainly feel them. Even this therefore, the most barba-rous, inhuman shadow of reason which sophism could invent to deceive and betray us, vanishes away. *Grant, great God*, that the light of truth may dis-pel every other error. May you, my countrymen, be convinced of your true interests, and with your wonted magnanimity steadily pursue them. May you be endowed with patience to bear present small evils in preferance to future great ones; and may you have fortitude to resist the importunities and arguments, to refute the fallacies of those schemers, who with a spe-cious appearance would decoy us into ruin. For however they may gild the bitter pill they want us to swallow, and whatever shew of reason drawn from our necessities, they may produce to make us swallow it, still these truths stand uncontroverted, that a multiplied paper currency, is a never failing source of national debt, and that THERE ARE NO BOUNDS TO NATIONAL DEBT BUT NATIONAL DESTRUCTION.

CIVIS.

The precise occasion for these "Political Enquiries" is unknown, but at
the time of their composition these themes would have been very much
on Morris's mind. As events moved toward American independence,
people's thoughts naturally turned to questions of the purposes and ori-
gins of government. Morris had taken a leading part in the patriot cause
from his election to the first New York provincial congress in 1775, although for many months he remained hopeful that there could be a reconciliation. By 1776, that caution had evaporated. These short pieces are
clearly drafts, with many lines crossed out and as many more inserted.
Probably they were meant for Morris's private use, as he set about preparing himself for the problems of self-government that were ahead.[1]

Gouverneur Morris Papers, Rare Book and Manuscript Library, Columbia University, item 796. Included with the manuscript of these essays is an outline as well as a
page with the notation in Jared Sparks's hand: "On Government. Date uncertain."
Below this, in a fainter hand (perhaps that of Anne Cary Morris) is "and addresses to
the Legislators & People on various Subjects. Copies of articles. Minutes. Canal Reports." At the bottom of the page, upside down, is the notation "Political Enquiries"
in Morris's handwriting. These essays have been referred to by various titles, but
"Political Enquiries" seems to be the one favored by the author himself. I am grateful
to Art Kaufman for allowing me to consult his transcription of these essays, which is
appended to his dissertation (Arthur Paul Kaufman, "The Constitutional Views of
Gouverneur Morris" [Ph.D. diss., Georgetown University, 1992; Ann Arbor, Mich.:
University Microfilms, 2007]). This document, edited by Willi Paul Adams, was also
previously published in *Amerikastudien* 21 (1976): 327–31.

1. The "Enquiries" are analyzed at length in Kaufman, "Constitutional Views,"
39–79.

OF THE OBJECT OF GOVERNMENT

Is it the legitimate Object of Government to accumulate royal Magnificence, to maintain aristocratic Pre-Eminence, or extend national Dominion? The answer presents itself: Is it then the public Good? Let us reflect before we reply. Men may differ in their Ideas of public Good. Rulers therefore may be mistaken. In the sincere Desire to promote it just Men may be proscribed, unjust Wars declared, Property be invaded & violence patronized. Alas! How often has public Good been made the Pretext to Atrocity! How often has the Maxim Salus populi suprema Lex esto,[2] been written in Blood!

Suppose a man about to become the Citizen of another State and bargaining for the Terms. What would be his Motive? Surely the Encrease of his own felicity. Hence he would reject every Condition incompatible with that Object, and exact for its Security every Stipulation. Propose to him that when Government might think proper he should be immolated for the public Good: would he agree? To ascertain that Compact which in all Societies is implied, we must discover that which each Individual would express. The Object of Government then is to provide the Happiness of the People.

But are Governments ordained of God? I dare not answer. If they are, they must have been intended for the Happiness of Mankind. Hence an important Lesson to those who are charged with the Rule of Men.

OF HUMAN HAPPINESS

We need not enquire whether mortal Beings are capable of absolute felicity; but it is important to know by what means they may obtain the greatest Portion which is compatible with their State of Existence. Three questions arise: What constitutes the Happiness of a Man, of a State, of the World? The same Answer applies to each. Virtue. Obedience to the moral Law. Of avoidable Evil, there would be less in the World if the Conduct of States towards each other was regulated by Justice; there would be less in Society if each Individual did to others what he would wish from them; and less would fall to every Man's Lott if he were calm temperate and humane. To inculcate Obedience to the moral Law is therefore the best means of promoting human Happiness. Hence a maxim. No Government can law-

2. "The safety of the people should be the supreme law."

fully command what is wrong. Hence also an important Reflection. If Government dispenses with the Rules of Justice, it impairs the Object for which it was ordained.

But how shall Obedience to the moral Law be inculcated? By Education Manners Example & Laws. Hence it follows that Government should watch over the Education of Youth. That Honor and Authority should not be conferred on vicious Men. That those entrusted with office should not only be virtuous but appear so. And that the Laws should compel the Performance of Contracts, give Redress for Injuries, and punish Crimes.

OF PUBLIC VIRTUE

Which should be most encouraged by a wise Government public or private Virtue? Another question immediately arises. Can there be any Difference between them? In other Words, can the same thing be right and wrong? If an Action be in its own Nature wrong, we can never justify it from a Relation to the public Interest but by the Motive of the Actor. & who can know his Motive? From what Principle of the human Heart is public Virtue derived? Benevolence knows not any Distinctions of Nation or Country. Perhaps if the most brilliant Instances of roman Virtue were brought to the ordeal of Reason, they would fly off in the light Vapor of Vanity.

A Man expends his fortune in political Pursuits. Was he influenced by the Desire of personal Consideration, or by that of doing Good? If the latter, has Good been effected which would not have been otherwise produced? If it has, was he justifiable in sacrificing to it the Subsistence of his Family? These are important questions; but there remains one more. Would not as much Good have followed from an industrious attention to his own Affairs? A Nation of Politicians, neglecting their own Business for that of the State, would be the most weak miserable and contemptible Nation on Earth. But that Nation in which every Man does his own Duty, must enjoy the greatest possible Degree of public and private Felicity.

OF POLITICAL LIBERTY

Political Liberty is defined, the right of assenting to or dissenting from every Public Act by which a Man is to be bound. Hence, the perfect enjoyment of it presupposes a Society in which unanimous Consent is required to every public Act. It is less perfect where the Majority govern. Still less where the Power is in a representative Body. Still less where either the executive or judicial is not elected. Still less where only the legislative is elected. Still less where a Part of the Representatives can decide. Still less where such Part is not a Majority of the whole. Still less where the Decisions of such Majority may be delayed or overruled. Thus the Shades grow weaker and weaker, till no Trace remains. But is it not destroyed by the first Restriction?

In England, a Majority of Citizens does not elect the Majority of Representatives. A certain Part of those Representatives being met, the Majority of them can bind the Electors. The Decisions of these Representatives are confined to the legislative Department. And the Dissent of the Lords or of the King sets aside what the Commons had determined. The Englishman therefore does not, in any degree, possess the Right of dissenting from Acts by which he is affected, so far as those Acts relate to the Executive or judicial Department. And in respect to the legislature, his political Liberty consists in the Chance that certain Persons will not consent to Acts which he would not have approved. And is that a Right which, depending on a Complication of Chances, gives one thousand against him for one in his favor? Right is not only independent of, but excludes the Idea of Chance.

Of Society

Of these three things Life Liberty Property the first can be enjoyed as well without the aid of Society as with it. The second better. We must therefore seek in the third for the Cause of Society. Without Society Property in Goods is extremely precarious. There is not even the Idea of Property in Lands. Conventions to defend each others Goods naturally apply to the Defence of those Places where the Goods are deposited. The Object of such Conventions must be to preserve for each his own share. It follows therefore that Property is the principal Cause & Object of Society.

Of the Progress of Society

Property in goods is the first step in Progression from a State of Nature to that of Society. Till property in lands be admitted Society continues rude and barbarous. After the lands are divided a long space intervenes before perfect Civilization is effected. The Progress will be accelerated or retarded in Proportion as the administration of justice is more or less exact. Here then are three distinct kinds of Society: 1. rude and which must continue so. 2. progressive towards Civilization. 3. Civilized. For Instances of each take:

1. The Tartar Hords & American Savages. 2. The History of any European Kingdom before the sixteenth century and the present State of Poland. 3ly. the actual Circumstances of France and England.

If the forgoing reflections be just this Conclusion results that the State of Society is perfected in Proportion as the Rights of Property are secured.

Of Natural Liberty

Natural Liberty absolutely excludes the Idea of political Liberty since it implies in every Man the Right to do what he pleases. So long, therefore, as it exists Society cannot be established and when Society is established natural Liberty must cease. It must be restricted. But Liberty restricted is no longer the same. He who wishes to enjoy natural Rights must establish himself where natural Rights are admitted. He must live alone.

If he prefers Society the utmost Liberty he can enjoy is political. Is there a Society in which this political Liberty is perfect? Shall it be said that Poland is that Society? It must first be admitted that nine tenths of the Nation (the Serfs) are not Men. But dignify the Nobles with an exclusive title to the Rank of Humanity and then examine their Liberum Veto.[3] By this it is in the Power of a single Dissent to prevent a Resolution. Unanimity therefore being required no Man is bound but by his own Consent at least no noble man. If it be the Question to enact a law this is well. But suppose the Reverse. Or suppose the public Defence at Stake. In both Cases the Majority are bound by the minority or even by one. This then is not political Liberty.

Progress of Society. The Effect on Political Liberty

We find then that perfect political liberty is a Contradiction in Terms. The Limitation is essential to its existence. Like natural Liberty it is a Theory. $\underline{A}$ has the natural Right to do as he pleases. So has $\underline{B}$. $\underline{A}$ in consequence of his natural Right binds $\underline{B}$ to an oak. If it be said that Each is to

---

3. Literally, "I freely forbid it." Morris reflects the generally held Anglo-American understanding that the liberum veto meant that unanimous consent of the members was required to every act of the Polish Sejm (Parliament).

use his right so as not to injure that of another we come at once within the Pale of civil or social Right.

That Degree of political Liberty essential to one State of Society is incompatible with another. The Mohawks or Oneidas may assemble together & decide by the Majority of Votes. The six Nations must decide by a Majority of the Sachems.[4] In a numerous Society Representation must be substituted for a general assemblage. But arts produce a Change as essential as Population. In order that government decide properly it must understand the Subject. The objects of legislation are in a rude Society simple in a more advanced State complex. Of two things therefore one. Either Society must stop in its Progression for the Purpose of preserving political Liberty or the latter must be checked that the former may proceed.

Where political Liberty is in excess Property must always be insecure and where Property is not secure Society cannot advance. Suppose a state governed by Representatives equally & annually chosen of which the Majority to govern. Either the Laws would be so arbitrary & fluctuating as to destroy Property or Property would so influence the Legislature as to destroy Liberty. Between these two Extremes Anarchy.

Of Commerce

The most rapid Advances in the State of Society are produced by Commerce. Is it a Blessing or a Curse? Before this Question be decided let the present and former State of commercial Countries be compared. Commerce once begun is from its own Nature progressive. It may be impeded or destroyed not fixed. It requires not only the perfect Security of Property but perfect good faith. Hence its Effects are to encrease civil and diminish political Liberty. If the public be in Debt to an Individual political Liberty enables a Majority to cancel the Obligation but the spirit of Commerce exacts punctual Payment. In a Despotism everything must bend to the Prince. He can seize the Property of his Subject but the Spirit of Commerce requires that Property be secured. It requires also that every Citizen have the Right freely to use his Property.

Now as Society is in itself Progressive as Commerce gives a mighty Spring to that progressive force as the effects both joint and Separate are to diminish political Liberty. And as Commerce cannot be stationary the society without it may. It follows that political Liberty must be restrained

4. Representatives of the Six Nations to the common council.

or Commerce prohibited. If a Medium be sought it will occasion a Contest between the spirit of Commerce and that of the Government till Commerce is ruined or Liberty destroyed. Perhaps both. These Reflections are justified by the different Italian Republics.

CIVIL LIBERTY IN CONNECTION WITH POLITICAL

Political Liberty considered separately from civil Liberty can have no other Effect than to gratify Pride. That society governs itself is a pleasing reflection to Members at their Ease but will it console him whose Property is confiscated by an unjust Law? A Majority influenced by the Heat of party spirit banishes a virtuous Man and takes his Effects. Is Poverty or is Exile less bitter decreed by a thousand than inflicted by one? Examine that Majority. In the Madness of Victory are they free from apprehension? What happens this day to the Victim of their Rage may it not happen tomorrow to his Persecutors?

If we consider political in Connection with civil Liberty we place the former as the Guard and Security to the latter. But if the latter is given up for the former we sacrifice the End to the Means. We have seen that the Progress of Society tends to Encrease civil and diminish political Liberty. We shall find on Reflection that civil Liberty itself restricts political. Every Right of the Subject with Respect to the Government must derogate from its Authority or be thereby destroyed. The Authority of Magistrates is taken from that mass of Power which in rude Societies and unballanced Democracies is wielded by the Majority. Every Separation of the Executive and judicial Authority from the Legislative is a Diminution of political and Encrease of civil Liberty. Every Check and Ballance of that Legislature has a like Effect and yet by these Means alone can political Liberty itself be secured. Its Excess becomes its Destruction.

In looking back we shall be struck with the following Progression Happiness the Object of Government. Virtue the Source of Happiness. Civil Liberty the Guardian of Virtue political liberty the Defence of civil. Restrictions on political Liberty the only Means of preserving it.

3 Oration on the Necessity for Declaring Independence from Britain (1776)

Morris did not serve in the second New York Provincial Congress, which was elected in November 1775. The following spring, however, he was elected to the third. By this time he had abandoned any hope for reconciliation with Britain. If independence was coming, it was urgent for the colonies to assume full responsibility for governing themselves; as Morris argues in this speech, independence and self-government are effectively synonymous. The implication is clear. The Provincial Congress must stop thinking of itself merely as a protest body, and begin to think like a government.

It is not clear when this speech was made. Max M. Mintz argues that it was given May 24, 1776, when Morris is reported to have made "a long argument showing the necessity of the measure."[1] The first half of the manuscript is missing.

. . . Merchant, rather than the Husbandman, is to be delivered unto Satan to be buffeted. Furthermore I am convinced that heavy Duties and Impositions on Trade to a certain amount will more effectually injure the Husbandman himself, than any direct Tax you can possibly impose. Shall we secure ourselves by a covenant that the Money shall all be lodged in Provincial Treasuries, and granted away at the Discretion of our Assemblies? This indeed looks very well. But what shall we be the better, for having a

Gouverneur Morris Papers, Rare Book and Manuscript Library, Columbia University, item 797. A note in Sparks's writing on the last page indicates "probably early in 1776." Large portions of the speech are reproduced in Sparks, *Life*, 1:95–107. This document, edited by Willi Paul Adams, was also previously published in *Amerikastudien* 21 (1976): 320–27.

1. Mintz, *American Revolution*, 58. Kaufman discusses the difficulty of dating the speech, "Constitutional Views," 129–31.

Pile of Money in the Treasurer's Box? Sure we shall be as much distressed, by putting it there, as any where else. Neither can I perswade myself that it would even remain there long, for the Governors and their Assemblies might soon come to a good Understanding with each other, & then nothing can be easier than to share the spoils. Ireland will teach us the whole mystery of Government on this Head. Let me go a little farther. Is the bright Goddess of Liberty "whose Altar's Earth Sea Skies,"[2] is she only to be worshipped in the narrow Temple of Taxation? Advert (I beseech) you to first Principles. *Power can not safely be entrusted to Men, who are not accountable to those over whom it is exercised.* On this Rock I build. Now Tell me, the Tribunal before which we shall cite the Members of the British Legislature. None that I know of except the august seat of Heaven, & few Men will be found ready to go there in order to prosecute the Appeal. True it is we may make the last Resort to arms, but more of that presently.

Come, sir, don't let us be discouraged; undoubtedly you will find some State Carpenter ready to frame this disjointed Government & warrant his work. And if there should be some Flaws, considering the Protection you receive from Britain, you ought to put up with them. I know he will tell you so. Protection, Sir, is a very good Thing, yet a man may pay too Dear for Diamonds. There is a common story of a certain Juggler, who would undertake to cut off a Man's Head, and clap it on again so neatly as to cure him without a Scar. Much such a sort of juggling Business, is this Protection we are to receive. Great Britain will not fail to bring us into a War with some of her Neighbours, and then protect us as a Lawyer defends a Suit, the client paying for it. This is quite in Form, but a wise Man would rather I think get rid of the suit and the Lawyer together. Again, how are we to be protected? If a Descent is made upon our Coasts, and the British Navy and Army are three thousand miles off, we cannot receive very great Benefit from them on that Occasion. If, to obviate this Inconvenience, we have an Army and Navy constantly among us, who can say that we shall not need a little Protection against them? We may indeed put a Clause in the

2. Alexander Pope, "The Universal Prayer," line 50. Morris alters the quotation slightly. The stanza reads:

> To Thee, whose Temple is all Space,
> Whose Altar, Earth, Sea, Skies;
> One Chorus let all Being Raise!
> All Nature's Incence Rise!

Agreement, that Britain shall not use them to enslave us; and then all will be safe, for we cannot suppose they will break their promise.

Thus I find, Sir, that with the Help of a few Rheams of Paper, and a few Gallons of Ink, we may draw out a large Treaty, filled with cautious Items, and wise et ceteras. Then the whole affair is settled. America is quite independent of Great Britain, except that they have the same King. For altho the British Parliament is allowed to possess, in the Name of Supremacy, an immense Train of Legislative Powers; there are contained in the Agreement, strict Inhibitions from using any one of them. Thus it is settled I say for seven years. Not a Day farther. The very next Parliament, not being bound by the Acts of the former, the whole is in Law as to them a Nullity. Our Acknowledgement of Supremacy binds us as Subjects, and our most exquisite Restrictions being contrary to the very Nature of civil Society, are meerly void. Remember too, that no Faith is to be kept with Rebels.

In this case, or in any other case, if we fancy ourselves hardly dealt with, I maintain there is no Redress but by Arms. For it never yet was known, that when Men assume Power, they will part with it again unless by Compulsion. Now the Bond of continental Union once broken, a vast Load of Debt accumulated, many Lives lost, and nothing got; I wonder whether the People of this Country, would again chuse to put themselves into the Hands of a Congress, even if a *general* attack was made upon their Liberties. But undoubtedly the whole Continent would not run to arms immediately upon an Attempt against one of the Colonies, and thus one after another, we should infallibly be subjugated to that Power, which we know would destroy even the Shadow of Liberty among us.

These, and ten thousand other reasons Sir, all serve to convince me; that to make a solid & lasting Peace, with Liberty and Security, is utterly impracticable. My Argument therefore stands thus. As a connection with great Britain cannot again exist, without enslaving America, an Independence is absolutely necessary. I cannot ballance between the two. We run a Hazard in one path I confess, but then are infallibly ruined if we pursue the other.

Let us however act fairly. Let us candidly examine this Independence. Let us look back how much of the Journey is past and forward how much is yet to come. Many objects are hideous, only from the [illegible] at which they are viewed. Strict Scrutiny may sometimes give us the Demonstration of sense, that things frightful at the first Appearance, are nevertheless of great utility. The Perfection of Man is to be guided by Reason. And above all Men those who are intrusted with public Concerns, should as much as Possible divest themselves of every Prejudice and Passion. Without Passion or Prejudice therefore, let us coolly go round this Subject & examine it on every Side.

Here it will be necessary to determine in what it consists, which will naturally open our Attention to what further steps are necessary to the Completion of it. Then perhaps it may be proper to weigh the Consequences, as well for the future, as for the present Generation. Let us then imagine ourselves far removed from the present Age. Ignorant entirely of present Transactions, further than History delivereth them: And reasoning about Events, with philosophic Indifference. Or rather let us suppose ourselves elevated upon some vast Mountain, from whence we can see below us all the Glories of human Life, with all its Follies, and all its Cares. Some Mountain round whose Base roar Tempests and Storms, whilst the serenity of Wisdom blazes on the Summit. Call to your Aid the Magnanimity of true Statesmen, and you have gained this splendid Heighth.

Sir, I believe no such thing as perfect Independence, ever yet existed in any State. The Wants and Weaknesses of Cities, Kingdoms and Empires; like the Wants and Weaknesses of those Miserables who inhabit them, form mutual Connections, Relations and Dependencies [one line is obscured here] necessarily adapted to various Purposes. Independence then, applied to Communities, can mean nothing more than the Powers which separate Societies exercise among themselves. These relate to the Society compared either with its component Parts, or with other Societies. As to the first, it comprehends Legislation & distributive Justice. The second consists in Coining Money, raising Armies, regulating Commerce, Peace, War & Treaties. These, Sir, I take to be the grand Lineaments & Characteristics, which mark out Indepence. Go farther, and you will degenerate into quibbling Logicians. To them and Dictionary Makers let us leave all nicer Distinctions; and see how far America may, or may not, be termed an Independent State. First, as to Legislation; I do candidly confess, that I meet with no Laws which you have passed in the usual Stile of *be it enacted*; but your cogent Recommendations with the Penalties of Disobedience affixed, are far from unfrequent. Secondly, as to distributive Justice. At the first view indeed it seems not to have been your Object; because Writs run, and Judges sit as they were wont to do, and the King of England is (by Fiction of law) present at every Court on the Continent. Sir when this new Government was first organized, we found a very good Code of civil Laws in Being. The Wisdom of Ages hath been collected for their Perfection, and we must have been Loosers by a Change. But if you thought proper to shut up the Shops of Justice, not wantonly, but from evident Necessity, Will any Man pretend to deny, that the Law would from that single Breath become a dead letter? And if any other Government, should take a Step of this Kind without evident necessity, the Subjects of that Government would revolt at least as readily, as the Inhabitants of this Country. We do not find, there was any immediate and personal Act of the Prince necessary, for the exercise of the Law, unless perhaps the affixing a Bit of Wax now and then, to a Bit of Paper or Parchment, and I believe we may find Men in this Country, quite as well skilled in that Manufacture, as any English Workmen. If not, I am confident we may import as many Workmen as we please. But Sir, what says the Law to the present Resistance? We have Lawyers enough among us, to tell what the Law Books say. Many hard names are there stored up for such occasions, of which I believe the very gentlest and smoothest Kind, are riotously and routously.[3] Yet from the general Silence of Judges and Juries, I cannot but think that the People consider this House as the Sovereign Power, a Resistance of whose Commands, is that Resistance which all these hard words are levelled at. Let us consider the Matter a little more deeply. Pray, if we had found the People of this Country without any Law whatsoever, or (what amounts to the same Thing) if his Majesty should send a Frigate, to bring over his Governors Councillors Judges Great Seal, &ca, &ca, in such case should we hesitate a Moment, to provide proper Laws and proper Tribunals. Did we in such instances as the Law was deficient in, did we there hesitate? Or rather have we not a strict Tribunal for Congress Law, in every Committee? To affirm then, that the Distribution of Justice is not in the Hands of this House, argues great Want of Attention, & Ignorance of our public Proceedings. To make short of this Part of my Argument, I take the Masachusett's Bay as an Instance in Point, which renders further reasoning unnecessary.[4]

We find therefore, the Characteristical Marks & Insignia of Indepen-

3. *Routously:* in a disorderly manner, in the manner of a mob. In the common law, a rout was a movement toward accomplishing an unlawful purpose; it was intermediate between an unlawful assembly (three or more persons gathered for an unlawful purpose) and a riot (accomplishing an unlawful purpose).

4. The Massachusetts Government Act of 1774 had replaced the government under the 1691 colonial charter with one more directly under British control. Citizens of Massachusetts resisted the law by creating their own courts and other governmental institutions, as outlined, for example, in the Suffolk Resolves.

dence in this Society, considered in itself. Compared with other societies, the Enumeration is Conviction. Coining Money, raising Armies, regulating Commerce, Peace, War. All these Things you are not only adepts in, but Masters of. Treaties alone remain, and even this you have dabbled at. Georgia you put under the Ban of the Empire, & received her upon Repentance as a Member of the Flock.[5] Canada you are now treating with. France and Spain you ought to treat with, and the Rest is but a Name. I believe Sir the Romans were as much governed, or rather oppressed, by their Emperors; as ever any People were, by their Kings. But Emperor was more agreable to their Ears, than King. Some, nay many Persons in America, dislike the Word Independence. For my own Part, I see no reason why Congress is not full as good a word, as States General or Parliament, and it is a mighty easy matter to please People, when a simple Sound will effect it. But more of this presently.

We will now Sir with your Favor, turn to the Consideration of what advantages and what Disadvantages may result from taking this step, or rather from sliding into this unavoidable Situation. To determine with Precision upon this Head, we must seek for the Objects of Government. We need not wander far, but use your own emphatical Terms, Peace, Liberty, and Security.

Whether a State shall enjoy Peace or suffer War, depends upon two great leading Circumstances; the Probability of Attack, and the Means of Defence. As to the Probability of Attack, we must consider by whom it is to be made, in what Manner, and for what purpose. It is quite a hackneyed Topick, boldly insisted on, tho very lightly assumed, that the Instant an American Independence is declared, we shall have all the Powers of Europe on our Backs, as by a general Consent, to share out this Country amongst them.

Experience Sir has taught these Powers and will teach them more clearly

5. Georgia did not send delegates to the First Continental Congress, or initially to the second, which met May 10, 1775. On May 17, 1775, the Second Continental Congress voted unanimously to cut off trade with Georgia, the Canadian provinces, and East and West Florida. See *Journals of the Continental Congress, 1774–1789*, ed. Worthington C. Ford et al. (Washington, D.C.: U.S. Government Printing Office, 1904–37), 2:54. When Georgia's provincial congress accepted the provisions of the Continental Association on July 6, 1775, the Congress seated Georgia's delegation (*JCC*, July 20, 1775, 2:192–93).

every day, that an American War is tedious, expensive, uncertain & ruinous. Three thousand Miles of a boisterous Ocean are to be passed over, and the vengeful Tempests which whirl along our Coasts, are daily to be encountered, in such expeditions. At least three months expence must be incurred, before one Gun can be fired against an American Village; and three months more, before each shattered armament can find an asylum for Repose. A hardy brave People, or else a destructive climate, must be subdued, while the Troops exhausted by Fatigue, find at every Step that Desertion and Happiness are synonimous terms. Grant, that with a wasteful Dissipation of Blood and Treasure, some little Portion of this vast Country is conquered. Fortresses remain to be built, magazines provided, and Garrisons established, for the Defence of a broad Dessolation, not worth one Shilling to the Possessors. Or should it better please a maritime Power, (and we have none but those to fear) should it please them to carry on a naval War, pray where is the American Property, which will pay the Expenses of an European Armament?

Nations do not make War without some view. Should they be able to conquer America, it would cost them more to maintain such Conquests, than the Fee Simple of the Country is worth. They could gain Nothing but our Commerce, and that they may have without striking a Blow. Thus Sir it appears to my poor Discernment, an incontrovertible Truth, that no Nation whatever would incline to attack us. For after all, this Consideration must arise amongst them; that the surest Consequence of the most splendid victories, would be a bloody War with each other, about sharing the spoils.

But I cannot think it will ever come to this. For when I turn my eye to the means of Defence, I find them amply sufficient. We have all heard, that in the last War America was conquered in Germany. I hold the converse of this Proposition to be true, namely, that in, and by America, his Majesty's German Dominions were secured. The last, and every other War for more than a Century, has been determined more by the Wealth, than the Arms of contending Nations, and the great source of that Wealth, is in the Western World. It rises here, flourishes in Europe, and is buried in India. The Situation of this Continent formerly did, and still does enable us in a very great Degree, to check that Flood of Property, which thus glides along to the Eastward. The Rapacity of Adventurers will greedily seize the opportunity of becoming Rich, by preying upon the Merchandize of other People. And large Convoys to Merchant Ships, are equally expensive and inefficacious. I appeal to Experience. As to the Project of shutting up all the

Creeks and Harbours along this extensive Coast, this is calculated only for the Meridian of St. James,[6] and becomes daily an object of Ridicule, even to our Women and Children. I know the objection, that when we ourselves are a trading People, we may suffer equal Loss with our Foes. Altho I cannot admit this in its fullest Latitude, yet it hath some Weight. But it leads to a very obvious Consequence, that is to say, an American Navy. Gentlemen may either start or smile at this idea, as it chances to raise their Contempt or Admiration. Let us consider it. Would a Fleet consisting of ten Sixty, ten fifty, & ten forty Gun Ships, with ten Sloops of twenty and thirty of ten Guns, Would such a Fleet Sir make a respectable Figure in the Defence of our Coasts? Some Persons will say, Aye Aye, but where are you to get them. Why Sir, the materials are amongst us, and five Million Dollars will fit them all out for a six Months voyage. I shall be told, that is very pretty Scheming, and asked perhaps how the Expence of this Fleet is to be maintained. I would not lay heavy Imposts upon Trade. I am sure five p. Cent upon all Commodities imported into this Continent, would be a very trivial Tax, and there certainly are not less than twenty Millions of Dollars in value, annually imported. This would yield one Million, and that is sufficient to keep your Navy afloat. And with such a Navy, it would be still more inconvenient to attack this Country. See what Effects have followed from fitting out a few little insignificant Vessels, under the name of Privateers. The last mode of Defence, consists in having a respectable Army. I do not mean an armed Banditti, to become our Masters. The *Officers* of your standing army, should be regularly paid, & the Profession by that means cultivated. But the Soldiers should never be inlisted, except when actual service required it; & lest we should then be at a Loss for good ones, it should be provided by wholesome Militia Laws, that every Man in the Country should know the Duties of a Soldier.

Thus Sir, by means of that great Gulph which rolls its Waves between Europe and America, by the Situation of these Colonies always adapted to hinder or intercept all Communication between the two, by the Productions of our Soil which the Almighty has filled with every necessary to make us a great maritime People, by the Extent of our Coasts and those immense Rivers which serve at once to open a Communication with our interior Country and teach us the Art of Navigation, by those vast Fisheries which, affording an inexhaustible Mine of Wealth and Cradle of Industry, breed hardy Mariners inured to Danger and Fatigue, finally by the un-

6. That is, the British Court.

conquerable Spirit of Freemen deeply interested in the Preservation of a Government which secures to them the Blessings of Liberty & exalts the Dignity of Mankind. By all these I expect a full & lasting Defence against any and every Part of the Earth. While the great Advantages to be derived from a friendly Intercourse with this Country almost render the Means of Defence unnecessary from the great Improbability of being attacked. So far Peace seems to smile upon our future Independence. But that this fair Goddess will equally crown our union with Great Britain, my fondest Hopes cannot lead me even to suppose. Every War in which she is engaged, must necessarily involve us in its Detestable Consequences, whilst weak & unarmed we have no Shield of Defence, unless such as she may please (for her own Sake) to afford, or else the Pity of her Enemies & the Insignificance of Slaves, beneath the Attention of a generous Foe.

Let us next turn our attention to a Question of infinitely greater Importance, namely the Liberty of this Country. I speak here only of political Liberty, & this may I believe be secured by the simplest Contrivance imaginable. If America is divided into small Districts, and the Elections of Members into Congress annual, and every Member incapacitated from serving more than one Year out of three, I cannot conceive the least Temptation to an abuse of Power, in the Legislative and executive Parts of the Government. And as long as those Fountains are pure, the streams of Justice will flow clear and wholesome. But shall we pretend to say that we have political Liberty, while subject to the Legislative Control of Great Britain? Even freed from that, will not the silent efforts of Influence, undermine any Constitution we can possibly devise? And of what Importance is it to the Subject, whether a Love of Power, or Love of Money, whether avarice or ambition are the Causes of his unhappiness. If I were to chuse a master, it should be a single Tyrant, because I had infinitely rather be torn by a Lion, than eaten by Vermin.

The last Consideration, Sir, is Security, and so long as the System of Laws by which we are now governed shall prevail, It is amply provided for in every separate Colony. There may indeed arise an Objection, because some Gentlemen suppose, that the different Colonies will carry on a sort of Land Piracy with each other. But how this can possibly happen, when the Idea of separate Colonies no longer exists, I cannot for my Soul comprehend. That something very like this (I do not mean to offend) has already been done I shall not deny; but the Reason is as evident as the Fact. We never yet had a Government in this Country, of sufficient Energy to restrain the lawless and indigent. Whenever a Form of Government is established which deserves the Name, these Insurrections must cease. But who is the Man so hardy as to affirm, that they will not grow with our Growth, while on every Occasion we must resort to an English Judicature, to terminate Differences, which the Maxims of Policy will teach them to leave undetermined. By Degrees we are getting beyond the utmost Pale of English Government. Settlements are forming to the Westward of us, whose Inhabitants acknowledge no Authority but their own, and of Consequence no Umpire but the Sword. The King of England will make no new Grants, the Settlers will ask none. We occupy but a small Strip of Land along the Sea Coast, & in less than fifty years those Western Settlements, will endeavour to carve out for themselves a Passage to the Ocean. Are we then to build a huge Wall against them? Are we to solicit Assistance from Britain? Vain thought! Britain already sinking under a vast Load of Debt, and hastening to Ruin by the Loss of Freedom (without which even the Interest of that Debt cannot be paid) She will have Enemies enough of her own. If we seize the present opportunity, we shall have no such Causes of Apprehension. Those Settlements, sensible of their present Weakness & our Power, will all be made under the authority of that Body, which is the Legislature of the Continent. They will constantly look up to it for Laws and Protection.

Sir, I am sensible that I weary you. I could enumerate many Advantages which would result from an Indepency, and which form no Part of what I have already mentioned. I could show, that a free and unrestrained Commerce would fill the Coffers of this Country with Wealth. That all Nations would resort here as an Asylum from oppression. No longer would we fly away across the pathless Deep to the Metropolis of Britain, & waste our Treasure in the Pursuit of Vice, then return to spread the infectious Poison among our Countrymen. Population would increase with Freedom; and our Children's Children should behold the Cultivation of that great Garden, which their ancestors had enclosed. Here could I expatiate with fond Delight, but I hasten to a Conclusion.

Nothing further remains therefore, than just to examine the Inconveniencies, to which an independent Form of Government would subject us. And what are they? A War with Great Britain. And in that very War are we already engaged. Perhaps some Gentlemen may be apprehensive of loosing a little of Consequence and Importance, by living in a Country where all are on an equal Footing. Virtue in such a Country will always be esteemed, and that alone should be respected in any Country. If these Gentlemen would reflect, that free republican States are always most thickly inhabited, perhaps they may be of Opinion with me; that the Indulgence of a few in

Luxurious Ease, to the Prejudice of their fellow Creatures, is at best not laudable; but when it tends to thin the Ranks of Mankind, and to encourage a general Profligacy of Manners, it is then criminal in the highest Degree.

I do not scruple to affirm, that all Dangers to be apprehended from an Independency, may well be obviated by this Assembly. If we so regulate our own Power, as to give perfect Freedom to our constituents, there is but little Danger of intestine Broils. For Mankind, however chargeable with Levity on other occasions, are by no Means prone to change their Form of Government, so long as it is meerly tolerable. And this leads me Sir to consider the last objection to Independence, which I shall take on me to mention. It is, the Reluctance which many Americans feel for this Measure.

This Reluctance Sir, is laudable for the greater Part. It is a patriotic Emotion. In some Cases, Religion has a Share in the Sentiment. It is said what Check have we upon the Members of Congress? If they abuse their Power and establish an Oligarchy, where are the means of Redress? How shall we know, that they will return willingly into the Ranks of Citizens, after so great Elevation? Is there not great Reason to fear, that the American Army may chuse a different Kind of Government, from the Rest of the People? And, say they, altho Providence has kindly interposed so far for our Preservation, how dare we expect his future assistance, when cancelling the Oaths of our Allegiance, we stain the Cause with Perjury?

To most of these Questions, we may make a satisfactory answer, without seeming to know that they were ever asked. As to Danger arising from the Love of Power among ourselves, I cannot believe there is any. Nor do I think it quite proper, for us all to abandon the Senate House, and leave the Business to entire new Men, while the Country continues in its present dangerous Situation. But the Instant we are determined to cut off the small Connection which remains with Great Britain, we ought by our Conduct, to convince our Countrymen, that a Fondness for Power does not possess the smallest Corner of our Hearts. And we should from this moment take Care, that the Gift of all Commissions be reserved to this House. This will cure the Inquietudes of the patriotic Breast. And for the Religionist, let the Change appear as it hath hitherto done, the Work of our Enemies and not of ourselves, we then stand acquitted; and Superstition will see, or think She sees, the Hand of God manifestly laboring to promote our Ends, and this fond Idea is sufficient to remove the Imputation of Guilt.

I do not mean however, to hire a Number of Men, to go and bawl Independence along the Continent. I would send ambassadors to the European Courts, and enter into Treaties with them. Every Thing like Independence, should form secret articles; the Rest I would give to the World as soon as it was completed. This measure will both discourage, and preclude, impertinent Enquiry. And when the People of this Country enjoy the solid Advantages which arise from our Measures, they will thank us for the Deception.

In God's Name! Why should we ballance? Have you the least Hope in Treaty? Will you even think of it, before certain Acts of Parliament are repealed? Have you heard of any such Repeal? Will you trust these Commissioners? Is there any Act of Parliament passed to ratify what they shall do? No, No, No. They come from the King. We have no Business with the King. We did not quarrel with him. He has officiously made himself a Party in the Dispute against us. And now he pretends to be the Umpire. Trust Crocodiles, trust the hungry Wolf in your Flock, or a Rattle Snake in your Bosom, you may yet be something Wise. But trust the King, his Ministers, his Commissioners, 'tis Madness in the Extreme.

Remember! For Heaven's Sake I conjure you Remember you have no legal Check upon that Legislature. They are not bound in Interest Duty & Affection to watch over your Preservation, as over that of their Constituents; yet those constituents are daily betrayed. What can *you* expect? You are not quite mad. Why will you trust them? Why force yourselves to make a daily Resort to Arms? O God! Shall we never again see Peace! Sweet smiling Peace! Is this miserable Country to be plunged in endless War? Must each revolving Year, come heavy laden with those dismal Scenes, we have already seen? If so, Farewell Liberty! Farewell Virtue & Happiness! Oh, farewell, for ever.

4 ✸ Public Letters to the Carlisle Commissioners (1778)

On January 20, 1778, Morris took his seat in the Continental Congress, then meeting in York, Pennsylvania. Almost immediately, he was sent on a fact-finding trip to Washington's army at Valley Forge and did not return until mid-April. On his return, he served on a number of committees simultaneously and chaired several. It was customary for the committee chairman to do the bulk of the work, and thus Morris was fully occupied—perhaps a welcome distraction given the lack of society in York.

In early May, copies of the treaty of alliance with France reached Congress; meanwhile, a British Commission appointed to negotiate with the Americans had set sail. Rumors had been circulating for some time that the British would offer to concede to a few American demands as a way of undermining the rebellion. Many in Congress were apprehensive that the commission's proposals would weaken American resolve, just when independence seemed within reach thanks to the French.[1]

Congress moved to get the propaganda advantage on the commission in May, sending a circular to the people, to be read in all the churches. Its draft, written by Morris, was approved on May 8.[2] On June 4, the commissioners, led by the Earl of Carlisle, landed in Philadelphia. They sent their first letter to Congress June 9. A newspaper and pamphlet war ensued, lasting through the summer and fall of 1778. As the commissioners and Congress sparred over the next several months, Morris not only drafted many of Congress's replies to the commissioners' proposals, but wrote them these public letters, using the pseudonym "An American."[3]

---

1. See the discussion of April 22, 1778, in *Journals of the Continental Congress, 1774–1789*, ed. Worthington C. Ford et al. (Washington, D.C.: U.S. Government Printing Office, 1904–37), 10:374–80.

2. The circular is in the *JCC* 11:474–81.

3. Mintz, *American Revolution*, 103; see chapters 5 and 6, pp. 88–137, for further information on Morris's activities in this period.

To the Earl of CARLISLE, Lord Viscount HOWE, Sir WILLIAM HOWE
(or, in his absence, Sir HENRY CLINTON), WILLIAM EDEN,
and GEORGE JOHNSTONE.
Trusty and well beloved servants of your sacred master,
in whom he is well pleased.

As you are sent to America for the express purpose of treating with any-body and anything, you will pardon an address from one who disdains to flatter those whom he loves. Should you therefore deign to read this address, your chaste ears will not be offended with the language of adulation, a language you despise.

I have seen your most elegant and most excellent letter "to his Excellency Henry Laurens, the President, and other Members of the Congress." As that body have thought your propositions unworthy their particular regard, it may be some satisfaction to your curiosity, and tend to appease the offended spirit of negotiation, if one out of the many individuals on this great Continent should speak to you the sentiments of America. Sentiments which your own good sense hath doubtless suggested and which are repeated only to convince you that, notwithstanding the narrow ground of private information on which we stand in this distant region, still a knowledge of our own rights, and attention to our own interests, and a sacred respect for the dignity of human nature, have given us to understand the true principles which ought, and which therefore shall, sway our conduct.

You begin with the amiable expressions of humanity, the earnest desire of tranquility and peace. A better introduction to Americans could not be devised. For the sake of the latter, we once laid our liberties at the feet of your Prince, and even your armies have not eradicated the former from our bosoms.

You tell us you have powers unprecedented in the annals of your history. And England, unhappy England, will remember with deep contrition, that these powers have been rendered of no avail by a conduct unprecedented in the annals of mankind. Had your royal master condescended to listen to the prayer of millions, he had not thus have sent you. Had moderation

The Pennsylvania Gazette, June 20, 1778; reprinted from *Letters of Delegates to Congress, 1774–1789,* ed. Paul H. Smith et al. (Washington, D.C.: Library of Congress, 1976–2000), 10:154–61.

swayed what we were proud to call *mother country*, "her full-blown *dignity* would not have broken down under her."

You tell us that "all parties may draw some degree of consolation, and even auspicious hope, from recollection." We wish this most sincerely for the sake of *all parties*. America, even in the moment of subjugation, would have been consoled by conscious virtue, and her hope was and is in the justice of her cause, and the justice of the Almighty. These are sources of hope and of consolation, which neither time nor chance can alter or take away.

You mention "the mutual benefits and consideration of evils, that may naturally contribute to determine our resolutions." As to the former, you know too well that we could derive no benefit from an union with you, nor will I, by deducing the reasons to evince this, cast an insult upon your understandings. As to the latter, it were to be wished you had preserved a line of conduct equal to the delicacy of your feelings. You could not but know that men, who sincerely love freedom, disdain the consideration of all evils necessary to attain it. Had not your own hearts borne testimony to this truth, you might have learnt it from the *annals of your history*. For in those annals instances of this kind at least are not *unprecedented*. But should those instances be insufficient, we pray you to read the unconquered mind of America.

That the acts of Parliament you transmitted were passed *with singular unanimity*, we pretend not to doubt. You will pardon me, gentlemen, for observing, that the reasons of that unanimity are strongly marked in the report of a Committee of Congress, agreed to on the 22d of April last, and referred to in a late letter from Congress to Lord Viscount Howe and Sir Henry Clinton.

You tell us you are willing "to consent to a cessation of hostilities, both by sea and land." It is difficult for rude Americans to determine whether you are serious in this proposition, or whether you mean to jest with their simplicity. Upon a supposition, however, that you have too much magnanimity to divert yourselves on an occasion of such importance to America, and perhaps not very trivial in the eyes of those who sent you, permit me to assure you, on the sacred word of a gentleman, that if you shall transport your troops to England, where before long your Prince will certainly want their assistance, we never shall follow them thither. We are not so romantically fond of fighting, neither have we such regard for the city of London, as to commence a crusade for the possession of that holy land. Thus you may be certain that hostilities will cease by land. It would be doing singular injustice to your national character, to suppose you are desirous of a like cessation by sea. The course of the war, and the very flourishing state of your commerce, notwithstanding our weak efforts to interrupt it, clearly shew that you can exclude us from the sea. *The sea your kingdom.*

You offer "to restore free intercourse, to revive mutual affection, and renew the common benefits of naturalization." Whenever your countrymen shall be taught wisdom by experience, and learn from past misfortunes to pursue their true interests in future we shall readily admit every intercourse which is necessary for the purposes of commerce, and usual between different nations. To revive *mutual* affection is utterly impossible. We freely forgive you, but it is not in nature that you should forgive us. You have injured us too much. We might, on this occasion, give you some late instances of singular barbarity, committed as well by the forces of his Britannic Majesty, as by those of his generous and faithful allies, the Senecas, Onondagas and Tuscaroras. But we will not offend a courtly ear by the recital of those disgusting scenes. Besides this, it might give pain to that humanity which hath, as you observe, prompted your overtures to dwell upon the splendid victories obtained by a licentious soldiery over unarmed men in defenceless villages, their wanton devastations, their deliberate murders, or to inspect those scenes of carnage painted by the wild excesses of savage rage. These amiable traits of national conduct cannot but revive in our bosoms that partial affection we once felt for everything which bore the name of Englishman. As to the common benefits of naturalization, it is a matter we conceive to be of the most sovereign indifference. A few of our wealthy citizens may hereafter visit England and Rome, to see the ruins of those august temples, in which the goddess of Liberty was once adored. These will hardly claim naturalization in either of those places as a *benefit*. On the other hand, such of your subjects as shall be driven by the iron hand of Oppression to seek for refuge among those whom they now persecute, will certainly be admitted to the *benefits of naturalization*. We labour to rear an asylum for mankind, and regret that circumstances will not permit you, Gentlemen, to contribute to a design so very agreeable to your several tempers and dispositions.

But further, your Excellencies say, "we will concur to extend every freedom to trade that our respective interests can require." Unfortunately there is a little difference in these interests, which you might not have found it very easy to reconcile, had the Congress been disposed to risque their heads by listening to terms, which I have the honour to assure you are treated with ineffable contempt by every honest Whig in America. The difference I allude to is, that it is your interest to monopolize our commerce, and it is our interest to trade with all the world. There is indeed a method of cutting this gordian knot which perhaps no statesman is acute enough to untie. By reserving to the Parliament of Great-Britain the right of determining what our respective interests require, they might extend the freedom of trade, or circumscribe it, at their pleasure, for what they might call our *respective interests*. But I trust it would not be to our *mutual satisfaction*. Your "earnest desire to stop the farther effusion of blood, and the calamities of war," will therefore lead you, on maturer reflection, to reprobate a plan teeming with discord, and which, in the space of twenty years, would produce another wild expedition across the Atlantic, and in a few years more some such commission as that "with which his Majesty hath been pleased to honour you."

We cannot but admire the generosity of soul, which prompts you "to agree that no military force shall be kept up in the different States of North-America without the consent of the general Congress or particular Assemblies." The only grateful return we can make for this exemplary condescension is to assure your Excellencies, and, on behalf of my countrymen, I do most solemnly promise and assure you, that no military force shall be kept up in the different States of North-America without the consent of the general Congress, and that of the legislatures of those States. You will therefore cause the forces of your royal master to be removed, for I can venture to assure you that the Congress have not consented, and probably will not consent, that they be kept up.

You have also made the unsolicited offer of concurring "in measures calculated to discharge the debts of America, and to raise the credit and value of the paper circulation." If your Excellencies mean by this to apply for offices in the department of our finance, I am to assure you (which I do with "perfect respect") that it will be necessary to procure very ample recommendations. For as the English have not yet pursued measures to discharge their own debt, and raise the credit and value of their own paper circulation, but, on the contrary, are in a fair way to encrease the one and absolutely destroy the other, you will instantly perceive that financiers from that nation would present themselves with the most aukward grace imaginable.

You propose to us a devise to "perpetuate our union." It might not be amiss previously to establish this union, which may be done by your acceptance of the treaty of peace and commerce tendered to you by Congress; And such treaty, I can venture to say, would continue as long as your ministers could prevail upon themselves not to violate the faith of nations.

You offer, to use your own language, the inaccuracy of which, considering the importance of the subject, is not to be wondered at, or at least may be excused, "in short to establish the powers of the respective legislatures in each particular State, to settle its revenue, its civil and military establishment, and to exercise a perfect freedom of legislation and internal government, so that the British States throughout North-America acting with us, in peace and war, under one common sovereign, may have the irrevokable enjoyment of every privilege that is short of a total separation of interests, or consistent with that union of force on which the safety of our common religion and liberty depends." Let me assure you, gentlemen, that the power of the respective legislatures in each particular State is already most fully established, and on the most solid foundations. It is established on the perfect freedom of legislation and a vigorous administration of internal government. As to the settlement of the revenue, and the civil and military establishment, these are the work of the day, for which the several legislatures are fully competent. I have also the pleasure to congratulate your Excellencies, that the country, for the settlement of whose government, revenue, administration, and the like, you have exposed yourselves to the fatigues and hazards of a disagreeable voyage, and more disagreeable negociation, hath abundant resources wherewith to defend her liberties now, and pour forth the rich stream of revenue hereafter. As the States of North-America mean to possess the *irrevokable* enjoyment of their privileges, it is absolutely necessary for them to decline all connection with a Parliament, who, even in the laws under which you act, reserve in express terms the power of *revoking* every proposition which you may agree to. We have a due sense of the kind offer you make, to grant us a share in your sovereign, but really, gentlemen, we have not the least inclination to accept of it. He may suit you extremely well, but he is not to our taste. You are solicitous to prevent a total separation of interests, and this, after all, seems to be the gist of the business. To make you as easy as possible on this subject, I have to observe, that it may and probably will, in some instances, be our interest to assist you, and then we certainly shall. Where this is not the case, your Excellencies have doubtless too much good sense as well as good nature to require it. We cannot perceive that our liberty does in the least depend upon any union of force with you; for we find that, after you have exercised your force against us for upwards of three years, we are now upon the point of establishing our liberties in direct opposition to it. Neither can we conceive, that, after the experiment you have made, any nation in Europe will embark in so unpromising a scheme as the subjugation of America. It is not necessary that everybody should play the Quixotte. One is enough to entertain a generation at least. Your Excellencies will, I hope, excuse me when I differ from you, as to our having a religion in common with you: the religion of America is the religion of all mankind. Any person may worship in the manner he thinks most agreeable to the Deity; and if he behaves as a good citizen, no one concerns himself as to his faith or adorations, neither have we the least solicitude to exalt any one sect or profession above another.

I am extremely sorry to find in your letter some sentences, which reflect upon the character of his most Christian Majesty. It certainly is not kind, or consistent with the principles of philanthropy you profess, to traduce a gentleman's character without affording him any opportunity of defending himself: and that too a near neighbour, and not long since an intimate brother, who besides hath lately given you the most solid additional proofs of his pacific disposition, and with an unparalleled sincerity, which would do honour to other Princes, declared to your court, unasked, the nature and effect of a treaty he had just entered into with these States. Neither is it quite according to the rules of politeness to use such terms in addressing yourselves to Congress, when you well knew that he was their good and faithful ally. It is indeed true, as you justly observe, that he hath at times been at enmity with his Britannic Majesty, by which we suffered some inconveniences: but these flowed rather from our connection with you than any ill-will towards us: At the same time it is a solemn truth, worthy of your serious attention, that you did not commence the present war, a war in which we have suffered infinitely more than by any former contest, a fierce, a bloody, I am sorry to add, an unprovoked and cruel war. That you did not commence this, I say, because of any connection between us and our present ally; but, on the contrary, as soon as you perceived that the treaty was in agitation, proposed terms of peace to us in consequence of what you have been pleased to denominate an insidious interposition. How then does the account stand between us. America, being at peace with all the world, was formerly drawn into a war with France, in consequence of her union with Great-Britain. At present America, being engaged in a war with Great-Britain, will probably obtain the most honourable terms of peace, in consequence of her friendly connection with France. For the truth of these positions I appeal, gentlemen, to your own knowledge. I know it is very hard for you to part with what you have accustomed yourselves, from your earliest infancy, to call your colonies. I pity your situation, and therefore I excuse the little abberations from truth which your letter contains. At the same time it is possible that you may have been mis-informed. For I will not suppose that your letter was intended to delude the people of these States. Such unmanly disingenuous artifices have of late been exerted with so little effect, that prudence, if not probity, would pre-vent a repetition. To undeceive you, therefore, I take the liberty of assuring your Excellencies, from the very best intelligence, that what you call "the present form of the French offers to North-America," in other words the treaties of alliance and commerce between his most Christian Majesty and these States, were not made in consequence of any plans of accommoda-tion concerted in Great-Britain, nor with a view to prolong this destruc-tive war. If you consider that these treaties were actually concluded before the draught of the bills under which you act was sent for America, and that much time must necessarily have been consumed in adjusting compacts of such intricacy and importance, and further, if you consider the early noti-fication of this treaty by the court of France, and the assurance given that America had reserved a right of admitting even you to a similar treaty, you must be convinced of the truth of my assertions. The fact is, that when the British Minister perceived that we were in treaty with the greatest Prince in Europe, he applied himself immediately to counteract the effect of these negociations. And this leads me with infinite regret to make some obser-vations, which may possibly be by you considered in an offensive point of view.

It seems to me, gentlemen, there is something (excuse the word) disin-genuous in your procedure. I put the supposition that Congress had ac-ceded to your propositions, and then I ask two questions. Had you full power from your commission to make these propositions? Possibly you did not think it worth while to consider your commission, but we Americans are apt to compare things together, and to reason. The second question I ask is, What security could you give that the British Parliament would ratify your compacts? You can give no such security, and therefore we should, after forfeiting our reputation as a people, after you had filched from us our good name, and perswaded us to give to the common enemy of man the precious jewel of our liberties; after all this, I say, we should have been at the mercy of a Parliament, which, to say no more of it, has not treated us with too great tenderness. It is quite needless to add, that even if that Par-liament had ratified the conditions you proposed, still poor America was to lie at the mercy of any future Parliament, or appeal to the sword, which certainly is not the most pleasant business men can be engaged in.

For your use I subjoin the following creed of every good American. I believe that in every kingdom, state, or empire there must be, from the necessity of the thing, one supreme legislative power, with authority to bind every part in all cases, the proper object of human laws. I believe that to be bound by laws, to which he does not consent by himself or by his representative, is the direct definition of a slave. I do therefore believe, that a dependence on Great-Britain, however the same may be limited or qualified, is utterly inconsistent with every idea of liberty, for the defence of which I have solemnly pledged my life and fortune to my countrymen; and this engagement I will sacredly adhere to so long as I shall live. Amen.

Now if you will take the poor advice of one, who is really a friend to England and Englishmen, and who hath even some Scotch blood in his veins, away with your fleets and your armies, acknowledge the independence of America, and as Ambassadors, and not Commissioners, solicit a treaty of peace, amity, commerce and alliance with the rising Stars of this western world. Your nation totters on the brink of a stupendous precipice, and even delay will ruin her.

You have told the Congress, "If, after the time that may be necessary to consider this communication, and transmit your answer, the horrors and devastations of war should continue, we call God and the world to witness that the evils, which must follow, are not to be imputed to Great-Britain." I wish you had spared your protestation. Matters of this kind may appear to you in a trivial light, as meer ornamental flowers of rhetoric, but they are serious things registered in the high chancery of Heaven. Remember the awful abuse of words like these by General Burgoyne, and remember his fate. There is one above us, who will take exemplary vengeance for every insult upon his Majesty. You know that the cause of America is just. You know that she contends for that freedom, to which all men are entitled. That she contends against oppression, rapine, and more than savage barbarity. The blood of the innocent is upon your hands, and all the waters of the ocean will not wash it away. We again make our solemn appeal to the God of Heaven to decide between you and us. And we pray that in the doubtful scale of battle we may be successful, as we have justice on our side, and that the merciful Saviour of the world may forgive our oppressors.

I am, my Lords and Gentlemen, *The friend of human nature, And one who glories in the title of,*

An AMERICAN.

To the EARL of CARLISLE.

My Lord,

As you, in conjunction with your brother Commissioners, have thought proper to make one more fruitless negociatory essay, permit me, through your lordship, once more to address the brotherhood. It is certainly to be lamented that gentlemen so accomplished should be so unfortunate. Particularly, my Lord, it is to be regretted that you should be raised up as the topstone to a pyramid of blunders.

On behalf of America I have to intreat that you will pardon their Congress for any want of politeness in not answering your letter.[4] You may remember, that in their last letter they stated certain terms as preliminaries to a negociation. And I am sure your lordship's candor will do them the justice to acknowledge that they are not apt to tread back the steps they have taken. In addition to this it so happens that they are at present very indifferent whether or not your King and Parliament acknowledge their independency; and still more indifferent as to withdrawing his fleets and armies.

You mistake the matter exceedingly when you suppose that any person in America wishes to prolong the calamities of war. No, my lord, we have had enough of them in all conscience. But the fault lies on you or your master, or some of the people he has about him. Congress when Sir William Howe landed on Staten-Island, met him with their Declaration of Independence. They adhered to it in the most perilous circumstances. They put their lives upon the issue; nay their honor. Now in the name of common sense how can you suppose they will relinquish this object in the present moment?

I am fully of your lordship's opinion, when you decline any dispute with Congress, about the meaning of the term Independence. They would have infinite advantage over you logically, but what is worse, they are politically in capacity to put upon the term just what construction they please: Nay, my lord, eventually Great-Britain must acknowledge just such an independence as Congress think proper; they are now in the full possession and enjoyment of it. How idle in you to talk of insuring or enlarging what is out of your power and cannot be encreased.

The Pennsylvania Packet, July 21, 1778; reprinted from *Letters of Delegates to Congress*, 10:327–29.

4. The Commissioners had sent a second letter to Congress July 11, 1778.

You give two reasons for not withdrawing your fleets and armies. The first is, that you keep them here by way of precaution against your ancient enemies. Really, my Lord, I was at a loss for some time to comprehend the force of this reasoning, or how a body of men in this country and a large fleet could protect you against an invasion from France. And I am even now perhaps mistaken, when I suppose your sea and land forces have been kept here to draw the attention of your enemies to this quarter, and leave their coast exposed, that so you may have an opportunity of invading France. If this was the object, it hath had the desired effect. Your armies are doubtless assembled in readiness for the descent, which, considering the unprovided state of that country, cannot but prove successful; and therefore I congratulate your lordship on the fair prospect you enjoy of seeing your Sovereign make his triumphant entry through the gates of Paris.

Your second reason for staying here is to protect the Tories. Pray, my lord, ease your mind upon that subject. Let them take care of themselves. The little ones may be pardoned whenever they apply. The great ones have joined you from conscientious or from interested motives. The first in having done what they thought right will find sufficient comfort. The last deserve none. I offer you this consolation, my lord, because we both know that you cannot protect the tories, and because there is every reason to believe that you cannot protect yourselves.

You have, it seems, determined your judgment by what you conceive to be the interest of your country, and you propose to abide by your declarations in every possible situation. I rather imagine that you are determined by your instructions; but if otherwise, surely, my lord, you are not to learn that circumstances may materially alter the interest of your country and your conceptions of it. The decision of some military events which you did not wait for, would put you in a situation to speak to Congress in much more decent terms than those contained in your last letter.

But you want to know, my lord, what treaties we have entered into. In pity to your nerves Congress have kept this knowledge. It will make the boldest among you tremble. As we are not about to negociate at present, there is no need of the communication. However, to satisfy your curiosity as far as an individual can, I pray you to recollect, that the Marquis de Noailles told you his Court, when they formed an alliance with America, had taken eventual measures. You cannot but know that a French fleet is now hovering on the coast near you—draw your own conclusions, my lord.

It is a most diverting circumstance to hear you ask Congress what power they have to treat, after offering to enter into treaty with them, and being refused. But I shall be glad to know by what authority you call on them for this discovery. The Count de Vergennes had a right to it, but the Earl of Carlisle certainly has not.[5] Let me add, my lord, that in making the request there is a degree of asperity not suited to your situation. When you were in the arms of victory we pardoned an insolence which had become habitual to your nation. We shall revere it if preserved when you are reduced to the lowest pitch of wretchedness. But in the present moment, when you certainly cannot terrify, and have not suffered so as to deserve pity, such language is quite improper. And it forces from me certain facts which I am sorry to mention, as they shew your masters to be wicked beyond all example.

When they found that an alliance was actually on the carpet between his Most Christian Majesty and these States, they offered to cede a part of the East-Indies, to give equal privileges in the African trade, and to divide the fisheries, provided they might be at liberty to ravage America. And when that would not do, they told the French Ministry that it was absurd to treat with Congress; that they were faithless; nay, that the bargain was actually struck for the purchase of America, and money, to the amount of half a million, sent over to pay the price. These, my lord, are facts—facts which will hang up to eternal infamy the names of your rulers. The French, my lord, laughed at the meanness and falshood of these declarations. But they suffered themselves to appear to be deceived. They permitted you to flounder on in the ocean of your follies and your crimes. You and your brethren, I find, are directed to play the same game here; to call our allies faithless; to tell an hundred incoherent fictions about our treaties, the substance of which you confess yourselves at this moment ignorant of. And what is the very complication of absurdity, you pretend to tell Congress the manner in which the negociations were carried on, when Mr. Deane, the principal negociator, on their part, is on the spot to give information.[6] For shame. For shame. It is for these reasons that Congress treat you with such utter contempt.

There is but one way left to sink you still lower, and, thank God you have found it out. You are about to publish! Oh my lord! my lord! you are indeed in a mighty pitiful condition. You have tried fleets and armies, and proclamations, and now you threaten us with news-papers. Go on, exhaust

---

5. The Count de Vergennes was the French foreign minister.

6. Silas Deane had returned in mid-July, following his recall to face accusations of mishandling funds.

all your artillery, But know, that those who have withstood your flattery and refused your bribes, despise your menaces—Farewell. When you come with better principles, and on a better errand, we shall be glad to meet you: Till that moment, I am your Lordship's most obedient And most humble servant,

An AMERICAN.

To the Earl of Carlisle, September 19, 1778

To his Excellency the Earl of CARLISLE.

MY LORD,

Through the medium of a newspaper, I see a declaration and requisition, signed by yourself and your brethren Clinton and Eden, together with an apologetic Epistle from Governor Johnstone.[7] As these papers are transmitted by *your* Secretary, and reflect light upon each other, your Lordship will excuse a few animadversions on them addressed to you. My intention is, to undeceive you in some matters you seem to have mistaken, and to state the true ground on which you stand with respect to America. This I attempt from a sincere desire of peace; considering it as a blessing, the loss of which can never be compensated by the splendors of victory.

Your first error, a leading one, which hath tinged the complexion of all your national acts since the early commencement of the controversy, is a supposition that Congress do not speak the sense of the people of America. Of all the people they do *not*, but of a considerable majority they certainly *do*. Considerable for the numbers, property, principles, temper and character of those who compose it.

The number, according to my best estimation, is at least two-thirds of the whole; and the remaining third are of very little political consideration. They consist of a few who adhere to you from principle, a few more from interest, and a very few (now) from fear, as Indians worship the Devil. The remainder are attached to *no* side, unless indeed they could discover with

The Pennsylvania Packet, September 19, 1778; reprinted from *Letters of Delegates to Congress*, 10:667–74. The manuscript is in the Gouverneur Morris Papers, Rare Book and Manuscript Library, Columbia University, item 798.

7. These were issued August 26, 1778.

absolute certainty which is the *strongest* side, being, as they term it *moderate men*. Add to this, that your American friends, from their religious notions and other circumstances, are generally averse to war.

The majority are further considerable from their property. It is by no means a figurative expression to say that the land of America is against you. This may seem extraordinary after what you have heard, especially if you have had the *honor* of a conversation with some of those traders who have lately, taken it into their heads to call themselves the *Gentlemen* of America. But if your Lordship will condescend to enquire for the ten greatest land-holders of the state of New-York on the whig side of the question, you will find that no forty tories throughout the whole Continent have an equal property; considered as to the extent, the fertility, or the value in coin.

The principles of your opponents are republican, some indeed aristocratic; the greater part democratic, but all opposed to Kings, from a thorough conviction by reason, by history, and above both by experience, that nine times in ten they are the scourges of mankind.

The temper of this majority is not only vigilant and irascible, but much roused and exasperated. Exasperated by the injustice, the treachery, the cruelty of Great-Britain. Respect, my Lord, for your feelings forbids that odious detail which justifies these charges. Should you doubt, ask Sir Henry. Ask the officers in your regiments and on board your ships. Let them paint the violations, the burnings, the massacres, the starvings they have been witness to. And if this evidence is insufficient, invocate the manes[8] of those wretches who died at Philadelphia in the paroxisms of madness and despair, from reflecting on the horrors they themselves had executed.

Lastly, the character of those who compose the majority in America is of no small importance. Many of them are the most respectable members of the community; others again are distinguished by superior talents; and a great number are of that aspiring cast who look on high, and will neither be thrown out in pursuit of their favourite objects, nor dropped into insignificancy. To these things, I add the perseverance of the lower class in a cause which they think, with me, is just and righteous. At the Valley-Forge I was an eye witness to the sufferings of our soldiery: Many of them lay literally on the earth naked without fire and without food. It is to their honor that they did not mutiny; that they did not desert; that they did not even

---

8. *Letters* reads "invocable the Manes." In ancient Roman religious practice, the *manes* were the deified souls of ancestors; in later usage it came to mean departed souls more generally.

complain. The sentiment expressed by these brave citizens was, "We know every measure is taken to relieve our wants, and if we are distressed, it is because distress is unavoidable." Of such a majority, my Lord, the sense is spoken by Congress. To convince you of it, look at their publications; see how frequently, how fully, how directly they appeal to the people. Can you lay your finger on any falsehood sanctioned by their authority? Have they ever descended to meanness or artifice to cajole or to deceive their constituents or even their enemies? I know that your Gazetteers have charged all these things upon them; but, my Lord, I can hardly suppose that you was sent hither to read or to write news-papers.

A second error which hath affected your national conduct, is an opinion that Congress lead the people. The direct contrary is so much a fact, that the business of Congress is, in a great measure, to discover the sentiment of the people and clothe it in words. Whenever any step is to be taken, they ask, what is the opinion of the people? For should they go beyond the ground on which they are supported by popular favour, that instant their power is at an end. To prove this further, I ask if the people have ever refused obedience to the matters proposed by Congress? Have the accumulated distresses of the present war, distresses almost beyond example, prevailed on them to desert their Congress? Nay, have all your efforts impaired the credit of our continental money, resting, as it did, merely on the public opinion and confidence in Congress?

An error of another kind appears in the papers now before me. From them it is manifest that you really misinterpret the language, and mistake the meaning of Congress. You seem to suppose, that when they declared it *incompatible with their honor to hold intercourse with George Johnstone, especially to negociate with him upon affairs in which the cause of liberty and virtue is interested*, they indirectly receded from their determination to have nothing to say to any of you till you sent away your fleets and armies, or acknowledged the Independence of America. It is a maxim, my Lord, that a positive act cannot be repealed by implication. The plain language of the resolution, therefore, is this, "Perhaps the British Commissioners may have collateral matters to urge, such as the exchange of prisoners, &c. If he who hath insolently tendered bribes to us should join in any application of this sort, we cannot listen to it. Let us therefore give our enemies a timely notice, that they may square their conduct accordingly. Let us not leave them the shadow of a reason to charge us with any disingenuous procedure."

From the best information, I take on me to assure your Lordship, that not the remotest idea was entertained of departing from their resolutions.

The candour which dictated this last determination, is entitled to a very different language from what it hath met with. But since the conduct of Congress is stigmatized with the charge of duplicity, it may not be improper to shew the entire consistency of that Body, notwithstanding the many changes it hath undergone of the individuals. This will corroborate my former position, that they are simply the mouth of a people steadily attached to, and determined to support their rights and liberties.

The declaration of Independence will form a principal part of the present question. But, though much hath been, and much more may be speculated on the right of a people to become independent, it will perhaps ultimately turn on their power. You yourselves tender to Congress every thing they may ask short of a total separation of interests: Therefore, you offer to confine the union simply to the person of the Prince. Supposing it accepted, then without enquiring whether Americans might afterwards choose a King for themselves, clearly the English might, or else as clearly their now King is an usurper. If the people of Britain should exercise this right, then America continuing under her old King, would be independent. But a contract which one party can break, and the other cannot, is void; and therefore America could of right break the bargain as well as Great Britain; and therefore either party might at pleasure be independent of the other. And if America could of right declare herself independent after the agreement, certainly she could before. But further; from your own shewing, we are not subjects of the Parliament: If subjects therefore, we are subjects of the King. Again, it is agreed that if we do not like a King, we can send him away and take another in his stead, for our fathers did so before us. Therefore, as the greater contains within it the lesser, so we could do just one half of the proposition, viz. get rid of one King without getting another; and this is precisely what we have done. Take it lastly as a question of force, and then we fight to determine the moot point of which side are rebels. So much for the right to Independence.

In the commencement of this controversy, Congress prayed to be placed in the situation of sixty-three. This was practicable at that time, for nothing more was necessary than on your part to repeal the impolitic acts you had passed. You refused; they pressed it earnestly. For tho' the situation of sixty three was not very eligible, yet, as the event of war was uncertain, and the costs and the miseries but too certain, it was prudent and right to urge this request. Still you refused and appealed to the sword, and prosecuted and persecuted us to obtain what you now acknowledge you had no right to ask. Thus then were we plunged into a war against our inclinations, and of consequence could not be bound by any offer made with a view to avoid it. Besides, the situation of sixty three was no longer attainable: For, though the paper acts of your Parliament could have been repealed, yet the bloody acts of your soldiery could not. You could not pour back into the veins of our citizens the blood you had wantonly spilt. Previous to the year sixty three, points which should always have remained in oblivion, had never been started. But the question of supremacy once made in the rude language of arms, a decided line of authority and subjection became necessary to a future union. Desirous of avoiding the further calamities of war, we intreated you to pursue the measures necessary for reconciliation. This you refused, pertinaciously adhering to your first postulatum of *unconditional submission*, and with a view to the great object of *solid revenue*. You therefore urged the war, and applied to every little Prince in Europe for troops: We deprecated it, and did not even seek an alliance with any foreign power, knowing well that such alliance would close the door of reconciliation forever with all the bars of national faith and honor.

The situation of America was at length such by your obstinacy, that the evils Congress laboured to avoid were to become certain. At the same time it was a decided fact, that the interests of England and of America were directly opposed to each other. It was your interest to restrict our commerce, and it was our interest to extend it: It was your interest to take our money, and it was our interest to keep it. In a word, it was your interest to tyrannize, and it was our interest to be free. We therefore could not trust you, and you would not trust us. The King and his Ministers no body would trust. So that a re-union became every day more problematical.

The great fleets and armies you had employed, and the pains you had taken to deprive us of all military stores, obliged us to seek foreign aid, and it was clear that no Prince would assist us while we acknowledged ourselves to be rebels. Thus it was certain that we should experience the horrors of war, notwithstanding we had offered a part of our rights to avoid them. It was highly probable that without help we should be conquered. The object of reconciliation was distant and precarious at best, and by no means worth the blood and treasure necessary to attain it; and therefore, the people of America, through their Congress, declared themselves free and independent, as the only mode left to obtain their great end of peace, liberty and safety.

The war continued, and success seemed to be yours. Swoln with the hopes of conquest, you disclaimed every thing which looked like concession. At length the fate of the brave unfortunate Burgoyne recalled you to your senses: You sent to Congress the draft of your conciliatory bills.[9] They, at that time, knew nothing of what their Commissioners had done in Europe. They saw, however, that your concessions proceeded from weakness, and were dictated by necessity. They knew your insincerity, and therefore wisely determined to have nothing to say to you till you acknowledged our independence, or withdrew your forces. Between this period and your Lordship's arrival, Congress received a copy of the treaties with his Most Christian Majesty. In answer to your letters therefore, they informed you, that after you had complied with the alternative just now mentioned, they would consent to a treaty with your Prince, not inconsistent with those already entered into. At length a war hath broken out between your sovereign and France, which, if I am rightly informed, will again alter the situation of affairs as far as they relate to negociation. From this detail your Lordship will perceive that the most perfect consistency hath been maintained on our part. We have acted from a conviction of your force and your violence, of your weakness and your insincerity.

I come now to a matter of some delicacy, which I shall nevertheless, treat with freedom, and hope your Lordship's pardon for the unpolished terms of a republican. In your declaration you state a series of facts (as you call your assertions) to shew the insincerity of France. My Lord, you are deceived, or you mean to deceive; for the assertions you make are not founded in truth. Not only so, but you grossly mistake our disposition; for were every thing you say admitted, it would not produce the effect you wish for. You say, it is well known to the whole Continent of America, that public intimation of the conciliatory propositions was given in November last—Permit me to undeceive your Lordship. The direct contrary of what you say is perfectly well known to the people of America; and further, they know your Ministers breathed nothing but conquest and war at that period. You say, it is equally well known that the preliminaries of a French treaty, sent by Mr. Simeon Deane, did not bear date earlier than the sixteenth of December. The people of America do not enquire into such trifling circumstances. It is very immaterial to us when Mr. Simeon Deane went to sea, or why he put back, or when he came out again: If these things had been of consequence, we know that Congress would have published them. One thing, however, is very clear to me, that you know not when those preliminaries, as you call them, were dated, nor indeed any thing about them. Let me ask one question: Are you certain, my Lord, that when Mr. Simeon

9. Burgoyne surrendered on October 17, 1777.

Deane first sailed he had any papers whatever with him?[10] You suppose that difficulties arose in the negotiation with France, for want of power in the American Commissioners. No such thing, my Lord; they had powers as ample as they could wish. Our Congress know better than to send their servants on a fool's errand. Perhaps your Lordship may find it convenient to recommend their example by the old adage of *fas est et ab hoste doceri.*[11] You roundly assert, that the conciliatory propositions were a subject of discussion in all the debates upon the state of the nation from the twentieth of January. I hope[12] your Lordship will revise, and correct that sentence, before the next edition of your declaration. A reputation for veracity may be of service to you at some time or other. You assert also, that no treaties were sent from France before the eight of March: Your Lordship's intelligence is not to be depended on. From better evidence I assure you, that dispatches containing the treaties were sent by the way of Corunna much earlier. The gentleman who brought them left Paris immediately on conclusion of the treaty, which by the bye is not antidated.

I have said above, that the affair of Saratoga determined your conduct; I mean, my Lord, that it opened the scene of American politics at St. James's, at Versailles, through-out all Europe. You have laboured to prove that France did not act from motives of Generosity but of interest. You have failed; but I will admit the conclusion, though I deny the premises; and then I add, that if she had consulted any thing besides her interest, America would by no means have been pleased with the alliance. The generosity of statesmen, my Lord, is but another name for caprice, and we wish no connection with the capricious. It is the interest of France to be allied to America; it is the interest of America to be allied to France. The rulers of the two nations see their interest and pursue it. What more can be desired? Did you expect, when you told the Congress a long story about reviving free intercourse and mutual affection, with other the airy forms, ideal nothings, to which you had given a local habitation and a name; did you suppose them such coxcombs as to pay the least attention unless, at the

10. The course of events here is murky. In late 1777, a Captain Folger sailed from France with dispatches from the commissioners, including preliminary terms of the treaty, but when those letters were opened, they turned out to have nothing but blank paper. There were strong suspicions that the British were behind the substitution. Simeon Deane later brought the final copy of the treaty.

11. It is proper to be taught even by an enemy.

12. "Those" in the newspaper and *Letters;* "I hope" in the manuscript.

same time, you could convince them it was their interest? No, you did not. Your conduct shews you did not. Unfortunately you applied to the private interest of the Members, instead of the general interests of their constituents. We wish to be at peace with all the world, and therefore we will make peace with you *when you are properly authorized to speak*, and have proper terms to offer. In the mean time, if you like fighting better, why we will fight with you.

My Lord, you are come hither for the very modest purpose of persuading a free and independent nation to surrender their rights and privileges: You are confessedly incompetent to the business of subduing them and are therefore to proceed by what you call reasoning. Now, as public addresses are not always the most clear and intelligible compositions, in order to simplify the matter, I will suppose you in conference with such an honest farmer as myself: You ask me *to become a subject of the King of Great Britain; and what shall I get by that? Security of your person and property.* My person and property are secure already. *He will make laws for you and govern you.* I had much rather make laws for myself and govern myself. *But he will regulate your trade.* Pray what is that? *Why he will tell you where your ships* SHALL *go, and where they shall* NOT *go, and what they* SHALL *carry, and what they shall* NOT *carry.* But I had rather our merchants should send their ships where and with what cargoes they please; I fancy they know as much of trade as your King, and how to get the best prices and the cheapest goods. *Aye, aye, but this is for the sake of a union of force, and for the interests of the whole British empire.* My good friend, the force of America is already united, and I have nothing to do with the British empire. *Yes, you have; for unless you comply with these terms, the King of England will conquer you.* I do not think he is able. *He will try however; and therefore, if you do not instantly submit your person and property to his disposal, you are answerable to Heaven for all the miseries of the war he shall carry on for that purpose.* I do not believe a syllable of the matter. I wish your King would mind his own affairs, and not trouble other people. But if he will send armies hither to fight, we must e'en fight. And so I wish your Lordship a good morning. I am, my Lord, with the most profound veneration, Your Lordships most obedient, and most humble servant,

AN AMERICAN.

To SIR HENRY CLINTON, &c. &c.

May it please your Excellency.

I have been favoured with the sight of your letter to the Congress, dated at New-York, the 19th September, 1778, on which I shall take leave to make a few observations.

It was suggested to me to notice the requisition you sent upon the same subject, some time since, as a Commissioner, in conjunction with your brethren, Eden and Carlisle. I avoided it, because I was certain your Excellency would offer me another and a better opportunity. You will, however, pardon me for referring to that paper on the present occasion.

Let me observe, Sir, that fraud and hypocrisy, however they may be mistaken for policy by weak minds, are of a very different family, and have not the slightest connection. The use of them is at all times dishonourable, sometimes dangerous. They may serve one turn and for one moment, but they frequently fail even of that short purpose, and impede a man in all his future operations. If ever there was an opportunity for using these weapons successfully, you had it with us; for we reposed the highest confidence in British integrity, and we had an affection for the nation. But you have so imprudently dissipated our good opinion, that when you aim a great stroke the means are wanting.

When your officers broke their paroles, we imputed it to a defect of principle among them individually from the want of education and other circumstances of that kind, which, considering the characters of some, is not to be wondered at. And when we heard that these persons were not only countenanced but caressed, we did not believe it.

We know tolerably well the insidious manners of your court, for they were painted by your own citizens, and we had reason to believe their assertions. We found the design to enslave us was persisted in through every change of Ministers and measures, and professions in a long course of years. But we did not, we could not believe that their baneful influence had so deeply affected every order of your state. And though the conduct of Lord Dunmore, in tendering freedom to all the slaves who should butcher their masters and repair to his standard, was sufficient to have opened our

The Pennsylvania Packet, October 20, 1778; reprinted from *Letters of Delegates to Congress*, 11:85–91.

45

eyes.[13] Yet our partiality in your favour led us to attribute this to the profligacy of his private character, and to a predeliction for Negroes, arising from his natural propensity to the females of that complexion.

In short, I have known some of the best friends to America behave coldly to their friends, for believing the relation now too well attested, of your conduct to those unhappy men who capitulated at Fort Washington.[14]

At length conviction came, though slow, yet full. To mention the instances in which you broke faith with the public and with individuals, would be to write the history of your three campaigns, with all the attiral[15] of proclamations and protections. But it would be for the honour of human nature to bury this history in oblivion. It is sufficient for the present to observe, that we became fully convinced you were no longer to be trusted.

Honest men, after they have been defrauded, acquire that wholesome suspicion which others inherit. The only difference indeed is, that the former reason from facts, the latter from feelings. Of consequence mutual diffidence took place to the greatest degree; and it is perhaps as laughable a circumstance as any of the others that you made at this time, and under such auspices your conciliatory propositions, which of all things required the greatest confidence. But to return.

It was predicted by every discerning man, that the troops of the convention would be used against us the instant they were out of our power. Your former conduct justified the inference, and considering the many infractions you made in it from the very commencement of the treaty, Congress had good right to have declared the stipulations on their part void. Principles, however, of national honour induced the determination of that Body strictly to comply with the convention. Luckily for America General Burgoyne, by declaring in a letter to Congress that they had broken it, gave an additional ground, known and acknowledged among nations, for suspending it until a ratification from the court of Great-Britain. It is observable, that even then the suspension was carried by a very small majority,

---

13. In November 1775 the Royal Governor of Virginia, the Earl of Dunmore, issued a proclamation offering freedom to any slave of a patriot master who would fight for Britain.

14. Fort Washington, on the northern end of Manhattan Island, was captured by the British on November 15, 1776, along with all its equipment and over two thousand American soldiers. Many of the prisoners were put on British prison ships in New York harbor, where the poor conditions killed a significant portion of them.

15. In the newspaper, "attiral"; in *Letters*, "attirais."

although every Member present was convinced you did not mean to pay the least regard to it. They reasoned (but with what force it becomes not me to determine) that it was better to convince the world by one more experiment of your want of integrity. Luckily however, they were overruled; and you have daily given additional proofs of the wisdom of that cautionary measure.

On the requisition by yourself and others, Commissioners, &c. dated at New-York, the 26th August, the following doubts arise:

1st. Why was it not made sooner, since clearly the Commissioners had as much power to ratify it before, and their King was as much in need of his troops.

2d. By what authority did the Commissioners intermeddle in a business by no means in contemplation at the time of their appointment, and (as will be shewn hereafter) clearly out of their power, especially when you the proper person was on the spot, and only made one of them.

I am informed that the solution given in Congress at the time was, that the Commissioners had received a ratification of the convention, together with orders to make an application of that kind, with a view to two objects:

1st. If possible to obtain the prisoners, and then declare the convention void by reason of the suspension, and of their want of authority.

2d. At least to lead Congress into some kind of treaty or correspondence with them on the subject, and thereby indirectly into an acknowledgment of an authority in the Commissioners to treat with us as subjects of Great-Britain.

This is confirmed substantially by your letter; for it cannot be supposed that your Ministers have less pride or wisdom than heretofore. If therefore their Commissioners had been possessed of sufficient authority, they would hardly have sent you that express and recent authority you mention to have received since the date of their requisition. It is worthy of observation that this date is the 26th of August, and Your authority the twelfth of June, between which is an interval of eleven weeks. It is evident that Your Ministers in the critical situation of their country, would give this paper every possible dispatch. Six weeks or seven, at farthest, were sufficient to transmit it from Whitehall to New-York. Hence it is evident, not only that you had received that paper before the date of the requisition, but also that it was on that ground the requisition was made.

What right had the Commissioners to interfere in it? They were appointed for the single purpose of persuading us to become subjects to the King, being a kind of missionaries to propagate monarchy in foreign parts, and what connection this has with a military convention, no man can discover. They had no authority to speak to Congress on national grounds. They were not Ambassadors, Ministers Plenipotentiary, nor any thing of that kind. They were not appointed by letters of credence but by commission under the great seal, not from the mere motive of the Prince, but by Act of Parliament. In short, the whole mission was on domestick principles; when therefore the people of America refused to become subjects to the King of England, their authority, if any they had, ceased, nor could they possibly have had authority to the purpose they pretended. It was given them neither by their commission, nor by the act on which that commission was grounded, nor could it possibly have been in contemplation when that act was passed; and your letter shews demonstratively, not only that they had not any such authority, but that your King and his Ministers did not think they had.

But what kind of authority is your's? Why it seems you have sent a paper, purporting to be the extract of a letter from Lord George Germaine, and that is a true extract, we have the word of one Smith, your secretary. And what is this extract? Why it seems it is a signification of your Monarch's pleasure? And what is it that will please him? Why that you give assurances, &c. All this appears from the paper. But why will it please him? Because he would get some troops without being under the necessity of keeping the convention. For does it follow, that because he desires you to give assurances, that therefore he gives assurances? Does it follow because your secretary hath signed a piece of paper as an extract, &c. that therefore it is an extract? I believe it is, but I also believe that your court would deny it if they could get any thing by it. Does it follow, if this is a true *extract*, that the whole letter taken together is not of a different complexion? Does it follow, that it is the King's pleasure you should do so because Lord George Germaine says it is? In a word, will any assurances given by you under such flimsy authority, amount to that explicit ratification which was demanded by Congress? A demand then justified by the conduct of General Burgoyne, and which the chicane used since, hath rendered it absolutely necessary to [insist]16 on.

The position then, Sir Harry, is clear, that when Carlisle, Eden and Clinton made their remonstrance and requisition, and when you made your demand, neither they or you had given or could give that satisfaction for keeping the convention which Congress had a right to demand: Of conse-

16. Bracketed in *Letters;* only the first two letters are legible in the newspaper.

quence you could not expect the troops would be suffered to depart from our shores. This being the case, let us consider the requisition. I say what did you and your brethren mean by your eulogy upon the faith of cartels, military capitulations, conventions and treaties which you have sported with so often? What did you mean by calling on us by the sacred obligations of humanity and justice, to do what, confident with a regard to either, or even to our own safety you knew was impossible? What did you mean by a threat of retaliation, you who have exhausted the mores of military barbarity? What were you to retaliate? A weakness almost amounting to pusilanimity in declining to avenge the injuries you have done? Do you think it possible to affright us by an idea that you will pay no regard to cartels or capitulations? You never yet have done it: Those who surrender to you know they are exposed to the sword or to languish in confinement.

You have dared to say, "all breach of faith, even with an enemy, and all attempts to elude the force of military conventions, or to defeat their salutary purposes by evasion or chicane, are justly held in detestation, and deemed unworthy of any description of persons assuming the characters or stating themselves as the Representatives of nations," and yet at that moment you are employed in the very attempt by evasion and chicane to elude the convention of Saratoga.[17] You had surmounted, possibly after many compunctious struggles, at least for the honour of human nature I hope so, but you had surmounted every sense of justice, of humanity, and of honour. Let me congratulate you on this new victory over the sense of shame. In this view you have gained at length the victory over yourselves, and may stand forth the first of philosophers in your kind, you may boast to be leaders of those, who cloathed with the dignity of national character, display the story of their own disgrace.

It is to be lamented, that on an occasion so solemn, and of such serious consequences to your reputations, we cannot derive an idea of your wisdom, equal to that which your fortitude hath impressed. It would have been

---

17. The Saratoga Convention was the result of the surrender negotiations with General Burgoyne after his defeat at the Battle of Saratoga in October 1777. It provided that the troops under Burgoyne's command would be allowed to return to Europe on condition that they not bear arms against the United States again. In January 1778, Burgoyne accused the Americans of adding new conditions, after which Congress refused to honor the convention until it was ratified by the King, which would amount to a *de facto* recognition of independence. Apparently the King had told Carlisle to ratify, but Congress did not believe that the ratification was authentic.

glorious indeed, could you have shown a capacity to deceive all mankind with the same facility that you set their opinions at defiance. But unfortunately this is not the case, for you have taken upon you to remonstrate against the *unjust detention* of the Saratoga troops. Did you consider the force of the term? If the detention is unjust, the convention is broken, if we have broken the convention you are no longer bound by it, if no longer bound in equity, a ratification extorted by the *unjust* detention will be void. To have released them therefore on this requisition, other objectionable circumstances being removed, would by implication have admitted you a ground whereon to build a release from your engagements; wherefore the requisition taking it conjunctively with the remonstrance contained in it, as it shews the mind an opinion which you possess so presumptively it demonstrates the conduct you mean to hold, and therefore compels Congress to a greater caution and circumspection, being in fact a supplement to that letter of General Burgoyne which I mentioned before.

We come now to your letter of the nineteenth of September. One word more as to chronology. Your offer it seems is not only by express but *recent* authority, &c. If this epithet means any thing, we are to conclude that the authority was then just received. Indeed you take pains to induce that belief. But the extract you send us is dated the 12th of June, that is more than three months prior to your letter. Did you imagine the Congress had such implicit faith in your dictums, as to believe you had but just received that letter? The imposition is too glaring to pass on men of much less sagacity. What could have put it in your head that it is *unprecedented* to take no notice of demands by those who have no right to make them? The Lord Chief Justice of England is an officer at least as well known in the constitution of your kingdom as these newfangled Commissioners. Suppose the Earl of Mansfield had written a letter to Congress demanding the convention troops, do you think a neglect of this demand would have been quite *unprecedented?* And yet he had full as good right to make the demand as those Commissioners; else why the express and recent authority to you? You will not surely pretend that it was sent in consequence of the neglect you complain of, for there again chronology is against you.

But let us examine this express authority. I take it such authority can be derived but two ways respecting those to whom it relates: These are dependent on the points either of sovereignty or subjection.

First then as to the sovereignty. Conceding that America is an independent power, then clearly your authority ought to be expressed in a letter of credence to Congress, which it is not.

Secondly, as to the subjection. If, as you say we are subjects, then on general principles you are not bound to keep faith with rebels. But further, your laws have expressly determined this matter by a case in point, showing that capitulations and conventions with rebels are merely void, so that the least which could be expected is an act of Parliament. But

Thirdly, on the ground both of sovereignty and of subjection, leaving that great point *in dubio*, the authority should have been derived under the great seal and sign manual.

In lieu of all this you send an extract of a letter from a Secretary of State, which neither with foreign nations, nor even with your own subjects is worth a pinch of snuff; and thus you have thought proper to dubb with the sounding title of an express and recent authority from the King.

In order however to piece out the deficiencies of your ratification, you have insinuated a threat of certain consequences which are to follow from withholding a compliance with your demands. You are really a most diverting correspondent. What in the name of common sense can you mean by this and by your former menace of retaliation? Is it that if ever we are so weak as to make any agreement with you, you will break it? We always expected as much, we have told you so repeatedly, and this is one of the capital reasons why we reprobate all connection with you. Is it that you will to the utmost of your power lay waste our country? You have done this already, not excepting the territory of those poor creatures who had a confidence in your promises and an affection for your cause. Is it that you will burn our habitations? You made no small figure in that kind of business before the convention was made. Is it that you will murder prisoners in cold blood? Why even that practice, bad as it is, you are by no means unaccustomed to. This part of your letter reminds me of a speech which one of your excellent poets hath put in the mouth of a mad King. He too takes upon him to threaten those whom he cannot injure, and exclaims, "I will do such things! What they are yet I know not."[18]

To conclude, Sir Harry, though you are my enemy, I will express to you a wish, prompted by philanthropy; it is this, that the things you have done, and the things you have meditated to do, may not totally reduce you to the situation of that unhappy creature.

I am, with the greatest respect, Sir, your most obedient and humble servant,

An AMERICAN.

18. *King Lear,* act 2, scene 4.

5 ✥ Proposal to Congress Concerning the Management of the Government (1778)

Sometime after his return from visiting the Army at Valley Forge, Morris turned his attention to a systematic overhaul of Congress's way of doing business. The result is this document, which may have been prepared for delivery as a speech, although there is no record of it being delivered. A number of these proposals later were incorporated into other reports, including the report on the treasury department (chapter 6, below).

The proposal gives an insight into the wide range of issues Congress faced in mid-1778 as its attention turned to the reality of a long war. It also shows the extent to which Congress concerned itself with the minutiae of execution. Morris's proposals for creating a more effective executive establishment were, however, well ahead of his colleagues' thinking. Some reforms were made piecemeal, including the appointment of a superintendent of finance and establishment of a secretariat of foreign affairs. But it took nearly three years before those reforms were carried out.[1] It was not until 1781 that the Confederation began to conduct its business more efficiently. It would take almost a decade before most of the country would accept the need for the vigorous executive that Morris foreshadowed here.

Reprinted from *Letters of Delegates to Congress, 1774–1789*, ed. Paul H. Smith et al. (Washington, D.C.: Library of Congress, 1976–2000), 10:202–13. The manuscript is in the Gouverneur Morris Papers, Rare Book and Manuscript Library, Columbia University, item 805. Although the manuscript has been dated 1779 by archivists, the *Letters* editors date it to June–July 1778; Morris's biographers are unanimous in giving it a 1778 date. See Mintz, *American Revolution*, 130; Kline, *New Nation*, 109–15; Sparks, *Life*, 1:161.

1. Jack N. Rakove, *The Beginnings of National Politics: An Interpretive History of the Continental Congress* (New York: Alfred A. Knopf, 1979), 300.

To the Congress.

In the present Situation of our Affairs it must be evident to every Observer that America must be victorious if she can prosecute the War since it is impracticable for Great Britain to pursue it much longer. Now America can prosecute the War so long as she can keep an Army in the Field, but to keep an Army it is necessary to have Men to clothe, arm, Feed & pay them. To all these Purposes Money is the great Thing needful. A Paper Circulation may depreciate to such a Degree as no longer to answer the Purposes of Money. And this hath been the Case in a great Measure from the Want of Attention, Management and Method. To look thro the Causes of our Misfortunes may lead to the Cure. The Want of Men arises from sundry Sources. 1st. the short Enlistments at the Commencement of the War. 2ly. the Advance in the Price of Labor & Commodities. 3dly. the enormous Bounties given by several of the States. 4thly. the great Sums paid for Substitutes in the frequent Calls of the Militia. 5thly. from the Want of Discipline by which Means Soldiers not only desert in great Numbers but no Attention being paid to their Manner of Living by their Officers they loose their Cloaths become sickly & finally die or are rendered unfit for Service. 6thly. from the Want of Cloathing, Blankets and the like & lastly from the Defects of the Hospitals by which many die & the Sufferings of those who survive prevent ReEnlistments.

The Money also hath depreciated from several Causes as 1st. From the very Nature of it it was a Matter of very great Doubt among many whether it would not finally sink in the Hands of the Possessor hence the Aspect of our Affairs hath a manifest Influence upon its Credit. 2ly. From the many different Kinds of Paper Money Counterfeits became easy and therefore Men were less inclined to receive it. 3dly. The great Wages given to our Soldiery, The frequent Calls of Militia and after that every other Cause which hath caused great Emissions tends by the Quantity of the Money to lower it's Value. 4thly. The great Prices given for Commodities the natural Produce of the Country by the Servants of the Public from the Want of due Arrangement in the several Departments. 5thly. The Want of Oeconomy & Frauds in those Departments. 6thly. All those Laws which were framed to regulate Prices from that of Gold & Silver down to every other Article the necessary Consequence of which was to exclude such things or at least the greater Part of them from Commerce and therefore to raise the Price of the Remainder from the Scarcity, from the Plenty of Paper Money & from the Risque of breaking the Law. 7thly. From the Depreciation once begun arose a Depreciation consequent upon it distinct from other Causes since from thence the Possessors of Commodities would ask more than what would otherwise have been the Market Price foreseeing that tho' that Price might be the just Value at the Time of Sale it must soon become less, others also from this Depreciation would be led to engross and moneyed Men continually receiving their Debts in nominal Money of decreasing Value would be led to *realize* (or purchase any thing not perishable such as Land, Gold, Silver, Iron & the like) all which was taken out of the Circle of Commerce. 8thly. No Taxes having been laid and the Authority of the Governments in many Instances shaken it became doubtful with many whether even any Attempt would be made to redeem any Part of it and therefore, 9thly. When the Continent offerd to loan their own Money there being no visible Funds to pay the Interest Men were disinclined to trust them.

In order to restore the Value of Money it becomes necessary to lessen the Quantity & Kinds to provide Ways and Means to procure Funds for carrying on the War and to use Oeconomy in the Expenditures.

(1) To lessen the Quantity & Kinds of Money I would propose that every State should instantly by Law cry down their own Emissions and redeem them with Continental Loan Office Certificates and be duly charged by the Continent with the Interest of such Certificates.

(2) If Credit can be procured in Europe (of which more presently) to absorp a considerable Quantity of the Paper by selling Bills of Exchange.

(3) To gain a Credit to our Funds in Order to procure Loans and here

1st. The Payment of the Bills drawn for the Interest of the Debt will have a considerable Influence but it is necessary to extend that Influence into foreign Countries & gain Credit there, for which Purpose I propose

2ly. That the States should each pass an Act restricting their several Limits within a certain Line to be drawn for that Purpose and declaring that the Residue shall appertain to the Congress of the united States in Consequence of which Cession the States which really Part with Territory to receive a Compensation by the Abatement of some Part of their future Quota of the Continental Debt. From this Land I would set off a well sized State for our own Soldiers, for Deserters from the Enemy and for such Gratuities as Con-

gress or their public Ministers may chuse to make from a proper
Distribution of which Land the Men of great Influence in Europe
may be brought to favor our Cause. The Remainder should be divided into other large Districts by Natural Boundaries and be called
by separate Name which should denominate our Funds and supposing these names to be A, B & C any Man in Europe who put into
the Fund A should be entitled at any Time to so much Land in that
Country as could be purchased there at that Time for his Debt by
which Means we should be able to give Security for the Principal of
our Debt which no Nation in Europe can do.

3dly. It should be an Additional Article in the Confederation
that an Acknowledgement of 2½ per Cent should be paid on the
Value of all Commodities imported into America from any Port
not within one of the united States and that this Acknowledgement
and also every other Duty for the Regulation of Trade or otherwise
laid should be paid to the Continent as a sinking Fund for the Principle & Interest of Debts by them contracted during the War. This
Acknowlegement alone would produce from the American Commerce in 1772 £125.000 Stg. equal to 1,250,000 Dollars of our present
Money at least and if we add 250,000 for what would arise from
other necessary Duties over and above the Cost of collecting the
Whole this would make 1,500,000 Dollars which would be the Interest of a Debt of 25,000,000 Dollars at six per Cent. The Post Office
also properly regulated would in Time produce a very considerable
Remedy without Burthening the Community it being rightly observed that this is the most agreable Tax ever invented. But as these
would yield little or nothing at present I would propose

4thly. that a Capitation Tax of one Dollar upon every Inhabitant
be paid as a sinking Fund at present and that this be faithfully and
honestly applied notwithstanding any Exigency to pay the interest &
Part of the Principle or where the Interest is payable in Europe there
the Principle of the public Debts at the same time taking Care that
the Debt of highest Interest be paid first.

(4) In Order to raise the Value of the Money which is always a saving
to the public it will be proper.

1st. To take off all Restrictions upon the Sale of every Commodity
Gold and Silver not excepted.

2dly. As soon as a State of the public Debts can be made out after adopting the other Plans proposed to publish such State and thereby undeceive the Public who think it much greater than it really is.

3dly. To devise a proper Mode of calling all those to Account who have received any public Monies and provide Checks in the further Issues of which more hereafter.

(5) In providing Money for the public Exigencies I would observe that from January to January Congress should Vote a particular Sum, for Instance 20,000,000 Dollars of which 10,000,000 should be raised by the several States by Tax and the Remainder on Loan in America and as at present 27 Livres Tournois are equal to 15 Dollars supposing Exchange to fall so low as that a Dollar shall be worth two Livres then a Credit of 20,000,000 Livres Tournois will enable us to buy up a Sum of Paper Money equal to the whole Tax by which Means the Cash will be in the public Coffers in Advance and the Credit of the Money at Home just as high as we chuse to make it for by this Means the public will not be indebted to its own Subjects one Shilling more after borrowing 10,000,000 Dollars than before, and the circulating Medium will be 10,000,000 less and as the foreign Debt is to be paid in Produce whenever the Money is made valuable the Produce will become cheap & the Debt consequently small, for Instance, 5 Livres as above will purchase 2½ Dollars which in the State of New York will purchase one Bushel of Wheat but the Money being made valuable as above the Wheat may be bought for one such Dollar, that is for the same Money two Bushels and an half of Wheat may be purchased which in France will sell for twenty Livres Wherefore 5 Livres borrowed and invested in Paper now will pay twenty Livres hereafter or in other Words the Debt is lessened ¾ tho By pursuing the above Plan with Judgment it will be very easy to regulate the Value of our Money which ought not be very high for the following Reasons. 1st. The Pay of our Soldiery is now fixed at 6½ Dollars per Mo. which at par Exchange is 1/Stg. per Day but at present about 4d½ or less If Exchange be lowered to 2½ Livres for 1 Dollar in Paper the Pay of the Soldiery will be 6d per Day. 2dly. The Money being below Par thus much, that is 2½ instead of 5, We shall by paying our Interest in France give in Effect 12 per Cent which will finally bring all our Money into our own Coffers so as that our Subjects will eventually

be our Chief Creditors the Good Reasons for which in sinking the Debt are obvious. 3dly. It will enable us to regulate our Contracts for Supplies to the Army as we please of which more hereafter. Many other Reasons will shew themselves in the Course of time.

These Means being pursued to get Money and render it valuable the next Consideration is to be cautious in the Expenditures without which it is impossible to provide Funds even could we mortgage the Mines of Potosi.

(1) The Treasurey Board, the Navy Board, and the Commercial Board, I am unacquainted with but I must confess that I wish to see all this Business executed by Commission[er]s.

1. The Treasury Board should consist of three Parts, the Treasurer, Auditor & Comptroller. The Auditor should be a Gentleman of Great Industry, Accuracy & Integrity & have in his Office at least six Gentlemen each of them a good Accomptant & faithful which six should form two Chambers, one of Dues the other of Claims. The former should adjust all Accompts brought into the Treasury for Payment, the other All Accompts unsettled where it is supposed that the Public Money lies in the Hands of Individuals. These Accompts being Adjusted should be laid before the Auditor (who should be impowered by the several States to call Persons to accompt by particular Process) and he should examine them & mark them thus Audited for the Sum of   this   Day of   177   , and sign it, He and the several Chambers under him always taking Care that exhorbitant Prices are not allowed if charged. Copies of these Accounts should be kept in his Office marked filed & Entries made in his Books of the Sums audited and on what Accounts and make Monthly Returns of such Entries made to Congress, then the Accounts with the Vouchers referred to should be handed over to the Comptroller whose Business it should be to examine them anew and see from whom and to whom the Sums audited are payable & pass the same and make proper Minutes thereof in his Books and draw Bills on the Treasurer comformable to the Manner in which such Accompts are passed (to which the treasury Seal is to be put) and make monthly Returns to Congress of the Accompts by him passed. The treasurer is simply to receive and pay Money taking Care that he pay it only to those duly authorized to receive it, to keep the Check Accompt of the Loan Office & the like and ought also to render monthly Accompts to Congress.

The Navy Board or Board of Admiralty ought as I conceive to be submitted to five Intelligent Sea Officers well acquainted with maritime Affairs and otherwise qualified as Men of Business. Untill our naval Affairs are a little more reduced to System it must require Great Knowlege in Sea Affairs upon a large Scale to qualify a Man for a Seat at that Board. Nor shall we find for many Years Persons duly qualified to act in it from having made such things the Object of their Attention as a Branch of political Science. These Persons should from Time to Time make Report as should the Board of War, the treasury Board & the like to an Executive of which more hereafter.

The Commercial Board should consist of the five most intelligent Merchants to be met with. At present it will be their Duty to attend simply to the Commercial Concerns of the Continent but such a Board ought to exist for the Purpose of continually collecting, comparing & examining the Commerce of the Several States, the Course of Exchange &ca &ca by the Help of which they would be enabled to give Information from Time to Time what Laws, Treaties & Regulations would be proper and beneficial, what Number of Seamen could be had in Emergencies & the like.

The Board of War being at present in Commission I shall say Nothing upon that Chapter only that Men of Experience, of Business & acquainted with the Resources of America should be always upon that Board which for many Years Yet to come will have infinite Concerns to attend to. For whether we have Peace or not I state it as certain that we must have some Soldiers & many Magazines of Artillery, Field Equipage, Ammunition & military Stores &ca.

I will here take an Opportunity to observe upon what must strike the Observation of every Gentleman acquainted with our public Affairs. It is that a Body such as the Congress is inadequate to the Purposes of Execution. They want that Celerity & Decission upon which depend the Fate of Great Affairs. Other Reasons not less cogent might be adduced Wherefore it might be proper especially during the War to have either a Committee of three or a single officer such as Chief of the States Who should superintend the Executive Business, receive the Reports of the several Boards of the Secretary for foreign Affairs and the like and prepare the whole in the Form of Memorials for the House where there Authority is necessary & where it is not there to perform the necessary Acts.

(2) The Next Thing which demands a most serious Attention is to involve all the military Affairs of the Continent into one Department which would prevent a Variety of Abuses by which the public is injured in many Respects but particularly by the Destruction of Vast Sums of Money. Thus there are at present a Commissary's Depart-

ment, a Quarter Masters Department & an Hospital Department
to the Northward and no army besides the several Departments
clash in Purchases double, treble or quadruple the Number of Persons are employed in procuring the same Articles and the like not
to mention the absolute sinecures &ca but the Detail is infinite.

(3) As to the several Staff Departments of the Army viz the Quarter
Master's, Commissaries & Hospital in their order.

1. The Quarter Masters Department is open to such an Endless Train of
Frauds from the very Nature of the thing that it is impossible to devise any
adequate Checks. A thing which hath never as I can learn been done by any
Army. The only Way to keep it within any Bounds is by examining the Accounts frequently, the Vouchers accurately, taking Care that the Purchases
and Expenditures agree & that Losses, Casualties & the like be properly
ascertained, after all the Head of the Department is most to be depended
on if he is vigilant, industrious & honest he may do much towards preventing Frauds. Further a constant Return should be required of his Deputies,
their Pay & Appointments &ca. where they are &ca. This Detail should be
monthly. I would observe particularly that the Article of Forage alone is
ruinous without accurate Managemt. Wherefore there should always be in
the Army a Forage Yard and Rations of Forage delivd. with Accuracy as also
at the several Magazines and Receipts taken without which the Expenditures should not be allowed. At present any of the Depy. Qur. Mrs. may purchase on the Contl. Acct. & sell on his own Acct. without being detected.

2. The Commissaries Department upon which but too much is to be
said. Generally I will venture to affirm that every Step is capitally defective.
Let me be indulged in a small Detail. *A* who is a Commissary of Purchases
buys 100 Cattle whose Average Weight is in Beef 400, Hide & Tallow 100,
in the whole 50,000 wt. for these he gives Certificates at 25 per Ct. Advance
upon the Market Price supposing that to be 1/ then his Certificates are at
the Rate of ⅓, and to color it the Cattle estimated and marked accordingly
to weigh on an Average 600. 50,000 wt. @ 1/ is £2,500 to which add ¼ or
£625, the Price Charged is £3,125, the Difference he pockets by purchasing
the Certificates at a Discount by the Intervention of a third Person. These
Cattle are driven at the Public Expense during all Seasons favorable or
unfavorable to the Camp. When they get there they consume Forage for
which the Army is always in great Distress, grow lean, some of them die,
some when killed returned unfit for Use, some sent out of Camp into the
Country to be fattened, of the Beef, some putrifies almost all the Tallow is

lost, a great Part of the Hides lost, many of them much damaged, the Heads are thrown away, the Entrails & Filth serve to generate putrid Diseases, the Horns are lost, the Feet from which Oil to curry all the Hides might be extracted are also thrown into the general Mass of Corruption, finally the Beef itself in the Hot Weather renders the troops liable to Diseases of a bilious Kind. I say Nothing of the purchases of Spirits, of Vinegar, of Bread, of Pease &ca. &ca.

The Remedy I would here propose is 1st. To contract within particular Districts of Country with Individuals for the Cattle of that District as thus to be delivered at some Place on the Banks of the Rivers Susquehannah, Delaware or Hudsons (where it is to be presumed the Enemy could not penetrate) at a certain Time from so many thousand to so many thousand Wt. of Beef, the Beef to be weighed as thus, the four Quarters, the Hide & the rough Tallow at so much per Pound. At these Places should be the public works necessary and Magazines of Salt, Nitre, Allum, Pot or Pearl Ashes, Barrills &ca. &ca. The Cattle should be here killed the Beef cut into Mess Pieces of 4lb. each and 50 Pieces put in a Barrill with a proper Proportion of Salt, Nitre (or Pot Ashes) & Allum to preserve it. The Hides taken proper Care of. The Tallow made into Candles & Soap. The oil extracted from the Feet. The Tripe taken Care of and the Heads made into portable Soap. It is worthy of Observation that those who contract with the Crown in Ireland clear nothing but the Horns & Hoofs by their Bargain. It may be said that the Transportation of Provisions would be by this Means rendered too expensive to which I answer that the Transportation should be by Water as much as possible and if there be 40 Miles Land Carriage for the Provision of 20,000 Men it will require daily twenty good Teams being eighty Horses whereas the same Men would require 40 large Oxen per Day and with 5 Days Provision before Hand there would be a constant Demand of Forage for 400 large Cattle instead of eighty Horses.

As to Purchases of Flour they may I am confident be better made by Contract than at present as may the Baking Business for which the Contract should be that the Quarter Master provide ovens & Fuel and that the Contractor deliver so many Pounds of Bread as he shall receive of Flour.

Spirits & Whiskey ought by a Resolution to be Fixed at a certain Standard in the Delivery to Soldiers for otherwise great Frauds may happen of which more hereafter.

Vinegar which I will venture to say is absolutely necessary to an Army should be procured by Contract in very large Quantities at different Places by which Transportation would be saved and the Article itself if not used one Year be infinitely better the next. So much for the Purchases but in the Issues a still more terrible Scene opens upon us, to trace which let us suppose a Regt. to consist of 500 Rations daily & take the year @ 350 Days, & examine the Perquisites, private & public Frauds.

1st. Perquisites.

500 Rat. Salt Prov. 50 Days is 130 Blls. in each of which is ¼ of a Bushel of coarse Salt @ 40 Dlls per B. 1300   Dlls.

20 Rat. daily on an Average to the Sick in the whole 10,000 @ ⅕ of a Dollar 2000

Perquisites.   3300

Private Frauds.

500 Gills of Rum or Whisky for abt. 250 Days, 125,000 from which deduct ⅓ (sometimes more) and add Water leaves 40,000 say 32,000 or 1000 Galls @ 4d per Gall is 4,000

For Rat. not delivered, scant Weight & Measure &ca &ca say 20 Rat. for 350 Days, 9000 @ ⅕ 1,400

Private Frauds.   5,400

Public Frauds.

500 Rat. fresh Beef @ 1¼ for 300 Days & usual Allowances for Wastage is abt. 200,000 from which the Real Weight killed viz 240,000 deduct ⅙ for false Returns of Wt. by issuing Comy. of Brig. is 40,000 @ ⅛ 5,000

Absent on Detachments, With Leave, Deserters &ca. always some wherefore suppose the whole Regt. abt. 10 Days in the Year during which time they draw Provisions elsewhere is 5000 @ ⅕ 1,000

For setling back Rations they give (due Bills) wherefore the whole Quantum being issued & due Bills given to such as do not draw the whole say 20 Daily for 250 Days. 5,000 @ ⅕ 1,000

Public Frauds.   7,000

The Account then stands thus

Perquisites	3,300
Priv. Frauds	5,400
Public do.	7,000
	15,700.

15,700.   Peculation on 500 daily, or 157 on 5

Suppose 100,000 Rat. daily issued is three Million Dollars. If to this be added the Frauds in purchasing, Losses from Mismanagemt. &ca. which may be fairly stated at two Millions more this will be five Millions, or 50 Dollars on each Ration supposing them worth ⅓ each to the Public then for a Year it is 120. Now if as the Case is at least 3 Rat. be delivered out on the Continent for every soldier actually in Service then each Soldier must be estimated at 360 Dollars per Annum to feed him from which is peculated & wasted in different Ways to the Amount of 150 Dollars, on the whole it will appear that at least 5 times as much is paid as is necessary. But to remedy this.

1. I observe that for this Purpose as well as many others, it is absolutely necessary to procure Muster Masters and Adjutant Generals well acquainted with their Business and possessing Industry and strict Integrity. These Officers are the great Checks of an Army particularly the former who should at every Muster make Return to the Genl. & to the Board of War noting in the same all Differences between the Musters and the Returns.

2. The Officers of every Rank except Genl Officers should be confined to the drawing of but one Ration which if not drawn should not be paid for and a Subsistence Money equal to their present Rations should be allowed in Lieu of what they are now entitled to Under this Head also we may comprehend another Abuse & the Remedy. No Officer should be allowed to keep a Soldier as his Servant but should be allowed the Sum of 8 Dollars per Mo. to pay & subsist his own Servant.

3. No Ration should be allowed to the sick but the same ought to be specifically drawn for by the Surgeon who in his sick Return should also return the Provisions drawn for to the End that the Orders if improper may be corrected by his Superiors and such Orders should be copied by the Clerk of the flying Hospital weekly & transmitted to the Commissary General. From this Regulation also the frequent Absence of Surgeons from their Regts. would be prevented a thing much to be lamented at present.

4. No Rations should be drawn unless for those present fit for Duty and where officers on Command & Detachments not joined &ca. draw Provisions either of Commys. or Inhabitants, they should be charged with the same and obliged to pay therefor unless within a Month Copies of their Receipts are by them filed with the Commissary Genl. or his Deputy or Agent, this being the only Means of checking the Waste occasioned by Detachments.

5. The present Pernicious Practice of serving out Rations to Artificers in Places where they can find Subsistence should be stopped since among

many other Evils which arise from it the Infinity of Commissaries is by no Means the least.

6. The Quarter Masters in drawing Provisions should be obliged to make duplicate Returns of their respective Regts. & of the No. of Rations drawn and duplicate Receipts of the specific Articles & one Copy of each should be filed with the Adjutant Genl. who should weekly annex to the same a Copy of the Weekly Return of such respective Regt. & send the same to the Comy. Genl. who should be allowed proper Clerks of the Check to examine and check the same.

7. When any Spirits shall be delivered out below the Standard the Qur. Master should be obliged to make up in Quantity the Defect of Quality.

3dly. of the Hospital Department I will venture to affirm generally that it is replete with Abuses of the greatest Consequence.

1st. in the very great Number of Persons employd in it which partly arises from the Number of Departments into which it is divided.

2ly. In the Ignorance of many of its Members owing to the Promotion of improper Persons to higher office originally than they had Right to expect &

3ly. In the Want of Method and Arrangement throughout or rather in the pernicious Systems adapted.

As this Business is not that to which I am most adequate, so on the other Hand I will venture to say that from Inquiry & Attention I have put myself in a Situation not to be quite ignorant of it. By the last Returns prior to which a great Number were discharged it appears there were in Pay of the Cont. 1 Director Genl., 3 Deputy Directors Gen., 2 Assistant Deputy Directors Genl., 3 Phisicians Genl., 3 Surgeons General, 3 Phisicians & Surgeons Genl., 3 Apothecaries General, 30 senior Surgeons, 36 junior Surgeons, 56 Surgeons Mates and seven Apothecaries Mates over and above all the Regimental Surgeons & Mates & over and above what may be in the Southern Departt. Here it is worthy of Remark that from 1st Jany. to the 1st May all the Sick of our Army were Attended by 1 Senr. & 2 Junr. Surgeons as also 3000 Patients innoculated. To remedy the Evils in this Business, I would propose to institute a Medical Board to consist of a chief Director Genl., Inspector Genl. & chief Phisician & Surgeon. These three should examine all medical Men Candidates for Office & give Certificates according to their talents. Moreover the Chief Director should mark out the several Places for erecting Hospitals, who should attend at them and the like.

The Inspector Genl. should visit & examine the Hospitals from Time to Time & the Conduct of those whose Business it might be to take Care of them & the like, and the Chief Phisician & Surgeon should receive regular transcripts of the Diseases & Wounds with the Prescriptions & Operations & examine the same. Under these Gentlemen should be one Purveyor and three Assistants, one Commissary & such Deputies as Occasion might require, 4 Surgeons & Phisicians, 8 Senior Surgeons, 16 junior Surgeons & 32 Mates, 1 Apothecary, 2 Assistants & as many Mates as Circumstances might require. These with occasional Detachments from the Regtl. Surgeons in Times of great Sickness would be amply sufficient for an Army of fifty thousand Men if one-fifth were constantly in Hospital besides Accidents. By this also Men of Science might be got into the Service, a thing which would save the Lives of many brave Soldiers.

4. The Cloathier Genls Department will require considerable Attention but for this Purpose it will be proper to appoint a special Committee to examine into this Matter & report some Method of putting Cloathing into the Hands of the Regt. Paymasters with the Prices to be charged the troops.

Finally as to every Department.

It should be an unalterable Decree that whenever any Person in the public Service either in the Quarter Masters, Commissaries or Medical Departments shall be guilty of trading or of following any other private occupation such Person should be discharged & forfeit all the Pay & Appointments of his Office.

And to all this let it be added that exact Discipline in an Army is essential to Oeconomy & without it no possible Arrangments can be effectual.

G.M.

6 ❧ Report of the Committee on the Treasury (1778)

Creating an effective public administration from the materials available to Congress in 1778 was a formidable problem, as the previous document suggests. Not only was there no executive to speak of, but there were no systematic procedures for doing simple things like paying for supplies. Congress was paying bills and considering other issues as they were presented, and thus was always at the mercy of events. Morris's proposal for organizing the Treasury would be a small step toward regularity. It exhibits both his attention to the details of administration and the degree to which Congress's procedures were unsystematic, even at this late date.

The Committee to whom was referred the Report from the Treasury of the fifteenth of April last beg leave to report:[1]

That it appears necessary to organize the several Treasury Departments immediately, for the following Reasons:

1st. Because the Adjustment of the Finances of the United States, now much deranged, cannot be made without arranging that Office, which will in all Instances more or less affect them.

2dly. Because until this be done, it will be impracticable to call the several States to account, and even Individuals, much less to have those frequent Accounts, which can alone check Fraud and regulate the Expences of a Community.

3dly. Because the Attention which Congress are under the Necessity of paying to the particular Disbursements of the public Money, together with the Variety of other Business, which as well as this ought to be transacted

Reprinted from *Journals of the Continental Congress, 1774–1789*, ed. Worthington C. Ford et al. (Washington, D.C.: U.S. Government Printing Office, 1904–37), 11:779–84. The manuscript, not in Morris's hand, is in the Gouverneur Morris Papers, Rare Book and Manuscript Library, Columbia University, item 1324.

1. For the prior deliberations on this subject, see *JCC* 10:351, note 1. Morris's committee was appointed July 30, 1778, and delivered this report August 13.

elsewhere, prevent them from applying to the greater Affairs of the Continent. And,

4thly. Because the Arrangement of every Department should have an ultimate Reference to the Manner of doing Business at the Treasury, and therefore until that be fixed, the other cannot be adjusted.

That it appears to your Committee the following Particulars should be attended to in the Business referred to them:

1st. That no more Persons should be appointed than are necessary: Since Numbers increase the Expence, delay Business, and give greater Room for Corruption and for the Concealment of Frauds, Indolence or Inattention.

2dly. That there be proper Checks devised to prevent as much as possible those who are intrusted with the public Monies from converting it to their own Use. And those who are to examine the public Accounts from Collusion with the Creditors of the public, or with its Debtors.

3dly. That Congress may be enabled to see with Precision the Manner of Expenditures, and the Amount. And know the state of the public Debts, and the Produce of the public Revenue.

Under these Ideas your Committee submit to the Consideration of Congress the following Arrangement, viz:

That for conducting the Affairs of the Treasury there be three [principal]² Officers, a Comptroller, a Treasurer, and an Auditor; That each of them be allowed the sum of   Dollars per Annum, and the sum of   Dollars per Annum for the Expence of an Office and Clerk.

That it shall be the Duty of the Comptroller to keep the Seal of the Treasury. That he shall receive the Accounts transmitted to him by the Auditor with the Vouchers, which he shall examine, and thereon shall determine to whom the several Sums audited are payable, and whether the same are payable by the United States; in which case he shall draw a Bill on the Treasurer in the following form annexed, and marked A.,³ to which he shall affix the Treasury Seal: and if the same are not payable by the United States, then he shall redeliver the Vouchers thereof to the Auditor and mark them "not passed." That he shall keep regular Books containing the Accounts by him passed, in which Books a separate Account shall be opened between the United States and each Individual or State, and shall transmit monthly Accounts to Congress of the Monies by him drawn for and in whose favor.

2. Inserted by [Henry] Laurens. [*JCC* note.]
3. The forms are omitted here. See *JCC* 11:784–86.

That he shall affix the Treasury Seal to all Loan Office Certificates, and shall deliver them to the Treasurer, whose Receipt for the same he shall file; and shall transmit monthly Accounts thereof to Congress specifying therein the Dates and Amount of such Certificates. That he shall receive from the Treasurer Receipts for the Monies by him received and shall thereon give a Discharge in the Form annexed and marked B., which he shall sign and affix thereto the Treasury Seal, and transmit the same to the Auditor to be indorsed, rendering a monthly Account as aforesaid. That he shall receive of the several Loan Officers monthly the Certificates which shall not have been by them employed, and shall give thereof a Receipt in the Form annexed and marked C., which he shall sign and transmit to the Auditor, to be indorsed, rendering monthly Account as aforesaid. That where a Resolution of Congress shall direct the Payment or Application of Monies he shall from Time to Time draw Bills on the Treasurer agreeable to such Resolutions in the Form annexed and marked D., which he shall sign and thereto affix the Treasury Seal, and transmit the same to the Auditor to be indorsed, rendering monthly Accounts thereof as aforesaid. That he shall keep a Book for the Entry and Record of Loans made to the United States by Persons who shall choose to put Money in [a Fund to be called the Confederal][4] Fund; and, upon receiving the Treasurer's Receipt therefor, shall make Entry thereof in the Form annexed and marked E.; a copy of which Entry under the Seal of the Treasury shall be given to the Party, and when he shall receive a Power of Attorney from the Person in whose Name the Entry is made, in the Form annexed and marked F., duly authenticated by a Writing in the Form annexed and marked G., which Authentication shall be under the Hand and Seal of such public Ministers or Officers as Congress shall from Time to Time direct, he shall file such Power of Attorney and authentication. And whensoever and as often as the Attorney therein named shall by Indorsement in the Form annexed and marked H., transfer all or any part of the Stock of his Principal, he shall make an Entry thereof in the Form annexed and marked I., opposite to the Entry above mentioned and marked E.; and also an Entry in the Form annexed and marked K. And he shall make regular Entries of the Interest arising on such sums as aforesaid on the Debit Side of the said Accounts or Entries, and whenever and as often as any Interest shall be paid thereon, he shall make Entry on the Credit Side of the same Accounts; of all which

4. Inserted by Laurens. [*JCC* note.]

Sums so lent and being due, together with the Interest payable and paid, he shall monthly render an Account to Congress.

That where an Account shall be transmitted to him from the Auditor on which Monies shall be due to the United States, he shall hear the Party, if he chuse to be heard thereon, and shall then fix the Day of Payment and shall thereof notify the Auditor and Treasurer in the Form annexed and marked R.

That it shall be the Duty of the Treasurer to keep the Monies and Loan Office Certificates of the United States. That he shall issue the Monies upon Bills for that Purpose to be drawn by the Comptroller under the Treasury Seal, and shall file Duplicates of the Receipts for such Monies with the Auditor, and render Accounts thereof to Congress monthly. That upon Receipt of Monies paid into the Treasury, he shall give his Receipt therefor in the Form annexed and marked L., of which he shall also render Accounts monthly to Congress. That he shall monthly issue Loan Office Certificates to the several Loan Officers, and take Receipts for the same in the Form annexed and marked M., to which shall be annexed Schedules containing Lists of the Certificates issued, and which Receipts he shall transmit to the Auditor to be by him entered and indorsed, and shall transmit Accounts thereof to Congress monthly. That he shall also receive such Monies as shall be put into the [Confederal][5] Loan aforesaid, and give a Receipt in the Form annexed and marked N., of which he shall also render monthly Accounts to Congress.

That it shall be the Duty of the Auditor to audit all Accounts brought against the United States, and also to call all Persons to account who may be indebted to the said States; that for these Purposes there be two chambers of Accounts, the one to be called the Chamber of Claims, and the other the Chamber of Debts, each to be composed of three Persons, who shall each of them have a Salary of   Dollars per Annum.

That the Chamber of Claims shall digest and state all Accounts brought against the United States, examine the Vouchers, &c., as the Auditor shall direct and shall take Care that Articles furnished and Services done be not overrated, or if so, then to reduce them, after which they shall transmit the same to the Auditor with the Vouchers, marking the said Accounts *examined*. Thereupon the Auditor shall again examine the Accounts and compare them with the Vouchers and reduce any Demands which may be ex-

5. Inserted by Laurens. [*JCC* note.]

orbitant, and having caused them to be entered in his Books, mark them in the Form annexed and marked O., and transmit them [with the Vouchers]⁶ to the Comptroller. That the Chamber of Debts shall digest and state all Accounts of Persons who are, or are supposed to be indebted to the United States, and also all those who may be called to Account in Manner hereafter mentioned; that they shall conduct their Business in like Manner as the Chamber of Claims, and the Auditor shall in like Manner as before examine and enter the Accounts; and where Monies are due to the United States shall mark the Accounts in the Form annexed and marked P., and transmit the same to the Comptroller to be filed, and render monthly Accounts to Congress. That when an Account shall be returned to the Auditor of Articles not passed, he do deliver the same with the Vouchers to the Party, and make Entry thereof and render Account as aforesaid. And where Discharges shall be transmitted to him of Persons who have paid Money into the Treasury, he shall enter the same in his Books and endorse them thus "Entered of Record in my Office, the   Day of   177   . T. U. Auditor." And where Receipts of Loan Office Certificates shall be transmitted to him, he shall enter the same in his Books, and indorse them thus "Entered to the Credit of A. B., Loan Officer within mentioned, the   Day of 177   in my Office. T. U. Auditor." And where the Comptroller shall transmit to him Drafts on the Treasurer according to Resolutions of Congress, he shall enter them in his Books and indorse them thus: "Entered to the Debit of   in my office. T. U. Auditor." That where any Person hath received public Monies which remain unaccounted for, or shall be otherwise indebted to the United States, or have an unsettled Account with them he shall issue a Summons in the Form annexed and marked S., in which a reasonable Time shall be given for the Appearance of the Party according to the Distance of his Place of Residence from the Treasury; and in case he shall not appear, then on Proof of the Service in due Time, or of other sufficient Notice of the Summons, a Requisition shall issue under the Treasury Seal, but shall be made out in the Auditor's Office in the Form annexed and marked T., which shall be directed to the executive Power of the State or States, in which the Party shall reside or be.

That it be recommended to the several States to enact Laws for the taking of such Persons, and also to seize the Property of Persons, who being indebted to the United States shall neglect or refuse to pay the same. Notice

6. Inserted by Laurens. [*JCC* note.]

whereof shall be given by the Auditor to the Executive Authority of the respective States in the Form annexed and marked V., the which Notice shall be under the Treasury Seal.

That the several Officers of the Treasury above mentioned do, before they take upon them their said Offices, take an oath faithfully and honestly to execute the same.

That the Loan Office Certificates be dated on the tenth Day of every Month respectively, and that Monies be received in the Loan Offices until the twentieth day of every Month and no longer.

That on the three last Days of every Month the Auditor and Treasurer and the Comptrollers do no other Business than to prepare their monthly Accounts for Congress.

That a Committee be appointed to prepare proper Books and other Blanks for the Use of the Treasury.

7 ❀ Some Thoughts on the Finances of America (1778)

After his report on reorganizing the Treasury in August 1778, Morris turned his attention to the daunting problems of public finance. Congress and the states had resorted to currency finance in order to carry on their operations, and by 1778 the paper was depreciating rapidly. Congress grappled with the problem throughout the fall of 1778 and winter of 1779. On September 19, 1778, the committee on finance delivered a report, authored by Morris, for bringing the government's finances into better order.[1] The proposals, which included levying taxes for Congress's use, were controversial and for the most part shelved.[2]

This paper was probably prepared in the course of that effort. Morris's memorandum at the end sounds a rare note of frustration: "prepared for Congress but not compleated because . . . many had adopted a system they were determined to persevere in." One of his suggestions, however, was acted on fairly promptly. Congress decided to "lay the state of our Finances" open to France and Spain. The result was the "Observations on the Finances of America," which Morris drafted along with the diplomatic instructions for Franklin. Congress adopted both the instructions and the "Observations" in late October 1778 and forwarded them to Franklin.[3]

Gouverneur Morris Papers, Rare Book and Manuscript Library, Columbia University, item 818. Sparks dates the manuscript as "'79 or '80," though I think 1778 is more probable.

1. *Journals of the Continental Congress, 1774–1789*, Worthington C. Ford et al., eds. (Washington, D.C.: U.S. Government Printing Office, 1904–37), 12:928–33.

2. Kline, *New Nation*, 118–21.

3. *JCC* 12:1048–52. The "Observations" may be found in the *Papers of Benjamin Franklin*, ed. Claude A. Lopez et al. (New Haven: Yale University Press, 1988), 27:642–46. The Franklin papers also have the diplomatic instructions and an account of the controversy over their adoption (27:633–42).

The Question of Finance naturally resolves itself in common Cases into two others, viz. the Manner of getting Money and the Manner of spending it. Either of these in the oldest and best organized States is considered as an Object of the greatest Magnitude which can be submitted to the Consideration of the most instructed and most comprehensive Mind. The Congress must consider both. They labor on this Occasion under some particular Disadvantages. The Country is new. It's Resources are of Consequence not very accurately known and improper Culture may blast the Germ of future Wealth. The Governments being distinct the Machine is proportionately complex and consequently every Effort will be slow and every System liable to great Derangement. The administration of the States having by no Means attained to vigor and Regularity the public Wealth cannot be brought to a Point with Vivacity and Effect. However great may be the Talents of Gentlemen Attention hath been of Necessity wanting to many and the Opportunities of Instruction to all. Besides these there is one capital Object which never occurred fully before & which of Consequence cannot be examined by the Light of Experience. In speaking therefore of our Paper Money we must reason by analogy and consequently without Certitude. From all this however results one striking Maxim. That we must proceed with Caution.

To the many Obstacles which lie in our Way We have to oppose Freedom. The Power of this is great but Knowlege is necessary to direct it's Activity and it's Force. Whoever then turns his Attention to the Great Object of Finance tho his Intelligence may be defective is still entitled to Forgiveness for efforts which are well meant.

Disquisitions of this Kind have Nothing wherewith to tickle the Ear and charm the Imagination. They must consist of Reasonings from common Place Observations and dry arguments founded sometimes on Facts and what is still worse sometimes on Hypothesis. These cannot be adorned by a series of Calculations. But we live to serve others not to please ourselves.

We must then in the first Place seriously attend to the Nature and to the Effects of our Paper Money. Secondly to our Situation and consequent Wants. Thirdly to the proper Means of Getting Money and Lastly to the necessary Precautions in expending it. Above all Things, we must divest ourselves of Prejudices from whatever Source they may arise. We must deliberate with Calmness. We must act with Decission. We must persevere.

In considering our Paper, we must observe that Money as such derives it's

Value from a general Consent that to facilitate the Commerce of Mankind it shall represent all commercial Property. Gold and Silver are the only universal Money because they alone have this general Consent. Paper then is the Representative of Gold and Silver, and derives it's Value from a Consent founded on the former. This Consent arises from a Confidence that at a certain Time and Place the Quantity of Specie mentioned in it will be actually paid. From these Circumstances it follows that when that Confidence is lost the Consent ceases and consequently the Paper becomes of no Value.

Bills of Exchange were the first Paper Money and are precisely in that Situation. The South Sea Paper in England and the Mississipi in France verify the Observation. So do Bankers Notes or Bills and it may safely be affirmed that if any Bank in Europe either public or private should stop Payment for half an Hour it's Bills would no longer be what they now are a circulating Medium of Trade. This Kind of Paper then is of Consequence either precisely what it purports to be or it is Nothing.

The Advantages of it arise from its greater Portability and the Impracticability of diminishing it in Substance or Alloy. The Disadvantages from the Danger of being counterfeited. Paper Bills therefore of large Amount not liable to be counterfeited ought among an enlightened & commercial People to have the Preference over Specie. And this is precisely the Case.

If a Legislature to prevent the Consequence above stated should utter a Paper Medium payable at a distant Day it would or would not be received according to the Want of such Medium among the People. And when received it's Value would depend on the Consideration $1^{st.}$ of the Want $2^{ly.}$ of the Distance of the Day of Payment & $3^{ly.}$ of the Certainty or Uncertainty of such Payment.

If no Day of Payment be assigned then another Consideration will be the Ability of the State and the Integrity of it's Rulers both of which will influence the Currency and the Value of their Paper. If by Increase of the Quantity or from other Causes either the Ability of the State or the Honesty of the Government should be brought into Question one of two Consequences would certainly follow. Either that the Paper would not circulate at all or that it would circulate with great Rapidity. But if a general Belief should prevail that the Government would not redeem it, the Circulation must cease. If on the contrary, a general Confidence prevailed in the Government, and Doubts as to the Wealth of the State then as the probable Day of Payment would be necessarily postponed it would from this Circumstance become of less immediate Value and from the Decrease of that Value it would obtain a most rapid Circulation, each Individual apprehending that the Loss might happen in his Hands.

If the Legislature were by Law to declare such Paper a Tender in Extinction of Debts this would so far check the Rapidity of Circulation as the Debtor would find it to be in his Hands Money against his Creditor to all Intents and Purposes and of Consequence every new Contract would make a new Fixture of the Valuation. Whenever the Quantity of such Money became too great for the Purposes of Commerce, it would necessarily loose of it's Value but the Proportion of Loss would depend on an incidental Circumstance.

If on the Face of the Bill the Value should be estimated at a certain ideal Sum such as Pounds Shillings and Pence the decreasing Value would be less perceptible than if a certain specific Coin should be stated such as Guineas Dollars and the like. But in Proportion as the Loss became perceptible would that Loss increase because the Confidence necessary for Support of the Paper would be so far withdrawn. It would not however loose it's Value entirely except in two Cases. One is a Certainty that the State could no longer exist as such, the other a Certainty that should it exist the Government will never redeem their Emissions.

If neither of these Cases be supposed then the Value would depend $1^{st.}$ upon the Quantity and the probable Quantity considered relatively to commercial Property $2^{ly.}$ upon the Certainty or Uncertainty of it's Genuineness $4^{thly.}$ upon the Property and probable Property of the State and $5^{ly.}$ upon the supposed Ability of the Government to command it.

The Question supposes a free State, because the Case would not exist under an arbitrary Government for the plain Reason that such great Confidence never was and cannot possibly be placed in a Prince or his Ministers. This Assertion is Warranted by Experience. The Observations before made will perhaps appear to be also confirmed by the same unerring Guide if proper Allowance be made for adventitious Circumstances all of which cannot and ought not to be taken into View on general Positions seeing that they have only a casual and temporary Existence. It may therefore upon the whole be affirmed that the Instant a Belief should obtain that Congress would not redeem their Money that Instant it would cease to be of Value notwithstanding the Laws making it a Tender and as a Corallary from this Position, that every Thing which might contribute to support such opinion would depreciate and every Thing to discountenance it would appreciate the Continental Bills.

It is said above that the Value will depend upon the Quantity &ca. it therefore becomes necessary to examine what is the proper Sum of circulating Medium for these States. This is an Object of Calculation and as such Calculation will frequently require a Comparison between Currency and Sterling Money it is necessary to fix some Standard. This will be Taken by estimating Dollars at 4/8 Sterling.[4] If the Exchange be calculated on Gold they will stand at 4/6 at least in some of the States but they weigh as much as an English Crown and pass currently throughout America for 112 half Pence or 4/8 wherefore 30 Dollars will be considered as of the Value of £7 Sterling.

The Imports to America from England only exclusive of Linnens for 8 years preceding the year 1765 amounted to £15.283.833. .1. .4 Sterling. The Exports therefore at a more advanced Period of American Population cannot be estimated below the annual Sum of ....£2.000.000^Stg

For Linnens from England and the Imports from
Scotland and Ireland add ½ the above Sum.......................1.000.000
Imports from Great Britain and Ireland   £3.000.000
For Articles Imported from elsewhere such as West India
Produce, Wines, India Goods, Gun Powder, Hempen
Cloths, naval Stores, Groceries, Silks &ca
must be added at least ⅓ of the above Sum 1.000.000
The Total Imports therefore will be £4.000.000
But lest this might by some Possibility be too
high for the greater Certainty deduct 500.000
    Remains...£3.500.000
    Equal to .... D^lls. 15.000.000
A Sum was exported sufficient to pay for this and all the Expences
of the double Transportation and Insurance Merchant's Profits
Port Charges Factorage and Duties both at Home and abroad
besides which the Country as such continually became richer
notwithstanding the continued annual Expence of Clearing the
Wilderness. The Exports therefore cannot be stated lower than ½
as much more or... 22.500.000
    Total of Imports and Exports.................................... D 37.500.000
The Inland Commerce arising meerly from the external must
necessarily be at least equal to it 37.500.000

4. That is, 4 shillings, 8 pence.

Total of Commerce depending on foreign
Trade .... D 75.000.000
The Internal Commerce arising from other Causes such as different
Manufactures Trades and Professions besides meer Husbandry. The
Sale of Lands. Expences of travelling. Rents Money on Interest &cᵃ·
cannot be less than as much more or   75.000.000
Total annual Commerce .... D 150.000.000
But as the whole Trade of a State is not carried on in one Day a Sum of
Money equal to the whole is not necessary and on the other Hand as no
Person can every Day use all his Money so more is necessary in Circulation
than what is barely equal to the Commerce of the Day. If a Medium of ⅕
or 73 Days be taken for the Money of the State to change Hands then the
above Sum must be divided by 5 which will give for the proper circulating
Medium about 30.000.000 of Dollars.

As this is a Matter of Importance it may require some further Attention.
It is not possible perhaps to determine the precise Sum but the Object is
to discover it nearly so as not to exceed. Suppose the Continent to contain 3,000,000 souls, which at 6 to every Family will be 500,000 Families.
Divide this Community into rich and Poor and ¹⁄₅₀ or 10,000 would be rich
if ½ of these be taken there will be 5000 rich 250,000 in the intermediate
Ranks and 240,000 poor or Slaves. The Sum above stated to be imported is
15.000.000 Dollars if of this ⅓ be applied to the Rich (i.e.) those who have
the Benefit of the Labor of 49 Families it will be 5.000.000 among 5000
or annually of foreign Articles each 1000 Dˡˡˢ· If one fifth of the Remʳ· or
2.000.000 Dollars be applied to the Poor it is 2.000.000 among 240,000 or
annually of foreign Articles each . . . 2⅓. If the Remainder or 8.000.000 be
applied to the middling Ranks it is 8.000.000 among 250,000 or annually
of foreign Articles each . . . 32.

Again the Sum stated for internal Commerce distinct from that which
arises from the Imports and Exports is 75.000.000.
If 5.000.000 be applied to the rich it will be to each Family 1.000.
If 10.000.000 be applied to the Poor it will be to each Family 44 1/6.
If the Remʳ 60.000.000 be applied to the middling Ranks it is for each
240.
Lastly the whole Commerce is stated at 150.000.000 if then the rich and
the Poor be alike excluded from any share and the intermediate Ranks
alone considered there will result to each Family an annual Commerce of
600 Dollars which is by no means exagerated for tho it may exceed that of

common Farmers or Mechanicks it is very short of that of the most trifling Retailer.

But as a Corollary of the several Facts above stated the circulating Medium is placed at 30,000,000 Divide this Sum among 500,000 Families and it amounts to 60 Dollars each & this Sum if a medium Rank be taken is small to carry on the necessary Commerce of Life. If it be objected that so much was not formerly in Circulation, it may be answered that this hath never been proved. And if it had been it is not decissive because great Part of the former Commerce was carried on upon Credit for Want of a sufficient Medium.

Some considerable Time before the War the Legislature of the Colony of New York emitted 500,000 Dollars which never circulated beyond that Colony but rapidly within it. Sometime after the Emission this Sum did not form more than ¼ of the Circulating Medium if so much as the Payments made &cᵃ· served to demonstrate. The Medium therefore of that Place could not be less than 2,000,000. But if the comparative Wealth of New York were placed at ⅒ of that of the whole Continent the Estimate would be very high and consequently at the Time when the Want of a sufficient Medium was loudly complained of it could not have been less than 20,000,000. The above Estimate therefore may be considered as within the Bounds of Truth rather than beyond them.

It hath been said that the Value of our Paper Money would depend 1st upon the Quantity and probable Quantity considered relatively to commercial Property. If the Quantity did not exceed 30,000,000 but in all Likelyhood would exceed it in some short Time this would affect the Value because Persons possessing Property would either demand so much for it as to secure themselves against the Effects of the Increase or they would refuse to sell thereby decreasing the commercial Property. If there were no such Probability of Increase then any Measures which would Decrease the commercial Property or any natural Incidents to the same Effect would necessarily Decrease the Value of the Money, and so would any Cause whatever producing uncommon Rapidity in the Circulation while on the other Hand and Measures tending to bring into Commerce more Property & to lessen the Rapidity of the Circulation would increase the Value.

Hence the following Conclusions are drawn. First. That not only the Increase but the probable Increase of the Paper Money lessens its Value and on the contrary the Decrease or probable Decrease would enhance that Value. Secondly. That any Acts limiting the Prices of or discouraging either the Sale or the Production of any Articles tend to a Depreciation and on the contrary full Permission to sell every Thing at any Price ample Encouragement to Husbandry and Manufactures together with Taxation so far as it may bring even Lands into Commerce must appreciate. & Thirdly. That every Circumstance either natural or adventitious bringing into Question the future Value of the Money by increasing the Rapidity of Circulation decreases its Value and every Thing which by making the Holder secure of an after Compensation renders him less solicitous to part with it will produce an appreciation.

It hath been said also that the Value will depend upon the Certainty or Uncertainty of it's Genuineness. Hence it follows that if the Paper is easily to be counterfeited it will be less valuable than otherwise and if actually counterfeited the Value will be still less: 1$^{st.}$ Because the counterfeit Money will increase the Quantity 2$^{ly.}$ Because Every Person selling a Commodity will demand as much over and above the ordinary Price as would secure against the Danger of receiving Counterfeits notwithstanding the necessary Precautions. To determine how far the continental Paper hath been counterfeited it may be observed that Specie is now at the Rate of 6 for 5 which would suppose the Medium increased to 180.000.000 at least. If Deductions be made from this for all the Causes of Depreciation distinct from Quantity it will appear that a very considerable Sum must be in Circulation over and above 100.000.000 which is the full amount of all the Emissions as well by the Continent as the several States. Perhaps if the Counterfeit be placed at 15.000.000 after Experience will discover that the Estimate is at least not too high. To provide against Counterfeits it is necessary that the Forms be simple and few. The Act difficult and if not perfectly well performed easily discernible. If then the several States were instantly to redeem their Emissions it would so far be of good Consequence. But it is also necessary to detect those now existing. And to accomplish this the Mode which naturally presents itself is that the several Bills chiefly counterfeited should from Time to Time be called in and redeemed with new Paper not so open to the Villainy. If this Mode is adopted it will become necessary to prepare such Bills and that they may speedily be obtained and for the Reasons which have been before mentioned as also to secure at once a sufficient Sum which the Continent should not exceed. They might be as follows:

1.000.000 of .... 40 Dollars each ....D. 40.000.000
1.000.000 of .... 30... 30.000.000

```
1.000.000 ............... 20 ......................................... 20.000.000
1.000.000 ...............15 .............................................15.000.000
1.000.000 ............... 10 ........................................ 10.000.000
1.000.000 ................ 5 ............................................. 5.000.000
1.000.000 Sheets of 120 ..................................... 120.000.000
```

If this Mode were adopted 30.000.000 might be called in at the End of six Months, 30.000.000 more at the End of nine Months and the Remainder at the End of a Year.

It hath also been said that the Value of the Money will depend on the Property and probable Property of the State. Wherefore every Loss of Territory will render it less and every Accession more valuable. But here the Increase will never be proportionate to the Decrease for the former will operate simply from it's natural Weight the latter from the Fears of the People affecting the whole Mass of Circulation. Hence it follows that great Expence to acquire Territory of little Value will if attended with the greatest Success be of no good Consequence and that the Expence in defending Territory is necessary. But even this is to be considered in the Degree and with Relation 1st to the Practicability because where not practicable it ought on every Principle to be not attempted 3^{ly} As to the Consequence 4^{thly} as to the Effects of Loss in the general Opinion & 5^{thly} as to the comparative Value or Importance & Expence.

Lastly it hath been said that the Value of the Money would depend upon the supposed Ability of the Government to command the Wealth of the State. This is founded on a Distinction between the Riches of the State and of Individuals. The latter produces the former only where it can be commanded by the Government. Now Obedience to Government frequently arises from the Lenity of its administration. A Demand of two may be granted where three would be refused. The ability abovementioned is only to be evinced by the Effects of Taxation. Taxes therefore should be as Moderate as is possible all Circumstances considered, because the Ill Consequences of their unproductiveness will be greater than the good of all which they really produce.

In a natural State of the Country at least two thirds of the Money would be in the Hands of the Wealthy beyond their Proportion and so as not to be reached by Taxation. The Remainder divided equally not more than one half could be taken without greatly distressing the lower Orders of the Community. If then the Medium were 30.000.000 the Sum of 5.000.000

being ⅙ might be raised and if so then 35.000.000 would be the proper circulating Medium because the Taxation and Expenditures by Government would make a new Commerce to that Amount. In the present Situation of Affairs it might not perhaps be prudent to Attempt more than ⅐ particularly as a far greater Proportion of the Money is in the Hands of a few Individuals. To determine then the Quantum of Taxes to be raised the Medium whatever it be may be divided by 8 and that Sum considered as the Extent of what the Taxes can produce at present.

This being premised with Relation to our Paper Money a System new great and extraordinary the possible Extent of which together with all the Effects perhaps no Man can at present determine. We come next to our Situation and consequent Wants. Engaged as we are in a War which hourly becomes more extensive and inhabiting a Country whose Coast is immense and in every Part accessible bound by Treaties and Engagements on the one Hand and pressed by Debts to the very Brink of Bankruptcy on the other. We are to carry on the War and for that Purpose to arm clothe feed and Pay an Army. We are to create a Marine. And we are either to pay our Debts or at least satisfy our Creditors. For the two last Purposes and also to arm and Cloathe our Army, as well as for some other Purposes which will appear hereafter the Sum of about 1.500.000 £ St^g· will be necessary in Europe for which we should endeavor to get Credit as speedily as possible. For other Services it will appear that about 1.750.000 £ St^g· would with the least Tolerable Management have sufficed at the Commencement of the War. If then the Articles necessary be considered as so scarce at present that they are doubly Valuable it will amount to £3.500.000 St^g· or at the Par 15.000.000 Dollars and if the Depreciation can be so far remedied as to bring the Money to half its preferred Value then 30.000.000 Dollars will be sufficient for the next year's Expenses with any Tollerable Management. At least the Expenditures ought to be confined within that Sum. Wherefore our wants will induce us to obtain if possible 1.500.000 £ St^g· in Europe and 30.000.000 Dollars here.

To obtain a Loan of Money in Europe several Methods present themselves to all of which there are Objections. The first is to endeavor to get Money of Individuals on the general Credit of the Public. But this requires either that the Credit should be very good or the Interest so high as finally to crush us. And to good Credit solid Securities for the Principle and unquestionable Funds for the Interest are indispensibly necessary. This Mode therefore in our present Circumstances may be considered as ideal or ruinous. A Plan hath been digested to obtain Money in present to be paid (without Interest) the double in future for which the Western Country to be mortgaged as a Security.[5] But to this it is objected that this Country is not and in all Probability will not be subject to the Control of Congress. And however true it may be that each of the united States would find the Measure to arise from true Policy it is not probable that the proper Laws would be passed in Season especially as private & local Interests are deeply interested. It may also be attempted to obtain Money by undertaking to make Remittances in the staple Commodities of the Country for Extinguishment of the Debt. But the Lender will in such Case insure himself commercial Advantages at least as oppressive to us as exhorbitant Interest. Our own Merchants will enhance the Value of our Remittances so much that the Public will pay at least twice as much as they ought. Any Agents who can be employed will find it too much for their Interest to sacrifice or for their Ease to neglect the Public Business. And the Means of Transporting will be so difficult and the Danger so great that this Mode cannot be prudent. Many other subaltern Methods may be hinted as to the Manner of making European Loans which greater Knowlege of the Subject may inspire. But perhaps none can be pointed out which will be effectual without it be to obtain the Guarantee of some of the greater Powers of Europe. For this purpose two present themselves viz. France & Spain. The former will certainly want all her Credit for her own Purposes and perhaps if she should spare us a Part it would not among the monied Interest of Europe be of so much Consequence as her great Power and Resources would at the first View indicate. Her Countenance however and Intrigues would be of much Service. The latter certainly must have very great Credit and be enabled very much to serve those whose Cause she espouses. If then France and Spain would be prevailed on jointly to push our Credit and to guarantee for us a Loan of 1.500.000 St$^{g.}$ and at the same Time the latter would grant us a Subsidy of 3.000.000 St$^{g.}$ payable in ten annual Payments It would produce the most happy Consequences. A Question arises here whether this is practicable. To which no conclusive Answer can be made untill after a fair Experiment.

Spain hath not as yet acknowleged our Independence but her Connection with France her Preparations for War and her deep Interest in curtailing the exhorbitant Power of Britain together with the Desire of wiping off the Ignominies of the last War will not permit a Doubt that she is disposed to do it. On the other Hand the Power of these States consequent on their Independence. The enterprising Spirit of the People. The Vicinity of her im-

5. Morris presented this plan to Congress on September 19, 1778.

mense Empire. And the contagious Influence of the Example speaks loudly
to her Caution. The unbounded Western Claim of some States stimulates
her Suspicions. And the Ports of Augustine and Pensacola with Florida are
Objects of national Interest and Ambition. To induce Spain then in the first
Instance to declare it is necessary to quiet her Suspicions by establishing a
Boundary. And this might be the Mississipi to the West and the Latitude
of　　　　to the South.

The former of these Boundaries will perhaps be readily agreed to. The
Propriety of the latter is not quite so obvious. It must be considered then
as it affects the Northern States the Middle States the Southern States and
the united States. The Northern States will always be drained of Men and
consequently of Riches by Migration to the Southward and in Proportion
as that Region is extensive and unwholesome will be their Loss. The middle
States (i.e.) those who have great Western Territory will find their Security
for the Obedience of their Ultramontane Subjects to rest upon carrying
on as much as possible their Commerce which will depend greatly upon
Keeping the Mouth of the Mississipi in Possession of an unenterprising
People not adicted to Commerce. Besides this the great Staple of Tobacco
will then be much more confined to the States of Virginia and Maryland
than would otherwise happen. The Southern States are most deeply interested because the Attempts of Spain would in the first Instance free them
from a very Troublesome Neighbour. A Country which would otherwise
be their Rival in the Articles of Rice and Indigo will thereby be doomed
to continue Wild as on the one Hand it is the clear Policy of the Spanish
Court to inhibit Cultivation and on the other their Subjects have greater
Views in the Western Country than on the Atlantic. The numerous Indian
Nations who are their very troublesome Neighbours will find full Employment against the Spanish whose Temper will certainly lead them into continued Hostilities and lastly the Trafick which may be indirectly carried on
thro that Province with new Spain will bring them a continued Ballance in
Specie. The united States would derive Advantage in every point of View
1st immediate because it would bring to their Aid a most powerful Ally &
give a decided Superiority on the Ocean by which alone the important
States of Quebeck and Nova Scotia can be brought into the Confederacy.
Because it would spare the enormous Expense for Defence of the Southern
States or Conquest of that Country And because it may reflect the most
useful Light on the Affairs of their Finances. 2^{ly} Remote because it would
take away a Country which would certainly drain the Remainder of many
useful inhabitants. Because it would facilitate the Yearly Subsidy proposed

and thereby greatly Aid their military Operations & Because it would tend to ensure the Obedience of the great and valuable Western country.

Further to interest the Courts abovementioned in our Favor it would be necessary to lay the State of our Finances fully before them and shew the utter Impracticability of carrying on the War vigorously on our Part without their Interposition in the Manner proposed.

If the Plan abovementioned should be agreed to by those Courts then of the 1.500.000 borrowed 500.000 should be applied to the Payment of our foreign Debts &ca. and the remaining 1.000.000 in procuring in the North of Europe 20 good Ships of War to carry each 44 Guns of twenty four Pound Caliber and in Cloathing for our Army as well Officers as Soldiers. The Ships should not draw above 25 Feet Water. To pay the Interest of the Sum borrowed 90.000£ should be appropriated from the Subsidy of 300.000 and of that Subsidy the Remainder should be employed for such Uses as Circumstances might require and if not otherwise called for be applied in sinking the Principle of our Debt or lowering the Interest.

Some thoughts on the Finances of America intended for the Congress but not compleated because of much intervening Business of various Kinds & because Many had adopted a System they were determined to persevere in.

8 ❋ To the Quakers, Bethlemites, Moderate Men, Refugees, and Other the Tories Whatsoever, and Wheresoever, Dispersed (1779)

By late 1778, serious factional divisions had appeared in Congress, particularly in the controversy over Silas Deane's service as a U.S. commissioner in France. Deane was accused by one of his co-commissioners, Arthur Lee, of misappropriating public money and of engaging in commercial activities of his own while an official representative of the country. The dispute became public in December 1778 with the publication of a series of articles by Thomas Paine, the secretary of Congress's committee on foreign affairs, in the *Pennsylvania Packet*. Further, in early 1779 a series of disputes between Congress and the State of Pennsylvania came to light, among them a personal rift between Morris and Joseph Reed, the president of the state. In light of this evidence of divided councils, Morris wrote to assure those who still doubted the American cause that the factional disputes had not diminished Congress's ability to work with the states or its determination to win the war.

※

To the Quakers, Bethlemites, Moderate Men, Refugees and other
the Tories whatsoever, and wheresoever, dispersed.

Peace.

I entered into the American contest from a love of my fellow-creatures. Lamenting as a Philosopher the consequences of my conduct as a citizen, while I strove to expel despotism I wept over the victims of ambition. That principle which first prompted me remains uneffaced, nor can I except from amongst men, even those who are my enemies. Equally capable of free-

The Pennsylvania Packet, or General Advertiser, February 27, 1779. Reprinted from *Letters of Delegates to Congress, 1774–1789,* ed. Paul H. Smith et al. (Washington, D.C.: Library of Congress, 1976–2000), 12:114–20.

dom with others it is my earnest prayer that *you* may equally deserve it. The effects of prejudice are known, and humanity calls on us to remove it if possible; for the same bosom which flows with indignation against guilt, melts in pity of ignorance. But I intreat you to remember, that men who shut their eyes against the light, as they will deserve, so will they receive a double measure of punishment.

That it is the will of Heaven, mankind should be free, is evidenced by the wealth, the vigor, the virtue and consequent happiness of free States. And the idea that providence will establish such governments as he shall deem most fit for his creatures without their efforts is palpably absurd. Did he overturn the walls of Jerusalem by the mere breath of his mouth, or did he stir up the Romans to add Judea to their other provinces? In short, is not his moral government of the earth always performed by the intervention of second causes? How then can you expect that he should *miraculously* destroy our enemies, merely to convince you that he favours our cause? Sufficient notifications of his will are always given, and those who will not then believe, neither would they believe though one should rise from the dead to inform them. Trace the progress and mark the incidents of the war, and you will see evident tokens of providential favor. For whether our success be owing to the folly of our opponents or to any other immediate cause, we are equally indebted for it to the bounty of Heaven. Many of our measures which you perhaps justly considered as unwise, have by an amazing coincidence of circumstances become the corner-stones of independence. And on the other hand, many of the enemy's most brilliant successes which made your hearts to sing for joy, have produced to you nothing but bitterness and woe.

I am led to these reflections and to this address, partly from perceiving and more from being informed, that you derive pleasing hopes from the following circumstances. First, the taking of Georgia. Secondly, the calumnies against Congress, and supposed divisions among them. And Thirdly, the symptoms of discontent, lately exhibited by the Executive Council of Pennsylvania. I shall take notice of these in their order, make some short observations on public affairs, and then leave you to judge. I exhort you to read with attention, and to determine with that coolness which is due to a subject so important to your welfare, perhaps your existence.

The expedition against Georgia was dictated by the necessities of the British army, and the danger of their own dominions. In the first case they expected considerable supplies of rice for an army, and for islands in a starving condition. In the second they labored to establish a barrier between these States and East-Florida, the better to secure that latter, and thereby in case of a war with Spain check the free navigation of the gulf of Florida, thro' which the treasures of the new world are conveyed to Europe. The consequences are, first, to inspirit your brethern in the Southern States, and thereby to purge them of men who would have been pernicious members of a free society. These men will be justly stripped of that property and those rights which they have not spirit to contend for, and by banishment, poverty and lasting remorse expiate the guilt of endeavoring to subjugate their fellow-citizens. Secondly, this expedition will rouse the States of North and South-Carolina. They will derive from it that energy which is acquired in a state of war, and which produces obedience and subordination so necessary to society in a state of peace. But thirdly, what is of more importance to such of you as dwell in the middle and eastern States, is, that by dividing the force of your friends, whatever may be the lot of those wretches who are doomed to wrestle with a baneful southern clime, it renders their army at New York less efficient and consequently less capable of assisting you.

As to the calumnies against Congress and supposed divisions in that body, you are greatly tho' not altogether mistaken in the latter fact, and at any rate draw from it very false conclusion. The late abusive writings shew indeed the illiberality of the respective writers, but by no means impeach those against whom they are directed. Being equally indifferent to the several performers, I wish not to balance their respective merits. This is certain that Billingsgate language marks at most a Billingsgate education, and among those who know the real value of such performances, the reputation of a virtuous citizen will not suffer more from the scurrility of a news-paper, than from the nervous diction of an oyster-wench. The licentiousness exhibited on these occasions, demonstrates the existence of liberty, which is a pleasing consideration to those who have a value for it. And altho' such productions may offend individuals, yet they are not without use to society, in like manner as the blasts of winter tho' keen are wholesome. We may further deduce from it the falacy or rather falsity of what was once a favorite position among you, that people did not dare to utter their sentiments, neither is it unworthy of your attention that the various attacks upon Congress have not drawn the least notice from that body. From hence it is to be concluded that they have a well founded confidence in themselves, for did the shaft stick, it would make the body sore. And nothing is truer than this, that little minds are more resentful than great ones, and truth more resented than falsehood. From some acquaintance and good information I will venture to add, that the present Congress considered in the double view of abilities and integrity is at least as respectable as any which hath yet been assembled. Let it not be concluded from this, that I conceive the individuals of that body to be of a superior nature. They like other men are subject to passions, prejudices, weaknesses and the influence of the elements, and since the Deity chose one Judas among twelve disciples, it cannot be wondered at if among a much greater number some few should be charged with peculiar pravity. But this by no means militates against the general observation.

To say there are divisions in Congress is only saying in other words that it is a popular Assembly. Different views of the same subject naturally lead men to differ in sentiments. Personal connections excite personal emotions, and the conflict of such emotions sometimes produces personal altercation. The heats inevitable on such occasions seldom evaporate within the walls of one house, but stimulate to bitter observations easily credited, because they flatter a self-importance which is uneasy at any kind of superiority. Perhaps you will ask how it happens that such things did not exist formerly? They did; but the public dangers and distresses taught men to keep more secret those things which they readily divulge in an hour of greater security. The appearance of such divisions therefore in personal matters are striking marks of national prosperity, and you will find, that however the members of Congress may disagree about who shall be in and who shall be out, they will be firmly united in refusing to accept the independance Great-Britain is about to offer, and insist on a clear, explicit and pointed acknowledgment of it in the most extensive sense previous to any treaty whatsoever.

For what regards the dispute between the Executive Council of this State and Congress it is, as far as your views may be served by it, the most trifling of all trifling things.[1] Stimulated by a laudable zeal to discover public abuses, their suspicions were turned on one to whose gallantry America is much indebted.[2] Greatness and weakness are sometimes nearly allied.

---

1. A number of disputes had arisen between Pennsylvania and Congress, in some of which Morris himself figured prominently. For a detailed list of Pennsylvania's complaints, see Joseph Reed's letter to Congress, read into Congress's journal on April 15, 1779 (*Journals of the Continental Congress, 1774–1789*, ed. Worthington C. Ford et al. [Washington, D.C.: U.S. Government Printing Office, 1904–37], 13:453–55).

2. Benedict Arnold, whose financial dealings while military commander of Philadelphia led to a court martial in June 1779.

That spirit which carried him in triumph over the fields of honor, induced a want of respect for Magistrates to whom he did not deem himself accountable. Charity bids us believe that conscious innocence inspired an elevation which he would not have felt under the pressure of guilt. Perhaps also it was regard to the privileges of his brother soldiers which rejected submission to other than a military tribunal, when his conduct as an officer was arraigned. These and many other reasons doubtless suggested themselves to the Council, and had they been at liberty to obey those dispassionate sentiments which embellish their high office, his refusal might perhaps have been disregarded. But on the one hand attachment to the interests of America, and on the other divisions in their state and doubts about their authority, which naturally rendered them more jealous of it than those to whom dignity and power are familiarized, these motives would not permit a moment delay in pursuing the interests and vindicating the majesty of the people. Perhaps there may have been some little personalities concerned, tho' the reverence which is due to the Supreme Executive of an independent State, opposes the idea. But be this as it may, Congress seems to have viewed the matter somewhat differently from the State. Conscious of possessing the love and respect of their countrymen in arms as well as of others, they were not open to angry impressions, which indeed are of little use either in public or private life. Affection also for an army which hath served them so faithfully, so generously, might raise some prejudice in favor of it's members; as an indulgent parent smiles at the petulant vivacity of a favorite child. They did not therefore catch the resentments of the Council, and tho' determined to support the authority of a State, they were not eager to blemish the reputation of a worthy soldier. The Council probably influenced by good reasons which they will undoubtedly declare at a proper time, came to certain resolutions which they have published and transmitted to the several States. But this little feverish ebullition, and the ridicule which many have attemted to cast upon it, can do no good to you. The Assembly of Pennsylvania which by their constitution is of real importance, acts in perfect harmony with the Congress. And depend upon it, whatever your leaders may flatter you with, the Whigs of Pennsylvania will not engage in any dispute with the representative body of America to the prejudice either of the acknowledged rights of that body, or of the privileges of those brave citizens who have drawn their swords in the cause of Freedom.

And even if any such dispute should exist, can you suppose, that in case of necessity, the President of that State would hesitate a moment to head his militia? That he would not instantly take the field with his wonted alacrity? That he would not fight under the banners of America with his former zeal? Those who know him know better. It would be equally absurd for you to suppose that the Council are disposed to promote public divisions, in order to favor the negociations of the enemy. Do not dwell on the mysteriousness in Doctor Berkenhout's affair.[3] It is nothing new that an artful man should impose upon the unsuspicious. Honesty and knowledge are very different things, and of the two the former is the most amiable.

As little ground have you for hope in the depreciation of the Continental money. You know that this is in a great degree to be attributed to the arts of interested men whose efforts to acquire it shew their conviction of it's value. I know it hath been a fashionable doctrine, that after the emissions should amount to a certain sum, the bubble, as the phrase was, would burst. But the absurdity of this to men acquainted with human nature was evident. The reasons are needless, because we may appeal to experience to shew whether there is the least danger of this event. When two emissions were called in, and every method, consistent with justice and good faith, taken to stop their circulation; those who had principally contributed to depreciate the money were the very persons who continued to receive the vicious emissions. For as soon as it became a question, whether they should lose not the value, but merely the use of so much money, they made every effort to uphold the credit of it. A few days ago, when a report prevailed of the arrivals of some favorable intelligence from Europe, such of you as are in this city cannot but remember the rapid fall of every article, specie not excepted. Hence the deduction is clear that the money issued by Congress is intrinsically worth what they contend, but is depreciated by the quantity in some degree, and more by the arts of engrossers. Take the familiar proposition, that a country will easily bear taxation to the amount of some given part of the circulating medium, suppose a tenth, tho' in fact one fifth may be raised among a free people, and you will see that, let the paper medium be increased to any degree, it may be sunk in a short period.

Not pretending to great knowledge of national secrets, and little desirous of communicating whatever of this kind it hath fallen to my lot to know, I shall reason with you on these things as I have reasoned for myself, and I trust the event will verify my conclusions. And first I consider it to be manifestly the interest of every Court in Europe to foster our indepen-

3. John Berkenhout, M.D., was a British scientist who had met with the American commissioners in France, and later was a British agent in the United States. He was a figure in the controversy over Silas Deane.

dence because it is in effect the dividing a great empire, whose power was formidable, and whose insolence was insupportable.

Beginning with Russia; iron, potash and such other commodities as that country produces in common with this, will now have equal advantages at the London market, because no bounties will in future be granted by Parliament to the produce of these States. Sailcloth and the other articles produced there and consumed here will come hither directly from thence, and in direct return they will take our rice and tobacco, the commercial advantages of which are evident, not to mention the increase of naval force they may expect from it. Add to these solid reasons of national interest the personal character of the Empress.[4] This is strongly marked by benevolence and the love of that fame which results from contributing to the happiness of mankind, a disposition evidenced by giving to her subjects all the liberty they are at present capable of. These considerations will naturally lead you to the answer filled with disdain which she gave to a proposal of the British Ambassador requesting her troops to subdue us. "My glory shall never be tarnished by the infamy of oppressing those who only contend for freedom and justice." They will also account for her refusal to accede to subsequent propositions from our enemies the most disgraceful to them as well as apparently advantageous to her.

The spirit of the State reasons abovementioned applies generally all the Northern Courts, and it must be observed that the lesser will be very cautious how they contravene the views of the greater. As to Denmark her imbecility is the best possible reason why she should not side with the weaker party, especially when she holds the little of her West-India possessions as a tenant at will to the maritime powers.

Sweden, the faithful ally of France, if she acts at all, will certainly take part in our favour, and with twenty ships of the line ready at a moment's warning, is in capacity to afford us no inconsiderable aid.

Prussia and Austria, equally desirous of becoming maritime powers, equally desirous to obtain for that purpose a share of the American commerce, and actually at war with each other, will neither of them be willing to send force against America. Nor will the smaller German Powers dare to weaken their dominions, by the loss of a single soldier, whilst the Emperor and King of Prussia are armed in motion, and in capacity to swallow them up.

Of the United Netherlands and Italy nothing need be said, unless that

4. Catherine the Great.

at least a strict neutrality may be depended on from them; the reasons of which are too obvious.

France is already at war with Great-Britain for American Independence; and those who know the connection between the Courts of Versailles and Madrid, their enmity to that of St. James's, and their national interests, cannot but perceive that Spain will soon be joined in this contest, unless it be terminated agreeably to our wishes.

Hence then it is evident, either that we shall immediately conclude a safe and honorable peace, or that Great-Britain must carry on the war alone, and unsupported against France, Spain and America, in which case the two former will give every aid in their power, to our trade and finances, so that on the whole no well founded doubt can exist, that the Continental currency will rise greatly in its value, and that the independence and safety of America will be established on the firmest foundation.

Convinced as you must be of these things, what ought your conduct to be? You cannot pretend to plead conscience on this occasion, because the success of our measures being apparent, it is on your own principles the will of God, to which you are conscientiously bound to conform. If you oppose your countrymen you may indeed incourage the enemy, and thereby lengthen out the contest, in which case you yourselves shall determine, whether you will not in some degree be answerable for the consequences. You have seen enough of war to wish a termination of it. You have sense enough to perceive that you can live happily under those governments which you wished in vain to prevent. You ought to fear that if the enemy perform their threats of wasting our country, your persons may become obnoxious to the vengeance of your fellow-citizens, and your estates be applied to compensate the ravages committed on theirs. Take then the counsel which I again declare to you is dictated by humanity. I wish sincerely the happiness of all mankind. I wish sincerely the prosperity and glory of the United States. And as sincerely I wish for peace. May Heaven grant it to us, to you and to all.

AN AMERICAN

After Congress snubbed the Carlisle Commission, George Johnstone returned to Parliament to defend his conduct. He gave a long speech in the House of Commons on November 27, 1778, in which he blamed just about everyone for the commission's failure. He blamed the North ministry for advocating nothing but coercion and the opposition for wanting nothing but concession. For good measure, Johnstone also blamed the French and the Americans. He reminded the House that he had long recommended a policy that combined force with negotiation, and argued that such an approach would have succeeded. Finally, he defended himself against charges that he had tried to bribe Joseph Reed, the president of Pennsylvania.

Johnstone's speech was summarized in the *Pennsylvania Packet* on February 11, 1779, and then published in full on March 9. All of Morris's quotations come from the full version. Even as busy as he was with Congress's business, Morris clearly thought it was vital to give a swift response to Johnstone's speech.

For the *PENNSYLVANIA PACKET.*
To *GOVERNOR JOHNSTONE.*

Sir,   *Philadelphia, March 4, 1779.*

Having seen your speech on American affairs at the opening of the session, I cannot avoid making some observations upon it; for although it contains important facts and sensible remarks, yet it is not without some mistakes.

You say, *the cause of America is wicked, because we are united with France for the express purpose of reducing your country.* The object of our alliance with the

The Pennsylvania Packet, or General Advertiser, March 11, 1779. Reprinted from *Letters of Delegates to Congress, 1774–1789,* ed. Paul H. Smith et al. (Washington, D.C.: Library of Congress, 1976–2000), 12:146–52.

Most Christian King, is simply to secure that Independence without which our liberty would be but a name. And although you are too weak to maintain the present contest, yet you are too powerful to be conquered. Neither is it the interest of the House of Bourbon on the one hand, or of America on the other, that you should. Britain would be as troublesome a province to France, as America to Britain: Either would distract and enfeeble their masters. But, assuming your fact, is it *wicked* to attempt the reduction of a nation which hath lately shewn itself the common enemy of man? which hath drenched this country in the blood of its inhabitants, for the *impious* purpose of reducing them to unconditional submission. Impious, as *you* have repeatedly declared, as *they* have "with singular unanimity" directly acknowledged. Is it *wicked* to crush a court and a ministry profligate beyond conception, and deceitful beyond example?

You aver, *that the treaty with France is not ratified in a constitutional manner.* You are mistaken even on your own ground. Still more are you mistaken on the ground assumed by your government; for they confessed the authority of Congress to form treaties, by the very application which brought you hither.

You are equally wrong in supposing, that the objects of your commission were frustrated by delay. The draught of the bills arrived in season, and the sentiments of Congress were expressed on them so early as the twenty-second of April, previous even to the knowledge, much less the ratification of a treaty with France. They were expressed with an *unanimity* which, on such occasions, is not *singular.*

You say, *it was always your view that force should accompany the concession.* What concession do you mean? The acts of Parliament gave no more than what you frequently contended for as our *right*, and to assert that there is concession in giving a man his own, is hardly common sense, but certainly not common honesty. The idea of vigorous coercion in the moment of treaty, is a genuine British idea. It is a good one, provided the offers to be made in treating are generous and honest; but if insidious and unequal, it is marked with the spirit, not of a man, but a tyrant. That preparation for war is the best means of obtaining peace, is an old and true adage, but there is an essential difference between peace and dominion. Those in either country who seek the former on safe and honourable terms, will be gratified; those who aim at the latter will inevitably be, as they ought to be, most grievously disappointed.

The opprobrious language you make use of is but little ornamental to your eloquence, and would flow with more propriety from the pen of an hireling than the mouth of a statesman. That the Congress in their proceedings have a respect to the people, is true; that they attempt to deceive the people, is untrue. Shew, if you can, a falshood sanctioned by their authority. If you cannot, retract a charge which must recoil upon you. Whoever hath informed you that the newspapers are under the direction of Congress, was mistaken, or meant to deceive: And when you shall have the pleasure of perusing some late Gazettes, you will see not only that the Congress and its Members, but some other very respectable personages, are handled with sufficient freedom to contradict your charge. Be cautious, however, that you do not draw false conclusions from these publications. The Americans being really free, are subject, like other people, to the intemperatures of freedom. The conversations and conduct of your adherents, have seemed to flow from the following dilemma: If the newspapers do not blame measures and traduce characters, there is tyranny; if they do, there is disunion. But the natural interpretation is, that the former arises from public confidence and a sense of decency, the latter from personal emotion and the irritability of little spirits.

For what relates to the charge brought against you by General Reed, you will certainly acquit Congress of disingenuity, after you have seen what hath been stated on that occasion. Whether their zeal led them into declarations, which those who are accustomed to the business of corruption will consider as hasty and unnecessary, is not for me to determine, having had no *transactions where other means besides persuasion have been used.* This, however, you may be certain of, that it was no *political* stroke to avoid the question about General Burgoyne's troops. Nor will the harsh epithets which you and others so liberally bestow upon Congress, by any means impeach them. Pardon me, Sir, for observing, that on this occasion the charge of duplicity lies against you and your brethren in commission. To enter into the arguments would be tedious; but if you will suppose us to be, what we have declared ourselves, independent, then I pledge myself to meet you on the ground of national right, and shew that the Congress have acted with perfect consistency and integrity. At present I shall only observe, that you had no authority whatever to offer a ratification of the convention of Saratoga, and that you knew you had not at the moment in which you made the offer.[1] At the same time I fully agree with you, *that policy founded on injustice*

1. The Saratoga Convention had been negotiated by General John Burgoyne and General Horatio Gates after Burgoyne's defeat, and provided that the British and allied soldiers captured at Saratoga would return to Europe and not fight against the

and dishonour is contemptible in private life, and where the dignity of people is con-cerned, abominable meanness.

That you was received at Philadelphia with joy; that they wished the continu-ance of the British army; that they made golden promises of thousands and tens of thousands to join you, is extremely probable. They made the promises as an inducement for you to comply with their wishes, and their wishes were founded on their hopes and their fears. But as a negociator, it was unpar-donable to rest your creed on the opinions of those who were confined in Philadelphia.[2] Your friends would naturally resort thither from other parts of the state, and consequently afford but a partial sample of the remain-der. Your enemies would not readily avow their sentiments under a military government, which had not been exercised with too great lenity. And as for the inhabitants of your gaols, their ideas like their information, would naturally be much circumscribed. Nor can it be wondered at, if in the lin-gering tediousness of long confinement, worne away with want, and broken with the insolence of petty tyrants, their spirits should be so depressed as to adopt any means of relief which might offer. Had you consulted the British Generals; had you consulted former experience, you would have known that all reasoning on such foundations is illusory; all promises by such men ineptious; all reliance on either absurd.

But it seems you are persuaded, *that had you been at liberty to have acted in the field, your most sanguine expectations would have been fulfilled.* Those, Sir, who had *sanguinary* wishes and expectations, would have been gratified; those who delight in human woe, might have beheld with satisfaction the fields of carnage. If there be any who can derive pleasure from the pangs of a helpless widow, or the tears of fatherless children, they might have been satiated with the savage feast. But you are deceived if you suppose that losses, defeats or distress, could have induced a submission to unreasonable terms. America *has profited from her own example in the low state of affairs be-fore the action of Trenton,* and believe me, the object is too large to depend on the fate of a battle, a siege, or a campaign.

You seem to be of a different opinion, whilst leaving the plain road of facts, you wander through the fields of supposition, to shew the propri-ety of your former conduct, and what you propose in future. *Suppose,* you

---

United States again. After a dispute over the terms arose in early 1778, Congress re-fused to honor the convention until the king ratified it—a de facto recognition of American independence.

2. Philadelphia was occupied by the British when Johnstone arrived.

say, *Admiral Keppel had beaten Mons. the Count d'Orvilliers*, that is; *destroyed half his fleet*, which he was prevented from doing by *the accidents of wind and weather; suppose Admiral Byron's Squadron had not met with a storm;* if Clinton had not been ordered to leave Philadelphia, &c. Why did you not at once suppose you had fairly conquered America, as well as that Byron had met no storms, Kepple [*sic*] no unfavourable gales, and Clinton no ridiculous commands. Incidents like these, should always be supposed by wise men. Wise men, Sir, will never stake the fate of an empire on the uncertainty of the winds, the turbulence of the waves, and the fluctuations of human opinion. Suppose d'Estaing had arrived in the Delaware before Philadelphia was evacuated, and that by the united efforts of his fleet and the American armies, you had shared the fate of the unfortunate, insulted Burgoyne. Suppose the Count, instead of leaving Rhode-Island had staid till the storm abated and then went to Sandy Hook to wait for the shattered fleets of Howe and Byron. Suppose he had in force have met the latter alone. Your suppositions, it seems, would have laid the topic of Independence asleep, and silenced its supporters; but mine would have placed the opposers of it in the most ridiculous light imaginable.

For the encouragement of friends and the terror of foes, you declare your unalterable resolution *to die in the last ditch*. The GREAT NASSAU made the same declaration, and in the mouth of a hero contending for freedom after the loss of many battles, against superior force and almost exhaustless resources, it hath a dignity and elevation which description cannot reach. But when it is used to color obstinate perseverance in a ridiculous war, for the sake of a bubble, a feather or a name, it is hardly in the compass of language to descend to such a deep profund. In what ditch, my good Sir, would you die? Shall the rich current which glides through your veins dash along the roaring Susquehanna, swell the great Potowmac, or fill the bay of Chesapeak? Shall it empurple the Canadian snows, shall it fertilize the arid sands of Florida, or stain the rocks of Nova Scotia, hard and unpitying of the generous sacrifice? The gentle Tweed can never be witness of his Johnstone's fate, for, indeed Sir, if you stay at home, we cannot possibly martyrise you. But seriously; why are you so apprehensive for Canada, Nova-Scotia, the Floridas, and West-India islands? It is not the interest, and therefore hardly the wish of our allies, that we should become dangerous to Europe, though it is their and our determination to render the United States secure. Neither can we harbor a desire after extended empire, when the pernicious effects of it on you are so recent. Besides, we have not men to squander on the unhealthy climates of Florida and the West-Indies.

But why are you so inconsistent? You state us as very low and weak. If the fact be so, whence do you derive your apprehensions? You consider your nation in capacity still to subdue us. Why then do you harbor any fears? If our resources are really exhausted, if it is not in imagination to paint our contentions, divisions and sufferings, can you suppose that we shall continue the war for future improbable acquisitions?

You ask, *What reason America can have for not explicitly declaring her intentions of conditionally renouncing her connections with France upon your declaring her independency?* The answer is plain. Because she is honest. Would you go farther? Because she is wise. If she faithfully abides by her treaties, other nations will court her alliance. Suppose, for the sake of those fanciful advantages to be derived from *an union of force* with you, and to avoid *the evils of war in a dubious contest*, America had been guilty of breaking her faith; would you have relied on her promises? While you strove to make her so *wicked*, could she rely on yours? Not to mention the criminality, is there a greater absurdity, than at the very moment when you would lead men to repose confidence in *your* faith, to shew a sovereign contempt of it, by persuading them to violate *theirs?*

You say, that *your riches are greater than at the commencement of the last war,* but admit *the embarrassment of your funds.* Is Governor Johnstone yet to learn, that money and riches are very different things when applied to nations? Have you more men? Have you more manufactures? Have you more plenteous productions of the soil? Three millions of subjects are lost. Fifty millions of debt are incurred. All Europe is against you.

Your warlike operations, you say, *are less extensive in Germany, the East Indies, Portugal, North-America and the West Indies.* Who gave you the prescience to determine where and how the war shall rage? Are the East-Indies annihilated, that they can be no longer the theatre of your battles and your crimes? What has become of Gibraltar and Minorca? Have you abandoned the shores of Africa? Have you let the miserable Electorate of Hanover to farm? Have you conquered America? Or does it require a lesser operation for that purpose, than it did, with the assistance of your colonies, to reduce Canada? You certainly are of a different opinion; for you think 25,000 *men are necessary in America exclusive of what are in Canada and Halifax:* These I suppose amount to about 3,000. Add to the account 12,000 which you ought to have in the Floridas and West-Indies, and it will make 45,000 men. You can neither send or maintain so large a force at such a perilous distance. New winds again may blow, again may storms arise, and fresh blunders be again added to the catalogue of national absurdities. Should a convoy be lost or a fleet destroyed, figure to yourself your *so excellent, so beautiful, and so well appointed army*, in all its *comeliness*, and in all its *grace*, panting for a piece of pitiful pork, or surrendering for the lack of musty biscuit. You speak of the American Tories as *a shrewd, cunning, sensible people, who will not join the weak and wavering*; and will they, think you, join the ruined and undone? Alas! Surrounded as you are with dangers and distresses of every kind, prudence seems wholly to have abandoned you: And like a ruined gamester, having lost so much as almost to have lost your senses, you would stake your clothes, your wife and your children on the desperate hazard, till nothing remains for you but *to die in a ditch.*

You are led to suppose, from some riots which happened between the French sailors and lower kind of inhabitants in the brothels of Boston, that *the indignant spontaneous passions of the people are indisposed to the French alliance.* Suppose (since you are so fond of suppositions) that an English fleet should have arrived at the *loyal* town of Boston, would the officers and seamen have been received with open arms, and pressed and caressed by the inhabitants? Suppose an English seaman and soldier should come to blows for a prostitute, would you, from this circumstance, apprehend a defection of your invincible fleet or graceful army? However *spontaneous* might be their passions, you would hardly draw that conclusion.

It is said above, that peace may be had on terms safe and honorable for Britain and America. It may be added for every other party who may be concerned in the war. What do you want with Gibraltar and Minorca? As badges of sovereignty and of ancient glory, they may feed your pride, but they empty your purse; for your Levant trade is a losing game, and will, from our independence, be more so every day. These places are like thorns in your neighbour's sides, who, for that very reason, cannot be your friends. If you mean peace, they can do you no good; and therefore it is your interest to get rid of them on the best terms you can. Jamaica is, indeed, a valuable possession; but as it raises the jealousy of others and creates enemies to you, you should keep it no longer than until you can obtain something better in lieu of it. Your privilege of cutting logwood in the Bay of Honduras, is useless, now that so much better is brought from Campeachey. And considering their situation, you cannot long possess the Floridas, or wish to hold the Bahamas. Why not then abandon all these things to Spain, who can give you territory of far greater value, and may perhaps extricate you from the *embarrassment of your finances.*

Nova Scotia, inhabited as it is by emigrants from the eastern states, and commodious for their fisheries, is useless to you, tho' necessary for us.

Nor can you suppose we shall think you sincere, if, in a treaty of perpetual peace, you insist on keeping Halifax to check our fisheries and fetter our commerce. Bermuda is so dependent on us, that you cannot wish to hold it in terrorem at a certain national expence, when it can be of no national advantage. Especially as compensation may be made you, in various ways, for ceding these things. Among other benefits you may hope from the cession are these, the saving of men and money; neither of which you abound in. A return of the sweets of American commerce, which a continuance of hostilities may deprive you of for ever; and a certain and firm guarantee of all your American possessions. Great-Britain and Ireland condensed within themselves, will become more powerful than with their late domains. Being not so easily attacked, their defence will be less expensive. They will be more capable of offence, because their force will not be employed in the protection of distant possessions. You can have nothing to apprehend from us, because our system is from its nature, and must be from necessity, pacific and commercial. You will become more populous, because you will not suffer the same waste of men from emigrations, garrisons, &c. By admitting a representation from Ireland, your government might be simplified so as to become active and efficacious. It is no paradox to say, that your manufactures would be in a more flourishing situation. Those in which you cannot rival other nations, might languish; but those which are natural to you, and being derived from your own resources, do not depend upon fortuitous incidents: These would be benefited by the accession of that money, labor, and ingenuity, which is now directed to other objects. And as these manufactures are not precarious, the wealth of a country might safely be rested upon them. It is a mistake, that exclusive privileges are advantageous. The character of a monopolizer is as odious, applied to a nation, as it is to a man, and as unprofitable as it is contemptible. But I beg pardon, Sir, for political disquisitions to so refined a politician, and for mentioning the means of peace to one enamoured of war. To the force of necessity; to the embarrassment of your finances; to that wheel of fortune which you wish not to be thrown out of, and whose revolutions will place your country as low in this as she was high in the last war; to these I leave you. When all other views are precluded, then you will see your true interests, and then you will join in a prayer for peace with Your most obedient and humble servant,

An AMERICAN.

10 ✵ "An American" Letters on Public Finance
for the *Pennsylvania Packet* (1780)

Morris's tenure in the Continental Congress ended in November 1779.
He decided to stay in Philadelphia and establish his law practice there;
he also embarked on a number of business ventures. But he did not give
up his interest in public finance. The essays that follow were published in
early 1780, partly in response to a set of "Letters on Appreciation," published in the *Pennsylvania Packet* in January of that year.[1] Max Mintz argues that the ideas Morris puts forward in these letters are the origin of
some of the proposals that later appeared in Robert Morris's "Report on
the Public Credit." That report, drafted by Gouverneur and submitted
to the Continental Congress in July 1782, is arguably the most important
document on public finance before Hamilton's 1791 report of the same
title.[2]

Partial drafts of several of the essays are in the Gouverneur Morris Papers, Rare Book
and Manuscript Library, Columbia University. Where discrepancies appear between
a manuscript and the newspaper, I have used the manuscript reading.

1. The "Letters on Appreciation" appeared on January 20 (Letters 1 and 2) and
January 25 (Letter 3); they were later published as a pamphlet. The pamphlet has
sometimes been attributed to Morris [e.g., American Antiquarian Society of Early
American Imprints, series I (Evans), no. 16820].

2. Mintz, *American Revolution*, 155–56, and Clarence Ver Steeg, *Robert Morris: Revolutionary Financier* (Philadelphia: University of Pennsylvania Press, 1954), 123–31. See
also Kline, *New Nation*, 242–45. Robert Morris's report, dated July 29, 1782, appears
in the *Journal of the Continental Congress* on August 5, 1782 (*Journals of the Continental Congress, 1774–1789*, ed. Gaillard Hunt [Washington, D.C.: Library of Congress,
1914], 22:429–46).

To the INHABITANTS of AMERICA.
MY COUNTRYMEN,

A considerable time hath elapsed since I determined to publish a few sentiments on the finances of America, but was restrained by the epidemical madness of the times, which for certain causes not worth enquiring after, would hardly have borne with me. At present there appears to be a sincere desire of attending to reason from any quarter, and at present if ever plain honest reason appears necessary, for after the many unsuccessful efforts which have been made it is not rash to assert, that to draw forth the resources of our great country on free and equitable principles, is no easy task.

The various opinions entertained, propagated and supported relative to your Paper Currency, differ so widely that they cannot all be right. Perhaps not one of them is strictly or entirely so. Unfortunately it happens on such occasions, and indeed on too many others, that mankind reason from their prejudices, their circumstances, and their interests. Thus in the most important affairs, like grown persons at the dancing school, we have much to unlearn, as well as to learn, before we can think and move with ease and grace. We must cast off our prejudices, rise above our circumstances and divest ourselves of a pitiful regard to our interests whether pecuniary or political. Hard task indeed!

The writer of these papers pretends to no extraordinary virtue or abilities. He has thought on the subject and he meant to think consistently and uprightly, but he may be mistaken, he may be deceived, he may be unequal to the task he hath attempted, as he hath no ambition of a literary reputation, and no leisure to acquire it, ornaments of style are not to be expected. The actual state of America, differs from that of any other country, instances therefore drawn from former ages, or foreign nations, are not always applicable. General maxims ought for the same reason to be well considered. But with these salutary cautions, taking experience for our guide, and candor for our friend, let us crawl along in the search of truth, with a disposition to pardon human error in others, but suspect it

Pennsylvania Packet, or General Advertiser, February 17, 1780. Courtesy American Antiquarian Society. Parts of this letter are in items 812 and 815, Gouverneur Morris Papers, Rare Book and Manuscript Library, Columbia University.

in ourselves, with a desire to be convinced where solid cause of conviction shall appear, notwithstanding the little cavils of little cavillers, and above all things with an inflexible determination to pursue the public good in spite of all opposition from local or private interests.

In this place before I proceed further, let me pay the tribute justly due to the author of certain letters on free trade and finance, who hath written more good sense on that subject than hath appeared from any, or perhaps every other quarter.[3] That the writings are not more generally read and approved of, is perhaps owing to this circumstance, that they contain nothing of novelty to recommend them to prurient curiosity. For in politics as in physics and religion, the plain old sober dictates of science and truth, are neglected, nay despised, for new maxims, new doctrines, new cures, and new tricks. Hence the tribe of schemers, mountebanks, and itinerant preachers, with their attendant herd of rogues, fools and enthusiasts.

The nature of money is among those great political topicks, which require no small share of industry to be fully acquainted with. Nor is the difficulty removed, when paper is substituted in the place of gold; it requires much attention to make proper distinctions, and free ourselves from that connection of different ideas, which habit has rendered almost inseparable. To avoid confusion, the word *money* will, in these papers be equally applied to every kind of it. *Specie* to what is called hard-money, that is coined bullion, and the Bills of Credit will be called by the simple name of *paper.*

Money is the child of commerce, and of consequence it differs in different places, according to the actual state of society. Specie, in some nations, is not money. Paper is so in very few. The first and rudest commerce is by barter, and wherever that obtains, it marks either a very savage State, a very absurd Legislature, or a very tyrannous Administration. The difficulty of comparing the value of different things, renders a common measure necessary. If for instance, among a rude people, any individuals wished to interchange bows and arrows for coarse cloth, it would be difficult to discover how much of the one must be given for the other. It would not be so difficult to estimate the ingenuity, labour and materials expended on each of them. These form the true value; but even these do not admit of a regular and exact comparison. Some other thing therefore, of common use, production or estimation, such as oxen, sheep, corn, &c. must be taken for the

---

3. Morris is probably referring to a series of "Essays on Free Trade and Finances" which appeared in the *Pennsylvania Packet* in late 1779 and early 1780. The third and last essay was published in two parts, on January 6 and 8, 1780.

common measure, or money. Among nations still more barbarous, where there is no agriculture or tame animals, natural productions used either as food or ornament, become the money of the country. Such as cocoa nuts in the islands of the pacific ocean, and wampum among the Savages of North America. In the advanced state of society, precious metals are adopted, because they are not subject to decay, because their value may be reduced to a certainty, and because they may be divided and subdivided with accuracy. The precious metals are first used as bullion, that is to say, they pass according to their quantity and fineness, in which case, every trader must have a scale to try the weight, and an assay to determine the alloy. This practice formerly obtained through Europe, and continues in some places at this moment. But as it is very inconvenient, the government of civilized States have provided particular marks, to distinguish the value of every piece, and this is called money, in contradistinction to bullion. In a more advanced state of society, it is found to be dangerous, difficult and consequently expensive, to transfer considerable sums of specie from place to place; to remedy this, Bills of Exchange have been invented which are the first kind of paper. The great value of specie, the ease with which a person may be robbed of it, and other circumstances occurring in the rapid progress of civilization, introduced the practice of lodging money in public or private banks, and accepting notes in lieu of it. These are the second kind of paper. Finally, bills have been issued by public authority to pass in lieu of specie, the government covenanting with individuals that at some future period the one shall be given for the other. This then is the third kind of paper, with respect to which it is remarkable, that some governments have had the boldness to compel their subjects to accept it, even when the period of redemption was not fixed, and what is still more remarkable, those laws have been followed neither by insurrection nor yet by the absolute ruin of the paper itself, or even by a general clamor. Thus, as in a strong natural body, where the principle of life is vigorous and energetic, the worst aliments will be digested and become nutritious; so in society, where a thorough confidence in their rulers pervades and animates the whole State. The most impolitic institutions will be corrected by the manners of the people, and rendered subservient to useful purposes. But alas, in the one case as in the other, persisting in error brings on evils of an alarming nature, which the ablest management will hardly alleviate. To quit the metaphor. A course of blunders on the part of government will at length destroy that confidence which is the source of their authority. Then a thousand and a thousand things which were easy before will become impracticable. Then they must bid adieu to fine spun plans and beautiful theories. However reluctant, they must bid adieu to imaginary strokes of finance. With nice distinctions between a breach of promise in words and in deeds; they must no more amuse the casuistical fancy. No more must they soar in aerial heights sublime. In short, they must be content to move slowly along in the plain path of common sense and common honesty, or they will soon cease to move at all.

Money is only the sign of wealth, and its value is derived from credit or opinion. Corn used as money is at once a necessary of life, a commodity and a sign of wealth; specie applied to the same purpose, is both a commodity and money. But paper is money simply and purely, being neither a necessary of life nor a commodity. He who in the first case sells his property for corn, gives it some little credit as money, more as a commodity, and much more as a necessary of life. He who in the second case sells his property for specie, gives it credit as money from a conviction, that the whole commercial world will receive it again; he gives it also some credit as a commodity. But he who sells his property for paper, gives it credit as money alone, for if others will not in their turn, receive his paper, it is absolutely good for nothing.

The experience of ages had long since declared, and our own experience hath severely demonstrated, that all tricks played with money, such as debasing the coin, and others of that cast, have greatly injured the government, as well as individuals. The reason of this appears, from the foregoing considerations, which prove that credit is the foundation of money. Take away the former; and the latter falls in shapeless ruin. Barter is introduced, commerce is fettered, mutual confidence among men is shaken, confidence in the government is lost. No one will trust it for a month, nor with a shilling. The State cannot make vigorous exertions. Oeconomy in the administration, becomes impracticable. Confusion arises. The country lies in prey to its enemies, or hangs as a weight about the neck of its friends. A thousand little shifts and mean expedients take place of manly decisive wisdom and fortitude, while the butterfly dignity of government, is crushed beneath the hand of insult, or blown away in the breath of ridicule.

It is a vulgar error, that specie is better than good paper. If paper were emitted in such form, that it could not be well counterfeited, under such circumstances that it would not depreciate, and for sums not expressed by any particular coin, it would be preferable to specie. 1st. Because the value being purely arbitrary, it would also be determinate, and consequently a more certain measure of value by the same rule that the distance of forty miles is more certain and determinate than a day's travel, and nine inches than a span. 2dly. Because it would not be liable to gradual waste by the wear, nor to adulteration or diminution. 3dly. Because it could more easily be transported from place to place. And 4thly. Because when destroyed, the community would be at no expence to replace it, which is always the case with specie. To this may be added some other advantages, which not being so obvious shall in this place be omitted.

The credit of paper issued by a State depends upon the idea of the wealth of the State, the ability of the government to call it forth, and the integrity of those whose duty it may be to apply it. These are the ultimate objects of such credit, though the immediate object is the idea of what it will fetch at the market, just as the ultimate credit of a bank paper depends upon the wealth of the banker, and his disposition to pay or the legal means of compelling him. Suppose the credit good as to its ultimate object, still the paper may depreciate by a super-abundance of quantity, by a probability of farther increase, and by the very circumstance that it hath depreciated. For upon the instant that money becomes of uncertain value, men are unwilling to use it as the medium of their commerce, just as they would decline to buy or sell by weights and measures which are continually varying.

An inquiry into all the causes by which our paper hath depreciated would be perhaps amusing, and though laborious, it would not be without utility; but the data on which calculations must be made are too uncertain. It is not for instance at all fixed what would be the necessary circulating medium of the continent, nor even what was the circulating medium heretofore. Were I to hazard an opinion, I should fix both much higher than any estimate I have yet seen. Indeed the present value of the paper cannot otherwise, I believe, be rationally accounted for. No rule of depreciation can be drawn from the quantity by any direct numerical process. Moral causes of various kinds are to be added to the account, and these act with a velocity continually increased by their own action. Even if the quantity alone gave rise to the depreciation, the manner in which it operates appears much mistaken. Suppose in a very sultry day it should be found that, the consumption of this city being ten thousand pounds of flesh, and no salt to be had; does any man believe that this super-abundance would lower the price only one twentieth? Would, for instance, the beef, part of which at six o'clock had been vended at five pence, sell at nine o'clock for five pence three farthings? Would it not more probably fall to three pence, or even two pence? It is not my object to dilate unnecessarily; the intelligent reader when the game is started can himself hunt it down, and the unintelligent had better quit a subject he can never understand. But further, it would be a mistake to suppose that a super-abundance of money acted with no greater force as to its price than the super-abundance of a commodity. The consumption of a commodity is for the most part equable, or if it varies it will be greatest when there is the greatest plenty, and the demand is in a ratio compounded of the consumption and the quantity. A super-abundance of money, on the contrary, instead of increasing really lessens the demands for it, because fewer commodities are offered for sale, and every person striving to turn his money, it is applied with increasing velocity to every saleable object. Now there is no reason in the world why one barleycorn, if an infinite velocity be given to it, could not measure in a moment the immensity of space. Money, therefore, being the measure of wealth, operates like nature with a momentum[4] equal to its quantity multiplied into its velocity.

Here let us pause; and while we contemplate the huge object, which by a combination of natural, moral and political causes, is driven forwards impetuously towards general ruin over the prostrate morals of society and amid the imprecations of the widow, the feeble, the fatherless, the aged, the undefended, let us pause and endeavour to investigate those other causes which with contrary influence have impeded, checked, stopped, and almost inverted its progress; causes, which if left to their free operation, will say to this deluging flood in the imperative tone of authority, so far shalt thou go and no farther.

And here it is to be observed, that although in the first instance depreciation will generate a further depreciation, yet at length that further depreciation will cure itself. For there is something in money which leads it, like the power of gravitation in fluids, to seek continually the natural level. Of consequence, therefore, when by any accident money is raised too high, it immediately descends, and, if left to itself, after many undulations will come to a fixture. The increased depreciation having raised the prices of all articles, it is soon found that the circulating medium is too small for the purposes of commerce. Money then becomes relatively scarce. The opposite cause produces an opposite effect and runs to the opposite extreme, until at length it finds that mean where the value is in direct proportion to the quantity. This reasoning, however, does not apply to a medium constantly increasing, an exception which will be afterwards noted, but is mentioned in this place because otherwise conclusions might be too forcibly drawn from what had been before stated.

I have spoken of paper hitherto without marking particularly the effects

---

4. In the manuscript, "momentum"; in the newspaper, "momenture."

which follow from the idea of redemption. But now let us advert for this purpose to our own paper. Suppose a full confidence prevailed that in twenty years it would be appreciated to its nominal value; then every man possessed of forty dollars would believe that if he kept it twenty years it would be worth forty dollars in specie. Now if we reckon a compound interest at six per cent. forty dollars payable twenty years hence will be worth at present about twelve and a half, which deducting two and a half leaves ten. Wherefore it would follow, that he who purchased paper at the rate of four for one, would have the best possible security to receive a compound six per cent. interest on his money, with an ultimate additional profit of twenty-five per cent. at the end of twenty years. Our paper then, computing it at forty for one, is depreciated ten times more than it would be if the ultimate objects of credit were unimpaired. Whether the public diffidence arises from an idea of the poverty of the State, the weakness of government, or their want of integrity, is not as yet the subject of enquiry. Let it suffice at present to observe, that the favorable or unfavorable opinion on these topics must necessarily retard or accelerate the progress of depreciation.

To these two general principles may be added some others of lesser import, which will meet the attention of the contemplative reader. Quitting then this subject for the present, the next object deserving of notice is to examine the effects of those laws made with the express design of supporting the credit of our paper.

I am your friend,

An AMERICAN.

February 24, 1780

To the INHABITANTS of AMERICA.
My COUNTRYMEN,

To combat opinions generally received and supported by great authority, is a task which the prudent would wish to avoid. A man generally gets but little by his labour, and is for the most part, esteemed to be a madman or

Pennsylvania Packet, or General Advertiser, Februrary 24, 1780. Courtesy American Antiquarian Society.

a fool. Nay, it is well if he comes off at so cheap a rate, for there is a certain dogmaticalness of disposition inherent in human nature, which makes each individual a Pope to himself, and leads him to talk, write and fight with equal obstinacy, to defend his own infallibility, and destroy that of his neighbour.

I should gladly avoid unnecessary opposition to received maxims, being by nature and education so much more attached to ease, than fond of distinction, as fully to agree with a late reverend writer, "That if the army of Martyrs is to be recruited, or a new one raised, I will have no hand in the business one way or t'other."[1] It is, however, necessary to understand the nature of our political complaints, before we can apply a remedy, and for this purpose, attention to facts is better than the best hypothesis. Among the first efforts to support the credit of our paper, was the law for rendering it a lawful tender, and that which inflicted pains and penalties on those who should refuse to receive it as equivalent to specie. The learned Doctor Price, from the bosom of the British capital, hath ventured to assure us of the utility of such laws, and thence inferred, that our paper is much better than that which is issued by the Bank of England.[2] His hypothesis may be good, his reasoning on it very good, and his conclusions fairly drawn; but stubborn fact stands opposed to them. This shews at least, that we ought a little to distrust hypothetical propositions.

Shall I be pardoned, for asserting in contradiction to Doctor Price, that a law to make paper a tender, is injurious to it? Will the reader bear with patience an attempt to prove my position? I am aware of the objection that heretofore such laws did not injure the paper then issued, but surely it would be illogical to assert, that every thing of an injurious nature, must do actual injury, or that a weak opposition is no opposition at all. It must be remembered, that the paper emitted through the several States shortly previous to the present war, was strongly requested, nay, demanded by the people. The rapid extension of our commerce, rendered it necessary, notwithstanding a more general credit was given throughout America, than in almost any other country. Add to this, that it was proper to make some money a legal tender, for the meer purposes of jurisprudence, and it was

1. The quotation is from Laurence Sterne, *Tristram Shandy*, chapter 3.XI; Sterne has "augmented" rather than "recruited," and the concluding phrase is "I would have no hand in it, one way or t'other."

2. Richard Price, 1723-91, Welsh philosopher and clergyman, was a prominent British supporter of the American cause.

very indifferent what kind of money that was. From these reasons arose an universal consent among all ranks of men, to receive the paper of government, and therefore the ill effects of the law, were no more perceptible, than the weight of an ounce against fifty pounds. Yet there is no doubt but that when the scales are even, the weight of an ounce would cause one of them to preponderate. When the purposes of commerce do not require an increase of the circulating medium, and when of consequence the people do not desire it, nothing can be more unjust than to compel a man to receive for a pound of silver, a piece of paper, which the government do not mean to repay with another pound, in less than twenty years. Suppose the government should seize a man's flock of fifty sheep, and give him a promissory note to pay fifty sheep twenty years hence, would not this be considered as a horrible tyranny. And where is the difference except in value, between taking a pound of silver, or a pound of mutton, one sheep, or fifty sheep. Suppose again, that after taking the stock of A in the above arbitrary manner, there should be a power given to him, to seize as many sheep from his neighbour B, and to pay for them by the same promissory note, and so on, from B to C and from C to D, through the whole community. Would not such a law of itself, be sufficient to occasion a general revolt, and where is the difference between seizing sheep, and seizing the value of them; or between paying for goods with a note for sheep, and a note for the price of them in silver and gold.

That such laws have not had the effects above stated, is to be attributed to the causes already assigned, and further, we may observe that while the paper is in full credit, and a man can get from his neighbour the specie specified on the face of it, we do not perceive the injustice. But this perception instantly recurs when the paper depreciates. Besides we know, that a great part of the community would have resisted long ago, if they had dared. Many have eluded it, all now join in reprobating it; and the only difficulty as to the repeal, seems to be about the manner.

This law therefore, must appear from the considerations already stated, to be either useless or unjust. Useless before the paper depreciates, unjust afterwards. Useless as to the obtaining a currency for it, because no law could do that, without the general consent of society, and unjust by forcing the acceptance of it, above the natural value. But it is not sufficient, to have proved it simply useless or unjust. I must go farther, and attempt at least to shew that it is pernicious. And to do this let us suppose that without such law government should at any time go on and issue paper until all the channels of commerce were compleatly filled: The paper would at that moment be on the eve of depreciating from its quantity, and would depreciate unless a wise and timely stop was put to the emissions. In this situation of things let us suppose the government become apprehensive of a depreciation, and in order to prevent it enact a Tender Law.

Before we take one step farther, let us remember, that nothing is more pernicious in money-matters than to have what are called State secrets concerning them: Such secrets are very indifferently kept in Republics. A representative Body will never permit any individual to keep their secrets for them, and they may rely on it, the people at large have not delegated their curiosity, but will be at least as prying as their superiors. Nay, they will assert an equal privilege with them, to reason on public affairs, and are not always the worse reasoners of the two.

In the case above put, the people will instantly know the principle on which the law is enacted, or at least they will suspect it. Though government should keep its motives secret, they will immediately infer even from passing such a law that the paper stood in need of aid, and ask this dangerous question: if the legislature were not convinced that the money would not pass without their interposition, why did they interpose? From that moment each individual receives it with suspicious reluctance, and pushes it with eagerness to his neighbour. The debtor begins to pay his debts by selling property at an advanced price to some money-holder solicitous to realize. The creditor accustomed to live from the interest of his funds, and finding no one who will covenant to give him that interest, is obliged to turn speculator or beggar, and becomes one or the other according to his opportunities and abilities, or the degree of his indolence or activity. The circulation thus rapidly increased, and the quantity of vendible property diminished, depreciation is a natural and necessary consequence.

But this is not all. When men begin to reason on a subject, neither tyrants nor mobs can hinder them, on the contrary every effort to prevent it carries them rapidly to conclusions, even without regard to premises. For the argument is still the same, if the thing will bear consideration, why not let us consider it? In reasoning therefore on the Tender Law, they see its injustice; the debtor who is benefited by it, and whose clamors masked under the garb of patriotism, give it vigor and activity. The fraudulent debtor sees the injustice as clearly as his defrauded creditor. Both of them therefore agree in their sentiments of the legislature.

There is nothing more dangerous than the tyrant's plea of necessity. It is an argument which applies with equal force to every thing, and that government is indeed unhappy which is obliged to recur to it. If necessity can induce the breach of one moral tie, it can of another. If it will justify fraud, it will excuse murder. Let those in authority beware of it. Let them take care how they obey the calls of necessity, even though urged by the voice of the whole community, when that necessity is to commit evil. If they do obey it, however pleasing their conduct may be for a moment, they will soon find, that like the book of the Revelations, though sweet in the mouth, it is better[3] in the belly, and that the people will, sooner or later, despise those who have sinned against their own consciences to please the people. In the case before us, each individual will consider, that the redemption of the paper depends on the men who have made it a lawful tender: And he will tremble to think of what necessity may lead to at a future period. Thus one of the ultimate objects of credit is impaired, confidence in the integrity of government.

Of the same class with this, are all other laws made to support the credit of paper. On their very face they carry the strongest arguments against it. No artful preamble can evade—still less can it answer the great question: Why enact it? Why these pains and penalties to compel the exchange of a round dollar for a square one, if the exchange would take place without them? Shall the word necessity stop the clamorous mouth of enquiry? Alas! It only shews that the folly of the law is equal to its iniquity. It shews that the paper and the specie are not of equal value, at the very moment it attempts to force an exchange. It shews too, that they have made an attempt, which from the very manner of making it, must prove ineffectual. Thus in the same moment, the people lose their confidence both in the integrity and in the wisdom of government: So that another of the ultimate objects of credit is impaired.

Here let us stop, and leave to a future opportunity the consideration of those laws for limiting prices, which may be called regulations. They deserve a separate place, for they have not only the disadvantages above stated in common with the Tender and Exchange Laws, but some others of no little moment peculiar to themselves. Whether these are equal to the advantages expected from them, and whether any such advantages really do or can arise will then perhaps appear. It will appear to the candid enquirer. If there be a prejudiced reader, he will perhaps liberally dispense the term knave, blockhead, or some other of the pretty little appellations at present

---

3. Morris or more likely the typesetter has made a crucial typographical error here. The quotation from Revelation 10:10 is: "and it was in my mouth sweet as honey: and as soon as I had eaten it, my belly was bitter."

used by witty writers and polite critics. But he will at some time or other acknowlege that such flowers of rhetoric may be very properly spared, and that the interests of society, like those of heaven, can better be served by solid reasoning than florid declamation, much less abuse.

It will be useful in this place to consider attentively the nature of our paper, because the many writings relative to it, like the lace and fringe on Peter's coat, have almost hidden the original cloth.[4] The paper is a promissory note for so much specie from the government to the holder of it: Consequently it is a promise of as much labor and as much of the necessaries and even luxuries of life as that specie would purchase. It is like a similar note from an individual, excepting that the day of payment is not fixed, a circumstance which, among others, hath tended much to impair the credit. Suppose the individual A, being possessed of a great landed estate, with necessary stock and utensils so as to derive from it a considerable income, hath promised his neighbour B to pay him one hundred bushels of wheat at some future day: When the day arrives ought he not to pay? Suppose the promise had been made in 1775, payable in 1780? Would it be just for him to say, one hundred bushels of wheat were worth in 1775 one hundred dollars, here, take you one hundred dollars which I have obtained by the sale of two bushels? Would a Court of Justice support him in this chicanery? A promise to pay money is nothing more or less than a promise to pay what that money will purchase; and that which is unjust in an individual is unjust in a nation.

But what is the contract which results simply from issuing paper? The government promise, on the part of all the land, labor and commodities of the country, to the individual who shall accept the paper in lieu of his property, that an equal quantity shall be returned to him in exchange for that paper. If the individual voluntarily accepts the proffer of government, a contract is made, and that contract ought to be fulfilled scrupulously and exactly, not nominally and apparently. But suppose the individual is unwilling to trust the government, and suppose they compel him to accept their paper, does this diminish their obligation to repay it? In other words, shall government take advantage of their own wrong? Is a trespass more justifiable than a breach of promise? Or is a man less guilty of the violation of a contract because he forcibly compelled his neighbour to make it? Suppose,

---

4. In Jonathan Swift's satire *A Tale of a Tub*, the lace and fringe on Peter's coat symbolized the embellishments on the pure doctrine of Scripture (the coat itself) by the Catholic Church.

to carry the matter still further, the individual should incline to ask more of the paper for his property when so obliged to receive it than he would have accepted in specie, and that in such case government should again interpose and force the acceptance of it at an equal rate with specie, would not this also increase the obligation? Laws of this sort, although they impair the value of the paper, increase the duty and multiply the obligations of the State to redeem it. An individual, when called on for money, would best maintain his credit by punctual payment; but if instead thereof he should give notes, bonds, mortgages, judgments, promises, vows and oaths, each step would diminish the faith of his creditors, although it would increase his legal and moral duties to satisfy their demands. If such debtor should daily increase his expences, neglect his occupation, and suffer his affairs to run fast into confusion, none but usurers would deal with him, and those only on the most exorbitant terms. But should he drop a hint that he intended to become a fraudulent bankrupt, from that moment all confidence in him would be lost, and every person who had been so unfortunate as to trust him would endeavour speedily to realize a part of his demand by accepting a large discount. If he happened to be privileged against legal process, the mischief would be increased, and his note for a guinea might sell for a crown, a shilling, or even a groat.[5] Similar causes will always produce similar effects, and honesty and credit are alike in public and in private life.

It has for some time past been a fashion to fear that the money would appreciate; that it would appreciate too fast, and the like. These ridiculous apprehensions have found admittance to graver places than will readily be imagined. The experience of many months hath shewn them to be groundless; but now it is contended that appreciation would be a greater injustice to the public in favor of the money-holders, while at the same time it is contended that depreciation was a just and wise tax.[6] These propositions when contrasted have no very favorable aspect, and unless I am much mistaken, they will both appear to be false when separately considered.

To recur then to the case above put. Suppose on the death of the debtor his heir should oeconomize his affairs, become industrious and thrifty, pay the debts his father had contracted, retrench the old expences and avoid new ones: Would not his credit increase? Would not the notes which had sold for a groat rise to the value of a shilling, a crown, and at length a guinea? Although he might perhaps honestly buy his father's notes at their

5. A groat was worth four pence.
6. This was the position taken by the author of the "Letters on Appreciation."

depreciated value, might he as honestly insist on having them at his own price, or not paying them at all? And when the value of them rose, would he be justifiable in forcibly keeping it down? Although he might alledge that what his father had received only a groat for should be repaid with a groat. He would hardly contend that the note given for one guinea should not be repaid with another, merely because it had afterwards been negociated at an under value. If to him who had purchased such a note for a groat it should be said that he ought not in justice to demand a guinea, would he not reply, that when he paid his groat the chance of getting any thing was so dubious that the full value of the note was paid? If his reprover should pretend to be a friend of the deceased, and charge his opponent with an usurious disposition, might not the creditor very properly ask of such a friend, why he had not himself given for the same note a shilling? Might he not ask which was the most sincere in professions of friendship, he who had given a groat or he who would give nothing?

I do not mean to apply this doctrine with all the strictness it would admit of. I do not pretend that the modesty of subjects should serve as a model or rule for the fortitude of their rulers. I am very sensible that government have more enlarged views of objects than can be taken in by the weak optics of private information. Above all things I am far from wishing to hazard the shadow of censure on my superiors. I would, however, pray of them not to consider the breach of moral duties among the common resources of a Financier. I do not contend that our paper will appreciate; I certainly do not fear that it will. This however I do contend, that any effort of the State to prevent the appreciation would, according to the rules of private justice, be wrong; and if public acts are to be tried by a different standard, I confess it is a standard I am unacquainted with.

But it will be said that depreciation hath made engrossers nominally rich, and that appreciation would realize their hoards. The demerits of engrossers will be examined at a future period. Admitting, however, that the effects of their conduct are as pernicious as the cause is despicable, and admitting them to be as nefarious as it shall please any body to describe them, still the point in dispute is far from decided. If they are guilty of one crime, must government to punish them be guilty of another? How is this on the private scale? May A cheat B, because B cheated C? I know it is easy to exclaim against engrossers, but it is much more useful to reason. Putting the immorality of this business out of the question, government I fear would not find their account in it, for the political pursuit of engrossers, tories, &c. very much resembles fox-hunting, which, whatever sport it may give to the huntsmen, and however it may purport the defence of geese and chickens, is always attended with more cost than profit.

Suppose by some sudden stroke from heaven the money could instantly be appreciated: Who would not gain by it? Certainly not the engrosser. He has it not. His occupation consists in keeping any thing and every thing but money. Suppose the appreciation takes place by degrees, in the common course of levying taxes, then all will by degrees gain and lose: They will gain on the appreciation of the money; they will lose in the price of commodities. But the engrosser will gain least because he has least money, and he will lose most because all commodities would be brought to bear their natural proportion to each other, and of consequence those which by monopoly had been raised higher than their due level would necessarily in the reduction of prices be most reduced.

Thus, then, it is evident, that any attempt to prevent the appreciation of our money would be equally impolitic and dishonest. Let us next examine whether depreciation was a just and wise tax.

I am your friend,

An AMERICAN.

FEBRUARY 29, 1780

To the INHABITANTS of AMERICA.

My Countrymen,

It is among the advantages of a government, administered on free principles, that a man may not only follow what occupation he pleases, but hold also the opinions, and publish the doctrines which are most agreeable to him. As many seem inclined to use this last privilege, particularly with relation to your finances, all have the opportunity of chusing a system ready made, if they will not be at the trouble of framing one for themselves. It is however by no means a matter of indifference, what system is generally adopted, and particularly whether or not it be an honest system; for though we should admit, that a considerable present profit may be derived from

Pennsylvania Packet, or General Advertiser, February 29, 1780. Courtesy American Antiquarian Society. Parts of this letter are in items 813 and 815, Gouverneur Morris Papers, Rare Book and Manuscript Library, Columbia University.

knavery, we must agree that a lasting loss is incurred. So that in effect a sum obtained on fraudulent principles, pays heavier interest than even an usurer would have exacted.

Chartres, who was one of the most notorious as well as one of the greatest rogues that ever lived, often said, he would give ten thousand pounds for a good character.[1] It seems that by repeatedly ruining the widow and the orphan, with other enormities, his bad reputation was so firmly established, that he could no longer find men foolish enough to become his dupes. Government will soon arrive at the deplorable situation of Chartres, if they suffer themselves to be drawn into an imitation of his conduct.

These things being premised, let us proceed to examine, whether the depreciation hath been a wise and just tax. I involve these things together, because I wish to inculcate a thorough conviction, that in all cases, but more particularly in matters of finance, that which is wicked can never be wise.

The proposition that depreciation is a good tax, involves two others. First that a tax on money is a good one, and secondly, that the depreciation is a good mode of laying and collecting it. To give both these a fair examination, we will for the present admit the former to be true. In order to determine the latter, let us suppose the State is about to issue its paper, and should say openly to the people, we here offer you our note for a guinea, but we intend to make so many others of the same kind, that it shall not eventually be worth more than a groat. What would such a note sell for in the first instance? Perhaps nothing, but certainly not above four pence, because it is evident, that no man would give more for it in present, than it would be worth in future. The intention of the State, therefore would be defeated at once, and they would have the mortification to find that the whole course of intended depreciation, would be run in an instant.

Suppose that instead of fixing the future value at a groat, they were to leave it indefinite. Then what would the note sell for? It would sell for nothing; because, even those who inclined to believe in it at all, would conclude differently, as to the eventual value. But as the eventual must be the standard of the immediate value, consequently, the latter would be as indeterminate as the former; and therefore, it could not possibly serve as a medium of commerce. If for instance, the individual A, believed it would be worth half a guinea, B a crown, and C a shilling. If A wanted to buy of B, the price would be too high, and if of C, it would be still higher. But as each

---

1. Colonel Francis Chartres (1675-1732) was a notorious rake. He is featured in Hogarth's *A Harlot's Progress*.

of them would trade for specie on equal terms, he would refuse the paper for the sake of a more certain medium.

It may be said that experience hath contradicted this reasoning. If her sentence is against us, we must be wrong, but perhaps, that sentence is mistaken. We must remember, that when the money was first issued it was to a people used to place confidence in paper. It was accompanied with promises, similar to those which they had been accustomed to rely on. It was made for a purpose they had much at heart. Their enthusiasm would hardly give time for reflection. The circulation of it at the value specified was a necessary consequence, and that circulation having taken place, the few who had not confidence, found it would purchase of the many who had; wherefore, as it served to satisfy their immediate wants, they also would naturally receive it. Add to this, that the general determination of the people, and their good opinion of the Congress was so great, that no person dared openly suggest a doubt of the future redemption. For whatever solid reasoning such doubt might have arisen from, or been supported by, it certainly would then have been placed to the account of disaffection. Nay, it is more than probable, that if any man out of Congress, had hazarded the idea of an intentional depreciation, the people would have washed out such an insult on that respected Body, with the blood of the offender. There is then an infinite difference between the two cases. But if we consult experience in a more similar instance, we shall find, that her unerring decree is decidedly in our favour. What was the conduct of those who really entertained doubts as to the future value? Did they not shut up their stores, conceal their goods, leave their grain unthreshed, and the like? Were not the first regulations made expressly with the view of punishing disaffected persons? And were not the terms tory and monopolizer very early considered as of the same import? But this is not all: We must all remember the late situation of things, when by an attempt made in some publications to shew the propriety of redeeming our paper at a depreciated rate, the rapidity of depreciation was so accelerated as to give an appearance of reason to the very doctrines which occasioned it. Under these circumstances, many persons refused to traffic for any other money than specie; but since that period, when the paper had obtained a more fixed value, the same persons received it with equal, and in some instances with greater readiness.

The reader's own judgment and reflection will convince him without further proof, that if the intended depreciation were declared, it would fail of the effect. Let us next suppose it to be concealed, and then the first idea which presents itself is the violation of public faith.

It hath been already observed, that our paper is a promise made by Government on the part of those who possess the land, labour, and commodities of the country. This idea cannot be too well fixed in our minds. When A purchases a commodity of B what does he give? Not specie but the promise of Government for so much specie at a future period. Not only in the act of emitting therefore is this promise made, it is reiterated by the public officers who convey it from the Treasury to individuals; nay, more; it is confirmed in every private bargain. If A being indebted to B assigns in payment a promissory note, which C had given him, C becomes B's debtor instead of A; but as this is purely optional, C makes no new contract with B, who relies upon the original promise made to A. On the contrary, if A delivers in payment a promissory note of Government, that is, if he pays the debt with paper, then the Government having by law compelled B to accept their paper in extinguishment of A's debt, they of consequence make a new contract with him for the redemption of it. This being the case, what can be more dishonest than to continue issuing such notes, in order to reduce their value. If the baleful effect be produced, it is of no consequence in what mode the cause operates. To poison is as wicked as to stab, nor was it ever yet heard of, that the guilt of murder could be atoned by the clean and clever manner of performing it. The iniquity of breaking public promises directly is evident. Can the breaking them indirectly mend the matter? Or in other words, will the weight of a crime be lessened by the addition of hypocrisy?

But further, it is confessed on all hands that taxes should be raised from individuals in proportion to their wealth. Depreciation on the contrary raises its tax in the greatest possible disproportion. He who by the successful efforts of twenty years unremitted industry, had gained a little competence in money, is taxed at least nineteen shillings in the pound, while his neighbour who possesses a country almost equal to that of a German Prince is not taxed a shilling.

Again: If Government can ever be justified in making a difference as to the proportion of taxes to be paid, that difference should be in favour of its best and most faithful subjects, but depreciation operates most on those who have received most of the paper, and he who never would receive it at all, eludes the tax entirely.

Lastly, a wise government will always encourage and reward industry and frugality, and for the same reason, it will discountenance and punish idleness and dissipation, but if the theory and practice of depreciation be established and adopted, then it will follow, that he who laboured most and wasted least, would pay the heaviest tax, and he who wasted most and laboured least, would pay the lightest.

This new doctrine, then, of depreciation, founded on the supposed propriety of taxing money, involves in it as necessary consequences, that those who should receive it, from their confidence in, and attachment to government, would be defrauded, and those who should refuse it, would benefit by the fraud. That those who had industriously added to the wealth of the State, would lose the fruits of their industry, for the sake of the lazy and dissolute; and that those who had been compelled to accept the paper, would be as effectually robbed by the two acts of government taken together, as they would have been by the one act of a highway-man or house-breaker.

I shall forbear to mention the frauds which public officers are excited to commit, by a knowledge that the depreciating money placed in their hands for the public service, may by a seasonable investure for private purposes, produce an amazing profit, and yet their accounts appear to be perfectly square and just. On this subject I feel too much to speak with temper, besides it is not my object to inflame but to inform. Peace be with them, if bosoms like theirs can harbour peace.

But let us now suppose, that all objections to the mode could possibly be obviated, still there remains another question, whether the pre-supposed tax on money is a good one? This again divides itself into two points, first, whether it be right to lay a tax on specie? And secondly, whether if so, it be also right to tax the paper which represents it? These questions should be examined with accuracy, because they bid fair to occur frequently in the course of our public affairs. Admitting then, for the present, that a tax on specie is right, let us examine the other.

Taxes should be laid and levied upon the wealth of the State. If in any society, the wealth, that is the land, labour and commodities were worth 9,900,000 dollars, and if there were in it 100,000 dollars circulating specie, as this sum would when sent abroad, bring home an equivalent in other commodities, the wealth of the State might be estimated at 10,000,000. Suppose in this situation of things, the government should issue a million of paper, would the State be richer than before? Would it produce more of the necessaries of life, or maintain a greater number of men? Certainly it would not, nor on the other hand, would the wealth of the State be diminished, should the whole paper be instantly destroyed. But during the circulation of it, every commodity would nominally be dearer, perhaps at twenty prices, consequently the nominal wealth of that state would be 200,000,000. A tax, therefore, of six pence in the pound, on every man's property, would sink the whole. Let us suppose that in such a State, during the circulation of the paper, a part of the people, either from diffidence as to the value, opposition to Government, or any other cause, should constantly avoid receiving it, or when received immediately dispose of it, what would be the consequences of a tax on the paper under all these circumstances? In the first place the burden would not fall on the wealth of the State, but meerly on the sign, or measure of that wealth. For instance, if A and B being possessed of equal property, A had sold to B and received paper, B who had the wealth would pay nothing, A who had only the sign would pay all. In the second place the burthen would not fall on the whole people, but only on a part, and that the most friendly to government. In the third place, the doubts and difficulties as to receiving the paper would be encreased, because the tax would operate as a premium to the money-holder, to dispose of it, and as a penalty upon his neighbour, for receiving it. Thus while government by one law compel the reception of their notes, they by another prohibit it. Of consequence the notes and the government too would vaguely fluctuate on the surface of popular opinion, and like a shattered bark with tattered sails and broken oars, whose rudder is lost, they would become the sport of those waves which could not fail to overwhelm them.

The objections above stated have certainly some weight; but another and a weightier objection still remains. To elucidate it let us suppose, that a merchant had issued his promissory notes to the amount of 10,000*l*. and when called on for payment, instead of vending a part of his property, should offer his creditors, ten fifteen or even nineteen shillings in the pound. If he was able to pay the whole he certainly would be considered as a knave, and if not as a bankrupt. Where is the difference between paying only nineteen shillings in the pound, and a tax of one shilling in the pound laid by government on its own notes? Would not the conclusion in both cases be the same? If a tax of one shilling can be justly laid, why not a tax of ten? Why not of nineteen? Why not sink the whole at a single stroke? Can a satisfactory answer be given to such questions? If it cannot, what will become of that public confidence on which not only the paper but the government itself must be supported? For the security of their rights mankind unite in the social state. For these they place the sword in the hand of the Magistrate. For these they have often resumed it. Let me not be misunderstood. I do not pretend to blame the private sentiments of any individual, much less any collective body, and infinitely less the deliberative act of any State. I know all the indecency of presuming to set up private judgment as the measure of public conduct. I shall therefore most sedulously endeavor to avoid it. I wish to avoid the shadow of offence to any, but I wish to give salutary caution to all. I earnestly wish to remove the cloud of prejudice and display the radiance of truth.

I am your friend,

AN AMERICAN.

MARCH 4, 1780

To the INHABITANTS of AMERICA.

MY COUNTRYMEN,

I know not what success these papers may have, but if they answer the intentions of the writer, they will have a good one; as a great part of his time hath been spent in the public service, it became his duty to think attentively on public affairs; and he now considers it as his duty to give you those reflections which were originally made for your benefit. He does not pretend to convince your servants. To be convinced is not their business, as everybody knows. But if his opinions are founded on arguments which have weight with you, your voice will not be unattended to.

Having already endeavoured to shew, that depreciation is a bad mode of collecting a tax on money, and that a tax on paper is a bad one. It still remains to determine, whether paper being out of the question, it is right to tax specie. To tax it as a commodity, is just. To tax it as a luxury, is wise. To tax it as money, is impolitic and unjust. He who hath invested 1000*l.* in plate, ought to be taxed the same proportion on that sum with him who hath invested 1000*l.* in land. He may also be taxed for it in a further sum, as being one evidence of that great wealth, which cannot perhaps be reached in any other manner than laying high rates on those luxuries which are the visible signs of it. But the man who hath 1000*l.* of specie in his chest, or hath lent that sum to his neighbour, ought not to be taxed for it. Now as

Pennsylvania Packet, or General Advertiser, March 4, 1780. Courtesy American Antiquarian Society. Portions of this letter are in items 813 and 815, Gouverneur Morris Papers, Rare Book and Manuscript Library, Columbia University. The March 11 letter, which follows, includes a list of errata in this one. Those errors have been corrected here.

these propositions may appear extraordinary, and, as it is a very favorite maxim with some, that bonds in particular ought to be taxed. I shall examine the question on the ground both of justice and policy.

If there be no law to regulate the rate of interest, it will regulate itself by the average relation which the wants of the debtor bear to the abilities of the creditor. Suppose this should be about 6 per cent. and suppose A and B to possess lands of equal quantity and value adjoining to each other, and to have equal skill and industry in the management of them. Let the value of each tract be 1000*l*. Let A be possessed of 1000*l*. in money, to stock and improve his farm. And let B hire 1000*l*. from C for the same purposes at 6 per cent. In this situation of things, A's property will be worth 2000*l*, and B's 1000*l*. Let us then further suppose, the annual produce of each farm to be 200*l*. and a tax of one per cent. to be laid on the land stock, &c. in possession of each: Then A would pay 20*l*. and remain master of 180*l*. from which if we deduct 120*l*. for the interest of his own property, it would leave 60*l*. as the reward of his skill and industry. In like manner, B would pay 20*l*. tax, he would also pay 60*l*. to C for the interest of his money, which would leave in the hands of B 120*l*. and if from that we deduct 60*l*. for the interest of his own property, it would leave a like sum of 60*l*. as the reward of his skill and industry. A and B therefore for the same labors would have the same reward.

But now let us suppose, that the government should lay a tax of one per cent. on C's bond. As this would neither diminish the wants of debtors nor increase the abilities of creditors, the average relation before-mentioned would remain the same; and therefore the rate of interest being effectually the same to the creditor, would become greater by the one per cent. tax to the debtor. Of consequence B would pay for the money he had borrowed 7 per cent. and therefore his net profit would be reduced from 60*l*. to 50*l*. Thus then a difference would be made in favor of A, the rich man, against B the poor man. But further in the case above stated; C's bond would only represent the cattle and utensils on B's farm. Taxing the representative, therefore, as well as the thing represented, would lay a double tax on the poor, and leave it single on the rich. Perhaps we shall be asked, whether the monied man ought not to be taxed. I answer, that if a tax is laid on all other property, then, whenever he purchases any thing with his money, in the price of that he will pay the tax laid on it. Whoever borrows his money in order to purchase with it, must do the same, and will therefore give a lesser interest, which operates a tax. But while it lies in a man's chest, it is useless to him, wherefore it ought not to be paid for, and the moment it goes out, that moment it pays the tax inseperable from the price of the commodity purchased.

But when the above arguments press hard, and shew what injuries the poor will sustain. We shall be told of laws to regulate the rate of interest. Without observing as I might, that these laws do not operate with all the efficacy which is imagined; it will be easy to shew the injustice of the tax from another quarter. If one penny per pound be laid on candles, and the chandler is at liberty to reimburse himself by the addition of a penny per pound to the price. Then if one shilling per day be laid upon hackney horses the owner ought to be at liberty to increase the daily fare of his horses one shilling. And if he who lets horses, is at liberty to increase the hire, by reason of the tax, surely he who lets money to buy those horses, ought to have the same liberty.

In every case then the tax on money would be unjust, and if unjust then from the principles before established, it must also be unwise. But this general deduction may not appear sufficiently conclusive to those who are pleased with the character of great politicians. A character which the world hath very erroneously bestowed on men of finesse and intrigue. Men who consider attentively the end they have in view, but are not very scrupulous about the means they make use of. As these men have sometimes a great deal more to say in public affairs than is absolutely necessary. I shall mention some arguments against the tax in question, on the ground of policy and expedience, which may perhaps be more agreeable to their temper and disposition.

Supposing the tax to operate the effect intended, then the money holder finding he could not make the proper and necessary advantage from letting his money, would naturally make use of it himself, and thereby deprive the industrious poor of that use, or if from any local or particular circumstances he could not so apply it, he would quit the state and take his bond with him, in which case the tax would be utterly unproductive. The State therefore would derive no benefit from the law, but would sustain an annual loss by payment of the interest. To evince this let it be supposed, that in time of full freedom and peace, Pennsylvania should not tax bonds or money, and every other State in the Union should tax them. Would not every monied man repair to Pennsylvania? Would not Pen[n]sylvania be enriched by the money of the whole Continent? And would not every other State pay her a tribute for the use of it?

It is very common that those who labour, should feel some enmity towards those who do not. It is also very common for those who feel supposed grievances, to take the most direct road for getting rid of them. Mankind are generally wrong in both instances, but never more so than in the question now before us.

Unless the rewards of industry are secure, no one will be industrious; for the motive which prompts the toils of a laborious man, is the hope of enjoying what those toils may produce. This produce is wealth, and whether it be in one shape or in another, so long as it is employed for the purpose of increasing the commodities in a country, so long is it beneficial and no longer. Thus, if the farmer hath not the right to dispose of his grain, he certainly will not labour to raise it, after he hath raised it, if it be applied to feed cattle in order to produce more grain, or to feed men whose labours produce other things, it is beneficial to the State; but not if it is suffered to decay in his granaries. If he sells it and places the money in his chest, the money is unproductive, but if that money be let to a farmer or mechanick, who is thereby enabled to increase his productions, it is beneficial to the State. If instead of this, it is invested in the purchase of uncultivated land, so as to become eventually advantageous to the purchaser, by a rise in the value of the land, that land lying uncultivate, is as unprofitable to the State, as the money would be while lying in a chest. If several purchasers should obtain all the uncultivate land lying contiguous to settlements, they might by monopolizing increase the value of it to themselves, but they would destroy the value of it to the State: Their wealth would be greater; the wealth of the State would be less. The poorer and more industrious part of the Community therefore, which in a political point of view is certainly the more valuable and respectable part, these are injured by the one use of money, as opposed to the other in two different ways. Negatively, because for the want of materials they cannot extend their industry so far as they otherwise would. Positively, because they would pay dearer for the necessaries of life, in proportion as the land was dearer, from which those necessaries were raised, and because, as the aggregate wealth of the State would continue the same, while the relative wealth of the rich became greater, the relative wealth of the poor must necessarily become less.

To deduce from hence the pernicious consequences which would follow to our Republican Constitutions, is needless, neither are they within my present plan. But as doubts may remain with respect to the force of these arguments, we will make a short appeal to experience. And here let it be premised, that in mentioning different States, I mean not to draw any odious comparisons, but simply to shew effects as they have followed from their causes. The land of Holland is very high, interest very low. There are constant emigrations from other countries to Holland. In America the land is very low, interest very high. There are constant emigrations from other countries to America. In Ireland land is high and interest is high. There are constant emigrations from Ireland. Again: In New York land was monopolized; in Pennsylvania it was not. Money in Pennsylvania was at six per cent; in New-York at seven. In Pennsylvania the country was well cultivated, and manufactures were brought to great perfection; in New York the country was not well cultivated, and manufactures were hardly introduced. What was the reason of these differences? The poor man in Pennsylvania bought a farm for one hundred pound, and paid on that sum six per cent interest; The poor man for a like farm in New-York, gave one hundred and fifty pounds, and paid seven per cent. The manufacturer in Pennsylvania gave six per cent. for the money which purchased rude materials, and fed his workmen with flour at sixteen shillings per cwt. raised from a farm of one hundred pound cost; the manufacturer in New-York gave seven per cent. for his materials, and fed his workmen with flour at seventeen shillings per cwt. raised from a farm of one hundred and fifty pound cost. The farmer bought an ax in Pennsylvania for nine shillings, from a smith who gave six per cent. for iron and coals; the farmer in New-York gave ten shillings for an ax, to a smith who paid seven per cent. for iron and coals. Lastly, to the foreigner who wanted flour, the merchant of Pennsylvania offered seventeen barrels in exchange of a piece of gold; which the New-York merchant would only give sixteen barrels for: The Pennsylvania merchant therefore having outbid the other, purchased the piece of gold, and added it to that money, the abundance of which brought interest down to six per cent. in Pennsylvania, and to three per cent in Holland.

From what has been said, it clearly follows, that two uses of property being given, the one to let it out on interest to the industrious, and the other to purchase uncultivate land; the former is far more beneficial to the community than the latter. Now, as a tax on money must produce the latter, if it produces any thing, therefore such tax must be unwise. But this is not all. To raise a tax with ease and cheapness, it must be raised in money, tho' not on money. It can therefore only be raised out of the circulating medium of the country. But it has already been shewn, that a tax on money would tend to banish it from the State. Hence it follows, that the circulating medium being decreased, to raise a given sum would not only be more difficult, but a greater share of the commodities of the country must be sold to procure it. Or in other words, the tax being nominally the same, and as to other States effectually the same, would as to the particular state be much greater.

The general odium against monied men is therefore very ill founded, although individuals among them in all countries are justly deserving of public scorn. We ought however, in political reasoning, to distinguish very carefully between motives and actions. The motives of an individual may be bad, and yet his actions may be politically good, while on the other hand, his motives may be good, and yet his actions politically bad. Inordinate ambition may stimulate a rich man to spend his fortune in the public service, and misguided zeal may induce a pious man to beggar his children by endowing a convent.

But to return. Monied men being odious, the plain method of dealing with them seems to be by taxing their money, and this is particularly agreeable, when that money hath been acquired in a mean or wicked manner. But this is far from operating the desired effect. I have shewn, that supposing the tax could be rendered effectual, it would produce injury to the State in general, and to the poor in particular. To all this, let me add, that the tax never can be rendered effectual. Money is of too subtile and spiritual a nature to be catched by the rude hand of the law. It will continually elude the grasp of the Legislator. He will at length discover that he hath followed a jack olanthern, in politics over many weary ways and perhaps very muddy ones too, yet still continues as far from the object as ever. How will you find a man's money, is the question? I know there is a trite reply very ready with some folks. But what should we think of a government that would offer to every one of its subjects a reward for perjury, exactly proportioned to his wealth. And what difference is there, except in the name, between such an offer and laying a tax, the quantum of which is to be determined by the oath of the party? Men who are honest may flatter themselves that perjury would not in general be committed. I wish such men would examine the records of a Court of Chancery, or the history of Holland, or any other country in which such tax has been laid. There is no instance where it has not failed upon fair experiment, and no experiment which has not been injurious to public morals. If however the advocates for such a measure persist in their idea, of the integrity of mankind, I confess it is an amiable prejudice, and I will not strive to remove it. This however must be admitted, that some men would by perjury elude the law, and this being admitted, it follows clearly, that the law would be a tax upon honesty and not upon money.

A tax then on specie is unjust and unwise; a tax on paper is more unwise; and more unjust! And of all the modes in which it can be laid or collected. Depreciation is the worst. Thus stands the matter in fair argument, but to every argument used on these occasions, there are some who answer by repeating the terms monopolizer, forestaller,[1] regrater,[2] engrosser, Bloodsucker, and so forth. Thus a conjurer it is said, can raise the devil by the help of certain cabalistic terms, which it would puzzle the very devil himself to understand. Let the money sink say some, and you will punish those villains who are grown rich by the public distress.

There are undoubtedly bad men who have acquired wealth by odious methods, and to take it from them might gratify the public resentment, they justly merit. But Legislators ought not to be swayed by passion. Be these men ever so nefarious, it is not very clear that government hath a right to break their faith, in order that they may punish acts of moral turpitude, by exacting a penalty which no law had inflicted. Perhaps it would be better to leave the punishment of such miscreants to the anger of Heaven, than to incur that anger by committing one crime to avenge another. Besides, among those who have mended their circumstances during the war, a part, and not the smallest part, have done so by plunder taken from the enemy, at the risk of their fortunes, and of their lives, others by adventrous foreign commerce, and some indeed by engrossing. But certainly among those who hold the paper. Persons of the class last mentioned, have not at most, above a hundredth part. To ruin our money then, in order to ruin them, even supposing the one to be both a necessary and desireable consequence of the other, would do at least ninety-nine times as much harm as good. Harm to the honest merchant! Harm to the brave seaman! To the industrious Whig farmer or mechanick! To the helpless orphan, to the distressed widow, and to the generous foreigner, who hath entrusted to us his property in the hour of distress, through difficulties and dangers innumerable. The man who advocates a measure of this sort, must be deceived, or he must be our foe.

I am, your friend,

An AMERICAN.

---

1. One who buys up goods before they reach the market.
2. One who buys goods in order to resell them; a retailer.

To the INHABITANTS of AMERICA.

My Countrymen,

Having already considered the nature of our currency, some effects of depreciation, and the propriety of taxing money, before we attempt to shew how the value of our paper is to be fixed, how supplies are to be raised, and how oeconomy is to be introduced in the various departments, consistently with the principles of liberty and justice, we must consider the laws against monopolizers, together with those which are called regulations. And here let me repeat, that bad motives may produce actions beneficial to society, and let me add, that infamous characters are oftentimes necessary. The office of hangman must be executed as well as that of Judge, and the villain who informs is so far an useful villain. We ought therefore to be cautious how we listen to the dictates of hatred or contempt, and still more cautious how we obey them.

We have the evidence of history and experience, to shew that laws against monopolizers have been ineffectual. History goes further, and shews that such laws have been injurious. And when we look for the reason why they have been injurious, reason will perhaps inform us, that their object was to prohibit acts of public utility. These propositions may surprize some minds, and that surprize will be increased if these propositions are demonstrated. Thus in the infancy of science, when Toricelli asserted the existence of a vacuum, he was heard with the utmost astonishment and indignation.[1] With equal indignation and astonishment we now hear that Toricelli's assertion was considered as a crime. Since thousands of our fellow-men have been mistaken in former times, let us believe it possible that we of the present day, may in our turns be mistaken. And in this belief let us examine a matter of no small importance, with the calmness and attention it undoubtedly merits.

The principles of a monopolizer I abandon to his foes. His principles are not our present object. Neither is it our business to consider that species of monopoly, by which a few individuals under some particular name or de-

---

Pennsylvania Packet, or General Advertiser, March 11, 1780. Courtesy American Antiquarian Society. Portions of this letter are in item 815, Gouverneur Morris Papers, Rare Book and Manuscript Library, Columbia University.

1. Evangelista Torricelli, 1608–47, was the inventor of the barometer.

scription, enjoy any branch of commerce to the exclusion of their fellow subjects. The monopolizer we now speak of, is he who being possessed of wealth, invests it in the purchase of articles which will probably become more scarce and dear, than at the time of purchasing them. I say possessed of wealth, for, as to those who speculate on the money of other people, I believe that very little is to be apprehended from them, because men soon learn not to give credit, when that credit is to be used against them. Indeed it is somewhat surprizing, that any man would part with his goods for any thing but cash. Both private interest and public good are opposed to the idea. Private interest, because the seller on credit, risques and suffers the depreciation. Public good, because credit takes away the use of money, and therefore enables the same quantity to go farther as a circulating medium, and when that is redundant, increases the redundancy. Besides which, the purchaser on credit, always found it his interest to depreciate the money.

The articles engrossed, may be of two kinds, either foreign or domestic. And foreign articles may be either luxuries or things of common use. As an example of the former, let us take the article of rum, and let us suppose that by means of a monopoly, it were raised to double the real price for which it was bought. I say the real price, because the depreciation hath been such, that many articles are nominally higher than they were, though they have fallen considerably in the real price, by which I mean the price either in wheat or gold. Supposing then, that the price of rum were doubled, the consequence would be, that as the consumption of the article would be lessened, fewer native commodities would be exported to pay for rum, and therefore a balance be created on foreign commerce in favour of the country. If, for instance, it were necessary to send away sixty bushels of wheat, to purchase a hogshead of rum, then every hundred hogsheads of rum saved, would be a clear saving of six thousand bushels of wheat. The country therefore, could pay six thousand bushels of wheat more in taxes, or support as many more men, as those six thousand bushels could maintain. I shall not contend that distilled spirits are unwholesome, and the like. Arguments against luxury, however just, are beside our system. But this at least must be allowed, that a man would not be less healthy, or less happy, at the end of the month, because he had not drank a gallon of rum in it. By this operation then, of the engrosser, and all others like this, the community is greatly enriched without any injury to individuals.

Let us next consider the effect of monopolizing foreign articles of common use. Let us take cloth as the article monopolized and suppose the price of that also to be doubled. In this case as in the other, less of the article would be consumed. The society at large therefore, would be better supplied from the stock on hand, for when the price rose, every man who was not under a necessity of buying, would wear his old coat rather than get a new one: He therefore who really wanted a coat would be able to procure it, for though there might be enough for a part of the people, yet there might not be enough for all of them, and if there was enough for all, the engrosser would not find his account in it, because, as only a part of the people would buy, part of the article would remain unsold to his great detriment. Add to this, that the increased price would encourage the importation of more, and thereby hasten and increase his loss. Neither can it be justly objected that the poor would suffer. For altho' it is true that they would pay a great advance for their coats, yet they would reimburse themselves by an equal advance on the price of their labour, particularly in this country where the demand for labour is so great. But even if they should not entirely reimburse themselves, yet surely it is better for them to pay a greater price for their cloaths than to go entirely naked, which must inevitably happen to many if the price of the cloth were not increased.

Hence therefore it is evident, that the engrossing foreign luxuries and even foreign necessaries, would be useful to the community, when separately considered. But the engrossing foreign articles in general is attended with other advantages. The speculator, by purchasing immediately of the importer, for cash, enables him immediately to send his ship upon another voyage, and stimulates his industry by the quick sale of his goods. Besides which, it keeps prices more steady, because when the thing is cheap the speculator buys, and when it grows dear he sells; wherefore importations become equally useful to the whole community, whereas otherwise they would benefit that part only which lies near to the sea ports. And however pleasing it might be to them that they should have this superiority over their fellow citizens, they would soon find their error. For if those at a distance could not obtain the things they wanted in exchange of those they had to sell, they certainly would bring nothing to market, and the citizen would feel that the want of beef can be but indifferently compensated by the temporary cheapness of salt, neither would he be able to quiet the clamors of his children for bread by the saving of two pence on the price of a dram. Add to this, that if the merchant could not obtain country produce, he would be obliged to discontinue his importations.

But perhaps it may be doubted, whether speculation tends to fix prices, and indeed the current of opinion, notwithstanding the clear reason of the thing, seems to set very strongly the other way. This is owing to the depreciation and some other particular circumstances which have attended the present war. Neither is it all surprizing, that under such circumstances effects should be attributed to improper causes. For the true causes were as remote and intricate, as the effects were apparent and oppressive. But if we turn our eyes to times and countries, in which these circumstances have not existed, we shall see the truth of the proposition above laid down in the clearest manner imaginable. We shall find that in our own country and within our own memory, if we except those articles which from their nature and that of the trade to obtain them were not liable to much alteration, such as hardware and the like, if I say we except these articles, the prices of those which were in any degree objects of speculation, were much more fixed and determinate than any other. Indeed this must be so, for speculators govern their purchases and sales by the average price of their sales and purchases, or which comes to the same thing, by the average price of the commodity, all risques, costs and charges considered. Thus, for instance, if the average price of rum were 45–90 of a dollar per gallon, the speculator would buy at 44, and sell at 46.[2] Thus in Holland, which is as it were a nation of speculators, prices are more fixed and determinate than in any other country. Any commodity or cargo which is carried thither, may be immediately sold on good terms; and any commodity or cargo which is wanted from thence, may be immediately bought on good terms. The concurrence of speculators, desirous of buying, brings up the cargo to be sold within a small per centage of the average price; and a like concurrence of speculators, desirous of selling, brings down the cargo to be bought in the same degree. From these circumstances it happens that so many cargoes are carried there, and so many others brought away. And also that the subsistence of the people, not the tenth part whereof is raised in the country, is fixed in its price to the tenth part of a farthing. Lastly, we shall find that Bills of Exchange, which were not speculated on in America, were more fluctuating here than anywhere else, but in Holland where bills are most speculated on, there exchange has but a small variation. It is the merchant's business to know the effects of his fluctuation, but rely on it, that the husbandman will feel them, and to his sorrow.

2. The decimal standard for the U.S. dollar was not adopted until 1792 (although Morris himself would suggest a decimal system when he served as assistant superintendent of finance in the 1780s). The fractions here are 90ths of a Spanish dollar, a unit that frequently appears in contemporary documents such as the *Journals of the Continental Congress.*

Engrossing articles of home produce has the same effect on the farmer which that of foreign articles has on the merchant, for a ready market not only prompts the farmer to make the articles engrossed, but the ready money enables him to make them. This kind of monopoly tends also to fix the price of home produce, in like manner with that of foreign articles. But it is of more importance, because, as home produce is the fund on which the laborer subsists, fixing the price of it, fixes the price of labor, and fixing the price of labor, fixes the price of every thing which labor can produce.

These then are the consequences which attend speculation on native and on foreign articles, when separately considered. A further advantage follows from it, in a more general point of view; which is, that it facilitates the interchange of commodities between the merchant and the husbandman. From the engrosser of home produce, the merchant is sure of getting a cargo to export, without the cost or trouble of collecting it before hand, neither of which might be quite convenient to him; and from the engrosser of foreign produce, the husbandman or country store keeper is sure to find the commodities he wants, without waiting at a great expence the arrival of any particular vessel. Add to this, that without such a class of men in a community, the consumption even of useful things would sometimes from the plenty, run to licentious and pernicious excess, while at others, industry would languish from the scarcity or want of them. Thus, the commodities of a country, like the rains which fall on its surface, when collected in reservoirs, and dealt out by degrees, produce an increase of riches to the whole community. But without that precaution, they frequently deluge and waste the soil they should have refreshed and fertilized, then leave it exposed to the glowing heats of summer, until it is scorched into a barren desart. We shall, perhaps, be told, that the engrosser's motive, is private interest: Undoubtedly it is, and so is that of the merchant, the farmer, or the mechanic. But while from their labors, society derives a benefit, why not permit them to labor?

Admitting, however, that it were necessary to punish speculators, and prevent speculation, framing laws against them would be but a poor expedient to accomplish it. Many reasons might be adduced to shew this, but it is sufficient to observe, that though often attempted, it never was effected by the laws of any government which ever yet existed. Such Laws have invariably produced the effects they were intended to obviate. On the contrary, if we repeal these laws, and let monopolizers alone, they will soon punish and prevent each other. For when all are at liberty to act as they please, many would speculate in the same articles, and as secrecy is essential to their operations, not one of them could know the quantity engrossed. But the price rising with the demand, would increase the quantity brought to market and lessen the consumption, so that at length they would all find it necessary to sell, and the instant they began, they would also find it necessary to undersell each other, in which case those who bought in last would be so undersold by those who bought in first, that they would have no little cause to repent of their bargains.

Hitherto I have considered monopolizing as a very practicable thing, and I shall still do so, while we pursue our enquiry to the most odious of the whole tribe of engrossers: I mean the man who engrosses the bread of the State. In order to form a proper judgment in this instance we must remember, that while there is no probability of a scarcity, the engrosser will not purchase, or if he does he will most probably lose, whence by the bye, we deduce this corollary, that he must be a man of great knowledge and foresight as well as of great wealth and credit. But to proceed, we will suppose a state in which at some particular season, they should raise no more bread than just what would be necessary for the whole people. Now what would be the conduct of Government if they knew this circumstance? Would they not prohibit waste, secure all they would lay their hands on and appoint trusty persons to take care of it? Would they not deliver it out in small quantities, and in a word imitate the master of a ship, who during a long voyage puts both his passengers and his crew upon short allowance? This is certainly what many Governments would attempt, and in a State not much larger than a ship, they might possibly succeed, tho' not in an extensive and populous State, at least not without the aid of miracles. For a moment let us pause, and picture to our fancies the feelings of virtuous men, composing such a Government. We shall behold the venerable fathers of the people, their eyes fixed on the meagre form of Famine, who in all his horrors rapidly advances. We shall behold them torn with anxiety, for their careless and improvident children. Solicitous, but unable to avoid the impending evil; their bosoms swell with concern, and every countenance is marked with the deep lines of care and dejection. Already they anticipated the agonies of the poor. What pleasure then it must give them, to be told that their wise laws and their vigorous administration have rendered property secure. That there are men who possess considerable wealth, and are ever intent on the means of increasing it. That these men are sensible of the approaching dearth—That they have already purchased the harvest of the year, as if by consent, though unknown to each other—That they will watch night and day to keep off the vermin which might consume, and the accidents which might destroy it—That they will gradually increase the price, and thereby lessen the consumption—and that they will at the same time be prevented by the fear of each other from raising it extravagantly high. So that upon the whole, though the people will be somewhat impoverished, they will not be starved.

Perhaps, on hearing these glad tidings, the senate might be filled with that resentment which the motives of an engrosser seldom fail to excite, and might point at his devoted forehead the thunders of legal vengeance. But they should remember that resentments are unworthy of their high office. That these men, tho' indeed prompted by the execrable thirst of gain, have already enabled the husbandman to increase his tillage, and have encouraged his labours. That not only from their efforts hath the impending danger of want been averted, but the fair prospect of plenty expanded to the view. That considering the nature of the commodity in which they had dealt the expence they had necessarily incurred, and the great risque they had been exposed to, the profit was far from being very exorbitant. That if they should repeat the experiment, as many of them certainly would, those who undertook it would thoroughly regorge their former gains. That even those gains were far less than it would have cost, for public purchasers, public superintendants, and public distributors with their endless attirail of directors, deputies, defendants, appendants, purveyors, masters, clerks, aids and assistants; and in short that they have been the cheapest stewards the public could possibly have employed. Above all things government should never forget that restrictions on the use of wealth may produce a land monopoly, which is most thoroughly pernicious, and that if the rights of property are invaded, order and justice will at once take their flight, and perhaps forever.

That speculators should have incurred the public odium, is natural, for their principles deserve it. It is true, they prevent a real want, but in order to do this, they create an artificial scarcity. Those, therefore, who know that such scarcity is artificial, and who feel the effects of it, and who not only act but reason too from their feelings, will always revile and reproach the avaricious authors of their calamities. Amid all these revilings and reproaches however it is somewhat remarkable that King Pharaoh and his prime Minister Joseph, are the first monopolizers which history gives us any account of. It is remarkable that the commodity they speculated upon was bread. That the King made every penny by it which he possibly could.

That his whole plan was founded on a miracle. And that no censure whatever is passed on the use he made of that intelligence which the deity had imparted to him.

But further, before we attempt to punish, or prohibit monopolizers, it is worth while to consider, whether it is possible for them to have any very considerable influence, either one way or the other. If people in general monopolize, these two things may be relied on: First, that the cause must originate in some radical defect of commercial policy; and secondly, that it is impossible to execute a law for punishing the delinquents. If only a few individuals monopolize; then let it be considered, what immense property would be necessary to effect any great purpose. When we hear that a man is worth a million dollars, it sounds high. But we must not suffer ourselves to be seduced by sounds. Such a man could not purchase above twenty thousand bushels of wheat. Now this is not more than was formerly in the power of a very small dealer, and it would go but a very little way towards monopolizing the wheat of one State, much less the whole Continent. Besides this, we know that most men among us, who possess large personal property, are engaged in other business. Few of them are even suspected of engrossing, and that few can do very little in effect, though the name may be very great. Nor is this all, for money, notwithstanding, the quantity emitted, is so scarce at present, that the richest can hardly get enough for their necessary occasions. Much less can they expend it in schemes of speculation. And if they would, and did so expend it, they would certainly loose by the business. But as for the effect of laws to prevent engrossing, we shall find, that salt and flour, the two capital articles, for which people in power have shewn most solicitude, are dearer than any other article whatever. Wine on the contrary, about which they seem to have given themselves no concern at all, is the cheapest thing at the market. We shall also find, that salt which hath lately been let alone, is even nominally cheaper than it was some time ago; and that flour itself bids very fair to be so, unless kept up by some aukward strokes of civil policy.

In order that we may have an adequate idea of the practicability of monopolizing, we must recur a little to calculation. This would be very extensive if we chose to go into it. But we may simplify it greatly, and yet derive the full effect from that mode of reasoning. On the lowest computation, there cannot be less than 200,000 bushels of salt consumed in six months, between Connecticut river and James river; nor less than 400,000 gallons of rum in the same time and space. Reckoning therefore the bushel of salt and the gallon of rum, each at 100 dollars, it would require 60,000,000 dollars to engross a six months supply of these two articles only, which sum is as much as could be raised by 120 men, each of which could command half a million for that purpose over and above his other necessary occasions. Where shall we find 120 such men, or where is the chance that not only these but all other articles should be monopolized? If this thing should really happen, it must be, because the great body of the people are engrossers. If this is the fact, then no laws can be executed against them, and indeed such an unnatural combination must be owing to very extraordinary circumstances, which no direct laws can reach. What these circumstances are, and how to obviate them will hereafter appear. We will therefore proceed to the examination of those laws which have been made against monopolizers under the name of regulations. Laws from which it is possible that more of our sufferings have originated, than from any other cause.

I am, Your friend,

An AMERICAN.

MARCH 23, 1780

TO THE INHABITANTS OF AMERICA.
MY COUNTRYMEN,

It is a painful as well as an invidious task to point out errors, but it is a necessary task. In States as in men, improper treatment of slight maladies will occasion great ones. And though many have died of disease, yet not a few have died of the Doctor. At the commencement of this contest, it was not our fortune to have persons among us thoroughly versed in State affairs. Attentive to their private duties, the citizens of America had no leisure or inclination to study, what there was no use or necessity for them to know; so that your servants were compelled to act, in the very moment when they would have wished to learn. That they have erred therefore is not to be wondered at, for it was human, but that they have erred no more is almost miraculous.

Those who think our present Rulers inferior to their predecessors, judge hastily and perhaps rashly. It must be remembered that our circumstances

Pennsylvania Packet, or General Advertiser, March 23, 1780. Courtesy American Antiquarian Society. No manuscript for this letter has been found.

are different from what they were. Different qualifications therefore are necessary to superintend them. A ship assaulted in mid-ocean by conflicting elements, requires the aid of intrepid seamen. When near her haven she can best be served by a dexterous Pilot. If those at the helm know not how to steer, it is better by far to assist than to revile them. Since in a common bottom we have freely embarked, let our common counsels be freely contributed. If we are friends to the public, let us shew that friendship by our candor in the examination of public affairs. Let us strive to discover what measures were erroneous, meerly that in future we may learn to avoid them. And let us not blame those now in authority for the erroneous measures of those who went before them, but liberally dispense to others that charity of opinion, which according to the common vicissitudes of life, we shall in our turns most surely stand in need of.

When this war began, we were so much opposed to the tyranny of Great-Britain, and so much disgusted with the abuses of her administration, that, by a very natural progress of the human mind, we felt a repugnance even against those useful institutions which our enemies had adopted. It was therefore a kind of merit to do every thing the reverse of what they did. A general rule to which many and great exceptions ought undoubtedly to be made.

A dislike to contracts and contractors was among the number of those which were then imbibed. Whether the Rulers of America were themselves tinctured with the prevailing prejudice, or whether they thought it was wise to give way to the popular stream, is not worth an inquiry. Certain it is, that they might at that time have made as many contracts as they pleased, upon very good terms, and thereby secured every necessary article, stipulating no other payment than their paper. I shall not now state the many advantages which would have resulted from adopting that mode of obtaining supplies, because men are pretty generally convinced of them. I shall simply observe, that it had been sanctioned by the constant practice of all wise nations, particularly by the King of Prussia, the greatest economist in Europe; and that if we had followed their example, it would have been the interest of the contractors with all their Agents and deputies to keep down prices, or in other words, to keep up the value of the paper. I mean not to draw invidious comparisons, but I must be permitted to say, that there is a wisdom in rendering private interest subservient to the public welfare. Let me add, that had contracts been made, there would not have been even the appearance of necessity to render the paper a lawful tender, or to regulate prices.

Another and a capital error, was the prohibition laid on all commerce. By that the use of money was lessened, at the moment when the quantity of it was increased. America, deprived of manufactures from abroad, was compelled to make them at home, in a season when the demand for labor was increased by the demand of men for the army: The merchant was obliged to sell his ships, and dismiss his seamen in foreign countries, when ships and seamen were necessary to distress the enemy. And the farmer being deprived of a market, had no longer any incitement to his industry; from which must necessarily follow a scarcity of his productions.

A third great error, in the line of finance, was the regulation of prices. Its operation on the money has already been mentioned, but this was only one among many evils. It disgusted the people at a time when their good will and affection was most necessary. It gave a woeful impression of the new governments, by laying down a violation of the rights of property as the corner stone on which they were to be erected. It discouraged commerce, manufactures and agriculture, or rather it left to the husbandman, tradesman and merchant no encouragement at all. It tended to lock up all commodities, compelling the whole community to become monopolizers. It introduced the tedious and expensive mode of trading by barter. And it sapped the foundations of civil authority, for the temptation of interest to contravene or elude the law was too great to be resisted. Hence the breach of it became general, and that taught the dangerous lesson, that laws may be broken with impunity. Of consequence, the legislature fell into contempt, because it was made manifest that they were not possessed of this superior wisdom and power, which are the sources of reverence and respect.

From the breach of regulations of the first kind arose a contest between the government and the people. A contest always dangerous, but particularly so at such times as those in which it happened. This contest produced regulations of the second kind, enforcing the former by pains and penalties, and impowering persons to seize at limited prices. As the legislatures felt a necessity of assigning reasons for these laws they pretty generally agreed to *whereas it is necessary to carry on this just and necessary war, and whereas it is necessary to support the army who are engaged in it.* From such recitals followed, first, a very disagreeable impression of the justice of a war which was to be maintained by injustice, instead of fair, equal, and general taxation; and secondly, a variance between the people and the army, or at least an abatement of their warm and cordial affection towards each other. For on the one hand, the people felt a degree of coldness for those who were held up as the cause why their property was wrested from them; and on the other hand, the army could not but be disgusted at a people who would not otherwise than by force give bread to their protectors. Besides all this, the British were greatly encouraged to carry on the war, by a hope of obtaining that assistance among us which their refugee adherents had promised. For to make the second kind of regulations as palatable as possible, in compliance with the ruling whimsey of the day, they were all of them levelled at the disaffected, the enemy had therefore the declared opinions of our own legislatures in their favour. Many good Whigs were in some degree intimidated by this bugbear of disaffection, and the Tories were proportionably strengthened and consoled. The enemy ought indeed to have examined the true cases which produced the declaration of our legislatures, before they confided in it; but they might safely confide in the tendency of the laws to which it served as a pretext. For a little reflection must have convinced them, as it ought to have convinced us, that, whatever abundance there might be in the country, our aukward mode of collecting supplies would not only render it difficult to obtain them in the instant, but infallibly produce a future deficiency.

These second regulations were the worst children in the whole family of regulations. The tyranny of the former laws now appeared in its proper garb. The invasion of the rights of property was clothed with every necessary circumstance of violence. And the industrious men who bro't from abroad or produced at home those things which we stood in need of, were subjected to all the insult, and no little degree of the infamy of felons. Good God! What should we think of a legislator who would declare, that it was a crime to procure bread for the hungry, or clothes for the naked, and enact, that those who should in future commit that crime, should have their houses and barns and stores broken open, their property seized, their persons insulted, and their reputation stigmatized with the odious appellations of Monopolizer and Tory? Change but the terms, and we have had such laws. We have had them, even in the hour of our wants and distresses.

Here let us pause, and ask of plain common sense, what must be the necessary effect of this strange policy. The answer is short, Dearth and dearness. An answer to which melancholy experience hath affixed the seal of truth. What then have we left to hope, unless it be that salutary reflection, tho' late, may come at last? That it may teach us to avoid those rocks and shoals from which we have hitherto narrowly escaped, and on which thousands before us have been miserably shipwrecked?

It was hardly possible to have embittered the bitter draught which these laws had prepared for the people; yet even that was accomplished by the manner of enforcing them. Men of old approved character, who respected their neighbours and were by them respected, would not descend to it. The executors of these new laws therefore, were men who, like the laws themselves, were new. They were men, raised to the low office of persecution. And yet from necessity they were entrusted with money—but we will draw a veil over this part of the picture.

There were other pernicious consequences which flowed from these laws. Property being shut up from market, it required a number of persons to collect it for the public use whose labour was lost to society. Add to this, the great train which became necessary in order to bring it forwards, and the still greater train which they required to feed and supply them. The quantity of unproductive labour necessarily maintained from these causes is almost beyond calculation, and the unnecessary expence is in proportion to it. But this is not all. These persons are maintained, either by fixed salaries or by commissions. If by the former, they have no incitement to be industrious. Their salary goes on as fast while they are idle as it does while they labour. And whether they sleep or wake, whether the army be well or ill supplied, is equally to them a matter of indifference, save only, that indolence is more agreeable than toil, rest more pleasing than fatigue, and sport more delightful than care. If the public servants are maintained by commissions, in this case they may become as much too attentive, as they are too negligent in the other. There was one Judas among twelve disciples, and one Peter. There was one who betrayed his Lord, and one who denied him. Two out of twelve! I have not the slightest intention to accuse or abuse those which have been or which are employed. I verily believe that they are in general much better than could reasonably be expected, and I know that some of them are highly deserving; but certainly it is dangerous to set the interest of individuals in opposition to that of the Community. Yet this danger inevitably followed from the baneful system of regulations. And what is still worse, while one set of servants are stimulated by commissions to enhance prices, another set of them are lulled by salaries to omit the necessary exertions in forwarding what is procured.

These are the appendages on a system of regulations. These are the fruits of that notable system, which in spite of reason and of history was adopted, and in spite of feeling and experience adhered to. A system of injustice, where injury is sharpened by insult. A system, which if it could be rendered effectual, would, contrary to the declared wishes of its advocates, truly realize the money which moneyed men possess. For strange as it may seem; the same persons, in the same day, on the same occasion, and almost in the same breath or sentence, will tell us: That those who buy and refuse to sell, abound in money. That this money ought not to be realized. And that prices should be so regulated, as that this money would purchase twice as much as it otherwise would do.

But what are these regulations in the event? Are they not a tax, and a very unequal one? They certainly are intended to operate a tax, and on those near to the seat of war, who already suffer enough of its disadvantages. A tax levied on every man in proportion to his industry, and with every circumstance of rigorous injustice. A penalty on commerce, an incitement to engrossing, an discouragement of labor, a reward of indolence. What can such a system produce, except want and distress? Ask of the farmer, why notwithstanding the regulations, he ploughed and sowed, or the merchant, why he imported, their answer is the same, a hope that, by the next harvest or the next arrival, the regulations would be no more; and a confidence that, at the worst, all regulations might be eluded. Happy it is for us that they may, or long since industry ceasing, the fruits of it would have been no more, and pinched with want, persecuting and persecuted by each other, we should have sunk self-subdued beneath the yoke prepared for us.

But to every argument that can possibly be used, we shall receive the empty answer of declamation. Spite of constant and of sore experience we shall receive it. For those who recommended regulations because of the supposed impracticability of paying the prices of 1776, and increased their vociferousness with the increased prices of 1777, and grew still more extravagant with the extravagance of 1778; those same persevering politicians will doubtless support the same dogmatical positions, notwithstanding the contradiction of three successive years. And still they will argue, and though confuted they will argue still; and still find breath and words and noise, to puff and rave and roar as vigorously, as boldly, and as loudly as ever. From the din of such bellowings let us turn away, and consult the sacred oracle of experience.

By the fruit we may know the tree, and sad fruit indeed hath this tree borne. Who would have suspected, three years ago, that, in the midst of a war against the greatest naval power, our native productions should become dearer than foreign commodities? Yet even this thing hath come to pass. The whole system of commerce hath been inverted, the laws of property invaded, the laws of justice infringed, every absurdity practiced, and every impossibility tried, to get a little beef and a little bread, which would almost have come forward of themselves if things had been left to their natural course, if honest labor had been permitted to heap the blushing clusters of plenty in the lap of freedom. And now, after straining and working this cumbrous machinery of grinding regulations for three long tedious and oppressive years, what at last have we squeezed from it to recompence our toil? What but the dry husks of penury? Nothing! Nay worse than nothing. For it is notorious that, when we began this war, our country was full of provisions, that our annual exportation and consumption have been much less than they used to be, and that at present we are miserably poor and base.

Thus then when we look back on the path we have trodden, we shall find penal laws on refusing the paper, and penal laws on receiving it, penal laws on industry, and penal laws on honesty, penal laws to produce monopoly, and penal laws against it, contradiction staring in the face of contradiction, and one half the people employed in exacting all these contradictory penalties from the other half; while one system of finance hath rapidly succeeded to another system of finance, and one Utopian mountain been piled on top of another mountainous Utopia. This is not the coloring of a fervid imagination, neither is it painted for the purposes of ridicule. I have not sought after the faults which I have found; they lay in my path. I might have mentioned others, but I wish them to be hidden, and even these I would have concealed, but it was necessary to point them out, that they may be avoided, and it was just to direct public enquiry to the true sources of public misfortune. Yet not with a desire to draw down censure on those who have erred with upright intentions. Let me then repeat, that we ought not hastily to conclude our present rulers inferior to their predecessors. Let me intreat those rulers to profit by the many striking examples before their eyes. And let me remind them, that, with such examples, they will be doubly answerable for their own conduct.

I am your friend,

AN AMERICAN.

To THE INHABITANTS OF AMERICA.

MY COUNTRYMEN,

Having in some former letters lightly touched a few principal causes of our pecuniary misfortunes; I shall now proceed to shew how the public credit is to be established, supplies drawn forth, and oeconomy introduced. These things are the great desiderata of American politics, they have long been so, and yet they are not only practicable, but very easy, if those whose business it is, will obey the dictates of plain sense and common honesty. If they will fairly bid adieu to finesse and subtility. Neither is any degree of patriotic enthusiasm necessary. Enthusiasm is too frail and shortlived a thing to place any reliance on. He whose labors have added a blade of grass to the common stock, has done more to recruit the finances of his country, than all the enthusiasm of all the enthusiasts in it. Under a proper administration therefore, nothing further is requisite than that the people should be actuated by that regard to private interest, which has been ineffectually written and preached and prayed against, from the fall of Adam to the present hour. It is frequently asserted, that we have nothing to fear, but from the state of our finances, and that patriotism has given way to the love of gain. Happily for us, one of these evils may be overcome by the help of the other. I beg therefore, it may be understood, that I have an utter contempt for every scheme which supposes the least degree of patriotism in the people. On the contrary, I ask no more than that every man get as much as he honestly can. Neither would I desire him to sell a single barley corn if he does not chuse it. On these plain requisitions shall I build, taking man as he is, without pretending to be wiser than his Maker, or supposing my countrymen to be better than those of other people.

Some indeed there are, whose sacrifices in a virtuous cause, would entitle them to any thing the world can give, if the world could give any thing comparable to the internal sense of rectitude. And there is one among them, whose modesty in declining applause, is only equalled by the great and good qualities which deserve it.

Names like these, shall be recorded in the annals of time, on materials

Pennsylvania Packet, or General Advertiser, April 11, 1780. Courtesy American Antiquarian Society. The manuscript is item 819, Gouverneur Morris Papers, Rare Book and Manuscript Library, Columbia University.

more durable than the brazen monuments of glory. Names like these, will render the title of American dear and sacred to succeeding generations. But it would be a cold and uncharitable idea that other nations are barren of talents or virtue. Let us then believe that we stand on the common level of humanity; and let us adopt those things which experience hath shewn to be useful among men.

Some time ago nothing more was necessary to fix the value of our paper, than that government should have undone what had been ill done. Had this been the case, the people would soon, by general consent, have brought it just where it ought to be, nor would they then have complained that it was too high or too low. One object of these papers, was to inculcate that conviction which the writer felt of the inutility of all projects, and to prevail, if possible, that no more should be tried. But the time is past, and nothing shall be said on that subject, not only because it would wear the appearance of acrimony satire or reproof, all of which are very far from his intentions, but because some things which have since taken place, have rendered this easy remedy inefficacious, wherefore there can be no use in displaying its advantages. It has now become necessary, not only to wipe off the blots and blunders of the former day, but to adopt a regular, equitable and prudent system, such as will stand the test of time and the shock of fortune. Not a little temporary expedient to eke out a starvling campaign. A life of expedients is a life of folly and meanness, it is feeding on the beggarly scraps and parings of revenue, instead of the full feast.

In matters of finance there are certain principles to be combined together, the want of which in any system would render it miserably defective. Thus all plans of this sort should be founded in the nature of man, not on ideal notions of excellence. They should be such as will tend to produce public wealth and prosperity, not such as for a present supply will dry up the resources of future taxation. And they should be such as are consistent with the principles of freedom and virtue, not such as will overturn the liberty of the present generation, under a falacious hope of securing that of posterity, or destroy the morals of the people, to come at their wealth.

To these general maxims must be added some others more particularly adapted to our situation. And first our plan should be plain and simple, so as to be understood by every body, and convince every body. Nothing can be more contemptible than the affectation of secrecy and mistery on this subject, for manly sense and truth and justice disdain concealment. Diffident in our paper as the people are at present, they must know all deeply concerned in it, they ought to know all, and inquisitive wise and free they will know all. Any thing therefore which cannot be fully communicated, will not answer the purpose.

Secondly, the plan must be strictly just. Mean paltry pitiful shifts of villainy cannot more effectually injure the character of an individual, than tricks and deceptions will ruin the reputation of a republican government. If kings deceive, yet when the faithless monarch dies, new hopes from a virtuous successor inspire new confidence, but a dishonest republic is irreclaimable, and no prudent men will trust it. But if integrity is necessary in general, how much more so in particular circumstances of distrust, and how indispensible when in such circumstances a part of the community labor to impeach the general credit. If there be an object in the world for which the very existence of a republic should be staked, it is for the preservation of her public faith, particularly an infant republic just emerging from subjection, and claiming the aid, alliance, and confidence of other powers. The government of such republic should guard her honor with the delicate solicitude of Caesar, so that it should not only be unsullied but unsuspected.

The last object I shall mention, is the preservation of our Foederal Union, which in my poor opinion will greatly depend on the management of our revenue. The articles of confederation were formed in a moment when the attachment to Congress was great and warm. The framers of it therefore seem to have been only solicitous how to provide against the power of that body, which by means of their provident foresight and care, now exists almost by meer courtesy and sufferance. This is an evil which cannot at present be remedied; but if in addition to this a number of long accounts and quotas and propositions be left for settlement, until the enemy are removed at a distance, and the fear of them also removed, these will afford so much matter for litigation, and occasion such heart-burnings, and give such room for the intrigues which Great-Britain has already attempted, and which will doubtless be carried on by her or some other foreign power, that our Union will become, what our enemies long since declared it was, a meer rope of sand. Congress then, like the travellers coat in the fable, after having been hugged close through the stormy hour of danger, will be cast aside as an useless burthen in the calm, and sunshine of peace and victory. Surely the consequences of such a measure, the struggles, the convulsions, the miseries need not be pictured to a sensible and discerning people.

Having premised these general observations, I shall proceed to sketch a few outlines of a plan which may perhaps be so improved as to produce the desired effect. I shall give the outlines only, for altho' much will depend on the detail, yet entering into detail would too much distract the readers attention, besides it is the business of proper ministerial officers whom we shall take notice of hereafter.

Our first object should be, how to fix the value of our circulating paper medium, for untill this be in some measure accomplished, it is impossible either to tax with effect, expend with oeconomy or even act with justice. It becomes therefore both our duty and interest, while at the same time the subject is so delicate that the utmost caution must be used to prevent even the appearance of force or injustice.

The circulating paper is of three kinds, one bearing a stirling interest, one an interest in currency, and the third no interest at all. The two first do indeed go by a different name from the last, being called Loan-Office Certificates, but on inspection it will appear that these Certificates are transferable from hand to hand and payable to the bearer in like manner with the Bills of Credit, and the fact is, that they are actually so transferred.

Posterity will be at a loss for the motives which dictated the form of these Certificates, unless memorandums are kept for their use. I sincerely wish that every thing of this sort may be buried in oblivion, and therefore shall say nothing about them. But it must be remarked that instead of taking money out of circulation more of it was thrown in, tending to depreciate the other by reason of the quantity, and also of the difference between them, that one bore interest and not the other. But the Certificates were at first in the lesser repute of the two, for causes not necessary now to be enumerated; as the fact is fresh in every ones memory. At that time it was truly ludicrous to see the solicitude of many well meaning men, to pay the public debts with these Certificates instead of the common paper, and even to give an advance in purchases to those who would accept of them. Nay, it was no uncommon argument in favor of a large grant; that some considerable part of it was a warrant which was to be liquidated by Loan Office Certificates. Strange as it may seem, it is nevertheless true, that a hope was then cherished by some persons, that the depreciation might be checked by these Certificates, which would, they imagined, be hoarded for the sake of the interest. This reasoning was founded on what was called a parallel instance among the Eastern States, relatively to their old tenor and new lawful reasoning which was deemed conclusive, although the reluctance with which the Certificates were accepted, and the discount at which they were sold, clearly evinced the contrary, and although it was at the same time a common argument of the same persons in favor of their present form, that unless they were transferable, people would not lend money to the public.

But it was evident from another quarter, that they must have depreciated, because they manifestly depended on a paper which was itself depreciating with no little rapidity. Thus then, was an interest given on the circulating medium of the country, to answer no one valuable purpose. A measure laudable, perhaps for the generosity, if with the exuberance of public revenue, the Treasury were running over, but savoring much of prodigality in some other circumstances. For not to mention the paper which has been expended for the interest of the Certificates, issued subsequent to March 1778. Those previous to that period, cost us above eight millions livres in France, for less than eight millions of paper here, which might have been made at less expence than the Certificates themselves, and to better purpose.

To remedy the ill effects of the Loan-Office Certificates; people should be induced to exchange them for a funded debt. In order to do this, (assuming what we shall hereafter attempt to prove, that sufficient taxes can be raised for the purpose) I propose, that the full value of each Certificate, at the time when the loan was made, should be estimated in specie; and every holder, who chose to bring in his Certificate, by a given time, should be considered as a creditor to the public for that value, with five per cent. interest, payable half yearly in specie during the war, and both principle and interest, to be paid within ten years after the conclusion of it. This stock should not be subject to any tax, neither should it be transferable without certain legal formalities.

This measure, it is conceived, would be equitable, effectual and beneficial. Equitable, because the public would, by that means, perform all which, by an equitable interpretation, they can be supposed to have promised. The reduction of interest from six to five per cent. would be partly compensated by the security against taxation, and partly by the payment of specie in this country, which sells for a fourth more than specie in Europe; so that the reduction of one sixth would still leave a difference of one half per cent. interest, in favor of the creditor, where that interest is now payable in Europe; but the difference is still more considerable, where the interest is payable in paper. There may perhaps, be some particular instances, where injury would happen; yet it is as small an injury as can possibly be expected in a general calamity; add to this, that it would be optional in the creditor, either to hold his certificate, or to exchange it, and there is no maxim of law or equity, more solid than this, that no injury is done to him who acts from perfect volition.

This measure would be effectual, because very few, if any, would be disposed to risque their Certificates on the present uncertain contingencies, when they might easily be fixed on the solid base of specie. And the very formalities necessary to a transfer, would be an additional security, especially to foreigners. For there is a manifest folly in supposing that they would willingly entrust their property in our funds, for a Certificate, which, in the hands of their factors, was as so much money, and might pass out of those hands again the instant after, thereby depriving them of the possibility of recovering anything from the public, in case those factors became insolvent.

Sundry advantages would, it is conceived, flow from the adoption of this plan. For first, a considerable sum of paper would be taken out of circulation. Secondly, the stock when funded, would, as an object of commerce, represent part of the circulating medium, and raise the value of the remainder. Thirdly, the Bills of Credit would no longer suffer by a comparison between them, and a medium bearing interest. Fourthly, a considerable saving would be made on the interest now payable in Europe; and the public monies there, might be applied as they most undoubtedly ought, to purchasing necessaries for the army. And fifthly, the public confidence would be in some degree regained, which of all objects is the most valuable.

The Certificates being disposed of, our next point, is to give a fixed value to the Bills of Credit, or rather to fix a standard, below which, they could not fall. Let then, every holder of the paper, be entitled, not compelled, to bring it in, at the rate of forty for one, (if this number should be thought most proper, though I confess, I should have rather chosen twenty, for reasons which I will not trouble the reader to peruse,) and let him be credited in like manner, for a stock in specie, on the same terms with the holders of the Certificates. Let the paper so brought in, be burnt in his presence who brought it. And further, let it be covenanted, that all the paper shall be sunk in five equal annual payments, after the war, or redeemed with specie, at the expiration of that term.

That this proposition would be equitable, will appear from two considerations. First, that the covenant to pay the whole sum in five years after the war, is fully conformable to the original promise on the face of the bills; and secondly, that the liquidation of forty for one, is not an infraction of that promise, but a new engagement for the benefit of those who hold the money, if they themselves choose rather to take that fixed value in the present, than to risque the future redemption. In which case, they can have no more reason to complain, than any other creditor, who allows a discount on a debt for prompt payment. That it would be effectual, if the funds for payment are good, can hardly be doubted, because no man would give forty-one paper dollars to purchase a silver one, if it might be had of government for forty. On the contrary, the conviction that all the paper would be sunk in five years after the conclusion of the war, would rather tend to raise it above that level. Those who declaim against appreciation, will affect to dread the consequences of this step. But waving what hath been said in a former paper, on the justice of permitting an appreciation, it will at least be admitted, that we had better get rid of our present evils, than continue to labour under them, meerly from the apprehension of a future mischief, which, if it could really arise, may always be cured with the greatest facility, or rather a mischief which would cure itself.

So much for the equity, efficacy, and effect of these propositions. But before they can operate, it must be made evident that they are not meer paper, as most of the promises hitherto made, have proved to be. In other words, taxes must be laid and raised in specie, sufficient to discharge the principle and interest of the debt to be funded. I know it is a common assertion, that there is not coin enough in the country, to pay such a tax. The common assertion of men, who busily sow the seeds of a heavier future taxation, while at the same time, before that taxation takes place, they contribute to banish what specie there is, by excluding it from circulation, and laying embargoes on the produce of the country. Supposing therefore, the fact to be as they state it, certainly the policy of their conduct is very contemptible. It would be better to raise such tax as can be paid, and such tax would be sufficient, because the only real object of taxation, after liquidating our debts, is to produce the means of maintaining the army, and the sum necessary for this purpose will depend upon the amount of the circulating medium compared with the real wealth of the country. If there be a great medium, a greater sum will be necessary, and a great sum can be paid. If the medium be small, the public necessities and public revenue will be proportionately small. The ways and means of raising taxes, therefore, will be our next object, previous to which, we must enquire what sums are necessary to be raised, and first, what will be the real amount of the funded debt abovementioned.

There are two reasons why this cannot be done with exactness. First, that there are as yet no accurate accounts to be obtained of the sums put into the several Loan Offices. And secondly, that we have not the means of determining precisely, the depreciation in the several parts of the continent,

monthly, from the first of January 1777, to the present time. In order however, to come at it as nearly as possible, I shall state the amont of the several
Loans half yearly, from the best accounts and estimates I have been able to
procure, and I shall state the average value of the first half years Loans, at
one for one, the second, at two for one, and so on in geometrical proportion. The account will then stand thus:

Loans to	July	1777,	3,480,081, at one, are	3,480,081
	January	1778,	3,278,790, at two, are	1,639,395
	July	1778,	5,553,017, at four, are	1,388,254
	January	1779,	5,448,776, at 8, are	681,097
	July	1779,	14,298,433, at 16, are	893,652
	January	1780,	7,052,710, at 32, are	220,397
Total amount of Loans,			39,111,707, of the val. of	8,301,876

This account is by no means exact, as to the amount of the Loans, neither
is that of their value of all accurate. Nor would it be proper to make such
an average estimate of the depreciation, because as far as it is applicable to
private or public justice, the estimate ought to be as minute and precise as
possible. But if this account should be near the truth, and it is not far from
it, if also the average should be within bounds, and it certainly is not excessive, then the sum found will be tolerably well ascertained for the purposes
of political calculation.

As for the Bills of Credit, supposing that one half of them were brought
in, which certainly would not happen if sufficient provision were made for
liquidating the whole. This half, or one hundred millions, at forty for one,
would be two millions and an half, which, with the sum above stated, would
be ten millions eight hundred and two thousand eight hundred and seventy
six dollars. But as mistakes on one side of this account would be very dangerous, we will suppose that the whole circulating medium were funded,
which would add two millions and a half more, and that the Loans since last
January are worth about two hundred thousand. This would bring the debt
to twelve millions and an half, to which we will add two millions and an half
more, in order to provide for any possible deficiencies in the calculation,
which ought to be somewhat more than merely just to the creditor, lest it
should look like doing him an injustice. We shall then have to provide for
a debt of fifteen millions, bearing five per cent. interest, or seven hundred
and fifty thousand dollars annually. To pay this debt in ten years, requires
an annual sum of two millions, and to this sum we will add five millions

more, for the expences of the war, making in the whole seven millions, or
one million five hundred and seventy five thousand pounds sterling. A sum
so small, that not to raise it in a contest like the present, for the defence of
all which is dear and sacred to man, would be the deepest ignominy.

I am your Friend,

An AMERICAN.

APRIL 15, 1780

To the INHABITANTS of AMERICA.
My Countrymen,
The inefficacy of all measures hitherto taken with our finances is so evident, that to dwell on them would be a tedious absurdity. To the many
intrinsic defects peculiar to each, we must add a general defect which
pervades the whole. The plans adopted for aiding our paper, have been
themselves but meer paper; having no substantial connection with the universal money of commercial nations. Of consequence, they subsist and act
independently of that universal medium; so that as the paper-money ultimately rests upon a paper tax, it cannot, by that means be brought at all
nearer to specie than it was before. Hence, a tax in specie becomes necessary, to regulate the present value of our paper.

In considering of ways and means, I shall first state the taxes and their
produce, secondly the appropriation, and thirdly the mode of collection.

And first, I propose a tax of two dollars per hundred, in specie, for every
hundred acres of appropriated lands within the United States; to continue
until ten years after the conclusion of the war; with a proviso, that any person who should bring in the value of twenty dollars, either in bills or certificates, according to the estimate mentioned in a former paper, should be
freed from this tax for one hundred acres, and be intitled to receive annually, after the war, one dollar in specie for ten years, and so in like manner
for any greater number of acres; the paper or certificates so brought in to
be destroyed in his presence.

Secondly, I propose a tax of two dollars, in specie, on every man able to

Pennsylvania Packet, or General Advertiser, April 15, 1780. Courtesy American Antiquarian Society. The manuscript is item 820, Gouverneur Morris Papers, Rare Book
and Manuscript Library, Columbia University.

bear arms, and not actually in the Continental army, as a military officer or as a soldier. This tax also to continue until ten years after the war, with a proviso nevertheless, that it may be paid during the war, either in specie or paper, at the rate of forty for one, but in specie alone after the peace.

Thirdly, I propose, that quotas be laid for raising the annual sum of forty millions, payable in paper only, and to continue until five years after the conclusion of the war. I propose quotas, if that mode should be deemed preferable to any other, as it probably may be by some persons however unreasonable. But if it should be found inexpedient, as on experience it undoubtedly will, then, in lieu of it, this sum should be raised by an addition to the other taxable articles, or such of them as shall be most proper.

Fourthly, I propose, that a perpetual tax of five per cent. be laid on all exports, and one dollar per ton annually on all vessels above twenty tons; and that it be an additional article of confederation, that every State lay what regulations and restrictions they may think proper on trade, but that the fiscal produce thereof be paid to the United States.

Lastly, I propose, that the following rates be laid, payable in specie or in paper at forty for one, to wit, one dollar per head on all horses above a year old, and half a dollar per head on all cattle above a year old, and one dollar each for every glazed or sash window, in a house having more than ten windows. These rates to continue only so long as the public exigencies shall require.

Having stated these taxes, our next object is to enquire into their probable produce. This can only be determined, at present, by a rude estimate, which deserves more the name of a guess than a calculation: It must therefore be made within bounds, especially as the cost of collection is supposed to be deducted. And first as to the land-tax.

From Passamaquadi Bay, in the latitude of forty-five degrees north, to the mouth of St. Mary's river, in the latitude of thirty-two degrees north, and sixteen degrees west long. from Passamaquadi, is in a direct line, along the surface of the globe, about thirteen hundred miles. This line, however, is too much extended for an oeconomical calculation; we will therefore restrain it to the length of one thousand miles, from Casco Bay to the mouth of Savannah river, and we will take an average breadth of one hundred and fifty miles, which is far from being the extent of appropriation in many States, tho' it exceeds that of some others. This length and breadth will contain one hundred and fifty thousand square miles, or ninety-six million acres. But we must make a deduction, first for bays, rivers, lakes and other lands covered with water; secondly, for mountains, wastes, deserts, marshes and other lands not yet appropriated; thirdly, for highways, cities and public territories; fourthly, for lands in possession of the enemy or otherwise not within the power of the States; and lastly, for the expences of collection. This deduction will be nearly, if not intirely equal to one half of the superficial content. Wherefore we will take off forty-six million acres, and calculate only on the remaining fifty millions; which, at two dollars per hundred, will give a revenue of one million.

The number of inhabitants within these States hath usually been estimated at three millions, and perhaps they may amount to it, the proportion of men able to bear arms is as one to five, so that the number of such men, in America, ought to be about six hundred thousand. But from this number we must, for very obvious reasons, make a considerable deduction; wherefore the number of taxable polls, may be stated at half a million, so that the tax of two dollars each, will amount to one million.

As to the quotas, if the tax of forty millions in paper, be laid that way, then it will be the business of the States to apportion it; but if it be not so laid, then it will be distributed on articles, which experience shall have demonstrated to be sufficiently productive, wherefore this tax may also be considered as amounting to one million.

The amount of our exports cannot be precisely ascertained, but there are good reasons for placing them as high as seven millions sterling before the war, which we will for greater certainty reduce to thirty million dollars. The many natural and artificial reasons which have conspired to lessen the amount of our exports, operates so forcibly that, with melancholy truth, we may now reduce them to one tenth of what they were, or three million. But on the other hand, the inhanced prices will perhaps raise the value of this about one third, so that we may state it at four millions, which at five per cent, gives two hundred thousand; in which sum the tonnage is supposed to be included.

If there is difficulty and uncertainty in numbering the acres, and the men of America, the cattle and horses will be estimated with still greater difficulty and uncertainty. Without any calculations therefore, I shall suppose the horses above a year old, to amount to one million, and the horned cattle of the same age to two million. These numbers are, I have reason to believe, within bounds, and, if so, then the tax on each will amount to a million, being equal to the land and poll tax.

How many houses there may be having above ten windows, and how many windows there may be in such houses, no man can accurately determine, but the wealth of the Americans, compared with that of other nations, gives room to suppose, that here are a much greater proportion of houses liable to the tax now under consideration in this, than in any other country, and of those houses which are subject to it, there are probably a greater number with above thirty windows, than under twenty. The average therefore might be stated at twenty five, but we will take it at twenty, and state the houses at one hundred thousand, wherefore this tax would produce two millions.

The account of the whole will stand thus:

1. Land,	50,000,000	acres, at	2	per cent.	1,000,000
2. Men,	500,000	at	2	per poll,	1,000,000
3. Quotas,	40,000,000	dollars, at	40	for one,	1,000,000
4. Export,	4,000,000	at	5	per cent.	200,000
5. Horses,	1,000,000	at	1	each,	1,000,000
6. Cattle,	2,000,000	at	1–2	each	1,000,000
7. Windows,	2,000,000	at	1	each	2,000,000
					7,200,000

Of these taxes the three first should be appropriated, as a sinking fund, to the full and final discharge of the public debts, and cancelling of the paper. And on this head it is to be observed, that as the sum payable for this purpose during the war would be at the most not above seven hundred and fifty thousand, so there would be a further appropriation of the residue, being two million two hundred and fifty thousand, which should be to the expences of the war. Two hundred and fifty thousand of this surplus would be in specie, which should be set apart for secret service, and the support of our countrymen in captivity. It is also very probable that a further sum of specie would result from these taxes, and if so, then it would be proper that our army and navy would be paid in that kind of money; though no promise should be made, because it is unwise and unjust to make promises which the course of accidents may prevent us from performing. But further it is to be observed, that as the sum arising from the land and poll tax might exceed two millions, and as the funded debt would probably fall short of fifteen millions, so there would remain a ballance above what is necessary to sink that debt; this ballance therefore would admit of a further appropriation, as the pledge for payment of such further domestic loans, as the exigencies of the war might require. And lastly, as forty millions of paper annually, would be sufficient to sink two hundred millions in five years, and as these two hundred millions would be lessened by the part brought in and funded, as also by the waste and loss attendant on our frail and perishing medium; so there would remain a considerable surplus, which might be appropriated to sinking such monies as might be issued to make up deficiencies in the circulating medium, if it should be found deficient.

The fourth of these taxes, on exports and ships, ought in reason and propriety to be appropriated to the support of our navy, under which head must be comprehended packet-boats and the like. As it must be the wish of every good American, that our navy should flourish, encrease and endure, so we should take care that the fund to support it be certain, growing, and perpetual. Here then let me indulge in a short digression, while an imagination fond and fervid for the general welfare, anticipates the rising glories of our country. That moment, when the rapid growth of her agriculture, commerce and fisheries, shall multiply her exports, in proportion to the energetic principles of freedom, which give them stability, vigor and animation, thence shall arise a naval force, which, governed with oeconomy and directed by prudence, shall protect our native shores, and wave, in dignity, our peaceful and commercial flag over the remotest verges of the ocean.

The fifth, sixth, and seventh of these taxes should be appropriated to the support of the war, and should continue until the various accounts and expenditures of it be finally liquidated and adjusted; among which accounts must be taken that of foreign loans already made, or which we may hereafter be necessitated to make. But after this final adjustment, these taxes may all be decreased, or one or more remitted, so as to leave only what is necessary for the half pay of the army, and the support of such fortifications and troops as may be necessary during the peace.

It will appear that in this estimate and appropriation no notice is taken of two objects, namely, the general civil list, and the support of government in the several States. The latter of these, is properly an object of internal policy to each State. I will however drop a sentiment with relation to both these things. And, as to the first, the post-office, if properly regulated, would produce a revenue sufficient for the greater or general civil list, by which is meant the support of the civil officers and officers of Congress, both foreign and domestic. As to the second, or lesser civil list, this would be fully provided for by a light stamp duty, in addition to the fees and perquisites of office. It is hard to conceive taxes more easy and more beneficial than these, for they defray the expences of government, by facilitating the commerce and securing the property of individuals. Some readers may not see the force of the latter part of this observation, but those who know that frauds and forgeries have been frequently detected, by means of the stamps affixed to deeds and other instruments, will readily perceive it; and all will feel the difference between a stamp act made by our own legislatures, and a stamp act imposed by a foreign power. Roads, bridges, and inland navigations, will, if I may be allowed the expression, provide for themselves. In other words, they are most equitably and most effectually maintained by tolls and turnpikes; which with a proper administration will leave a surplus to support the poor. These different things are mentioned meerly to shew the propriety of the other taxes and the appropriation of them. Let us then further advert to this reason and propriety in themselves, and in relation to each other.

I know that almost innumerable objections will be raised against these propositions. We shall be told, that the business of Congress is not to lay rates but quotas, that is to say, they have a right to demand money by guess, but not on fair and equal principles. We shall be told, that the land-tax would fall heavy on the rich, the poll tax on the poor, and the other taxes on all. That some of these taxes would fall heavy on the merchant, and some on the husbandman; some on the city, and some on the country. If all this be admitted, it would only shew that these taxes would be heavy to the whole community, and all agree that heavy taxes must be raised, I mean all good whigs; but every one will strive to ease his own shoulders of the burthen. All complain of the evil, yet nobody inclines to look it in the face, which is the only reason why it exists. Congress call on the States to raise quotas, of which an equitable account is to be made by and bye, that is, they will, by the wealth of a State twenty years hence, determine what it is to pay in the present moment. After a month's debate, on a subject of such magnitude that all agree it cannot admit of a moment's delay, Congress at length give their fiat, and then the States take up the resolutions. The first thing the States do, is to complain of the apportionment and the second to make excuses why they cannot pay. At length however, in imitation of the very thing they complain of, the States also quota their districts or counties. These, in their turn, guess at the wealth of individuals, or compel the individuals to declare it on oath, which is infinitely worse. Thus guess generates guess, delay produces delay, and murmur succeeds to murmur; till when, with grumbling discontent, a little pittance is paid; one half its value is swept away, by the rapid current of depreciation. In the mean time the war is left to support itself, as if the army could be fed and clothed, our enemies beaten and subdued, or our liberties secured and established, by idle debates, vain reproaches, or quibbling subtilties.

Without adverting, therefore, to the little cavils which may abundantly be made against any and every plan, I shall assign a few reasons in favor of these imposts, generally and particularly. And we are to observe generally, 1st. That the land labor and commodities of our country were originally mortgaged for our debts, and must eventually redeem them. 2dly. That unless taxes are laid on specifick articles, they cannot consist with freedom; because freedom is to be governed by laws, and slavery by men, he therefore who pays a tax levied on a specifick thing is free, because he is governed by the law, but otherwise he is not free, being governed by the will or the whim of the assessor or collector. 3dly. That no other taxes can consist with justice, for it is just that men and states should pay in proportion to their respective wealth; that is to their land labor and commodities, not the opinions of others. Lastly. That as no other taxes can consist with private freedom and justice, so by no other means can the rights and liberties of the several States, and the general superintendence of Congress subsist together. If Congress can compel the least State to pay as large a tax as the greatest, their rights and liberties are no more; and a prevailing faction in Congress may commit the most horrible injustice. If every State has a right to deliberate and determine for itself on the propriety of the quota allowed to it, the authority of Congress is a shadow, our union a thread, and our force an idea.

We will next consider these taxes in their successive order; and here we must remember, that land is the ultimate object of human avarice, for which there is the greatest contest among States and among men. On this, then, let the tax be laid. Let the landholder pay for the defence of his land. A monopoly of the soil is pernicious or even destructive to society, let taxes, therefore, compel the owner, either to cultivate it himself, or sell to those who will cultivate it. Land can neither be carried away nor concealed, no care therefore is necessary to secure, no art to discover it. Other objects may elude the grasp of the Legislature, but this is always open to their inspection, always subject to their authority. There is indeed an objection, that some lands are better than others. This objection would be more solid if it were proposed to tax land alone, still however it has weight; but a part of it will be removed when we reflect, that if it is unjust to tax the bad land of A, as high as the good land of B; it is equally unjust, to tax the cost and labor which C, has expended, to render his farm better than that of D. And the objection will almost vanish when we consider, that if a valuation were made, it would be very partial and unequal in the present moment, but more so in the space of a few years; not to mention the time and expence, neither of which can be spared. To this may be added, that the above tax, tho' unequal at first, would soon become equitable, by the changes of property and the efforts of industry.

As to the tax on polls, we must remember that labor is scarce and dear at present in this country, beyond any other country and any other period, so that it is difficult to procure soldiers with every possible exertion. If therefore a tax be laid on men, they must either work to pay it, or become soldiers to avoid it, either of which is a desirable consequence. Add to this, that a poll tax will fall on the rich rather than on the poor, especially such a poll tax as that now proposed, because, from the nature of the thing, the laborer must be paid for by his employer, and the slave by his master.

The tax on exports is not liable to the objections against the two former, but will perhaps startle those who expect to discourage foreign articles by laying duties on importation, and to encourage native productions by bounties on exportation. This subject would lead me too far, I shall therefore quit it with a few short but leading objections. 1st. The consumer of the article pays the tax, with the profits of the merchant and retailer. 2dly. Taxes must either be paid from the surplus produce which remains to the country after maintaining its inhabitants, or some of those inhabitants must be starved. 3dly. The cheapness of the necessaries of life is the source of population, and together with it forms the wealth and strength of a nation. And 4thly. A tax on exported commodities will equalize all others, and fall precisely on the wealth of each individual. To evince these positions, let us suppose that the farmer, who consumes in his family about forty gallons of imported spirits annually, is to be taxed five pounds. To obtain this sum, a duty might be laid on spirits of two and six pence per gallon, but the merchant who paid this two and six-pence, in the first instance, would take a fifth profit, or perhaps more, which would bring it up to three shillings on the retailer, who, in his turn, would take a third, or more, and thereby increase it to four shillings, wherefore the farmer's tax on forty gallons would amount to eight pounds instead of five. If the tax were laid on the produce the farmer brought to market, then he would pay the five pounds and no more, not to mention the advantage of being taxed in the very moment when he sold his commodities. Besides this, he would pay nothing on his own necessary consumption. If he did not bring his surplus produce to market, it would be so much the cheaper in the country, and therefore the means of subsistence, and consequently labor and manufactures would be the cheaper. Something would at length be exported, and the five per cent. on this something would operate backwards, a gentle tax, on all those who had contributed to its production and improvement. The propriety of carrying all duties to the general account, will appear from the single consideration that as the consumer pays the tax, so when one State carries on the commerce of another, that other would be indirectly taxed by those who carry on their trade, over and above their general proportion.

The tax on horses and cattle will encourage the breeding of good stock, which next to the culture of our lands ought to be one great object of our policy. Horses must be very indifferent which are not worth on average forty dollars each, and cattle which are not worth twenty, the tax therefore would be but two and a half per cent. on their value.

Lastly, As to the tax on windows, I can only say, that I know of none which bids so fair to be proportionate to the wealth of the subject, and which will, at the same time, so well bring the city and country on an equal footing of taxation.

There lies I know an objection to all these taxes, which indeed applies with equal force to all others, that the advanced prices near the seat of war, will better enable the inhabitants of that part of the Continent to pay, than those more remote. It is true that there is such an advantage, but I can safely venture to promise on the part of those who enjoy it, that they will readily give it up to such as are more desirous of being in the neighbourhood of the enemy. To determine however the weight of our burthens, let us, before we quit this subject, make an estimate of the taxes which, in consequence of the above plan, would be levied from a rich man, a wealthy husbandman, and a poor laborer.

	Dol.
The Rich Man would pay,	
For himself and thirty laborers or slaves,	62
For ten thousand acres of land,	200
For sixty horses,	60
For one hundred and twenty cattle,	60
For thirty-six windows,	36
	418.

For his quota of 40,000,000 paper, in proportion to the above sum 2786 2–3, or   69 2–3.
Proportion on exports according to the poll tax   12 3–5.
         500 1–15.

	Dol.
The Wealthy Husbandman would pay,	
For himself and three more,	8
For three hundred acres of land,	6
For eight horses,	8

For sixteen cattle,	8
For twelve windows	1 2
	42.
For his quota as above 280, or	7
Proportion on exports as above,	1 3-5
	50 3-5
The Poor Laborer would pay,	Dol.
For himself,	2
Or he would inlist and pay	0.

These then are taxes which are far from being oppressive. We will next proceed to inquire into the proper mode of collecting them, but we must first take notice of two objections which may be urged, altho' contradictory to each other.[1] One that the land tax being payable in specie alone would depreciate the paper, the other, that the circulating medium would not be sufficient to pay the taxes. Neither of these objections are solid. The land tax would not depreciate the paper, because there is a means of paying it in paper, so as to render every landholder security to himself for the paper he possesses; and because the other taxes will amount to more than two hundred and forty millions of paper, so that when the certificates alone are funded, even if no bills are brought in, still the tax will exceed the whole paper medium by one fifth. The second objection admits of an answer equally short and clear. If the circulating medium is too small, one of two things will certainly happen; either the value [w]ill rise, or more money will be demanded by the people. If the value rises, less of it will answer the purposes of government. If more is required, government may emit more, without any danger of depreciation. It might, however, have been prudent to obviate it, by raising the paper higher than forty, but, since these taxes are not all to be raised in the same moment, as will more fully appear when we speak of the collection, the paper will serve to pay more than would at first view be supposed. At any rate we had better labor under the weight of taxes, and suffer the want of a circulating medium too, than permit our last struggles in this glorious contest to become feeble and ineffectual.

I am your Friend,

An AMERICAN.

---

1. Morris seems to have intended to continue this series, but no further letters appeared.

As Congress struggled with its financial problems in 1780, it was seriously handicapped by its inability to levy taxes and thus support the paper money it had issued. In March 1780, Congress decided to retire all of its existing paper currency and replace it with a new issue. It exchanged old money for new at a rate of 40 for 1, thus bringing down the value of its paper from $200 million to $5 million. The old money would be retired at a rate of $15 million a month by having the states tax it out of existence.[1]

The Pennsylvania General Assembly moved quickly, giving a first reading to a bill for carrying out Congress's plan on March 23, just five days after Congress acted. The bill was published for public comment in the *Pennsylvania Packet* on March 25. It ultimately passed the General Assembly on June 6. A supplementary bill received its third reading November 29, 1780, and was published in the *Packet* December 2. This letter was probably written soon afterward.

⋆⟫⟩⟨⟪⋆

RIGHTEOUSNESS ESTABLISHETH A NATION.[2]

To the general Assembly of the State of Pensilvania.
Gentlemen:
    I crave Leave to submit to you some Considerations on a Bill lately published entitled "a supplement to an Act entitled an Act for funding and redeeming the Bills of Credit of the united States of America, &ca."[3] I shall

---

Gouverneur Morris Papers, Rare Book and Manuscript Library, Columbia University, item 817. Sparks's note on the last page says "Banks—1782-85? probably published." I have not been able to find a published version, however.

1. E. James Ferguson, *The Power of the Purse: A History of American Public Finance, 1776-1790* (Chapel Hill: University of North Carolina Press, 1961), 51.

2. Proverbs 14:34: "Righteousness exalteth a nation: but sin is a reproach to any people."

3. The act was reported by committee and ordered published on November 29,

for the Sake of Perspicuity class these Considerations under two Heads, 1ˢᵗ·
on the Bill now published, 2ˡʸ· on the Measure to which it relates.

As far as the Bill is designed to operate a Tax, I shall make but one Remark, which if well founded may be useful on all such Occasions. To levy
Taxes by Quotas is pernicious. In the first Place, as far as assessors or other
such Officers may be concerned in apportioning the Quotas on Individuals, it is parting with the Powers of legislation in the most valuable Instance,
and conferring it on Men very inadequate to the Duty; because he who tells
me how much I am to pay is the Man who taxes me, & not he who tells me
how much my County must pay: In the second Place such Taxes operate
unequally and therefore unjustly, and what is almost as bad inefficaciously.
If the Property in Bucks County is worth £100,000, and that in Northampton only £50,000, the Taxes on the one, should be just one half of those on
the other. But, as it is next to impossible to ascertain what either of those
Counties is worth, it is in like Manner next to impossible that the Quotas
laid should be proportionate. Now if a man in Bucks County pays on his
Property five per Cent Tax, and a Man in Northampton six per Cent, this
is unjust. Further, when such unequal Taxes are laid, they must in some Instances fall disproportionately on the Poor: In such Case, if the poor cannot pay them then they are ruined. If, on the contrary, the poor can pay
them, then the whole Tax is less efficacious than it ought to be. Because
if the true Proportion of a poor Man be two Shillings, & he pays disproportionately four Shillings, it follows that if the rest of the Community
were taxed after the same Rate, the Revenue would be double & the Poor
not more oppressed than at present, or in other words, that the Revenue
is one half less than it ought to be. Lastly, if it be considered, that Assessors and other the like Officers will be elected by those of most Interest in
the Counties or Districts, and that those of most Property have generally
speaking the most Interest, it would follow, that the wealthy will for the
most Part appoint the Assessors; and then, as is natural, those Assessors will
favor the Persons by whom they are appointed. I am aware of an objection
viz. that Men of Property in Pensilvania do not now govern these Elections. But the evident Reason is because they do not now exert themselves
for that Purpose.

As I do not meddle with State Affairs, I should not have troubled you
Gentlemen with the foregoing Observations, but that another Part of the

___
1780, and published in the *Pennsylvania Packet* on December 2. On December 26, the
Packet reported it as having passed the Assembly, along with several other bills.

Bill appears of a very fatal Tendency. This has forced me as a good Citizen to take Notice of that Part & if in so doing I had been silent as to the Rest it might have been thought that I approved of it.

The Bill proposes to make the new continental money a lawful Tender. I must be indulged one Question. Do you believe that without any such Clause it would be of equal Value with Specie? If you do why do you labor to compel the Currency of it? Surely if it is good Money, he who would refuse it need undergo no greater Penalty than not to receive it. Evidently then you do not think it equal to Gold and Silver. If so, is it not unjust to compel Men to receive it? But Gentlemen this is not all. Do you really believe that making it a lawful Tender would give it a Currency? If you do you are mistaken. Most Men have paid off their old Debts and have now the Leizure to be honest. And all Men dread a new depreciating Medium. The Language of your Constituents is this <u>do not give us a new Emission but if you do at least secure it against Depreciation.</u> It is practicable to grant the former Part of their Prayer but I fear that the latter is impracticable. Do not then mistake the Sense of the People but believe that the same Spirit which dictated the late Association to fix the Value of continental Money will dictate a like Association against the present Plan.[4] The Cause is in both Cases the same <u>The Dread of a depreciating Medium.</u>

But it is needless to waste Time on this Head. You are yourselves convinced that making this Money a lawful Tender will not answer the End and therefore have added the Pains and Penalties contained in the last Clause of the Act.[5] For God's Sake Gentlemen consider well of this Clause. How will it apply to the Feelings of Mankind? A fond Father hears that his virtuous Son is a Prisoner with the Enemy. Taken in Battle bravely fighting for the Liberties of his Country. He hears that this captive Son the Staff of his Age languishes in Bondage with distressful Want. He receives a Letter suppli-

4. It is not clear what group Morris has in mind. There were a number of merchants' groups that had formed to resist state and congressional pressures to impose price controls. A Philadelphia group had published its "Representation" in the *Pennsylvania Packet* on September 10, 1779; one of its signers was Robert Morris. They argued that currency stability would achieve the same purpose as price controls, but with less hardship on sellers and creditors. A Connecticut group formed in June 1780 and was reported in the *Packet* July 6, 1780. The price controls are discussed in Margaret G. Myers, *A Financial History of the United States* (New York: Columbia University Press, 1970), 29–30.

5. The bill barred anyone refusing the paper currency from collecting for the debt in question, and further penalized any assignment of the debt.

cating for the Means to procure a little Bread. The Father sells a Part of his Property & to obtain Specie he sells it cheap. Mark the Consequence. He is dragged from his hospitable Mansion. Indicted. Arraigned. Convicted. Condemned. At one fell stroke Half of his wealth is gone forever. He is immured with in the damp Walls of a Goal.[6] Forced into Fellowship with the Dregs of Men. A prey to Vermin Filth & Disease, bending beneath the Weight of Years, and pining to behold a long lost Child, his Grey Hairs are brought with Sorrow to the Grave. Think you that a Law pregnant with Consequences like these can possibly be executed in the State of Pensilvania? Believe me there are Bounds to every Thing human, nor can the Authority even of a free Legislature exceed those Bounds. Should you enact this Law without the last Clause it will be eluded and with the last Clause it will be rejected. Emit the new Money as you please it will be governed by the same Principles and share the same Fate with the old.

Having said thus much as to the Bill I crave your Indulgence for a few Words on the Measure to which it relates. I mean the issuing of the new Money. There is either Money enough already for the Purposes of Commerce and Taxation or there is not. If there is not I shall be glad to learn the Reason why it happened that at the same Time hard Money was exported the Depreciation continued and the Prices of different Articles remained as high as ever and indeed rather rose than fell. Surely this is a Demonstration that at least there was Money enough. If then there be Money enough how can we flatter ourselves that if more be issued it will not depreciate? It is no easy Matter just now to say what is the real Rate of Exchange but in Deference to the Associators I will state it at 80 for 1. I take 80 rather than 75 as it is a round Number and I believe quite near the Truth. Now Gentlemen your Bill is for the issuing 1,250,000 Dollars wherefore according to the Resolution of Congress of the 18th of March 25,000,000 of Dollars continental are to be called in. These at 80 for one are 312,500 Dollars. Your Bill therefore carried into Effect would encrease the present Circulating Medium by the Sum of 937,500 Dollars hard money. Is there a Possibility of doing this without Depreciation? If not is it possible that the proposed Law should be executed? Or if it be executed is it possible that any Commerce should be carried on? Is not this the first commercial State on the Continent? What is to become of us if our commerce is ruined? Turn back Gentlemen to this Resolution of forty for one. What was the evident De-

6. "Goal" in the manuscript, presumably a mistake for "Gaol," since the word "common" precedes it but is crossed out.

sign? Was it not to prevent Appreciation? Against whom then was it to operate? Was it not against those who held the Money? And who held the Money? Did not the commercial States hold it? Pardon me one Moment. A Man in New Jersey brought Continental Bills to Philadelphia to purchase Salt and put them off at the Rate of four for one. These Bills necessarily continued in Philadelphia because the Ballance of Trade is in our Favor. Afterwards that very Man by his Representative declares he will redeem that Bill at the Rate of forty for one. Our loss then is ninety per Cent & that which has happened may happen again.

But the Question is what shall we do with this Resolution of the 18th of March. Even if no satisfactory Answer could be given to this Question it does not follow that we should ruin ourselves. But I will attempt to answer it satisfactorily. Congress asks us to bring in 25,000,000 Dollars to be destroyed, and they ask us to provide Funds to destroy in six Years 1,250,000 Dollars, equivalent to Specie with 5 p. Ct. Interest.

The Demand therefore stands thus.
In the Year 1781 25,000,000 at 80 for 1 equal to 312,500
To sink 1,250,000 Dollars with five Per Cent Interest
in six Years requires annually 249,536
Total for this year according to the Resolutions of
the 18th March 562,036

The sum to be issued, is to be expended at the Rate of 12/p^r Bushel for Wheat, wherefore the Demand is, in Effect, 781,250 Bushels of Wheat, which may certainly be purchased for less than as many Dollars in Specie, if the new Money be not issued. I shall therefore consider the demand as for so many Dollars. Then I pay

To destroy 25,000,000 at 80 for 1 as above 312,500
To defray the Expenses of the current year.................781,250
       Total...1,093,750
Let a Part of this be paid by the Taxes to wit..............293,750
Let the Rem^r be borrowed viz. 800,000

and to pay this, let a further tax of 162,691 Dollars be mortgaged for six Years. The whole Tax then of the present Year will be 456,441 Dollars; and of the five ensuing Years 162,691. The Difference therefore between the present Mode and the former is, this Year, 105,095 Dollars, and the five succeeding Years each 86,845 Dollars. I am sensible of two Objections which lie against my Proposition. One is that there is not Money enough in the State to pay large Taxes, another that the loans could not be made. To these I answer 1st that we cannot untill the Experiment is made determine what Money is in the State. But if the plain Position be admitted that the Demand for Money will determine the Need of it I shall presently take occasion to shew how the Want, if any, may be supplied. 2ly As to the Practicability of procuring a Loan. I would propose that the Bank be incorporated, the Funds abovementioned mortgaged to them, the Faith of the State pledged to support them, and they [illegible] and directed to make the Loan, or so much of it as the Exigencies of the State might require. I do not believe the whole would be necessary for the Purposes stated. Further, as to a Part of the Loan, to wit 312,500 Dollars, I would propose that Continental Money be received at the Rate of 80 for one, & as to the whole of it, I would propose that the Subscribers pay [several illegible words] the Day of Subscription ¼ in three Months ¼ in six Months and the Remaining ⅙ in nine Months, but that it bear Interest from the Day of Subscription. Lastly I would by Law declare that the Notes of the Bank not under three Pounds payable on Demand without Interest should be receivable in some of the Taxes as Specie. I say some of them, because there are some in which Specie alone should be received. These Notes would supply the Place of Money, if there was a want, and on the Contrary if there were no want, they would be immediately brought in for Payment. Now Gentlemen I shall close my observations for the present because I believe you have too much good Sense not to make every proper Reflection—

A Citizen

12 ❀ Observations on Finances: Foreign Trade and Loans (1781?)

This paper is difficult to assign a date. No published version has been found, nor has the "former paper" Morris cites in the first sentence. The conclusion—that Congress needs an independent revenue—could describe his thinking at any time from 1778 until the Constitutional Convention nine years later. Sparks wrote on the manuscript "1780? Probably printed," but it was not published with the other public finance essays in the spring of that year. For much of the remainder of 1780 Morris was recuperating from the loss of his leg in mid-May.[1]

If the paper dates from Morris's service in Congress, it may be from as early as 1778, when he was preparing a plan for the country's finances. His committee report of September 19, 1778, recommends both seeking a loan in Europe and the imposition of a poll tax and an import duty.[2] Against that is a deleted passage from the manuscript that includes the sentence: "I believe we have engaged a Financier as good as any we would have found even if we had gone into foreign countries to look for him." Assuming the Financier is Robert Morris, the paper must date from sometime after Morris was appointed Superintendent of Finance in spring 1781. By this time Congress had proposed an impost as well. Thus this may be a draft of a speech or newspaper essay prepared by Morris sometime in the first half of that year. Perhaps, however, it was simply a working document for his own use, for a friend in Congress (possibly Robert Livingston), or for use in the Finance office. Some of these ideas were embodied in the Report on Public Credit of July 29, 1782, which Gouver-

---

Gouverneur Morris Papers, Rare Book and Manuscript Library, Columbia University, item 814.

1. Mintz, *American Revolution*, 141–42.

2. *Journals of the Continental Congress*, ed. Worthington C. Ford et al. (Washington, D.C.: U.S. Government Printing Office, 1914), 12:929–33.

neur drafted for Robert Morris.[3] The passage about Robert Morris may have been deleted when Gouverneur became Robert's assistant in June 1781.

Having shewn in a former Paper the advantage from foreign Loans it may now be worthwhile to consider that Subject in a few of its different Relations. Some approved old writers going upon certain Principles which they assumed as Facts but which were very disputable & even erroneous had drawn a Conclusion that foreign Loans were impolitic. Among these Principles is the leading one that bringing Specie into a Country is advantageous and carrying it out pernicious. This Principle must be examined because it influences opinion in the Business now before us. It is either true or false according to Circumstances but generally speaking it is false. It is supremely false as to Spain and Portugal. In Great Britain the Importation of Bullion is useful the Exportation more so. In America bringing it in is useful only because it must be brought in before it can be carried out. All this shall be demonstrated. In Spain and Portugal Manufactures languish because Labor and Subsistence are too high. Carry Money out of those Countries faster than it is brought in reduce the Medium by Degrees and Labor would grow cheaper. In Consequence Subsistence would be more abundant and in Consequence of both they would carry on Manufactures for themselves. To dwell on this Part of the Subject is unnecessary because it will receive Light from what follows. In Great Britain to import Bullion is useful. It is a Commodity or rather a raw Material which Industry renders more valuable. It circulates thro all the Different Tribes of Commerce Husbandry and Arts. It leaves the Island again mingled with a thousand different Things and in a thousand different Forms Watches Gilding Lace Embroidery, &ca. The Importation of Specie in this View is like the Importation of Spanish Wool. A vast Quantity of it is exported in Bullion to India. This is also useful because it prevents the too great Increase of it which by raising the Price of Labor in Comparison to other Countries would ruin many of their Manufactories. The same observations apply to France. In Respect to America this Matter ought to be well understood. Let us suppose a Man possessed of Gold to any Amount & that he laid it

---

3. The report is in *JCC* 22:429–46.

in his Chest. There it would produce Nothing. Suppose he laid it out to buy Tools and hire Labor for the clearing of Land. There it would become productive. But whatever Labor he hired some other Person might want if Labor were in Demand. The Evil therefore would equal the Good when considered in a general Point of View. Suppose then he brought a Man from abroad and Tools for him to work with sending out his Gold for the Purpose. Here would be a clear gain to the Country. Suppose the Value of a Man's Labor to be annually ten Pounds over and above his Subsistence. Suppose one Million Pounds could be sent out of the Country and in Exchange for it twenty thousand Men brought in. This would give an annual Revenue of two hundred thousand Pounds whereas Keeping the Money in the Country would give no Revenue at all. But it may be said if so much Money were sent out Commerce would suffer for the want of a Medium. The People would glow clamorous. It is true and they would as heretofore ask Government to issue Paper Money. This would supply the Place of the Gold. The Country would gain by the Exchange. Here then is another Source of our Prosperity and yet nine Men out of ten would cry the Ballance of Trade is against us we are ruined.

It has been said above that many old Writers concluded foreign Loans to be pernicious. These have been followed by a Train of Politicians who prophesized the Ruin of Great Britain from the Increase of the national Debt. They have ventured at different periods to fix the Era of national Bankruptcy by the amount of the day, a Variety of Sums from fifty to two hundred millions. They have been constantly mistaken. The national Debt and national Prosperity have increased together. Expensive Wars are injurious and if they are unnecessary as well as expensive so much the worse. But the Expense being stated borrowing a Part is better than taxing the whole & that is the Reason why Great Britain has for a Century past contended successfully agst superior Force and Resources. But this Proposition must be received with some Limitations. Holland has sunk beneath her Debts. First her Loans were all domestic. Secondly her Country was incapable of greater Improvement. Thirdly her Commerce could be extended only as a Carrier which is the least profitable Mode of employing Money. Hence her Subjects became Lenders to others at a low Interest because they could not find means to invest their Funds to advantage.

France and Britain have borrowed in Holland and they have gained the Difference between the Profits arising from the use of Money and the mere Interest. Besides the Money payable from Britain & France to Holland, if it goes in Cash must raise the Price of Labor in the latter and lower it in the former. Of Consequence the Manufactures of Holland must pine and decay while the others flourish till eventually the Ballance is paid in Goods instead of Money & this has already happened.

There is another Thing worthy of Notice. The Loans which Great Britain has made have prevented her from suffering as much as her Neighbors by the Wars she has carried on and at this Moment her Credit enables her to make Head against an opposition greater than she ever yet experienced. The Subjects of her Enemies are five Times as numerous as her own & with the single Exception of Great Britain herself they are more wealthy and powerful than any proportionate number of People in the World. Yet she opposes them under peculiar Circumstances of Disadvantage. This is by Means of her immense Credit. A Credit partly arising from the very Debts which it was supposed she would sink under. It is true that she must be ruined by the Event of this present war because this Country being cut off the Theatre for Improvement no longer remains. She must therefore soon fall into a Situation similar to that of Holland and the amassed Wealth of her Individuals become a Food for the Improvements Wars and Luxuries of other Countries. Had America continued in Union with her, it is probable that This Misfortune would not have happened.

To apply these Observations to our Country the Reader is requested to cast an Eye at the Map of America and think for himself. His Conclusion from the whole must be that to make Loans for a Part of our Expenditures and to establish our national Credit ought to be two great objects of our Policy. To impress this Conclusion still more forcibly let him reflect that in half a Century our Population will probably amount to fifteen Millions. There will be many more then than now to bear the Weight of Burthens which may now be laid.

But before we can borrow it is necessary that Credit be established and this cannot be done after the severe Shocks it has received without considerable Efforts.[4] It requires no great knowledge of Finance to determine

4. The rest of this paragraph is an insertion replacing this lined-out text:

I do not pretend to any great Knowledge of Finance. But I believe the Situation of this Country requires that its affairs be managed by Good Sense and Integrity without the Affectation of Mistery or Science and therefore I believe we have engaged a Financier as good as any we would have found even if we had gone into foreign Countries to look for him. Indeed if one may judge by all the Strokes of Finance which have been practiced in this or any other

that good Sense and Integrity will be of more use on this occasion than the Parade or Affectation of Mistery & Science. It is a plain matter and may safely be rested on plain Principles.

Thus it is very clear that no Man who knows the value of Money will lend it to a Person unable to pay or who is privileged against legal Process. It is equally clear that where a man can give good Security and will pay a high Interest he can command Money. It follows therefore that if Congress are to borrow They must have certain Revenues granted to them in such Manner that they can mortgage them to the public Creditors and thereby put them out of their own Power and that of the States too untill the Debts for which they are mortgaged shall be finally paid. It is the Business of Congress and of the several States to determine the proper Sources from which this Revenue is to be drawn but it must be granted & It ought to be drawn from the same Articles throughout the Union & at the same Rates. It ought to be such as will increase with our Wealth and Population. It ought also to be such as foreigners can easily form an Idea of.

If this be done Money may be had abroad Taxes lessened at Home & the War be supported with Ease to the People. We shall become more rich and more powerful than we otherwise should have done. We shall command Resources which might otherwise be employed by our Enemy. And what is of equal Importance with all the Rest We shall convince that Enemy whose Hopes are confessedly founded in the derangement of our Finances that we are able to carry on the War both longer and easier than he is. That of Consequence he must eventually sink in the Contest & therefore that it is necessary for him to ask Peace. In which Case we and not he shall dictate the Terms. If all this be desirable let the previous Measures be taken. <u>Let the States give to Congress a permanent productive Revenue.</u>

Country it is no small advantage not to have been bred to the Business. Without pretending to dictate on this Subject I would submit it to the public Discernment on very plain Principles & then the public Servants may do as they please for I will not abuse them if they do not employ me or take my advice.

13 ❖ Ideas of an American on the Commerce Between the United States and French Islands As It May Respect Both France and America (1783)

When Morris arrived in France in early 1789, he already had a reputation for knowledge of economics and finance. In large measure, this reputation rested on several letters that he had written in 1783 and 1784 concerning American trade with the French West Indies, which had been circulated among French policy makers.[1] Morris himself was inclined to make light of the letters; in any case he was in France on private business and had no desire to become involved in French policy discussions:

> I find . . . that fortunately the Comte de Puisignieu prevented the Publication of my Letter to Monsr. de Chatellux. This Letter is after all, in my Opinion, a very trifling Thing and I cannot conceive the Reason for so much Applause as has been given to it. . . . I tell him I have no Wish to talk with their Ministers on public Affairs but if he [Monsieur de Malesherbes][2] chuses to ask my Ideas it will be my Duty to give them after his very particular Attention to me. In Effect I had rather leave our Affairs in the Hands of our Minister [Thomas Jefferson] and give *him* my Ideas.

The English originals of most of these documents seem to have been lost. What survive are a draft of the letter to Chevalier de la Luzerne, included here, and a French translation of a letter to the Marquis de Chas-

Gouverneur Morris Papers, Rare Book and Manuscript Library, Columbia University, manuscript 834. The manuscript is damaged. Where conjectures are possible, I have included them in brackets; otherwise, missing words are indicated by empty brackets. This appears to be a draft of a paper sent to the French minister, the Chevalier de la Luzerne, in October 1783. It is excerpted in Sparks, *Life*, 1:261ff. According to Kline, *New Nation*, 284, the proposal Morris makes here was substantially embodied in the French Arrêt of August 1784.

1. Diary entry of March 2, 1789 (Morris, *Diary of the French Revolution*), xxxvii.
2. Chrétien-Guillaume de Lamoignon de Malesherbes (1721–94), French statesman and uncle of Chevalier de la Luzerne.

tellux. There are also summaries of two letters to Chastellux and the letter to Luzerne among Thomas Jefferson's papers.[3]

Ideas of an American on the Commerce between the United States and French Islands as it may respect both France and America—
It is [considered] by some, to be for the Interest of France to [prohibit] to her Islands the Importation of Flour from this Country, and the Exportation of Sugar &ca. in American Bottoms. That such Regulations will be injurious to the Commerce of the United States, that Artifices will be used to elude them, and that animosities may be excited between the two Powers, is evident. But let us consider whether it [will] advance either the Commerce, the Revenue, or [the] Navigation of France to tread in the Path lately marked out by Great Britain.[4]

It is said, that the Merchants of Bourdeaux are desirous of confining to themselves the Flour Trade of the Islands. But these Merchants should consider that their Commerce in Wine, already very important, may derive considerable Benefit from the Consumption of this Country. That if America cannot vend her Commodities, she cannot purchase those of other Countries & that the Inability to purchase must restrain us, *first*, in Articles which are *not* necessary, and next, in [Articles] which *are* necessary. In the first Case, we must bear the Want, and in the second we must supply it by our own internal Efforts. Let it then be considered as a general Rule with Respect to this Country, *that so long as she can obtain Vent for her gross articles of raw Produce, she will procure Manufactures abroad, and that she will expend for Luxuries, in proportion to her Wealth.* But to conciliate the Interests of [French] Merchants with the Interests of this Country, and of the Islands,

3. Jefferson summarizes the letters to Chastellux of October 7, 1783, and May 14, 1784, as well as the paper to Luzerne. This summary is published in *The Papers of Thomas Jefferson* (Princeton: Princeton University Press, 1953), 7:351–53. Another letter to Chastellux, dated June 17 and 24, 1784 (GM wrote the first paragraph on the 17th and completed the letter on the 24th; there is also a postscript dated July 1), is preserved in the archives of the French Foreign Ministry. See Ministère des Affaires Étrangères, *Mémoires et Documents, États-Unis* II, 120–23, Manuscript Division, Library of Congress.

4. An Order in Council of July 2, 1783, excluded all but British ships from commerce with ports in the British West Indies.

suppose a light Duty, of about one Livre per Quintal,[5] were laid on the Import of Flour from any foreign Country to the french Islands. This would give sufficient Preference to the Produce of France, & secure to the Islands a permanent Mode of Supply, prevent Distress in the Case of Hostilities. It would also produce no inconsiderable Revenue to the Crown.

With Respect to the Islands themselves, it is conceived that they must flourish in Proportion to the Facility with which they can obtain Subsistence. From this Country they cannot receive any European Manufactures, because they can get such things cheaper directly [from] France, & besides which [it] might be provided by an Edict that every Vessel importing contraband Articles should be confiscated, with her Cargo. If the Subsistence of the Islands be cheap, their Produce will be delivered proportionately cheap; & Lands will be cultivated which would not otherwise bear the Expence of Cultivation. As, by this Means, both the Population and Produce of the Islands would be encreased, *they would consume more of the Commodities of France, and pay for them more readily.* Therefore it may be considered as certain, that every Thing [which] can contribute to subsist the Islands cheaply, must increase the Commerce & Wealth of France. And it is a clear Corollary, *that the Navigation & Revenue must increase in as great (if not greater) Proportion.* The quantity of Produce being encreased in the Islands, the Revenue arising from that Produce must encrease & the Consumption of the Produce and Manufactures of France being increased, the [Revenue] from that Produce and those Manufactures must also encrease. In like Manner the Produce being encreased, the number of Ships and of Seamen to transport it must be encreased. But further, the Produce being made cheaper by the Cheapness of Supplies, the Demand for it is raised in those Countries which have no Islands, & a Preference obtained over the like Produce from other Countries. The Commerce [in] Sugar between france and the North of Europe will therefore be invigorated, and the Navigation extended in Proportion. On the other Hand it may be worthy of Consideration, in france, that the Sugars of Portugal brought from the Brazils, may soon obtain a Preference (in foreign Markets) over french Sugars, by being delivered at a cheaper Rate.

But will it be prudent for france to permit the Commerce with America, to be carried on in American Bottoms? This also is an important Question.

---

5. A *French quintal* was 100 livres, or about 49 kg; the *English quintal* was equal to a hundredweight, either 100 pounds (45.36 kg) or 112 pounds (50.84 kg). The quintal has since been redefined as 100 kg.

An objection to it is, that if the Americans are permitted to carry away the Produce of the Islands, for their own Use, they will take more than they want, so as to elude any Restrictions [   ] on them; and if they are permitted, generally, to carry the Produce of the Islands, they will become the sole Carriers of the Islands. To obviate this objection therefore some have proposed that this Trade should be carried on only in french Bottoms. But (all smuggling out of the Question) let it be considered whether this would be a judicious Plan. *The Commerce with the Islands cannot be carried on in Vessels from Europe to America thence to the Islands, and thence again to Europe.* Nor, supposing the circle to commence at any other of those three points (America for Instance) can it be carried on in that Manner. The articles carried from hence to the Islands must (from the [Nature] of the Navigation among the Islands & on our own Coast) be sent in small Vessels, navigated by few Men. These being not only permanent, but perpetual Reasons; we may well conclude that the Preference formerly given to small Vessels will continue. Such Vessels however are not calculated to carry the Produce of the Islands to Europe, and will suffer as much in a Competition with large Vessels, for that Business, as they will gain in the other [Competition] just mentioned. If then the Islands are to be supplied from hence, by the Intervention of large Vessels from Europe, the Cost of those Supplies will be encreased, and all the Evils consequent thereon must take Place. As this is a Matter which depends a little on Calculation it may be proper to state the general Propositions on which such Calculations are to be founded. And, first, the Produce which is carried directly from America to Europe, employs many [more] Ships than can be employed in bringing articles from Europe to America. Thus, the Tobaccoes exported from the Chesapeak, will require two hundred large Ships, which two hundred Ships are sufficient to bring the annual supplies from Europe for all America— yet Tobacco is among the most valuable Articles of Export in Proportion to its Bulk. Certainly it does not employ above one fifth of the Shipping which plies between Europe and America. It follows from hence, *that [a] far greater Part of the Vessels coming from Europe to America must be empty;* and this was so notoriously the Case with Respect to the Tobacco Trade, that Goods were freighted from Britain to the Chesapeak for very little, and sometimes for nothing. As tobacco may be carried hereafter to France in french Bottoms, the same Thing will probably happen in the Freight of Goods from France to that Country.

In the second Place it must be considered, that a Ship sailing directly from France to the Islands, can perform her Voyage with great Certainty by a given Time, because of the tropical Winds; but the Voyage to this Country is more uncertain, and much longer.

In both Cases then let it be supposed that she is empty; or, in other Words, that the Ship is risqued, her Crew employed, and the Necessity of Repairs and Refreshments incurred, without any Thing on board, whose Freight can pay the Expence. Now it will be found, that if two Ships sail together, one [for] this Country, and one for the Islands, the Ship coming hither, to fetch a Cargo for the Islands, will have expended (by the Voyage) so much more than the other as will nearly am[oun]t to one fourth the Value of the Cargo to be taken from hence & then she must perform a Voyage (which is always long in such Ships) before she can get to the Islands. *The Difference of this Expence is such, as must advance the Price of Supplies carried in that Manner, one fourth [more] than the same Supplies carried from hence in the common Mode.* Here then is an Expence incurred, without any Use whatever; and it must be borne either by the Merchant who fits out the Ship, or by the Planter who consumes the Produce. If therefore a free Competition is allowed, it is an Expence which will not be incurred at all; or in other Words, *No Merchant will send a Vessel from Europe to carry over products [to the] Islands and take their Produce to Europe.* The Corollary is, that *No Merchant will send a Vessel from hence to the Islands to take Freight to Europe and return from thence to America.* For the Circle is the same, let it commence at whatever Point it may. There is indeed one Case in which American Vessels will take Sugar &ca. to Europe. When a Vessel is built in America, to be sold in Europe, it may sometimes be convenient to send her to the Islands for a Freight, but this will happen only to a Part of the Vessels built for Sale, and can therefore very little interfere in the French carrying Trade. By giving full Permission to this Commerce, France will derive the advantage of having greater numbers of American Ships offered for Sale in her Harbors, which is not a trivial Consideration.

It appears then, that natural Causes will always prevent any material Interference from this Country, in the Carriage of Produce from the Islands, if that Trade be entirely laid open to us. In fact, if we take a View of America (beginning at the South) we shall find that untill we get to the Delaware, so far from being able to carry for others, those States are, and always will be, obliged to employ others to carry for them. The Reason is clear. They have not that Class of People among them from which Seamen are formed, all the Maritime Parts being inhabited by a few [Landholders], Masters of numerous Slaves. Going on Northward, we shall find that the States of Pensilvania & New York must, for a long Period to come, employ

Numbers of foreign Seamen to navigate their Ships, used in the Carriage of their own Produce. No Interference then can arise, but from the Eastern States, and if we deduct from the Shipping of those [States] employed in transporting [   ] Lumber Oil & Live Stock to the Islands, such as are necessary to bring back the Supplies of West India Produce, which they stand in Need of, & such as will be employed in carrying that Produce to the Southern and middle States (there to be freighted home with the articles of Southern Growth consumed to the Eastward) the Remainder is too trivial to be worth Notice.

To make undue Restrictions on the Commerce therefore with a View to encrease thereby the numbers of French Seamen, will defeat the very Purpose intended. For, by allowing a free Trade, the Produce of the Islands will be so much encreased, that with every possible Deduction for what may be carried in American Bottoms, there must be a very great Increase of french Shipping to carry off that Produce. The Benefits in a Commercial Point of View will be reciprocal. Each Nation will derive an addition of private Wealth and of public Revenue, and the Number both of French and American Seamen will be encreased. Which Circumstance ought to be a pleasing Consideration to both Countries, as the Time may not be far distant in which they may at Sea be joined under the same Banners as lately they were at Land.

14 ❧ Address to the Assembly of Pennsylvania on the Abolition of the Bank of North America (1785)

Robert Morris's 1781 appointment as superintendent of finance brought the beginnings of order to America's finances. In May 1781, the Continental Congress approved Morris's proposal for a national bank, and in December of that year Congress incorporated it as "the President and Company of the Bank of North America."[1] It was not clear, however, that Congress had the authority to issue a corporate charter, and as a result several states also issued charters. The Bank chose to organize itself under the charter issued by the Pennsylvania Assembly on April 1, 1782. But the charter had met with substantial opposition in the General Assembly, and by 1785 the Bank's opponents felt strong enough to bring a proposal for its repeal. The bill was introduced April 4, 1785, and occasioned considerable debate both inside and outside the Assembly. Both Gouverneur and Robert Morris argued against the repeal. The Morrises saw the Bank as an essential tool in managing the country's finances, as did Hamilton and as others would later. Their arguments were unsuccessful, however; the charter was repealed September 13, 1785.

Gentlemen,

Whether the Bank shall be abolished or established, is one of those important questions, which will in course attract your notice. The heat of disputation will then give birth to many arguments. But disputants do not always convey information. There is, no doubt, a great majority of mem-

Reprinted from Jared Sparks, *The Life of Gouverneur Morris, with Selections from his Correspondence and Miscellaneous Papers* (Boston: Gray & Bowen, 1832), 3:437-65. A draft is in the Gouverneur Morris Papers, Rare Book and Manuscript Library, Columbia University, item 838.

1. On the creation of and controversy over the Bank of North America, see Bray Hammond, *Banks and Politics in America from the Revolution to the Civil War* (Princeton: Princeton University Press, 1957), 48-64.

bers, who will vote according to their dispassionate judgment; and such men will naturally wish to form opinions on plain reasons plainly delivered. To them, therefore, this paper is addressed. And, in order that we may have a clear view of the object, let us consider, first, whether admitting the institution of the Bank to have been pernicious, a law to abolish it would be wise; and, secondly, whether it is really a pernicious institution.

First, then, admitting the institution of the Bank to have been pernicious, would a law to abolish it be wise? The answer to this question depends on two points. First, whether such a law would be effectual; and secondly, whether it would be prudent. An inquiry whether the law would be effectual involves a doubt of your power, and may, therefore, offend the weak or illiberal, but wise representatives of free citizens will listen with candor and form a dispassionate judgment. They know that the boasted omnipotence of legislative authority is but a jingle of words. In the literal meaning it is impious. And whatever interpretation lawyers may give, freemen must feel it to be absurd and unconstitutional. Absurd, because laws cannot alter the nature of things; unconstitutional, because the Constitution is no more, if it can be changed by the Legislature. A law was once passed in New Jersey, which the judges pronounced to be unconstitutional, and therefore void. Surely no good citizen can wish to see this point decided in the tribunals of Pennsylvania. Such power in judges is dangerous; but unless it somewhere exists, the time employed in framing a bill of rights and form of government was merely thrown away.

The doubt which arises on this occasion, as to the extent of your authority, is not founded on the charter granted by Congress; but supposing the incorporation of the Bank to have been the same in its origin as that of a church, we ask whether the existence and the rights acquired by law can be destroyed by law. Negroes have by law acquired the right of citizens; would a subsequent law take that right away? It is not true that the right to give involves the right to take. A father, for instance, has no power over the life of his child, nor can a felon or traitor, pardoned by act of grace, be by repeal of that act condemned and executed. Should an act be passed to cancel the public debts, would that act be valid? Where an estate has been granted by law, can it be revoked by a subsequent law? Could the lands forfeited and sold be resumed and conveyed to the original owners? Many such questions might be put, and a judicial decision, either affirmative or negative, would be inconvenient and dangerous. Look then to the end ere you commence the labor.

Secondly, admitting your power, ought it, in prudence, be exercised. You will certainly consider, that, as a violation of private property, it must sully the reputation of the State. Good men are careful of their own reputation, and protect that of their country, from sentiment. Wise men are confirmed in this sentiment, by reflection and information. Facts are sometimes better than arguments. It is then a fact, that applications made by citizens of Pennsylvania to borrow money in Holland have been defeated by those attacks already made on the Bank. It is also a fact, that the credit of our merchants has been greatly injured, in foreign countries, from the same cause. This is the argument which foreigners use. If your government so little respects the property of their own citizens, as to overturn an institution like the Bank, how can our property be safe among you? It will not be easy to answer that question, and you know, gentlemen, that your merchants cannot give credit, unless they can get credit; and you know also how important credit is to the frontier inhabitants, at least, if not to those of the more settled country.

Deeply, therefore, are we interested in preserving unsullied fame. But if this consideration has not sufficient weight, reflect on the domestic consequences of abolishing charters. What is practice today becomes precedent tomorrow. And sure it is worth some serious thought, whether this dangerous practice shall be introduced. Every man is interested in the establishment of such precedent, as a member of some religious society, or of particular corporations for the promotion of science, or the purposes of humanity. Attention to the changes of human affairs, like meditation among the tombs, teaches solemn and affecting lessons of wisdom and moderation. Look back to the disputes which convulsed this commonwealth twenty years ago. Mark the succeeding revolutions. See how friendships and how enmities have changed. See how power has been wrested from one, and grasped by another. This generation will soon pass away. Who can designate the men that will sit in seats of authority twenty years hence, or five, or one? You are here today and gone tomorrow. Beware then how you lay the foundation for future encroachments. While justice is the principle of government, to be innocent is to be secure. Be not then seduced by the momentary bauble of power; for place it where you will it is dangerous, and the tyrannous use of it is always tyranny. Those who live by the sword shall die by the sword. The violent must, of necessity, become victims of violence. Should the next election give power to those who may now be oppressed, what bounds shall be set to unbridled resentment? May not all charters be at once laid low, by a general law declaring the existence of corporations to be incompatible with the public welfare? Since, then, these consequences may follow, we may reasonably doubt whether a law to abolish the Bank would be wise, even if the institution had been pernicious. But is it really a pernicious institution?

This question is of great magnitude. Some objections against the Bank may perhaps be well founded. Let us examine them. They are,

First, that it enables men to trade to their utter ruin by giving them the temporary use of credit and money.

Secondly, that the punctuality required at the Bank throws honest men into the hands of usurers.

Thirdly, that the great dividend on bankstock induces monied men to buy stock rather than lend on interest.

Fourthly, that rich foreigners will, for the same reason, become stockholders so as that all the property will finally vest in them.

Fifthly, that the payments of dividends to foreigners will be a constant drain of specie from the country.

Sixthly, that the Bank facilitates the exportation of coin.

Seventhly, that it injures the circulation of bills of credit.

Eighthly, that the wealth and influence of the Bank may become dangerous to the government.

Ninthly, that the directors can obtain unfair advantages in trade for themselves and their friends.

And tenthly, that it is destructive of that equality which ought to take place in a free country.

These objections, though artfully made and industriously circulated, do not consist very well together. For if it be true that the Bank enables men to overtrade themselves, by the use of money at an easy rate; it cannot be true that it throws men into the hands of usurers, who exact for the use of money an exorbitant rate. If it be true, that foreigners will buy out stockholders, even as is said at fifty per cent advance, so as to become proprietors of the whole; it cannot be true that the money of our rich citizens will be vested in bankstock, and none remain for loans. If it be true, that the Bank facilitates the exportation of coin; it cannot be true that it injures the circulation of bills of credit, which bills are always expressly emitted to supply the real or supposed want of specie. If it be true, that the use of money obtained by discounts at the Bank ruins the trader; it cannot be true that the directors and their friends would gain any advantage by it. If it be true, that the Bank has a tendency to lock up in its vaults the money of rich citizens; it cannot be true that it facilitates the exportation of coin. If it be true, that foreigners will continually bring in money to buy the principal of the stock;

it cannot be true that the country will continually be drained of specie by paying the dividend on that principal. If it be true, that the funds of the bank must finally vest in foreigners; it cannot be true that it is destructive of equality among the citizens.

Thus much in general. Let us now consider each objection by itself; and FIRST, that it enables men to trade to their utter ruin, by giving them the temporary use of money. It is true that the Bank has given facility to commercial people, of which some have made an imprudent use, by engaging in rash and ruinous enterprises. But this abuse of commercial advantages cannot be prevented, otherwise than by the destruction of commerce itself, or by confining the trade, as in China, to an exclusive company. Neither of these modes would suit the genius and temper of Pennsylvania. We must therefore, as in former times, leave the foolish to suffer the consequence of their folly, and not punish, for their sakes, the sober and discreet. The convenience merchants derive from being able to obtain money for short periods, and on easy terms, is of the greatest consequence to them. And it would be a marvellous thing indeed, if the use of water were prohibited, because some people choose to drown themselves.

SECONDLY, it is said that the punctuality required at the Bank throws honest men into the hands of usurers. This objection will admit of nearly the same answer with the last. If men, who borrow for a short term, will engage the funds borrowed in long speculations, thereby depriving themselves of the means of payment, who is to blame? Is it the benevolent lender, or the foolish and dishonest borrower? Why did he incur the debt and undertake the payment? Or why divest himself of the means? But say, that a man is, by misfortune, in want of a considerable sum, without which his credit would suffer. The Bank advances the sum for forty days, and saves him from ruin. If within that period he collects his funds, and repays the advance, has he derived no benefit from the Bank? If at the end of forty days he should be unable to pay, is the situation worse than it was? If in that case the Bank renews the discount for forty days more, which has usually been done, is not the benefit increased? And if after all, when it will trust him no longer, he apply to usurers, which he must otherwise have done in the first instance, is the Bank to blame? But the man it seems has been unfortunate, and is ruined, which ruin the Bank did delay, but could not prevent.

Now what is the conclusion drawn from these premises, and how is it drawn? Why thus. Misfortune is the cause of loss. Imprudence is the source of disappointment. Loss and disappointment demand supplies of cash. Usurers exact enormous interest. Bad voyages, wild speculations, mismanagement, and usurious interest, produce ruin. Therefore the Bank must be destroyed. It must be destroyed, because it would not continue to trust men who were no longer trustworthy. Before this objection be repeated, let these men, or at least one of them, be openly named; so that the directors may have an opportunity fairly to combat the charge; and then, if they do not show that the party received every indulgence he had any right to claim, expect, or even hope for, let the charge be established. But until this opportunity be given, let not the voice of slander be heard in the sanctuaries of legislation.

Rely on it, gentlemen, that however calumny may cast the aspersion, no proof will ever be adduced. It might therefore be abandoned to merited contempt. But since such pains have been taken to inculcate a false idea, that the Bank promotes usury, let us recur to facts. Before the establishment of the Bank, usury had been carried to an alarming degree. Men of the greatest property, who happened to be here from the neighboring States, were forced to pay as high as ten per cent for one month's anticipation of their remittances; merchants who met with misfortune were driven to the greatest distress, and the public could not obtain advances upon any terms. Under these circumstances the Bank was instituted; and there are many in this city and elsewhere whom it saved from destruction. The number of usurers and the rate of usury were soon diminished. But as there still remained some objects, whose distresses the Bank could not relieve, *because most of its funds were employed in the public service*, so there still remained some usurers to prey on those distresses. In proportion as the number who want money is increased, or which comes to the same thing, as the means of obtaining money are diminished, in the same proportion will usury abound and flourish. This the usurious know, and therefore they have never intermitted their efforts to destroy the Bank, as the sure means of increasing and securing their unrighteous gains. Beware then, gentlemen, that you be not dupes to the artifice of such wretches. It is indeed but a slender and despicable artifice; a poor attempt to persuade you, that an institution which lends for one half per cent per month drives folks to borrow at ten per cent. And on this ground they suggest, that the best mode of preventing men from giving ten per cent for a month's use of money, is to disable them from obtaining it on any other terms.

THIRDLY, it is said the dividend on bankstock induces monied men to buy it rather than lend on interest. The object of this assertion is to persuade you, that the difficulty of borrowing money arises merely or chiefly from the Bank, which is not true. For first, it is notorious that few stockholders are of that class, who were in the habit of lending on interest. Such as are foreigners or inhabitants of the neighboring States, and these it is said own half the stock, would not lend their money in Pennsylvania, even if circumstances favored such loans. A considerable part of the remaining half belongs to small stockholders, who would not send their money into the country. And a far more considerable part is the property of merchants, who would be obliged immediately to employ their funds in their own business, if deprived of those facilities which the Bank affords. After making these deductions from the capital of the Bank, the remainder, belonging to those who would and could lend, will be inconsiderable. But such as it is, to whom would it be lent? Not to farmers, who pay interest irregularly, and from whom the principal cannot always be recovered without legal process. No, it would be lent to merchants, and the greater part to such as, through necessity, give more than legal interest. Can it be believed, while usurers get ten per cent per month for the use of money, and pledges in hand for security, that the twenty or thirty thousand dollars, now vested in bankstock, which belong to men not engaged in active business, would be lent on bonds and mortgages for six per cent per annum? It is true that money cannot be borrowed, and it is also true that the purchase of bankstock is more profitable than lending on interest. But trace the evils complained of to their true sources, and it will be found that they flow from that usury, which has been occasioned by the peculiar circumstances of the times, and from that opposition which has been excited against the Bank. Why is money scarce and not to be borrowed? Why is it so desirable to own bankstock? An answer to these two questions will lead to the solution of a third. How is money to be made more plenty, and to be obtained with more ease?

First, then, why is money scarce and not to be borrowed? It is a melancholy truth, that during the late war many were ruined by payment of their debts in paper greatly depreciated. Some, who received the paper while it was valuable, put it in the loan office. Some purchased land. And some kept it till it was good for nothing. It is evident, that these persons, who before the war were lenders of money, have no money to lend now; and that every shilling so paid and disposed of must be deducted from the sum formerly at interest in Pennsylvania. The remainder of that sum is still in the hands of those, who borrowed it ten years ago, and cannot be lent before it be paid. It may perhaps be said, that some merchants made money during the war. But it will be found that the gainers were few, the losers numerous; and that taking the merchants collectively as a body, they are poorer by millions. The reason therefore why money is not to be borrowed is, that no one has money to lend, and even admitting that there should be a few who can lend, there are none who will; for the following reasons. Those who want are always willing to borrow, but those who owe are not always willing to pay.

If therefore the laws of a country, or the administration of those laws, countenance unreasonable delays of payment, the owners of money, or anything else, will not dispose of their property on credit, unless they be tempted by great interest, or great profit. And such as disdain usurious dealing will not be tempted at all. A prudent peaceable man would rather buy stock in the British funds, and receive regularly but five per cent, than take a mortgage at six on the best estate in Pennsylvania. Because he may suffer for years a detention of both interest and principal, and because he apprehends some things which have happened already, and may therefore happen again. For instance, he trembles lest a long train of paper emissions, with a legal tender at the tail of them, should cancel his debt for a tenth of the value. He fears also, that a tax on his bond may reduce the precarious interest of six per cent to four, and even oblige him to pay the two per cent tax, though he cannot recover the six per cent interest. Thus we find, on fair investigation, that money is scarce, because, in one way or another it has been taken or withheld from the owners; and that money is not to be borrowed, from a well grounded apprehension that, when due, it will not be repaid.

Let us then, in the second place, inquire why it is so desirable to own bankstock. Three causes present themselves. First, that the dividend gives something more than legal interest, although by extension of the capital, and contraction of the business, it yields less than formerly. Secondly, that this dividend is payable with rigid punctuality at the end of every half year, so that the proprietors can count with certainty on their income to defray their expenses. Thirdly, that in case of unforeseen demands the stockholder can, for legal interest, command a temporary accommodation; and if unfortunate events should oblige him to collect all his resources, he can speedily sell and thereby command the value of the stock. To these three reasons, which strike every person at first sight, must be added a fourth as applying more directly to the charge, that the benefits of bankstock incline men to purchase it rather than lend. After the peace, when the advantages of the Bank had been felt, and the property of stock had become secure, an opposition was raised by some of the same persons who are now the opposers, but on ground somewhat different. For then, instead of considering a bank as pernicious, it was declared to be so highly beneficial that they must needs have two.[2]

They did indeed complain of the old Bank. But for what? Not because the capital was so large as to threaten general ruin, but because the directors would not open a subscription to make it larger. And what was the modest request of that day? Why truly such an extension of the capital, as might enable those, who had waited for events in perfect ease and safety, to enjoy the same advantages with those who had borne the burthen, and ran the risk of the contest. It was indeed a hard case, that many worthy gentlemen, who would not have given a shilling to save the State, should be obliged either to pay five hundred dollars for a share in a bank which had cost but four, or to lend their money on bond and mortgage to the farmers of Pennsylvania. A very hard case! And so loudly did they complain of it, that at last many sensible members of Assembly were prevailed on to believe it would be a good thing to have two Banks, two shops to go to; for that was the fashionable phrase. And they were the more easily led into this opinion, because it was laid down by some in high station, for whose sentiments they had acquired a habitual respect. But that respect may perhaps be diminished, if those who pronounced decisive judgment two years ago that two banks were necessary, should now as positively pronounce that no bank at all is necessary; and wonderful to relate, go cackling round the country, that one bank is pregnant with ruin to the State. The language of truth is uniform, and these sudden changes of hasty opinion show so great a want of temper and knowledge, that those who really mean the public good will quit such blind guides, and think for themselves. The consequence of the noise made at that time must be well remembered.

The Assembly were plagued with long arguments on both sides, which might as well have been spared, and then all at once the thing was hushed up and accommodated. Because such of the promoters of the new bank as had money found out that most of their new friends had none. Because they all found out, that the scheme did not promise so much either of profit or security as was imagined. And because they had not too much confidence in each other, being like Nebuchadnezzar's image composed of discordant materials. They agreed, therefore, to abandon their project, on certain con-

---

2. In spring 1784 a group of Philadelphia merchants who had tried without success to become stockholders in the Bank of North America nearly persuaded the Pennsylvania General Assembly to charter another bank. They abandoned their effort after the Bank agreed to enlarge its capital. Hammond, *Banks and Politics*, 52.

ditions acceded to by the old Bank, one of which was to extend the subscription; and this it is which has converted all the surplus money of the State into bankstock. For otherwise, let the price of a share have risen ever so high, nay had it gone to four thousand instead of four hundred dollars; not one penny would have been added to the bank capital. But in proportion as stock rose, the dividend would have been less valuable, till at length it would have been more profitable to lend at six per cent, than to purchase bankstock. For instance, if the dividend on a share of four hundred dollars had continued to be forty dollars, and the price of such a share had risen to be eight hundred dollars, then the purchaser would have got only five per cent for his money, instead of six.

Thirdly, then, let us inquire how money may be rendered more plenty and easier to be obtained. And first, the surest way to render money plenty is to bear the evils of scarcity. To make it plenty, according to the desire of some, would be as in the continental times to make it no money at all. For when it can be obtained without labor, and found without search, it is of no use to the possessor. Those nice politicians, therefore, who try to make money so plenty that people may get it for nothing, will find that their money is good for nothing. The scarcity constitutes the value. And when that scarcity is such that men will do a great deal for a little, it will become plenty; for those will always have most money, who will give most for it. The complaint that money is scarce is generally made by the idle or the unfortunate; by those who will not, or those who cannot give anything in exchange for money, except bare promises which they cannot or will not perform.

Now such men would suffer more from the want of cash in Amsterdam or London, where it is most plenty, than in any part of the State of Pennsylvania. If folks are idle they must be relieved by labor, and if poor by charity. Till this be done, the complaint that money is scarce will continue, and though very loud, will not be very just. There was, for instance, a grievous complaint of the want of money at the close of the war; and yet every man who had a bushel of wheat could get eight or nine shillings for it. People in general plunged into extravagance, and laid out their coin for foreign fripperies, and the merchants unable to remit for payment of these things in produce, except on ruinous terms, sent away the coin; so that in two years there has been more money exported from this country, in which a scarcity was then complained of, than is necessary for a circulating medium. The several States are now issuing paper, that what little specie is left may also be exported, instead of the wheat, corn, rice, and tobacco. Flour has long been cheaper in London than in Philadelphia. We buy fine coats, and handsome buckles, and a thousand other handsome fine things in London, and then when called on to pay, though our barns be full of wheat, we will not sell it as formerly for five shillings the bushel, but sit down and cry because money is scarce. The wagon is in the mud, and we beg Hercules to pull it out without putting our own shoulders to the wheel. The Legislature must relieve us, for we will not relieve ourselves. And against what do we want to be relieved? Why against our idleness, extravagance, and folly.

But, secondly, another means of making money plenty is to render it less necessary. For this purpose enforce the punctual payment of debts, so that those who trust can be sure of recovering in season from those, whom they have trusted. This will produce two happy consequences. First, that men will no longer run in debt for idle gewgaws, which they must pay for with their substance when pay day comes. Executions for debt will then be as wholesome warnings to the extravagant, as executions for crimes are to the profligate.[3] Secondly, a man who wants to buy land or needful goods on credit will then obtain the credit desired. The punctuality of his payments will extend his credit. Those payments will also enable the merchant to comply with his engagements, which will, in like manner, extend his credit at home and abroad. In proportion to the punctuality of remittances, the merchant will get longer credit, and on better terms; and thus money will be plentier because the trading people, who have always a preference in such things, will be relieved from the necessity of borrowing.

Thirdly, another means of making money plenty, is to enforce a collection of taxes, make solid provision for paying the interest of our debts in coin, and introduce order and economy into the administration of affairs. This will restore the public confidence, and then the value of certificates will rise, and the possessors be able to dispose of them for cash. Thousands will thereby be relieved, who are now in great want of money, and under the dire necessity of getting it from usurers, or going to gaol.

Lastly, these plain and simple measures will make money not only plenty but easy to be obtained. Because industry and frugality, which want but little, will thereby be introduced; and we can always command money when we are not in want of it. As to those blades who must forever want, because they spend their time in streets and taverns, and occupy themselves with State affairs, instead of their own affairs, and who dress and feast and will

---

3. Presumably Morris intends "execution" in the general legal sense here, as when a sheriff or other officer enforces a court's judgment, rather than capital punishment.

not work, but wish to borrow; let them meet the rebuff given by an old philosopher to one of their predecessors. "Friend, borrow of thy back and belly, they will never ask thee for the money, but I should be very troublesome."[4]

A FOURTH objection made against the Bank is, that rich foreigners will be induced to become stockholders, so as that all the property will finally vest in them. This objection has some weight, and, if it be allowed to operate as a bar to measures of public utility, will save a deal of time and trouble to the government, though it may not conduce to the prosperity of the State, and must prove injurious to those by whom it is made. People in general seem now to expect some permanent provision for the interest of the public debts, and if that should happen, foreigners will purchase a considerable share. The Dutch are said to hold about thirty millions sterling in the British funds, bearing an interest of four per cent, and they lent five million guilders to Congress at five per cent, when no funds were provided, and during the war. Hence we may with certainty infer, that they will buy up the certificates bearing six per cent, when placed on a solid footing. Is that a sufficient objection against providing for the public creditors? And if not in one case, why in the other? The practice some men have of affirming today, and denying tomorrow, is neither decent nor becoming. A grievous complaint is made of the want of money, and yet as grievous a complaint of the only means to obtain any. We have it not at home, and we must not receive it from abroad. Do these gentlemen suppose it will rain money now, as it did manna of old? And because they have the same perverseness with the children of Israel, do they expect the same miracles? To experience a want of public credit is, they say, terrible; but to destroy the only means of supporting public credit is, they say, desirable. Let us appeal to facts.

No country on earth enjoys extensive credit which has not a public bank. We have ourselves experienced its good effects, when we were in the greatest distress. And shall we now be told that the Bank must be destroyed, and yet public credit be supported? People who speak in this way show great ignorance, or something worse. They ask how a bank contributes to public credit; and, if no reply be made, think they have gained a victory, when they have puzzled an opponent. For the sake of those who love truth, and not with any hope of making such men sensible either to shame or conviction, their question shall be answered. The Bank may be likened to that which

4. The saying is attributed to Francis Bacon. See James Spedding, Robert Leslie Ellis, and Douglas Denon Heath, *The Works of Francis Bacon* (London, 1892), 7:178.

bears the same name, a bank or dam for collecting the waters. After a head is raised, some part turns the wheels of the mill, and some part waters the adjacent grounds. Take the bank away, and the water will still flow, but not with the same beneficial effect. If revenues were appropriated to the interest of the public debt, and other important objects of government; should any delay take place in collections, a similar delay of payment would also happen. The want of punctuality would lessen the value of stock. And, on the other hand, if collections were more rapid than the payments, much money might be taken out of circulation, and lodged in the public coffers. The consequence would be, either that commerce must suffer as, at present, for the want of it, or that the State must procure more money than is necessary; which might not be very easy, if we may judge from past experience. But with the aid of a bank, the same stream turns the wheel, and fertilizes the ground, being prudently applied to either purpose as occasion requires. And so the same sum of money will not only supply the business of the merchant and of the State, but the funds proceeding from trade, and those arising from taxes, will, when thrown into the same mass, mutually aid the operations of each, and jointly secure the objects of both. Nor is there the least danger that foreigners will hold even a great proportion of the bankstock. Bankstock will always be most useful for the mercantile man who lives on the spot. Because he, and he alone, can at once receive the dividend, and when occasion requires have, by loan for a short time, the use of his money; so that he will naturally outbid the foreigner. And as the object of the foreigner must be to secure a certain annual income from his funds, make but the interest of the public debt as regular and safe as the bank dividend, which by means of the Bank is easily done, and the foreigner will as naturally wish to exchange his bankstock for an amount of funded loan office certificates yielding more annual interest, as the merchant will to exchange such an amount of certificates for bankstock. And so far from any danger to the State, by the interest of foreigners in their funds, there is a great security. Every foreign creditor is an advocate for us with his own government, in times of public calamity, and is induced to lend more as the means of securing what has been already lent; especially if he has been regularly paid the interest of his capital.

The FIFTH objection against the Bank is, that the payment of the dividend to foreigners will be a drain of specie from the country. This has already been answered in part; but farther, a man who has bought a piece of ground wants to borrow money for the purpose of clearing, fencing, draining, and cultivating it. He would not relish the advice of a neighbor, who might tell him not to borrow, lest the payment of interest should drain him of cash. He might indeed be glad to get the money at a low interest, or for no interest, but he would certainly get it if he could; and by industrious attention, and a prudent application of it, he would pay both principal and interest from the profits of his farm. And thus by degrees, a wilderness is converted into beautiful cultivation. From the discovery of America to the present hour, we have been paying interest for what we owe on the other side of the Atlantic. Our debt and our prosperity have gone hand in hand. And yet when people now complain of the difficulty of borrowing money, they must be told it is for their advantage not to obtain the principal, because they will not, in that case, be obliged to pay the interest. If a farmer in Pennsylvania has to pay annually five pounds for the use of a hundred pounds borrowed, is it of any consequence to him whether the lender lives in Philadelphia, New York, Boston, London, or Amsterdam? Twenty bushels of wheat will do the business. And when he has parted with them, whether they are eaten in Philadelphia, or sent to Lisbon, is none of his affair. On the large scale, indeed, it might be convenient that wealthy men should cross the Atlantic to become citizens of Pennsylvania; and so they will, if equal just laws, and a mild firm administration give that security to property, without which it is a curse instead of a blessing. But if bad laws be made, or the good laws be badly executed, and if solid establishments can be overturned by every capricious breath, the wise and the good will avoid us as they would the pestilence. Then indeed there will be a constant drain of wealth, for none will leave property in a country where it is insecure.

But farther, though we admit that borrowing does every year carry a sum out of the country for payment of interest, it will not follow that the country is impoverished by the amount of that sum. When a farmer wants necessaries, and has not cash, he must either take them on trust, or borrow money on interest. Everybody knows that the difference between buying with ready money, and buying on credit, is much greater than the interest on the price of the goods, and therefore it is cheaper for the farmer to borrow, than to run in debt at the store. Just so it is with the country. Most of the articles we want, when purchased at the first hand, must be immediately paid for; and when merchants abroad lay out their cash to buy goods, and after, sell them to us on credit, we pay, in the price of such goods, not only an interest on the purchase money, but for the trouble foreign merchants take, and the risk they run. To all this is added a handsome commission, and then a round profit into the bargain. Thus, for instance, since it has been the practice to buy tea with cash at the first hand, we get that article for nearly one half of what it used to cost. Let any man therefore calculate the difference between paying fifty pound per annum, instead of a hundred, in price, and six per cent, or even ten per cent per annum, for interest on the fifty, and he will be convinced that we are recompensed five fold for the dividend paid abroad.

On the whole, the matter stands thus. The merchant whose business it is, and who must for that reason be the best judge, tells you that the advance of money by foreigners for bankstock, and the facility which the Bank can thereby give to commercial operations, enable him to carry on business more advantageously, though he sells imported commodities lower, and buys produce higher, than before the war. The farmer, who perhaps neither comprehends nor cares for the reasons on which this assertion may be founded, prudently brings it to the test of experience. The tree, says he, is known by its fruits. Let me examine the facts. He does so, and finds that most of the articles imported can be purchased for much less than formerly, and that he can get half as much again for his wheat. So that duties properly laid on articles, the consumption of which is chiefly unnecessary, and sometimes pernicious, would pay the interest of the public debts, and not cost the consumer more than before the war. Thus, without imposing new burthens, full relief may be given to the public creditors, and they be thereby enabled more cheerfully and more easily to sustain their share of such burthens, as circumstances may hereafter require. All which advantages we must, it seems, forego, and preclude ourselves from the possibility of establishing public credit, lest foreigners should derive an interest on lending us money. Overturn the Bank, say they, and perhaps you may get a little of their money. Kill the goose that lays golden eggs, and you may wear her feathers.

SIXTHLY, it has been said that the Bank facilitates the exportation of specie. Of all the charges in the world, this is the last which one would have expected. The operations of the Bank depend, as every body knows, on the quantity of specie in its vaults. When that is gone, the Bank is done, just as the mill stands still when the pond is dry. And therefore to suppose the directors would facilitate the exportation of coin, is the most absurd of all suppositions. Truth is, the directors of the Bank are extremely solicitous to prevent the exportation of coin, and happily for the State have the means in their power. The bank capital is about a million of dollars, part of which is in their vaults, and the remainder lent for short periods. The amount of their loans is supposed to be twice as much as their capital. A part of the sum lent is in bank notes, the remainder in coin. Now, therefore, when the directors find that cash is exported, which they do at once, by perceiving that any considerable sum goes out of the Bank in a week more than is received, they are not merely led by inclination, but driven by necessity, to lessen or to stop their discounts, according to the nature of the case and the degree of the evil. This stoppage has the effect, for not only the money is prevented from going abroad, but if the stoppage continue, it is brought in from every quarter. The operation is so powerful, that on one occasion many thousand dollars were brought to the Bank, and there, taken out of those packages in which they were, next morning, to have been shipped to London.

In this place it may be proper to notice the strange opinion, that in the present state of trade a bank is injurious. This opinion seems to have been founded on the idea, that because money is collected in the Bank, it may easily be taken out of the Bank. And so indeed it might by an armed force, but those who have tried the experiment in any other way, have been disappointed. The money is collected in bank, it is true, but how is a man to get it out? Either he must sell property for the purpose, and then it is of no consequence whether the payment comes out of the Bank, or out of the Treasury, or where it comes from. The owner may dispose of it as he thinks meet; and we might as well say, that David Rittenhouse facilitates the exportation of money, when he pays for arms or clothing to a merchant who sends it to Europe, as lay that blame on the Bank.[5] The other mode of getting at money in bank, is by borrowing for the short period of forty days, and if the borrower ships it off, he will be obliged, when the forty days expire, to hunt for it, and will sometimes pay dearly for his trick. Perhaps it will be found on examination that some of those, who complain of being driven to deal with usurers, had been dabbling in this way, and proved too cunning for themselves, as cunning men generally do.

So far is the Bank from being injurious to the present state of trade, that the converse of the proposition is true, viz. that the present state of trade is injurious to the Bank. And it would have been ruinous to the commonwealth, but for the seasonable checks given by the Bank, which checks are among the causes of the present complaints. They say the Bank facilitates the exportation of coin, and that therefore they complain; but in truth the Bank prevented them from exporting the coin, and therefore they complain. While a man spends more than he earns, his coin must go to pay the

5. David Rittenhouse (1732–96) was a Pennsylvania astronomer, mathematician, and inventor. He was the first director of the U.S. Mint.

difference, and he will have less of it when the year ends than when it began. Just so it is with a country. We import great quantities of goods; we either cannot or will not give produce on moderate terms to pay for them, and yet we grumble that our cash runs low. We will not acknowledge our own imprudence, but accuse the Bank, which has alone resisted the general torrent; by which means Pennsylvania is better off than any of the neighboring States.

A SEVENTH objection against the Bank is, that it injures the circulation of bills of credit. This is a popular argument, and therefore it is made. But as to the truth of the assertion, the authors do not trouble their heads about it.

Their maxim is, let us lay it on, and let them take it off as they can. Some will stick. Suppose this kind of morality were extended a little, and when these charitable kind hearted people walk the streets, one of their proselytes should bedaub them with the contents of the kennel, hugging himself in the idea *that some will stick*, would they not find the practice of their own principles rather unpleasant? Pray how has the Bank injured the circulation of paper money? Why the paper is not received in bank as specie. And did ever any man suppose it would, or could be so received? If it had, would not the directors have been guilty of an infamous breach of trust? Could they have excused themselves to those of whose specie they had the custody? The Bank might indeed have given currency to the bills, as long as their coin lasted, by exchanging one for the other; and no one can doubt that in this case the coin would, as fast as exchanged, have been packed up and sent to our good friends and favorites in London. Under such circumstances, those candid gentlemen who prayed and voted for paper currency, and afterwards refused to receive it, would perhaps have played their patriotic game quite through. And we may reasonably suppose too, that when the coffers of the Bank were filled with their emissions, they would have found as good reasons to abolish the paper, as they now do to abolish the Bank. If a refusal to give money for bills of credit be an injury, what shall be said for those who, though patrons of the plan, would neither give money nor anything else for the bills? It would be difficult to make an apology, if the generality of the refusal were not a sufficient reason for each individual.

Let us then be candid, and far from reprehending the practice, calmly seek the cause. Paper can only circulate on a par with specie, from a general belief that it is equal to specie. The faith makes the thing. If there be not such a general belief, it cannot be equal to coin, because it will not so generally answer the purpose. The holder may think, as in the continental times, that his three pound bill is worth eight dollars, and be very angry that his neighbor is not of the same opinion. But unless he can persuade the person whose goods he wants, that the paper is really equal to the silver, his own conviction will be of small avail. Admitting then, for argument's sake, that every merchant in Philadelphia did really and truly believe the new bills to be worth what they specify; still they could do nothing with them, unless the farmers, whose produce they want to purchase, had the same belief, and would sell that produce for paper as freely as for gold. Because the merchants being either in debt, or wanting to purchase goods in foreign countries, can make no other use of the paper than to buy such things as may be sent abroad. And further, they must be able to buy not only such things, but at such prices, as may answer in foreign markets. If, therefore, the country gentlemen will agree to sell wheat for five shillings the bushel in paper money, merchants will be as solicitous to receive, as they are now to avoid paper. But while produce continues at the present prices, wise merchants will not sell but for specie, which they can export safely, because they must lose by sending away produce; a practice which some have pursued to their ruin.

Having thus hinted at the true means to give paper a brisk and lively circulation, candor requires that a few words be said in favor of the landed interest, on whom the blame might otherwise be thrown. Supposing, therefore, the charge to be made against an honest farmer, he would perhaps make the following reply. How can it be expected, that I should repose confidence in a government, who for eight years past have been the victim of that confidence? A piece of my land was sold for continental bills; these are all sunk in the gulf of depreciation. Part of my property was seized by officers of Congress, and part was sold to officers of the State. For all this I have nothing but useless certificates. When everybody had grown sick of the old money, Congress issued new, and though experience was against the measure, yet relying on their wisdom, I took the new bills cheerfully; but found, to my sorrow, that the new travelled in the same road with the old, and the only difference was that they travelled faster. The bills issued about that time, by the State, had what they call funds for redemption, but they soon fell to six for one. I have observed too, that when these bills become of little value, the government joins in and agrees to the depreciation; so that every one who receives them is sure to suffer in the end. Now, therefore, until I have eight years' experience that government may safely be trusted, I cannot forego the benefit of that experience, which I have bought so dear.

By trusting government, one half my substance is gone; the other half must be kept to provide for my family.

These reasons, or reasons like these, are not confined to any one body of men, either merchants, husbandmen, or manufacturers. They pervade all ranks and degrees. The citizens of Pennsylvania will not give free circulation to the State paper, because they have not confidence in the government. We know that confidence cannot otherwise be established, than by the steady pursuit of just measures, for a number of years. It is self evident and every man must feel as well as see it. Every man therefore can judge of the excellent sense of those, who cry, down with the Bank, if you could give circulation to the bills. Break a promise made three years ago, by way of inducing men to rely on the promise you make now.

But EIGHTHLY, it is said that the wealth and influence of the Bank may become dangerous to the government. It is a political monster whose property may be ten millions of dollars, whose duration is perpetual. These circumstances are so terrible, that some are for putting the poor monster to instant death, while others in their great goodness would only give him a hectic,[6] which should work his dissolution in a dozen years. Of each in turn, but first of those who would limit the duration of the Bank to a few years, and limit the capital to what suits their own ideas of propriety. These are really the worst of the two, for their half way conduct would be every way wrong. Such a law would be as unjust, and have every essential circumstance of violence, as the immediate dissolution of the charter. And however they may deceive themselves into an opinion of their own lenity, not a man among them would either as juryman or judge admit it to be a good defence against a charge of murder, that the act had been performed by a slow poison. Public credit must suffer alike in both cases, for in both the rights of private property will be alike violated.

What then are the advantages held out? Why it seems, that if the charter be limited to a short period, the legislature can, at the expiration, renew it on such terms and conditions as may to them seem meet. And these terms or conditions must of course be some benefit to the commonwealth, which could not otherwise have been obtained. And to prove these things, the Bank of England is quoted. But the choice of an example is rather unlucky, for that limitation of their charter, which one cunning Minister introduced, other cunning Ministers have at different times taken advantage of, till at

6. That is, a hectic fever, or consumption.

last all the substance of the Bank has been squeezed out. And for what purpose? Was it to open navigations? To clear new roads? To extend a lucrative commerce? No, it was to support the power of the Minister for the time being, and feed the expense of those ruinous wars, which the people would not otherwise have borne. Standing then on the ground of their experience, let us look forward to the probable consequence of such a limitation in Pennsylvania. Suppose the period arrived when the charter is to expire. Is it certain the State would then want aid from the Bank? If not, the object of the limitation is gone. But even supposing the State should stand in need, what temptation could they offer to obtain relief? Not a prolongation of the charter, because the supposition implies a breach of the contract made when the Bank was first instituted, and therefore no reliance could be placed on any subsequent contract. For if the Bank should lend to the government, then the canceling of that debt would be an additional motive for dissolving the Bank.

Nor is this suspicion injurious, for one act of moral turpitude is always the prelude of another. But admitting that the Bank would purchase a few year's existence; from whom would the purchase be made, and for what price? The directors of that day would naturally cast their eyes on the leading members in Assembly, and open the negociation with them. Men of great wealth and influence, should any such arise, would make use of the Bank to extend and increase their authority. They would watch this moment to obtain seats in Assembly. And if a majority could be prevailed on to vote with such leaders, the purchase would be made of them, and the price would be some private gain, and not the public good. In like manner, if the capital be limited, it is not the State, but great men in the State would receive the benefit of an enlargement. And why should the capital be limited within narrower bounds than at present? It is notorious that if the directors had not been under compulsion, they would not have extended the subscription beyond the first four hundred thousand dollars.[7]

It is notorious also, that every addition to the number of shares lessens the value of each. And therefore we have the best security in the world, the interest of the proprietors themselves, against an increase of the capital. In like manner there is every reason to believe that the Bank will continue to afford that aid to government, which has never yet been withheld when it could with propriety be granted. And if they should extend their capital, a thing so contrary to their interest, it can only be on some trying occa-

7. Morris again alludes to the political pressure put on the Bank in 1784.

sion, to support the government of which they are citizens, and preserve the ship in which all are embarked. The charter being held sacred, as chartered rights ought ever to be, applications for aid by the State will be plain and manly transactions, not dirty jobs. The Bank will candidly state their means, the extent to which they are willing to go, and the security they are willing to accept. They will perhaps, on such an occasion, point out the ill treatment they have received, when funds appropriated by the Assembly to payment of a former loan were diverted to another object; and in their quality of citizens, as well as that of directors, they will perhaps go a little farther, and state with becoming firmness the dangers, which must ensue if any individual shall dare to alter appropriations of public money made by legislative authority. But surely this can do no harm. Calm reflection will therefore convince a candid man, that the wealth and influence of the Bank can only become dangerous to the State, by laying it at the mercy of great men in the State. For it is utterly inconceivable that four or five hundred stockholders, of all ranks, parties, and denominations, should join in choosing directors who would attempt to overturn the government. On the contrary it is a truth vouched by uniform experience, from the earliest ages, that the monied interest of a country will ever oppose, check, and counteract all changes, and convulsions of government; because that interest is sure to be the victim of confusion and disorder. This last consideration applies forcibly also to the arguments of those, who would now dissolve the charter.

Let them further consider, that the business of banking is not, of necessity, to be carried on by public banks alone. One or more individuals may form a banking company, whose operations will be extensive and lucrative, in proportion to the degree and extent of their credit and connexions. Over such a bank, or such banks, there can be no control. The citizens of Philadelphia will have no vote in choosing directors, nor will any person be particularly interested in observing their conduct. Dissolve the National Bank in March, and by the first day of May a private bank will rise on its ruins. The merchants of Philadelphia will pour in their coin, with as much confidence as they now do into the National Bank; and experience has so clearly shown the advantage of such an institution, they will not, cannot be without it. If therefore the enemies of the Bank will look around, and see who are the men that will probably set up such a private bank, it may do more towards bringing them to a right judgment, than the most conclusive arguments.

The NINTH objection is, that the directors can obtain unfair advantages in trade for themselves and their friends. And it must be owned, that there is some force in this objection. But it cannot be alleged that the supposed advantages are unfair. Some advantages are necessarily attendant on the place of a director, and some inconveniences are as necessarily the appendages.

It is not possible that things should be otherwise, and the only check is in the annual election, by which the stockholders have an opportunity of testifying their sense of each director's conduct. This will always prevent any great mischief. For the Bank being an institution in which the money of many acts for the benefit of all, by being jointly applied to each in his turn, every stockholder is a sentinel, bound by his private interest to discover unfair practices, and sound the alarm, when undue advantages are obtained, because the preference of one must operate the exclusion of another. After all, however, we must acknowledge, that this evil will in some degree prevail, for we know that nothing on earth is perfect. But must we forego a great advantage to all, because a greater advantage will result to a few? We might as well object to the existence of government, because it must be administered by fallible men, and confer on them superior eminence and authority, or to the use of money, because it is sometimes applied to vile purposes, as object to a money government or bank, because the labors of a director are compensated, or more than compensated, by commercial advantages.

LASTLY, then, let us consider whether the Bank be destructive of that equality, which ought to take place in a free country. And the first question is, whether by equality is meant equality of property, or equality of rights. If it be the former, then it may perhaps be doubted whether the opposers of the Bank would themselves agree to an equality, that is to say, a general division of property among all the citizens of Pennsylvania. This might suit eight or ten thousand gentlemen, who came over last year from Ireland and Germany to give us the honor of their good company. But will the substantial freeholder, or wealthy mechanic be willing to pay for that good company such an exorbitant price? We have in general, it must be confessed, been ready enough to give a preference to strangers over our own brethren and countrymen, but there is reason in everything. If an equality of rights be meant, then the objection vanishes, for any man may purchase the right of a stockholder in the Bank for less money, than he can purchase a farm, even in the back counties. So that he may be a stockholder on easier terms than he can be a freeholder. And if it suits one man to be a stockholder, and the other to be a freeholder, neither ought to grumble at the right or possessions of the other. But if, which is most likely, the objectors mean here, under a plausible cry raised about equal rights, to cover the dictates of envy at superior fortune and success in the world, then they had best consider again, whether by overturning the public Bank they would not assist in setting up a private bank. And whether such private bank would not bring very great accessions of wealth to those, whom they particularly dislike.

You, gentlemen of the Assembly, who are the guardians of Pennsylvania, and bound by every principle which can actuate honest men to promote her welfare and prosperity, it is with you to consider this great object in all its lights. The objections raised will doubtless be varied. The answers given will certainly be disputed. Perhaps the arguments in support of the Bank are not so strong as the advocates believe. One thing however is certain, that consequences of the last importance to your constituents must follow from your decision. If therefore the event be doubtful, nay if the destruction of this charter should not be absolutely necessary, pause a moment and consider most deeply what you are about to do. How can we hope for public peace and national prosperity, if the faith of government so solemnly pledged can be so suddenly violated? If private property can be so lightly infringed? Destroy this prop, which once gave us support, and where will you turn in the hour of distress? To whom will you look for succor? By what promises or vows can you hope to obtain confidence? This hour of distress will come. It comes to all, and the moment of affliction is known to Him alone, whose divine providence exalts or depresses states and kingdoms. Not by the blind dictates of arbitrary will. Not by a tyrannous and despotic mandate. But in proportion to their obedience or disobedience of his just and holy laws. It is he who commands us that we abstain from wrong. It is he who tells us, *"do unto others as ye would that they should do unto you."*

15 ❦ The Constitution of the United States (1787)

Morris was, by his own admission, a surprise choice to represent Pennsylvania at the Constitutional Convention, but he proved to be one of its most active members. On September 10, 1787, the convention adjourned to allow the Committee of Style and Arrangement to put its handiwork in order. By eighteenth-century custom, the committee chair, William Samuel Johnson of Connecticut, would be expected to do the work; but by all accounts the work was done by Morris. He reduced the convention's twenty-three articles to seven, ordered the contents, and wrote the Preamble as well as the letter transmitting the document to Congress.[1] Responding to Jared Sparks, Morris's biographer, in 1831, James Madison recalled Morris's role:

> The *finish* given to the style and arrangement of the Constitution fairly belongs to the pen of Mr. Morris; the task having, probably, been handed over to him by the chairman of the Committee, himself a highly respectable member, and with the ready concurrence of the others. A better choice could not have been made, as the performance of the task proved. It is true, that the state of the materials, consisting of a reported draft in detail, and subsequent resolutions accurately penned, and falling easily into their proper places, was a good preparation for the symmetry and phraseology of the instrument, but there was suffi-

Reprinted from *The Constitution of the United States*, 18th ed. (Washington, D.C.: Commission on the Bicentennial of the United States Constitution, 1992). The names of the signers have been omitted.

1. The standard documentary source on the Constitutional Convention is *The Records of the Federal Convention of 1787*, ed. Max Farrand, rev. ed. (New Haven: Yale University Press, 1911–87). Farrand compiles the Convention's resolutions at 2:565–80; the August 6 draft presented by the Committee of Detail is at 2:177–89. The draft letter to Congress is in 2:583–84, and the final version at 2:666–67. The final version of the letter, reprinted here, differs only in capitalization and punctuation from Morris's draft. It may also be found in the *Journals of the Continental Congress*, ed. Worthington C. Ford et al. (Washington, D.C.: U.S. Government Printing Office, 1904–37), 33:502–3.

cient room for the talents and taste stamped by the author on the face of it. The alterations made by the Committee are not recollected. They were not such, as to impair the merit of the composition. Those, verbal and others made in the Convention, may be gathered from the Journal, and will be found also to leave that merit altogether unimpaired.[2]

A false story about Morris apparently gained currency from a speech of Albert Gallatin's about a decade after the convention.[3] Gallatin claimed that Morris had tried to enlarge the powers of Congress by inserting a semicolon after "lay and collect taxes, duties and excises" in Article I, section 8. The insertion, so the story goes, was designed to make the next clause—"to provide for the common defense and general welfare"—an independent power. According to Gallatin, one of the Connecticut delegates detected Morris's "trick," and the convention "restored" the original language. No such dialogue occurs in the records of the convention, however, and a letter from Madison in 1830 indicates that the semicolon did not appear in any other copy the convention had. Madison concludes that it was "an erratum of the pen or press," not a trick of Morris's.[4]

The Constitution of the United States of America

We the People of the United States, in Order to form a more perfect Union, establish Justice, insure domestic Tranquility, provide for the common defence, promote the general Welfare, and secure the Blessings of Liberty to ourselves and our Posterity, do ordain and establish this Constitution for the United States of America.

2. *Federal Convention of 1787*, 3:499.

3. Speech in the House of Representatives, June 19, 1798 (*Federal Convention of 1787*, 3:379).

4. Letter to Andrew Stevenson, November 17, 1830 (*Federal Convention of 1787*, 3:492). The report of the Committee of Detail on August 6 also has a semicolon after "excises" but follows it with the commerce power. The semicolon may have been carried over inadvertently in copying.

ARTICLE I.

Section 1.

All legislative Powers herein granted shall be vested in a Congress of the United States, which shall consist of a Senate and House of Representatives.

Section 2.

The House of Representatives shall be composed of Members chosen every second Year by the People of the several States, and the Electors in each State shall have the Qualifications requisite for Electors of the most numerous Branch of the State Legislature.

No Person shall be a Representative who shall not have attained to the Age of twenty five Years, and been seven Years a Citizen of the United States, and who shall not, when elected, be an Inhabitant of that State in which he shall be chosen.

[Representatives and direct Taxes shall be apportioned among the several States which may be included within this Union, according to their respective Numbers, which shall be determined by adding to the whole Number of free Persons, including those bound to Service for a Term of Years, and excluding Indians not taxed, three fifths of all other Persons.]* The actual Enumeration shall be made within three Years after the first Meeting of the Congress of the United States, and within every subsequent Term of ten Years, in such Manner as they shall by Law direct. The Number of Representatives shall not exceed one for every thirty Thousand, but each State shall have at Least one Representative; and until such enumeration shall be made, the State of New Hampshire shall be entitled to chuse three, Massachusetts eight, Rhode Island and Providence Plantations one, Connecticut five, New York six, New Jersey four, Pennsylvania eight, Delaware one, Maryland six, Virginia ten, North Carolina five, South Carolina five and Georgia three.

When vacancies happen in the Representation from any State, the Executive Authority thereof shall issue Writs of Election to fill such Vacancies.

The House of Representatives shall chuse their Speaker and other Officers; and shall have the sole Power of Impeachment.

---

* Changed by section 2 of the Fourteenth Amendment.

Section 3.

The Senate of the United States shall be composed of two Senators from each State, [chosen by the Legislature thereof,]* for six Years; and each Senator shall have one Vote.

Immediately after they shall be assembled in Consequence of the first Election, they shall be divided as equally as may be into three Classes. The Seats of the Senators of the first Class shall be vacated at the Expiration of the second Year, of the second Class at the Expiration of the fourth Year, and of the third Class at the Expiration of the sixth Year, so that one third may be chosen every second Year; [and if Vacancies happen by Resignation, or otherwise, during the Recess of the Legislature of any State, the Executive thereof may make temporary Appointments until the next Meeting of the Legislature, which shall then fill such Vacancies.]†

No person shall be a Senator who shall not have attained to the Age of thirty Years, and been nine Years a Citizen of the United States, and who shall not, when elected, be an Inhabitant of that State for which he shall be chosen.

The Vice President of the United States shall be President of the Senate, but shall have no Vote, unless they be equally divided.

The Senate shall chuse their other Officers, and also a President pro tempore, in the absence of the Vice President, or when he shall exercise the Office of President of the United States.

The Senate shall have the sole Power to try all Impeachments. When sitting for that Purpose, they shall be on Oath or Affirmation. When the President of the United States is tried, the Chief Justice shall preside: And no Person shall be convicted without the Concurrence of two thirds of the Members present.

Judgment in Cases of Impeachment shall not extend further than to removal from Office, and disqualification to hold and enjoy any Office of honor, Trust or Profit under the United States: but the Party convicted shall nevertheless be liable and subject to Indictment, Trial, Judgment and Punishment, according to Law.

* Changed by the Seventeenth Amendment.
† Changed by the Seventeenth Amendment.

Section 4.

The Times, Places and Manner of holding Elections for Senators and Representatives, shall be prescribed in each State by the Legislature thereof; but the Congress may at any time by Law make or alter such Regulations, except as to the Places of Chusing Senators.

The Congress shall assemble at least once in every Year, and such Meeting shall be [on the first Monday in December,]* unless they shall by Law appoint a different Day.

Section 5.

Each House shall be the Judge of the Elections, Returns and Qualifications of its own Members, and a Majority of each shall constitute a Quorum to do Business; but a smaller number may adjourn from day to day, and may be authorized to compel the Attendance of absent Members, in such Manner, and under such Penalties as each House may provide.

Each House may determine the Rules of its Proceedings, punish its Members for disorderly Behavior, and, with the Concurrence of two thirds, expel a Member.

Each House shall keep a Journal of its Proceedings, and from time to time publish the same, excepting such Parts as may in their Judgment require Secrecy; and the Yeas and Nays of the Members of either House on any question shall, at the Desire of one fifth of those Present, be entered on the Journal.

Neither House, during the Session of Congress, shall, without the Consent of the other, adjourn for more than three days, nor to any other Place than that in which the two Houses shall be sitting.

Section 6.

The Senators and Representatives shall receive a Compensation for their Services, to be ascertained by Law, and paid out of the Treasury of the United States. They shall in all Cases, except Treason, Felony and Breach of the Peace, be privileged from Arrest during their Attendance at the Session of their respective Houses, and in going to and returning from the

* Changed by section 2 of the Twentieth Amendment.

same; and for any Speech or Debate in either House, they shall not be questioned in any other Place.

No Senator or Representative shall, during the Time for which he was elected, be appointed to any civil Office under the Authority of the United States, which shall have been created, or the Emoluments whereof shall have been increased during such time; and no Person holding any Office under the United States, shall be a Member of either House during his Continuance in Office.

Section 7.

All bills for raising Revenue shall originate in the House of Representatives; but the Senate may propose or concur with Amendments as on other Bills.

Every Bill which shall have passed the House of Representatives and the Senate, shall, before it become a Law, be presented to the President of the United States; If he approve he shall sign it, but if not he shall return it, with his Objections to that House in which it shall have originated, who shall enter the Objections at large on their Journal, and proceed to reconsider it. If after such Reconsideration two thirds of that House shall agree to pass the Bill, it shall be sent, together with the Objections, to the other House, by which it shall likewise be reconsidered, and if approved by two thirds of that House, it shall become a Law. But in all such Cases the Votes of both Houses shall be determined by yeas and Nays, and the Names of the Persons voting for and against the Bill shall be entered on the Journal of each House respectively. If any Bill shall not be returned by the President within ten Days (Sundays excepted) after it shall have been presented to him, the Same shall be a Law, in like Manner as if he had signed it, unless the Congress by their Adjournment prevent its Return, in which Case it shall not be a Law.

Every Order, Resolution, or Vote to which the Concurrence of the Senate and House of Representatives may be necessary (except on a question of Adjournment) shall be presented to the President of the United States; and before the Same shall take Effect, shall be approved by him, or being disapproved by him, shall be repassed by two thirds of the Senate and House of Representatives, according to the Rules and Limitations prescribed in the Case of a Bill.

Section 8.

The Congress shall have Power To lay and collect Taxes, Duties, Imposts and Excises, to pay the Debts and provide for the common Defence and general Welfare of the United States; but all Duties, Imposts and Excises shall be uniform throughout the United States;

To borrow money on the credit of the United States;

To regulate Commerce with foreign Nations, and among the several States, and with the Indian Tribes;

To establish an uniform Rule of Naturalization, and uniform Laws on the subject of Bankruptcies throughout the United States;

To coin Money, regulate the Value thereof, and of foreign Coin, and fix the Standard of Weights and Measures;

To provide for the Punishment of counterfeiting the Securities and current Coin of the United States;

To establish Post Offices and Post Roads;

To promote the Progress of Science and useful Arts, by securing for limited Times to Authors and Inventors the exclusive Right to their respective Writings and Discoveries;

To constitute Tribunals inferior to the supreme Court;

To define and punish Piracies and Felonies committed on the high Seas, and Offenses against the Law of Nations;

To declare War, grant Letters of Marque and Reprisal, and make Rules concerning Captures on Land and Water;

To raise and support Armies, but no Appropriation of Money to that Use shall be for a longer Term than two Years;

To provide and maintain a Navy;

To make Rules for the Government and Regulation of the land and naval Forces;

To provide for calling forth the Militia to execute the Laws of the Union, suppress Insurrections and repel Invasions;

To provide for organizing, arming, and disciplining, the Militia, and for governing such Part of them as may be employed in the Service of the United States, reserving to the States respectively, the Appointment of the Officers, and the Authority of training the Militia according to the discipline prescribed by Congress;

To exercise exclusive Legislation in all Cases whatsoever, over such District (not exceeding ten Miles square) as may, by Cession of particular

States, and the Acceptance of Congress, become the Seat of the Government of the United States, and to exercise like Authority over all Places purchased by the Consent of the Legislature of the State in which the Same shall be, for the Erection of Forts, Magazines, Arsenals, dock-Yards, and other needful Buildings;—And

To make all Laws which shall be necessary and proper for carrying into Execution the foregoing Powers, and all other Powers vested by this Constitution in the Government of the United States, or in any Department or Officer thereof.

Section 9.

The Migration or Importation of such Persons as any of the States now existing shall think proper to admit, shall not be prohibited by the Congress prior to the Year one thousand eight hundred and eight, but a tax or duty may be imposed on such Importation, not exceeding ten dollars for each Person.

The privilege of the Writ of Habeas Corpus shall not be suspended, unless when in Cases of Rebellion or Invasion the public Safety may require it.

No Bill of Attainder or ex post facto Law shall be passed.

No Capitation, or other direct, Tax shall be laid, unless in Proportion to the Census or Enumeration herein before directed to be taken.*

No Tax or Duty shall be laid on Articles exported from any State.

No Preference shall be given by any Regulation of Commerce or Revenue to the Ports of one State over those of another: nor shall Vessels bound to, or from, one State, be obliged to enter, clear, or pay Duties in another.

No Money shall be drawn from the Treasury, but in Consequence of Appropriations made by Law; and a regular Statement and Account of the Receipts and Expenditures of all public Money shall be published from time to time.

No Title of Nobility shall be granted by the United States: And no Person holding any Office of Profit or Trust under them, shall, without the Consent of the Congress, accept of any present, Emolument, Office, or Title, of any kind whatever, from any King, Prince or foreign State.

* See Sixteenth Amendment.

Section 10.

No State shall enter into any Treaty, Alliance, or Confederation; grant Letters of Marque and Reprisal; coin Money; emit Bills of Credit; make any Thing but gold and silver Coin a Tender in Payment of Debts; pass any Bill of Attainder, ex post facto Law, or Law impairing the Obligation of Contracts, or grant any Title of Nobility.

No State shall, without the Consent of the Congress, lay any Imposts or Duties on Imports or Exports, except what may be absolutely necessary for executing it's inspection Laws: and the net Produce of all Duties and Imposts, laid by any State on Imports or Exports, shall be for the Use of the Treasury of the United States; and all such Laws shall be subject to the Revision and Controul of the Congress.

No State shall, without the Consent of Congress, lay any duty of Tonnage, keep Troops, or Ships of War in time of Peace, enter into any Agreement or Compact with another State, or with a foreign Power, or engage in War, unless actually invaded, or in such imminent Danger as will not admit of delay.

ARTICLE II.

Section 1.

The executive Power shall be vested in a President of the United States of America. He shall hold his Office during the Term of four Years, and, together with the Vice-President chosen for the same Term, be elected, as follows:

Each State shall appoint, in such Manner as the Legislature thereof may direct, a Number of Electors, equal to the whole Number of Senators and Representatives to which the State may be entitled in the Congress: but no Senator or Representative, or Person holding an Office of Trust or Profit under the United States, shall be appointed an Elector.

[The Electors shall meet in their respective States, and vote by Ballot for two persons, of whom one at least shall not be an Inhabitant of the same State with themselves. And they shall make a List of all the Persons voted for, and of the Number of Votes for each; which List they shall sign and certify, and transmit sealed to the Seat of the Government of the United States, directed to the President of the Senate. The President of the Senate shall, in the Presence of the Senate and House of Representatives, open all the Certificates, and the Votes shall then be counted. The Person having the greatest Number of Votes shall be the President, if such Number be a Majority of the whole Number of Electors appointed; and if there be more than one who have such Majority, and have an equal Number of Votes, then the House of Representatives shall immediately chuse by Ballot one of them for President; and if no Person have a Majority, then from the five highest on the List the said House shall in like Manner chuse the President. But in chusing the President, the Votes shall be taken by States, the Representation from each State having one Vote; a quorum for this Purpose shall consist of a Member or Members from two thirds of the States, and a Majority of all the States shall be necessary to a Choice. In every Case, after the Choice of the President, the Person having the greatest Number of Votes of the Electors shall be the Vice President. But if there should remain two or more who have equal Votes, the Senate shall chuse from them by Ballot the Vice-President.]*

The Congress may determine the Time of chusing the Electors, and the Day on which they shall give their Votes; which Day shall be the same throughout the United States.

No person except a natural born Citizen, or a Citizen of the United States, at the time of the Adoption of this Constitution, shall be eligible to the Office of President; neither shall any Person be eligible to that Office who shall not have attained to the Age of thirty-five Years, and been fourteen Years a Resident within the United States.

[In Case of the Removal of the President from Office, or of his Death, Resignation, or Inability to discharge the Powers and Duties of the said Office, the Same shall devolve on the Vice President, and the Congress may by Law provide for the Case of Removal, Death, Resignation or Inability, both of the President and Vice President, declaring what Officer shall then act as President, and such Officer shall act accordingly, until the Disability be removed, or a President shall be elected.]†

The President shall, at stated Times, receive for his Services, a Compensation, which shall neither be increased nor diminished during the Period for which he shall have been elected, and he shall not receive within that Period any other Emolument from the United States, or any of them.

Before he enter on the Execution of his Office, he shall take the following Oath or Affirmation: "I do solemnly swear (or affirm) that I will faith-

* Changed by the Twelfth Amendment.
† Changed by the Twenty-Fifth Amendment.

fully execute the Office of President of the United States, and will to the best of my Ability, preserve, protect and defend the Constitution of the United States."

Section 2.

The President shall be Commander in Chief of the Army and Navy of the United States, and of the Militia of the several States, when called into the actual Service of the United States; he may require the Opinion, in writing, of the principal Officer in each of the executive Departments, upon any subject relating to the Duties of their respective Offices, and he shall have Power to Grant Reprieves and Pardons for Offenses against the United States, except in Cases of Impeachment.

He shall have Power, by and with the Advice and Consent of the Senate, to make Treaties, provided two thirds of the Senators present concur; and he shall nominate, and by and with the Advice and Consent of the Senate, shall appoint Ambassadors, other public Ministers and Consuls, Judges of the supreme Court, and all other Officers of the United States, whose Appointments are not herein otherwise provided for, and which shall be established by Law: but the Congress may by Law vest the Appointment of such inferior Officers, as they think proper, in the President alone, in the Courts of Law, or in the Heads of Departments.

The President shall have Power to fill up all Vacancies that may happen during the Recess of the Senate, by granting Commissions which shall expire at the End of their next Session.

Section 3.

He shall from time to time give to the Congress Information of the State of the Union, and recommend to their Consideration such Measures as he shall judge necessary and expedient; he may, on extraordinary Occasions, convene both Houses, or either of them, and in Case of Disagreement between them, with Respect to the Time of Adjournment, he may adjourn them to such Time as he shall think proper; he shall receive Ambassadors and other public Ministers; he shall take Care that the Laws be faithfully executed, and shall Commission all the Officers of the United States.

Section 4.

The President, Vice President and all civil Officers of the United States, shall be removed from Office on Impeachment for, and Conviction of, Treason, Bribery, or other high Crimes and Misdemeanors.

ARTICLE III.

Section 1.

The judicial Power of the United States, shall be vested in one supreme Court, and in such inferior Courts as the Congress may from time to time ordain and establish. The Judges, both of the supreme and inferior Courts, shall hold their Offices during good Behaviour, and shall, at stated Times, receive for their Services a Compensation which shall not be diminished during their Continuance in Office.

Section 2.

The judicial Power shall extend to all Cases, in Law and Equity, arising under this Constitution, the Laws of the United States, and Treaties made, or which shall be made, under their Authority; to all Cases affecting Ambassadors, other public Ministers and Consuls; to all Cases of admiralty and maritime Jurisdiction; to Controversies to which the United States shall be a Party; to Controversies between two or more States; between a State and Citizens of another State; between Citizens of different States; between Citizens of the same State claiming Lands under Grants of different States, [and between a State, or the Citizens thereof, and foreign States, Citizens or Subjects.]*

In all Cases affecting Ambassadors, other public Ministers and Consuls, and those in which a State shall be Party, the supreme Court shall have original Jurisdiction. In all the other Cases before mentioned, the supreme Court shall have appellate Jurisdiction, both as to Law and Fact, with such Exceptions, and under such Regulations as the Congress shall make.

The Trial of all Crimes, except in Cases of Impeachment, shall be by Jury; and such Trial shall be held in the State where the said Crimes shall have been committed; but when not committed within any State, the Trial shall be at such Place or Places as the Congress may by Law have directed.

* Changed by the Eleventh Amendment.

Section 3.

Treason against the United States, shall consist only in levying War against them, or in adhering to their Enemies, giving them Aid and Comfort. No Person shall be convicted of Treason unless on the Testimony of two Witnesses to the same overt Act, or on Confession in open Court.

The Congress shall have power to declare the Punishment of Treason, but no Attainder of Treason shall work Corruption of Blood, or Forfeiture except during the Life of the Person attainted.

ARTICLE IV.

Section 1.

Full Faith and Credit shall be given in each State to the public Acts, Records, and judicial Proceedings of every other State. And the Congress may by general Laws prescribe the Manner in which such Acts, Records and Proceedings shall be proved, and the Effect thereof.

Section 2.

The Citizens of each State shall be entitled to all Privileges and Immunities of Citizens in the several States.

A Person charged in any State with Treason, Felony, or other Crime, who shall flee from Justice, and be found in another State, shall on Demand of the executive Authority of the State from which he fled, be delivered up, to be removed to the State having Jurisdiction of the Crime.

[No Person held to Service or Labour in one State, under the Laws thereof, escaping into another, shall, in Consequence of any Law or Regulation therein, be discharged from such Service or Labour, but shall be delivered up on Claim of the Party to whom such Service or Labour may be due.]*

Section 3.

New States may be admitted by the Congress into this Union; but no new State shall be formed or erected within the Jurisdiction of any other State; nor any State be formed by the Junction of two or more States, or parts of

---

* Changed by the Thirteenth Amendment.

States, without the Consent of the Legislatures of the States concerned as well as of the Congress.

The Congress shall have Power to dispose of and make all needful Rules and Regulations respecting the Territory or other Property belonging to the United States; and nothing in this Constitution shall be so construed as to Prejudice any Claims of the United States, or of any particular State.

Section 4.

The United States shall guarantee to every State in this Union a Republican Form of Government, and shall protect each of them against Invasion; and on Application of the Legislature, or of the Executive (when the Legislature cannot be convened) against domestic Violence.

ARTICLE V.

The Congress, whenever two thirds of both Houses shall deem it necessary, shall propose Amendments to this Constitution, or, on the Application of the Legislatures of two thirds of the several States, shall call a Convention for proposing Amendments, which, in either Case, shall be valid to all Intents and Purposes, as part of this Constitution, when ratified by the Legislatures of three fourths of the several States, or by Conventions in three fourths thereof, as the one or the other Mode of Ratification may be proposed by the Congress; Provided that no Amendment which may be made prior to the Year One thousand eight hundred and eight shall in any Manner affect the first and fourth Clauses in the Ninth Section of the first Article; and that no State, without its Consent, shall be deprived of its equal Suffrage in the Senate.

ARTICLE VI.

All Debts contracted and Engagements entered into, before the Adoption of this Constitution, shall be as valid against the United States under this Constitution, as under the Confederation.

This Constitution, and the Laws of the United States which shall be made in Pursuance thereof; and all Treaties made, or which shall be made, under the Authority of the United States, shall be the supreme Law of the Land; and the Judges in every State shall be bound thereby, any Thing in the Constitution or Laws of any State to the Contrary notwithstanding.

The Senators and Representatives before mentioned, and the Members of the several State Legislatures, and all executive and judicial Officers, both of the United States and of the several States, shall be bound by Oath or Affirmation, to support this Constitution; but no religious Test shall ever be required as a Qualification to any Office or public Trust under the United States.

Article VII.

The Ratification of the Conventions of nine States, shall be sufficient for the Establishment of this Constitution between the States so ratifying the Same.

Done in Convention by the Unanimous Consent of the States present the Seventeenth Day of September in the Year of our Lord one thousand seven hundred and Eighty seven and of the Independence of the United States of America the Twelfth. In Witness whereof We have hereunto subscribed our Names.[5]

Letter to Congress

In Convention, September 17, 1787

Sir,

We have now the honor to submit to the consideration of the United States in Congress assembled, that Constitution which has appeared to us the most adviseable.

The friends of our country have long seen and desired, that the power of making war, peace and treaties, that of levying money and regulating commerce, and the correspondent executive and judicial authorities should be fully and effectually vested in the general government of the Union: but the impropriety of delegating such extensive trust to one body of men is evident—Hence results the necessity of a different organization.

It is obviously impracticable in the foederal government of these States, to secure all rights of independent sovereignty to each, and yet provide for the interest and safety of all—Individuals entering into society, must give

5. The names of the signers have been omitted.

up a share of liberty to preserve the rest. The magnitude of the sacrifice must depend as well on situation and circumstance, as on the object to be obtained. It is at all times difficult to draw with precision the line between those rights which must be surrendered, and those which may be reserved; and on the present occasion this difficulty was encreased by a difference among the several States as to their situation, extent, habits, and particular interests.

In all our deliberations on this subject we kept steadily in our view that which appears to us the greatest interest of every true American, the consolidation of our Union, in which is involved our prosperity, felicity, safety, perhaps our national existence. This important consideration, seriously and deeply impressed on our minds, led each State in the Convention to be less rigid on points of inferior magnitude, than might have been otherwise expected; and thus the Constitution, which we now present, is the result of a spirit of amity, and of that mutual deference and concession which the peculiarity of our political situation rendered indispensable.

That it will meet the full and entire approbation of every State is not perhaps to be expected; but each will doubtless consider, that had her interests been alone consulted, the consequences might have been particularly disagreeable or injurious to others; that it is liable to as few exceptions as could reasonably have been expected, we hope and believe; that it may promote the lasting welfare of that country so dear to us all, and secure her freedom and happiness, is our most ardent wish.

With great respect,
We have the honor to be,
SIR,
Your Excellency's most
Obedient and humble Servants,
GEORGE WASHINGTON, PRESIDENT.

16 ❖ American Finances (1789)

Morris had long wanted to go to Europe, and in 1788 his business ventures with Robert Morris at last gave him a reason to do so. Robert's fortunes began their long decline in 1787 when his London agent suddenly defaulted. Gouverneur's mission was to try to pick up the pieces as best he could, and especially to save the large contract with the Farmers-General of tobacco in France. Besides this damage control, he intended to pursue some other ventures, including purchasing the American war debt to France and selling land in New York.[1]

On his journey to Europe, Morris spent some time collecting his thoughts on American affairs.[2] On arriving in Paris, he had extensive discussions with Thomas Jefferson, then American minister to France, on American affairs and particularly on finance. This paper was one result of those conversations. It was completed sometime that spring, and enclosed with the letter to Robert Morris of May 8.

The establishment of a new Constitution in America, while it raises the hopes of all true friends to liberty, cannot remove the apprehensions of many, who are intimately acquainted with the affairs of the United States. Those gentlemen, therefore, who are called to act a part on that first great theatre of American legislation, to which the eyes of all are directed with expectation and anxiety, will feel the importance of the duties they are to perform, and, impressed with such feelings, they will not perhaps withhold a moment's attention to the ideas of an individual, who has no other claim to their notice, than a zeal for the public welfare.

Reprinted from Jared Sparks, *The Life of Gouverneur Morris, with Selections from his Correspondence and Miscellaneous Papers* (Boston: Gray & Bowen, 1832), 3:469–78. The title is the one given by Morris in his letter to Robert Morris.
  1. Miller, *Envoy to the Terror*, 10–14.
  2. GM to Robert Morris, May 8, 1789, quoted in Sparks, *Life*, 3:469.

Among the subjects, which must occupy the deliberations of Congress, those of Finance will demand a principal share. To make effectual provision for the foreign debts, and for those which are due to their fellow citizens, to obtain the sums requisite for current service, to establish on a firm basis the national credit, these are objects which must contribute to reputation abroad, tranquillity at home, security everywhere. All will agree in the propriety of revenue for these important purposes, and so long as the government shall confine itself to general theoretic propositions, universal assent may be expected, but the instant any step is taken towards the necessary end, opposition from some quarter or other will certainly arise; and although the progress towards that end must not be retarded by slight obstacles, yet some may be encountered, which cannot be surmounted, and which ought therefore to be avoided.

The national treasury has an exclusive right to all duties and imposts on commerce, but the commercial States have already laid duties, and incorporated them into their domestic systems of revenue and administration. Some have appropriated them as a fund for payment of the State debts, others, to the discharge of debts due by the Union, which thcy havc adopted. If then these revenues be taken from the States, without any provision for their relief, it would excite disgust among many friends of the new Constitution, and furnish weapons to its enemies. A plausible pretext would be given for opposition to such of the State Legislatures as are inclined to oppose. They would excuse whatever systems they might adopt, upon the ground of necessity, and thus every vice in such systems would adroitly be charged to the account of Congress.

There is a concurrent jurisdiction, respecting internal or direct taxes, but each of the States has laid hold of that, which accords best with the prejudices of its citizens, and is consequently least repugnant to their feelings. Hence the needful resort to this species of revenue will either increase the burthen upon those things which now bear it, or falling on new objects excite apprehension, perhaps disgust, and even opposition. It is the vice of direct taxation, that collectors ask money from those who generally speaking have none to give, and the payment being involuntary produces complaint. But while there exists a party disposed to propagate and magnify every ground of disgust and disaffection, a more than usual degree of caution becomes needful on the part of government.

Another great difficulty arises from the extent and variety of the United States. These render it almost impracticable to tax them equally, because the same sum drawn from like objects in different places would not be proportionate to their respective value. And even if it would, there is a further inconvenience, which arises from the necessity of apportioning direct taxes in a manner fixed by the Constitution. This, which seems to force the Congress into requisitions, leads thereby to perpetuate that ineffective system, whose result will always be a grievous disappointment, and thence much disorder in the finances, and thence national impotence and extravagance.

A difficulty of another kind and of no little magnitude arises from that want of confidence in the government, which so long and so generally prevailed. It is a truth not perhaps sufficiently attended to, that the loss of credit always involves a loss of authority. How indeed can it be otherwise, since both are founded on opinion? That sudden, prompt, and as it were joyful obedience, which is the offspring of respectful confidence, cannot be hoped for in the first moment. The operations, therefore, will be heavy, and those speculations in the public funds, which have drawn the money from commerce, husbandry and the arts, to a business lucrative to individuals, but destructive to the community, will increase the natural difficulty of collecting taxes in America. It must not be forgotten also, that the want of a ratio for apportioning taxes, and adjusting old accounts between Congress and the States, may be seriously felt.

Thus the difficulties arise, present themselves, and demand deliberate attention. To obviate them, let us suppose first, that all accounts with the States be settled without any view to the various contributions demanded. That every sum paid into the public treasury, or value supplied, with the interest, be carried to their respective credits, and the balances which may be due to each, after deducting the payments or advances made to them, be constituted a debt from the Union to the States, bearing interest at six per cent. This would quiet all clamor and heart-burning about quotas and proportions for the past, and it would become a fund from which the States would not only pay the principal and interest of debts due to their particular creditors, but provide also for the administration of their own internal affairs, without the necessity of imposing taxes for either purpose. Consequently all the sources of revenue would at once be laid open to Congress without impeachment. The means of paying this debt to the States will come into contemplation hereafter.

Suppose, secondly, that duties were laid similar to those, which Congress called for in the spring of 1783. It is needless to inquire here whether any alterations therein would be prudent, whether salt would be a proper article to be added, and the like, for everything of that sort is mere matter of arrangement, to be adjusted in consequence of conversation and reflection among the different Representatives, who will doubtless adopt what appears best at present, and make such amendments hereafter as experience may dictate. It seems, however, to be an opinion both general and well founded, that these duties would produce annually from one and a half to two millions of dollars. In order then to establish the public credit abroad, a loan might be opened in Europe for payment of the debts to France, to Spain, to foreign officers, and to the Farmers General, as also for various contingent matters, which will occur in the course of the investigation. These objects would require a sum, which, together with the present loans in Holland, may be stated at about twelve millions of dollars, the interest of which at five per cent would be six hundred thousand; consequently the duties would leave about a million surplus. But instead of appropriating a specific sum of these duties to such loans, it might be best to appropriate the whole, declaring that the surplus should be carried to the aggregate fund. The terms and the manner of such loans, with many other details, are matters of administration, which will be considered presently. It is from the surplus of these loans, after paying the various demands abroad, that the current expense of the war should be taken, because the taxes to be imposed for that object cannot be productive until a future period. But besides the current expense, it is probable that there will still remain a surplus, which may be usefully applied towards establishing the public credit, by taking up some of these unrepresented effects, which now float about the continent, and will, so long as they exist in their present depreciated state, impair confidence and prevent domestic anticipations. But this also is a matter of administration.

Suppose, thirdly, that a general tax were laid of one twentieth of the produce payable in kind, but redeemable by the taxable at one half of the value at the place of delivery. A thousand objections rise at once, and yet the idea may merit consideration. There are circumstances, which render a measure of this sort more applicable to America, than to any other country. Let it then be examined, premising that the surplus, if any, beyond the contribution of the State, as fixed by the Constitution, is to be paid into the State Treasury. Hence it results that the State Legislature may safely and usefully be entrusted with various matters of internal administration, which relate to it. Thus, there can be no danger in leaving them to enumerate the objects on which the tax is to fall, and to fix the value of each; for if by defective enumeration, or valuation, the sum prove deficient, Congress may increase the ratio of demand, or lessen the redemption price. And leaving the enumeration to the States, enables each to give indirectly a protection to the cultivation or manufacture, which it may wish to introduce.

In like manner the States can have no inducement, by fixing too few or too many places of delivery, either to burthen the people or to increase the expense of collection; for it is understood that each taxable person should deliver at the place of delivery the proportion allotted to him either in articles or cash. They would have every reason to provide that the collectors and receivers should sell and dispose of the articles at the best price, and therefore as the receivers should be appointed by the Union, with authority to appoint the collectors within their respective districts, and the whole expense of collection should be paid by a certain commission on the amount the States might be entrusted with, making many regulations respecting their conduct, they would naturally watch that conduct with a useful jealousy. The States might also be entrusted, at least in the first instance, with determining in what mode the share of each taxable should be ascertained. The estimation ought to be, and probably would be, the just value of each article at the place of delivery, and as the individual could commute it for one half of that value, the payment would generally speaking be in money. For this is an inverse progress to the plan which has usually been pursued, of laying taxes in money, and making them payable in produce above its value, which always brings in produce instead of money.

A tax of this sort would be perfectly just, and seldom or never oppressive;[3] for a good crop can bear a large tax, and when the crop fails the tax is avoided. Every day's experience would meliorate the collection, and thereby render it both more productive and less burthensome. The circumstance of having receivers and collectors of the Union throughout the country, would be no serious objection, although it might at first furnish a topic of declamation to many unfriendly dispositions. It would, certainly, tend to procure for the Union better lights, than they now possess, and these persons would always be at hand to explain the operations of Congress, so as to avoid this representation and consequent disaffection. By this means also the collection of taxes might go on for the ensuing year, at the same time with the enumeration of the people, and the one would be completed in season to regulate the other.

The appropriation of this tax might be first to the current service; but in this place it is proper to observe, that the civil list might be paid by taxes on

3. In the original this phrase was "seldom or ever oppressive."

legal proceedings in the national courts, and from the post office, so that those, who derive the immediate and evident benefit from government, would immediately and evidently contribute to its support. The military and naval establishments, with what relates to them, would by this means be first in the appropriation of the direct tax. And therefore these important services would certainly be provided for.

The second appropriation might be to pay the interest of the debt above mentioned from the union to the several States. This circumstance would greatly facilitate and accelerate the collection. The balance, if any, might go to the aggregate fund.

Lastly, this aggregate fund, which should contain the remainder of all receipts, whether ordinary or extraordinary, ought to be chargeable with the interest of the domestic debt, and the balance, after deducting contingent expenses, should be applied as a sinking fund, in discharge of the public debts generally. The mode of this application is also an object of administration. But it may not be amiss to observe here, that in proportion as the public debt shall be lessened, and by the extension of commerce the public revenue increased, a part of the duties may be applied to the construction and support of a Navy, for the protection of that commerce on which it depends.

Success in matters of administration must depend on the powers and abilities of the administrators to take advantage of circumstances as they arise, and use them for the public benefit. But setting aside all question as to integrity, and notwithstanding the good effect of ministerial responsibility, the conciliation of public confidence is so important, that it will always be wise to guard in such manner against abuses, as that the public mind may be tranquillized. On no subject perhaps can it be more needful to take precautions of this sort, than on that of finance both for the public security and for the reputation of the Ministers. It might therefore be wise to provide, that the terms on which loans are to be made, and the manner of making them, should be discussed and decided on, not only by the officers of the Finance department, but by the President and the other principal officers of State, such as the Secretary at War, and of Foreign Affairs. These taken together might be very safely entrusted with the appropriation of the revenue to purposes generally described in the law, and as their determinations would be secret, the public would derive every advantage of wisdom, activity, and integrity from such an arrangement. And in the same view of this great subject it occurs, that as some matters must, after all possible care in the framing of instructions, be left to the discretion of the agent or Minister employed in Europe, it would not perhaps be quite useless to direct, that in affairs of major importance, he should consult with the other public Ministers abroad. But as this is more properly within the purview of the Administration, than of the Legislature, the idea shall not be pursued.

The absorption of those unfunded effects, which are at present in circulation, appears to be a measure of indispensable necessity to the establishment of public credit, but the ways and means are not very evident. To purchase them up might be well, when funds are at command for that purpose, but a formal act of the Legislature to that effect would defeat itself, and at the same time be charged by some with injustice, which charge, whether well or ill founded, will always be both unpleasant and injurious. To receive them on loan, would increase the public debt considerably, and prove of but little relief to the holders, who having only small sums would be obliged to sell to those who have money, and who would by that means profit considerably by their dispersed and indigent situation. Perhaps it might be well to make them receivable in the direct taxes, at the rate of one half the amount annually for two years, and the administration above mentioned under general powers might in the mean time apply the surplus of any loans abroad, and also the effects of any anticipations which would be obtained, in purchasing them up, which, after a provision made for them, would be a justifiable procedure. Every saving resulting therefrom would be felt within two years at farthest, and the taking of them out of circulation would be felt immediately. To prevent, at the same time, any material defecit of the revenue, the estimates for the service of the first two years should bear, each, one half of this unfunded debt, and afterwards a like amount might be carried annually to the head of Marine, and thus this operation would only postpone for a little time the naval establishments of the United States.

A third object of administration is mentioned above, viz. the application of a sinking fund to the discharge of the public debts. Perhaps America offers the fairest field for this business of any country on earth, especially if the above hints should be converted into any regular plan. The debt due by the States would in such case be represented by a debt due to them from the Union. Every purchase therefore of stock from the State creditors would enable a set off by the Union in alleviation of its debt to the State, and as the only revenue which would prove deficient would be that, which this last debt would be founded upon, and as this deficiency could only arise from the neglect of the States themselves, the Administration of the Union would on every principle be justifiable in beginning their operations at that end.

From looking back on this sketch, a general and consoling idea arises, viz. that the people of the United States by paying to the public treasury one fortieth of the annual produce of their property and their industry, and by allowing one shilling on the pound on their consumption of foreign productions, which is in effect a bounty on domestic manufactures, would establish their credit on the most solid foundation, bind their union by the most indissoluble ties, quiet the apprehensions by which they have so long been agitated, and secure, as far as human prudence can do it, the future enjoyment of freedom and happiness.

17 ❊ Observations on Government, Applicable to the Political State of France (1789)

The Estates-General convened on May 5, 1789, amid royal pageantry and unrealistic expectations. Morris attended the opening session with Thomas Jefferson and later commented to Mrs. Robert Morris:

> Here drops the Curtain on the first great Act of this Drama in which Bourbon gives Freedom. His Courtiers seem to feel what he seems to be insensible of, the Pang of Greatness going off.[1]

Throughout that summer Morris was frequently asked his advice on constitutional issues, since it was well known he had a part in writing the new American Constitution. His initial reluctance to give advice to the French (see the headnote to chapter 13) faded as he became convinced that the French were about to replace one despotism with another.

Around the end of July, as Morris was preparing to travel to England on some more of Robert Morris's business, a member of the Estates-General asked him "to throw together some Thoughts respecting the Constitution of this Country."[2] This is probably that document, although the original apparently has not survived. Morris wrote it on July 25 and spent the next few days alternately translating it and consummating his relationship with Adele de Flahaut. That translation also does not seem to have survived; the version here is Sparks's back-translation from an unknown French original.

Reprinted from Jared Sparks, *The Life of Gouverneur Morris, with Selections from his Correspondence and Miscellaneous Papers* (Boston: Gray & Bowen, 1832), 2:463–71. The title is Sparks's.

1. Morris, *Diary of the French Revolution*, 1:68.
2. Morris, *Diary of the French Revolution*, 1:161.

That the French have not those manners, which are suited to a free constitution, is a reflection by no means dishonorable to that nation. It applies with equal force to all others, whose political situation is similar. Voltaire has called his countrymen, *lâches courtisans mais braves guerriers*.[3] Had the despotism been more complete, that moral painter would perhaps have said *vils courtisans et lâches guerriers*.[4]

But whence this deprivation of morals in arbitrary governments? The Almighty, for wise purposes, has formed man in such manner, that he lives not in himself, but in the opinion of others. In monarchies he looks upwards, and each contrives how best to gain the good opinion of his immediate superior. Begin then at the point of the pyramid, where the crown is placed, and in each degree of descent you will find that, to flatter the prevailing folly or the ruling vice, obtains the good opinion of the superior, and opens the way to fortune. The vulgar, who are at the base of the pyramid, dazzled by the splendor of the great, suffer their opinion to be captivated by show, and adore the idol that is raised for their devotion. With them a golden calf commands the respect, which is due to the Lord of Hosts.

In a republican government, those who wish to be great must begin by obtaining the good opinion of their equals. For this purpose they must be virtuous, or appear so; and the appearance has, generally speaking, the same advantages, as to the community, with the reality; because the example is the same, and because the opportunities of ruining the nation, by vices long concealed, are not frequent. But remark, that the possession or appearance of virtue will not alone suffice. In this kind of government, as in the other, the prevailing follies and vices must be flattered. The Roman must be brave, the Athenian polite, the monk devout; and each must prefer the interest of his society to those of mankind, and the rules of his Order to the principles of justice. In pursuing these reflections, we shall find the source of an important maxim, which Montesquieu has advanced; *That laws and manners have a mutual influence on each other.* To fit us for a republic, as for any other form of government, a previous education is necessary. But what is education? Let us not confound things. Education of the head, learning, pedantry, superstition; these are what the college confers. Education of the heart, manners, these we derive from the society around us.

---

3. Cowardly courtiers but courageous warriors.
4. Despicable courtiers and cowardly warriors.

Hence the Dutchman is avaricious, the Englishman proud, the Frenchman vain; and yet each has read the same Livy, the same Cicero, the same Horace.

The education, even the scholastic education, of a free government is more virtuous, because the tutor is obliged to sacrifice to public opinion; and the pupil does not see a horrible contrast of divine precepts and diabolical practices. In free governments, men are obliged to pay inviolable regard to their promises, because falsehood is a crime which cannot be concealed, and which, as it exposes to infamy, is sure to impede the march towards that greatness, which can only be obtained by public favor. This is a trait of infinite consequence, because men, being able to trust each other, perform cheerfully the part allotted to them, either for the acquirement or for the defence of liberty.

Lastly, in free governments the laws being supreme, and the only supreme, there arises from that circumstance a spirit of order, and a confidence in those laws for the redress of all injuries, public or private. The sword of justice is placed in the hands of the constitutional magistrate, and each individual trembles at the idea of wresting it from his grasp, lest the point should be turned upon his own bosom, or that of his friend. In despotic governments the people, habituated to behold everything bending beneath the weight of power, never possess that power for a moment without abusing it. Slaves, driven to despair, take arms, execute vast vengeance, and then sink back to their former condition of slaves. In such societies the patriot, the melancholy patriot, sides with the despot, because anything is better than a wild and bloody confusion. Those, therefore, who form the sublime and godlike idea of rescuing their fellow creatures from a slavery, they have long groaned under, must begin by instruction, and proceed by slow degrees, must content themselves with planting the tree, from which posterity is to gather the fruit.

But to quit metaphor, which, though it may enforce sentiment, very rarely conveys a clear and precise idea; and leaving these general observations, in order to apply more particularly our investigations to the facts immediately before us, it must be remembered, that, as each individual is governed by the opinion of the public, so each contributes to the formation of that very opinion. Thus, a thing not unfrequent in moral action, the effect becomes, in form, the cause. Those things then, which command the public opinion, command the public. A reverence for religion gave power to its ministers. Again, destroy at once an opinion, without raising at the same time another, you destroy all which stands connected with that opinion. Bring the people to despise their priests, and their religion is gone, unless you introduce enthusiasm to drive out superstition. The French have a blind deference for their nobles, and a warm attachment for their Prince. Bring them to detest the one and despise the other, what have you gained? A multitude ungoverned, and very soon ungovernable. Will you preach to them as a philosopher, the dignity of man, the empire of reason, the majesty of the laws? You might as well talk of the centripetal and centrifugal forces in the solar system, or the reflection and refraction of the rays of light. To such fine discourses, you will receive your answer from some decollated victim at the *Place de Grève*.[5]

And what end are we to look for as the result of unbridled licentiousness? History tells us of but one. Reason can discover but one. Experience proclaims that it is despotism. If then from history, from reason, from experience, we may derive one lesson, as to our political conduct, we must agree in the propriety of preserving those objects, which now command the reverence of opinion, till time shall raise a new generation, educated in different opinions. Leave to the people a corps, which they may consider as the common enemy, and which may, from that circumstance, unite them in a steady and constant support of the rights of mankind, the object for which they long contend will be endeared by the contest. By degrees they will *feel*, that which now they only *think*, and they will *love* that liberty, which they at present *admire*. A body constantly opposed to the popular wish, nay, constantly laboring to oppress, will save them from their most dangerous enemy. It will save them from themselves. They and their representatives will always be as desirous of oppressing the nobility, as that nobility can possibly be of debasing the people.

In the legislative struggle, where each having a veto neither can prevail, the good of all must be consulted, to obtain the consent of each. It is not the number of chambers in which laws are discussed which is important, but the spirit which prevails in the discussion; and that prevailing spirit will depend on the prevailing interest. The pride of nobility is offensive; but to whom? Not to the humble. Pride stimulates the *great* to rise. And pride prompts the *little*, who cannot rise, to pull down the mighty from his seat. Reduce the noble, against whom envy now points her arrows, reduce him to the common level, *there remains no other mark but the Prince*.

But in destroying orders, do you destroy the natural inequality of man, or the artificial inequality of society? In attacking one effect, do you re-

5. Until 1802, the name of the plaza in front of the Hôtel de Ville in Paris.

move the general cause? If you cannot alter the nature of man, why not consent to treat him according to that nature? Suppose all distinctions gone, and one body of representatives appointed for this great kingdom, on whom will the choice fall? This question demands a solemn pause. In the answer is involved all future consequences. Will not the rich and the great be chosen? Have wealth and grandeur lost their influence? Have the people of France attained to that philosophic contempt of splendor and riches, which induces men to perish inactive, and starve with tranquillity? The rich and great, possessed of power which is only not absolute because there is a king, will they not desire to remove the only obstacle to the increase of their greatness? Or will pity restrain them from those impositions on the people, which will increase their wealth? Will not a very slight reflection convince us, that the methods pursued by some to overturn the authority of the great, must tend eventually to fix that authority, and to give legal sanction to what is at present perhaps an unjust usurpation? Is it not most wise to put all these enemies in one body together, and not suffer them to elude the vigilance of observation, by dressing in the popular garb? Why suffer the wolves, (if wolves they be) to occupy the place, which should be reserved for the shepherd?

Again, let us not in our zeal for momentary reformation, lose sight of the probable consequences. Where the national character is base, the national government cannot be pure. Let the legislator then always bear in mind an attention to the means of preserving and exalting the character of his nation. This is particularly needful, when we would form a free constitution. In absolute monarchies, as has already been observed, the Prince gives the tone to all subordinate ranks. Cyrus commands the brave Persians, and Darius the voluptuous. But a free people take, by degrees, their distinctive traits, which are indelible. You would destroy the nobility of France. You say, that the respect paid to a titled fool is misplaced, and that the Condé of today should not be decorated with the insignia of his heroic ancestors. You reason on the equality of mankind, till you believe in it yourself, and become convinced that the whole nation are of your opinion. They think that they believe the same thing, and yet they are deceived. Such rooted sentiments are not to be in a moment eradicated.

But suppose it were as you imagine. Your nation, no longer influenced by the splendor of rank and titles, will pursue more steadily the objects of ambition and avarice. Remember that you are to be free, and have much to apprehend from ambition. You will of course render the acquisition of power difficult, the possession precarious, the abuse fatal, and consequently the pursuit will be confined to those few, whose souls are formed with loftiest views, and who can be happy only in command. Such men there are in all societies, and such will risk all things, and suffer all things, to obtain their darling superiority. The great mass, however, terrified at the rugged ascent, at the uncertain stand, and the tremendous fall, will prefer a humbler walk in life.

Suppose then, that you have arrived at the philosophic situation, where a love of power is repressed, and a love of titles annihilated. You have cut down ambition, and torn up vanity by the roots. What then? Why then the great, rich, fertile, commercial kingdom of France is to be under the base dominion of avarice. Everything is to be rated at its price in gold. And do you imagine that liberty will be the only exception in such a general sale? God has formed man with a variety of passions, but man would be wiser than his Creator, and simplify the principles of human action. Alas! in proportion to his success, will be his misfortune. What shall we think of the musician, who cuts three strings of his violin, and plays upon one? And yet he may plead in excuse, that an instrument with but one string is more easily kept in tune.

Suppose for a moment that man could be reduced to this standard, and that a wise legislature were about to form a constitution of government for such men. Would he not foresee and anxiously provide against the dangerous consequences of that overruling, base, inordinate propensity? And in the midst of this anxiety would he not rejoice to meet with some one, who could awaken the bosoms of his countrymen to new and livelier emotions; to those passions, whose quick and energetic action briskly agitates the national manners, and dissipates all stagnant and putrescent scum? Would he not thank the man, who should give to youth the headlong fury of love, and to manhood the insatiate thirst of applause? When these restless passions prevail, they chase ambition and avarice from the stage. By the prodigality of youth, riches are as lightly squandered, as they were busily or basely collected. And ofttimes the victorious general in catching at a feather lets fall his sword.

But farther, let us suppose an excellent constitution established. This alone is not sufficient. Next year perhaps it will be destroyed. We ought, therefore, to provide as well for the preservation as for the establishment. And how is that to be done? Quit your philosophic closet, and look abroad into the world. Behold those numerous swarms of human insects, all busy, all intent upon some pursuit. What is it, which animates them? Observe a little nearer and you will see that it is interest. No matter whether well or ill understood, no matter whether the object be salutary or pernicious, it is still self-interest, or if you please self-love, which, to obtain that desired object, sets all in motion. Be pleased then to consider, that in society there will always be a great number, who, from their natural propensities or peculiar situation, must feel a direct interest in the overturning of actual establishments.

Here then is a constant cause, which must have its effect, and produce a constant and persevering effort to destroy the constitution. The acting individuals will change forever, but the action will forever be the same. As in a siege, the bullets are successive, but the direction and operation continual. How are we to obviate the fatal consequences, of this evil, which is unavoidably interwoven into all possible societies? We may venture to say with geometric certitude, that to a force constantly acting, a similar force must be opposed. To balance this permanent interest, another must be raised equally permanent. An order of men with distinct privileges will feel a constant and regular desire to prevent innovations and change. But a hundred mouths are open to exclaim, why prevent any change? Have not the people a right to alter the constitution and laws as they think proper?

Such questions require no answer with men acquainted with affairs, and to others it is difficult to give an answer which will be understood. Perhaps it is best to ask this other question, why should we have any laws at all? No man will deny, that a government greatly defective and oppressive ought to be changed, and that laws manifestly cruel and unjust ought to be abrogated. But a very little experience will convince any thinking man, that frequent variations in the law are a serious evil, and that frequent changes in the form of government are the most afflicting misfortune. From these must follow a loss of commerce, a decay of manufactures, a neglect of agriculture, and thence poverty, famine, and universal wretchedness. It is not worth while then to dispute about the inherent right, which man enjoys to plunge himself into this situation, for surely all will agree, that to exercise such right is madness in the extreme.

But another violent cry is raised from a different quarter. What beautiful and pathetic dissertations have we not heard, about the natural equality of mankind! A thing, which the writers themselves do not believe in, or they would never have taken so much pains to show their own superiority. How unjust that we are not all born Dukes! True; but still more unjust that we are not all born Kings. Is the establishment of distinct orders in a monarchy necessary to the national happiness? If it be, let the establishment be made, or being made, let it be preserved. But you complain that you do not possess nobility. The road is open. Deserve it. But many are noble who never deserve it. True. And many are rich by no better right. You will not violate the laws of property, because it is necessary to the national prosperity that they be held sacred. If then the privileges of a distinct order be equally necessary, why will you violate them? But you will not impair the rights of property; why then will you take away from the son those privileges, which his father bought? Surely the one property should be as sacred as the other. And if you respect the eminence, which was bought, can you despise that which was earned? If you acknowledge the titles paid for with gold, will you deny those which were purchased with blood?

Lastly. Examine the history of mankind, and find, if possible, the instance where a monarchy has existed in which the people were free without an intermediate order. If there be none such, consider the vast sum which France must stake upon a new experiment. The happiness or misery of twenty millions. But is it a new experiment? Has it not been tried? And have not events demonstrated, that all such trials terminate in despotism?

18 ❖ Memoir Written for the King of France, Respecting the New Constitution (1791)

By mid-1791 the National Assembly had been deliberating a new constitution for France for two years. Along the way, however, it had taken some radical steps, including abolishing the feudal system, issuing the Declaration of the Rights of Man and the Citizen, and nationalizing the property of the Catholic Church. The Civil Constitution of the Clergy, issued in July 1790, made the church subordinate to the state. At each step, King Louis XVI responded in ways that were ultimately counterproductive. On June 20, 1791, the royal family, who by this time were virtually prisoners in the Tuileries, tried to flee the country. They were captured at Varennes on June 25. After some debate, the king was reinstated July 15.

By the end of August, it was clear that the National Assembly would soon finish work on the constitution, and equally clear that the king's fate depended on how he handled the situation. Most of the king's advisors favored simply accepting the constitution. Morris advocated a firmer line, accepting the document but making the king's reservations known. The following two documents were prepared by Morris for the king. The first is a memorandum on the political situation, which according to Sparks was "given to M. de Montmorin on the 31st of August, 1791."[1] The sec-

Reprinted from Jared Sparks, *The Life of Gouverneur Morris, with Selections from his Correspondence and Miscellaneous Papers* (Boston: Gray & Bowen, 1832), 2:512–25. Sparks adds this note: "On the original manuscript is the following endorsement, in the handwriting of Mr Morris; 'Memoir given to M. de Montmorin on the 31st of August, 1791. He gave it to the King after the step was taken, which this Memoir was to influence. The King returned it with a request to have a translation.' The King took the oath to accept and maintain the constitution on the 14th of September." The manuscript has disappeared since Sparks's day. See Morris, *Diary of the French Revolution*, 2:248.

1. Armand Marc, Comte de Montmorin (1745–92), had been minister of foreign affairs and the navy. He resigned after the flight to Varennes but continued to advise the king.

ond is a speech written for the king. Morris records in his diary that he read the speech to Montmorin on August 27, and that Montmorin made it clear he would not use it.[2]

⊹⟩═══⟨⊹

Memoir Written for the King of France,
Respecting the New Constitution

In the present posture of affairs what is the King to do?

This question is important, and, to decide it properly, three things are necessary. First, a retrospect of the past; secondly, an examination of the present; and thirdly, a rational investigation of the future.

It may be said, in general, that few Kings have shown a more tender regard for their subjects; and an eloquent discourse might be made, in which some striking incidents of the present reign might be placed in a strong light, but this would be attended with inconveniences. There is little dignity in praising one's self, and still less in begging future favor on the score of past kindness. Men in general are not very grateful for benefits bestowed on themselves, and no one thinks himself bound, in his own particular, to return good offices performed for a whole nation. All agree in considering the good done as so much gained, and in looking forward for as much more as they can contrive to obtain. A discourse of this sort, therefore, would be attended with no profound effect. The fine phrases in it would be applauded, and at the next moment the speaker might be insulted. Such things have already happened.

In reviewing the past, therefore, we must not seek for occasions or means to make his Majesty applaud himself. Still less should he beg the poor pittance of gratitude at the hands of the ungrateful. But it is important for him to show that he has acted consistently. And yet this should be accomplished in such manner, as to produce the effect without appearing to intend it; because such appearance would place him in the situation of one, who defends himself before his judges, and a King should never forget that he is accountable only to God. It is a general fault in his discourses, since the States-General were first convened, that too great court is paid to popularity. The consequence of such proceeding is, that the monarch purchases momentary favor *for his Ministers,* at the expense of royal authority.

2. Morris, *Diary of the French Revolution,* 2:246–47.

The people revere only those who show superiority without contempt, and that calm wisdom which their breath can neither reach nor ruffle.

To render a short view of the past in some degree useful, it may be proper to show what the King might have done at particular periods. For instance, when he determined to convoke the States-General, he might have given to the kingdom such a Constitution as he pleased; and if he had chosen a tolerable form of government, those who now exclaim against all monarchic power, would have raised statues to Louis the Sixteenth. But, by the manner of convoking the States, some questions were left undecided, which necessarily tended to create dissension; and from thence must have resulted, as a necessary consequence, one of two things; either that royal authority would preserve sufficient force to decide the question during the contest, in which case (if that authority was exercised) one of the parties would be thrown into opposition, so as to obstruct the good intentions of the King; or else, that the royal authority not having sufficient force, one of the parties would overpower the other, in which case a future scene of violence must succeed, and suspicions arise tending to multiply those acts of injustice, which ever attend the steps of a predominant faction. These things ought to have been foreseen, because in such circumstances they are inevitable, and nothing is so vain as the expectation to allay the heats of party, by sprinkling on them a few soft sentences or pretty phrases.

When the States-General were assembled, the King might still, by his speech at the opening, have given them whatever form he pleased; and it is the more surprising, that this opportunity was neglected, as the many discussions of every kind, which had taken place on that subject, ought to have pointed out the evil, and led to the best remedy which remained. This measure would have been attended, however, with the first inconvenience above mentioned. Possibly it was with a view to avoid such inconvenience, that it was thought prudent to wait until the strength of the parties should be fairly tried, and then to join the strongest. But the mischiefs resulting from such a line of conduct were self-evident. First, it contains an acknowledgment of weakness, and that, in matters dependent on public opinion, always creates the thing which it confesses. Secondly, it contains a proof of bad faith, and of course precludes the hope of zealous assistance from anybody. And thirdly, it must prevent the royal authority from being brought into action, until that action should be evidently useless; and consequently the King could not command the party which he might join, under such auspices, but they would command him. Whatever might have been the reason for neglecting to organize the States-General on that day, this at least is certain, that such neglect showed timidity, and of course invited the danger which it feared, for this also is inevitable in matters dependent on opinion.

The *Séance Royale* of June 1789 was held too late. The force, which might have been crushed before it appeared dangerous, was then too great for the power which attempted to oppose it. The subsequent measures showed an ignorance of the actual state of things, which, though great, is more pardonable than is now imagined, because an intimate knowledge of man, and of the nature of his existence, in the approach towards freedom, are necessary to decide on all the energies of human character, and on the effects which result from a sudden display of its powers. But, although the cause of those counsels by which his majesty was swayed at that time, may be overlooked, the consequences can never be forgotten. The Assembly acquired thereby the reputation of courage, consistency, and power, and of course became master of the empire.

Here commenced a new epoch. Men acquainted with the violence of popular assemblies, could not doubt that they would arrogate to themselves all power. Resistance was evidently ineffectual, and of course must have the consequence of increasing their power, and inflaming their wrath. And since an attempt to reject their decrees must, in the nature of things, be unsuccessful, it only remained to choose one, of two things, either to accept the decrees in silence, or to make suitable remarks. Had a clear view been obtained, of those events which were unavoidable, the choice would perhaps have been different from what it was. These events are, first, the assumption of all power by the Assembly, and consequent abuse of it. Secondly, corrupt and unjust conduct on their part. Thirdly, the relaxation of order, and of course the introduction of anarchy. Lastly, as the necessary result of these, a thorough contempt of the Assembly among all ranks and degrees of men.

To provide beforehand the means of profiting by these events, such observations should have been delivered on each decree, such explanations given of its tendency, and such prediction made of its consequences, that when the Assembly should have reached that point of disrespect, at which they could not but arrive, the simple repetition, in a methodical manner, of what had been already said, would convince the nation that their King was both wiser and better than their representatives. This conviction would naturally lead them to restore his authority. A different determination, however, was adopted, which had always this inconvenience in it, that when his Majesty should find it necessary to reject the *whole* work he had previously adopted in detail, he would not be able to preserve that frankness and nobleness of character, which he might have done, had he given the reasons for his dissent to each *part* of that work. Still, however, he had it in his power to show, when a proper occasion might offer, that he had acted only under the influence of a controlling necessity, and been in fact a passive instrument in the hands of the Assembly. But his speech to that body in February, 1790, deprived him of this last advantage, at least in a considerable degree, and it forms at this moment the most disagreeable circumstance in the whole of his conduct.[3]

In the month of June last, the Assembly had approached very near to that period which they must reach, and as far as it is possible to decide where there is no absolute evidence, the chance is, that, by the present day, the royal authority would have been considerably exalted on their ruins, if the King had not taken the ill-advised step which he did. This step could not eventuate well; for in the supposition that he had reached Montmedy, or any other place *in the kingdom*, he would still have been brought back, unless he had sufficient force to protect himself, and the question as to that point must have depended upon the event of a civil war. If he had gone *out of the kingdom*, the same situation would have occurred.

Nothing, therefore, but the favorable event of a bloody contest could re-instate him, and there is every reason to believe that the event would have been unfavorable. First, the kingdom would have been united in opposition, and the conquest of France is, perhaps, beyond the strength of all Europe combined. Secondly, the feebleness of the constitution would have been instantly remedied, by general consent, from a general conviction of the necessity. Thirdly, the bankruptcy, which is now perhaps unavoidable, would have been charged to the King, as arising from his flight, and subsequent hostility. Fourthly, by confiscations a considerable addition would have been obtained to the stock of public lands, so as to alleviate the taxes, which by means of the bankruptcy would be less heavy than before. And, fifthly, since in the course of the contest, discipline must have been estab-

---

3. In his speech of February 4, 1790, Louis expressed his approval of the National Assembly's goals and left the impression that he would approve of its future actions. The result was a temporary harmony that emboldened the assembly to enact measures that the king ultimately could not approve, such as the Civil Constitution of the Clergy. For Morris's warning that the king should not try to "place himself at the head of the revolution," see his letter to the queen of January 26, 1790, in Sparks, *Life*, 2:472–73.

lished in the army, it is more than probable, that foreign powers would have been obliged to acknowledge such form of government as the National Assembly might have adopted. The best thing, therefore, which could have happened, is that which actually did happen; and the proof of what is said above, respecting the events which would have taken place if his Majesty had remained quietly at home, exists in the present state of things, after he had, by his departure, done so much to increase the power of his enemies.

Being now at the second subject of contemplation, viz. the present state of things, it is proper, if possible, to look at them with the same calmness, that posterity will enjoy in making the same examination. This is one requisite quality in the character of a statesman.

The members of the Assembly begin to feel the inevitable consequences, which follow from the want of wisdom and virtue. To gratify the little interest, or pitiful vanity, or base fear of the moment, the leaders have urged forward measures which they could not but know were pernicious. As to the great herd, they must, in every such Assembly, be profoundly ignorant of the business they are engaged in; and although there is not a *petit maitre* among them, who would employ a shoemaker that had not long worked at his trade, each has the unaccountable pretension to be, without any sort of experience, an able legislator and profound politician; as if it were an easier thing to make a constitution than a pair of shoes.

The great bulk of the people have already signified their impatience, that the session of the Assembly has continued so long; and although very few of their acts failed to produce applause at the moment, from some quarter or other, there is in regard to the whole constitution a solemn silence. The parts were fitted to the fashion of the day, and that fashion has changed. No man approves. And no man of understanding can approve. The rich tremble, and there is throughout all ranks a vast anxiety. How will this end, is the general question; and it proves a general conviction that the constitution is not the end.

The paper money, whose depreciation has long been sensible in the greater circle of commerce, begins now to be felt in those smaller concerns which interest the poor. The price of bread rises, because the produce of the earth cannot remain cheap, while all other articles grow dear. Every day the number of those who feel the necessity of providing against this evil increases; and their efforts, by showing more clearly its nature and extent, accelerate its progress. Hence the inquiry grows general, Where are the blessings promised by the revolution? Why are we not in the enjoyment of them? With whom lies the fault? Is it with the King? Is it with the Assembly? Is it with the emigrants? The nation begins to cry out like a sick savage, I suffer; what ails me? Who has put the pain in me which I feel? The next question will be, "How am I to get it out?"

The situation of the colonies affects deeply the commercial interests of the kingdom, while at the same moment commercial property melts away from the powerful operation of paper money. These things give awful notice to the mercantile cities, that all is not well. The licentious conduct of the army, notwithstanding the attempts to conceal it, excites alarm rather than indignation; which is worthy of remark, because it proves a general sense of weakness and general apprehension of danger. The situation of the Finances is deplorable, and produces also its effect, though not yet in full force. The flattering prospect of restoring an equality between the receipts and expenditures vanishes. The absurdity of establishing order in this department, by introducing disorder into every other, becomes evident; and it is possible, by tearing away the thin veil with which it is at present covered, to make a very deep impression. By striking forcibly at the centre, a shock may be given at the remotest extremities of the empire; and as the evil is inevitable, the stroke is sure.

These circumstances mark a moment, in which the public mind is open to new impressions; and it is of vast consequence to make such impressions as will tend to produce good, and avoid a part of the impending evil. But this leads to the third point of consideration.

A full and complete view of the future course of things would generally lead to a wise conduct. But such knowledge cannot be obtained by man. All that he can do is to form rational conjecture. And for this purpose he must divest himself, as much as possible, both of hope and fear.

It seems to be evident, that the measures taken for securing a peaceable and orderly administration of justice and police are greatly inadequate. Hence violence and injustice must continue to prevail. And as the administration is both expensive and ineffectual, there is in that alone sufficient cause to ruin the finances, were they otherwise in good condition. But if the administration were most vigorous, still a circulation of the immense sum of twelve hundred millions in paper money, would inevitably produce disorder. The effects of such money are, first, a loss of value as to exterior commerce and connexion. Secondly, a similar loss in respect to all manufactures depending in any degree on raw materials of foreign growth. Thirdly, from the combined effect of these two losses results a loss of value, in regard to other manufactures. Fourthly, a rise in the price of the necessaries of life becomes at last inevitable, because the husbandman, in exchanging the things he has for those he wants, by the intervention of money, must of course raise the price of the one, in proportion to the price of the other.

Besides, it must be remarked, that as the value of paper money is dependent on opinion, every event, which affects public opinion, must accelerate the progress of depreciation. Moreover, the expenses of government arise in a great measure from the purchase of different commodities. It follows, therefore, that such expense must be increased as the value of the money diminishes. And since the same diminution forms a reason with every citizen not to sell an object of intrinsic value, until the moment when he wants the money, it becomes his interest to delay the payment of his taxes to the last moment, so as to obtain the highest price for his commodities. Consequently, in proportion as the wants of government increase, its means must diminish. The increase of the price of every article will give to each citizen, who is held to the payment of a fixed sum, and whose means of payment are derived from the produce of the earth, a balance in money which he will perceive to be of little use; and as he will regret the sale of his goods for such money, which grows worse every day, he will of course hold back from the market his remaining merchandize.

On the other hand, all those who are in the receipt of fixed sums, being obliged to economize, by reason of the decreased value of their income, a great number of persons, whom they formerly employed, must remain idle. The heads of manufactories also, who are in the habit of selling on long credit, will at each payment suffer considerable loss, and that must incapacitate them from continuing their operations, whereby a number of workmen will be thrown out of employ. The cities and towns will, from the operation of these causes, be burdened with a great number of people, and at the same time straitened in subsistence. Then will arise a cry against those, who monopolize grain; attempts will be made to regulate the price of bread, and a train of popular excesses will succeed, all tending to increase the evil from which they arise.

This is the probable state resulting merely from a paper currency, but there are other, and abundant sources of evil. While the government possesses a sufficiency of this paper, it is easy to preserve an appearance of paying the public creditors, although in fact they receive but three quarters of their due, but as soon as the paper is all gone abroad, and can be brought back only by the effect of taxation, and when that effect, dependent at best on a feeble and disjointed administration, is weakened by the causes already pointed out, it will become indispensably necessary to suspend again the payments, and this will be the more pernicious, as the abundance of paper money, and its consequent loss of value, destroy all private credit, and thus increase in every way the suffering of those who are deprived of their due. This will also affect the mercantile credit of the whole kingdom, and thus it is probable, that about the time when the revolt of the colonies begins to be severely felt on the seacoast, the capital will be convulsed by a general bankruptcy.

Such a state of things would naturally excite commotion in the army, whatever might be the state of its discipline; but an army already familiarized to revolt, dissolute, debauched, and rapacious, will probably make the people feel, long before that period, the direful effects of military oppression. Whether these various miseries will all arrive, and whether they will take place at the same moment, or only in succession, cannot be decided with precision, but it seems to be inevitable that, from some or all of these causes, an opportunity will present itself, in which the King will be able to act as he pleases, if he shall be possessed of the public confidence. But if he does not possess it, he may be the victim of follies, which others have committed.

Here then recurs again the question; What is the King to do? And with it, a partial answer offers. Let him take such steps now, as will obtain and secure the public confidence hereafter. But how? Shall he reject the constitution? No; for then he would be charged with all the future evils, as resulting from that rejection. Shall he then accept it in the same silence, with which he has received the different parts? No; for then it will be impossible to convince the world, that he acts with good faith, because he has already declared his conviction, though in general terms, that the constitution is bad. Shall he then acknowledge that he has been deceived, and finds it now to be a good constitution? No; for this would be false, and, therefore, in all cases unjustifiable. Besides, it would make him in some sort responsible for events, which he ought in all cases to avoid. Shall he then repeat, in general terms, that he finds the constitution bad, but yet accepts and swears to maintain it? No; for this will involve an appearance of falsehood, meanness, and contradiction. What then shall he do?

Circumstances seem to point out his conduct with a decisive force. He ought to accept, assigning as a reason therefor, the mischiefs which would inevitably follow from his refusal and he should remark at the same time, that the omnipotence of the Assembly, and the deserted state to which he is reduced, leave him no alternative. He may even infer, from a modest doubt of his own judgment, and the decided adherence of the nation to the

Assembly, that it is his duty to submit to the public will so strongly pronounced. This idea, contrasted with their self-sufficiency, will, at a future period, when his opinions are justified by events, work strongly in his favor.

On the constitution itself he is bound, by the strongest ties of duty and interest, to make clear and pointed observations. It is a duty to himself, because he will thereby justify his departure in June last, though he had in February, 1790, declared his antecedent adherence; for he will be able to show, that the constitution is so bad, that he ought not to adopt it, unless in the last necessity. It is a duty to his subjects, because it must occasion their misery, and therefore he ought to show, that such is the unavoidable consequence of a form of civil polity so crude and monstrous; and, indeed, all his observations should be raised on that single basis, for which purpose he should introduce them, by declaring that the government ought to be calculated merely for the benefit of the people. Lastly, it is a duty to God. It is to his high Tribunal, that the monarchs of the earth must render a solemn account of their conduct; and he requires of them, that it be regulated by the principles of truth and justice, which alone endure forever, and which forever establish the peace and prosperity of empires.

His Majesty's observations should be powerful, clear, and convincing. A weak blow recoils, but a strong one penetrates. The present is a decisive moment in his fate. He must conquer or perish. If he does not mark his disapprobation, he is disgraced; and if he shows it faintly and weakly, he is ruined. Every kind of intrigue will doubtless be set on foot to induce him to be sparing in his censure. The reason is clear. The friends of the several members of the Assembly fear their disgrace; and they know, that, if they can avoid the stroke of the moment, time and circumstances will enable them to recover their influence. Already they agree in blaming the constitution in general terms, but if you descend to particulars, each will defend the most blameable parts, and censure only some light and trivial things, which he happened to oppose. Each one, therefore, labors to obtain the royal sanction to his particular opinions, and the only reward which the King and his counsellors will obtain from their generosity, will, as heretofore, be a momentary applause bestowed on the composition of his speech, and in the next half hour, pointed ridicule for being the dupes to superior address.

It must be remembered, that the Assembly will soon be dissolved, and nobody will then be accountable for their misconduct, even at the bar of public opinion. But the King remains; and unless human nature is greatly changed, he has no method of acquiring the favor of the next Assembly so certain, as that of blaming the present, because by this means he provides for them an excuse beforehand, for the evils which must arise under their administration. And he ought also to provide beforehand against the attempts, which they may make to destroy his authority. Above all things, it is important for him, that when any misfortune arises, the people may say, "*this is what our King has warned us of, not in vague and indefinite terms, but clearly and pointedly. Happy would it have been for us, had we put our trust in him, instead of an Assembly, which has plundered him and ruined us.*" It is proper also for his Majesty, after pointing out, in the most forcible manner which the needful brevity will admit of, the manifold vices of the constitution, to state the general outlines of a better, and that in such way as to secure the support of men of wealth and influence. By this means he will obtain the suffrage of the enlightened part of Europe, and that will have great weight with the vanity of this nation.

In the course of the events which follow, should he pursue the steps now pointed out, a favorable opportunity will offer to effect the great good of the nation, although it is impossible exactly to show that opportunity now, with all its incidental circumstances, each of which will not fail to influence the conduct of the moment. But if he shall have conciliated the good opinion of the nation, which can alone be secured by the general persuasion of his wisdom and virtue, many things now deemed impossible will then appear easy.

A number of little accessory measures are purposely omitted in this place, but one great means is to require the abolition of the decree, prohibiting a choice of Ministers among the members of the Assembly; and in all cases to choose Ministers remarkable for their attachment to the constitution. And should the next Assembly find it necessary, as they certainly will, to invade that constitution, he ought to exercise his veto, assigning as a reason that he will not violate his oath. At length, when the various evils shall be so accumulated, that the business can no longer go on, it is not impossible that the Assembly, acknowledging their own incapacity as arising from the state in which they are now placed, may themselves confer a dictatorial power on the King.

If nothing of this sort should happen, a moment may arrive, in which the King may proclaim a new constitution, and call on the people to proceed to the elections under it, if they approve; and should the day of election be near at hand, and the time for deliberation short, (a thing which necessity would justify,) the example of Paris in electing would be followed throughout the kingdom, and a change be thereby effected. The conduct of Paris might be influenced by a single circumstance, viz. a suspension of the payments, and a view of restoring the public credit by a more vigorous government. Various other modes of changing the constitution might be mentioned, but as has already been observed, the proper measures to be pursued must be pointed out by the circumstances of the moment. All, which man can properly do, is to fix his object, and then steadily pursue it, in consistence with the everlasting rules of justice, and according to the situation in which he is placed.

19 ✵ Observations on the New Constitution of France (1791)

Morris prepared this speech for the king's use in accepting the National Assembly's Constitution of 1791. It reflects the understanding of the king's political position developed in the previous document.

SPEECH FOR THE KING OF FRANCE

Gentlemen,

It is no longer your King who addresses you. Louis the Sixteenth is only a private individual. You have just offered him the crown, and informed him on what conditions he must accept it.

I assure you, Gentlemen, that if I were a stranger to France, I would not mount the slippery steps of the throne. But the blood, which flows in my veins, does not permit me to be insensible to the fortunes of the French. Descended from a long line of Kings, the remembrance of those who are no more, the rights of future generations, and my paternal love for the people whom Divine Providence has once placed in my care, everything, in fine, forbids me to abandon my post. I must at least maintain it, so as to secure you from anarchy, and from civil war. In this perilous position, I have taken counsel only of my own conscience. It is this, which has decided me to accept your Constitution. May it ensure the tranquillity of the kingdom, and contribute to its prosperity!

France, in granting you its entire confidence, has placed you in posses-

Reprinted from Jared Sparks, *The Life of Gouverneur Morris, with Selections from his Correspondence and Miscellaneous Papers* (Boston: Gray & Bowen, 1832), 2:491–512. The manuscript is in the Gouverneur Morris Papers, Rare Book and Manuscript Library, Columbia University, item 840. Portions are also included in Morris's *Diary of the French Revolution*, 2:248–52. All of the quotations from the Constitution are in French in the manuscript, as is the concluding paragraph. I have used Sparks's translations and punctuation.

sion of the whole power. You have therefore become responsible, before the throne of the Almighty, for the happiness of this immense people, whose fortune is in your hands. I have been a King. Nothing remains to me now, either of authority or of influence. Yet I have a last duty to fulfil. It is that of imparting to you my reflections on your work. I pray you to hear them with serious attention.

Observations on the Constitution.

Previous to any examination of the Constitution, it is proper to acknowledge, in the most explicit manner, the eternal maxim of reason and justice, *that all government ought to be instituted and exercised for the benefit of the people.* And, parting from that principle, we should in any particular society seek that form of government, which is best calculated to protect its citizens against foreign invasion, and secure domestic tranquillity, with the enjoyment of liberty and property.

You have determined on a hereditary monarchy, and by that means you have the certainty, that the chief executive magistrate must ever desire the prosperity of France. A King of France can have no interest distinct from that of the people. Their happiness, their power, and their glory must necessarily be the source of his. Every other public person may have other objects; but your King can aggrandize himself only by increasing the wealth and influence of the nation. He may be mistaken, and he may be misled, but he cannot be bought. It is the misfortune of his situation to see with the eye and act with the hands of others; it is, therefore, evidently his interest, that the representatives of the people should watch over his Ministers, and that they should be punished for misconduct, whether arising from incapacity or any other cause. He cannot but wish also for a strict and, regular administration of justice, since that is alike necessary to his glory and to the national prosperity.

These are among the advantages of hereditary monarchy. Whether you have provided against the evils to which it is liable, and secured the good of which it is susceptible, is a question deeply interesting to France, and to the human race.

You begin with a declaration of the rights of man, but since the instruments of this sort, which have hitherto appeared, have occasioned much metaphysical discussion, it may well be supposed, that a King whose occupations require a knowledge of man, such as he exists, and not such as he may be imagined in abstract contemplation, is little fitted to decide on the merit of such compositions. There seems, however, to be some inconvenience in joining it to a constitution, because if the constitution secures those rights, whatever they may be, it is unnecessary, and otherwise it is useless; but there is in every case the risk of seeming contradictions. Controversies may thence arise, and whoever may be the judge of such controversies, becomes thereby arbiter of the constitution.

To show that this inconvenience is not imaginary, it will perhaps suffice to recall to your recollection the first article of your declaration, that *"men are born and exist free and equal in rights."* You have decided, however, that the representatives shall be distributed among the eighty three departments, according to the three proportions of *Territory, Population,* and *Direct Taxes.* It results, therefore, that a given number of men, in one of the departments, will have the rights of electing more representatives, than the same number in another department. They might then imagine, that they are not equal in the very important right of choosing the members of the Legislative body.

You have also declared, that *"the law is the expression of the general will; that all citizens have the right of concurring personally, or by their representatives, in its formation; and that, all citizens, being equal in the eye of the law, are equally admissible to all dignities, places, and public employments, without other distinction than that of virtues and talents."* On the other hand you have established, *"that to be an effective citizen, it is requisite to pay, in some part of the Kingdom, a direct tax, at least equal to the value of three days' labor, and that no one can be an elector unless he unites with the necessary conditions for being an effective citizen, that of paying a direct tax of ———— days' labor."* In reconciling these various clauses, it may be doubted whether the first is to be regarded as an inalienable right, or if, on this hypothesis, the second is a just modification of it.

You have also declared, *"that for the maintenance of the public forces, and for the expenses of the government, a general tax is indispensable, and that it ought to be equally distributed among all the citizens, according to their ability";* and yet by your constitution you delegate *"exclusively to the legislative body the right of imposing public taxes, of determining the nature and quality thereof, and the mode of collecting them."* Now, as many taxes, and particularly those which are called indirect, are distributed among the citizens, not according to their ability, but according to what they consume, and even to their most urgent necessities, it may happen, that your declaration may become, in regard to imposts for a part of the citizens, the ground of a serious complaint.

Without farther considering the collateral circumstances, it is proper now to examine the organization and the distribution of the legislative, executive, and judiciary powers. According to the declaration of rights *"every society wherein the separation of powers is not determined has no constitution."* That the separation of powers is of great importance cannot, indeed, be denied. It is necessary then to examine, whether you have provided for it in such a manner, that no one of them can encroach in the others. Commencing with the LEGISLATIVE POWER, you have decreed as follows;[1]

Art. I. The National Assembly, forming the Legislative body, is permanent, and is composed of only one chamber. In case of the King's refusing his assent to the decrees of the Legislative body, this refusal is only suspensive, and when the two legislatures, succeeding that which shall have presented the decree, shall have successively presented the same decree in the same terms, the King shall be considered to have given it his sanction.

Art. II. The Legislative body cannot be dissolved by the King. The representatives of the nation are inviolable. They can for a criminal deed be arrested in the act, or by virtue of an order of arrest, but notice shall be given thereof without delay to the Legislative body, and the prosecution cannot be continued until after the Legislative body shall have decided, that there is ground for accusation.

Art. III. The Legislative body has the right of police in the place of its sessions, and in the compass around, which it shall have determined upon. It has the right of disposing of the forces, which by its own consent are quartered in the city, when it shall hold its sessions; and the Executive power cannot introduce, or quarter, any body of troops of the line within the distance of thirty thousand toises[2] from the Legislative body, except by its requisition or authority.

Art. IV. The Constitution delegates exclusively to the Legislative body the power of prosecuting before the High National Court, the responsibility of the Ministers, and principal agents of the Executive power. No Minister in place, or out of place, can suffer a criminal prosecution for an act of his administration, without a decree of the Legislative body.

Art. V. Whenever the King shall have pronounced or confirmed the suspension of Administrators or Sub-administrators, he shall inform the Legislative body thereof. That body can either remove the suspension,

---

1. The quotations from the Constitution in this document either are from an earlier draft or are paraphrased from the document approved on September 3, 1791.

2. A *toise* was six *pieds* (feet), or about 1.95 meters.

or confirm it, or even dissolve the culpable administration, and if there be cause send all the members of it, or a part of them, to the criminal tribunals, or issue a decree of accusation against them. The tribunals cannot summon the members of an administration before them for official acts.

ART. VI. When, after two appeals, the judgment of the third tribunal shall be questioned, upon the same grounds as the two first, the case cannot be farther acted upon in the tribunal of appeal, (Tribunal de Cassation) without having been submitted to the Legislative body, which shall issue a decree explanatory of the law, to which the tribunal shall be bound to conform. The Minister of Justice shall state to the tribunal of appeal, through the medium of the King's Commissioner, the acts by which the judges may have exceeded the bounds of their power. The tribunal shall annul them, and if there is ground for impeachment, notice shall be given to the Legislative body, who shall grant the decree of accusation, and send the accused before the High National Court.

ART. VII. War cannot be decided upon without a decree of the Legislative body. It belongs to the Legislative body to ratify treaties of peace, of alliance, and of commerce, and no treaty can take effect without such ratification.

By the first article, the whole legislative authority is vested in a single chamber of representatives, and consequently the leaders of a majority in that Assembly may dictate such laws as they think proper. The King may indeed suspend the decrees for a given period, but history furnishes instances of nations, which have for a longer period been under the influence of faction, and if France should ever be in that situation, the King, by suspending the decrees, would only prolong the disorder without avoiding the mischief. A dangerous law may be adroitly framed, so as to suit the popular taste, and the rejection of it might be represented as a ministerial despotism. It is, therefore, to be feared, that if the Assembly should wish to encroach on the executive authority, a *suspensive veto* would make but a feeble resistance. The time, for instance, may arrive in which a law obliging Ministers to obey such Committees, as shall be appointed to superintend their respective departments, will be represented as essential to the public safety. Rumors of disaffection may be spread abroad, and the people be led to suspect the intentions of their King, even though his whole life should have been a constant endeavor to procure their happiness. It will then give them pleasure to see the power taken from him, who is essentially their friend, and bestowed on those who have no other object but their private interest.

On the other hand, what are the evils to be apprehended from giving to the first executive magistrate an absolute veto? He cannot, without the consent of the Assembly, extend his own authority; and if that consent be supposed, it is a matter of indifference whether his veto be suspensive or absolute. In a well ordered society, new laws are seldom necessary, either for the purposes of police, or of distributive justice; and if they were, how can we doubt of the King's consent? The laws for imposing taxes, and for the public defence, will naturally also receive his assent. It is only, therefore, in the case of an attack upon his constitutional authority, that a right of rejection would be exercised. The knowledge that such right exists would frequently prevent the attempt, in like manner as the hope of eventual success, where the rejection is only for a limited time, would frequently invite it. In the one case, peace and order may be expected; in the other, turbulence and tumult.

By the second article it is provided, that the Assembly shall exist, and the persons of the members be held sacred, so long as a majority may think proper. If, therefore, such majority should harbor dangerous designs, there seems to be no means of terminating their session, nor of punishing the guilty, but by general insurrection, or civil war. It is of the nature of absolute power to corrupt the heart, and if there be temptation and indemnity, guilt may ensue. Should a faction be hired by our enemies to sacrifice the national interest and honor, to withhold the needful means of defending the State, or of supporting its credit, the King has no constitutional method of appealing to the people, neither can any tribunal punish the traitors, without the consent of their accomplices. History informs us, that, both in ancient and modern times, the leaders of popular Assemblies have been bought by foreign powers, and that thus nations unconquerable by arms, have become the victims of seduction.

By the third article it is provided, that the Assembly shall command such number of troops at the place of their sessions, as they think proper; consequently, they may possess themselves of the means at once to awe the people, and imprison the King. His person will be in their hands; his life at their disposal; and though he may have the courage to disregard his own life, yet his wife, his children, the dearest objects of his heart, remain also in their power. If, then, some future Assembly should be desirous of changing the form of government, and of assuming greater powers than those, which you have thought proper to delegate, it seems that neither of the other departments, nor even the people themselves, have any means of resistance.

By the fourth article, the Ministers and other agents of the executive authority are exposed to criminal prosecution by the Assembly, and secured against such prosecution from every other quarter. Therefore, should the Assembly incline to make encroachments, the Ministers in opposing them would have much to fear, but by submission would be sure of indemnity.

By the fifth article, the authority of the King over those charged with the administration is rendered subordinate to that of the Assembly. He is, as it were, the public accuser. The Legislative body is authorised to judge *their* conduct, and consequently to judge *his*. Administrators protected by the leaders of the Assembly, if such should ever exist, may not only disregard his orders, but even dictate to him the conduct he shall pursue. If the taxes should be either burthensome or disagreeable to several departments, and the administration prove remiss in collecting them, the executive power is in the sad necessity of seeing the public interest sacrificed by their neglect, or of rendering itself odious by more vigorous measures. In both cases the Ministers will be at the mercy of the Assembly, who may accuse them for not having suspended the administration, or, by taking off the suspension, degrade the executive authority. Under such circumstances of absolute dependence, the Minister, although appointed by the King, must obey the orders of those, who can influence a majority of the Assembly, and consequently that part of the executive authority now in question, though vested nominally in him, resides really in them. And the administrators, certain that they cannot be cited before the tribunals, unless previously accused by the Assembly, will frequently consider rather how to please those whom they have cause to fear, than how to perform their duty to the State.

By the sixth article, the judiciary power, in the last resort, is given to the Assembly; for a decree declaring what the law is in a given case, is only another name for a judgment in such case. The *Tribunal de Cassation* being obliged to conform, its subsequent proceedings are merely ministerial, to clothe the decree in the form of a sentence, and to cause the execution. From hence it results, that the people will no longer enjoy that security in their property and possessions, to which they are entitled; for it may happen, that many judgments of the *Tribunal de Cassation* will have been submitted to, before the case supposed in the article occurs, and that afterwards the Assembly may decree contradictorily to the tribunal, in which case the preceding judgments will doubtless be questioned. Moreover, as it is not to be supposed that a numerous Assembly will consist of persons skilled in legal discussions, it may happen that their explanatory decrees will affect the whole system of jurisprudence. There is reason to fear also, that their decisions may be influenced by the acts of intrigue, or other motives. The Assembly having reserved to itself the sole right of accusing the judges for misconduct, timid or corrupt judges will decide in favor of those, who have influence with the Assembly, and against the poor and unprotected.

By the seventh article, the Assembly has reserved to itself the rights of war, peace, treaties, so that the King is merely their agent, with this difference, that (not being previously instructed) he must act under the uncertainty of being approved or disavowed. From the changeableness of the representatives, the opinion of the Assembly must be unstable. Moreover, it is hardly to be expected, that persons taken from the ordinary occupations of life, will possess the information needful to judge of foreign politics, and its various combinations. The opinions of men, also, depend much on their respective habits and professions. Some, therefore, would sacrifice everything to the honor of the nation, some its commerce, and some its tranquillity.

By collecting together in one point of view the various powers given to the legislative body, it appears that they have the right to make laws and decide in the last resort, both on the application and execution of them; that they have the supreme right of war, peace, and treaties; that they have an existence dependent only on their own will, power to protect themselves from the pursuit of justice, and the command of such force as they may think proper; of course all power not already vested in them is exposed to their assumption. It may indeed be said, that there is no just reason to suppose the representatives of a free people will prolong their political existence, assume extraordinary powers, or become instruments of foreign ambition; but history informs us, that such representatives have existed, and therefore they may again exist. And since the formation of a constitution and laws presupposes human depravity, we must calculate on the effects of those passions, which have ever influenced the conduct of mankind.

The next in order is the EXECUTIVE POWER, about which you have decreed;

> ART. I. To the King is delegated the care of watching the external safety of the kingdom, to maintain its rights and possessions. It belongs to the King to conclude and sign with all foreign powers, all treaties of peace, of alliance, of commerce, and other conventions, which he shall judge necessary to the welfare of the State, under the ratification of the Legislative body.
>
> ART. II. The King appoints two thirds of the Rear Admirals, half of the Lieutenants General, Field Marshals, Captains of vessels, and Colo-

nels of household troops; the third of Colonels and Lieutenant Colonels, and the sixth of Lieutenants of vessels.

ART. III. Administrators are agents elected for a period by the people, to exercise under the superintendence and authority of the King the administrative duties. The King has the right of annulling acts of Administrators of departments, contrary to the laws, or to orders issued to them, and can in case of obstinate disobedience, or if they compromise by their acts the public safety, or tranquillity, suspend them from their offices. He shall inform the Legislative body thereof, and that body may remove or confirm the suspension. The executive power directs and superintends the collection and the disposition of the taxes, and gives all necessary orders to that effect.

ART. IV. The officers of the National Guards are elected for a period, and cannot be re-elected, except after an interval of service as soldiers.

In considering the executive power of a State, it is proper to examine the object, for which such power is instituted, because the means should always be proportioned to the end. Now the object is to defend the State, and enforce obedience to the laws. To accomplish this, the members of every department must be perfectly obedient to the chief, who then, and then only, can be responsible for the conduct of affairs. It results also from the nature of this authority, and from that accountability, which the nation has a right to require, that it should be derived from one head, and that in every instance, there should be one principal, or superior. For if a Council, or Committee, be charged with the whole, or any part of the executive department, it may happen, first, that so much time will be consumed in deliberations, that the business will be neglected. Secondly, that their conduct will vacillate according to the attendance of the different members. Thirdly, that the needful secrecy cannot be preserved, since not only each member, but the Secretaries and Clerks also must be privy to their decisions, because the will of a Board is expressed only by the record of its deliberations. Fourthly, that it will be difficult, if not impossible, to render them accountable, since each will give plausible reasons for his vote, so that though the general conduct be manifestly wrong, no one in particular can be convicted. Whereas it is, as has been already noticed, essential to the public safety, that Ministers should be punished as well for incapacity as for misconduct.

It has already been noted, also, that perfect obedience is necessary from every inferior, but to obtain it, the chief should have power to appoint and to remove the subordinate officers. In common life this is necessary to every man, who employs others either in his own affairs, or in those committed to his management. And if this be needful in those small concerns, where the principal can daily superintend his agents, how much more so for him, who must employ many for various purposes, and at considerable distances; for a King, in short, whose duty it is to protect the French against foreign invasion, and to maintain their internal tranquillity; a King, who, in the pursuit of their interest, which is one and the same with his own, must at every step encounter the opposition of private views.

By applying these evident principles of common sense to the four articles just cited, it will appear how far your constitution is calculated to confer on the people of France those benefits, of which a hereditary monarchy is susceptible. By the first, the right of war, peace, and treaties, is granted to the Assembly, and the King must act not only in subordination to their will, but also in uncertainty as to what that will may be. From hence results the difficulty, if not impracticability, of making any treaty at all. Who will enter into stipulations with a Prince, who cannot bind these whom he represents? The communication of powers is a usual preliminary, even to the conversations which precede a treaty. Suppose, for instance, that the King, apprehending the aggression of several powers allied against France, should endeavor to form with other powers a defensive alliance, each of these might be obliged to reject his overtures from regard to its own safety, because the treaty being made and submitted to, the Assembly would, if not approved of, expose it singly to the vengeance of the enemies. Similar observations apply to treaties of commerce.

That the nation may be effectually guarded, it may sometimes be necessary to attack, in order to disconcert measures otherwise injurious, if not fatal. Without looking abroad, the history of France furnishes numerous examples in support of this truth. But it is now impracticable, for an application to the legislature must disclose the design, and would be considered also as an aggression, consequently it would have the evils of such a measure without the advantages. Besides, although a majority of the Assembly might judge the war to be necessary, many of that majority might wish to delay it, that their particular speculations of commerce or finance might be previously arranged; not to mention the advantages, which a foreign Prince might derive from intrigue and corruption.

Lastly, in the course of a war many leading members of the Assembly may have such an interest in the continuation of hostilities, as to prevent the restoration of peace, though necessary to the kingdom. Thus the King, whose position enables him to discover, and whose interest obliges him to promote the national advantage, is rendered incapable of acting, or at best subservient to others, some of whom must be incapable of judging, and even have an interest opposite to that of their country.

The second article relates to the organization of the military force, which, in all governments, is an object of most serious attention. The idea of a society, each member of which is a soldier, cannot be applied to modern States; especially to those, whose power is dependent on commerce and the arts. If our fields and shops be abandoned by the manufacturers and husbandmen, famine and poverty must inevitably ensue. A part of the society must, therefore, be selected to guard the whole. The experience of all ages has proved, that if this part which forms the army, be not well disciplined, it will oppress the kingdom, but cannot defend it. Vain is the attempt to supply by numbers the want of order and subordination, without which, licentious bands must be alike detested by the people, and despised by their foes. The expense of such an army will increase in proportion to its inutility, and thus the public taxes become a public fraud, seeing that those who contribute have a right to expect from the appropriation of their money the greatest benefit which it can produce.

If, however, with the organization which you have devised, it be practicable to establish a strict discipline, it will remain for you to consider whether your army may not become a dangerous instrument in the hands of its chiefs. If only the superior grades feel a dependence on the King, they may be induced to second the views of an ambitious General, and it will be easier for them to lead the troops they command against their country, if the officers are named by election, or seniority, than if they are dependent on the King; for it is not even to be hoped, that an army, which has lost respect for its Prince, will long retain it for a popular Assembly. It has been complained of as one of the ancient abuses, that the command of the troops was given almost exclusively to a privileged order.

It resulted from hence, that, actuated like all others by their own interest, they opposed every attempt to change the existent establishments, so that France preserved a greater degree[3] of freedom, than other monarchies; and if the ancient regime had been unexceptionable in other respects, this part would have been eminently useful, for it is certainly wise to interest the army in supporting the constitution. And it is among the advantages of a hereditary monarchy well organized, that numerous and disciplined armies may be maintained without danger to liberty; a thing which in Re-

---

3. In Sparks, "decree"; in the manuscript, "degree."

publics has seldom happened. If ever a design should be formed to subdue France by the arms of Frenchmen, the conspirators must wish for officers without property or connexions, because such men when inured to war will readily follow the standard of him, who can hold out great hopes and expectations; whereas, those who have property of their own, and whose relatives and connexions share in the administration, will not risk the advantages they possess in the great game of revolutions. A resistance, similar to that, which has often irritated you, may on other occasions, and opposed to other efforts, become an impenetrable shield to the liberty of France.

The third article relates to that branch of executive authority, which respects internal affairs. Here it is proper to distinguish between the different duties of administrative bodies. So far as relates to the concerns of a particular department, or district, they are certainly useful, and most certainly they should be chosen by the people for short periods. A great mass of local knowledge and minute attention will thus be usefully employed, and an honest and industrious administration be probably obtained. But when the execution of the laws, the collection of taxes, and the preservation of order, are committed to such bodies, disappointment may be expected. The people in their choice will naturally prefer men of easy temper, and such as are disposed to gratify their wishes. If, therefore, riots or insurrections should happen, the administrators will not always act with requisite vigor; and as they are not personally affected, by the penury of the public treasury, they will sometimes give way to the solicitations of those, who wish to delay their contributions. Being independent of the King, his Ministers will have but little influence on their conduct; and, of course, cannot be accountable for the consequences. But yet on that conduct everything depends. It is not necessary to mention, what all the world knows, that unless order can be restored the Constitution must perish; but it is proper to give a glance at the finances.

The sum of Assignats, which you have decreed, will ere long be expended, and if the mass be increased, the credit will be diminished, and consequently the value.[4] This resource, then, is almost exhausted in every respect. If the taxes you have laid be not sufficient, or not seasonably collected, a considerable deficit must ensue, and it must fall either upon the interior administration, or the public force, or the creditors of the State. The interior administration must in all cases be supported, since anarchy is the

4. *Assignats* were originally a type of bond issued against the value of the confiscated church property, and evolved into a form of paper money.

worst of all political evils. It will only, therefore, remain to decide between your creditors, and your troops. If the payments be again suspended, that last stab to public credit will perhaps prove fatal, and a bankruptcy ensue, after the immense sacrifices of every kind to avoid it. If, on the contrary, the army be not paid, it is easy to see the consequences.

The public resentment will in either case, perhaps, be directed against the Ministers, and perhaps against the King. Such injustice is not uncommon, and might cheerfully be submitted to could it remove the cause of complaint; but, on the contrary, by increasing the disorder, it will increase the mischief. Let then these important truths be duly considered. Where there is no authority, there can be no accountability. Where the executive power is feeble, anarchy must ensue, and where anarchy long prevails, despotism must succeed; not indeed in the descendants of your ancient Kings, for they will probably be the earliest victims.

On the fourth article no particular observation will be necessary, but only a general application of those, which have been already made. You will on the whole decide for the French nation, whether the authority given to the King be sufficient to produce that peace and safety to the people, for which alone that, or any other power, ought to be instituted.

Thirdly, of the JUDICIARY. *The judiciary power is delegated to judges, elected by the people for a period.*

It is proper to distinguish between inferior and superior judges. The former may be appointed for a time, because it will be difficult to find proper persons to fill those numerous places; but it is to be desired, that the superior judges should hold their offices during good behavior, and their salaries also. Those, who are charged with the important duties of administering justice, should, if possible, depend only on God. Their impartiality is of the last importance to every member of society, but principally to the most numerous class, who by that alone can be shielded from oppression. It seems important, also, in every point of view, that they should not be named by popular election.

To make a proper choice of judges, as of other officers, those who choose should have not only a competent idea of the duty to be performed, and of the talents required, but an interest also in making a good choice. Will this be the case in a popular election? Will not those, who have suits depending, endeavor to get such men named, as will best answer their purpose? Will not the elections be governed in a great degree by intrigue? Must not the opinion of the voters be in general formed from the information of others?

Will not the rich exert themselves to have such judges chosen, as will be instruments of their despotism? And what instrument so dangerous as an iniquitous judge! It is yours to decide, whether this mode gives reasonable ground to hope for proper appointments; and you will consider that to the great mass of French population, the making of the laws will ever be of minor importance, since the needful security of property must confine their wealth within the narrow circle of their wants. But if, in this confined state, their little all be at the mercy of a partial judge, that tranquillity of the soul, which liberty should confer, exists not for them, and that which is to others a blessing, becomes to them a curse. And when their unavoidable dependence on the rich, increased by the influence of such judges, compels them under the pressure of that double weight to re-elect their oppressors, then, humiliated and degraded even in their own eyes by the possession of privileges they cannot exercise, they will find themselves enslaved by the excess of liberty.

Such are the observations, which present themselves on the partition of powers, which you have adopted. Many less matters are not noticed, because it is not intended to criticise your work, but to make a last effort for the happiness of the French. There is one, however, which compels to a painful expression the heart of a father. You have decreed, *that females are excluded from the regency.*[5] Alas, in entrusting the charge of the Constitution to wives and mothers, was it possible to forget that maternal love is the only sentiment, which resists all trials, which occupies the heart of a mother until death, and expires only with her latest breath. Can a mother betray the interests of her child, and are not the interests of this child your own?

It remains only to make some remarks, as to the kind of government, which our situation and our manners would seem to require. This beautiful country, profusely blest by the munificence of nature, bears on its bosom the means of exhaustless wealth, and presents in the genius of its people a source of infinitely varied enjoyment. Hence she will ever be viewed with cupidity by her neighbors, and be exposed to those interior ills, which wealth cannot fail to produce in the advanced stages of society. France has also been the protector of inferior powers, from the epoch of the revolution in Switzerland and the Netherlands, to that in which she secured the liberty of the new world. She must then have a vigorous internal adminis-

5. In the manuscript, the rest of this paragraph after the word *decreed* is in French.

tration to control the vices inseparably attached to prosperity; and, at the same time, she must possess such naval and military force, and such constitutional activity and decision, that she may protect her possessions, succor her allies, and repress the audacity of her foes.

A high toned monarchy seems, therefore, to be designated as the only government, which may consist with her physical and moral state. And, accordingly, her history, from Charlemagne to the present hour, proves, that her happiness has always been proportioned to the vigor of her administration. Nature, stronger than man, has preserved the monarchy amid the shocks of various revolutions, so that the royalty has remained, though the race of Kings has been changed.

Admitting, then, the necessity whose existence is proved both by reason and experience, it remains to consider by what means freedom can be secured against the power, which time and circumstances will confer on the King, if that office be not abolished in the attempt to establish a government, which consists neither with our manners nor with our situation. And on this occasion, it is proper to rise above the prejudices of the moment, and speak the language of truth to a bewildered nation. They will discover in it the paternal love of a King, which, founded on principles of religion, is beyond the reach of human power, and has resisted the flatteries of a court, and the indignities of a gaol.

Will numerous representatives, chosen for a *short* period, prove a sufficient barrier against royal authority?[6] Where the members are few, the election is more nice, and the competition of candidates presents a greater choice. Hence the individuals, of which such body is composed, will be less liable to deception and seduction. The post being more rare, is thereby more esteemed and sought after, and at the same time more difficult to be obtained or preserved, and hence a greater dependence of the representatives upon the people. A body not numerous is also more under the dominion of reason, and less exposed to the powers of eloquence, and the wanderings of enthusiasm. Persons chosen for a short period, may feel themselves little interested in supporting the privileges, which they must speedily cease to enjoy, and may therefore betray their trust for the attainment of more permanent or more lucrative situations. That ambition, which prompts a factious leader to wrest authority from a weak prince, might render him the

6. There were 745 representatives in the National Assembly under the 1791 Constitution, elected for two-year terms.

slave to one of stronger mind, and accordingly we learn from history, that the same men have been alternately the leaders of a faction and the flatterers of a court.

It seems, therefore, wise to provide for the stability of the Constitution, by the unchanging principles of private interest, and therefore to oppose against the efforts of a hereditary monarch, the resistance of a hereditary Senate, whose members should possess great landed property. Let it not be imagined, that this would restore abuses justly complained of. A patriot King cannot wish to be surrounded by needy dependents, who first deceive and then betray him; who obtain from his bounty the wealth, which they abuse, and by their pernicious art, render even his virtues the scourge of his people. But he may, in a just abhorrence of despotism, desire an institution, which has ever been considered as its most dangerous enemy.

Such a body, if unchecked by a King on the one hand, and by representatives of the people on the other, would doubtless be oppressive. It has already been so in France. The excess of royal authority has in its turn been also injurious; but the levity, the injustice, and the disorder of a government, merely popular, must be equally subversive of public and private happiness. It is by a just combination of the three, where each having an absolute veto on the others the particular interest of neither can prevail, that the general interest of the whole society will best be known and pursued, and this great nation raised to that station of happiness and glory, which nature seems to have intended.

This form of government has undoubtedly its objections, in common with every other; and since human institutions cannot but partake of the weakness of man, it is in vain that we seek perfection among imperfect beings. In the immense range of affairs, the extremes unite in evil. Reason and happiness are found in a just medium. The wise man stops there, and he who passes farther is lost.[7]

You have heard, gentlemen, the observations which it has always been my design to offer you, when an occasion should present. I have constantly acted with reference to your will, because I have made it my duty to consider you the organs of the will of the nation, and I have ever recognized in the people the right of being governed according to their wishes.

You require of me, gentlemen, and of every public functionary, an oath never to make any change in your constitution. I will take this oath; but I pray you to consider with me for a moment the consequences it involves.

---

7. The manuscript ends here. The last paragraph of the manuscript is in French.

My observation is perhaps superficial, and my fears vain; and the hopes of others may be as well founded as they are brilliant. But no one of us is infallible; there is no one but God, who, having foreseen all, can have preordained all. It is at least possible, that the seeds of evil may be concealed in the constitution, and that nothing but time and circumstances may be wanting to cause their development.

If this happens, as there will be no means of changing it, those to whom the people will have confided their interest will have only the sad alternative of violating their oaths on the one hand, or their duty on the other. It is also possible, that a great majority of the nation may one day be opposed to this form of judgment. Should we not preserve the right of change to this majority? Can we with justice oppose its will? Reflect, gentlemen, on this alternative, and let me urge you to continue your session for a time. Let us together make trial of your work; do not bind yourselves not to change your decrees; for no one is too wise to improve himself in the school of experience. If, after this trial, the Constitution answers your expectations, you will place it with the more confidence in the hands of your successors. If, on the contrary, you find parts of it to be feeble, or ill-adjusted, you will have it in your power to amend them.

But if you still persist in your determination to conclude your task without delay, at least grant the prayer which I make you in behalf of twenty-four millions of Frenchmen, of future generations, nay, of the human race. Deign in mercy to point out the means, by which the people can express their will, without being exposed to the perilous convulsions, which we have so lately experienced.

Whatever may be the result of your deliberations, I repeat to you, gentlemen, that I submit to them unreservedly. Let us then banish all suspicion; it cannot but be injurious to the interests of the empire. I give you my confidence, and I demand yours. Let us then labor in concert for the liberty and prosperity of the French nation.

But that this labor may not be suspected, and may meet with no opposition, I require of you, gentlemen, that you repeal the decree, which prevents me from choosing in the National Assembly the agents of the executive power. I would have it permitted me to nominate, as Ministers of the Constitution, those among you who have shown themselves its most zealous partisans. I would have the choice I shall make obtain your approbation, so that invested with the full force of public opinion, the Ministers may meet no obstacles in the execution of your plan. This appears to me the more proper, inasmuch as to the Ministers will appertain the exercise of royal power, and as you may naturally wish, that, in giving success to your work, they may show in the most striking manner how much I have been deceived in my opinion. I hope you will perceive, gentlemen, in the request I make to you, an unequivocal proof of the sincerity of my conduct; of that sincerity, which the French have a right to expect from their King, and which for his own honor a King ought ever to exhibit.

20 ❀ Notes on the Form of a Constitution for France (1791?)

Sparks says of this document, "The date of this paper has not been ascertained. The only copy, which has been found, is in the French language and in Mr. Morris's handwriting, with the following endorsement on the envelope, '*Notes on a Form of a Constitution for France.*'" There are no internal clues about its composition; clearly it differs fundamentally from the Constitution adopted by the National Assembly in 1791, but it reflects views that Morris had expressed consistently since 1789. Possibly this is the document Morris mentions in his diary on December 7 and 13, 1791, which encompassed a "Form of Government" and "general Principles" to accompany it.[1]

On December 14, Morris mentions the draft to the Minister of the Marine, de Lessart, but that seems to be the last mention of the document. Morris received word that Washington had nominated him to be minister to France in January 1792, and after that he generally stopped giving advice on French politics.

―――

I. PRINCIPLES.

The government of a nation should be constructed and administered so as to procure for it the greatest possible good.

The first duty of every State, as well as of every individual, is to provide for self preservation.

Treaties made between nations ought to have in each a sovereign authority, otherwise war could never be terminated except by conquest.

Reprinted from Jared Sparks, *The Life of Gouverneur Morris, with Selections from his Correspondence and Miscellaneous Papers* (Boston: Gray & Bowen, 1832), 3:481–500. The manuscript seems to have disappeared since Sparks's time.

1. Gouverneur Morris, *Diary of the French Revolution*, 2:322–25.

The tranquillity and liberty of nations can only be sustained upon the basis of justice.

The position of a State, its climate, the extent of its territory and the habits and manners of its citizens, have an influence in determining the proper form of government.

The form of the French government is monarchical, and imperious circumstances demand its preservation.

Monarchies should be hereditary, because an elective monarchy is incompatible with order and liberty.

The vigor of the executive power should be proportioned to the external dangers, to the extent of the empire, and to the circumstances resulting from its commerce, from its riches, from the inequality in the distribution of wealth, and from the luxury thence arising.

In order to preserve the integrity of the executive power, it is necessary that the chief should be an integral part of the legislature.

It is essential to the free exercise of the executive power, that the chief be inviolable, but it is likewise essential to the rights and interests of the citizens, that his agents be responsible for his conduct.

It is important to distribute the power in a State, so that all persons entrusted with it be interested to discharge their duties.

The necessary extent of the executive power and the inviolability of an hereditary chief, require precautions against abuse which might result therefrom.

It is requisite then to form a legislative body, whose members shall be specially interested in the maintenance of the established order of things.

Such a body should be protected against all temptation, as well as against all violence, consequently its members should be immovable and even hereditary.

Such a body should possess only moral powers, and that it may be able to resist authority on the one hand, and license on the other, it is proper to invest it with all the power of opinion.

To preserve to the people public liberty, to guaranty their civil rights, to watch over the administration of their affairs, and to control great criminals, the nation should be represented in the legislature.

None should be represented, however, except citizens, whose age gives assurance of mature judgment, whose condition guaranties moral independence, and whose connexions insure their attachment to their country.

The right of suffrage, like every other, ought to depend only on general rules; it is proper therefore to establish these on principles in accordance with good morals and social order.

That the representatives may express imperatively the national will, it is proper to constitute them a separate body.

Imposts bear upon the mass of the citizens; therefore, the right to levy them belongs exclusively to the representative body.

That the citizens may discharge their duties and preserve their rights, it is proper that they be acquainted with both; therefore the State should provide for public education.

The education of young citizens ought to form them to good manners, to accustom them to labor, to inspire them with a love of order, and to impress them with respect for lawful authority.

Religion is the only solid basis of good morals; therefore education should teach the precepts of religion, and the duties of man towards God.

These duties are, internally, love and adoration; externally, devotion and obedience; therefore provision should be made for maintaining divine worship as well as education.

But each one has a right to entire liberty as to religious opinions, for religion is the relation between God and man; therefore it is not within the reach of human authority.

Social rights and obligations are reciprocal. The right to be protected in the possession of life, liberty, and property, imposes the duty of not infringing on those of others, and even of protecting them.

It results therefrom, that, social liberty is not the permission for each one to follow his own inclination, but the obligation in which all are placed to perform their duty.

So social liberty exists not only within the limits, but by the limits, which the law prescribes.

The law is the will of all, and the rule of each.

The interpretation of the law ought then to be uniform, because the nation cannot require two opposite things, nor can the citizens conform to two opposite rules.

The interpretation of the law ought to be as fixed as the law itself, because the duty of conforming to it demands the means of understanding it, as well as of knowing it.

In the formation of the law, regard should be often had to the convenience, to the faculties, to the interests, and to the habits of the citizens, sometimes even to their prejudices, but in the interpretation of it, nothing but justice should be regarded.

The interpreters of the law ought to enjoy an independence proportioned to the extent and importance of their functions.

The judges ought to be as immovable as the law which they interpret, impartial as the justice which they dispense, and firm as the authority which they represent.

To guaranty the independence of the judiciary power, on which depends civil liberty, and to insure to the system of jurisprudence the necessary stability, it is proper that the Court of Final Appeal should be an integral part of the legislature.

Decisions of cases are the interpretations of the law; consequently they are of general interest; the facts on the contrary concern only the parties.

The choice of arbitrators is a natural right, but submission to legal authority is necessary to social order. Now every society has the right of providing for what concerns the general interest, so that in permitting the parties to choose the judges of facts, the State reserves to itself the power to name the judges of right, who are the interpreters of the law.

In the social, as in the savage state, there are certain subjects which are within the reach of every one, and consequently each citizen can decide in regard to them, but there are others for which it is necessary to refer to those learned therein; therefore reason and justice require, that the natural right of private judgment should to a certain extent be abridged.

II. Executive Power.

The executive power belongs to the King; consequently he has the right to appoint to all places and employments whatever, except those respecting which it is otherwise provided by this Constitution.

To the King belongs the power of making war, peace, treaties, and other conventions with foreign powers.

To the King belongs the right of granting to foreigners the privileges of French citizens, under such conditions or restrictions as he shall think proper.

Every oath of fidelity shall be taken to the King, in the manner following. *I promise in the name of God to be faithful to the King of the French.* But such oath can have reference only to the royal authority as recognized by the Constitution; so that to obey an order of the monarch, contrary to the laws and the Constitution, is to violate the oath of fidelity.

The King is commander in chief of all the forces both land and maritime, and of the national militia.

Justice shall be rendered in the name of the King.

The person of the King is sacred and inviolable.

Royalty is hereditary in the male line, in the order of primogeniture.

Regencies shall be established by the legislature.

III. King's Ministers and Council.

To the King belongs the choice and the dismissal of Ministers.

Ministers are responsible for their conduct, and to that effect each one shall countersign the orders of the King relating to his department, without which the order shall be void.

The Chancellor shall countersign every act, to which the seal of State is affixed, and shall be responsible therefor.

The Ministers are,

First, the Chancellor. His duty is to superintend distributive justice, education, and morals.

Secondly, the Minister of the Interior. His duty is to superintend the execution of the laws, and the preservation of public peace.

Thirdly, the Minister of Finance. His duty is to superintend the finances of the State, the receipts and the expenditures.

Fourthly, the Minister of Commerce. His duty is to superintend agriculture, manufactures, commerce, and the colonies.

Fifthly, the Minister of Foreign Affairs. His duty is to cultivate the relations of the State with foreign powers.

Sixthly, the Minister of War. His duty is to superintend the land forces and their operations.

Seventhly, the Minister of Marine. His duty is to superintend the navy, the maritime forces and their operations.

Eighthly, the Secretary of State. He is entrusted with the general charge of affairs.

Ninthly, the President of the Council. He presides at the Council in the absence of the King.

The two last are not essential, and the King may fill the places or leave them vacant at his pleasure.

The Ministers form together the Council of State, and each one shall be responsible for the advice, which he shall there give.

IV. Administration and Police.

There shall be in each department an administrative body to superintend the affairs, which are peculiar to such department, in the manner which shall be prescribed by the legislature.

The administrative body shall be composed of twelve members named by the electors of the department. The Grand Bailiff shall preside over it either in person or by his deputy. The commission of the Grand Bailiff shall be countersigned by the Minister of the Interior. The Bishop of the department and his Vicar are also members of the administrative body. Each department shall be divided into six districts, each of which shall choose two members (*administrateurs*) for four years, and it shall be decided by lot after the first election which of the two shall retire from the administration at the end of two years, so that subsequently one half of the members shall be elected every two years. To constitute an administrative body, it is requisite that the Grand Bailiff, or his deputy and six other members, should be present.

In each department there shall be a Government Attorney (*Procureur Syndic*) appointed by the King. He shall assist at the sessions of the administrative body, and shall have there a voice in consultations, but not in decisions. He is to attend to the crown lands, to the ground rents, and to the casual forfeitures to the treasury.

The King shall appoint each year justices of peace to preserve the tranquillity and maintain the police of the departments. The number of such justices shall depend on the will of the King. Their warrants shall be countersigned by the Minister of the Interior, and their authority shall be prescribed by the legislature.

V. Public Forces.

To the King belongs the appointment and the discharge of the Military officers. It is, notwithstanding, just and wise for him to prescribe for himself a regular system of promotions, and to preserve to each his rank, and nothing but the interest of the nation ought to induce a deviation from the general principles of the military administration.

The legislature shall determine upon the formation and organization of the public forces, upon the duties of the officers, soldiers, marines, and of the militia, upon the offences and penalties, and upon the manner of judging and punishing.

The commissions and warrants of the land forces and of the militia shall be countersigned by the Minister of War.

It is proper for the officers to be holders of property, because those to whom the State entrusts its forces should be interested in its preservation.

The commissions and warrants of the maritime forces shall be countersigned by the Minister of Marine.

VI. Revenue and Debts of the State.

The legislature shall regulate the imposts, but the collection thereof shall be made by royal authority.

The warrants of the collectors, and other principal agents of the treasury, shall be countersigned by the Minister of Finance. The other agents shall be appointed in such manner as the legislature shall order.

The land taxes and the casual forfeitures shall nevertheless be collected by the constable of the department, his sergeants and deputies, according to the writs issued to him by the Government Attorney, the whole to be done in the manner which the legislature shall prescribe; and nothing shall be paid, either for the collection of the land tax, or for the remittances to be made by the Government Attorney.

The legislature shall regulate whatever relates to the public debt; and no loan can be made without its consent.

VII. Education and Worship.

In each department there shall be a Council of Education and Worship, which shall be formed by the Bishop and the Professor of the department and six Rectors, one for each district. All the members of the Council shall be appointed by the King, but cannot be turned out; and their appointments shall be made under the seal of State.

The Bishop, or in his absence the Professor, shall preside at the Council, and three Rectors as least must assist thereat.

By the advice of the Council, the Professor shall appoint the preceptors, and the Bishop shall appoint the curates.

The Bishop shall appoint and dismiss his vicar at his own free will.

The places of preceptor and curate shall be removable according to the regulations of the legislature.

For the maintenance of worship, for providing for education, for the relief of the poor, and to defray the expenses of the hospitals, the tithe shall be collected in the manner prescribed by the legislature; but by the orders and under the superintendence of the administrative body, who shall distribute the same. The Government Attorney shall be the treasurer of the tithe, of which a tenth part shall be paid to the Bishop, who shall pay the fifth part to his vicar. One third of the residue shall be applied by the administrative body to the poor and to the hospitals, one third to public worship, and one third to public education. But a tenth part of this last third shall be paid to the order of the Chancellor, towards defraying the expenses of a National Academy, of which the Chancellor shall be always President, and shall appoint by the orders of the King the instructors. In everything else relating to the Academy the legislature shall direct.

VIII. COMMERCE AND COLONIES.

The King shall make all the appointments in the Colonies, in the manner determined upon by common consent. The commissions and warrants shall be countersigned by the Minister of Commerce, who shall also counter-sign the warrants of the Government Attorneys of the departments, of the Comptrollers of Customs, and of the Consuls in foreign countries.

IX. RELATIONS WITH FOREIGN POWERS.

Ambassadors, and other Ministers and diplomatic agents, shall be appointed by the King. Their credentials and instructions shall be counter-signed by the Minister of Foreign Affairs. The expenses thereof shall be paid out of the civil list, and when extraordinary expenses are incurred for secret services, the legislature will reimburse the same if it sees fit.

Treaties and Conventions with foreign powers shall be recorded at the King's Council, and signed by the King in his Council, with the advice of the majority of his Ministers, who are bound to countersign it before the treaty can take effect. It shall then become the supreme law of the State, and the Ministers who shall have signed it shall be all and each responsible therefor.

No treaty of commerce can take place without the previous consent of the Minister of Commerce, which shall be given and confirmed by his sig-nature before the treaty shall be submitted to the Council.

The decisions of the Admiralty Courts respecting prizes taken at sea, shall be made in accordance with the ordinances of the King in his Council, because they affect the external relations of the State, and depend on the rights of war; consequently the appeal from the Admiralty shall be made to the Council in such manner as the ordinances shall prescribe.

The judges of the Admiralty Courts shall be appointed by the King, and their commissions shall be countersigned by the Minister of Foreign Af-fairs. They are removable.

The royal attorneys in the Admiralty Courts are also removable. They shall be appointed by the King, and their warrants shall be countersigned by the Minister of Marine.

X. Legislative Power.

The legislative power shall reside always in the Senate and National Assembly, which, in concert with the King, shall make all laws, ordinances, and regulations whatever, which they shall judge necessary to the defence, preservation, and prosperity of the State.

The Senate shall be composed of ninety Senators, hereditary in the male line in order of primogeniture. They shall be appointed by the King, that is to say the King shall appoint forthwith fifty, and others according as circumstances may appear to him to require it. The patents of the Senators shall be issued under the seal of State, and registered at the chancery. They shall never have any other title than that of French Senator. The King shall appoint from among the members of the royal family Senators for life, of which the number shall never exceed nine, and they shall have no other title than that of French Senators; but the Prince Royal shall be always a Senator without the nomination of the King. Thus the Senators of the royal family may be ten in number including the Prince Royal, whose title however shall not be Senator, but only Prince Royal.

The King shall appoint twenty Ecclesiastical Senators, among whom shall be all the Archbishops; their title shall be Bishop Senator. Finally, the twenty-four Superior Judges hereafter mentioned shall also be Senators, but shall not have the title thereof.

No one shall have a seat in the Senate before the age of thirty years, except the Prince Royal, who shall have a seat there at sixteen years, and a voice in the decisions at twenty years, but shall never have a voice in consultations.

The Chancellor shall preside in the Senate, and when he is not there, the President shall take his place. The President shall be nominated by the King at the opening of each session, from among the hereditary Senators.

The Senate shall choose its other officers, such as registers, sergeants, and doorkeepers.

Every Senator shall lose his place for the crime of high treason, and for dishonorable actions or scandalous conduct, according to the decision of the Senate. A Senator cannot be judged except by the Senate.

The King can appoint to the Senate the son of one, who has lost his place, but he cannot reinstate a Senator degraded by a decision of the Senate.

The Senate judges of accusations brought by the National Assembly, because the complaints of the nation, through the medium of its Representatives, ought not to be submitted to any inferior tribunal.

In order that the accusations of the representative body may be judged in the most solemn manner, the King shall appoint from among the hereditary Senators a constable of France to preside over the Senate; but this office shall cease with the occasion which gives birth to it. The appointment shall be made to the Senate *vivâ voce.*

The King cannot pardon him, whom the Senate upon the accusation of the representatives shall have condemned. The Senate is judge in the last resort of all cases and causes, which shall be brought to it by appeal, according to the regulations of the legislature.

The Ecclesiastical and Royal Senators shall not assist the judiciary sessions, and the judges shall have only a voice in the consultations.

The Senate can never for purposes of legislation consist of less than forty members, hereditary or others. To fulfill its judicial functions, at least thirty hereditary Senators are necessary.

The National Assembly shall always consist of four members for each department, eight for Paris, and four for each of the cities hereafter named, and of those to which the legislature shall grant a representation.[2]

In great cities the citizens, who are not holders of property, have the stability necessary to form for themselves an opinion upon public affairs; in the country, on the contrary, they are reduced by circumstances to second the ambition of the rich, and consequently to destroy the equilibrium upon which depends the importance of the middling class and public liberty.

The cities which shall henceforth have representatives are Dunkirk, Lisle [Lille], Dieppe, Amiens, Havre, Rouen, Metz, Strasbourg, Lyons, St Malo, Nantes, Bordeaux, Bayonne, and Marseilles.

One hundred members shall suffice to form a Chamber of Representatives, because circumstances may often prevent members from being present, and the urgency of affairs sometimes does not permit any delay.

The Representatives shall be chosen for eight years, and it shall be decided by lot in each city and department, after the first election, which of the members shall retire from the Assembly at the end of two years, which of them shall retire at the end of four years, and which at the end of six years, so that consequently one quarter of the Representatives shall be

---

2. In 1790 the National Assembly created 83 *Departments* to replace the provincial structure of the ancien régime. Morris's assembly would thus have 396 members.

elected every two years, and when the place of a Representative shall become vacant, the vacancy shall be filled by an extraordinary election.

The electors of the departments are the male holders of property. The legislature shall determine on the value of the property. No one shall vote before he is married, and has attained the age of twenty-five years.

The elections shall be made in the districts and in the manner which the legislature shall point out. The list of voters of each district shall be sent to the department which shall examine the same, and the Grand Bailiff shall certify to the chancery, by the advice of the administrative body, the person elected. And in case of a disputed election, he shall send the lists to the National Assembly, to which alone belongs the right of judging of its members and of elections.

The electors of the represented cities are those who pay taxes; but after the first election, the cities may grant the right of citizenship to whomsoever they may see fit, provided he shall have attained the age of twenty-five years, shall be married, and of good character. Persons thus admitted by the cities are the only citizens, who have the right to vote for representatives of cities and municipal officers. And this right is inalienable except in cases of conviction of crime.

The municipal officers in the cities above named shall be chosen in the manner pointed out by the legislature, which shall determine upon the organization of the municipal bodies, and upon the cities to which such bodies ought to be granted. But in all cases the Mayors shall be appointed by a warrant from the King, which shall be countersigned by the Minister of the Interior.

The National Assembly shall choose its President at the commencement of each session, for the entire session, and all the other officers necessary shall be chosen in the same manner.

The expenses of the Representatives of each department and city shall be paid by the electors of the cities and departments represented, at a rate regulated by the legislature, and the assessments shall be respectively made by the administrative and municipal bodies.

Every law, or ordinance having the force of a law, other than those specially indicated in this Constitution, may be agreed to by the majority of the Senate and of the Chamber of Representatives, and shall then be presented to the King for his sanction.

Each Chamber has the right of making the alterations it may see fit in acts before assenting to them, and to each belongs the originating of laws, except those of revenue of which the originating belongs exclusively to the

Representatives; so the Senate can never have the right of changing anything in relation to imposts, but only of consenting or not consenting.

The style of the laws shall be, "The King, by common consent with the Senate and the French Nation, orders that, &c." But the style of the laws which levy imposts shall be, "The nation grants to the King for the necessities and honor of the State the imposts, which the Senate has consented to, and which his Majesty accepts, to be employed for the objects designed by the people in granting them; it is therefore ordered by common consent, &c."

The laws being presented to the King, he shall signify by his Chancellor, to the Senators and Representatives assembled in the Chamber of the Senate, the royal will. If the King does not agree, his refusal shall be expressed by these words, "The King will consider." If he agrees to the law, the form shall be, "The King consents, and will cause to be executed." But if it is a question of a law, which grants an impost, and which the King accepts, the form shall be, "The King accepts and will cause to be executed."

The laws shall be registered at the Chancery, and then sent by the Chancellor to the Keeper of the Records, to be printed under his inspection, and the originals to be deposited among the archives of the State. The Keeper of the Records shall send to the Constable of the department two printed copies of each law, that he may make proclamation thereof, and send one copy with the certificate of having proclaimed it to the Government Attorney, and the other copy with a similar certificate to the Register of the department.

The King shall assemble and prorogue the two Chambers; but if the Ministers suffer more than a year to intervene between two sessions, the Chambers shall assemble themselves by their chief, and the King cannot prorogue them before the expiration of six months without their consent.

Each Chamber can adjourn itself from day to day, but not for more than five days at a time.

Each Chamber shall have the right of police within its interior, and in what relates to it, and that of punishing its own members; the whole according as the legislature shall determine.

The members of the Senate and of the Assembly cannot be arrested during the session, nor in the space of time fixed by the legislature before and after the session, except for crime.

XI. JUDICIARY POWER.

The Judges shall be named by the King; their commissions shall be issued under the seal of State, and they shall receive a fixed salary from the public treasury.

The Judges are either Superior or Inferior.

The Superior Judges are not removable, and are twenty-four in number, of which twelve are stationary, and twelve circuit judges.

No one can be appointed a Superior Judge before the age of thirty-five years.

The stationary Judges shall be divided into four Chambers, or Courts, of which each shall have a supreme judge. The first Court shall judge all disputes upon fiscal concerns; the criminal code is the department of the second; the third shall determine cases which relate to real estate; and the fourth, all other cases.

The King shall appoint a crown lawyer for each Court, whose duty is to attend to the fiscal concerns of the nation. His warrant shall be counter-signed by the Minister of Finance.

The King shall appoint a Royal Attorney, whose duty is to prosecute every violation of public order. His warrant shall be countersigned by the Minister of the Interior.

A single Judge shall suffice to hold an ordinary session, but to decide fully upon a subject two at least shall be necessary.

Cases shall be judged by the Stationary Tribunals in the same manner as by the Circuit Courts.

The Judges of Assizes shall be divided into six circuits, and there shall be in each department two annual Assizes, one in the Spring, and the other in the Autumn. A single Superior Judge shall suffice to hold an Assize, with two of the Judges of the department hereafter mentioned, the Superior Judge presiding.

The Assize Courts shall judge all the complaints and cases whatsoever of the department, whether civil, criminal, or fiscal. There shall be an appeal from the decisions of the Judges, whether upon the principles or the adventitious circumstances, which shall be made, according to the nature of the case, to one or the other of the Stationary Tribunals.

The Stationary Tribunals shall likewise hold their sessions twice a year, in the Spring and in the Autumn, to decide on cases which are within their respective jurisdictions. They shall hold two other sessions in Winter and in Summer, to judge the various appeals which shall be made to them.

There shall be also an appeal from the decisions of the Stationary Courts to the Court of Appeals, over which the Chancellor shall preside, and at which at least twelve Superior Judges shall assist.

There shall be also an appeal from the decisions of the Appeals Court to the Senate, the whole according to the forms and conditions, and under the restrictions which the legislature shall prescribe.

When the subject of discussion in a civil matter involves the examination of accounts, or by the absence of witnesses out of the kingdom, or by other reasons it happens that the Assizes cannot render justice, then the cause may be either commenced in the Court of the Pretor, or be brought there, and appeal shall be had from the Pretor to the Chancellor, and from the Chancellor to the Senate, whether upon the facts or upon the judgments rendered, as well upon the principle as upon the form, the whole in the manner which the legislature shall determine upon.

The Pretor shall be appointed in each department by the Chancellor, and shall be removable. Every dispute in matters of business and of accounts is within his jurisdiction. He shall appoint four Commissioners; the facts shall be established by a Commissioner, and they shall be examined afterwards by the Pretor if he sees fit; and in view of the appeal granted on the facts, the depositions of the witnesses shall be written before the judgment.

There shall be in each department four Inferior Judges appointed by the King, who shall be removable, and their warrants shall be countersigned by the Chancellor. The Inferior Judges or two of them, with one or more Judges of Assize, shall hold the Assizes. A single Judge of a department can decide on the forms and adventitious circumstances to accelerate the proceedings, and obtain an earlier decision upon the principles of the case, but an appeal may be had from his judgment to the Assize Court, and thence a further appeal.

The register shall be named in each department every three years by the Assize Court sitting in the Spring, from among three persons, who shall be presented by the administrative body.

Every transfer or hypothecation of real estate, must be made before the Register, certified by him, and registered by the Government Attorney in the archives of the department; and every deed must be so registered, and the copy of the registry certified by the Government Attorney shall be available in justice; the whole to be according to regulations which the legislature shall establish.

Decisions in Assize Courts on facts shall be by juries of twelve respectable persons, and the witnesses shall all be publicly examined in presence of the jury and of the parties.

To form the juries, the electors shall choose every two years in each district forty-eight persons from among the holders of property in the district, and the list of them shall be registered at the administration and at the registry of the department. The Constable shall make for each case a list of forty-eight persons, according as the Court shall direct, and shall cause them to be summoned to appear under penalties, at the time and place designated, for judging the case. Each individual shall have the right of challenging six of the jurors without cause, and others for sufficient cause, and of the remaining number, twelve shall be drawn by lot to sit in the case. It is necessary that the verdict of the twelve composing the jury be unanimous.

The Constable shall likewise summon, when necessary, twenty-four persons for a grand jury of the department; and no person shall be judged at the Assizes for crime or offence, until he shall have been previously accused by the grand jury. The grand jury shall decide by a majority, but twelve voices are requisite for an accusation.

A person belonging to the grand jury cannot be summoned for another jury.

The King shall order extraordinary Assizes whenever circumstances require it.

To judge of criminal cases the Constable shall summon forty-eight persons, and the accused shall have the right of challenging twelve without cause, and others for sufficient cause. The twelve of whom the jury consists must be agreed to acquit or condemn.

Each person before taking his place as member of a jury shall make oath to give impartial attention to the case, and to speak the truth according to the evidence.

In every suit, before submitting it to the jury, the statements of the parties must be reduced to direct affirmations and negations, that the jury may be able to decide by yea and nay. And for this purpose in every complaint and every defence the facts must be precisely stated with the time, place and circumstances, that the opposite party may admit or deny them positively, and prepare their proofs.

There shall be in each department a Constable appointed by the King every year. His warrant shall be countersigned by the Minister of the Interior. He shall appoint in each district a serjeant, and such number of tipstaffs as he may think proper. To the Constable shall be addressed every writ, sentence, order, or letter of execution whatever, to execute the same. To him belongs particularly to keep the peace of the department, to cause the police to be performed, and the laws to be respected. It is his duty to suppress insurrections, and the citizens are required forcibly to assist him, his serjeants and tipstaffs, when called upon in the name of the King.

The Constable is governor of all the prisons of the department, and he shall appoint the deputy governors, jailers, and other necessary officers.

The legislature shall determine upon the rights honorary and pecuniary of the Constable, of the Government Attorney and Register, in such manner that these officers, their substitutes and agents, shall not be chargeable to the treasury. For it is right, that the citizens should pay the expenses resulting from the execution of the laws, when they have recourse to the protection which they afford; and it is right, that he, who will not render to any one his due, should defray the expenses which his bad faith makes necessary; finally, it is right, that the good and peaceable citizens should be protected in the enjoyment of their property, at the expense of the malevolent and unjust.

To avoid as much as possible lawsuits and quarrels, there shall be conciliatory tribunals for the resident inhabitants. The conciliatory tribunal shall be composed of one Justice of Peace and of two respectable citizens of the neighborhood, whom the Justice of Peace shall summon. This tribunal shall hear the statements of the parties but not the witnesses, and shall recommend means, of accommodation.

If accommodation cannot be had, the Judge shall give to each of the parties a certificate of having appeared, that he may be able to proceed; and if the parties have agreed on the facts, it shall be declared by the same certificate. The facts upon which they have agreed shall likewise be stated, in order to abridge the process of law when it cannot be avoided.

The Justices of Peace shall have such other authority, as the legislature shall grant to them; and the legislature shall establish from time to time all the tribunals, which shall be deemed convenient, useful, or necessary, and shall regulate all proceedings that shall be necessary for the most perfect distribution of justice, and to protect the property, rights, and privileges of all the citizens.

21 ❧ Remarks upon the Principles and Views of the London Corresponding Society (1795)

Morris left France in October 1794 and spent the next four years traveling in Europe. In mid-June 1795 he arrived in England, where he stayed for a year. Although he did some touring in the country, much of his time was spent in and around London, where he met and conversed with just about everyone of consequence.

In the 1790s various groups advocating reform of Parliament and other more radical political changes had grown up in England, among them the London Corresponding Society. Although not the most radical group, it had a large following—in 1795 it held a rally that attracted one hundred thousand people. Such a group was considered a threat by the government, and on several occasions its leaders were prosecuted. On October 29, 1795, King George III's carriage was attacked as he rode to Parliament, which led to further arrests.

Perhaps in response to the aftermath of the attack on the king, on November 23 of that year the society published a four-page pamphlet, *To the Parliament and People of Great Britain, An Explicit Declaration of the Principles and Views of the London Corresponding Society*. Morris returned to London that day from a tour of the northern parts of England, and wrote and published this brief reply sometime in the next month.

Remarks Upon the Principles and Views of the London Corresponding Society (London: Printed for J. Debrett, Piccadilly, 1795). The pamphlet is in the British Library collection, (c) British Library, 1102.i.30. The manuscript is in the Gouverneur Morris Papers, Rare Book and Manuscript Library, Columbia University, item 843. The manuscript version has been followed here; differences between the manuscript and the pamphlet have been indicated. Morris is responding to *To the Parliament and People of Great Britain, An Explicit Declaration of the Principles and Views of the London Corresponding Society*, dated November 23, 1795. That pamphlet is in several collections, including the British Library and the Library of Congress.

The London Corresponding Society have published *An Explicit Declaration of their Principles and Views*, by way of *Appeal to a Public deluded by their Calumniators*. Hence it may be fairly supposed, that this Paper is intended to express the Sentiments of those honest and moderate Members who have in view none but fair and honourable objects. The Writer of it has endeavoured to reconcile, to *their* satisfaction and that of the world, *their* Principles with those of the British Constitution. It may be well, therefore, to examine this Political Creed, the first article of which sets forth their *firm attachment to the Principles of Equality, accurately defined and properly understood*, and then proceeds to define *social* Equality.

It is presumed that they did not advert to the difference between *Equality* in its general sense, and the particular limitation[1] of it, by the epithet *social*. The former, in contradistinction to the latter, can only exist between the political aggregations of Men: these are said to be equal; and yet experience shews, that among Nations, however equal in right, the strongest gives the Law: and it would probably be found, if two men of full age were placed, by way of experiment, on a desert island, so as to realize (in some measure) the idea of what is called a *state of Nature*, that the stronger would compel the weaker to obey him; and thus in *this* state of Nature, that which Theorists call *natural Equality*, would be reduced (in practice) to the relation of Tyrant and Slave. Luckily that same state of Nature is not the natural state of Man. He is a social animal. His *rights*, therefore, and his *duties*, are *social*. Consequently, to talk of his *natural* rights, in contradistinction to the *social*, seems about as proper as to talk of his *angelic* rights, or his *bestial* rights, or of any thing else *as his*, which does not and cannot belong to him. And let it not be supposed that the common expressions (such for instance as the natural rights and duties of Parent and Child) apply to the distinction here mentioned. Those also are social rights and duties; and so far are they from what are called *The Rights of Man*, or *Perfect Equality*, that they imply command and support on the one side; gratitude and obedience on the other. Nay, it is from this special relation, and the long period through which it continues to exist, that man is not only, like other gregarious animals, *naturally* a social Creature, but he is so *necessarily*. And let it be further observed, for the consideration of those who amuse themselves and their neighbours by the discussion of political theories, that no creature can have rights inconsistent with its own nature.

1. In the manuscript, "limitation"; in the pamphlet, "distinction."

Man, therefore, being a social Creature, can have no rights inconsistent with the social state. And if any such be attributed to him, the conclusions drawn from them, by sound logical deduction, must go to the subversion of civil society. So, on the other hand, when a proposition is stated which militates against the existence of society, it is evident that such proposition cannot be true. And therefore, if it be in the nature of a deduction by just reasoning from supposed premises, it will follow that the premises must be false.

To return then to the Creed: this *social Equality* is said to consist, 1st, in the acknowledgment of *equal Rights*. Hence it would appear that *social Equality* and equal Rights are distinct matters, for surely a thing cannot consist in the acknowledgment of its own existence. It would indeed be a strange answer, if a Child should ask what is a Lion, to tell him it is the acknowledgment of a Lion. As far as one not initiated may venture to judge, the import of the term *equal Rights* would seem to be, that every one should have the same rights with every other: or that no one should have more or greater rights than his fellow-citizens. Taking this as the interpretation, it will be proper in the next place to enquire what is meant by the term *Acknowledgement*. And this, it is presumed, is taken from the phraseology of Disputants, and means the admission or confession of the adverse Party, founded on conviction. Now that Party, being in the present case the Government, and those who adhere to it, this first branch of the definition of *social Equality* amounts to a declaration, on the part of the Corresponding Society, to the following effect: "There is an end of that social Equality to which we are firmly attached, unless it be admitted as a maxim, that *no one Member of the Community has a greater right, or a greater number of rights, than any other Member*."

Social Equality is said to consist, secondly, in *equal Laws for the security of those Rights*. Now, the first question which occurs for consideration, is, what must be understood by the term *equal Laws?* Taken as a figure of rhetoric, it might mean equitable Laws, or Laws equitably administered, or both. But in the present case it must mean something else, or something more, since it forms a part of the definition of Equality, and is to be the security of equal Rights; for equitable Laws, equitably administered, do *proportion* penalties, damages, and the like (as far as may be), to the ranks and situations of Men, as well as to the circumstances attending their actions, and the resulting degrees of criminality. Now this proportion is the direct opposite to Equality. Proceeding on principles totally different, and founded on a supposed inequality of rights and ranks, it gives to one man greater damages than to another for the same injury, and inflicts heavier fines on different penalties for the same offence. All which, however equitable, is by no means equal: and Laws which operate these effects, though they may be just Laws, certainly are not equal Laws. This term, *equal Laws*, seems rather to relate to a position in one of those Bills of Rights which have lately sprouted up in different parts of the world, to the great annoyance of His Majesty's liege Subjects. But here it is proper to pause and explain.

There is an Instrument, commonly called the Bill of Rights, which contains a Declaration of some of the Rights of Englishmen. This is a Piece of great value. It was drawn up with much wisdom and discretion, and may be considered as a solemn Legislative Exposition, so far as it goes, of the British Constitution; setting forth sundry advantages to which the People are *entitled* by that Constitution, and which, of course, form *their Rights — the Rights of Englishmen*. And although it be a dangerous thing to lay down general Propositions, and therefore unwise to do so when no occasion calls for it, yet considering how prone Men are to abuse Power, it might be well, perhaps, that in every free Government, some clear statement were made, by public Authority, of the principal Privileges to which its Citizens are entitled. The World might thereby become acquainted with the Rights of Swiss Men, of Dutchmen, of American Men, and of Frenchmen, as well as of Englishmen. And Citizens of the World, in their journey through life, might put up at the Inn where the entertainment was most agreeable to them. But this is very different from those fantastic productions, each of which has been pompously proclaimed as the *only* solid foundation for all Government: each purporting to be a Declaration of the natural, indefeasible, imprescriptible, &c. &c. &c. Rights of Man, to doubt of which is a political heresy. It has happened with respect to these things, as it usually does in such cases, that they differ considerably from each other; and of course it is evident, at the first blush, that they cannot all be true. And, indeed, it was a strange thing to see the modern State Conventions, like the ancient Church Councils, in violent dispute about what other People should be bound to believe.

It is declared in one of those same Bills of Rights, (a French one, consequently one of the best authority, being a late Edition) that Men are equal in the presence of the Law, whether it protects or whether it punishes: it may therefore be fairly supposed, that by the term *equal Laws*, in the Creed, is meant Laws which, without respect to persons, operate alike upon all, and in whose presence all are equal, whether the question relate to Punishment or to Protection; consequently, the same fine for the same offence to be laid on the Duke and on the Duke's Footman—a pleasant thing for the Duke! and if the Nuptial Couch of each should have been sullied, then each to receive the same Compensation—a good thing for the Footman! These, it is to be presumed, are the *equal Laws* fitted to the Preservation of those *equal Rights* which are in the contemplation of the Society. Indeed, such *equal Rights* being *acknowledged*, these *equal Laws* must naturally result from them.

The third, and last part of the definition of social Equality, is "*equal and actual Representation*, by which *alone* the invasion of those Laws," the equal Laws, "can be prevented." Thus then the Trinitarian definition of social Equality is completed, by, 1st, an acknowledgment of equal Rights; 2dly, equal Laws to protect those equal Rights; and, 3dly, equal Representation to protect those equal Laws; and it is in this last that we find the damning clause of the Creed; for it declares, that by equal and actual Representation *alone*, &c. &c. just like St. Athanasius's, whoso doth not believe, &c.[2] The Indian, more modest, tells you, the sky rests on the earth, the earth on an elephant, the elephant on a tortoise, and then leaves you at liberty to believe in his System, or in that of NEWTON, though he thinks it somewhat absurd, that you should prefer the principles of attraction to his elephant and his tortoise.

Immediately after their definition, the Society go on to declare, that in their ideas of Equality, they never included the Equalization of Property, or *the invasion of personal Rights and Possessions.* And this Declaration is made with such warmth of expression, that it would be unfair not to believe it.

The Second Article of the Creed, somewhat in the manner of POPE's famous couplet:

> For Forms of Government let Fools contest;
> Whate'er is best administer'd, is best;

says, that "to dispute about forms and modifications of Government, marks a weak mind, which, in pursuit of shadows, forgets the substance"; and it declares, that "the objects to which the Society directs its attention, are the

---

2. Athanasius (ca. 293-373) was bishop of Alexandria and a leading figure in the controversy over Arianism. The Athanasian creed, probably composed about two centuries after his death, concludes: "Haec est fides catholica, quam nisi quisque fideliter firmiterque crediderit, salvus esse non poterit" (This is the Catholic faith, and whoever does not believe it faithfully and steadfastly cannot be saved).

peace, social order, and happiness of mankind, *all of which may be sufficiently secured by the genuine spirit of the British Constitution.*" Now then let the different parts of their Declaration be compared together.

Upon examining the definition of Equality, it appears primarily to consist in the admission as a principle, that no one Member of the Community has a greater right, or a greater number of rights, than any other Member; but it is said, nevertheless, that the invasion of personal Rights is not included in that idea. How can this be, if by *personal* Rights be meant a right of any person or persons which all others have not in common with him or them, and which does not therefore form a part of the *common* Rights? Nay, how can this be, if it be only admitted in *general*, that all have *equal* Rights? If John and Tom have equal Rights, then every thing which Tom possesses more than John, is not by *right* but by *wrong*. And consequently, whenever it is established that their Rights are equal, all Tom's pretensions fall to the ground: and it must appear that what he calls his *personal Rights*, are a *mere Usurpation*. His Grace the Duke of NORFOLK is Hereditary Earl Marshal, and the first Duke in England, a Member of the Legislative Senate, and Supreme Court of Appeals, in what is called *his own right*, and these his *personal Rights* will descend to his Heirs, if no Revolution be effected.

The Corresponding Society declare, that it is not their intention to invade his or any other man's personal Rights; but, having previously established in their Creed, that none such can exist, it follows that they are not invaded, but merely annihilated. And so indeed are the Rights of the whole House of Peers, as well as some others which it is not proper to mention.

Again, it is said, that the invasion of those equal Laws which secure those equal Rights, can *alone* be prevented by *equal and actual Representation*; and yet it is said, that the essential objects to which the Society have always directed their attention, can be sufficiently secured by the *genuine spirit* of the British Constitution. Hence it follows, that the genuine spirit of the British Constitution consists in equal and actual Representation. Let this be compared with the present state of things, and, putting aside the case of Boroughs (which, be they what else they may, are certainly to be noticed as possessions), this at least will be admitted, that in the choice of County Members, where each sends two, the Freeholders of a small County have, as such, a greater individual share of the Legislative Authority than those of a large County. It is true, that by proportioning the number of Representatives to the number of Inhabitants, all would be put upon a footing of Equality; but surely this could not be done without an invasion of *personal Possessions*. The great complaint of the Corresponding

Society is, that a small part of the Nation possesses a power to legislate for the whole, and their great object is to abolish this, which they consider as an abuse, and to introduce as of right, Universal Suffrage, under the name of equal and actual Representation. But yet, say they, we do not mean to invade personal Possessions. We will take away from the few the power they possess, and divide it among the whole Community; but God forbid that we should invade any man's Possessions. What would be thought of a civil Murderer, who should tell you, *don't be alarmed, I have no intention to take away your life, but only to kill you?* or of a gentle Robber, who should say, *bless me, why so much apprehension, I don't mean to deprive you of your Property, but only to share?* The Corresponding Society did not mean any of these contradictions, but the misfortune is, that these, and many more, must arise from attempting to conform the Principles of any Government, however free, to the old exploded System (now newly vamped up) of the Rights of Man. That is to say, from attempting to erect any social Fabric on the foundation of Principles declaredly[3] unsocial. And let it not thence be concluded, that the Members of this Society are Sons of Sedition. The chance is, that very few of them are so; nay, that the *Marats* and *Robespierres*, the *Borgias* and *Catilines* among them, are, as yet, good, honest Men, and justly offended that such appellations should be applied to them; for it is only by degrees that they will be led to crimes at which they now shudder. True it is, that the existence of that Society is pernicious; but yet their intentions are probably innocent. It is to be wished, however, that they would reflect seriously on what they are about. In the fervour of their zeal for Liberty, they may (like the Jews of old), crucify the God they adore. And if so, the mild spirit of expiring Freedom will exclaim, though in agony, "Pity them, Lord, for they know not what they do."

---

3. In the manuscript, "declaredly"; in the pamphlet, "evidently."

The only man among his contemporaries for whom Morris could be said to have unqualified admiration was George Washington. They first became acquainted in the very early stages of the Revolution, but Morris's respect for Washington grew into something approaching hero worship during the years he spent in the Continental Congress. Those years included the winter of the encampment at Valley Forge, where Morris saw the suffering of the troops and the determination of Washington at first hand.

Just a few days before Washington died, Morris had written to urge him to come out of retirement again for the good of the country. John Adams's deeply unpopular presidency had divided the country and the Federalist party. To Morris, Washington was the only one who could save the country from dissolving into an unhealthy factionalism. Thus for him the loss of Washington was not only personal, but public.

Sed quisnam merito divinas Carmine Laudes
Concipere, aut tanto par queat esse Viro?

AUREL. BRAND.[1]

Americans,
    Assembled to pay the last dues of filial piety to him who was the father of his country, it is meet that we take one last look at the man whom we have lost forever.

Oration, Upon The Death of General Washington, by Gouverneur Morris. Delivered At The Request Of The Corporation Of The City Of New-York, On The 31st Day Of December, 1799. And Published by their Request (New-York: printed by John Furman, opposite the City Hall, 1800). American Antiquarian Society Early American Imprints, series I (Evans), no. 38002. Courtesy American Antiquarian Society.
    1. "Who but that man deserves to receive divine praises in song, or can be so great

Born to high destinies, he was fashioned for them by the hand of nature—His form was noble—His port majestic—On his front were enthroned the virtues which exalt, and those which adorn the human character. So dignified his deportment, no man could approach him but with respect—None was great in his presence. You all have seen him, and you all have felt the reverence he inspired; it was such, that to command, seemed in him but the exercise of an ordinary function, while others felt a duty to obey, which (anterior to the injunctions of civil ordinance, or the compulsion of a military code) was imposed by the high behests of nature.

He had *every* title to command—Heaven, in giving him the higher qualities of the soul, had given also the tumultuous passions which accompany greatness, and frequently tarnish its luster. With them was his first contest, and his first victory was over himself. So great the empire he had there acquired, that calmness of manner and of conduct distinguished him through life. Yet, those who have seen him strongly moved, will bear witness that his wrath was terrible; they have seen boiling in his bosom, passion almost too mighty for man; yet, when just bursting into act, that strong passion was controlled by his stronger mind.

Having thus a perfect command of himself, he could rely on the full exertion of his powers, in whatever direction he might order them to act. He was therefore, clear, decided, and unembarrassed by any consideration of himself. Such consideration did not even dare to intrude on his reflections. Hence it was, that he beheld not only the affairs that were passing around him, but those also in which he was personally engaged, with the coolness of an unconcerned spectator. They were to him as events historically recorded. His judgment was always clear, because his mind was pure. And seldom, if ever, will a sound understanding be met with in the company of a corrupt heart.

In the strength of judgment lay, indeed, one chief excellence of his character. Leaving to feebler minds that splendor of genius, which, while it enlightens others, too often dazzles the possessor—he knew how best to use the rays which genius might emit, and carry into act its best conceptions.

So modest, he wished not to attract attention, but observed in silence, and saw deep into the human heart. Of a thousand propositions he knew to distinguish the best; and to select among a thousand the man most fitted for his purpose. If ever he was deceived in his choice, it was by circum-

---

a man?" The quotation comes from a poem of Aurelio Brandolini (1454–97), "De Laudibus Laurentii Medicis" (In honor of Lorenzo di Medici).

stances of social feeling which did honour to his heart. Should it, therefore, in the review of his conduct, appear that he was merely not infallible, the few errors which fell to his lot, as a man will claim the affections of his fellow men. Pleased with the rare, but graceful weakness, they will admire that elevation of soul, which, superior to resentment, gave honour and power, with liberal hand, to those by whom he had been offended. Not to conciliate a regard, which, if it be venal, is worth no price, but to draw forth in your service the exercise of talents which he could duly estimate, in spite of incidents by which a weaker mind would have been thrown from its bias.

In him were the courage of a soldier, the intrepidity of a chief, the fortitude of a hero. He had given to the impulsions of bravery all the calmness of his character, and, if in the moment of danger, his manner was distinguishable from that of common life, it was by superior ease and grace.

To each desire he had taught the lessons of moderation. Prudence became therefore the companion of his life. Never in the public, never in the private hour did she abandon him even for a moment. And, if in the small circle, where he might safely think aloud, she should have slumbered amid convivial joy, his quick sense of what was just, and decent, and fit, stood ever ready to awaken her at the slightest alarm.

Knowing how to appreciate the world, its gifts and glories, he was truly wise. Wise also in selecting the objects of his pursuit. And wise in adopting just means to compass honorable ends.

Bound by the sacred ties of wedded love, his high example strengthened the tone of public manners. Beloved, almost adored by the amiable partner of his toils and dangers, who shared with him the anxieties of public life, and sweetened the shade of retirement, no fruit was granted to their union. No child to catch with pious tenderness the falling tear, and soothe the anguish of connubial affection. No living image remains to her of his virtues, and she must seek them sorrowing in the grave. Who shall arraign, Oh GOD! thy high decree? Was it in displeasure, that to the father of his country thou hadst denied a son? Was it in mercy, lest the paternal virtues should have triumphed (during some frail moment) in the patriot bosom? AMERICANS! he had no child—BUT YOU—and HE WAS ALL YOUR OWN.

Let envy come forward if she dare, and seek some darkened spot in this sun of our glory. From the black catalogue of crimes envy herself must speak him free. Had he (a mortal) the failings attached to man?—Was he the slave of avarice? No. Wealth was an object too mean for his regard. And yet economy presided over his domestic concerns; for his mind was too lofty to brook dependence. Was he ambitious? No. His spirit soared beyond ambition's reach. He saw a crown high above all human grandeur. He sought, he gained, and wore *that* crown. But he had indeed one frailty—the weakness of great minds. He was fond of fame, and had reared a colossal reputation—It stood on the rock of his virtue. This was dear to his heart. There was but one thing dearer. He loved glory, but still more he loved his country. That was the master passion, and, with resistless might, it ruled his every thought, and word, and deed.

We see him stepping, as it were from his cradle, into the fields of glory, and meriting the public confidence, at a period when others too often consume in idleness the moments lent for instruction, or (in pursuit of pleasure) waste their moral energies. While yet his cheek was covered with the down of youth, he had combined the character of an able negotiator with that of a gallant soldier. Scarce had he given this early pledge of future service, when he was called on for the quick performance—He accompanies to the western wilds, BRADDOCK who, bred in camps of European war, despis'd the savage. But soon entrapped in the close ambush, military skill becomes of no avail. The leaders, selected by unerring aim, first fall—the troops lie thick in slaughtered heaps, the victims of an invisible foe. WASHINGTON, whose warnings had been neglected, still gives the aid of salutary counsel to his ill fated chief, and urges it with all the grace of eloquence, and all the force of conviction. A form so manly draws the attention of the savage and is doomed to perish. The murdering instruments are levelled—the quick bolts fly winged with death, and pierce his garments, but obedient to the sovereign will, they dare not shed his blood. BRADDOCK falls at his feet; and the youthful hero covers with his brave Virginians, the retreat of Britons, not less brave, but surprized by unusual war.

These bands of brothers were soon to stand in hostile opposition. Such was the decree of HIM to whom are present all the revolutions of time and empire. When no hope remained but in the field of blood, WASHINGTON was called on by his country to lead her armies. In modest doubt of his own ability, he submitted with reluctance to the necessity of becoming her chief; and took on him the weight, the care and the anguish of a civil war. *Ambition* would have tasted here the sweets of power, and drunk deep of intoxicating draughts, but to the *Patriot*, these sweets are bitterness.

INDUSTRIOUS, patient, persevering he remained at the head of citizens scarcely armed; and, sparing of blood, by skill, rather than by force, compelled his foe to seek a more favorable theatre of war. And now all hope of union lost, America (by her declaration of independence) cut the last slender thread of connection.

She had hitherto been successful; but was soon shaken by adverse storms. The counsel of her Chief had been neglected. His army had been raised by annual enlistment. The poor remnant of accumulated defeat, retreating before an enemy flushed with success, and confident in all superiority, looked with impatience to the approaching term of service. The prospect was on all sides gloomy; and sunshine friends (turning their halcyon backs to fairer skies) sought shelter from the storm. But though betrayed by fortune, his calm and steady mind remained true to itself. Winter had closed the campaign. Solacing in the enjoyment of what their arms had acquired, the victors tasted pleasure unalloyed by the dread of danger. They were sheltered behind one of the broad barriers of nature, and, safely housed, beheld upon its farther shore, a feeble adversary, exposed beneath the canopy of heaven to the rigors of an unpitying season. It was hoped that, their term of enlistment expired, the American troops would disperse; and the CHIEF (in despair) throw up his command. Such was the reasoning, and such reasoning would (in ordinary cases) have been conclusive. *But that* CHIEF *was* WASHINGTON! He shews to his gallant comrades the danger of their country, and asks the aid of patriotic service. At his voice their hearts beat high. In vain the raging Delaware, vext with the wintry blast, forbids their march. In vain he rolls along his rocky bed, a frozen torrent whose ponderous mass threatens to sweep the soldier from his uncertain footstep, and bear him down the flood! In vain the beating snow adds to the dangerous ford a darkened horror! Difficulties and dangers animate the brave. His little band is arrived; WASHINGTON is within the walls — the enemy is subdued!

Fortune now smiles, but who can trust to that fallacious smile? Preparations are already made to punish the AMERICAN LEADER for his adventurous hardihood. And now he sees, stretched out before him in wide array, a force so great that in the battle there is no hope. Behind him the impassable stream cuts off retreat. Already from his brazen throat the cannon gives loud summons to the field. But the setting sun leaves yet a dreary night to brood over approaching ruin. The earth is shrouded in the veil of darkness; and now the illustrious Chief takes up his silent march, and in wide circuit leads his little band around the unwary foe. At the dawn, his military thunders tell them their reserve posted far in the rear, is in the pounces of the American Eagle. They hasten back to revenge; but he has already secured his advantage, and (by a well chosen position) confines them to inglorious repose. The armies now rest from their toil. But for him there is no rest. His followers claim the double right of returning to their homes, and he stands almost alone. He dares not ask for aid, lest the enemy, emboldened by the acknowledgment of weakness, should dissipate his shadow of an army. Nothing remains but to intimidate by the appearance of a force, which does not exist; and hide from his own troops their great inferiority. Both are effected by skill rarely equalled—never excelled.

Scarce hath the advancing season brought forward a few recruits when he begins offensive operations. His enemy foiled in each attempt to advance, is compelled to ask from the ocean some safer road to conquest. The propitious deep receives on his broad bosom the invading host, and bids his obedient billows bear them to some shore, where they may join the advantage of surprize with those of number, discipline, and appointments. The hope is vain! WASHINGTON had penetrated their views, and stands before them! He is unfortunate. Defeated, not subdued—he leads on again to new attack. The half-gained victory, snatched from his grasp, at the head of an inferior, twice beaten army, he passes the long winter in an open field, within one day's march of his foe.

Here he was doomed to new difficulties, and dangers unknown before. Faction had reared (in the American counsels) her *accursed* head, and laboured to remove him from the command. That measure would at once have disbanded his affectionate troops—the country around them was exhausted. He had no means to clothe or feed his army—none to change their position. Many perished—each day the numbers were alarmingly diminished, and reinforcement was dangerous, because it might encrease the famine. Under these circumstances, a new system of organization and discipline was to be formed, introduced, and enforced, while the soldier could seldom obtain even his poor pittance of depreciated paper.

> who then hath seen
> The gallant leader of that ruined band,
> Let him cry praise and glory on his head.[2]

It was in the solitary walk of night—it was in the bosom of friendship, that he could alone unburthen himself, of the vast woe which weighed

---

2. Morris adapts the opening chorus from act 4 of Shakespeare's *Henry V*:
> . . . O now, who will behold
> The royal captain of this ruined band
> Walking from watch to watch, from tent to tent,
> Let him cry "Praise and glory on his head!"

upon his heart—Here was indeed no common nor vulgar care. HONOUR—LIBERTY—His COUNTRY, stood on the dangerous margin of uncertain fate, and no human eye could pierce the dark cloud which hung upon futurity.

From this black night of gloomy apprehension, broke forth the sun of golden, glorious Hope! A mighty monarch had connected his fortunes with those of America—In her defence the flag of France was unfurled, and gratitude hailed the sixteenth Louis, protector of the rights of mankind. His powerful interference took off from what remained of the war, all reasonable doubt as to the final event. After a varied scene of adverse and prosperous circumstances, that event arrived, and a solemn treaty acknowledged your Independence.

Great was the joy and high the general expectation, for the political state of America was not duly considered. Her band of federal union had been woven by the hand of distrust. The different states had been held together, in no small degree, by the external pressure of war. That pressure removed, they might fall asunder. There existed various causes of discontent, which the intrigues of European policy might ripen into disgust. Those who shared in the public counsels were filled, therefore, with deep apprehension. The army, taught by years of painful experience, became a prey to sinister forebodings. Connected by the endearing ties of soldierly brotherhood, these gallant sons of freedom anticipated with horror the moment when they might be called on to unsheathe their swords against each other: and pour, in impious libation, the purest of their blood upon the altars of civil war. Some of the more ardent spirits, smarting from the past, and fearing for the future, had formed a wish, that the army might be kept together, and (by its appearance) accelerate the adoption of an efficient government. The sentiment was patriotic—the plan of doubtful complection—the success uncertain—but the prospect was fair if the CHIEF could be engaged.

He knew their wrongs! He knew their worth! He felt their apprehensions! They had strong claims upon him, and those claims were strongly urged. Supreme power, with meretricious charms, courted his embrace; and was clothed, to seduce him, in the robes of justice. If, therefore, ambition had possessed a single corner of his heart, he might have deliberated. But he was ever loyal. He bid a last adieu to the companions of his glory, and laid all his laurels at the feet of his country!

His fame was now complete, and it was permitted him to hope for ease in dignified retirement. Vain hope! The defects of the Federal compact are soon too deeply felt not to be generally acknowledged—America directs a revision by persons of her choice. He is their President. It is a question, previous to the first meeting, what course shall be pursued. Men of decided temper, who, devoted to the public, overlooked prudential considerations, thought a form of government should be framed entirely new. But cautious men, with whom popularity was an object, deemed it fit to consult and comply with the wishes of the people. AMERICANS! let the opinion then delivered by the greatest and best of men, be ever present to your remembrance. He was collected within himself. His countenance had more than usual solemnity. His eye was fixed, and seemed to look into futurity. "It is (said he) too probable that no plan we propose will be adopted. Perhaps another dreadful conflict is to be sustained. If to please the people, we offer what we ourselves disapprove, how can we afterwards defend our work? Let us raise a standard to which the wise and the honest can repair. The event is in the hand of God."[3] This was the patriot voice of WASHINGTON; and this the constant tenor of his conduct. With this deep sense of duty, he gave to our constitution his cordial assent; and has added the fame of a legislator to that of a hero.

AGAIN, in the shade of retirement, he seeks repose; but is called, by unanimous voice, to be the first magistrate of the United States. Scarce are the wheels of government in motion, when he is struck by the view of that enormous revolution which still torments and terrifies the earth. The flames of war were spread throughout Europe, and threatened to waste the globe. The delegated incendiaries found America filled with inflamable matter. All the bad passions, with some that were good, stimulated her to engage in the contest. But the President, still calm, discerning, and true to your truest interest, proclaimed, observed, and maintained an exact neutrality. In vain was he assailed from abroad—In vain solicited, excited, urged, by those around him. He stood immoveable! Vain also were the clamors of mistaken zeal, the dark efforts of insidious faction, and the foul voice of mercenary slander. You have all lately seen his firm administration, and all now enjoy the rich result of his inflexible wisdom.

Though he still turned with fond desire towards his domestic shade, he never left the helm during the fury of the storm; but remained till he had the well founded expectation that America might enjoy PEACE, FREEDOM, and SAFETY—and then at last he claims the right of age. A venerable veteran, in all honourable service, having consecrated to his country

3. This is apparently the only source for this quotation. See *The Records of the Federal Convention of 1787*, ed. Max Farrand, rev. ed. (New Haven: Yale University Press, 1911–87), 3:381.

the spirit of youth, the strength of manhood, and the ripe experience of laborious years, he asks repose. His body broken with toil must rest. No— He is called forth again—again must he gird on his sword and prepare for the battle! And see! fresh in renewed vigor, he decks his hoary head with nodding plumes of war, and mounts the barbed steed—With countenance erect and firm, his eagle eye measures the lengthened file. Wonderful man! he seems immortal—Oh no—No—No, this our pride, our glory, is gone— He is gone forever.

But yet his spirit liveth. Hail! happy shade—The broad shield of death is thrown before thy fame. Never shall the polluted breath of slander blow upon their ashes—We will watch with pious care the laurels which shade thy urn, and wear thy name engraven on our Hearts. Oh! yet protect thy country! Save her! She is an orphan—Her father is mingled with the dust.

No! HE LIVETH—HE SHALL LIVE FOREVER! And when the latest of your children's children, shall pronounce his dear, his sacred name, their eyes shall be suffused with the tear of GRATITUDE and LOVE.

23 ❧ Speeches in the Senate on the Repeal of the Judiciary Act of 1801

On April 3, 1800, Morris became a member of the U.S. Senate as a Federalist from New York. His Senate term lasted until March 3, 1803, and thus spanned the transition from Adams and the Federalists to Jefferson and the Democratic-Republicans—the first peaceful transfer of power between rival parties. But the transition had not been entirely free of bitterness. The Judiciary Act of 1801, passed in the lame duck session at the end of the Adams administration, was a particular irritant to the Jeffersonians. It had created a system of circuit courts with their own staff of judges, replacing the earlier practice of circuit courts composed of two Supreme Court justices and one District Court judge, a subject of much complaint by the justices. But the outgoing Adams administration had packed the new courts with Federalist judges—the "Midnight Judges" made famous by the case *Marbury* v. *Madison*. Repealing the Act thus became a legislative priority for the Jeffersonians when Congress reconvened in December 1801.

The repeal passed the Senate on February 3 by a 16–15 vote. The constitutionality of abolishing the circuit courts was later upheld by the Marshall Court in *Stuart* v. *Laird*, 5 U.S. 299 (1803).

Reprinted from Jared Sparks, *The Life of Gouverneur Morris, with Selections from his Correspondence and Miscellaneous Papers* (Boston: Gray & Bowen, 1832), 3:365–402. A partial draft of the second speech is in the Gouverneur Morris Papers, Rare Book and Manuscript Library, Columbia University, item 844. The speeches are also in *The Debates and Proceedings in the Congress of the United States*, 7th Cong. (Washington: Gales and Seaton, 1851), 36–41 and 76–92. The full text of the *Debates* is available from the Library of Congress website: http://memory.loc.gov/ammem/amlaw/lwac.html.

FIRST SPEECH ON THE JUDICIARY ESTABLISHMENT.

Delivered in the Senate of the United States, January 8th, 1802.

Mr. President,

I am so very unfortunate, that the arguments for repealing the law, to which this motion refers, have confirmed my opinion that it ought not to be repealed. The honorable mover[1] has thought fit to rest his proposition upon two grounds;

First, That the judiciary law, passed last session, is unnecessary and improper.

Secondly, That we have, by the Constitution, a right to repeal it; and, therefore, ought to exercise that right.

The numerical mode of argument he has made use of, to establish his first point, is perfectly novel, and, as such, it commands my tribute of admiration. This, indeed, is the first time I ever heard that the utility of Courts should be estimated by the number of suits, which they are called on to decide. I remember once to have read, that a justly celebrated monarch of England, the great Alfred, had enacted such laws, established such tribunals, and organized such a system of police, that a purse of gold might be hung upon the side of the highway, without any danger that it would be stolen. But, Sir, had the honorable gentleman from Kentucky existed in those days, he would, perhaps, have attempted to convince old Alfred, that he had been egregiously mistaken; and, that a circumstance, which he considered as the pride and glory of his reign, had arisen from its greatest defect and sorest evil. For, by assuming the unfrequency of crimes as the proof that tribunals were unnecessary, and thus boldly substituting the effect for the cause, the gentleman might have demonstrated the inutility of the institution, by the good which it had produced. Surely this kind of reasoning is, of all others, the most false and the most fallacious.

But, Sir, if with that poor measure of ability, which it has pleased God to give me, I march on the ground I have been accustomed to tread, and which experience has taught me to consider as solid, I would venture the assertion, that in so far as our judicial institutions may accelerate the perfor-

---

1. John Breckenridge of Kentucky (*Senate Journal*, January 6, 1802).

mance of duties, promote the cause of virtue, and prevent the perpetration of crimes, in that same degree ought they to be estimated and cherished. This, Sir, would be my humble mode of reasoning, but for the wonderful discovery made by the honorable mover of the resolution on your table.

To prove, that the law of last session was *improper*, as well as *unnecessary*, we have been told of the vast expense of our judiciary. We are referred to the *estimates*, which lie before us, for *proof* that it amounts to no less than the yearly sum of one hundred and thirty-seven thousand dollars. And then, attributing the whole expense to this particular law, it has been assumed in argument, that to repeal the law would operate a saving of one hundred and thirty-seven thousand dollars.

If, Sir, the data upon which the honorable member has founded his other arithmetical arguments are equally incorrect, the inferences drawn from them will merit but little attention. Of this whole sum, of one hundred and thirty-seven thousand dollars, (mentioned in the estimates of your Secretary of the Treasury) no less than forty-five thousand dollars are stated as the supposed contingent expense, to accrue for the attendance of jurors, witnesses, &c. From hence is fairly to be inferred the expectation, that much business will be actually done.

The expense, supposed to accrue from the law we are called on to repeal, is but thirty-two thousand dollars for salaries, and fifteen thousand for contingences, making together forty-seven thousand dollars. But let us not stint the argument. Let us make a generous allowance. Let us throw in a few thousands more, and take the amount at fifty-one thousand dollars. Let that sum be apportioned among the people of the United States, according to the census lately taken, and you will find, that the share of each individual is just one cent. Yet, for this paltry saving of a cent a man, we are called on to give up what is most valuable to a nation.

Undoubtedly, it is one great purpose of government to protect the people from foreign invasion, and to be in readiness for it a considerable armament may be necessary. The maintenance of naval and military force to protect our trade, and to guard our arsenals and magazines, will alone require much money; to provide which, you must raise a considerable revenue. That again will for the collection of it demand many officers, involving a still greater expense. All this must be paid, and yet all these provisions are for events uncertain. An invasion may, or may not, take place. Nay, if I may judge from certain documents, those who administer our affairs have little apprehension of such an event. I hope they may not be deceived. But, admitting that we have no danger to fear, or, which comes to the same thing, that we are properly secured against it; what else have the people a right to demand, in return for the whole sum expended in the support of government? They have a right to ask *that*, without which protection from invasion, nay government itself, is worse than useless. *They have a right to ask for the protection of law, well administered by proper tribunals, to secure the weak against the strong, the poor against the rich, the oppressed against the oppressor.* This, which involves but little expense, is all they ask for all their money. And is this little to be denied? Must the means by which the injured can obtain redress be curtailed and diminished, to save a poor and pitiful expense? You must pay largely to support but a small force, and much is to be feared from armies. They, indeed, may turn their swords against our bosoms. They may raise to empire some daring chief, and clothe him with despotic power. But what danger is to be apprehended from that army of judges, which the gentlemen have talked of? Is it so great, so imminent, that we must immediately turn to the right about the new corps, lately raised, of sixteen rank and file?

Gentlemen say that we must, and bid us recur to the ancient system. What is that system? Six judges of the Supreme Court, to ride the circuit of all America twice a year, and assemble twice a year at the seat of government. Without inquiring into the accuracy of a statement which the gentleman has made, respecting the Courts of England, (in which, however, he will find himself much mistaken) let me ask what will be the effect *here* of restoring that old system? Cast an eye over the extent of our country, see the distance to be travelled in making the circuits, and a moment's consideration will show, that if we resort to the old system, the first magistrate, in selecting a character for the bench, must seek less the learning of a judge, than the agility of a postboy. Can it be expected, is it possible, that men advanced in years, (for such alone have the maturity of judgment which befits that office) men educated in the closet, men, who from their habits of life must have more strength of mind than of body; is it, I say, possible, that such men can be continually running from one end of the continent to the other? Or if they could, can they find time also to hear, consider, and decide, on numerous and intricate causes? No, Sir, they cannot. I have been well assured by men of eminence on your bench, that they would not hold their offices under the old arrangement.

What is the present system? You have added seven district and sixteen circuit judges. These are fully competent to perform the business required, and the complaint is merely on the score of expense. No one has pretended that the business will not be done as speedily and as well. It is merely to save expense, therefore, that we are called on to repeal the law. But what will be the effect of this desired repeal? Will it not be a declaration to the remaining judges, that they hold their offices subject to your will, and during your pleasure? And what is the natural effect of that declaration? Is it not, that, dependent in this situation, they will lose the independent spirit essential to a due exercise of their authority? Thus, then, the check established by the Constitution, desired by the people, and necessary in every contemplation of common sense, will be destroyed. It has been said, and truly said, that governments are made to provide against the follies and vices of men. To suppose that governments rest upon reason, is a pitiful solecism, for if mankind were reasonable, they would want no government. From the same cause it arises, that checks are required in the distribution of power, among those to whom it is confided, and who are to use it for the benefit of the people. Here, then, let me ask, whether the people of America have vested all power uncontrolled in the National Legislature? Surely they have not. They have prescribed to it certain bounds, and in the natural supposition that these bounds might be transgressed, they have vested in the judges a check, which they supposed to be salutary and intended to be efficient. A check of the first necessity, because it may prevent an invasion of the Constitution by unconstitutional laws. And to secure the existence and the operation of this check, there is a provision highly important, whose object is to prevent any party or faction from intimidating or annihilating the tribunals themselves.

On this ground, then, I stand to arrest the victory meditated over the Constitution of my country. A victory meditated by those, who wish to prostrate that Constitution for the furtherance of their ambitious views. Not, Sir, the views of him who recommended, nor of those who now urge this measure (for on his uprightness, and on their uprightness I have full reliance,) but of those who are in the back ground, and who have further and higher objects. To them our national compact forms an insurmountable barrier. Those troops, therefore, which protect the outworks of the Constitution are to be first dismissed; those posts, which present the most formidable defence, are first to be carried; and then the Constitution becomes an easy prey.

Let us consider, therefore, whether we have constitutionally the power to repeal this law. And to this effect, let us hear the language of the Constitution. "The judicial power of the United States shall be vested in one

Supreme Court, and in such inferior Courts as the Congress may from time to time ordain and establish. The judges, both of the supreme and inferior Courts, shall hold their offices during good behavior, and shall at stated times receive for their services a compensation, which *shall not be diminished* during their continuance in office." On this, Sir, I have heard a verbal criticism, about the words *shall* and *may*, which appears to me wholly irrelevant. And it is the more unnecessary, as the same word, *shall*, is applied to the provisions contained in both members of the section. It says, "The judicial power *shall* be vested in one Supreme Court, and in such inferior Courts as the Congress *may, from time to time*, ordain and establish." The Legislature have, therefore, the undoubted right to determine what inferior Courts they will establish; but, when once *established*, a part of the judicial power *shall* vest in them. The words are imperative, and so they are as to the tenure of the office, which the Legislature in the exercise of this discretionary power may have created. The judges, it says, *shall hold their offices during good behavior.* Thus, upon the establishment of the tribunal, the Constitution has declared, that the judicial power shall vest and the office be held during good behavior. The second member of the section is equally imperative. It declares, that they *shall* receive a compensation, which *shall not be diminished* during their continuance in office.

Whether we consider, therefore, the tenure of office or the quantum of compensation, the language is equally clear and conclusive. After this simple exposition, gentlemen are welcome to every advantage they can derive from a criticism upon *shall* and *may*.

Another criticism has been made, which, but for its serious effects, I would call pleasant. The amount of it is, you shall not take the man from the office, but you may take the office from the man; you shall not throw him overboard, but you may sink his boat under him; you shall not put him to death, but you may take away his life. The Constitution secures to a judge his office, says he shall hold it, (that is, it shall not be taken from him) during good behavior; the Legislature shall not diminish, though their bounty may increase his salary; thus, the Constitution has made all possible provision for the inviolability of his tenure, as far as the power of language can extend; and, if not, I call on gentlemen to show the contrary, by giving us words more clear, more precise, more definite. If, after the strong positive expressions, any negative terms had been added, would it not have been improper? If the framers of the Constitution had said, the judges *shall hold* their offices, which *shall not be taken away*, would not this have been ridiculous? Would it not have almost amounted to what, in vulgar language, is called a bull?[2] Would it not have been inconsistent with the gravity of style proper for such an important and serious subject? Let us, I repeat it, Sir, be favored with the words, if any words can be used, more positive, more inhibitory, more peremptory, than those contained in this instrument. And is it not a mere contradiction in terms to say, we may *destroy* an office which we cannot *take away?* Will not the destruction of the office as effectually destroy the tenure, as the grant to another person?

But, we are asked if these laws are immutable. Unquestionably, Sir, the legislature have a right to alter, change, and modify, and amend, the laws which relate to the judiciary, so as may best comport with the interest, peace, and happiness, of the people. This right, however, is confined by the limitations which the Constitution prescribes. Neither the legislative nor the executive powers, nor both, can remove a judge from office during his good behavior. There is no power anywhere competent to this purpose; (saving always the right of a conqueror, for that is a power not derived from, but subversive of the Constitution;) and yet, it is contended, that by the repeal of the law, that office, from which he cannot be removed, may be destroyed. Is not this absurd?

But to prove it, we have been told, that whatever one legislature can do another can undo; that no legislature can bind its successor, and that a right to make involves a right to destroy. All this I deny on the ground of reason, and on the ground of the Constitution. What! can a man rightfully destroy his own children? When the legislature have created by law a political existence, can they by repealing the law dissolve the corporation they had made? You say you can undo whatever your predecessors have done. Your predecessors have borrowed money at high interest; can you now reduce that interest? They have funded the national debt; have you now a right to abolish that debt? Under a pressure of necessity, you have given an usurious consideration of eight per cent to obtain money; can you now, because it is onerous, annihilate that contract? When by your laws you have given to any individual the right to make a road or a bridge, and to take a toll, can you by a subsequent law take it away?[3] No; when you make a compact you

2. A ludicrous jest, or a statement containing a ludicrous inconsistency (*Oxford English Dictionary*).

3. This was the essence of the position taken by the Marshall Court in *Fletcher* v. *Peck* (1810) and the *Dartmouth College Case* (1819), holding in both cases that subse-

are bound by it. When you make a promise you must perform it. Establish the contrary doctrine, and mark what follows. The whim of the moment becomes the law of the land. You declare to the world that you are no longer to be trusted, that there is no safety, no security, in America. You erect a beacon, to warn all men of property that they do not approach your shores. Honest men will avoid you. They will fly from you. They will consider you as a den of robbers. How can you ask any one to put confidence in you, when you are the first to violate your own contracts? The position, therefore, that the legislature may *rightfully* repeal every law made by a preceding legislature is untrue, when tested merely by reason. Still more untrue is it, when compared with the precepts of the Constitution. The national legislature of America does not possess unlimited power, it has no pretence to omnipotence. It is restrained by the Constitution. And what does the Constitution say? "You shall make no *ex post facto* law." Is not this an *ex post facto* law.[4]

Gentlemen, to show that we may properly repeal the law of last session, tell us it is *mere theory*. For argument's sake it shall be granted. What then is the language of reason? Try it. Put it to the test of experience, after two or three years shall point out defects, or if they can now be pointed out, amend the law. What respect can the people have for a legislature, that hastily and without reflection meets but to undo the acts of its predecessor? Is it prudent, is it decent, even if the law were improper, thus to commit our reputation and theirs? Is it wise, nay, is it not highly dangerous to make this call on the people to decide which of us are fools? One of us must be.

Such, Sir, will be the effect of this hasty repeal on the public mind. What will it be on the injured man, who seeks redress in your Courts, and whom you have thus deprived of his right? You have saved him a miserable cent, at the price perhaps of his utter ruin.

The honorable mover of this resolution, Sir, in persuading us to adopt it, has told us not only what is, but what is to be.

He has told us that suits have decreased, and that they will decrease. Nay, relying on the strength of his preconceptions, he tells us, that the internal taxes will be repealed, and grounds the expediency of repealing the judi-

---

quent legislatures could not alter the terms of contracts agreed to by their predecessors. The Court later moved away from this interpretation, beginning with *Charles River Bridge* v. *Warren Bridge* (1837).

4. In *Calder* v. *Bull* (1798), the Supreme Court had held that the *ex post facto* clause of Article I, Section 10 (which applies to the states) extended only to criminal law.

ciary law upon the annihilation of those taxes. Thus, taking for granted the nonexistence of taxes which still exist, he has inferred from their destruction, and the consequent cessation of suits, the inutility of the judiciary establishment. And when he shall have carried his present point, and broken down that system, he will tell us perhaps, that we may as well abolish the internal taxes, for that we have no judges to enforce the collection.

But what, I ask, is to be the effect of these repeals, and of all these dismissions from office? I impeach not the motives of gentlemen, who advocate this measure. In my heart, I believe them to be upright. But they see not the consequences. We are told, that the States want and ought to have more power. We are told, that they are the legitimate guardians, from whom the citizen is to derive protection. *Their* judges are, I suppose, to execute *our* laws. Judges appointed by State authority, supported by State salary, looking for promotion to State influence, and dependent on State party. Are those the judges contemplated by this Constitution? There are some honorable gentlemen now present, who sat in the Convention when it was formed. I appeal to their recollection. Have they not seen the time, when the state of America was suspended by a hair? My life for it, if another be assembled they will part without doing anything. Never in the flow of time was there a moment so propitious, as that in which the Convention assembled. The States had been convinced, by melancholy experience, how inadequate they were to the management of our national concerns. The passions of the people were lulled to sleep. State pride slumbered. No sooner was the Constitution promulgated than it awoke. Opposition was formed. It was active and vigorous, but it was vain. The people of America bound the States down by this compact.

There was in it a provision tending to exhibit the sublimest spectacle of which my mind can form an idea. It was that of a great State, kneeling at the altar of justice, and sacrificing its pride to a sense of right. I flattered myself, that America would behold this spectacle, but that important provision has been repealed.[5] It gave way to the opposition of the States. It is gone. Another great bulwark is now to be removed, and you are told, that we must look to the States for protection. Your internal revenues are also to be swept away, so that no evidence, no exertion, no trace of the national

---

5. The Eleventh Amendment, ratified in 1795, overturned the Supreme Court's ruling in *Chisholm v. Georgia* (1793). The Court had ruled that the Constitution permitted federal courts to hear lawsuits against states by citizens of other states. The amendment withdrew the federal courts' jurisdiction over such cases.

power is to be perceived through the whole interior of America. And in order that it may be confined to your coasts, and be known there only at particular points, your sole reliance for revenue is henceforth to be placed upon commercial duties. In this reliance you will be deceived. But what is to be the effect of all these changes? I am afraid to say; I will leave it to the feelings, and to the consciences of gentlemen. But remember, the moment this union is dissolved, we shall no longer be governed by votes.

Examine the annals of history. Look into the records of time. See what has been the ruin of every Republic. The vile love of *popularity*. Why are we here? We are here to save the people from their most dangerous enemy, *to save them from themselves*. What caused the ruin of the Republics of Greece and of Rome? Demagogues, who by flattery prevailed on the populace to establish despotism. But if you will shut your eyes to the light of history, and your ears to the voice of experience, see, at least, what has happened in your own times. In 1789 it was no longer a doubt with enlightened statesmen, what would be the event of the French revolution. Before the first day of January, 1790, the only question was, who will become the despot. The word liberty, indeed, from that day to this, has been continually sounded and resounded, but the thing had no existence. There is nothing left but the word.

We are now about to violate our Constitution. Once touch it with unhallowed hands, sacrifice one of its important provisions, and we are gone. We commit the fate of America to the mercy of time and chance.

I hope the honorable gentleman from Maryland[6] will pardon me, if, from the section of the law he has cited, I deduce an inference diametrically opposite to that, for which he has contended. He has told us, that the last Congress, in reducing the judges of the Supreme Court from six to five, have exercised the right which is now questioned, and made thereby a legislative construction of this clause in the Constitution, favorable to the motion on your table. But look at the law. It declares that the reduction shall not take place, until, by death or resignation, there shall remain only five. Thus, in the very moment when they express *their opinion* that five judges are sufficient, they acknowledge *their incapacity* to remove the sixth. The legislative construction, therefore, is, that they have *not* the right which is now pretended.

The same honorable member has cited other cases from the same law,

6. Senator Robert Wright.

which if I understood his statement, amount to this, that Congress have increased the number of district judges; but surely this cannot prove, that we have a right to diminish the number. It will I think appear, Sir, that this law, so much complained of, is in no wise chargeable with maintaining the dangerous doctrine to be established by its repeal.

The whole argument in favor of the motion comes to this simple proposition, *let us get rid of these judges to save expense.* We can *repeal* the law, because we *made* the law; we have the *power,* let us *exercise* it. But, let me ask, Sir, if this argument will not go to prove anything. Will it not go to the abolition of the debts incurred by the last Congress? Shall it be said, that the cases differ because the debt results from a contract with the creditor sanctioned by the legislature? Sir, you have made a contract with the judges, sanctioned by higher authority. You indeed created the office, but when created, the Constitution fixed its duration. The first magistrate in our country, with this Constitution in his hand, applies to men of high character and great ability. He asks them to quit a lucrative and honorable profession, to abandon their former pursuits, to break their ancient connexions, and give their time, their talents, and their virtues, to the service of their country. What does he offer as a compensation? He offers a high and honorable office, to be holden by no capricious will, to depend on no precarious favor. The duration is to be terminated only by death or misconduct. The legislature has affixed a salary, which they may increase, but cannot diminish. Upon these proffered terms, the judge accepts. The contract is then complete. A contract which rests no longer on the legislative will. He is immediately under the protection of the Constitution itself, which neither the President nor the legislature can defeat. His authority rests on the same foundation with yours. It is derived from the same source. Will you pretend, that you are bound by your contract with him, who lent you money at eight per cent interest, and that you are not bound by your contract with him, who devotes his life to your service! Will you say that the consideration you have received is to make a difference, and that paltry pelf is to be preferred to manly worth? Is *that* to be respected, and *this* despised? Surely, Sir, the contract with a judge is, of all others, the most solemn. It is sanctioned by the highest of all authority. Can you then violate it? If you can, you may throw this Constitution into the flames. It is gone — It is dead.

SECOND SPEECH ON THE JUDICIARY ESTABLISHMENT.

Mr. President,

I had fostered the hope that some gentleman, who thinks with me, would have taken upon himself the task of replying to the observations made yesterday and this morning, in favor of the motion on your table. But since no gentleman has gone so fully into the subject as it seems to require, I am compelled to request your attention.

We were told yesterday by the honorable member from Virginia,[7] that our objections were calculated for the bystanders, and made with a view to produce effect upon the people at large. I know not for whom this charge is intended. I certainly recollect no such observations. As I was personally charged with making a play upon words, it may have been intended for me. But surely, Sir, it will be recollected that I declined that paltry game, and declared that I considered the verbal criticism which had been relied on as irrelevant. If I can recollect what I said, from recollecting well what I thought and meant to say, sure I am, that I uttered nothing in the style of an appeal to the people. I hope no member of this House has so poor a sense of its dignity, as to make such an appeal. As to myself, it is now near thirty years since I was called into public office. During that period, I have frequently been the servant of the people, always their friend; but at no one moment of my life their flatterer, and God forbid that I ever should be. When the honorable gentleman considers the course we have taken, he must see that the observation he has thus pointed can light on no object. I trust, that it did not flow from a consciousness of his own intentions. He, I hope, had no view of this sort. If he had, he was much, very much mistaken. Had he looked around upon those, who honor us with their attendance, he would have seen that the splendid flashes of his wit excited no approbatory smile. The countenances of those, by whom we were surrounded, presented a different spectacle. They were impressed with the dignity of this House; they perceived in it the dignity of the American people, and felt with high and manly sentiment their own participation.

---

7. Senator Stevens T. Mason.

We have been told, Sir, by the honorable gentleman from Virginia, that there is no independent part of this government; that in popular governments, the force of every department, as well as the government itself, must depend upon popular opinion. And the honorable member from North Carolina[8] has informed us, that there is no check for the overbearing powers of the legislature, but public opinion; and he has been pleased to notice a sentiment I had uttered. A sentiment which not only fell from my lips, but which flowed from my heart. It has, however, been *misunderstood* and *misapplied*. After reminding the House of the dangers to which popular governments are exposed, from the influence of designing demagogues upon popular passion, I took the liberty to say, that *we*, we the Senate of the United States, are assembled here "to save the people from their most dangerous enemy, to save them from themselves"; to guard them against the baneful effects of their own precipitation, their passion, their misguided zeal. It is for these purposes that all our Constitutional checks are devised. If this be not the language of the Constitution, the Constitution is all nonsense. For why are the Senators chosen by communities, and the Representatives directly by the people? Why are the one chosen for a longer term than the other? Why give one branch of the legislature a negative upon the acts of the other? Why give the President a right to arrest the proceedings of both, till two thirds of each should concur? Why all these multiplied precautions, unless to check and control that impetuous spirit, that headlong torrent of opinion, which has swept away every popular government that ever existed?

With most respectful attention, I heard the declaration of the gentleman from Virginia of his own sentiment. "Whatever," said he, "may be my opinion of the Constitution, I hold myself bound to respect it." He disdained, Sir, to profess an affection he did not feel, and I accept his candor as a pledge for the performance of his duty. But he will admit this necessary inference from that frank confession, that although he will struggle against his inclination, to support the Constitution, even to the last moment, yet, when in spite of all his efforts it shall fall, he will rejoice in its destruction. Far different are my feelings. It is possible, that we are both prejudiced, and that in taking the ground on which we respectively stand, our judgments are influenced by the sentiments which glow in our hearts. I, Sir, wish to support this Constitution, because I love it. And I love it, because I consider it as the bond of our union; because, in my soul, I believe, that on it

8. Senator David Stone.

depends our harmony and our peace; that without it, we should soon be plunged in all the horrors of civil war; that this country would be deluged with the blood of its inhabitants, and a brother's hand be raised against the bosom of a brother.

After these preliminary remarks, I hope I shall be indulged, while I consider the subject in reference to the two points, which have been taken, the *expediency* and the *constitutionality* of the repeal.

In considering the *expediency*, I hope I shall be pardoned for asking your attention to some parts of the Constitution, which have not yet been dwelt upon, and which tend to elucidate this part of our inquiry. I agree fully with the gentleman, that every sentence, every section and every word of the Constitution ought to be deliberately weighed and examined; nay, I am content to go along with him, and give its due value and importance to every stop and comma. In the beginning we find a declaration of the motives, which induced the American people to bind themselves by this compact. And in the foreground of that declaration, we find these objects specified; *to form a more perfect union, to establish justice, and to insure domestic tranquillity.* But how are these objects effected? The people intended *to establish justice.* What provision have they made to fulfil that intention? After pointing out the Courts which should be established, the second section of the third article informs us,

> The judicial power shall extend to all cases, in law and equity, arising under this Constitution, the laws of the United States, and treaties made, or which shall be made, under their authority; to all cases affecting Ambassadors, other public Ministers and Consuls; to all cases of admiralty and maritime jurisdiction; to controversies to which the United States shall be a party; to controversies between two or more States, between a State and citizens of another State, between citizens of different States, between citizens of the same State, claiming lands under grants of different States, and between a State, or the citizens thereof and foreign States, citizens or subjects.
>
> In all cases affecting Ambassadors, other public Ministers and Consuls, and those in which a State shall be a party, the Supreme Court shall have original jurisdiction. In all the other cases before mentioned, the Supreme Court shall have appellate jurisdiction, both as to law and fact, with such exceptions, and under such regulations, as the Congress shall make.

Thus then we find, that the judicial power *shall* extend to a great variety of cases, but that the Supreme Court shall have only *appellate* jurisdiction in all admiralty and maritime cases, in all controversies between the United States and private citizens, between citizens of different States, between citizens of the same State claiming lands under different States, and between a citizen of the United States and foreign States, citizens or subjects. The honorable gentleman from Kentucky, who made the motion on your table, has told us, that the Constitution in its judiciary provisions contemplated only those cases, which could *not* be tried in the State Courts. But he will, I hope, pardon me when I contend, that the Constitution did not merely contemplate, but did by express words reserve to the national tribunals a right to decide, and did secure to the citizens of America a right to demand their decision in many cases, evidently cognizable in the State Courts.

And what are these cases? They are those in respect to which it is by the Constitution presumed, that the State Courts would not always make a cool and calm investigation, a fair and just decision. To form, therefore, a more perfect union, and to insure domestic tranquillity, the Constitution has said, there shall be Courts of the Union to try causes, by the wrongful decision of which the Union might be endangered, or domestic tranquillity be disturbed. And what courts? Look again at the cases designated. The Supreme Court has no *original* jurisdiction. The Constitution has said that the judicial powers shall be vested in the *Supreme* and *Inferior* Courts. It has declared that the judicial powers so vested shall extend to the cases mentioned, and that the Supreme Court shall *not* have *original* jurisdiction in those cases. Evidently, therefore, it has declared that they shall, in the first instance, be tried by *Inferior* Courts, with appeal to the *Supreme Court*. This, therefore, amounts to a declaration that the *Inferior* Courts *shall* exist. Since without them the citizen is deprived of those rights for which he stipulated, or rather those rights verbally granted, would be actually withheld; and that great security of our Union, that necessary guard of our tranquillity, be completely paralyzed, if not destroyed. In declaring, then, that these tribunals *shall exist*, it equally declares, that the Congress *shall* ordain and establish them. I say they *shall*; this is the evident intention, if not the express words, of the Constitution. The Convention in framing, the American people in adopting that compact, did not, could not presume that the Congress would omit to do, what they were thus bound to do. They could not presume, that the legislature would hesitate one moment, in establishing the organs necessary to carry into effect those wholesome, those important provisions.

The honorable member from Virginia has given us a history of the judicial system, and in the course of it has told us, that the judges of the Supreme Court knew, when they accepted their offices, the duties they were to perform and the salaries they were to receive. He thence infers, that if again called on to do the same duties, they have no right to complain. Agreed. But that is not the question between us. Admitting that they have made a hard bargain, and that we may hold them to a strict performance, is it wise to exact their compliance to the injury of our constituents? We are urged to go back to the old system; but let us first examine the effects of that system. The judges of the Supreme Court rode the circuits, and two of them with the assistance of a district judge held circuit Courts, and tried causes. *As a Supreme Court* they have in most cases only an appellate jurisdiction. In the first instance, therefore, they tried a cause sitting *as an Inferior Court,* and then on appeal tried it over again *as a Supreme Court.* Thus then, the appeal was from the sentence of the judges to the judges themselves. But say, that to avoid this impropriety, you will incapacitate the two judges, who sat on the circuit, from sitting in the Supreme Court, to review their own decrees. Strike them off, and suppose either the same or a contrary decision to have been made on another circuit, by two of their brethren in a similar case. For the same reason you strike *them* off, and then you have no Court left. Is this wise? Is it safe? You place yourself in a situation, where your citizens must be deprived of the advantage given to them of a Court of Appeals, or else run the greatest risk, that the decision of the first court will carry with it that of the others.

The same honorable member has given us a history of the law passed the last session, which he wishes now to repeal. That history is accurate, at least in one important part of it. I believe, that all amendments were rejected, *pertinaciously* rejected; and I acknowledge, that I joined heartily in that rejection. It was for the clearest reason on earth. We all perfectly understood, that to *amend* the bill was to *destroy* it. That if ever it got back to the other House it would perish. Those, therefore, who approved of the general provisions of that bill were determined to adopt it. We sought the practicable good, and would not, in pursuit of unattainable perfection, sacrifice that good to the pride of opinion. We took the bill, therefore, with its imperfections, convinced that when it was once passed into a law it might be easily amended.

We are now told that this procedure was improper, nay, that it was indecent. That public opinion had declared itself against us. That a majority holding different opinions was already chosen to the other House; and that a similar majority was expected for that in which we sit. Mr. President, are we then to understand, that opposition to the majority in the two Houses of Congress is improper, is indecent? If so, what are we to think of those gentlemen, who not only with proper and decent, but with laudable motives, (for such is their claim) so long, so perseveringly, so pertinaciously, opposed that voice of the people, which had so repeatedly, and for so many years, declared itself against them through the organ of their Representatives? Was this indecent in them? If not, how could it be improper for us to seize the only moment, which was left for the then majority to do what they deemed a necessary act? Let me again refer to those imperious demands of the Constitution, which called on us to establish Inferior Courts. Let me remind gentlemen of their assertion on this floor, that centuries might elapse before any judicial system could be established with general consent. And then let me ask, being thus impressed with a sense of the duty, and the difficulty of performing that arduous task, was it not wise to seize the auspicious moment?

Among the many stigmas affixed to this law, we have been told that the President, in selecting men to fill the offices which it created, made vacancies and filled them from the floor of this House. And that, but for the influence of this circumstance, a majority in favor of it could not have been found. Let us examine this suggestion. It is grounded on the supposition of corrupt influence derived from a hope, founded on two remote and successive contingences. First, the vacancy might or might not exist; for it depended as well on the acceptance of another, as on the President's grant; and secondly, that the President might or might not fill it with a member of this House. Yet on this vague conjecture, on this unstable ground, it is inferred, that men in high confidence violated their duty. It is hard to determine the influence of self-interest on the heart of man. I shall not, therefore, make the attempt. In the present case it is possible, that the imputation may be just; but I hope not, I believe not. At any rate, gentlemen will agree with me, that the calculation is uncertain and the conjecture vague.

But let it now for argument's sake be admitted, saving always the reputation of honorable men, who are not here to defend themselves. Let it, I say, for argument's sake be admitted, that the gentlemen alluded to acted under the influence of improper motives. What then? Is a law, that has received the varied assent required by the Constitution, and is clothed with all the needful formalities, thereby invalidated? Can you impair its force by impeaching the motives of any member who voted for it? Does it follow, that a law is bad because all those, who concurred in it, cannot give good reasons for their votes? Is it not before us? Must we not judge of it by its intrinsic merit? Is it a fair argument, addressed to our understanding, to say we must repeal a law, even a good one, if the enacting of it may have been effected in any degree by improper motives? Or is the judgment of this House so feeble, that it may not be trusted?

Gentlemen tell us, however, that the law is materially defective, nay, that it is unconstitutional. What follows? Gentlemen bid us repeal it. But is this just reasoning? If the law be only defective, why not amend? And if unconstitutional, why repeal? In this case no repeal can be necessary; the law is in itself void; it is a mere dead letter.

To show that it is unconstitutional, a particular clause is pointed out, and an inference is made, as in the case of goods, where, because there is one contraband article on board, the whole cargo is forfeited. Admit for a moment, that the part alluded to were unconstitutional, this would in no wise affect the remainder. That part would be void; or if you think proper, you can repeal that part.

Let us, however, examine the clause objected to on the ground of the Constitution. It is said, that by this law the *district* judges in Tennessee and Kentucky are removed from office, by making them *circuit judges*. And again, that you have by law appointed two new offices, those of *circuit judges*, and filled them by law, instead of pursuing the modes of appointment prescribed by the Constitution. To prove all this, the gentleman from Virginia did us the favor to read those parts of the law which he condemns; and if I can trust to my memory, it is clear from what he read, that the law does not remove these *district judges*, neither does it appoint them to the office of *circuit judges*. It does indeed put down the *district courts*; but is so far from destroying the offices of district judges, that it declares the persons filling those offices shall perform the duty of holding the *circuit courts*. And so far is it from appointing *circuit judges*, that it declares the *circuit courts* shall be held by the *district judges*.

But gentlemen contend, that to discontinue the district Courts was in effect to remove the district judges. This, Sir, is so far from being a just inference from the law, that the direct contrary follows as a necessary result; for it is on the principle that these judges continue in office after their Courts are discontinued, that the new duty of holding other Courts is assigned to them. But gentlemen say, this doctrine militates with the principles we contend for. Surely not. It must be recollected, Sir, that we have repeatedly admitted the right of the Legislature to change, alter, modify, and amend the judiciary system, so as best to promote the interests of the people. We only contend, that you shall not exceed or contravene the authority by which you act. But, say gentlemen, you forced this new office on the district judges, and this is in effect a new appointment. I answer, that the question can only arise on the refusal of those judges to act. But is it unconstitutional to assign new duties to officers already existing? I fear, that if this construction be adopted, our labors will speedily end; for we shall be so shackled, that we cannot move. What is the practice? Do we not every day call upon particular officers to perform duties, not previously assigned to, nor required of them? And must the executive in every such case make a new appointment?

But, as a farther reason to restore, by repealing this law, the old system, an honorable member from North Carolina has told us, that the judges of the Supreme Court should attend in the States, to acquire a competent knowledge of local institutions, and for this purpose should continue to ride the circuits. I believe there is great use in sending young men to travel; it tends to enlarge their views, and give them more liberal ideas, than they might otherwise possess. Nay, if they reside long enough in foreign countries, they may become acquainted with the manners of the people, and acquire some knowledge of their civil institutions. But I am not quite convinced, that riding rapidly from one end of this country to the other is the best way to study law. I am inclined to believe, that knowledge may be more conveniently acquired in the closet, than upon the high road. It is, moreover, to be presumed, that the first magistrate would, in selecting persons to fill these offices, take the best characters from the different parts of the country, who already possess the needful acquirements. But admitting that the President should not duly exercise in this respect his discretionary powers, and admitting that the ideas of the gentleman are correct, how wretched must be our condition! These, our judges, when called on to exercise their functions, would but begin to learn their trade, and that too at a period of life, when the intellectual powers with no great facility can acquire new ideas. We must, therefore, have a double set of judges. One set of apprentice judges to ride circuits and learn, the other set of master judges to hold Courts and decide controversies.

We are told, Sir, that the repeal asked for is important, in that it may establish a precedent; for that it is not merely a question on the propriety of disbanding a corps of sixteen rank and file, but that provisions may hereafter be made, not for sixteen, but for sixteen hundred, or sixteen thousand judges, and that it may become necessary to turn *them* to the right about. Mr. President, I will not, I cannot presume, that any such provision will ever be made, and therefore I cannot conceive any such necessity; I will not suppose, for I cannot suppose, that any party or faction will ever do anything so wild, so extravagant. But I will ask, how does this strange supposition consist with the doctrine of gentlemen, that public opinion is a sufficient check on the legislature, and a sufficient safeguard to the people. Put the case to its consequences, and what becomes of the check? Will gentlemen say it is to be found in the force of this wise precedent? Is this to control succeeding rulers in their wild and mad career? But how? Is the creation of judicial officers the only thing committed to their discretion? Have they not, according to the doctrine contended for, our all at their disposition, with no other check than public opinion, which, according to the supposition, will not prevent them from committing the greatest follies and absurdities? Take then all the gentleman's ideas, and compare them together, it will result that here is an inestimable treasure put into the hands of drunkards, madmen, and fools.

But away with all these derogatory suppositions. The legislature may be trusted. Our government is a system of salutary checks. One legislative branch is a check on the other. And should the violence of party spirit bear both of them away, the President, an officer high in honor, high in the public confidence, charged with weighty concerns, responsible to his own reputation, and to the world, stands ready to arrest their too impetuous course. This is our system. It makes no mad appeal to every mob in the country. It appeals to the sober sense of men selected from their fellow citizens for their talents, for their virtue—of men in advanced life, and of matured judgment. It appeals to their understanding, to their integrity, to their honor, to their love of fame, to their sense of shame. If all these checks should prove insufficient, and alas! such is the condition of human nature, that I fear they will not always be sufficient, the Constitution has given us one more. It has given us an independent judiciary. We have been told, that the executive authority carries your laws into execution. But let us not be the dupes of sound. The executive magistrate commands indeed your fleets and armies; and duties, imposts, excises, and all other taxes are collected, and all expenditures are made by officers whom he has appointed. So far indeed he executes your laws. But these his acts apply not often to individual concerns. In those cases, so important to the peace and happiness of society, the execution of your laws is confided to your judges. And *therefore* are they rendered independent. Before, then, you violate that independence, pause. There are State sovereignties, as well as the sovereignties of general government. There are cases, too many cases, in which the interest of one is not considered as the interest of the other. Should these conflict, if the judiciary be gone, the question is no longer of law, but of force. This is a state of things, which no honest and wise man can view without horror.

Suppose, in the omnipotence of your legislative authority, you trench upon the rights of your fellow citizens, by passing an unconstitutional law; if the judiciary department preserve its vigor, it will stop you short. Instead of a resort to arms, there will be a happier appeal to argument. Suppose a case still more impressive. The President is at the head of your armies. Let one of his generals, flushed with victory, and proud in command, presume to trample on the rights of your most insignificant citizen. Indignant of the wrong, he will demand the protection of your tribunals; and, safe in the shadow of their wings, will laugh his oppressor to scorn.

Having now, I believe, examined all the arguments adduced to show the expediency of this motion, and which, fairly sifted, reduce themselves at last to these two things—restore the ancient system, and save the additional expense—before I close what I have to say on this ground, I hope I shall be pardoned for saying one or two words about the expense. I hope, also, that notwithstanding the epithets which may be applied to my arithmetic, I shall be pardoned for using that which I learnt at school. It may have deceived me when it taught that two and two make four. But, though it should now be branded with opprobrious terms, I must still believe, that two and two do still make four. Gentlemen of newer theories, and of higher attainments, while they smile at my inferiority, must bear with my infirmities and take me as I am.

In all this great system of saving, in all this ostentatious economy, this rage of reform, how happens it that the eagle eye has not yet been turned to the mint? That no one piercing glance has been able to behold the expenditures of that department? I am far from wishing to overturn it. Though it be not of great necessity, nor even of substantial importance; though it be but a splendid trapping of your government; yet, as it may, by impressing on your current coin the emblems of your sovereignty, have some tendency to encourage a national spirit, and to foster the national pride, I am willing to contribute my share to its support. Yes, Sir, I would foster the national pride. I cannot indeed approve of national vanity, nor feed it with vile adulation. But I would gladly cherish the lofty sentiment of national pride. I would wish my countrymen to feel like Romans, to be as proud as Englishmen, and, going still further, I would wish them to veil their pride in the well bred modesty of French politeness. But, can this establishment, the mere decoration of your political edifice, can it be compared with the massy columns on which rest your peace and safety? Shall the striking of a few halfpence be put into a parallel with the distribution of justice? I find, Sir, from the estimates on your table, that the salaries of the officers of your mint amount to 10,600 dollars, and that the expenses are estimated at 10,900; making 21,500 dollars.

I find, that the actual expenditure of the last year, exclusive of salaries, amounted to   25,154 44
   Add the salaries,   10,600
   We have a total of, $35,754 44
A sum which exceeds the salary of these sixteen judges.

I find, further, that during the last year they have coined cents and half cents to the amount of 10,473 dollars and 29 cents. Thus, their copper coinage falls a little short of what it costs us for their salaries. We have, however, from this establishment about a million of cents, one to each family in America. A little emblematic medal, to be hung over their chimney pieces; and this is all their compensation for all that expense. Yet, not a word has been said about the *mint;* while the judges, whose services are so much greater, and of so much more importance to the community, are to be struck off at a blow, in order to save an expense, which, compared with the object, is pitiful. What conclusion, then, are we to draw from this predilection?

I will not pretend to assign to gentlemen the motives, by which they may be influenced; but if I should permit myself to make the inquiry, the style of many observations, and more especially the manner, the warmth, the irritability, which have been exhibited on this occasion, would lead to a solution of the problem. I had the honor, Sir, when I addressed you the other day to observe, that I believed the universe could not afford a spectacle more sublime, than the view of a powerful State kneeling at the altar of justice, and sacrificing there her passion and her pride; that I once fostered the hope of beholding that spectacle of magnanimity in America. And now, what a world of figures has the gentleman from Virginia formed on his misapprehension of that remark. I never expressed anything like exultation at the idea of a State, ignominiously dragged in triumph at the heels of your judges. But, permit me to say, the gentleman's exquisite sensibility on that subject, his alarm and apprehension, all show his strong attachment to State authority. Far be it from me, however, to charge the gentleman with improper motives. I know that his emotions arise from one of those imperfections in our nature, which we cannot remedy. They are excited by causes, which have naturally made him hostile to this Constitution, though his duty compels him, reluctantly, to support it. I hope, however, that those gentlemen, who entertain different sentiments, and who are less irritable on the score of State dignity, will think it essential to preserve a Constitution, without which the independent existence of the States themselves will be but of short duration.

This, Sir, leads me to the second object I had proposed. I shall, therefore, pray your indulgence while I consider how far this measure is *constitutional*.

I have not been able to discover the expediency, but will now, for argument's sake, admit it; and here, I cannot but express my deep regret for the situation of an honorable member from North Carolina. Tied fast as he is, by his instructions, arguments however forcible can never be effectual. I ought, therefore, to wish for his sake, that his mind may not be convinced by anything I shall say; for hard indeed would be his condition, to be bound by the contrariant obligations of an order and an oath. I cannot, however but express my profound respect for the talents of those who gave him his instructions, and who, sitting at a distance, without hearing the arguments, could better understand the subject than their Senator on this floor after full discussion.

The honorable member from Virginia has repeated the distinction, before taken, between the supreme and the inferior tribunals; he has insisted on the distinction between the words *shall* and *may;* has inferred from that distinction, that the judges of the Inferior Courts are subjects of legislative discretion; and has contended, that the word *may* includes all power respecting the subject to which it is applied; consequently, to raise up and to put down, to create and to destroy. I must entreat your patience, Sir, while I go more into this subject than I ever supposed would be necessary. By the article so often quoted it is declared, "That the judicial power of the United States *shall* be vested in one Supreme Court, and in such Inferior Courts, as the Congress *may* from time to time establish." I beg leave to recall your attention to what I have already said of these Inferior Courts. *That the original jurisdiction of various subjects being given exclusively to them, it became the bounden duty of Congress to establish such Courts.* I will not repeat the argument already used on that subject. But I will ask those who urge the distinction between the Supreme Court and the inferior tribunals, whether a law was not previously necessary before the Supreme Court could be organized? They reply, that the Constitution says there shall be a Supreme Court, and, therefore, the Congress are commanded to organize it, while the rest is left to their discretion.

This, Sir, is not the fact. The Constitution says the judicial power shall be vested in *one* Supreme Court, and in Inferior *Courts*. The legislature can, therefore, only organize *one* Supreme Court, but they may establish as many Inferior Courts as they shall think proper. The designation made of them by the Constitution is, such Inferior Courts as the Congress may, from time to time, ordain and *establish*. But why, say gentlemen, fix precisely *one* Supreme Court, and leave the rest to legislative discretion? The answer is simple. It results from the nature of things, from the existent and probable state of our country. There was no difficulty in deciding that *one*, and *only one* Supreme Court would be proper or necessary, to which should lie appeals from inferior tribunals. Not so as to these. The United States were advancing in rapid progression. Their population, of three millions, was soon to become five, then ten, afterwards twenty millions. This was well known, as far as the future can become an object of human comprehension. In this increase of numbers, with a still greater increase of wealth, with the extension of our commerce, and the progress of the arts, it was evident, that, although a great many tribunals would become necessary, it was impossible to determine either the precise number or the most convenient form. The Convention did not pretend to this prescience; but had they possessed it, would it have been proper to have established *then* all the tribunals necessary for all future times? Would it have been wise to have planted Courts among the Chickasaws, the Chocktaws, the Cherokees, the Tuscaroras, and God knows how many more, because at some future day, the regions over which they roam might be cultivated by polished men? Was it not proper, wise, necessary, to leave in the discretion of Congress the number and the kind of Courts, which they might find it proper to *establish*, for the purpose designated by the Constitution.

This simple statement of facts, facts of public notoriety, is alone a sufficient comment on and explication of the word, on which gentlemen have so much relied. The Convention in framing, the people in adopting this compact, say, the judicial power *shall* extend to many cases, the original cognizance whereof shall be by the Inferior Courts; but it is neither necessary, nor even possible *now* to determine their number or their form; *that* essential power, therefore, shall vest in such Inferior Courts, as the Congress may, from time to time, in the progression of time, and according to the indication of circumstances, *establish*. Not *provide* or *determine*, but *establish*. Not a mere temporary provision, but an *establishment*. If, after this, it had said in general terms, that *judges* should hold their offices during good behavior, could a doubt have existed on the interpretation of this act, under all its attending circumstances, that the judges of the Inferior Courts were intended, as well as those of the Supreme Court? But did the framers of the Constitution stop there? Is there then nothing more? Did they risk on these grammatical niceties the fate of America? Did they rest here the most important branch of our government? Little important, indeed, as to foreign danger; but infinitely valuable to our domestic peace, and to personal protection against the oppression of our rulers. No. Lest a doubt should be raised, they have carefully connected the judges of both Courts in the same sentence; they have said, "the judges *both of the Supreme and Inferior Courts,*" thus coupling them inseparably together. You may cut the bands, but you can never untie them. With salutary caution, they devised this clause, to arrest the overbearing temper, which they knew belonged to legislative bodies. They do not say the judges simply, but the judges of the *Supreme* and *Inferior* Courts, shall hold their offices during good behavior. They say, therefore, to the legislature, you may judge of the propriety, the utility, the necessity, of organizing these Courts; but when established you have done your duty. Anticipating the course of passion in future times, they say to the legislature, you shall not disgrace yourselves by exhibiting the indecent spectacle of judges established by one legislature, removed by another. We will save *you* also from yourselves. We say, these judges *shall* hold their offices; and surely, Sir, to pretend that they can hold their office, after the office is destroyed, is contemptible.

The framers of this Constitution had seen much, read much, and deeply reflected. They knew by experience the violence of popular bodies; and, let it be remembered, that since that day many of the States, taught by experience, have found it necessary to change their form of government to avoid the effects of that violence. The Convention contemplated the very act you now attempt. They knew also the jealousy and the power of the States; and they established, for *your* and for *their* protection, this most important department. I beg gentlemen to hear and to remember what I say. It is this department alone, and it is the independence alone of this department, which can save you from civil war. Yes, Sir, adopt the language of gentlemen; say, with them, by the act to which you are urged, "If we cannot remove the judges, we can destroy them." Establish thus the dependence of the judiciary department. Who will resort to them for protection against you? Who will confide in, who will be bound by their decrees? Are we then to resort to the ultimate reason of kings? Are our arguments to fly from the mouths of our cannon?

We are told that we may violate our Constitution, because similar Constitutions have been violated elsewhere. Two States have been cited to that effect, Maryland and Virginia. The honorable gentleman from Virginia tells us, that when this happened in the State he belongs to, no complaint was made by the judges. I will not inquire into that fact, although I have the protest of the judges now laying before me; judges, eminent for their talents, renowned for their learning, respectable for their virtue. I will not inquire what Constitutions have been violated. I will not ask either when or where this dangerous practice began, or has been followed. I will admit the fact. What does it prove? Does it prove that, because they violated, we also may violate. Does it not prove directly the contrary? Is it not the strongest reason on earth for preserving the independence of our tribunals? If it be true that they have with strong hands seized *their* Courts, and bent them to their will, ought we not to give suitors a fair chance for justice in *our* Courts, or must the suffering citizen be deprived of all protection?

The gentleman from Virginia has called our attention to certain cases, which he considers as forming necessary exceptions to the principles for which we contend. Permit me to say, that necessity is a hard law, and frequently proves too much; and, let the gentleman recollect, that arguments which prove too much prove nothing.

He has instanced a case where it may be proper to appoint commissioners, for a limited time, to settle some particular description of controversies. Undoubtedly it is always in the power of Congress to form a board of commissioners for particular purposes. He asks, are *these* Inferior Courts, and must *they* also exist forever? I answer, that the nature of their office must depend upon the law by which they are created; if called to exercise the judicial functions, designated by the Constitution, they must have an existence conformable to its injunctions.

Again, he has instanced the Mississippi territory, claimed by, and which may be surrendered to, the State of Georgia, and a part of the Union, which may be conquered by a foreign enemy. And he asks, triumphantly, are our Inferior Courts to remain after our jurisdiction is gone? The case rests upon a principle so simple, that I am surprised the honorable member did not perceive the answer in the very moment when he made the objection. Is it by our act that a country is taken from us by a foreign enemy? Is it by our consent that our jurisdiction is lost? I had the honor, in speaking the other day, expressly, and for the most obvious reasons, to except the case of conquest. As well might we contend for the government of a town swallowed up by an earthquake.

General MASON explained; he had supposed the case of territory conquered, and afterwards ceded to the conqueror, or some other territory ceded in lieu of it.

Mr. MORRIS. The case is precisely the same. Until after the peace, the conquest is not complete. Every body knows, that until the cession by treaty, the original owner has the postliminary right to a territory taken from him. Beyond all question, where Congress are compelled to cede the territory, the judges can no longer exist, unless the new sovereign confer the office. Over such a territory, the authority of the Constitution ceases, and of course the rights which it confers.

It is said, the judicial institution is intended for the benefit of the people, and not of the judge; and it is complained of, that in speaking of the office we say it is *his* office. Undoubtedly the institution is for the benefit of the people. But the question remains, how will it be rendered most beneficial? Is it by making the judge independent, by making it *his* office; or is it by placing him in a state of abject dependence, so that the office shall be his today, and belong to another tomorrow. Let the gentleman hear the words of the Constitution; it speaks of *their* offices, consequently, as applied to a single judge, of *his* office, to be exercised by him for the benefit of the people of America, to which exercise his *independence* is as necessary as his *office.*

The gentleman from Virginia has, on this occasion, likened the judge to a bridge, and to various other objects; but I hope for his pardon, if, while I admire the lofty flights of his eloquence, I abstain from noticing observations, which I conceive to be utterly irrelevant.

The same honorable member has not only given us his history of the Supreme Court, but has told us of the manner in which they do business, and expressed his fears, that having little else to do, they will do mischief. We are not competent, Sir, to examine, nor ought we to prejudge their conduct. I am persuaded that they will do their duty, and presume they will have the decency to believe that we do our duty. In so far as they may be busied with the great mischief of checking the legislative or executive departments, in any wanton invasion of our rights, I shall rejoice in that mischief. I hope, indeed, they will not be so busied, because I hope we shall give them no cause. But I also hope, they will keep an eagle eye upon us, lest we should. It was partly for this purpose that they were established, and, I trust, that when properly called on they will dare to act. I know this doctrine is unpleasant. I know it is more popular to appeal to public opinion, that equivocal transient being, which exists nowhere and everywhere.

But if ever the occasion calls for it, I trust, that the Supreme Court will not neglect doing the great mischief of saving this Constitution, which can be done much better by their deliberations, than by resorting to what are called revolutionary measures.

The honorable member from North Carolina, sore pressed by the delicate situation in which he is placed, thinks he has discovered a new argument in favor of the vote, which he is instructed to give. As far as I can enter into his ideas, and trace their progress, he seems to have assumed the position which was to be proved, and then searched through the Constitution, not to discover whether the legislature have the right contended for, but whether, admitting them to possess it, there may not be something which might not comport with that idea. I shall state the honorable member's argument, as I understand it, and if mistaken pray to be corrected. He read to us that clause, which relates to impeachment, and comparing it with that which fixes the tenure of judicial office has observed, that this clause must relate solely to a removal by the executive power, whose right to remove, though not indeed anywhere mentioned in the Constitution, has been admitted in a practice founded on legislative construction.

That, as the tenure of the office is during *good behavior,* and as the clause respecting impeachment does not specify *misbehavior,* there is evidently a cause of removal, which cannot be reached by impeachment, and of course (the executive not being permitted to remove) the right must necessarily devolve on the legislature. Is this the honorable member's argument? If it be, the reply is very simple. *Misbehavior* is not a term known in our law. The idea is expressed by the word *misdemeanor,* which word is in the clause quoted respecting impeachments. Taking, therefore, the two together, and speaking plain old English, the Constitution says; "The judges shall hold their offices so long as they shall *demean* themselves well; but if they shall *misdemean,* if they shall on impeachment be convicted of *misdemeanor,* they shall be removed." Thus, Sir, the honorable member will find that the one clause is just as broad as the other. He will see, therefore, that the legislature can assume no right from the deficiency of either, and will find that the clause which he relied on goes, if rightly understood, to a confirmation of our doctrine.

Is there a member of this House, who can lay his hand on his heart and say, that consistently with the plain words of our Constitution we have a right to repeal this law? I believe not. And if we undertake to construe this Constitution to our purposes and say, that public opinion is to be our judge, there is an end to all Constitutions. To what will not this dangerous doctrine lead? Should it today be the popular wish to destroy the first magistrate, you can destroy him. And should he tomorrow be able to conciliate to him the popular will, and lead the people to wish for your destruction, it is easily effected. Adopt this principle, and the whim of the moment will not only be the law, but the Constitution of our country.

The gentleman from Virginia has mentioned a great nation brought to the feet of one of her servants. But why is she in that situation? Is it not because popular opinion was called on to decide everything, until those who wore bayonets decided for all the rest. Our situation is peculiar. At present our national compact can prevent a State from acting hostilely towards the general interest. But let this compact be destroyed, and each State becomes instantaneously vested with absolute sovereignty. Is there no instance of a similar situation to be found in history? Look at the States of Greece. They were once in a condition not unlike to that in which we should then stand. They treated the recommendations of their Amphictyonic Council, which was more a meeting of Ambassadors than a legislative assembly, as we did the resolutions of the Old Congress. Are we wise? So were they. Are we valiant? They also were brave. Have we one common language, and are we united under one head? In this also there is a strong resemblance. But by their divisions they became at first victims of the ambition of Philip, and were at length swallowed up in the Roman Empire. Are we to form an exception to the general principles of human nature, and to all the examples of history? And are the maxims of experience to become false, when applied to our fate?

Some, indeed, flatter themselves, that our destiny will be like that of Rome. Such indeed it might be, if we had the same wise but vile Aristocracy, under whose guidance they became the masters of the world. But we have not that strong Aristocratic arm, which can seize a wretched citizen, scourged almost to death by a remorseless creditor, turn him into the ranks, and bid him as a soldier bear our eagle in triumph round the globe. I hope to God we shall never have such an abominable institution. But what, I ask, will be the situation of these States, organized as they now are, if by the dissolution of our national compact they be left to themselves? What is the probable result? We shall either be victims of foreign intrigue, and, split into factions, fall under the domination of a foreign power; or else, after the misery and torment of civil war, become the subjects of a usurping military despot. What but this compact, what but this specific part of it, can save us from ruin? The judicial power, that fortress of the Constitution, is now to be overturned. Yes, with honest Ajax, I would not only throw a shield before it, I would build around it a wall of brass. But I am too weak to defend the rampart against the host of assailants. I must call to my assistance their good sense, their patriotism, and their virtue.

Do not, gentlemen, suffer the rage of passion to drive reason from her seat. If this law be indeed bad, let us join to remedy the defects. Has it been passed in a manner, which wounded your pride, or roused your resentment? Have, I conjure you, the magnanimity to pardon that offence. I intreat, I implore you, to sacrifice those angry passions to the interests of our country. Pour out this pride of opinion on the altar of patriotism. Let it be an expiatory libation for the weal of America. Do not, for God's sake do not suffer that pride to plunge us all into the abyss of ruin. Indeed, indeed, it will be but of little, very little avail, whether one opinion or the other be right or wrong; it will heal no wounds, it will pay no debts, it will rebuild no ravaged towns. Do not rely on that popular will, which has brought us frail beings into political existence. That opinion is but a changeable thing. It will soon change. This very measure will change it. You will be deceived. Do not, I beseech you, in reliance on a foundation so frail, commit the dignity, the harmony, the existence of our nation to the wild wind. Trust not your treasure to the waves. Throw not your compass and your charts into the ocean. Do not believe that its billows will waft you into port. Indeed, indeed, you will be deceived. Cast not away this only anchor of our safety. I have seen its progress. I know the difficulties through which it was obtained. I stand in the presence of Almighty God and of the world. I declare to you, that if you lose this charter, never, no never, will you get another. We are now perhaps arrived at the parting point. Here, even here, we stand on the brink of fate. Pause, then—Pause. For Heaven's sake—Pause.

24 ❧ Letters to the New York *Evening Post* on the Louisiana Purchase (1803)

When the Jefferson administration discovered that Spain had secretly given Louisiana back to France in 1800, they worried about having an ambitious and restless great power for a neighbor. As if to underscore those concerns, in fall 1802 the Spanish—then still in possession of the territory—suddenly suspended the American right of deposit in New Orleans, effectively closing the Mississippi to American commerce.

When Congress met in December 1802, Jefferson's Annual Message ignored the closure and treated Louisiana as a matter of indifference.[1] Congress did not take it so nonchalantly. Morris, who remained in the Senate until March 1803, spoke out against the administration's passivity and in favor of a set of resolutions by Senator Ross of Pennsylvania advocating a more assertive approach.[2]

It was not until early summer, well after Congress adjourned, that the news came that Napoleon had decided to sell Louisiana to the United States. Despite his differences with Jefferson, Morris approved of the purchase on the whole. It also pleased him that the purchase had been negotiated by his old friend Robert Livingston. James Monroe's involvement as Livingston's co-negotiator, however, was not so welcome to Morris. He and Monroe had clashed years earlier when Monroe succeeded him as U.S. minister to France. In a letter to Livingston, Morris sized up Monroe this way:

> It is possible that I am unjust to Mr. Monroe, but really I consider him as a person of mediocrity in every respect. Just exceptions lie against

1. Henry Adams, *History of the United States During the First Administration of Thomas Jefferson* (New York: Library of America, 1986), 288.
2. Morris's and Ross's speeches were later published as a pamphlet, and are available in the American Antiquarian Society's Early American Imprints, series II (Shaw-Shoemaker), no. 4995. Morris's speech is reprinted in Jared Sparks, *Life*, 3:403–34.

his diplomatic character, and, taking all circumstances into consideration, his appointment must appear extraordinary to the Cabinets of Europe. It is, in itself, a most unwary step, and will lower our government in public estimation.[3]

In these essays Morris resumes his old pseudonym, "An American," writing to express his disagreement with many of his fellow Federalists and give his qualified approval of the purchase.

AUGUST 30, 1803

TO THE EDITOR OF THE EVENING POST.
SIR,
　　Some essays have appeared in federal prints, which tend to raise a prejudice against the treaty by which Louisiana and New-Orleans have lately been ceded to the United States; this does not seem to be right, for it is the principle and the pride of a good federalist to support the government of his country in every thing not inconsistent with the public good, or with a sense of honour and justice. It becomes us therefore to wait patiently for the proceedings of the next Congress; we shall then know the opinions formed by our Senators and Representatives upon full enquiry, and we shall also be acquainted with some facts of which we are now ignorant. It may indeed be objected that the democrats are as busy in prepossessing the public mind with impressions favourable to this treaty, as they were during the administration of Washington in exciting opposition to that which was made with England by Governor Jay. But if the democrats behave ill, does it follow that we also should misdemean ourselves? Let it be remembered, that we possess not their priviledge of saying and unsaying, as may suit a present purpose. We claim confidence on the ground that we are actuated

---

3. Letter of April 23, 1803, *Diary and Letters of Gouverneur Morris*, 2:357. New York *Evening Post*, August 30, 1803, p. 2. Courtesy American Antiquarian Society. The editor prefaces the article: "A correspondent of the first respectability has sent us the following interesting essay, on a subject which must possess much importance in the minds of all reflecting men. The candid and liberal view he takes will ensure his essay a welcome with readers of every description."

by principle, by a regard for truth, and by that respect for the reputation of others which all men feel who have a proper respect for themselves.

Admit, for argument sake, that the treaty shall turn out to be a bad one, will it not be time enough to say so when we have formed a solid judgment, upon a knowledge of facts? And supposing it to be a good one, (which is surely a supposable case) will it not be better to rejoice without the pain of prefacing congratulation by retracting mistakes?

Let us give a slight glance at some of the most prominent objections. But first let it be premised, that to insinuate a charge of interested motives in our negociators, or either of them, is improper, without evidence, or at least a strong presumption. It is said that we do not want the western side of the Mississippi, having already land enough. It must be confessed, that we have enough, perhaps too much, and curious speculations may be made as to the probable effect of such vast possessions on our moral and political state, but we need not enter this wide field, for it will be readily admitted by considerate men, that our present extent is sufficient to produce the mischiefs (whatever they may be) which arise from wide dominion. The increase, therefore, of our territory gives no just cause for apprehension. But is it not, on the other hand, desirable to take from foreign powers every plausible pretext for coming within the bosom of America and forming establishments, which must be injurious to us, whether they be military, political, or commercial? There are some arguments respecting this river which it would be imprudent to press. Suffice it to say, that proper forts and garrisons at the mouth of it will give a security to our Empire which is not otherwise attainable.

The second objection is, that our honour is tarnished by purchasing what we might justly have taken, and might easily have held, in spite of any thing which could be done by France or Spain. There certainly is force in this objection, but it is proper to hear both sides before we condemn. To plunge a nation into war is easy, whereas, to get out of it on terms honourable and advantageous is frequently difficult, and sometimes impossible. It is true, that by vigorous measures we should probably have established a reputation favourable to our future repose; and it is also true, that paying for aggression, under whatever name, colour, or pretext, invites to, and may perhaps occasion renewed aggressions. But on subjects of this sort men generally reason according to their feelings. Besides, it is reasonable to suppose that the administration possess a knowledge of facts not within the compass of private information. At the time when this treaty was made, war between Britain and France was indeed inevitable — this we know; but there may be other facts of which we are ignorant, and which, when known, will give the business a very different complexion.

May it not, moreover, be said, that if we had taken this country it would have been lawful for France to take it back again at the first convenient opportunity; whereas, now that we have purchased, she is bound in honour to re-purchase if she should hereafter wish for the possession? And may it not be added, that we can, in such case, lawfully insist on a good round price, perhaps three or four times what it cost, seeing that such is the usual profit on land speculations? Nay, if these positions can be well established, may it not be argued that this treaty is a proper supplement to the act making provision for the "*whole* of the public debt?"

You will perhaps smile, Mr. Coleman,[4] at the idea of binding France by these, which you may call "Lilliputian ties"; and it must be acknowledged that the sword of the First Consul has occasionally cut asunder some bands of strong stuff. But is it fair to conclude from the transactions of France with absolute Princes, the conduct she will pursue towards her sister Republic? May it not also be said, that our fellow citizens will fight with a better stomach for what they have acquired by purchase than they would for a conquest, the right to which might be somewhat doubtful with men of tender conscience? And if to this it be objected, that altho' our independence was acquired by the force of arms, and our right of deposit at New-Orleans by peaceful treaty, yet an administration which would not have borne the slightest question as to our independence (unless perhaps from some sister republic,) felt most pacifically inclined when the right of deposit was infringed; let it be remembered, that men have different ways of viewing and estimating the same things. Hence it has long been a proverb, *De Gustibus non est disputandum:* in other words: Every man has his own way of riding his own hobby.

One clause has been somewhere mentioned, which will not, on examination, be found in the treaty. It is a stipulation as to what shall be done with the country hereafter. A stipulation of this sort would furnish to France a pretext, and perhaps a right, to meddle in our domestic concerns; it is therefore to be presumed, both from the talents and the patriotism of our ministers, that nothing of the sort exists. But if, unfortunately, such a clause should have slipt in, the wisdom of Government will unquestionably strike it out, and the First Consul will hardly insist on prescribing to us the manner in which we shall dispose of, settle, and govern our own territory.

The great objection remains to be considered. It is said we have paid too

---

4. William Coleman was editor of the *Evening Post.*

much for this country—that France, in the conviction she could neither take nor hold possession, had ordered the troops destined for that quarter to be disembarked before the treaty was made—that she would rather have given it to America than have suffered it to be taken, as it must have been, by England—that the French government, after having rejected haughtily every overture of Mr. Livingston, came all at once round, and made him the tender of Louisiana as soon as the King of England's Message to his Parliament reached Paris—and, that after all, Mr. Livingston had no power to strike a bargain, by reason whereof it was deferred till Mr. Munroe's arrival, so that this happy statesman might say with Caesar, *veni vidi vici.*[5] All this and much more is said, but is all this true; and if true is it the whole truth? Prudence requires that we suspend our belief till after the meeting of Congress. The Treaty will then be laid before the Senate, and with it the instructions to our ministers, their correspondence, &c. &c—such being the usage. It will then, most probably, appear, (according to assertions made on democratic authority) that Mr. Livingston was duly authorized. How else could he have made the overtures which are spoken of? It is indeed to be presumed that ample instructions were given to him long before, in which the various contingencies appertaining to the subject were ably discussed. The abilities of the President, and Secretary of State, leave little room for doubt. And however we may differ from those gentlemen, we cannot but acknowledge that they have a considerable share of talents.

But although, for the reasons already assigned, it is improper to examine the above assertions, we ought to give full weight to the observations made on the other side, viz—That the value of the acquired territory so far exceeds the price, that the United States cannot fail of eventual reimbursement. It must indeed be admitted, that the present sale of that land will prevent the sale of an equal quantity within our old limits; and of course, that the benefit to be derived is somewhat remote: But what are twenty or thirty years in the life of an empire? If it can be shewn, that we only make a small advance now, to secure an immense return forty or fifty years hence, what will become of the cavil about price? One objection, indeed, has been hinted, which, if founded, would be somewhat serious—It is, that all the valuable part of this country was granted before the cession, and that these grants are confirmed by a special clause in the treaty, so that the grantees will be able to undersell on the west, the United States on the east of the

5. The king sent several messages to Parliament in early 1803 regarding the need to prepare for war against France; the first was sent on March 8.

Mississippi. As to the supposed confirmation, nothing need be said about it, for the plain reason that such clauses are generally understood, even when not expressed. And as to the existence of the supposed grants, it remains to be proved. But whether they exist or not, what ground is there for apprehension? Can it be for a moment supposed, that provision is not made in the treaty for a case so palpable? When the instructions given to our ministers are produced, it will doubtless appear that it has been specifically provided for. The President's attachment to public property must have presented to him the idea by mere instinct. Neither great genius nor profound political science, was necessary, because the train of thought is so natural that it runs of itself from the pen. He would of course say to his plenipotentiary—"In authorizing you to give so large a sum for the acquisition of Louisiana, it is specially contemplated to reimburse the treasury by a sale of lands to be acquired. Now since it is possible that an abuse of his confidence, by those who surround the First Consul, may induce him to make such previous grants to individuals as would defeat this oeconomical plan; you must take especial care, by a precise clause in the treaty, to confine such grants within narrow limits. They must not exceed——— millions of acres; or if they should, a proportionate deduction must be made from the above sum: and should the grants extend to——— millions of acres, it will not be adviseable to make the purchase at all, you will in such case confine your views to the Island of Orleans." It is not pretended that these are the words of the instructions, but unquestionably the idea will be found in them clearly expressed; because should it even have escaped his excellency, it would not have escaped the studious reflection of his Secretary of State. Admitting, however, the bare possibility that both of them, occupied by domestic cares, should have nodded a little over foreign concerns; admitting too that Chancellor Livingston, in his eagerness to acquire fame, should have overlooked every smaller circumstance, can it be believed that the penetration of a gentleman, selected by the wisdom of government for this and other important missions, would not perceive that material defect? The acuteness of Mr. Munroe, would have seized the object instantaneously, and we cannot therefore have any ground for apprehension; more especially as there seems to be another clause in the treaty which would have suggested the precaution to the most inconsiderate. The claims of Americans to reimbursement, out of the price of this territory, for money due to them by France, is it seems limited to about four millions of dollars, nothing therefore could be more natural than to limit, in like manner, the claims of French grantees; the more so as it will otherwise be in the power of the French government to go on granting, provided their patents be dated before the last of April.

Monsieur Talleyrand is too well bred to date any of them on the first of that month. If then it be conceded that both the soil and jurisdiction of this vast country are acquired by the United States, the wisdom of the treaty so far as regards the quantum of price and other conditions onerous to us, must depend on that combination of circumstances with which the Congress will, it is to be presumed, be duly made acquainted, & on which that much respected body, will according to its constitutional rights and authorities, make sound and proper decisions. Some gentlemen indeed suppose that a veil of secrecy will be thrown over these transactions; but this seems unlikely, first, because a display of facts will tend it is supposed, to the honour of government; and secondly, because Members of Congress will not easily be persuaded to vote in the dark, when they may afterwards be called on for explanation by their constituents. On the whole, therefore, it seems to be the duty of every good Federalist, and indeed of every good Citizen, patiently to wait for the investigations which will soon take place. In all human probability, where every thing is known the great majority of the people will be of one opinion, and who is there as insensible to the interests of his country, as not to wish that this well founded opinion may be favourable to those who administer our affairs?

I am, sir, your obedient servant,

AN AMERICAN.

DECEMBER 24, 1803

To the Editor of the Evening Post
Sir,

Your flattering preface to my former Essay has induced me again to trouble you, and I am the more encouraged to do so as the Aurora folks have, I find paid me the compliment of attributing what I wrote to General Hamilton and Gouverneur Morris.[1] I thank them, not only for this mark

New-York Evening Post, December 24, 1803, p. 2. Courtesy American Antiquarian Society. The manuscript is in the Gouverneur Morris Collection, Rare Book and Manuscript Library, Columbia University, item 847.

1. The Philadelphia *Aurora* had published the essay on September 3, 1803, with a brief preface attributing the article "in all probability" to Hamilton, and a longer commentary following.

of approbation but for another not less unequivocal; the wrath with which they have replied. He who wears a tight shoe knows best where it pinches but his wry faces will indicate to a by-stander how it is with his toes.

In my former essay it is premised that to insinuate a charge of interested motives in our negotiators, or either of them, is improper without "evidence, or at least a strong presumption." Let it be added here that to make such charge is beneath the dignity of any man who has the honour to be a federalist. The ground on which it was made is curious. Chancellor Livingston, in a manner honorable to his talents & zeal insured the payment of a large sum due by the French government to American citizens. Among the creditors are, it seems, some of his relations, and because he has not excepted them from equal justice and common right he is charged with impure motives. The origin of this slander will be known by and bye; and if certain folks wish to preserve appearances, they should be a little more guarded in convivial moments—otherwise a newspaper zeal will not shield them from investigation.

As to the treaty itself, it is in my opinion, in its general scope and effect, a good one, and the Aurora folks are heartily welcome to as much of the praise as they can fairly take to themselves. Moreover, if in treading on this ground, their toes should be uneasy, they may pour out against federalism and federalists a curse as long as that of Ernulphus'; but let them not by sly and vile insinuation, endeavour to injure the man to whom they are indebted for this very treaty, on which they assume such great credit for political sagacity.[2]

> That democrats should snarl and bite,
> is in their nature—therefore right;
> But yet they ought to spare each other,
> for 'tis not right to bite a brother.[3]

I say again, sir, that I approve the general scope and effect of this treaty. We acquire West Florida including both sides the mouth of the Mississippi and Mobile Rivers. This is the great essential, and had it been unattainable but by twenty millions I should have been satisfied to pay my share even of that sum. The acquisition of the rest of Louisiana, if not so necessary, is

---

2. Ernulphus (Arnulf) was bishop of Rochester in the early twelfth century. His curse of excommunication (in Latin and English) takes up chapters 2.III–2.V of Laurence Sterne's *Tristram Shandy*.

3. Most probably Morris's own composition.

certainly useful inasmuch as we are thereby enabled to prevent any persons from occupying it until the colonization may be rendered advisable by the exuberance of our population. For these reasons I approve of the treaty and not because of "what was said by Morris, Mason, Wells and White," altho' I have the highest respect for those gentlemen. We federalists are in the habit of thinking for ourselves, and when a thing is well done, tho' by a rank democrat, we want neither a French cook nor a salt mountain to season it to our palates.[4] Apropos of that salt mountain. If Congress should, in their wisdom, make an appropriation to build a roof over it for the purpose of keeping off federal rain, might it not be well to construct a Dry dock under the same cover? This could be but a trifling addition to the expense, and then when our ships and frigates are packed up they can with great convenience be salted.

In my former communication I noticed the following among other assertions publickly made about this treaty: "It is said that the French government after having rejected haughtily every overture of Mr. Livingston's came all at once round and made him the tender of Louisiana as soon as the king of England's message to his parliament reached Paris, and that after all *Mr. Livingston had no power to strike a bargain*, by reason whereof it was deferred till Mr. Munroe's arrival; so that this happy statesman might say with Caesar *veni vidi vici*." Having thus stated the reports, I proceeded thus: "All this, and much more is said; but is all this true? and if true is it the whole truth? Prudence requires that we suspend our belief until the meeting of congress. The treaty will then be laid before the senate, and with it the instructions to our ministers, their correspondents,[5] &c. &c. such being the usage. It will then most probably appear that Mr. Livingston was duly authorized, *how else could he have made the overtures which are spoken of*." The answer of the Aurora folks to this paragraph is amusing. The poor fellows are so pinched, that in their agony they adopt the very observation which they writhe under, and roar out as follows: "First it is acknowleged that Mr. Livingston did make overtures, and of course, before the aggression of the Spanish Intendant; and secondly that the cession was in consequence of the king of England's speech. Here is saying and unsaying with a vengeance." To do them justice, however, they have by comparing dates fully

4. Among the information about the Lousiana territory that Jefferson supplied to Congress was that somewhere up the Missouri River there was a mountain of solid rock salt 45 miles wide and 180 miles long.

5. In the newspaper, "correspondents"; in the manuscript, "correspondence."

refuted the assertion that France ceded Louisiana *in consequence of the king of England's message*. This reply, had they stopt there, would have been neat, but, "this paragraph (say they) like four of the preceding, is evidently the result of communications between Mr. King and Mr. Hamilton." But surely so egregious a mistake in dates could not have been made by Mr. King, for he must have been well acquainted with facts. Calm reflection, therefore, had it been possible for men in their piteous condition to reflect calmly, would have absolved him from the charge. But I hear you exclaim, how could it enter into their noddles to make so strange a charge? Ah! There's the rub. Suppose, for a moment, that the facts stated are *substantially*, if not *circumstantially* true: They would, you know, in such case, naturally enquire how came this *American* to the knowlege of them? and then the squinting witch suspicion would as naturally whisper King must have told him—and then King and Hamilton being intimate friends the rest follows of course. They would, on slighter circumstances, charge a federalist with biting off his own nose. If then, we trace back their logic, we shall find it amounts to an admission that what I considered as wild assertion, was sober serious fact, viz. that Mr. Livingston was not authorized, and that the offer was made by France. Of this we have indeed further evidence from the same quarter. They say in the Aurora, after repeating the allegation (as if made by me) that Mr. Livingston had not power to strike a bargain, "And what then? admitting this, what does it prove?" "It proves that the administration was cautious in granting extensive powers—that it set on foot negociations and reserved to itself as long as was compatible to the state of things, the exclusive power to determine upon the terms proposed." And again, "The original negociation was commenced in Europe long before the act of the Spanish Intendant took place." And again—"If the United States had *no alternative* between the *acceptance* of the whole of Louisiana in the *utmost extent* as is ceded, or none, *which* of the *alternatives* ought to be preferred? We will undertake to say (what we believe to be) that such an alternative was given and that the choice of *our ministers* was made in that way." And in the message to both houses, "Previous to this period" (viz. the last session of congress, or the Spanish aggression, for by the felicity of expression peculiar to this writer,[6] it is doubtful which he means) "propositions had been authorized for obtaining the sovereignty of New-Orleans and of other possessions in that quarter interesting to our quiet to such extent as was deemed practicable, and the provisional appropriation of two millions of

6. Thomas Jefferson.

dollars intended as part of the price, was considered as conveying the sanction of Congress to the acquisition proposed." And again in the Aurora: "Mr. Marbois stated on the part of the first Consul that the *preliminary* to negociation should be that the claims on France by American citizens should be paid out of the first part of the Louisiana purchase money. There are only two other *preliminary* conditions, that the *whole* of Louisiana should be taken *as France originally held it*, and that the purchase should be fifteen millions of dollars." A host of observations presents itself, but to state them would be tedious, let it suffice that we have here direct acknowledgments, that altho' propositions had been authorized, or (in the other phraseology) negociations set on foot, no power was given to act. This it seems was reserved *as long as was compatible to the state of things*. But what state of things? It would seem from the other paper to be the *provisional appropriation*, which, (says the message-maker) was considered as conveying the sanction of congress to the acquisition proposed. Now by recurring to the report of the secret committee, we shall find that in the very outset they declare that the object of that appropriation was to *enable* the president to *commence* the negociation. They of course must have been ignorant of these propositions previously authorized, and of that original negociation commenced long before the Spanish aggression. The congress, however, sanctioned the acquisition proposed. But by whom proposed, and when, and to whom? Plain answers to these questions will probably discover the cause of that soreness which the Aurora folks feel; and the reason why they construe into irony, the simple suggestions of plain common sense. Taking it for granted that the president and secretary of state, men of acknowleged abilities, had fully instructed their ministers on a subject of such great importance, and in directing him to treat, had not only fixed the object & the terms they were willing to grant for its attainment, but had conferred on him the competent authority; assertions made to the contrary seemed to be not only malicious, but absurd. Under this impression, so natural to a man who does not pretend to diplomatic skill or court-intrigue but has been used to the strait forward way of doing business, I attempted to defend the administration against charges which had been publicly made. I was not indeed without apprehension that violent men of my own party might be displeased, but who would have suspected that the writer would have exposed himself to democratic fury? That he would be charged with "aiming to take Mr. Livingston by the legs and to beat down Mr. Munroe and the administration by *his* knocking out *his* brains." Such, however, is the melancholy fact. General Hamilton is charged (as author of my last essay) with this tremendous project, which will I trust, teach the wholesome lesson never to defend our administration upon principles of common sense. By-the-bye this eloquent flight of the Aurora folks would be no bad subject for a painter. In the foreground Gen. Hamilton holding Chancellor Livingston by the legs and swinging him round so as to beat out Munroe's brains, which, at the instant, fly in the form of grape-shot among the administration. These, of course, on the back ground in attitudes appropriate to their rank and station. The sturdy Secretary of war, for instance, might stand as Mars, and on the shield with which he covers himself, and his chief might be painted the head of the treasury department. But to return—it appears by what they will pardon me, for calling *their precious confessions*, that Mr. Livingston was not authorized to make a bargain; that if the propositions he *was* authorized to make, had been accepted, he was not even then authorized to bind his government; in short that he had only a right to say, will you sell, and what will you take? without being able to give any thing or even to declare that his master would give any thing. This may, for aught I know be diplomatic skill but it is presumed that neither the president nor his secretary would, in common life, have been so niggard of authority, if they had sent a negro to buy a pig. It appears also, that the proposition was at length made by France in the shape of three preliminaries. And let it be remarked in this place, that those three *preliminaries* contain in substance the whole treaty, except the grant of commercial privileges to France and Spain, and the covenant to admit the inhabitants of Louisiana into the American union. These two articles seem, from their account of the matter, not to have been asked by the First Consul, but rather to have been granted by our ministers out of pure love and kindness.

It being thus acknowleged that the offer was made by France, it only remains to enquire why it was made. By recurring to the papers presented by the British Ministry to the two houses of Parliament, it appears that on the seventh of April, Lord Whitworth delivered an official paper to monsieur Talleyrand, in which he peremptorily declares that Malta should not be evacuated and insists on satisfaction &c. Now with all humble submission to men who are well informed, I venture to ask how many days elapsed between the delivery of this note (which proved war to be unavoidable) and the determination of the first Consul to sell Louisiana? And how many days after that determination before it was communicated to Mr. Livingston? And how many days after that before the terms of the treaty were fixed between him and Monsieur Marbois? And how many days after that before it was drawn up in three pieces, such as we now see it? The signature took place on the thirtieth of April. Thus from the time when Lord Whitworth's paper was delivered to the time when the treaty was signed, is just twenty three days. Moreover it is believed that Mr. Munroe, bearer of the powers (*whatever they were*) did not reach Paris till the evening of the twelfth, was presented to Mr. Talleyrand on the fourteenth, lay sick a-bed for a week, signed the treaty on the 30th and was presented to the first Consul on the first of May. This was nimble negotiation. Whether beneficial or not will depend on the conditions which have been annexed to the first Consul's preliminaries.

The treaty contains two articles, which, from the history above given by the adepts, do not seem to have been insisted on by the French government. One of these secures certain commercial privileges to France and Spain, about which, I shall say nothing at present. By the other, viz., the third article, the inhabitants of the ceded territory are to be incorporated *in the Union* of the United States and admitted *as soon as possible*, according to the principles of the federal constitution, *to all the rights*, advantages and immunities of citizens of the United States. It becomes necessary here to repeat what I formerly said before the purport of the treaty was exactly known, "one clause has been somewhere mentioned which *will not on examination be found in the treaty*. It is a stipulation *as to what shall be done with the country hereafter*. A stipulation of this sort would furnish to France a *pretext* and perhaps a *right* to meddle in our domestic concerns. It is therefore to be presumed both from the talents and the patriotism of our ministers that nothing of the sort exists. But if unfortunately, such a clause should have slipt in, the wisdom of government will undoubtedly strike it out; and the first Consul will hardly insist on prescribing to us the manner in which we shall dispose of, settle, and *govern* our own territory."[7] Now mark the reply of the Aurora folks. "From the nature and principles of our government we boldly assert there is no such clause as *any way* to interfere with our *right* or independence as *sovereigns* of Louisiana from the moment it came into our possession. Why then this *malignant insinuation* by an affected denial?" Bravo! This is doing the thing handsomely: but let us reduce the proposition to its simple elements. It will stand thus. A clause which might in any way interfere with our right as sovereigns, is contrary to the nature and principles of our government, therefore no such clause either does or can exist, and therefore to insinuate any such thing is malignant. This I say is the plain and only meaning of the round declaration just cited, unless in-

7. See p. 336.

deed to elude the obvious import, they recur to a mental reservation and tell us they intended merely to say, that it consists with the nature of our government (that is of our administration) boldly to assert any thing without regard to decency or truth. Should they explain themselves in this way, nothing more need be said on the subject. But if the former be the true interpretation, it will follow that even in their opinion the third article is contrary to the nature and principles of our government. That is to say: it is not only accidentally but irremediably unconstitutional. Whether it be so or not I shall not presume to enquire, for since the principle adopted some time since, that Congress are exclusively the judges of their own power, any thing said on that subject might be deemed a breach of privilege. I leave the matter therefore with my superiors, presuming that if the clause be convenient it will turn out to be constitutional.

Let us then examine whether it be convenient. The reasons for putting it in the treaty, and the reasons for keeping it there, I pretend not to know and presume not to ask. Submitting with all due deference to the constituted authorities, I wait, with them, the course of events. But the day may come, perhaps it is not remote, when we shall feel the serious import of this measure. Those who favor the incorporation have certainly gained one step by stipulating for it with a foreign power; and as certainly, he, with whom we have made the treaty must from the reason and nature of things (what the Aurora folks may say to the contrary notwithstanding) have a right to insist on our compliance with the contract. In binding ourselves therefore to the performance of an internal and domestic act, we have conferred a right to meddle in our internal and domestic affairs. Now such is my idea of the importance of this right, that if I verily believe it wise to raise new states in that extensive region, and if I had the power to act according to my discretion, I would freely give the first Consul five millions of dollars to strike out that clause. Let Congress comply with it, not only to the letter, but to the utmost extent, according to their comprehension, still the French government may conscientiously believe that more remains to be done. The question must in some degree turn on the true intent and meaning of our constitution, of which the French government must therefore have the right to judge. The Congress may form one opinion and the first Consul another. Some of our fellow citizens may adopt his opinion. *The contract moreover is such that the breach of this condition destroys its effect.* If therefore we fail in the performance, our right to the territory is gone. But inasmuch as that performance, in its nature eventual, can only be compleated when all the inhabitants of the ceded territory shall be *incorporated in the union* and possessed of *all* the rights of American citizens, it follows that until that period, necessarily remote, shall arrive our *possessory right* remains subject to an *eventual claim* of France which she can make at the time most convenient. It follows also, that any half-dozen Frenchmen, settled if you please at the foot of the salt mountain, may claim the protection of France to obtain from the United States an admission into the Union, with a brace of senators. To be sure they may not be in those circumstances which are designated by the constitution, but who is the judge? Congress unquestionably, so far as regards our conduct, and as unquestionably, France so far as regards her conduct. It will perhaps be said that this is fine spun reasoning, and truly if it were, I might reply that France has never been deficient in fine spun reasoners when necessary to her views. The Empress of Russia had guaranteed an agreement between the catholics and dissenters in Poland, by which the former were to be admitted in common with the latter, to public office. By her armed interference under this guarantee began the partition of Poland. France has generally had the address to form her treaties in such way as to provide for future interpretations suitable to her interest. Let us examine the matter in this respect. We had heard a good deal about *the* treaty and were not a little surprised to find *three* treaties instead of one, or rather a *treaty* and two *conventions* about a single object. The whole affair consisted in the purchase of Louisiana for fifteen millions, four of which were to be paid to our own citizens, in extinguishment of their claims on the French government. To a man, who, as I said before, has been used to the strait forward way of doing business, this seems strange. If any one in common life purchased a tract of land, he would naturally, as evidence of his title, ask a deed which should specify the sum paid, and the land conveyed, in a plain and simple manner. But if the grantor should propose to put the grant in one paper, as a free gift with an eventual condition annexed to it, and the consideration money in two other papers, one of them having also the air of a free gift, and the other looking like the payment of an award, the grantee would not be a little surprised. And if he were a prudent man he would probably insist on having his title in the known and approved form.

The treaty begins by declaring a desire of the contracting parties to remove all source of misunderstanding relative to objects of discussion, mentioned in articles of a convention of 30th Sept. 1800 relative to the rights we claim by a treaty we made with Spain 27th Oct. 1795. The first article then recites the conveyance made by Spain, and that in consequence of it France has an incontestible right to Louisiana. Then the first Consul as *a proof of his friendship* gives it to the United States as *fully* and *in the same manner* as France had *acquired* it by the recited conveyance. Evidently therefore, if the Spanish conveyance was void, the United States would gain nothing by the Consuls *friendship* and *bounty*, especially as this french conveyance is without a *warranttee* of title, or a *guarantee* of possession, or a *covenant* for peaceable enjoyment.

The third article contains details uninteresting to the present enquiry, but the third already noted provides for the admission of the inhabitants of the ceded territory into the Union. The fourth, fifth, and sixth articles comprize like the second, details which may be omitted. The seventh on *the ground of reciprocal advantages to result from it to the contracting parties* gives certain commercial privileges exclusively to France and Spain, for twelve years. The eighth extends to France, forever, the right of being treated as the most favored nation *there*, whatever may be the case in *other Ports* of the Union. And the ninth, approves of a convention signed the same day *for payment of debts due to our citizens*, and of another convention signed the same day, *relative to a definitive rule between the parties*. Both of these conventions are by this article approved, and are to have their effect *as if* they had been inserted in the treaty. But it is *not* said *that they form a part of the treaty*. This is cautiously avoided.

We shall take up the conventions by and bye, at present it must be observed, 1st. That the commercial privileges, being granted on the ground of reciprocal advantage, form no part of the consideration for the grant. 2dly. That the grant itself is not in the nature of a sale, but of a free gift. And 3dly. That the only consideration for it, except what may be deduced from the preamble, is the condition that the inhabitants shall be admitted into our Union. It follows therefore, from the face of the instrument itself, that unless we comply with that condition *to the extent in which France may construe it*, we shall in her opinion have compleatly forfeited our right. Town, port, river, sugar plantations, and salt mountain, must all go together. In the mean time we hold by this *defeasable right* just what France was fairly entitled to by her treaty with Spain, and no more. So that if that treaty had previously become void, or been revok'd, we have no shadow of title. And if, under such circumstances, we take possession, no matter whether by force, by threats or by quiet surrender of the Spanish officer on the appearance of force, his Catholic Majesty can rightfully *at any time* dispossess us, and can properly call on his Allies (France included) for assistance. Since Spain is *in possession*, and therefore *presumptively the owner*, the following questions are not wholly impertinent. 1st. Can a nation assume any thing except peaceable possession as the evidence of right, on which to ground a transaction like the present? 2dly. If she may, within what limits does the doctrine prevail. 3dly. If it be unlimited, what shall prevent any two nations from interpreting at their pleasure treaties made by one of them with a third party, and disposing in consequence of towns, provinces and kingdoms? & 4thly. If this right be admitted, as by this treaty, it seems to have been, how are we to limit the exercise of it against ourselves? For instance, we take New-Orleans, and some time hence France and Spain, after examining our title, gravely determine that the treaty of St. Ildefonso,[8] from circumstances antecedent or subsequent or from articles in another treaty, or from some other cause which we know nothing about, had really given France no title, and therefore, as the First Consul had *by the very words* given us no more than France had acquired, we took nothing, but the title still continued in Spain. Thereupon they make a treaty in which, after reciting the Spanish title as we have recited the French title, his Catholic Majesty, as a proof of his friendship, gives the country to France. This may be done as soon after the conclusion of the present war with England as shall suit the convenience of the contracting parties. And if we complain and cry aloud to all Europe, we may very properly be told, that in making a treaty with France for territory in possession of Spain, we ought to have apprized the latter power of what was going forward; to have heard and weighed her objections, if any she had, and finally to have obtained her consent. That the situation of the country in the neighborhood of Spanish colonies did, in itself call on us to make a regular communication of our contract, even had Spain not been in the actual possession; and that having set the example of this strange traffic, we must take the consequence. Those who violate the law cannot claim the protection of the law.

If under these circumstances we complain that France has swindled us out of fifteen million of dollars, she may gravely tell us, 1st. That *caveat emptor* is a principle which should have taught us to examine the title. 2dly. That we should in common prudence have asked a guarantee; and 3dly. That it savors of insanity to talk of fifteen millions, when it will appear by the treaty that she had generously made us a valuable present, which we, according to the wise maxim, *never look a gift horse in the mouth*, had greedily accepted. And truly by looking at the treaty we shall find, that there is not one word in it about the fifteen millions, nor indeed about any consider-

8. The Treaty of San Ildefonso was the secret treaty signed in 1800 by which Spain gave Louisiana back to France.

ation whatever for the cession, which, on the contrary, appears *there* to have been perfectly gratuitous. We must then look for the consideration in the conventions, of which the first mentioned in the treaty *as the convention for payment of debts*, declares that the parties having by a treaty of the same date *terminated all difficulties relative to Louisiana*, and being desirous to secure the sums due by France to citizens of the United States, agree that a certain species of those debts shall be paid by the *United States*, to an amount not exceeding twenty millions of French livres, after the possession of Louisiana shall have been *given by the commissaries of France to those of the United States*. As to debts of any other description, or even those designated which may exceed the twenty millions, there is no provision whatever. This convention then proves, by necessary implication, that the twenty million livres forms no part of the consideration for Louisiana, because it declares in express words that all difficulties respecting Louisiana were already terminated. Indeed these twenty millions are evidently given on condition that a French commissary shall deliver peaceable possession of the country to an American commissary, and if the possession be not delivered by *French commissaries* but taken by *American soldiers*, the money is not to be paid. So that if under these circumstances we make such payment, it is an act done in our own wrong, from which, of course, we can derive no advantage.

The convention next noticed in the treaty as *a convention relative to a definitive rule*, declares that *in consequence of the treaty of cession of Louisiana*, the parties are willing to regulate definitively every thing *relative to the said cession*. And thereupon it is agreed that, over and above the sum for payment of debts, the Government of the United States shall pay France (in six per cent stock) sixty million of livres, *after Louisiana shall be taken possession of in the name of the United States*. Here then we find that the peaceable delivery of possession (one of the things not least important *relative to the said cession,*) is wholly lost sight of; and no matter how the possession be taken, whether peaceably or forcibly, by right or by wrong, we must pay. These sixty millions then are not given *for the cession* but for *something relative to it*. They are in effect promised as men sometimes pay lawyers, *not to side with the adversary*. It is so much *hush money;* and the plain English of the contract is, "*let us take Louisiana from Spain* under color of title from you *and we will pay you sixty million livres* to carry on your war with England." Can any reasonable man suppose that the difference of terms used in these two conventions as to the mode of obtaining possession, was purely accidental? Or can it be attributed to mere chance that no part of the eighty millions we are to pay is any where stated as the purchase money of Louisiana? Suppose this country to be wrested from us by Spain, aided by a powerful alliance, can we ask France to refund the money paid? Shall we not be told that in transactions of this serious nature mere talk of ministers can not be resorted to, but the ratified treaties, and that from the face of them Louisiana was a *free gift*, for which no other *consideration* was stipulated, or *even asked*, but the admission of the inhabitants among the American States?

But is it expedient to admit them? I must again say, that were it otherwise desirable, it would be dangerous when they come in by foreign patronage, and of course with foreign attachments. And I will take the liberty to express, as a free citizen, my opinion, that having purchased and paid for the country, we ought to have the right of governing it in the manner most suitable to our interest. It may, perhaps, be most convenient to hold *as colonies* those districts which from time to time we may deem it expedient to settle; but whether it be or not, we should have the sovereign right to give or to withhold a participation in our *national councils*. It is a strange policy to call in Frenchmen, Spaniards, and Indians, (for they also are inhabitants of the ceded territory) to decide on our highest concerns. This question is not between northern and southern, eastern and western states, but between United America and Foreign Nations. Analize this condition and we have purchased neither land nor subjects nor citizens, but masters. When, for instance, we give to New-Orleans and the territory around it the rights of a state, and make it a member of the Union, we diminish the share of each existing state in the national authority, and admit a voice in our councils which is not truly American. We must expect a strong predilection to a foreign country; and perhaps that very port for which we pay so much, may be surrendered by the inhabitants to its ancient master. Shall it be said that the enjoyment of freedom will be a pledge of their fidelity? Let those who hold that opinion look at our neighbours in Lower Canada. They chuse representatives to make their own laws; they pay no taxes whatever. The laws are well administered; and they have the protection of the habeas corpus. Yet I am warranted by the concurrent testimony of those who have travelled through their country, though I have not done so myself, to say, that they ardently desire the antient government of the Bourbons, and if an opportunity offered, would unanimously join the royal standard of France. Of us they speak under the name of Yankees, with hatred and contempt. That their brethren to the westward and southward have similar sentiments cannot reasonably be doubted; and the natural consequence it is not difficult to anticipate.

To pursue these the⁹ reflections would lead me too far. I therefore close with the sincere wish, that we may not have cause to mourn that portentous condition.

I am, sir,

Your obedient serv't.

AN AMERICAN.

9. In the newspaper the text read "these the reflections"; in the manuscript, "these reflections."

On July 11, 1804, Morris received word that "General Hamilton was killed in a duel this morning by Colonel Burr." When he went into town the next day, he discovered that Hamilton was still alive and rushed to his bedside, where he stayed until Hamilton died. That evening, asked to give the funeral oration, he replied,

> I promise to do so if I can possibly command myself enough, but express my belief that it will be utterly impossible. I am wholly unmanned by this day's spectacle.[1]

Morris records in his diary that as he thinks about what to say at the funeral he is mainly conscious of things he should *not* discuss: Hamilton's illegitimate birth, his attachment to monarchy, his public "avowal of conjugal infidelity," and the fact that he was killed in a duel. Further, there is no time for writing out an address or memorizing it. When he is finished speaking,

> I find that what I have said does not answer the general expectation. This I knew would be the case; it must ever happen to him whose duty it is to allay the sentiment which he is expected to arouse.[2]

Since there was no written text, this version is a reconstruction of Morris's address by William Coleman, editor of the *Evening Post*, with Morris's revisions.[3]

"Funeral Oration on the death of Gen'l Hamilton," Gouverneur Morris Papers, Rare Book and Manuscript Library, Columbia University, item 848. The manuscript is in another hand, possibly that of William Coleman. The oration was delivered July 14; a version based on the reporter's notes, which differs considerably from this text, was published in the New York *American Citizen* on July 16. The *New-York Evening Post* published this version on July 17, and the *New York Daily Advertiser* published the *Evening Post* version, with minor differences, on July 18.

    1. *Diary and Letters of Gouverneur Morris*, 2:373–74.
    2. *Diary and Letters*, 2:375.
    3. Ibid.

Fellow-Citizens,

If on this sad, this solemn occasion, I should endeavour to move your commiseration, it would be doing injustice to that sensibility which has been so generally and so justly manifested. Far from attempting to excite your emotions, I must try to repress my own, and yet I fear that instead of the language of a public speaker, you will hear only the lamentations of a bewailing friend. But I will struggle with my bursting heart, to portray that Heroic Spirit, which has flown to the mansions of bliss.

Students of Columbia—he was in the ardent pursuit of knowledge in your academic shades, when the first sound of the American war called him to the field. A young and unprotected volunteer, such was his zeal and so brilliant his service that we heard his name before we knew his person—It seemed as if GOD had called him suddenly into existence, that he might assist to save a world!

The penetrating eye of Washington soon perceived the manly spirit which animated his youthful bosom. By that excellent judge of men he was selected as an Aid, and thus he became early acquainted with, and was a principal actor in, the most important scenes of our Revolution.

At the siege of York, he pertinaciously insisted—and he obtained the command of a Forlorn Hope. He stormed the redoubt; but let it be recorded, that not one single man of the enemy perished. His gallant troops emulating the example of their chief checked the uplifted arm, and spared a foe no longer resisting. Here closed his military career.

Shortly after the war, your favour—no, your discernment called him to public office. You sent him to the convention at Philadelphia: he there assisted in forming that constitution which is now the bond of our union, the shield of our defence and the source of our prosperity. In signing that compact he exprest his apprehension that it did not contain sufficient means of strength for its own preservation; and that in consequence we should share the fate of many other republics and pass through Anarchy to Despotism. We hoped better things. We confided in the good sense of the American people, and above all we trusted in the protecting Providence of the Almighty. On this important subject he never concealed his opinion. He disdained concealment. Knowing the purity of his heart, he bore it as it were in his hand, exposing to every passenger its inmost recesses. This generous indiscretion subjected him to censure from misrepresentation. His speculative opinions were treated as deliberate designs; and yet you all know how strenuous, how unremitting were his efforts to establish and to preserve the constitution. If then his opinion was wrong, pardon, oh! pardon that single error, in a life devoted to your service.

At the time when our government was organized, we were without funds, though not without resources. To call them into action, and establish order in the finances, Washington sought for splendid talents, for extensive information, and above all, he sought for sterling, incorruptible integrity. All these he found in Hamilton—The system then adopted has been the subject of much animadversion. If it be not without a fault, let it be remembered that nothing human is perfect—Recollect the circumstances of the moment—recollect the conflict of opinion—and above all, remember that *the minister of a republic must bend to the will of the people.* The administration which Washington formed, was one of the most efficient, one of the best that any country was ever blest with. And the result was a rapid advance in power and prosperity, of which there is no example in any other age or nation. The part which Hamilton bore is universally known.

His unsuspecting confidence in professions which he believed to be sincere, led him to trust too much to the undeserving. This exposed him to misrepresentation. He felt himself obliged to resign—The care of a rising family, and the narrowness of his fortune, made it a duty to return to his profession for their support. But though he was compelled to abandon public life, never, no, never for a moment did he abandon the public service. He never lost sight of your interests—I declare to you, before that God in whose presence we are now so especially assembled, that in his most private and confidential conversations, the single objects of discussion and consideration were your freedom and happiness.

You will remember the state of things which again called forth Washington from his retreat to lead your armies. You know that he asked for Hamilton to be his second in command. That venerable sage well knew the dangerous incidents of a military profession, and he felt the hand of time pinching life at its source. It was probable that he would soon be removed from the scene, and that his Second would succeed to the command. He knew by experience the importance of that place—and he thought the sword of America might safely be confided to the hand which now lies cold in that coffin. Oh! my fellow citizens, remember this solemn testimonial, that he was not ambitious. Yet, he was charged with ambition; and wounded by the Imputation, when he laid down his command, he declared, in the proud independence of his soul that he never would accept of any office, unless in a foreign war he should be called on to expose his life in defence of his country. This determination was immovable. It was his fault that his opinions and his resolutions could not be changed. Knowing his own firm purpose, he was indignant at the charge that he sought for place or power. He was ambitious only of glory, but he was deeply solicitous for you. For himself he feared nothing, but he feared that bad men might, by false professions, acquire your confidence and abuse it to your ruin.

Brethren of the Cincinnati—There lies our chief! Let him still be our model. Like him, after a long and faithful public service, let us cheerfully perform the social duties of private life. Oh! he was mild and gentle. In him there was no offence; no guile. His generous hand and heart were open to all.

Gentlemen of the Bar—You have lost your brightest ornament. Cherish and imitate his example. While, like him, with justifiable, with laudable zeal, you pursue the interests of your clients, remember, like him, the eternal principles of justice.

Fellow Citizens—You have long witnessed his professional conduct, and felt his unrivaled eloquence. You know how well he performed the duties of a citizen—you know that he never courted your favour by adulation, or the sacrifice of his own judgment. You have seen him contending against you, and saving your dearest interests, as it were, in spite of yourselves. And you now feel and enjoy the benefits resulting from the firm energy of his conduct. Bear this testimony to the memory of my departed friend. I CHARGE YOU TO PROTECT HIS FAME—It is all he has left—all that these poor orphan children will inherit from their father. But, my countrymen, that fame may be a rich treasure to you also. Let it be the test by which to examine those who solicit your favour. Disregarding professions, view their conduct and on a doubtful occasion, ask, *Would Hamilton have done this thing?*

You all know how he perished. On this last scene I cannot, I must not dwell. It might excite emotions too strong for your better judgment. Suffer not your indignation to lead to any act which might again offend the insulted majesty of the laws. On his part, as from his lips, though with my voice—for his voice you will hear no more—let me entreat you to respect yourselves.

And now, ye ministers of the everlasting God, perform your holy office and commit these ashes of our departed brother to the bosom of the Grave!

This essay and the ones that follow all date from 1805 and seem to have been designed as school exercises. On the last page, Morris has endorsed this manuscript: "Oration on the Love of Wealth. June 1805, for young Fleming. The Subject had been anticipated by a Senior Student."

Of all the Passions or Propensities of the human Heart, none has been the Subject of more frequent or more severe Satire than the Love of Wealth; and none has exercised such constant and universal Dominion. Must the Bolts of Genius be hurled again at the Head of Avarice; or shall youth be permitted to burn a transitory Grain of Incense before the Idol of Age?

When we behold those Scenes of Dissipation which decorate every Circle of our festive Land, Scenes where the wrinkled Brow of Oeconomy is alike the Object of Scorn and Derision, we cannot but acknowlege there is no Need to declaim against a Passion devoted to general Contempt. But when we hear of the sly Usurer who turning a sanctimonious Eye to Heaven filches, with impious Hand, the monthly Impost of five per Cent which he has laid on the Necessities of unfortunate Men the revolted Soul can find no Terms to vent her Indignation. Such are the variant Sentiments imprest on the Heart by those Events which rise to View in every populous Town. Extreme in all Things, Fools neither seek nor find that golden Mean where Wisdom and Virtue hold their awful State. But who shall arrogate to himself the Praise of living under their holy Sway; or who presume to publish their sublime Decrees? Without pretending to a Claim, which would be imprudent in the Wariest, and in persons of our Age compleatly ridiculous, let me (tho timid) dare to examine whether this general Passion be essentially vicious.

To dwell on my Subject in the Abstract and enquire whether Man, in his primeval State, was stimulated by a Love of Wealth; or whether it befel him

Gouverneur Morris Papers, Rare Book and Manuscript Library, Columbia University, item 850.

(with other Mishaps) from the Indulgence of impious Curiosity, might involve us in a theological Maze as intricate as the questions of Freewill and Predestination. Let us therefore leave theological as well as metaphisical & political Science to those numerous and sage Professors who will doubtless enlighten the World whenever they shall have been so fortunate as to understand themselves. Let us keep a firm Footing in Fact, while the Land of Conjecture is surveyed patented parcelled out and retailed by the System Mongers of the World. That fairy Land which abounds in delightful Views and has never repaid the Expence of Tillage.

It may be well at the Outset to enquire in what does the Love of Wealth consist, or of what is it constituted. Among the Poor it is inseparably blended with a Love of Existence; for he who has nothing craves, and justly too, the Necessaries of Life. One Grade higher Men seek for those Conveniences and those thousand little Things which enter into the complex Idea of Comfort. If we pass on we come to that Station in which a Love of Wealth is confounded with a Love of Independence, and we cannot wholly quit the Votaries of Independence before we are surrounded by those who court Distinction and only toil for Riches because they court Respect. Should we rise a little more we shall find ardent Spirits who grasp at Gold as the Means of Power; and one Step further leads us again into the cold Abode of Penury where, our Circle compleated, we behold a palefaced Victim who submits to starve because he wants Courage to spend.

Which of all these shall we stigmatize for the Love of Wealth? Shall it be the Wretch whose daily Labor is required to earn his daily Bread, or him who seeks Comfort for the Wife of his Bosom and Children of his Bed that he may enjoy the Smile of domestic Felicity? Every Countenance tells me that to this Question the Heart says No. Well, then, shall we brand him who struggles to rise above a State of Dependence that he may display the natural Bent of his Disposition, or him whose chief Pleasure is derived from the Consideration and applause of his Fellow-Men? There is an honest Pride which pleads in Favor of the one, and a Consciousness of aimiable Infirmity which may excuse the other. Shall we not rather pity than blame that Being who glows with a Love of Fame but is cramped and shackled by the social Institutions of a Country which leaves no Road to Distinction except thro the Regions of Plutus? Unhappy State! Where Talents excite Envy instead of inspiring Respect, where Defamation is the Reward of Merit, where Virtue meets the Meed of Folly, where it is dangerous to deserve, and public Honors exclusively bestowed on worthless Minions become the true and indefeasable Titles to Contempt. As yet the Love of Wealth may seem more an Object of approbation than Aversion, and much of our Censure must be reserved for that Condition in which it becomes the Handmaid of Ambition or the Tyrant of Age. But Ambition is not our Theme. We are not called on to declaim against "Macedonia's Madman." Nor should we (if the Ashes of Alexander were committed to our Discretion) hastily condemn the Founder of so many Cities, who opened new Avenues to Science and new Channels to Commerce new Objects to the Arts and multiplied Sources of Enjoyment to Man. Thus then, after ranging thro this extensive Field we are at length confined to that forlorn Condition where, the Fire of Youth extinct each ardent Passion fled and the Vigor of Manhood unbrac'd a cold Heart bereft of all it's Joys clings to the hoarded Pelf which alone procures Respect Attention or Notice from the Mass of Mankind. Raise up the palsied Seer, give him again the bounding Pulse, let the weak artery spring elastic, pour fresh Fluid thro the Nerves, expand the contracted Chest, and flush the pale Cheek with Crimson, & soon shall the hated Passion fly, or rather confined within its proper Bounds the Heart shall beat high cheared by all the Virtues. We must not then blame the Love of Wealth, but pity the Absence of every other Love.

Let us be just. This Passion like all others useful laudable in the Degree, becomes pernicious only in the Extreme. To despise it in Youth is as much a Weakness as to cherish it in age. A Weakness less disgusting indeed but more dangerous. An inordinate Love of Wealth is the solitary Vice of Age and Decrepitude, but in Youth a boasted Contempt of Wealth is generally the Result of prodigal Dispositions, and too often the Cause of Acts which lead to Infamy. It is but the Excuse for that Idleness and those dissolute Habits which engender every Vice. From the rapacious Despot to the brawling Demagogue, thro all the Ranks of Life and all the Forms of Robbery Forgery and Fraud we find the same Cupidity for the Substance of others the same Waste of their own. Let such Men deride the regular Principles and sober Habits of Youth inured to virtuous Industry, of Manhood occupied by honest Cares and of Age rewarded by opulent Ease; but let us determine to scorn the Scoffer. Let us not be ashamed to love Wealth as it ought to be loved and seek it as it ought to be sought, that we may possess the Comforts which become our Station in Life, the means of that Independence which is essential to Freedom, and the Power of indulging a generous mind in Acts of Benevolence.

Morris endorsed this essay: "Oration on Patriotism. 1805 for young Hamilton."

+⟩══⟨+

Among the many Subjects which present themselves for the Exercise of youthful Talent none seemed so proper as Patriotism. I am sure that none can be more congenial to your Feelings; and tho my Genius be feeble, my Heart is warm with that Sentiment which glowed in the Breast of my Father.

But how shall I express or how define it? Must I exclaim with the Roman "Nescio qua natale Solum Dulcedine cunctos ducit, nec immemores non sinit esse sui."[1] Oh say what secret Charm twines round the Heart and bids it dote upon the natal Soil! Or must I believe it is a primal Sense which binds us to the Spot where we first inhal'd the Morning Fragrance, first saw the Light, first felt the Warmth of Day, first heard the Voice of parental Love, first tasted the Sweets of domestic Endearment. These delicious Ideas all press on the Heart, when Memory presents the Scene of infant Playfulness and the Joy of Youth. In the remotest Regions and in every State of Life, whether bustling among the busy Throng or lulled in the peaceful Shade, dissolving in the Lap of Luxury or struggling in the Grasp of Care, fanned by the vernal Breeze or cradled in the imperious Surge, still, dear Idea of the natal Soil still dost thou return. Neither Distance nor Time nor Pleasure nor Occupation nor Hope nor Fear, neither the Pursuit of Wealth the Turmoil of Ambition nor the Blandishments of Love can obliterate from the Heart thy fond Remembrance.

If we examine the various Countries and Climates of the Earth, we shall perceive the patriot Passion to be coextensive with the human Race. He feels it who basks on the burning Sand of Lybia, and he who shivers on the

Gouverneur Morris Papers, Rare Book and Manuscript Library, Columbia University, item 849.

1. "How I do not know, but the native soil sweetly charms all men and never allows anyone to forget her." Ovid, *Epistulae ex Ponto*, I.3.35–36.

frozen Shores of Lapland. The sedentary Belgian, the wandering Tatar, the sprightly Frenchman, the sober Spaniard, the proud Briton and obsequious Italian are all imbued with the Love of their Country. Nay in those alpine Regions where the Perseverance of helvetian Industry forces with Pain a scanty Subsistence from the rugged Soil, this Love seems to gather Strength from Circumstances, which would damp or extinguish it, if Reason were the Rule of Passion.

> And as the Child whom scaring Sounds molest
> Clings close and closer to the Mother's Breast,
> so the rude Tempest and the Thunder's Roar
> But bind them to their native Mountains more[2]

If then (with Ovid) we should acknowlege our Incompetence to define

> Those sweet Emotions which fond Memory lead
> To dwell enraptur'd on our natal Soil[3]

Still we must perceive and acknowlege that it is one of the many Propensities which designate Man as a social Being. Indeed when we contemplate ourselves we are struck at every moment with the Conviction that we cannot exist except in Society, and therefore we not only see but feel the Folly of those specious Reasonings, on a supposed State of Nature, which have led to wild Notions of Right and romantic Theories of Government. It is a State impossible, therefore not to be supposed; incompatible, therefore not to be admitted as a Ground of Argument: since Deductions from what is false and impossible must be fallacious and absurd. In the same Train of Reflection too we must see and feel that those queasy Principles of Philanthropy which Philosophers boast and which lead them to moan over the Miseries of a merciless Boor, or melt at the Recital of a Felon's Execution, but cannot prompt to relieve a Countryman in Captivity in Slavery in Chains, are as inconsistent with the patriot Passion as Ice with Fire.

This strong Passion swells the ingenuous Heart from early Youth till we bend over the Grave. Men of ardent Temper and Affections feel it for their

---

2. Morris seems to be quoting from memory from Oliver Goldsmith's "The Traveller": the third line should read "So the loud torrent, and the whirlwind's roar."

3. Morris may be quoting or translating this from memory, or perhaps it is his own composition; the exact quotation does not appear in Ovid. There are, however, many similar sentiments in the *Epistulae ex Ponto*, such as the passage quoted above, and in *Tristia*; cf. *Tristia* 4.2.57ff.

adopted Country; but who ever forgot his own? If there be a Wretch pre-eminently foul, whose Soul is beyond all Measure and Degree polluted, it is that Wretch who can see with Indifference the Ruin of his Country. But if among the countless Myriads of Mankind there be one solitary Individual who can wish for that Ruin, or who can malign his native Soil, "the Motions of his Soul are dark as Erebus and his Affections black as Hell. Let no such man be trusted."[4]

Yes! The Love of our Country is a primal Sense—the fair Impression of that Hand which form'd the human Heart. And with the characteristic Simplicity of creative Wisdom it is intimately blended with and strengthened by every other virtuous and honorable Sentiment. It is interwoven with the Bonds of connubial Tenderness, hallowed by the pious Sense of filial Duty, endear'd by the Charities of parental affection, nourished by the social Habits of Life, animated by the Fellowships of Youth, confirmed by the Amities of Age, and consecrated by the Mysteries of Religion. In the complex Idea of our Country is included Parents Wives Children Companions Friends, the Usages we respect, the manners we approve, the Language we speak, the Laws we love, and the Religion we venerate.

Such being the Principle Scope and Extent of the patriot Passion. We cannot wonder at the Effect. As it lasts thro Life "grows with our growth and strengthens with our Strength"[5] so it mingles in all our Projects and Concerns. Who can be indifferent to the Fate of his Country? In that Fate is involved the ambitious Man's Power, the rich Man's Wealth, the Peace the Honor the Safety of all. Is there a Spirit so poor as to hear without a Pang of his Country's Dishonor, so mean as not to exult in the national Glory, so feeble as not to dare in the public Defence? The Moment of Danger is the Proof of generous Minds. Then, when those Brawlers, who make Popularity a Trade, tremble and skulk, when Men of loud Boast are husht, and base Leaders hide, then the true Patriot steps forth to breast the

---

4. Morris is evidently quoting from memory Lorenzo's speech in Shakespeare, *Merchant of Venice*, act 5, scene 1:

> The man that hath no music in himself,
> nor is moved with concord of sweet sounds,
> is fit for treasons, stratagems, and spoils.
> The motions of his spirit are dull as night,
> and his affections dark as Erebus.
> Let no such man be trusted.

5. Alexander Pope, *Essay on Man*, epistle 2, line 136.

Storm. In the just Confidence of Worth he takes the Place assigned to him by Nature, and fills it with the due Measure of Talents and Courage. His Eye, beaming the Dignity of Virtue, commands. Clamor is silent. Envy obeys. For his Country he risques Wealth Life Honor, and asks for himself Nothing. The first Object is to serve and save his Fellow Citizens, the next is to enjoy (in common with them) common Rights protected by the common Law. Such was the great and glorious Washington. Wise firm collected, his Heart brave pure noble, his Conduct simple modest just, his Life consumed in patriot Exertions, his Reward the Shade of domestic Bliss and the Respect of his Fellow Citizens. This Respect was felt by all for I will not count those who vainly invok'd the Aid of Slander to tarnish the Lustre of his Fame. No—Let us anticipate on Time—Let them be forgotten—Let him be the Theme of Gratitude and Praise while in any human Breast there shall exist an American Heart.

The manuscript is clearly a draft, of which the first and last pages are missing. Sparks's note on the manuscript says "Fragment on Prejudice. Date uncertain." The Columbia library information indicates "probably 1805." Given its similarity of theme and treatment to the other essays from 1805 (which also include an "Oration on Music" not included in this collection), it seems likely it was written about the same time.

———

. . . can behold with Indifference Adultery Patricide and Treason "in the calm Light of mild Philosophy."[1] To such Men the Charities of domestic Life are but an idle Tale and Patriotism a feverish Dream. Centering every Thing in Self they sever all the Ties which connect us with Life and by the forced Expansion of social Sentiment to all Existence they render it too feeble for Use and even for Amusement. Till at Length by Force of viewing alike both good and Evil "in the calm Lights of mild Philosophy" cold Indifference destroys the Charm of Youth & the Consolation of Age and renders Being itself unsupportable.

The Truths necessary to Man are the common appanage of the human Race. So far as it was useful to see, Light is as given to all; but beyond that Verge the Darkness is compleat. There is no moral Herschel,[2] there is no metaphisical Telescope, there is no intellectual Baloon which can peer or soar beyond the general Limits. Common Sense and Common Sentiment are the strong Pillars on which repose the Arch of social Life and the Treasures of human Felicity. If filial Piety if connubial Fidelity if social

Gouverneur Morris Papers, Rare Book and Manuscript Library, Columbia University, item 852.

  1. Joseph Addison, *Cato*, act 1, scene 1:
          Thy steady temper, Portius,
          Can look on guilt, rebellion, fraud, and Caesar,
          In the calm lights of mild philosophy.
  2. William Herschel (1738–1822), British astronomer.

Subordination be indeed but Prejudice happy is the Land where Prejudice prevails. And most miserable they who casting off such Prejudice can be right. There is therefore an essential Difference between Prejudice and Error. The latter always wrong in itself is nevertheless to be pardoned when proper Means have been used to discover Truth. The former, however it may be indulged can never in Strictness be justified and is then compleatly odious when it invades the Rights or Happiness of Individuals or of Society.

Demo rails at Theophilus and, with no malevolence of Heart perhaps, holds him up to the World as a Bigot a Miser and a Tyrant. But Demo have you collected and collated Facts respecting him whom you traduce? Have you scrutinized the History of his Life to develope the Operation of his Mind and the Feelings of his Heart? No. Why then accuse him? Because I am convinced the Accusation is just. Convinced! But on what Ground? Why every Body says so, and what every Body says must be true. Not if every Body speaks on the same Ground with Demo. It happens that a thousand clamor and each perhaps will justify himself by the Clamor of nine hundred and ninety nine. But when the Hand of Time shall have drawn the Veil from before the Face of Truth it may appear that Theophilus was a Man pious charitable and kind. How then shall they excuse themselves by Whom he was slandered & persecuted? Perhaps by the poor Pretence that they were deceived. But if Pride will not permit them to impeach their own Infallibility they will boldly insist that Explanation is Artifice Demonstration a Cheat and Truth a Liar. Such is the natural Course of Prejudice fondled by Self-Love and made drunk with Pride.

But if the Effect of Prejudice were only to dishonor and to degrade there are perhaps Minds sufficiently base not to feel the humiliating Consequence. Yes there are Men who can patiently submit to deserved Scorn if they can but accumulate Treasure and indulge Sensuality. But let such Men know that Prejudice operates with an Influence as malign on Fortune as on Fame. False opinions lead to false Confidence false Operations and ruinous Results. He who will duly consider the different Relations in which he stands must be convinced that an unprejudiced Temper is favorable to Health to Fortune and to Reputation. Of Course he will feel it a Duty not only to others but to himself to examine with Industry Caution and Candor before he forms Opinions. For if the Mind revolts at the Idea of a Judge who acquits or condemns by hearing only the accused or the accuser how will it bear the galling Consciousness of having in like manner pronounced a rash and hasty Sentence not called on to decide by official Situation but acting under a self constituted Authority.

To dwell longer on this Part of the Subject might lead us too far. There is a Reverse to the Medal which may be worthy of Examination. As Men under the Impulse of Fear frequently run into Danger so it sometimes happens that the most prejudiced are those who have as they suppose thrown off all Prejudice. Those who from a Want of Reflection call for the Demonstration of Self evident Truths. Such Demonstration is in the Nature of Things impossible because we arrive at Truth only by the Induction of Consequences from evident Propositions. To invert this Course would prove the Certain by the Doubtful which is absurd. And to call for Proof of the certain is equally absurd for we can rationally ask Proof only where there is Doubt. Such Call therefore implies that the certain is doubtful. And when once it is admitted that self evident Propositions are Doubtful there is an End of reasoning because there is Nothing on which Reason can operate. He who demands Proof and thereby presumes a Doubt that two and two make four precludes himself from the Benefit of Arithmetical Calculation. He who holding in his Hand a Standard of Length denies the Accuracy of it's Dimensions can never apply it to the Purposes of Mensuration. And he who demands the Proof of those Duties whose Evidence is deriv'd from Sentiment destroys the Basis of all moral and social Obligation.

But if Prejudice be an opinion adopted without sufficient Reason then the Opinion that self evident Propositions require Proof is certainly a Prejudice because no sufficient Reason can exist for that which is manifestly absurd. It is therefore an Error founded on Prejudice and that Error is fatal. It is fatal because it destroys the Possibility of establish'd Truth. From that moment the False and the True lay Claim alike to Belief. And hence results that seeming Paradox so common in Life that the Infidel is of all Creatures on Earth the most credulous. He can believe in magic tho he has no Faith in Miracles and trust to Man while he renounces God.

These are the baleful Effects which too often arise from a haughty attempt to throw off what the Fastidiousness of Philosophy has been pleased to denominate vulgar Prejudice. Reason forsaking the humble Path which befits our frail Condition and pampered with the Vanity of that Foolishness which Man calls Knowlege establishes the primary Position that we must not believe what we cannot understand and then asks Explanation of things inconceivable and Demonstrations of Things indubitable.

> Man proud Man
> most ignorant of what he's most assured.
> His glassy Essence
> Plays such fantastic Tricks before high Heaven
> as makes the Angels weep.[3]

Yes. If there be any one Thing of which we are more assur'd than of any other it is that frail Existence which like Glass may be shiver'd in a Moment. And yet of that Existence what do we know? We move we Think; but in what consists the Power of Motion and of Thought we are as ignorant as the Earth on which we tread. Volition, Judgment, Sentiment, in what do they consist? How do they operate? Where are they placed? To these questions the Profoundest Philosopher can give no better answer than the poorest Babe. And yet he will presume to inquire into the Attributes of the Deity and to scan the Mode in which they operate on those Decrees which like God himself are eternal. And when Researches so presumptuous and so vain terminate as they must in grievous Disappointment he denies because he cannot comprehend. And will he also deny himself? Or can he comprehend himself?

It is a consolatory Reflection to the Great Mass of Mankind that the [the manuscript breaks off here].

3. Morris is quoting from Isabella's speech in Shakespeare, *Measure for Measure*, act 2, scene 2:

> . . . but man, proud man,
> Drest in a little brief authority,
> Most ignorant of what he's most assured,
> His glassy essence, like an angry ape,
> Plays such fantastic tricks before high heaven
> As make the angels weep; who, with our spleens,
> Would all themselves laugh mortal.

War in Disguise, or the Frauds of the Neutral Flags appeared in October
1805, the same month that Admiral Nelson won his great victory at Tra-
falgar. Nelson gave Britain control of the seas, and in *War in Disguise*,
James Stephen gave her a doctrine for using that power. Stephen, an
admiralty lawyer and former colonial official, argued that the French were
sustaining their economy during the war by shifting the trade with their
colonies from French ships to neutral ships. Like most colonial powers,
the French had previously adhered to mercantilist policies and allowed
this trade only in French ships. When war came, however, the French had
opened their commerce to neutral shipping. This meant, Stephen said,
they had "in effect, for the most part, only changed their flags, chartered
many vessels really neutral, and altered a little the former routes of their
trade."[1]

The solution, Stephen argued, was simply to shut down *all* commerce
in French goods, whether carried in belligerent or in neutral ships. This
would damage the French economy and hasten the end of the war. But it
was also a violation of neutral rights under international law. *War in Disguise* was an elaborate justification for this policy under the principles of
admiralty law. An American edition of the book was published in January
1806, and Morris's *Answer* followed in February. Meanwhile, Stephen's
argument had found a receptive audience in England. In May 1806 it became official policy with the first of a series of Orders in Council imposing a blockade of continental ports. Americans understood that the new

---

An Answer to War in Disguise; *or, Remarks upon the New Doctrine of England, Concern-
ing Neutral Trade* (New-York: Printed by Hopkins and Seymour, for I. Riley & Co.
February, 1806). American Antiquarian Society Early American Imprints, series II
(Shaw-Shoemaker), no. 10907. Courtesy American Antiquarian Society.

1. [James Stephen], *War in Disguise, or the Frauds of the Neutral Flags* (London,
1805; repr., New York: Hopkins & Seymour, 1806), 9.

policy was largely aimed at American commerce; ultimately this dispute would escalate into the War of 1812.

⸙

"Illud natura non patiatur, ut aliorum spoliis nostras facultates, copias, opes, augeamus: et unum debeat esse omnibus propositum, ut eadem sit utilitas uniuscujusque et universarum, quam si ad se quisque rapiat, dissolvitur omnis humana consortio."

—CICERO DE ORATORE. 3.[2]

PREFACE.

Those who are in the habit of approving or condemning, more from regard to persons than to things, wish to know the Author before they read a book. In the hope that these sheets may be impartially considered, the writer will not affix his name. He will, however, to obviate unfounded objection, so far gratify the curious, as to say, that he is not a Practitioner of the Law; he is not a Merchant; he has no interest in Trade; he holds no Office; and has no connexion with those who administer the Government.

AN ANSWER
TO
WAR IN DISGUISE, &c.

The Pamphlet, entitled "War in Disguise," on which we are about to make some remarks, is the production of no mean ability. We have been told, that it was written by direction of the English cabinet. This, however, we do not believe, since it shows a want of that caution and reserve, which usually mark the compositions of public men; our respect also for the British minister, will not permit us to suppose that, even hastily or in a convivial moment, he would assent to the general scope and tenor of this work; much less, that he would initiate its dangerous doctrine, after serious thought and

---

2. "Nature does not allow us to increase our capacities, wealth, and resources by robbing others; and this should be the single principle for all men, that the interest of each and all should be the same, for if each one appropriates things for himself, all human community will be dissolved." The inscription is in fact taken from book 3 of Cicero's *De Officiis*. Morris has combined the end of a sentence at 3.22 with a sentence at 3.26.

mature deliberation. We shall, therefore, treat the argument with freedom, unrestrained by any of that deference which delicacy would impose, if we believed ourselves addressing, even at second hand, the minister of a great monarch.

In effect, this pamphlet appears to be written in the spirit of a lawyer, stimulated by that of a merchant; and the author, supporting rather a generous client than a deliberate opinion, in the zeal of argument, overleaps the bound of reason. Nevertheless, though we are not blind to defects, we gladly pay our tribute of applause to great part of his work, especially to that which shows, in a manner equally clear and forcible, the mischiefs resulting from what is called the neutral carrying trade, or what might more properly be called, the covering trade. We fully agree with him, that it is inconsistent with neutral duties, and eventually hostile to neutral rights; that it derogates from the national honour, poisons the public morals, and is injurious alike to our interest and reputation. In this persuasion we believe that, to restrain it, the American Government will honestly and heartily concur in every measure of reason and justice. We acknowledge, with our author, the power of France. And though we shall not pretend to conceal our admiration of those qualities and talents which mark the Emperor Napoleon as the first man of the present age, we shall not deny, that such great power, in such able hands, may be dangerous to the liberties of mankind. We are thankful, therefore, to divine Providence that, in a position which fortifies the sentiment of inexpiable hostility by the double motive of interest and apprehension, he has placed a nation, whose incalculable resources enable her to display her valour in every quarter of the globe. Whether America should join in this arduous contest, is a question to be decided by those to whom she has intrusted her highest concerns. They will adopt such measures as they shall deem most advisable, under a consideration of every circumstance. And if, from the infirmity incident to man, they should pursue a line of conduct which may (because pacific) appear unwise to the ministers of his Britannic majesty, that conduct cannot justly be made the cause or the pretext of war. In holding out a menace, our author has not, perhaps, considered the ungracious appearance it gives to his argument. Neither has he duly appreciated the American character. The blessing of God on our first contest in arms, made this nation sovereign, free, and independent. Our citizens feel their honourable condition, and, whatever may be their opinion on questions of national policy, will firmly support the national rights. Our government must, therefore, be permitted to judge for itself. No minister, however splendid his talents—

no prince, however great his power—must dictate to the President of the United States. We may condemn his measures, but we respect his authority, because we respect ourselves. Let not this be considered as a false or fastidious display of national sentiment; neither let us be judged by those adventurers who, roaming about in pursuit of illicit gain, offer their conscience for sale at every market. England as well as America, has the misfortune to produce such men. Her achievements in war have not secured her against the scoffs directed at her pursuits in trade. But, while we disdain to join with the profligate Barrere[3] in stigmatizing, as hucksters, a gallant nation, we feel a right to expect a rcciprocation of candour and decency.

Having thus, in a way which the occasion seemed to require, discussed some preliminary matter, we shall approach the argument; and having explicitly avowed our opinion respecting the abuse of neutral trade, we shall as explicitly declare, that we consider it our interest to carry the British doctrine (on that subject) as far as reason and justice can, in any manner, permit. The geographical position of the United States, while it enables them to assail with peculiar advantage the colonial commerce of Europe, confines them in a great degree to that species of hostility, when at war with any of the commercial powers. To extend therefore the right of capture, by limiting neutral rights, should be a leading feature of American policy; especially as circumstances resulting from the same position, must so operate as to make us, when neutral, an exception to the general rule. But though our political and mercantile interests concur to favour the British tenets, we must not, by giving them an extravagant extension, transgress the bounds of reason and justice. For we fully agree with the writer before us, that "never in the affairs of nations was solid security or true prosperity, purchased at the cost of virtuous principle"; and we request that this maxim may, in considering the subject now before us, be present to every mind, and impressed on every heart.

The argument being leveled at America, we shall take little notice of instances brought from other countries, which cannot exist here; and as little shall we notice American cases which show that some corrupt individuals have covered as neutral, by false papers and false oaths, the property of a

---

3. Bertrand Barère de Vienzac (1755–1841), French politician and journalist. Barère switched sides several times in the course of the French Revolution and its aftermath. In 1798 he wrote a three-volume treatise, *La Liberté des mers, ou le gouvernement anglais dévoilé* [Freedom of the Seas, or the Government of England Unveiled], which was critical of the British government.

belligerent. We say, to the adverse belligerent, punish, if you please, by cost and confiscation; but respect the principles of Justice—punish not one for the crime of another—charge not on all the guilt of a few; neither, reviving the puritanical doctrine, that every thing is permitted to the saints, celebrate in Doctors' Commons your own canonization.[4]

The writer of War in Disguise, erects his fabric of argument on what he calls *the rule of the war of 1756*, "to which (says he) the neutral powers have all assented, in point of principle, by submitting to its partial application." He afterwards tries to persuade us that, considering Britain as the champion of the liberties of mankind, we ought, in aid of her exertions, to submit to his doctrine. But to urge our submission, on the ground of policy, in the same breath, when the submission of others is quoted as precedent to establish the controverted principle, is presuming a little too much on our want of discernment. Should we admit, for argument's sake, that a neutral, weak and unarmed, had (from motives of fear or pretexts of policy) submitted to the outrage of an armed and powerful belligerent; still we should deny that such right could be founded on such submission. What! does a wrong unresisted become a right? Can a momentary circumstance form a permanent rule? Will the silence of one prove the assent of all? Or, shall the tameness of pusillanimity fetter the conscience and conduct of the brave? Britain, beware! On your Channel's southern shore stands a power menacing and gigantic, who can show proofs of submission more general, to claims not more extravagant.

Thus much it seemed meet to say, on a supposition that the rule had been assented to in the manner above stated. But, in fact, it has not. The Dutch, for the confiscation of whose property a royal order was issued in 1758, of a very extraordinary nature, clamoured loudly, and made strong diplomatic representations. The practice (now called a rule) was complained of; the principle on which it was founded, was denied by that nation, against whom it was applied; and neither that nation, nor any other, has ever assented to it—and much less to the conclusions from it, which are now stated. To suppose the claim set up in 1758, by the British government, was any new principle in the law of nations, would alone destroy it; for there can be no new principle in that science. Whether it was a just conclusion from the old and acknowledged principles, will be considered in its place. But whether true or false, is immaterial as to other conclusions from the same premises. If

4. Doctors' Commons was the site of the civil law courts in London, comparable to the common-law Inns of Court. English Admiralty courts were civil law courts.

these be just, they want no incidental support, and if unjust, no incidental support can avail.

Our author, after citing his favourite doctrine in the words used by Sir William Scott,[5] in November 1799, says, "such were the principles of a rule first practically established by the supreme tribunal of prize, during the war of 1756, only because the case which demanded its application then first occurred; and it ought to be added, that *the decisions of that tribunal at the same period*, were justly celebrated throughout Europe, for their equity and wisdom"—to prove which he boldly cites Blackstone, Montesquieu, and Vattel. But here, instead of the caution of a statesman, we find (to use a gentle term) the address of an advocate. By recurring to Blackstone, we find that (after having mentioned that, in 1748, the Judges of the common Law Courts were added as members to the Court of Appeals in prize causes,) he adds, "such an addition became wholly unnecessary in the course of the war which commenced in 1756, since, during the whole of that war, the Commission of Appeals was regularly attended, and all its decisions conducted by a Judge whose *masterly acquaintance with the Law of Nations*, was known and revered by every state in Europe." That his talents were known and revered, is one thing: that his *decisions* were celebrated for their equity and wisdom, is another, and a very different thing. Blackstone, to prove the opinion entertained of the Judge's *knowledge*, quotes Montesquieu and Vattel. These do indeed applaud *the answer made in 1753*, by the English Court, to the reasons assigned by his Prussian Majesty, for not paying the Silesia Loan. But this was three years antecedent to the war of 1756. Montesquieu, writing from Paris in 1753, says of that State paper—"We consider it here as unanswerable." But what has this to do with the decrees of a Court made in 1758? The sprightly author of the Spirit of Laws, though bred in the Roman faith, was not so much a Catholic as to believe in the efficacy of Indulgences; still less did he pretend to pontifical power, and sanctify beforehand by the merit of a writer, in 1753, the decisions he might make as a Judge in 1758; decisions too, which, (if predicated on what is now said to have been the rule) were made in the very teeth of that argument which Montesquieu had so much approved. For the answer abovementioned of the English Court, lays down in the outset, and supports in the sequel, as an uncontrovertible maxim, "That whatever is the property of an enemy,

---

5. William Scott (1745-1836) was a distinguished English civil law jurist, and judge of the High Court of Admiralty from 1798. He was made Baron Stowell in 1821.

may be acquired by capture at sea, but that *the property of a friend cannot be taken, provided he preserves his neutrality.*"

The words of Sir William Scott, above referred to, are,

> The general rule is, that the neutral has a right to carry on, in time of war, his accustomed trade, to the utmost extent of which that accustomed trade is capable. Very different is the case of a trade which the neutral has never possessed, which he holds by no title of use and habit in times of peace; and which, in fact, can obtain in war, by no other title, than by the success of the one belligerent against the other; and at the expense of that very belligerent under whose success he sets up his title; and such I take to be the colonial trade, generally speaking.
>
> What is the colonial trade, generally speaking? It is a trade generally shut up to the exclusive use of the mother country, to which the colony belongs, and this to a double use—the one that of supplying a market for the consumption of native commodities, and the other, of furnishing to the mother country the peculiar commodities of the colonial regions; to these two purposes of the mother country, the general policy respecting colonies belonging to the states of Europe, has restricted them.
>
> With respect to other countries, generally speaking, the colony has no existence. It is possible that indirectly, and remotely, such colonies may affect the commerce of other countries. The manufactures of Germany, may find their way into Jamaica or Guadaloupe, and the sugar of Jamaica or Guadaloupe, into the interior parts of Germany; but as to any direct communication or advantages resulting therefrom, Guadaloupe and Jamaica are no more to Germany, than if they were settlements in the mountains of the moon. To commercial purposes they are not in the same planet. If they were annihilated, it would make no chasm in the commercial map of Hamburg. If Guadaloupe could be sunk in the sea, by the effect of hostility at the beginning of a war, it would be a mighty loss to France, as Jamaica would be to England, if it could be made the subject of a similar act of violence; but such events, would find their way into the chronicles of other countries, as events of disinterested curiosity, and nothing more.
>
> Upon the interruption of a war, what are the rights of belligerents and neutrals respectively, regarding such places? It is an indubitable right of the belligerent to possess himself of such places, as of any other possession of his enemy. This is his common right; but he has the certain means of carrying such a right into effect, if he has a decided superiority

at sea. Such colonies are dependent for their existence, as colonies, on foreign supplies; if they cannot be supplied and defended, they must fall to the belligerent of course: and if the belligerent chooses to apply his means to such an object, what right has a third party, perfectly neutral, to step in and prevent the execution? No existing interest of his, is affected by it; he can have no right to apply to his own use the beneficial consequences of the mere act of the belligerent, and to say, "True it is you have, by force of arms, forced such places out of the exclusive possession of the enemy, but I will share the benefit of the conquest, and by sharing its benefits prevent its progress. You have in effect, and by lawful means, turned the enemy out of the possession which he had exclusively maintained against the whole world, and with whom we had never presumed to interfere; but we will interpose to prevent his absolute surrender, by the means of that very opening, which the prevalence of your arms alone has effected: supplies shall be sent, and their products shall be exported: you have lawfully destroyed his monopoly, but you shall not be permitted to possess it yourself; we insist to share the fruits of your victories; and your blood and treasure have been expended, not for your own interest, but for the common benefit of others."

Upon these grounds, it cannot be contended to be a right of neutrals, to intrude into a commerce which had been uniformly shut against them, and which is now forced open merely by the pressure of war: for when the enemy, under an entire inability to supply his colonies, and to export their products, affects to open them to neutrals, it is not his will, but his necessity that changes the system: that change is the direct and unavoidable consequence of the compulsion of war; it is a measure not of French councils, but of British force.

Such is the language of that learned and profound civilian, for whom we sincerely feel, and frankly acknowledge, a high respect. But we as frankly *declare*, that if disposed to surrender our judgment to authority, we should seek the *private*, not the judicial opinions of Sir *William Scott*. His uncommon ability and honourable temper might command our confidence, in whatever he should say as a gentleman; but he will himself acknowledge, that he is not entitled to the same credit when speaking as a judge. The reason is obvious: Prize Courts are bound, from their nature and office, to decree according to the orders of their Sovereign. His right to establish, to alter, and to abrogate, the rules and principles of their decisions, is a necessary incident to his power of Peace and War. For it would be absurd and dangerous, that prize courts, by condemning what the Sovereign had directed them to acquit, should involve him in war; or should elude his declaration of war, by refusing to condemn prizes taken from his enemy. The business of a judge, in prize courts, is to weigh evidence so as to ascertain facts; to compare facts with the principles which are to govern his decision; to decree according to the law of nations, when not otherwise directed; and to assign such reasons for his decrees, as may best consist with the honour and dignity of his royal master. That no man can better perform, than Sir William Scott, these various, arduous, and important duties, will appear from the opinion just cited, in which every word is weighed. And when we come to consider the reasons and motives assigned in the pamphlet, to support the same opinion, we think it will appear that the Judge has shown no less wisdom in his silence, than by his expressions.

He begins, "The general rule is,"—We pause to put a question: The general rule of what? We answer, *of the King's Prize Court.* Sir William Scott would not commit his reputation, by saying it was a rule of the law of nations; for he knew that no such rule could be found in any good writer—and had he said it was a rule of the prize court, it would have been the indirect acknowledgment, that it is not a rule of the law of nations. But afterwards, in the same argumentative decree, he says, "much argument has been employed on grounds of commercial analogy—this trade is allowed—that trade is not more injurious—Why not that to be considered as equally permitted? The *obvious* answer is, that the *true rule to this Court is the text of the Instructions.*" This, if we understand it, is a full concession of the point in controversy; for the maxim, *where the reason is the same, the law is the same*, is peculiarly applicable to questions of this sort; but Sir William does not attempt, by distinguishing between the cases, to show a difference in the reason to justify a different decision. He refers to the instructions as an *obvious* answer to arguments from analogy. In other words, he says the cases are indeed similar, of course the reason is the same, but the sentence must be different, because those are decided by the law of nations and these by the instructions. This appears to us conclusive; but we will examine what is said to justify the instructions.

"The general rule (says Sir William Scott) is, that the neutral has a right to carry on in time of war his *accustomed* trade, to the utmost extent of which that *accustomed* trade is capable." The generosity with which he is kindly pleased to grant this indefinite extension of accustomed trade, is not a mere soothing compliment. He knew the objections to his definition of accustomed trade, which he slily confounds with accustomed *places* of trade. He knew that trade might be, and actually is, limited not only as to the *place*, but as to the *commodities:* he knew that the latter is not unfrequently the more important restraint; and he knew the objections to his rule were insurmountable, had he stopped at the first part of the phrase, confining the neutral, thereby, in time of war, to his accustomed trade. By substituting, in the course of his argument, the *port* for the *trade*, he contemplated the exclusion of neutrals from that commerce which his government wish to prevent, permitting at the same time that which they wish to encourage. Whether he has succeeded, will appear by applying his doctrines to facts. Take some commodity which England wants, Spanish wool for instance, an article necessary in the manufacture of superfine cloth. This can, by her navigation act, be imported only in British or Spanish ships. *In time of peace*, an American may indeed go from Cadiz to London, but he cannot take with him an article of the growth, produce, or manufacture, of Spain. In time of war, however, it becomes necessary to relax that rigorous system, and permit the importation of articles prohibited in time of peace. Sir William, therefore, would give to the *accustomed* trade every extent of which it is capable. But is it more an *accustomed* trade of the neutral to carry wool from Cadiz to London, than sugar from the Havanna to Hamburgh? If in the one case, he had been permitted to carry a single bale, or in the other, a single chest, the idea of extending his accustomed trade might apply; provided always, that, in fair argument, an occasional permission could be admitted as proof of a general practice, when indeed (being only an exception) it proves the contrary practice to be general. But does England permit the neutral, in time of peace, to import even that single bale of wool? She does not. May we not say then, in Sir William's own language, that, so far as regards our peace trade in wool between Cadiz and London, it is as if these cities were "in the mountains of the moon," that to the purposes of this commerce, "they are not in the same planet," &c. &c. And if this trade in wool does not in peace exist, as it certainly does not; if it be not, as certainly it is not, our accustomed trade, sure no extension of our accustomed trade can reach the carriage of wool.

Sir William's figures of earthquakes and mountains must not be considered as mere flowers of School-boy rhetoric. They are used by a man of sense, to dazzle the fancy and take off the attention from logical disquisition, by the amusements of poetry and eloquence. But if a French or Dutch privateer should capture a neutral taking wool from Cadiz to London, might not the French or Dutch Judge say (adopting the rule and parodying the language of Sir William Scott,) "what is this wool trade, generally speaking? It is a trade generally shut up against others to the exclusive use of England, and this to a double use; the one that of supplying a market for English commodities, and the other that of furnishing England with that peculiar commodity of the Spanish regions." He might indeed go a little farther, and, as an additional cause of condemnation, say the inhibition of that trade, in time of peace, forms part of the general system called the Navigation Laws, which Britain considers as the basis of her naval power, and has strictly adhered to for more than two centuries. Here then we take our first stand. We deny that municipal regulations established in peace, can in any wise limit the public rights of neutrals, in time of war; averring, and undertaking to prove by numerous examples, familiar to men conversant with the subject, that neutrals have ever carried on in war a commerce interdicted in peace; and that it never has been alleged, or even imagined, that in so doing they were liable to hindrance or molestation, much less to the seizure and forfeiture of ships and goods. We deny that strangers acquire rights against each other by the domestic regulations of commerce or police, which a sovereign may think proper to establish. A prohibition by England to import brandy from France, in any other than French or British bottoms, can, neither in peace nor in war, justify a Spaniard in taking a Dane bound to London with brandy. We insist that a limitation, as to the place where commodities may be laden, is of no greater import, than a limitation as to the commodities themselves. If there be any essential difference which can bear on the question, let it be shown: We see none, and appeal to the common sense of mankind. We insist, therefore, that the rights of a neutral are as perfect when the limitation of place is removed, as when the limitation of commodities is abrogated. His trade is in *both cases* alike; a new and unaccustomed trade. The restraints which France and Spain impose on the commerce of their colonies, give no rights to Britain; still less can she derive rights from the abrogation of those restraints. She pretends no right to make prize of an American carrying on, in time of peace, a contraband (and therefore unlawful) trade with Martinique—how then can she pretend a right to make prize of the same American carrying on in time of war, a permitted (and therefore a lawful) trade with that colony? Will the British government allow that America can rightfully make prize of a British smuggler on the Spanish Main, taken in the breach of Spanish law; or on the coast of Devonshire, taken in the breach of British law? Would she not truly contend, that we acquire no such right by the laws of England or of Spain? If, then, a third party acquires no right against those who trade in defiance of the municipal law, how can he acquire right against those who trade in conformity to the municipal law? Suppose France and Spain should revive the colonial monopoly, a relaxation of which is said to justify captures; would Britain have a right to take the smuggler in time of war, whom she could not touch in time of peace? And if not, by what perversion of reason and conscience can it be pretended, that a trade is innocent only while it is criminal, and criminal the moment it becomes innocent?

After the display of imagery, by which Sir William has skillfully masked his advance from the premises towards the conclusion, he states it as an indubitable right of the belligerent to take his enemy's colony. This no one will deny. But when he says, he has the certain means of carrying such right into effect, if he has a decided superiority at sea, as it is not a legal question, we may, without any want of deference to his opinion as a judge, take leave to differ with him. We entreat him to recollect that, with every *superiority* at sea his heart could wish, Britain has neither taken, nor is like to take, the French and Spanish colonies. Whatever may be her naval power, therefore, we must wait till time shall disclose the judgment of a higher tribunal than the British prize court, before we determine what she can take. But we readily acknowledge her right to try what can be done by attack or blockade, and equally acknowledge that neutrals have no right to step in and prevent the effect of either. The law of blockades is well known, but the present question does not turn on that law. Whenever Great-Britain, by force or otherwise, shall conquer a colony (which we suppose to be meant by turning the enemy "out of the exclusive possession,") we shall not dispute, or attempt to share, the rights she may have acquired; but we must be permitted to observe, that *attack* and *conquest* are definite words, of distinct meaning, which must not be confounded. It would be ridiculous to pretend that a Serjeant of Grenadiers, by firing his musket at a fortress, and stiling the bravado an *attack*, had acquired the rights of conquest. The learned judge will permit us also to observe, that as, in special regard to his situation, we do not blame, so we presume that he, as an accurate civilian, will not justify, the loose terms of "forcing a place out of the exclusive possession of the enemy"; or the application of such loose terms, as a ground for questioning the rights of that enemy in his own country—a country which he has held for centuries, and continues to hold. In short, we must insist on accurate language in the discussion of national affairs. If, by forcing a place out of exclusive possession, conquest be meant, let it be so expressed; and what remains will be a question of fact. If conquest be not meant, the terms (as applied) mean nothing. If France does not *exclusively* possess Martinique, let us know who is the joint tenant. If it be Britain, let her perform some act of ownership, issue some order, promulgate some law, for the government or administration, which will not be treated with contempt there, and with ridicule every where.

In pursuing his arguments, Sir William puts in our mouths, as addressed to England, this language: "True it is, you have, by force of arms, forced such places out of the exclusive possession of the enemy; but we will share the benefit of the conquest, and by sharing its benefits, prevent its progress; you have in effect, and by lawful means, turned the enemy out of his possession which he had exclusively maintained against the whole world, and with whom we never presumed to interfere; but we will interpose to prevent his absolute surrender," &c. Indeed, Sir William, we never have used, and never shall use, such language. You Englishmen can take liberties with your mother tongue, which you may not permit to others. When your Hibernian neighbours hazard any thing like a contradiction in terms, you call it a *Bull*. What you would say of us Yankees, on a similar occasion, we know not; but since it might expose us to ridicule, we shall not speak of your enemy as being turned out of possession before he has surrendered. For the rest, we never presumed to interfere with the French possession of Paris or St. Pierre, any more than with the English possession of London or Kingston; neither shall we presume to interfere with the belligerents in the conquests they may make from each other.

Sir William supposes us to say further: "You have lawfully destroyed his monopoly, but you shall not be permitted to possess it yourself." We make neither of these assertions, much less both of them together; not indeed readily understanding what is meant by the possession of a thing destroyed. If it be permitted to address England in our own words, we say: Great and generous nation! Proud of our common descent, we rejoice that you so nobly sustain the reputation of our valiant forefathers: speaking the same language, educated in the same habits, the same blood in our veins, the same love of liberty in our hearts, we sympathize in your sentiments, and exult in your glory: we know you will neither crouch under menace, nor be dismayed by danger: take care that you be not misled by flattery and intoxicated by success: listen to the language of truth in the voice of a brother: be persuaded that you can no more destroy your enemy's colonial monopoly, than he can destroy your navigation act: the necessity of war leads both you and your enemy to relax the system which each considers it for his interest to preserve in peace: we find our advantage in carrying on the trade which each of you permits, for his own advantage: and we entreat you to consider, that if you exclude us from a trade with the colonies of your enemy, because "it is not his will but his necessity, that changes his system," your enemy may, on like ground, exclude us from trading with you, in articles which your necessities require — Why then drive us to desperate conclusions, by insisting on principles, neither tenable in argument, nor useful in practice?

In truth, if the colonial trade be inhibited to the neutral, "because it is a direct and unavoidable consequence of the compulsion of war," every extension of his trade with a belligerent must be equally inhibited; for it cannot be doubted that such extension is a consequence of the war. We shall not waste time to refute distinctions between consequences direct and indirect, avoidable and unavoidable. As it will not be pretended that a neutral trade with her colonies is *indispensably necessary* to France, so it cannot be called an *unavoidable consequence* of the war. The different shades of convenience are considerations proper for the belligerent sovereign, in which the neutral has no concern, and about which he ought not to give an opinion.

Before we leave the argument of Sir William Scott, let us, however, make one remark. He certainly did not mean to justify the French Emperor, should he prohibit the neutral commerce with Britain: yet if such an idea had entered the Emperor's mind, might he not, at the head of his army near Boulogne, have proclaimed, "that it was his indubitable right to possess himself of Great-Britain: that he had the certain means of carrying that right into effect," &c. &c. and would the British government consider a conclusion, drawn from those premises, *that nobody should trade with England*, as worthy of serious refutation? Yet, where is the difference, (in reason) between the island of Britain threatened by France, and the island of Martinique threatened by England? If threats could acquire rights, the greatest bragger would be the richest man. We think too highly of England to believe she would rest her claims on the ground of gasconade. But if we turn from the threat to consider the danger, we appeal to the world, whether the danger of Martinique was greater than the danger of Britain. Nay, we appeal to the testimony of Britain herself, and produce before the tribunal of Europe her negociations with every court, soliciting aid to ward off the danger to which she was exposed, and the consequent danger to all, if she should be conquered.

From what has been said, it will, we believe, appear that the rule laid down by Sir William Scott, is unknown to the law of nations: that his arguments against extending neutral trade to the colonies and colonial productions of a belligerent, apply with equal force against every other extension of that trade: that these arguments, founded only on the power of a belligerent, will equally justify every other pretension of power — and, therefore, that, resolving justice into force, they are equally subversive of moral principle, and of those maxims of national law which have hitherto been held sacred by the civilized societies of man.

Before we proceed any further with the author of War in Disguise, we must take a moment to consider from whence a belligerent derives his right to make prize of a neutral; believing that in its source we shall find its limitation. It is, we confess, a too frequent practice to destroy the human race, merely to gratify the passion or promote the interest of a destroyer. But we believe no tyrant ever yet, in his wildest abuse of power, asserted a right to waste, at his pleasure, the lives and fortunes of mankind. It has not, that we recollect, been gravely stated to the world, as a rule of law, that the property of an innocent man may justly be taken from him whenever it is convenient to his powerful neighbour. Pirates indeed have practised according to that principle, but even pirates never published it as a code of maritime law.

It results from the state of war, that the property of an enemy may be acquired by capture at sea, but the property of a friend cannot be taken. If, however, the neutral divests himself of his proper character, and takes part in the war, he may justly be treated according to the character he has assumed. His property then becomes lawful prize. He might as well serve in the enemy's fleet or army, and, when made prisoner, claim his neutral privilege, as claim that privilege for his goods when employed in the war. If therefore he furnishes a belligerent with those means and implements of destruction, which, under the general term of contraband, are variously designated in the several treaties by which it has been defined; or if, when a belligerent has blockaded a town or place, he should attempt to introduce succor or subsistence, the property is lawful prize. In both cases he was engaged in direct hostility. But these cases excepted, there is no right of capture. A belligerent cannot rightfully complain of the remote and indirect consequences of a lawful act. Neither can he impute as guilt to a neutral, acts in themselves lawful, and which, having no direct tendency to injure the belligerent, imply no hostile intention of the neutral. To make this (if possible) a little more clear, take the following instance: If a neutral should let out his ship to transport soldiers for one of the belligerents, this would mark so distinctly his hostile spirit, as to justify capture and condemnation by the other belligerent. But suppose a neutral ship should meet a transport of the belligerent, sinking from stress of weather, and rescue the troops from impending destruction; would this expose the ship to condemnation? Surely not. Nature revolts at the idea: and a belligerent who should make prize under such circumstances, and justify the decree because of the consequential injury he might sustain from the salvation of his drowning foe, would render himself the object of general execration. The right, then, of capturing neutrals, does not arise either from advantages the belligerent may gain, or from injuries he might otherwise sustain. No: it arises, and in reason can only arise, from the guilt of the neutral himself. Where there is no crime there can be no punishment, and where there is no offence there can be no forfeiture. Miserable indeed must be the condition of man, if those who are invested with power can prescribe their convenience as a rule for the conduct of others; measure out rights and duties by their particular interest; bind up the conscience of such as cannot resist to the conclusions of their own reasoning, however false, and at their sovereign will and pleasure change innocence to guilt! Principles like these are fit only for beasts of prey, and for those enemies of the human race who may, like beasts of prey, be lawfully hunted down and destroyed.

In this place, though not absolutely necessary to our argument, yet not wholly impertinent, we take leave to say one word, on a subject which was agitated with no little spirit in the British parliament, during the French revolution. While the idea of making war against principles was opposed by much argument, and by more ridicule, on one side, it was supported on the other less vigorously than perhaps it would have been, had the public mind been prepared for the proper impressions. So long as opinions and principles are confined to the bosoms of speculative men, magistrates have no right to interfere, and much less foreign nations. When such opinions and principles, carried into practice, endanger the peace or morals of society, it becomes a duty in the magistrate to repress and punish. Still, however, the concern is of a private and municipal nature. But when a government avows and propagates principles hostile to the peace and safety of others, neighbouring nations should put themselves in a posture of defence; and if such government, regardless of their representations, carry these principles into practice, it is no longer their mere right—it is their bounden duty—to wage war and destroy the principles, by destroying those who avow them, and act agreeably to their dictates. No matter where, or how, or by whom, such principles are promulgated: no matter whether in French or in English, by a Nobleman or a Sans-Culotte: it is the duty of all nations to join for the purpose of suppressing doctrines hostile to mankind. In this faith, we proceed to consider what the writer of War in Disguise has alleged, in support of his supposed rule, and of the conclusions he would draw from it, to effect the destruction of our commerce.

In the first place, then, we contend that the British Courts themselves have repeatedly declared, by necessary implication, that there is no such rule in the law of nations. One word, however, as to the rule itself: Enemy's property taken at sea on board the ship of a friend, is lawful prize. But the enemy may conceal his property under a neutral appearance; and the pamphlet before us details some of many contrivances which the genius of traffic has devised for that purpose. It is the province of Admiralty Courts to investigate the question of property, and defeat, if they can, such contrivances. To this effect they justly presume every thing in favour of the captor; because the neutral, if honest, has sufficient proof in his power; whereas the captor is, from the nature of things, in a less favourable condition. Presumptions, according to the circumstances on which they arise, have different degrees of force, and may be strong enough to carry conviction against direct testimony. Still a court, notwithstanding such conviction, will not decree in the face of evidence. The neutral claim may become a subject of diplomatic discussion, and a decree against evidence would hardly be supported by the government under whose authority it was made. But a numerous class of cases may exist, in which the belligerent shall see himself continually and evidently the dupe of fraud and perjury. Under these circumstances, it is competent for him to establish rules, by force of which such cases shall be decided according to the fact, without regard to the testimony. He will in consequence issue an order broad enough to embrace his object; and his courts being bound to decree in conformity, the matter becomes a question between him and the neutral sovereign. If this last should insist, the belligerent must either recede, or take the alternative of war. But it is to be presumed that the neuter, convinced, by a fair representation of facts, that his subjects have fraudulently covered the property of an enemy, will assent to the measure of the belligerent. And if he does, other nations ought not to interfere, even though bound by treaty to support the neuter: because he is the best judge of what concerns his own honour, as well as of the measures best suited to his interest. But as they cannot rightfully interfere, so they cannot be bound by the assumption of one party, or submission of the other; neither can their silence be considered as an acquiescence, much less can it be construed into an assent.

From what has been said, it appears, that a rule, made under peculiar circumstances, for the direction of prize courts, though apparently at variance, may substantially accord with national law; seeing that the object of it is only to make prize of the property of an enemy. This appears to have been the course of reasoning adopted by Great-Britain, in the war of 1756. The Dutch carried to France, produce of French colonies, the property of

French subjects. Whatever may have been the appearance, such was the unquestionable fact; and certainly this property was lawful prize, by the law
of nations. But the Dutch claimed, under a treaty of near a hundred years'
standing, the right to secure the goods of an enemy against capture, by
virtue of their neutral flag. Proof, therefore, that the cargoes were French
property, was not sufficient to make them good prize, when claimed by the
Dutch in right of their treaty; wherefore it became necessary to strike at
the treaty itself. The arguments on this part of the subject, to show that
such cases were or were not contemplated by the treaty, are foreign to our
inquiry. Whatever may have been the preponderance of argument, it is an
historical fact, that those who then swayed the British councils, declared all
these cargoes to be lawful prize of war, and ordered the admiralty courts to
condemn them. They were accordingly condemned; and when the States
General complained, the British minister, (to cut a knot he could not untie)
directed Sir Joseph Yorke to declare that *his Majesty could not get out of the
war with safety if neutrals assumed a right of carrying on a trade with the King's
enemies, which was not allowed them in time of peace.* Thus we see that a measure, which (even if reconcileable to the law of nations) was a direct violation of positive compact, is justified by the plea of *necessity.* The rule (or,
to speak correctly, the practice) of the seven years' war, being therefore a
measure of necessity, can never be applied to ordinary cases; even against
the party whose weakness had submitted. To deduce consequences from it
now, is as logical as to conclude, that he who has once been acquitted for
killing a man in self-defence, has a right to kill every man he meets.

Having thus endeavoured to show how far the practice of England, in
the seven years' war, might have been supported by principles of national
law, had it not been contrary to express stipulations; let us see whether the
British courts have considered it as part of that law. The next war in which
England was engaged was the war of our Independence, and there (no instructions then existing to the contrary) the Admiralty courts regularly
acquitted neutrals taken under the circumstances which, in the preceding
war, had been followed by condemnation. Indeed, their decrees respecting
Dutch ships were strictly conformed to the treaty of 1668, which had been
broken on the ground of *necessity* in the war of 1756; but, the necessity no
longer existing, had revived in 1778, with original vigour. Evidently then
the British prize courts considered the decisions of the preceding war, as
resting solely on the King's special order, and that, not being derived from
the law of nations, they were of no authority in cases which arose after that
order had ceased to operate.

In the course of last war, three different instructions on this subject were given by his Britannic majesty, to his ships of war and privateers. The first, dated Nov. 1793, in the spirit of those issued in the seven years' war, directed them "to stop and detain for lawful adjudication, all vessels laden with goods the produce of any French colony, or carrying provisions or other supplies for the use of any such colony." The second, of Jan. 1794, directed them, to seize "such vessels as were laden with goods the produce of the French West-India islands, and coming directly from any port of the said islands to *Europe*." Finally, the third, of Jan. 1798, directed them to bring in for lawful adjudication, all "vessels laden with the produce of any island or settlement of France, Spain, or Holland, and coming *directly* from any port of the said islands or settlements, to any port in Europe, not being a port of his kingdom or of the country to which the vessel, being neutral, should belong." The courts conformed their conduct (at each successive period) to the instructions thus given; condemning only what fell within their direct and evident meaning. Hence it is evident, that they considered those instructions as infringing the rights which belong to neutrals, by the law of nations, and that the neutral right took effect, when the limitation was withdrawn: for in neither of these instructions was it declared, that vessels *not* within the description of those the ships of war were directed to seize, should *not* be taken. This was unnecessary: all such were acquitted of course. The prize courts, therefore, spoke to neutrals (by their decrees) this clear and distinct language: We acknowledge that, by the law of nations, you are entitled to the prohibited commerce, and should not hesitate to restore your captured property, but we are bound *by the text of the King's instructions;* where they do not apply, we shall restore, as we did during the American war; and as soon, and as far, as the instructions may be withdrawn, so soon and so far we will conform our decrees to the law of nations.

The author of War in Disguise, feeling the force of this conclusion, endeavours to obviate it. After acknowledging that the royal instructions become law, when promulgated, he adds, their force in the prize courts will not be disputed, "except that if a royal order *could be supposed* to militate plainly against the rights of neutral subjects, as founded on the acknowledged law of nations, the judge, it *may be contended*, ought not to yield obedience; but when the sovereign only interposes to remit such belligerent rights as he might lawfully enforce, there can be no room for any such question." He then assumes the thing to be proved, viz. that the practice of the seven years' war, which the government itself had defended on the ground of necessity, was founded on the law of nations, and endeavours to show that the instructions of 1794 and 1798, were merely remissions of the belligerent right. Those who wish to see his argument, may turn to the book, for we shall not spend time to refute what is palpably unfounded. He may, indeed, if he pleases, *contend* that judges are not bound to obey, for every thing may be *contended*, but the contrary has been *adjudged*. It has, in the strong and pointed terms of Sir William Scott, been *adjudged, that the text of the instructions is the true rule of a prize court.* But, notwithstanding this writer's attempt to reason on possibilities, against facts, he is obliged to acknowledge, that vessels and cargoes captured and condemned subsequently to the instruction of 1793, and previously to the instruction of 1794, were restored by the supreme tribunal, although within the letter and meaning of the former instruction. In so doing, says he, they may be *supposed* to have departed from the rule of the war of 1756. True: it may be *contended*, and it may be *supposed*. But on what other supposition could the supreme tribunal restore? If the captor's claim was founded on public law, merely promulgated by the royal instructions of 1793, and afterwards limited by the royal bounty in 1794, his right accruing in the interim was perfect. To deprive him of that perfect right, was an act of injustice and tyranny, which cannot be excused on any principle, even of policy; for though political considerations might induce the government to make compensation out of the public treasury to a *favoured* neutral, the captor was entitled to his *lawful prize.* A different course was pursued. The court of appeals *restored* the *prize;* and therefore not to a *favoured,* but an injured, neutral; for courts are the organs of *justice,* not *bounty,* and the captors (or at least some of them) received compensation from the public treasury. "All captors (says our author) whose *disappointment* would have been attended with *actual loss,* had reason to be satisfied with the national liberality and justice." From the conduct of the British government, then, this plain language is clearly to be inferred: The instructions of 1793, conformable to a practice in the seven years' war, were an infringement of neutral right, and gave to cruisers more than they were entitled to by the law of nations; consequently, more than they could reasonably expect or rightfully claim. As soon as the instructions are withdrawn, the unquestionable right of the neutral must be acknowledged. The captor, whose claim was grounded on *favour,* not *right,* cannot justly complain. But where he has incurred *actual loss,* let him be compensated. Without a tedious examination of cases cited by our author it is sufficient to observe, that they turn, in general, on the usual question, whether the property be that of a neutral, or the covered property of an enemy? Double papers, false papers, colourable pretexts, and the like, are all evidence of the latter; and, therefore, just cause of condemnation. But let us suppose that not only one case, but one hundred cases, could be adduced to show, that property of innocent men has been condemned by British judges, acting under British instructions: we ask, can the multiplication of instances justify, does it not rather aggravate, the wrong?

The charge against officers in the American customs, as lending the aid of government to the commission of fraud, ought not to have been lightly made. The author will find, on examination, that they act in mere obedience to the law, which has no view to fraud. The usual course of our trade has been to bond the duty and cancel the bond, on payment of a small part, when the goods are exported. If the duties had been paid, in the first instance, and repaid in the second, the case would not have been materially altered. It is not reasonable to expect that custom house officers of a neutral country, should go out of their way to insert unusual expressions in the clearances they give; especially when those expressions would be of no use to their fellow-citizens, but merely serve as a pretext for condemning their property. Is it just, is it decent, to insinuate against men in high public trust, a charge of abetting fraud, because they will not encourage plunder?

The author has laboured to show what is self-evident, that the frequent recurrence of a suspicious circumstance tends to strengthen suspicion. But when, to elucidate a position so clear, he likens neutrals to pick-pockets, we cannot consider it as a happy allusion. Neither can we admit that an illustration is an argument. And when, from that self-evident position, he attempts to show that the frequent recurrence of circumstances, naturally incident to fair transactions, gives ground to suspect fraud; we not only differ from him, but contend, on the contrary, that a suspicion of fraud would more naturally arise from the defect of those circumstances.

As little can we subscribe to his assertion, that the shipment of colonial produce to Europe, by the importer, is a proof that he imported with intention to make that shipment; inasmuch as Europe is the best market. Merchants aver that, in distant voyages, the best market can only be known by events; and that the American market is influenced by that of Europe. Indeed, it appears to us quite natural, that the price of exported articles should be governed by a view to the price likely to prevail, at their arrival in the country to which they are sent. It is equally natural that men of sanguine temper, counting on high markets, should be disappointed, to their loss. And it is notorious that many were ruined in America during the last war, by shipping West-India produce to Europe. Their imprudent speculations raised prices here at first, and afterwards the loss they sustained, together with numerous bankruptcies in the principal port of Germany, reduced prices below the reasonable standard. In that state of things, merchants who had imported with a view to the high price, rather than submit to loss by the decline, sent on their goods to Europe. Let any well informed merchant in the city of London be asked, whether this is not a true state of facts. And let any honest man declare, whether the frequency of such adventures, under such circumstances, conveys to his mind a suspicion of fraud. This we say, on the supposition that our merchants had not a right to import with a view to exportation; which we by no means concede. Neither will we admit that measures taken to conceal a lawful intention, for the purpose of eluding lawless power, impeach the integrity of those whose weakness has no other resource than concealment. Shall it be contended that because a prudent man riding near London conceals his purse and watch, the first highway-man he meets has a right to take them away?

Our author has shown, we think, in a satisfactory manner, that an American merchant can (if so disposed) furnish any evidence prize courts may ask, to prove such intention as they may prescribe; and we draw from his demonstration this clear corollary: that it is equally useless and offensive to abandon the clear and simple principles of public law, for the sake of these loose and unfounded notions. Has it been duly considered, that the inquiry into a merchant's intention, pushed to the extent now contended for, is a violation of our sovereignty? Has it been duly considered that the property, when once brought within our dominion, is as completely our own, as if it had been of our own growth and manufacture? Has it been duly considered that, even if acquired in contraband trade, the inquiry cannot properly be made after goods have reached our ports? It has been admitted that, from the time a ship leaves, and until she returns to the ports of her Sovereign, belligerents have a right (notwithstanding any intermediate entries, sales, or dispositions of the cargo, in the ports of other powers,) to consider it as one unfinished voyage, and to make prize, if, in any part of that voyage, she has violated the laws of war. If the belligerent may go on and follow her after she has again left the port of her Sovereign, as if still engaged in an unfinished voyage, when is the voyage to end? Is it to last as long as the ship? Must our government—but we forbear, for we are the advocates of peace.

We come now to that part of the work in which it is proposed that Britain should capture neutrals in the two-fold view of avoiding an inconvenience and gaining an advantage. The sum of what is said to that effect, may be comprised in these few words: my interest is reason, and my will is law; my advocate is power, and I myself am judge. We will, however, run over a few of his propositions.

To excite alarm, he begins by stating, as a singular and comprehensive truth, that, "with the exception only of a very small portion of the coasting trade of their enemies, not a mercantile sail of any description, now enters or clears from their ports in any part of the globe, but under neutral colours." This is a strong, and we believe, a true statement. The strong inference may be drawn, that no neutral vessel should be allowed to enter or sail from the ports of their enemy. The author, indeed, does not draw *all* that inference. He has the goodness to confine himself (for the present) to the colonial trade. But if the fact operates on the question, it goes to the full consequence. The advantage to France, the disadvantage to England, and the guilt of the neutral, (if guilt there be) is as great in supplying the produce of the United States, as in supplying the produce of the West-Indies. Bread, beef, and pork, are certainly more useful to the purposes of war, than sugar, coffee, and cocoa. And if the finances of France be the object in contemplation, our purchase of wine and brandy must be more beneficial than our sale of indigo and cotton. It would indeed be another new position in the public law, that a commerce of luxuries with the belligerent is forbidden, but that of necessaries permitted. Pursuing the same inverse ratio, contraband, no longer the subject of prize, will become the object of reward.

The author complains that "Hamburg, Altona, Embden, Gottenburgh, and Copenhagen, are supplied and even glutted, with the produce of the West-Indies, and the fabrics of the East, brought from the prosperous colonies of powers hostile to England." Premising that we know not of those French, Dutch, and Spanish colonies, which furnish the fabrics of the East, and believe that (with exception of China) the principal manufacturing countries are in possession of England; we take the liberty to recommend a little more caution in the next edition of War in Disguise. Sweden, Denmark, and Germany, may not relish a doctrine which would subject their supplies to British monopoly, and oblige them to pay not only the price, but the profit and duty, which Britain may think fit to impose. We somewhat doubt whether Russia would find her account in such an arrangement.

When our author, in the same querulous strain, tells us that the looms and forges of Germany are put in action "by the colonial produce of the enemy," we wish to know whether the honest Germans are to be persuaded to make common cause with England, for the purpose of stopping their own looms and forges! We did not know that the West-Indies supplied iron to German forges; but we know that our cotton may be worked as well in German as in British looms. Perhaps, in pursuing the same course of political justice, our export of American cotton in American ships, will be confined by British power to British ports.

Our author tells us, on the high authority of the French emperor himself, "that Martinique and Guadaloupe are flourishing so much beyond former examples, that since 1789, they have actually doubled their population." And this he attributes to the trade we carry on with those colonies. We neither dispute the fact nor the inference: nay, we venture to believe that Jamaica would also flourish beyond former example, if permitted to enjoy a free trade with the United States. We believe, moreover, that the British cabinet entertain the same opinion, and support a monopoly injurious to the colony for the exclusive advantage of England, in pursuance of the same system (whether good or bad) which the French had adopted. But we conclude, from the flourishing state of Martinique and Guadaloupe, now that the French monopoly is destroyed, that the commerce of those colonies is not, as formerly, for account of France; because if it were, they would not flourish more now than they did heretofore. Hence we consider it as demonstrated, by the very conclusion our author has himself drawn, that our flag is not, as he pretends, a mere cover of belligerent trade.

He has taken pains to prove that a commission to cover property, is more advantageous to the neutral, than trading on his own account; and thence he deduces a presumption that such neutral, engaging in unaccustomed trade, carries it on for the belligerent. This, like every other presumption, is to be weighed by the prize court; and we can safely leave it to their consideration. If, however, it be urged in justification of orders to be issued by the government, we are bound to declare, that, in our conception, the fact is different, and will support the adverse presumption. It seems to us an act of idiocy in the belligerent, to give more for covering his property than the profit of the adventure. This would be trading to a certain loss. And, however lightly our author may treat their morals, he will hardly charge either belligerents or neutrals with so great a mercantile sin. One would suppose that this subject, falling so much within the province of common arithmetic, no logic would be needful to show that men will not prosecute a trade that does not pay commissions. But since the author, in the same page, asks whence our merchants have derived "the means of purchasing the costly exports of the Havana and other Spanish ports?" it is proper to inform him, that our capital is greatly increased by trading *honestly* on our own account, with the colonies of the powers at war, instead of accepting *dishonestly*, a covering commission of small comparative value: that the capital and industry of America have greatly extended her credit; more especially on the exchange of London: and that British capital finds a valuable employment in subserving our commercial enterprise. If he will have the goodness to ask well informed men in Europe, they will tell him that for half a century the commerce of France and Spain has been supported, in a great degree, by Dutch and English funds. If he will read the parliamentary debates, for the last dozen years, he will see repeated assurances given by British ministers, that the French merchants have been long since ruined by assignats, requisitions, and forced loans; that the Spaniards are wholly exhausted by military expenses, contributions, and paper currency, and that the Dutchmen's purses have, in French presses, been squeezed to the very husks. After such decisive facts, vouched from such high authority, we must be pardoned for expressing, not merely surprise, but astonishment, that any man in England should suppose our trade with the French, Spanish, and Dutch colonies, is supported by the capital of France, Spain, or Holland.

But the writer of War in Disguise, after toiling hard to show, (what we venture to assure him is not a fact) that our commerce is but ostensibly neutral, comes forward, in page 102, to his main object: "After all (says he) let it not be supposed that *the important conclusions to which I reason*, depend on the fact, that the trade in question is carried on chiefly, *or in some degree*, on account of our enemies. *Were the contrary conceded*, very little, *if any*, deduction need on that score be made from the sum of the mischiefs here ascribed to the encroachments of the neutral flag." Thus the ground of right is completely abandoned, and the question is confessedly put on the ground of convenience. We enter here our solemn protest, on behalf of ourselves, of other neutral nations, and of all the societies of civilized man: We protest against the violation of principles laid down by the ablest writers, adopted by the wisest princes, and sanctioned by the consent of ages: We desire it may be distinctly understood, that, when we touch this argument in detail, we do not in the least or for a moment admit that it can ever be a proper subject of deliberation with honest men. No; it should be at once rejected in the gross, with general indignation. Since, however, all men are not honest, we hope for pardon in attempting to show that the arguments in support of that pernicious doctrine, are as weak as they are criminal.

In his 105th page, the author calls his reader's attention "to a single and highly important fact: the produce of the West-Indies (says he) sells cheaper in our enemy's ports, than in our own." This may be the fact of a moment, arising from some accidental excess of supply beyond the demand, joined to a *want of capital* to purchase on speculation. If so, it proves nothing. It may also be a general result of three distinct causes: 1st, Superior cheapness of the article at the place of purchase: 2d, Superior cheapness of transportation to the place of sale; and 3d, Inferior profit taken by the trader. The first cause has, we believe, existed for a long period antecedent to the present war; but if not, it goes to prove that the war has occasioned distress to the French and Spanish colonies, which could not be wholly alleviated by the neutral intercourse. The second and third causes, merely show our willingness to work for a moderate compensation. This perhaps is the great grievance. We prevent those immoderate gains which might be made, but for our competition. To remove it, the commerce of neutrals, the rights of neutrals, and the public law of nations must be destroyed. Powers of Europe, awake! America is to be plundered, in order that a tribute may be raised from your subjects, by the commercial rapacity of Britain. Is it for this you pour out the blood of those faithful subjects in her cause?

Another of our crimes is, that we diminish the profit of sugar refiners, arising, he says, *chiefly* "from an advance (pending the process) in the prices of the raw, and of course of the refined commodity." In other words, we by our industry, diminish the benefits which that *useful* class of citizens expect from *their monopoly*. Thus, by disappointing the engrosser, we render the article cheaper to the general consumption of British subjects. Our rights, therefore, must be invaded, and our property must be plundered, that refined sugar may become dear in England. And this argument is addressed to the good sense of Englishmen!

Having thus completed the list of grievances and of sufferings, with which the good people of England are afflicted, he proceeds to the benefits which accrue to their enemies. And first, says he, "the hostile treasuries are fed by the same means, with a copious stream of revenue, without any *apparent* pressure on the subject; a revenue which otherwise would be cut off by the war, or even turned into our own coffers." How a revenue could be turned into the coffers of Britain, by leaving the articles neutrals now export, to perish in the colonies of her enemies, we are not so happy as to comprehend or conjecture. Whether the weight of taxes be lessened by taking off only the apparent pressure, we leave to be determined by those who prefer appearances to realities. But we must take the liberty to say, that, in our humble apprehension, the real pressure of taxes can best be borne by foregoing the consumption of useless luxuries. We never have believed, notwithstanding the fashionable opinion, that power is the appendage of trans-atlantic possessions. We never have believed, that modern refinements and modern delicacies, form the strength and the sinews of a state; still less, that a great and brave nation can be ruined by taking from her the occasions of luxurious extravagance. When the French Emperor's power is attributed to an intercourse with his colonies, by the intervention of a neutral flag; we ask, whether it was by the aid of colonies that Henry the fifth wrested the sceptre of France from the gripe of her feeble monarch? Was it by the aid of colonies that Elizabeth destroyed the armada? Was it by the aid of colonies that Lewis the fourteenth made Europe tremble? Did the power of Spain, under Charles the fifth, rest on colonies? Have those colonies, now so flourishing, added (in modern times) a single nerve to Spanish strength, or a single ray to the old Spanish glory? Did Peter the great—did the immortal Catharine—rely on American islands, cultivated by African slaves, as the base of their colossal dominion? Or was it by the aid of colonial produce, that Frederick bore up against the hostility of almost all Europe? No: it was by genius and discipline, not by sugar and coffee, that he went triumphant through the seven years' war. How weak then the pretext, opposed to history and experience, that the power of France is dependent on a trade with her colonies: that to cut off the intercourse, maintained by intervention of neutrals, would enfeeble that vast empire; and, therefore, that it is lawful to pursue the doubtful consequence by immediate wrong. Surely, somewhat more than mere assertion should be advanced, not to justify, that is impossible, but to palliate such enormity.

When it is asked from what other source than the continuance of his colonial trade, the French emperor derives his treasure? although we hold ourselves not obliged to answer, because in fair argument the burthen of proof lies on the affirmant, we will assume the double task of showing 1st, some causes of Napoleon's power; and, 2dly, that it does not depend on the West-Indies. The power of England, under Cromwell; of France, under Henry Fourth; and of several other nations, indeed of nations in general, when emerging from civil war, has been, and ever will be, a problem of difficult solution to counting-house politicians. But when it is considered that the broad surface for cultivation remains; that the reduction of private fortunes lessens the expense of luxury; that the conversion of tenants into freeholders, (by confiscation and sale of large estates) leaves a disposable surplus for taxes in the hands of the cultivator; that the very destruction of aged and infirm persons, (by the cruelty and distress of civil convulsions) lessens the usual incumbrance on productive labour; that men inured to toil and accustomed to privations, can spare the fruit of their industry with less inconvenience than such as have been habituated to ease and enjoyment; and that, in times of disorder and violence, the spirit, genius, talents, and energies, of a nation, are called into action; and the proper characters thereby designated to fill the various departments of state, war, and finance, we shall no longer be surprised that a country so circumstanced, should yield, under the pressure of military government, more effectual revenue than can (in the usual course of things) be drawn from rich and luxurious nations. The numeric account may indeed be less, but the substantial effect will be greater: labour will be cheaper: and it is not guineas in bank, but men in arms, which form the power; and, therefore, the real wealth of a nation. Thus we find in the very circumstances relied on by some, to prove that France was tottering on the verge of ruin, a part of that resource which her sovereign employs with such dreadful ability. To this may be added the contributions drawn from other countries, and that pillage which has rendered Europe more productive to the French, than even India itself to the British armies. Conceiving that we have fulfilled our first engagement, we proceed to show, secondly, that the power of France does not depend on a commerce with the West-Indies. To do this, we call to our reader's recollection, a simple, well-known fact. St. Domingo, alone more productive than all the other French colonies put together, is completely lost.[6] If, therefore, the articles of colonial produce were the basis of French power, it would, instead of being increased so as to excite alarm, be diminished by at least one half. We appeal to the candour of impartial Englishmen, whether our reasoning, on this point, or that of our adversary, be most conclusive. But even admitting, that what is so clearly demonstrated were merely a matter of doubt, we ask whether conclusions from doubtful premises authorize the violation of unquestionable right?

Our author tells us, "a great part of the Spanish treasure shipped from South-America, may be *reasonably regarded* as nett revenue, passing on the King's account." We know not, neither shall we inquire, whether this presumption be well or ill founded, but will suppose the treasure in question to be the return for bills of exchange drawn by the Spanish treasury on their

6. The French colony of Saint-Domingue had proclaimed its independence as Haiti in 1804, after more than a decade of rebellion. In 1803 the Haitian army defeated an expeditionary force sent by Napoleon.

agents in Mexico, and sold to neutrals. This, we presume, is taking a case as strong as any the author could have contemplated; and we presume he would not hesitate to declare, not only that dollars paid on those bills should be taken from the neutral, as lawful prize, in the voyage from La Vera Cruz to New-York, but that if they should be landed at New-York, and exported to Hamburg afterwards, they should still be regarded as going towards their original destination; and still be lawful prize. Admitting this doctrine, for a moment, let us look for a similar case. During the last war, it was common for merchants in Hamburg to purchase bills drawn by agents of the British government for public account, to bring from England the dollars raised from the payment of those bills, to employ them in the purchase of similar bills, and so on, as long as the course of exchange would leave a profit. The same practice, under similar circumstances, would doubtless take place in the present or any other war. Would the dollars on their voyage from England to Hamburg, be lawful prize? Will Britain insist on the legality of such capture? Or, to go a little farther; if the Hamburg merchant should ship the dollars to India, would it still be lawful prize? Still infected by the original taint? If the enemy of Britain could take dollars, so circumstanced, as lawful prize, when going from Hamburg by sea, might he not as justly take them in any other place where he has lawful dominion? And has he not the right necessarily incident, and fully established by the common procedure in prize causes, to take any dollars he may meet with, and call on the neutral owner to show how they came into his possession? Let us take another case. There is in peace, (and if report say true, there is also in war,) a contraband trade between the Spanish colonies and Jamaica. The dollars, when going from those colonies, are unquestionably liable to confiscation; and it so happens, that each of them has a date which would either prove incontestibly, or at least raise the most violent presumption, that they had gone direct from the mines to Jamaica: would Spain, in time of full peace, be permitted to take British vessels leaving the port of Kingston, and confiscate dollars found on board, unless the owner could show they were not the fruit of contraband trade? That they were not imported with a view to re-exportation?

Among the heinous crimes this author has charged to neutral account, one is, that by becoming the carriers for France, French ships are unemployed; wherefore the Emperor can obtain them on easy terms of freight, when he wants them for his transport service. This is, indeed, an unheard-of offence; and the more injurious, as military conscriptions, impressment of seamen, and putting of property in requisition, are things wholly unknown in France.

The author also complains, that "by the licentious use of neutral flags, the enemy is enabled to employ his whole military marine in purposes of offensive war." It is unquestionable, that he who has neither commerce nor colonies to protect, is not called on to defend his colonies and commerce: an additional proof, by the way, that these distant possessions rather diminish than increase the power of a nation. Let us, in the true spirit of our author's reasoning, suppose that Britain, exercising the power attributed to her by the learned Judge, should take all the French, Spanish, and Dutch colonies; this would but so much the more concentrate their maritime power and enable them "to employ their whole military marine in purposes of offensive war." It follows, therefore, that her expensive expeditions to the East and to the West, would, if crowned with all the success her fondest wish might desire, only tend to strengthen her enemies. Already she bends under the weight of her vast dominion, and perhaps (at no distant period) may wish, like the wise Augustus, to circumscribe her empire; but while her government labours, by extending it, to produce the evil complained of, surely we may be permitted to carry on our lawful trade, even though it should in some small degree contribute to the unavoidable result of their own pursuits.

Another charge brought against neutrals, as being a consequence of their trade, is, that, notwithstanding those fleets, which cover the ocean, some little privateers in the West-Indies, now and then make prize of a British ship. The argument stands thus: Such is the power of the British marine, that if her enemies should fit out *merchant* vessels *they* would surely be taken: therefore, they do not fit out *merchantmen:* they are *obliged* to employ their seamen: therefore they fit out *privateers:* if neutrals did not trade with them, they would fit out merchantmen to be *certainly taken:* if they fitted out merchantmen to be taken, they could not fit out privateers to take other folks: therefore, it is the fault of neutrals, that they fit out privateers: moreover, *if* the British cruisers had a chance to make rich prizes, they *might* be more alert: if they were more alert, they *might* catch those privateers — those privateers are scarce worth catching; therefore, the British cruisers don't look after them: therefore, those privateers, not being hindered, now and then make a prize: therefore it is the fault of the neutrals, that such prizes are made: This reasoning is conclusive, therefore the consequences drawn from it are self-evident. The neutrals, in carrying on their commerce, could have had no view to their own advantage, which is only a remote and indirect consequence: therefore, they must have been moved by a view to the aforesaid fitting out of privateers, which is a necessary and direct consequence. To act with such a hostile intention, is to take part in the war: to take part in the war, exposes to confiscation: therefore, the neutrals are justly liable to confiscation. It might be proper to add, like lord Peter in the tale of a tub, this is clear reasoning, and may you all be d——d for a pack of rascals, if you pretend to dispute the conclusion.[7]

Another great injury complained of, is, that no prizes can be made on the enemy, "the only means by which a victorious admiral, when raised, as a reward for his illustrious actions, to civil and hereditary honours, can hope to support his well-earned rank, and provide for an ennobled posterity:" that the attempt to confiscate neutrals, as the law now stands, is generally a fruitless task, and at any rate attended with tedious litigation, "an evil peculiarly unpleasant to the ardent mind of a sailor:" that no captures, except those founded on the breach of a blockade, "which are of small value," can now be safely relied on: that this is a great discouragement to engaging in the sea service; and therefore, that this valuable class of men "ought not to be shut out from their ancient advantages, or be jostled by every neutral, in pursuit of their lawful game, and so sit down in poverty at the peace." Alas! poor Britain! Having destroyed the commerce of her enemies, she must weep, like poor Alexander, because there is no new world to conquer! The Barbary powers, when they have hunted down all the game of one christian nation, make peace and go to war with another, in pursuit of fresh game. These Barbarians have the candour to avow that *prudent* cause of peace, and this *honourable* motive to war. They have also the good faith to disclaim the law of nations, which they term, in derision, our Christian law. In the new shape the war has now put on, the kind sympathy of our author will, we presume, be extended from the sufferings of seamen to those of their brethren in the land service. With the same mild and gentle temper, from the same charitable and patriotic considerations, and in the same course of just and honourable argument, he will doubtless excite the British soldiers in Germany, to an indiscriminate plunder of friend and foe.

Another sore evil under the sun, is, that from a want of prey, the business

---

7. This exact phrasing does not appear to be in "A Tale of a Tub," but in section 4, Lord Peter says a number of similar things. For example, after he had told a story of a flying house, "And that which was the good of it, he would swear desperately all the while that he never told a lie in his life; and at every word, 'By G——, gentlemen, I tell you nothing but the truth, and the d——l broil them eternally that will not believe me.'" Jonathan Swift, *A Tale of a Tub, the Battle of the Books, and other Satires*, Everyman's Library (New York: E. P. Dutton, 1909), 80.

of privateering has been discouraged. This mild species of warfare, whose beginning is benevolence, and whose end is virtue, has decayed; but from no want of moral principle. Good men are still willing to seek wealth, by the plunder and ruin of industrious families; but their laudable zeal has expired, from the mere want of objects on which it might be displayed! True it is, that seamen who might have been engaged in this gentle occupation, are now employed in merchant vessels, or public ships of war. But the nation loses one inestimable advantage. The liberal use made of the means of war by men whose native energies had never been repressed by the pedantry of education, and who, in this pursuit of human game, were liberated from the restraints of law, used formerly to furnish occasions for the exercise of diplomatic skill. Thus the genius of statesmen was displayed, matter was furnished for conversation to the various coffee-houses of the metropolis, and, above all, the nation could easily be embroiled with her neighbours, so as to multiply the chances of providing for ennobled posterity of victorious admirals!

The increase of American shipping, though the last, is not the least of those evils our author complains of. America is growing into greatness, and the war seems favourable to her prosperity. That it is so in reality, may be doubted, without incurring the charge of scepticism; but certainly it has that appearance; an appearance alarming to those who would grasp at all trade, while complaining that, for the protection of what they already possess, the navy of Britain must be spread over every sea. To check this envied prosperity of America, blooming on the general felicity of mankind, it is proposed to make war; not in *disguise*, but open and flagrant, as it is unprovoked and unjust. And in order that a conduct so contemptuous of the moral sense, may want no circumstance of insult, not merely to the United States of America, but to every Sovereign in Europe, this war is now prompted, and is hereafter to be defended, on the principle that Great-Britain can in no other way fasten on the necks of other nations, the yoke of her commercial monopoly.

But our author would fain justify the conduct he has recommended, and to that effect, assuming the thing to be proved, (viz. the validity of his supposed rule,) he says, "If I should *dictate* to a neighbour, that in crossing *a certain field* which lay between our respective tenements, he and his servants should confine themselves *to a certain path which I had marked out* for the purpose, and if he should for years comply with the restriction, or *submit* to be treated as a trespasser whenever he deviated from it; I might *consistently* enough, if I found the passage a nuisance, *shut it up* altogether:

but it would be grossly *inconsistent* in him to deny *my right* to the field, and pretend it was *common* land." The reader will observe, that his right to the field is exactly the thing in controversy. If indeed the right were his, he might consistently shut it up. But if it were a piece of common land, and if, to avoid the assaults of a quarrelsome neighbour, I should for a while travel over it by the narrow path he had prescribed; and if, presuming on my pusillanimity, he should shut up that narrow path, might I not lawfully remove the obstruction, and call the neighbourhood to my assistance? The sea is a common right to all nations, and the right to trade is equally common. Neither the ocean, nor the commerce borne on its bosom, can be considered as the private property of any one nation: still less, will quaint allusions support extravagant claims.

The author has more semblance of reason, when he says, "it would be a most extraordinary and unprecedented situation for two friendly powers to stand in, if the one had a right to any thing which is *destructive* to the other." Here it is assumed, that one friendly power cannot justly do what is destructive to another; a position which must at any rate be so qualified as to reach only cases of *direct* and *evident* destruction. In such cases, the duty of self-preservation gives rights, founded on necessity, which we will presently notice: but these cannot arise from the mere apprehension of remote and contingent injury. The power of Venice, founded on her lucrative trade to Asia, was destroyed by Gama's discovery of the Cape of Good Hope; the commerce of India was thereby turned into a new track, and wholly lost to that republic. But if Venice had insisted that all nations should forgo the benefits to be derived from that discovery, because of the injury she might thereby sustain, the pretence would have been considered as equally insolent and ridiculous. Even in the limited sense of the above position, it admits of exceptions. If my friend puts himself in a situation where the exercise of my perfect right, though injurious, or even destructive to him, is, nevertheless, essential to my own preservation, he cannot expect that, to save him, I should sacrifice myself. But our author, after laying down his maxim, instead of applying it to the extreme case on which it was predicated, viz. national destruction, takes up a different and inferior case, viz. the ruining his *hopes* in the war, and giving his enemy a superiority at sea, which *may* render England a province of France. If then we take the rule, and the application of it together, it would follow, that a neutral must forego the exercise of his perfect right, whenever, in the opinion of a belligerent, it will ruin his *hopes*, or give to his enemy a superiority which *may* eventuate in conquest. And from this conclusion he goes to another conclusion, which certainly does not follow, viz. that if the neutral will not, in subservience to the belligerent's apprehensions, forego the exercise of a perfect right, the belligerent may lawfully seize and condemn his property. Thus he would make, not the necessity, but the apprehension of a belligerent, equivalent to the guilt of a neutral. That necessity gives rights, is certain; but these rights have their limits, as well as their foundation, in reason. Necessity will authorize whatever will be needful for self-preservation; but no more. The belligerent, therefore, may lawfully take goods going to his enemy, in the course of a lawful trade, provided they be either necessary for his own defence and existence, or that, under existing circumstances, it is dangerous to him that they should reach their destination. But this right, resulting from the unquestionable right of self-preservation, can by no means dispense with the duties of good faith and justice. These bind him, while pursuing his enemy, not to injure his friend: He must, therefore, if he take such goods, pay for them the highest price, with the charges resulting from capture and detention. Under this restriction, the neutral may repose some confidence in the reasoning of a belligerent on his own danger; for it is not to be supposed that he would wantonly exercise an expensive right. Having thus shown how far a belligerent may go, under the plea of necessity, let us suppose the doctrine contended for, by the author of War in Disguise, to be adopted into the law of nations, and trace the consequence. May not the French Emperor assert, that the wealth and power of Britain are avowedly founded on commerce; that a great and essential part of that commerce can, in time of war, be carried on by neutrals alone; that such commerce, therefore, contributing manifestly and directly to the power of his foe, is ruinous to his hopes in the war; and that, enabling England to subsidize continental powers, it may eventually give her, on land, the same superiority which she actually enjoys at sea? It cannot be denied that this reasoning is as conclusive, at least, as that of the pamphlet under consideration; neither can it be denied that one of the belligerents has an equal right with his adversary to reason about his own affairs. If then lucrative rights are to accrue from the apprehension of remote and eventual danger, what shall prevent him from putting in his claim? In his high station, an honourable pride may disdain claims founded in the avowal of fear; but, should he descend to such abuse of argument, would he not go to his conclusions with force and fairness, equal at least, to what his opponent can display?

Our author, after much of inferior matter, which we will not notice, because it would be tedious, and because it dissolves and vanishes on the application of sound principles, tells us at last: "after all that has been or can be said, on this important subject, one plain question will probably be felt decisive by every equitable mind. Quo animo? With what intention did the enemy open the ports of his colonies to foreign flags?" To this plain question, we make as plain an answer — the answer which our author himself would dictate. We verily believe it was not done out of any regard for us, but solely with a view to his own interest and advantage. And what then? Must I, to defend my right, prove that your enemy was actuated by pure love and kindness towards me? Since when, have states been governed by the dictates of a stark-naked benevolence? What sort of proof is expected? What semblance of proof can be given, that a sovereign has absurdly neglected the interest of his own subjects, to promote that of a stranger? In the common walks of life, we sometimes meet with ill-natured men, who are constantly cavilling at the conduct of others, and assign criminal motives to innocent or laudable actions. Such miserable motive-mongers are generally despised and detested; but here that hateful, contemptible, captious temper, is recommended as the standard of national justice — if, indeed, it be not a pollution of the sacred name of justice, even to mention the word in connexion with a proposal so enormously flagitious; with the deliberate plan to impute the prudent regard of *one* for his own interest, not to *him*, but to *another*, as guilt; to punish it as guilt. Here is a system audaciously proposed to the world, according to which, a neutral (in pursuing his lawful trade) shall be held not only to prove that he was himself actuated by such motives as a belligerent chooses to prescribe, but also to answer for the motives of an adverse belligerent: a system, according to which, if it should appear only probable, that such belligerent had not been either foolish or mad, but had in his public conduct consulted his own interest, the property of a neutral is to be sacrificed. Such is the closing argument, and such as it is, the writer fails not to triumph, and to conclude, "that the illegality of the commerce is as certain as its mischievous tendency; that to engage in it is to interpose in the war; and that the merchants who thus grossly violate the duties, have no claim to the rights of neutrality."

Having thus, by his sovereign will, stripped the neutrals of their rights, he calls in, to aid his argument, the ultimate reason of kings. He would extend the horrors of war to regions which it has not yet afflicted. He can view with indifference the scenes of plunder and the fields of blood: nor is he deterred from his fell purpose by the compunctious struggles of humanity. Yet even in the whirlwind of his wrath, though reason and conscience are silent, interest more vigilant whispers to his ear, "our trade might be materially injured by a war with the neutral powers." Attentive to that voice, and obedient to its monitions, he consoles himself in the hope, and avows the confidence, that a contraband trade now carried on between the English and their enemies, may be extended, by permissions under royal authority, so as to bring to British havens the commodities now transported in neutral ships, and vend British manufactures in the colonies of France and Spain. He holds out this resource, at once to calm apprehension and stimulate avidity. He excites his countrymen to seek in plunder an immediate profit and, lest they should be deterred by a view of that distress to which their manufacturing towns would be exposed, he shows how to obviate by guilt the consequence of folly. Fearful, however, that some timorous conscience might catch and spread alarm—fearful that the proud integrity of England should revolt at counsels which lead to crimes—he adds, "though I cannot undertake to defend the consistency of licensing to British subjects a trade with the enemy from which we claim a right to exclude neutral nations, yet, should those nations attempt to compel a surrender of that important right by cutting off our commerce, the remedy would be consistent and just." Thus the criminal circle is complete; and thus the plan becomes perfect. A plan not more profligate than absurd, and which would be ridiculous but for its atrocity. Yet in the moment of proposing this complication of all which can offend the reason, insult the pride, or alarm the conscience of man, he makes an appeal to God. "Let (says he) our humble confidence be placed in him at whose command nations and empires rise and fall, flourish and decay." Yes! yes! The fate of empire is in the hand of God: he will punish *here* offending nations, and has wisely ordained that the violent and unjust shall be the certifiers of their own destruction. England! you have solicited continental aid to ward off impending danger: your enemy has declared that his war is a general interest: that it is waged to establish a general right: that you are tyrants of the sea, and, in pursuit of gain, violate the first principles of justice. Is this the language of truth? If it be, how can you ask the aid of man? How can you supplicate the favour of God?

FINIS.

After his return from Europe in 1798, Morris maintained a steady correspondence with friends and acquaintances from the Old World. That correspondence often turned to the subject of investments—a subject on which Morris was acknowledged an expert—and especially investments in American land. Indeed, one of Morris's purposes in going to France in 1788 had been to sell land; by 1806, he was an experienced salesman. It is perhaps no coincidence that the lands he recommends here as good investments are in areas where he owned significant tracts.

Monday morning, 17th Nov. 1806

My dear Sir,

In answer to your inquiries respecting the United States of America, I send you the enclosed notes which you may communicate to any of your friends who may be prompted by curiosity or interest to seek information on the subjects to which you referred. You will, however, take notice, that I do not aspire at the character of an author, and therefore the hints now sent are not to be published.

I am,
With esteem and respect,
Your obedient servant.

Between the high colouring of exaggeration and the dark shade of detraction, it may be difficult to discern the truth in what relates to America. Not only the manners, which travellers estimate, as usual, by comparison with their own, have been exalted by some to the innocence of paradise and

Notes on the United States of America (Philadelphia: Printed at the office of the United States Gazette, 1806), pamphlet, 48 pages. The "Notes" also are printed in *The Port Folio*, 4th ser., vol. 2, no.3, September 1816, 185–203. It was also reprinted in French in the Swiss *Bibliotheque Britannique*, 1807. The text here follows the version in *The Port Folio*, except for the introductory letter, which appears only in the pamphlet version.

degraded by others to the corruptions of a brothel; but things which admit of more easy and accurate estimation, even the soil and climate, have been represented as variously as the temper, genius, and manners of the people.

"I am sorry, Sir, you kept such bad company in Spain," said a gentleman in Paris to one who indulged himself in the ridicule of Spanish customs. This flippant reply might be made to certain descriptions of American society, which border on caricature. But instead of resorting to repartee, which would here be misplaced, it seems proper to remark, that when strangers undertake to delineate the character of a nation from what they meet with in trading towns, great part of whose inhabitants are (like themselves) strangers, the portrait, however excellent in colour and expression, will hardly possess the merit of a good likeness. These painters should consider that a man who has a proper regard for his own character would be restrained from such great incongruity, if not by candour, at least by common sense. They should consider too that customs and manners must be taken together by him who would estimate them justly; because the best, when viewed in detail, may be made a subject of blame or ridicule. Finally they should know that long residence and an intimate acquaintance with the best company are pre-requisites to forming a just opinion and delineating a faithful resemblance. It is easy to conceive that one bred in the politer circles of London might not be pleased with the manners of Amsterdam, Hamburgh, or Philadelphia. The inhabitants of those towns have the humility to believe they want that high polish which courts alone can give. But what shall be said of youngsters just fledged and yet warm from the nest of Cambridge or Oxford, who discover in the best company of Berlin or Vienna a fund of contemptuous merriment? Who consider the gentlemen of Germany as bears, and those of France as monkies! When the count de Laraguais was asked, on his return from England, his opinion of its produce and inhabitants, he exclaimed, "Ah c'est le païs le plus drole qu'on puisse imaginer. Ils ont vingt religions, mais ils n'ont q'une sauce. Toutes les liqueurs sont aigres hormis le vinaigre. Ils n'ont de fruit mûr que les pommes cuites, et de poli que l'acier." *'Tis the strangest place you can conceive. They have twenty religions and but one sauce. All their liquors are sour except the vinegar. They have no ripe fruit but baked apples, and nothing polished but steel.*[1]

It would be well that this speech were printed on the title page of some

---

1. This quotation has been attributed to others, including Voltaire and Talleyrand, and most commonly to Francesco Caraccioli. The number of religions varies from twenty to a thousand, and the number of sauces from one to three.

books of travels in America which Englishmen have published, and in which (with no evil intention perhaps, but merely to display their genius and national superiority) they have degraded Americans below the most vile and vicious in Europe. That we, like others, have too good an opinion of ourselves may be true; but foreigners who on this ground charge us with ridiculous vanity should recollect the decision on a memorable occasion. "Let him who is guiltless cast the first stone." It may also be true that we have in the north the vices attached to commerce, and in the south those which result from domestic slavery; but we have the virtues which arise out of those conditions. He who travels through this extensive country, picking up rare incidents to portray manners in which the meanness of a Dutch huckster shall be combined with the profligacy of a Polish lord, may gratulate himself on the collection of materials for a biting satire. But should he put them together and publish the patchwork, it would perish before his eyes by the mortal disease of self contradiction. The American who claims for his country a proud exemption from the ills attached to humanity is less to be applauded for his zeal than pitied for his folly. Truth, however, will warrant the assertion, that our vices are not so great as might be expected from our condition. The Virginian is not cruel: the Yankee is not dishonest: the spirit of commerce has not destroyed the charities of life, and taken in the aggregate there is as fair a proportion of genius, virtue, and politeness in America as in Europe. Particular comparisons would be invidious. There is, however, one general trait which must strike the most cursory observer. The stranger of every country is received here with frankness and cordiality. He cannot, indeed, enjoy the venal respect of an inn, but may on the contrary be offended by a surly manner, amounting, sometimes to downright rudeness: for American tavern keepers too often take occasion to display their pride (which they falsely consider as a mark of freedom) to guests whom they are bound by duty as well as interest to serve and to please. No man of sound mind will defend or attempt to excuse this conduct which is equally ridiculous and brutal; but it may be accounted for by a simple fact. In the early settlement of a country, few are wealthy enough to keep an inn. Those few being of what the French would call *les notables* are persons of higher standing in society than the greater part of their guests. The commercial spirit has not yet bent their pride; but it will eventually, as in other countries, smooth the supercilious brow into a smile of welcome. Each reserving, as in other countries, the right to compensate his cringes to the rich by his contumely to the poor. Another disgusting trait of American manners is the insolent familiarity of the vulgar. But this does not arise from the greater stock of impertinence in our blackguards, but from the want of those restraints which they feel elsewhere. Let it, however, be observed, that the insolence complained of is perceivable only in the lowest, worst educated, and truly contemptible part of the people, or rather (to speak correctly) of the populace. Secondly, that the great majority of that populace is made up of imported patriots, the offcast and scum of other countries. And, thirdly, that these wretches abuse a momentary consequence, arising from the dearth of labour, to supply the increased and increasing demand of agriculture, manufactures, and trade. When peace shall confine commerce to its former channel, such fellows must take their flight or model themselves to the respectful demeanour which distinguishes the real people of America: than whom none are more civil and obliging when fairly treated. But he who displays in this country the insolence of an upstart will surely meet with mortification.

There is one striking characteristic in the manners of America, which is generally interesting. A traveller who would be introduced into the first companies of Europe, bating the case of uncommon merit or peculiar felicity, must show his stars, his ribbands, his military commission or noble descent. Above all, he must not show that he is a merchant or mechanic. But in America these passports and precautions are alike unnecessary. He who behaves himself well will be well received. He will be estimated at what he is worth. His money, if he has any, will procure him as much respect as elsewhere, provided no glaring vice or folly destroy its influence. Even then he may in America, as elsewhere, find societies to receive him when repelled by those who respect themselves. He will be estimated at what he is worth, and if he has merit, the honours and offices of the country are open to him.

The extent of the United States renders it impossible to speak of the climate but in reference to particular parts. It is so various that amateurs can please themselves. The Province of Maine offers to them the fogs of Britain, and by visiting Georgia they may bask in the heat of the torrid zone. But, cries an Englishman, have you any where a temperate climate. By this, especially if he comes from Lancashire, is meant a climate in which it would be difficult, but for the relative length of days and nights, to distinguish winter from summer, and in which it rains four days out of five. Those who seek such climate in America must go to the neighbourhood of Nootka Sound. But if by a temperate climate be meant an atmosphere warm enough in summer to ripen every fruit not peculiar to the tropics, without that intensity of heat unfavourable to health and industry, a climate not so cold in winter as to destroy the cherry, apricot, or peach tree, yet cold enough to give the earth repose from vegetation, and provide ice for the succeeding summer; that climate is found in the middle states of America. The winter along the sea coast, commencing about the middle of December and continuing to the middle of March, is variable. Sudden thaws are succeeded by sudden frosts. A south-east wind brings vernal air from the Gulph Stream, and a north-wester pours down frost from the mountains. Beyond these mountains, however, the cold is steady and not severe. From the middle of March to the middle or end of April, the weather, generally bad, is sometimes fine enough to deserve the name it bears of spring. May, though cloathed in blossoms, and sometimes in the beginning bound by frost, may generally be ranked among the summer months, and September has equal rights, although sometimes a slight frost supports the claim of autumn. Thus the summer is nearly five months long, and in that period five to fifteen days may be expected uncomfortably warm. The months of October, November, and great part of December, are fine. No man who has not enjoyed the autumn of North America can form an idea of weather so constantly pleasant. But the climate is changeable, say Europeans, and *therefore* unhealthy: to which it might be tritely replied, the climate is healthy, and *therefore* not changeable. All things figure by comparison. Climate among the rest. An insular position, especially if the island be small, free from mountains, and far from any continent, secures an equable temperature of the air. But if there be no sudden changes of heat and cold, there are frequent variations of another sort. Almost every wind brings rain or damp, drizzling, disagreeable weather. Such weather is scarcely known in the middle states of America. It rains and snows in earnest, after which the atmosphere resumes its usual brilliance. That the climate is favourable to human life is proved by the rapidity of population; to which emigrations from Europe do indeed contribute, but in such small proportion as to be scarcely worth notice. The instances of healthy old age are no where more numerous. They who contradict this fact insist that the proportion of those in America who reach the age of eighty is much smaller than in Europe. This remains to be proved. But if admitted, let it be considered that the population of Europe has increased but little in eighty years, whereas that of America, doubling in twenty years, was not, eighty years ago more than one sixteenth of the present number. Europe therefore ought to show sixteen times as many old men as America. To say that a climate is variable can form no objection unless the supposed mutability be injurious to health or vegetation. But if we descend from animal to vegetable life, the advantage of America over Europe is unquestionable; for there it is common to lose the fruit by unseasonable weather, a thing which rarely happens here.

Of the American soil it is impossible to speak justly without being very minute. There is, perhaps, none quite so bad as the heaths of Brabant, Westphalia, and lower Saxony. There is a great deal very good—some fields unexhausted by the constant harvests of a century without manure. To speak, however, as nearly as may be in general terms, if beginning where Hudson's River enters the sea, a line running south of Philadelphia along the falls of Susquehannah, Potomack, and Rapahanock be continued through North-Carolina, South-Carolina, and Georgia, the lands east of it are of indifferent quality, although there be many large tracts of excellent soil. West of this line to the mountains the land is generally good, but yet large tracts may be found which are bad. From New York to Boston the land between the mountains and the sea is rocky, and in some places the soil, generally fruitful, is meagre. There are fine vallies between the different ranges of mountains, and some of the mountains have excellent soil to the top. The great western valley from Quebeck to New-Orleans, is perhaps unequalled for extent and fertility. In ascending the St. Lawrence and descending the Alleghany and Ohio, the mountains on the left recede, and at length subside: those on the right lie at a vast distance beyond the western shore of the lakes. At the head of the St. Lawrence is that congeries of inland seas, whose waters, almost as transparent as air, preserve in this majestic stream its constant fulness. Those lakes, of which Ontario, the last, and by no means the largest, presents a surface of more than five thousand square miles, are of such vast extent, that no supposable quantity of rain can make any important change. Moreover, all the rivers they receive would not supply in a year the waste by evaporation in a month. They are unquestionably fed by springs, and as their surface varies very little, so the supply of water which they pour into the St. Lawrence is constant. Many considerable streams which sometimes overflow and are at other times much reduced, flow into that river; but the amount of what they furnish is so small compared with the volume from Lake Ontario, that in a space of fifty leagues from Cadaraqui to the mouth of Attawa River, the depth of water seldom varies a foot in a year.

The climate of this immense valley is uncommonly regular, fenced by a broad rampart of mountains against the mutability of the ocean, its seasons are determined by the advance and recess of the sun; and as causes must precede effects, the warmth of spring in the latitude of forty-five (which is the northern boundary of the United States) is seldom completely established before the first of May, neither does the cold reign of winter commence until the middle or end of November. A recent fact deserves to be noted here. During the storm which on the 23d and 24th of August 1806[2] made such dreadful ravage along the sea coast from New Hampshire to Georgia, it was (beyond the first range of mountains) calm and pleasant. In going from St. Regis southwardly up the river for forty miles, there is little change of latitude or climate: but there, having ascended the rapids, the influence of the lakes becomes perceptible. The winter is less cold and the summer more mild. Keeping on east of the lakes for about five hundred miles through eight degrees of longitude and three of latitude, the climate is nearly the same. All the fruits of a temperate climate flourish and come to great perfection in the open air except the peach, which has not yet succeeded beyond the latitude of Niagara, but at that place it is abundant. After getting on further south and losing the influence of the lakes, the climate is governed by the latitude, till at length, in the neighbourhood of New Orleans, are found the orange and sugar cane.

Some credulous people, seduced by flattering descriptions of America, have been led into ruinous speculations. They rashly supposed that man could here, as in a terrestrial paradise, live without labour and without law. These were the dreams of unripe judgment, and these were not the only illusions. It may dissipate some of them to inform Europeans that in America the professions of law, physic and divinity, are fully supplied. That the art of trading with small capital or no capital, is well understood. That the fine arts, little cultivated, receive but small encouragement. That those who wander from the path of industry will soon be entangled by want. That those who expect to live by contrivance will be greatly disappointed. The market is already overstocked with that commodity. Labourers and mechanics cannot fail of success if they be sober, honest, industrious and steady. But such men seldom emigrate. The idle and dissolute are better pleased than at home, because wages are high, and ardent spirits cheap, so that with tolerable management they can be drunk three days in the week. But this rogue's jubilee is almost over. The great demand for labour must cease with the war; and even while it lasts it would be better for such fellows to enlist in Europe. They can be as idle, will enjoy better health, and may live longer; for rum and whiskey are as fatal as the gun and bayonet. We frequently see an old soldier, but an old sot is very rare.

The influence of exaggerated description has in nothing been greater

---

2. "August 1806" in the *Port Folio*; "last August" in the pamphlet.

than in what relates to the land of America. Those awful forests which have shaded through untold ages a boundless extent; those streams, compared to which the rivers of Europe are but rills, streams which, deep and smooth, meander many hundred leagues through a soil waiting only the hand of culture to produce luxuriant abundance; those forests, streams and plains, dazzled the eye of reason and led the judgment astray. It should have been considered that great labour must be applied to destroy the forest before it can yield a harvest. That harvest too must with labour be gathered and prepared for market. At length embarked on the bosom of the flood, it must traverse extensive regions before it can be sold. It must pay (in freight) not only the expense of a voyage to the sea, but that of the boatmen on their return. Foreign articles also must bear a great charge of transportation; so that if the inhabitants can obtain from their produce the supply of their wants, little if any thing will remain to pay for land. He, therefore, who traces along the map the course of those majestic rivers should calculate a little before he counts on the advantage of their downhill navigation. The time will come, and perhaps it is not remote, when manufacturing towns will be established in those regions. The produce of the farmer will be then consumed by the artisan, and the articles he prepares will be used by those who till the soil. An intercourse more certain and more lucrative than foreign trade. But until that period arrives, every proposition respecting the western country should be examined with great sobriety.

Here the question may be asked, if it is in no case advisable to purchase American lands; and as this subject may hereafter occupy much of public attention, some moments bestowed on it may not be misapplied. Unquestionably the lands of America present a valuable object to those who are in condition to avail themselves of the advantage, provided they acquire the needful information and act prudently. The reason is obvious. Not much more than a century has elapsed since the land of America was worth little or nothing. At first it was worth less than nothing, for the original settlers were obliged to bring with them not only clothes and tools, but food, and must nevertheless have perished if the original stock of necessaries had not been frequently replenished by supplies from their native country. Land was then given away, and few would accept the gift coupled with the condition of settlement. As population increased, it became of more value, and as settlements extended, the value advanced slowly at first, then with accelerated velocity, so that in the last ten years it has been greater than in the preceding twenty. Several causes combine to produce this effect; as first a general rise in the price of all commodities, or, what is equivalent, a general decrease in the value of money owing to an increase of the quantity. This, however, is not so great as many have imagined; for the price of wheat throughout Europe, during the eighteenth century, has been on an average about one penny sterling a pound, and nearly as dear in the last period of twenty years as in the first. The expense of living arises in some degree from taxes imposed on consumption, and partly from the higher style of modern housekeeping. Admitting, however, the existence and the operation of this general cause, a resort must be had to others more efficient. For the better understanding of these, let it be observed that, from the progress of commerce and the useful arts, the price of land has increased in some parts of Europe, while it declined in others without any considerable change in the state of population, and that in general where population has increased the value of lands has also increased. Thus we have three distinct causes, commerce, manufactures, and population. These are permanent. Those which are fortuitous should not be noticed. Now these, permanent causes have been more developed in America than in any other country. The population has doubled every twenty years; the progress of manufactures is as rapid at least; and that of commerce is equal to both. The increase of American manufactures is scarcely suspected abroad or at home: but forty years ago hardly an axe or a scythe was made on the western side of the Atlantic. Carriages of pleasure, household furniture, and even butter, cheese, and salted provisions were imported. Things are in this respect greatly changed. Much is exported of the articles last mentioned, and even the manufacture of superfine cloth, now in its infancy, bids fair to become extensive, the wool of America being little inferior to that of Spain. The wide range of our commerce is generally known, but one circumstance which bears on the present object must not be omitted. That commerce, which twenty years ago was wholly supported by English credit, rests now principally on American capital, which is more than sufficient for the trade that will remain at a general peace. To apply these facts with mathematical precision would gratify only inquisitive minds fond of nice calculation, and would convert this hasty sketch from loose hints to abstruse speculation. It is sufficient, on the present occasion, to say that by these causes the value of land has been raised and from the continuance of these causes must continue to rise. Peace must operate to the same end, first, by lessening the demand of money to support commerce, and of course leaving more for the purchase and improvement of land; secondly, by a fall in the price of labour, because produce being the result of a combination between land and labour, the share of land increases in proportion, as that of labour is diminished; and thirdly, by the diminution of freight and assurance, which, facilitating the interchange of articles, foreign and domestic, gives greater intrinsic value to both. Judicious speculations in land have yielded more in the last ten years than in the twenty preceding, or the antecedent forty. Hence it is reasonable to believe that they will continue to be advantageous. But the question occurs, where and how are they to be made?

Those who would derive a great immediate revenue from land should purchase in the lower parts of South Carolina and Georgia, or in the vicinity of New Orleans. They must purchase slaves also, and superintend the planting of cotton, rice and sugar. The profit will be great, but the climate is not favourable to northern constitutions; the culture is unpleasant, and there are some inconveniences, such as occasional hurricanes and the danger to be apprehended from a revolt of slaves. This culture, moreover, requires previous instruction and experience. North of the district just mentioned, little revenue can be derived from land. The culture by slaves in Maryland, Virginia, and North Carolina, seldom pays five per cent. on the capital employed. But in these states, particularly the two first, a gentleman who wishes to enjoy the pleasures of a country life, coupled with its cares, who has no objection to become the master of slaves, and can submit to the inconveniences of a warmer summer than he has been accustomed to in Europe, with the consequent defect of verdure, may with little difficulty discover excellent situations. He will find among the gentlemen honourable temper, liberal manners, and frank hospitality; among the ladies beauty and accomplishment, joined to virtue and good housewifery. But he must not expect that his property will increase in value. This cannot happen until the labour of slaves shall have been replaced by that of freemen, a period which seems to be remote.

It has already been hinted that property on the rivers which empty into the Mississippi cannot attain to great money value until manufacturing towns shall grow up in that quarter. It is to be observed that the American cultivator generally pays more for his produce in labour than in the price of land. A first crop of wheat costs about twenty dollars per acre, exclusive of the land on which it is raised. The crop in countries favourable to it may be taken at from fifteen to five and thirty bushels: rarely on new land so little as fifteen and sometimes more than forty. It is evident that the expense and amount of a crop being the same, the value of land must depend on the price of its produce. Where wheat sells for a dollar, the crop usually pays for both clearing and culture—frequently for the land and sometimes more; but when it will not bring above a quarter of a dollar, the most abundant crop will scarcely defray the expense of tillage. Hence it follows, that if this great western region were as favourable to wheat as it is to Indian corn, it must for a long time be of little value. The scene for advantageous speculations in land, therefore, is confined on the south by the southern line of Pennsylvania, on the west and northwest by the Alleghany mountains, till we come south of Niagara, and then by Lake Ontario, and the river St. Laurence,[3] and on the north by the boundary of the United States. From this tract, however, must be excepted the province of Maine, in which, nevertheless, there are said to be some tracts of excellent soil, and which can certainly boast of fine harbours and fisheries. But taken in general, the country is not fertile, and the climate is not inviting, wherefore the current of emigration from New England sets westward. The northern parts of New Hampshire are inclement and mountainous. Good land there as well as in Vermont, is dear, and large tracts of it are not to be purchased, neither are such to be had either in Massachusetts or Connecticut, which states are so full of people that many thousands annually emigrate. Small tracts may be found which from the populousness of the neighbourhood will yield with good management a fair rent. Men possessing about ten thousand pounds sterling might establish themselves here, but not before they have dwelt long enough in the country to know the usages, manners, and disposition of the inhabitants as well as the climate, soil and circumstances peculiar to different positions. In general, those parts of Connecticut and Massachusetts which border on New York would be preferred; but it must be remarked that lands along the sound bear a price far beyond their value, and more especially those near the city of New York. North of Massachusetts along Connecticut river there is a charming country, but the climate becomes harsh in going northward, and rising at the same time to a greater elevation from the level of the sea. Men of the property abovementioned might perhaps find a few good positions in New Jersey, or the cultivated parts of Pennsylvania or New York. But in none of these places is there room for what is understood in America by land speculations. They must be confined to the unsettled parts of Pennsylvania or New York. Most of the former lie west of the Alleghany, and the remainder consists of several ranges of mountains with the vallies between them. These mountains are in general high, rough, and not unfrequently sterile. The vallies are narrow, and the access to them difficult. The land beyond the mountains falls under

3. The pamphlet consistently spells it "St. Laurence"; with this exception, "St. Lawrence" occurs in the *Port Folio*.

the general description of that which is watered by the western streams, although Pittsburg, already a manufacturing town, gives value to the neighbourhood. In effect, the lands conveniently situated in Pennsylvania are for the most part inhabited; still, however, good tracts may be found in the counties of Luzerne and Northampton, not too remote from the circle of commerce. The roads now laid out, and in part completed through the states of New York and New Jersey, to connect these lands with the city of New York, together with those which open a communication with Philadelphia to great part of them, must rapidly increase their value. The interior of the state of New York presents the fairest scene for operations on land, because it lies within the influence of commerce. A bare inspection of the map will show that in going round by water from Oswego, on Lake Ontario, to St. Regis, on the St. Lawrence, and thence by land to Lake Champlain, the whole course is within about fifty leagues of Waterford, a village at the confluence of the Hudson and Mohawk rivers, to which sloops ascend from New York. Thus, not to mention the facilities which the river St. Lawrence presents, produce, when the roads now in operation shall be completed, may be brought from the parts most remote to the tide waters of Hudson's river for twenty dollars a ton, without the aid which is derived from the Mohawk river and lake Champlain. In going west of a line from Oswego, to where Tioga river falls into the Susquehannah, we recede from the influence of commerce. The number of commodities which will bear transportation, is diminished by the distance. From Oswego to Albany, and from Tioga to New York, is about the same distance, and the Hudson running nearly parallel to the line from Oswego to Tioga, the facility of navigation through the whole intermediate space is nearly equal. It must not, however, be forgotten that a broad tract of mountains extends in a southwesterly direction from Lake Champlain to the northeastern corner of Pennsylvania. These render the space they occupy less valuable, and render the communications more difficult; but during the last five years, so many turnpike roads have been made, and so many more are now making, that the transportation will soon be easy throughout, saving always the effect of distance. Nature presents also great facilities for inland navigation. That of the Susquehannah has been practiced with success from above Tioga down to Baltimore. That of the Mohawk is so much improved that the merchant at Utica sells goods as cheap as at Albany, and gives nearly the same price for produce. It must be noted also that the mountains last mentioned do not form a continued chain, but lie in detached masses. Those who ascend the Mohawk river to Rome in a batteau are already on the western side of the mountains and can in the same boat descend by Wood Creek, Oneida Lake, and Oswego River, to Lake Ontario.

Hitherto the advantages to be derived from the navigation of the St. Lawrence have been unnoticed, but they are eminent, and the more so from that constant fulness of the stream which has already been mentioned. From the sea port of Montreal to the mouth of Lake Ontario, merchandise is transported for one dollar per hundred weight, a small addition to the value. The navigation downward is much less expensive, and by means of it, timber, which in clearing many parts of America must be destroyed, can be turned to good account. Many productions sell as high at Montreal as at New York; some higher. From the hills southeast of the St. Lawrence pour down numerous streams which give value as well as health and beauty to that country. The coincidence of these things, with an uncommon fertility of soil, have induced numbers to come in from the eastern states; and there is every reason to believe that all the land fit for culture will be speedily settled.

It remains to consider the manner in which operations of the sort now contemplated are to be performed. And first, the purchase may be either in large tracts of uncertain quality, or in small tracts, the soil of which is known to be good. He who purchases a small tract of choice land, must pay a large price, but he has the moral certainty of a speedy sale. He who purchases a large tract unexplored pays less, but much of it may be bad, and the sales will not speedily be completed. Opinions on this subject vary; but experience favours the purchase of large tracts at a moderate price. In this case there is less to be apprehended from the mistake or misrepresentation of surveyors, and frequently the proportion of good land is so great, that if made to bear the whole price, it will be as cheap as the small tract, leaving the inferior quality a clear profit. Moreover, when the best lands are sold and in cultivation, those which adjoin them find as good and sometimes a better market.

Supposing the purchase made, there are several modes of sale. First, the land may be sold as it was bought, in mass, at an advanced price, which is the easiest, but not the most profitable mode. Secondly, it may be retailed to settlers by an agent on the spot, who is to receive a fixed salary or a commission. The landholder who gives a salary to his agent is certain of nothing but the expense. He will generally be pestered with costly projects of roads, mills, and villages, which seldom answer any good purpose. The roads, if not laid out judiciously will not be travelled; in which case they soon grow up in bushes and become impassable. The mills must have millers, and the millers must have salaries, which they are careful to receive, but neglect their mills for the sake of hunting, fishing, or other idle pursuits; whereas the settler who builds a mill for his own account attends to it for his own interest. Houses built by a landlord are generally occupied by vagabonds. The industrious prefer living on their own land in their own houses. But bad settlers repel good ones. If the agent be paid by a commission, he will still hanker after expensive establishments, tending, as he supposes, to increase the sales, and at any rate to give him an air of importance. He will moreover pay too little attention to the moral character of settlers, which is nevertheless an important circumstance; for land always sells higher in the neighbourhood of sober, honest, industrious people, than in that of the lazy and profligate. Whichever of these two modes be adopted, the agent, if not perfectly honest, may sell the best land to friends, and share with them in a profit on the re-sale. To avoid these inconveniences, a third mode has been adopted. A contract is made with a capable person, and the lands are fixed at a price agreed on. He superintends the sale to settlers, which is not to be under a price also agreed on, and for his compensation receives one half of what remains after paying to the owner the price first mentioned with the interest. By this means, the interest of the agent is so intimately connected with that of his employer that he can seldom promote one at the expense of the other. Whatever mode of sale be adopted, these things are to be remarked: first, the choice of farms and of sites for mills, must be given freely to the first comers on moderate terms and long credit, because the future price will depend much on the improvements they make. Secondly, in the progress of settlement, prices must be raised and credit shortened, so that, having taken care that the first settlers were good, idlers and paupers may be kept off. Thirdly, the landlord must make no reservation of particular spots, because he would thereby disgust settlers and turn them away; whereas he can always get back any part which may strike his fancy, by giving a little more land in the vicinity, and a fair compensation for the expense of clearing. Besides, a choice of situation is more easily made after the country is opened than before. Finally, when the sales are sufficient to reimburse the capital employed, with the interest, it is wise to pause and let the effect of cultivation be felt. Purchasers become eager, and prices rise, so that what remains of good land will sell well: the bad should be kept. It will in a certain time become of great value, because settlers cut down and destroy timber as fast as they can, counting on the purchase of wood lots when their own farms shall be stript of trees. To get these lots they will pay three times as much for bad land as the good cost them; but the landlord had better not sell, but let them have wood at a low price, until they are all in want of fuel, and then a permanent revenue may be raised from the forest. This, by the by, is a better provision for posterity than to leave a large tract unsettled. In that case intruders go on, careless of title, whom it is difficult and expensive to remove.

There remains another mode by which lands may be disposed of, which has not been hitherto practised, and for which, indeed, the country was not ripe. A man may purchase from twenty to sixty thousand acres, and select for his special domain in the centre, as much as he shall think proper. After making an accurate survey, obtaining good information, and duly considering all circumstances, he may fix an agent at the place proper for a village, give away to good tradesmen some building lots, and (with each) a small lot for pasture, then sell four or five thousand acres in the neighbourhood, and stop the sales, directing his agent to let the remainder at a low rent for a term of one and twenty years, on condition to plant an orchard and put the land in good fence. These farms, at the expiration of the lease, would probably rent for one dollar per acre. The forest reserved in the centre would also become a source of revenue, to which effect, when the tenants come to want wood, it would be proper to let them take for nothing what lies down, and for a small consideration, the old and decaying trees, together with all which stand on the avenues to be pierced for beauty and convenience. These trees being cut in the summer solstice, and their cattle feeding gratuitously in the woods, the growth of under brush would be kept down. Those who adjoin the forest also, would, for their own sakes, keep up a good fence against it, and thus the landlord, making no expense and conferring favours, would find his park brought into excellent order.

This sketch has run to such length, that one important subject must remain almost untouched. Still, however, a few words on the government of America cannot be dispensed with. It is the fashion at present to decry republics, and so far as democracies are concerned, no discreet man will object to the censure. But pure democracy is rare, and is rather a destruction than a form of republican government. It is the passage to monarchy. It never did, and never can exist, but for a moment, and that too is a moment of agony. Let those then, who lavish their applause on monarchy, consider that the prevalence of democratic confusion can at last but establish their favourite system. Ere this can be done, however, America must be cursed with more mob than at present. A nation of landholders will not easily permit themselves to be ruled by the scum of other countries poured into their large towns to ferment under the influence of designing scoundrels. It seems more likely that they will, when taught by experience the danger of democracy, make such change in the government as circumstances may require. Causes must precede effects. The remedy cannot be adopted before the evil is felt. The sick may be prevailed on to take medicine though bitter, but those who enjoy health will not swallow drugs by way of antidote. That America, when fully peopled, may become a monarchy, is not improbable; but in the mean time she is free, prosperous, and happy. Some indeed there are, who, pluming themselves on the possession of a little wit or a little money, claim to be what they call the better sort of people, and deal out abundant invective against what they are pleased to denominate jacobinism, under which term they comprehend almost every tenet of freedom. These men tell us we should choose a king, as being a handsome capital to decorate the column of freedom. But that choice is not so easy a thing as they imagine. Where a crown descends from father to son by immemorial usage, there is no difficulty in making kings; but those who begin the trade have an up-hill road to travel, equally difficult and dangerous. The blackguards of a country will indeed readily hail king Log, though they prefer king Crane, in the hope of sharing the plunder of a spoiler; but the wealthy, the eminent, and the considerate, will not rashly choose a master, nor tamely submit to one which others have chosen. Admitting, moreover, that it were easy, is it desirable to establish monarchy? The idea of a French republic was no doubt ridiculous, and the attempt fruitful in abominations; to overturn monarchy in Britain would be as absurd and nearly as pernicious, and to propose a Russian or Prussian democracy, would be as wise a project as that of the Roman emperor, who wished to make a consul of his horse; but let those who are so proud of the monarchical trappings under which they prance, and who are so prodigal of censure on the opinions and feelings of America, show what has been done by royal governments to suppress that hideous spirit of jacobinism which is the theme of their abundant declamation. One nation has indeed stood forth the bulwark of mankind. But that nation is governed more by an aristocracy than by a monarch. According to the English law, the king can do no wrong—a modest expression of the fact, that he can do nothing. He can, it is true, choose ministers, but then his part is performed. The rest is theirs. Each and every of them for each and every act of government, is liable to be tried by the peers on impeachment of the commons. They are thus accountable to the aristocracy: for if the peers are clothed with the national dignity, it is the property which makes and sits in the house of commons. So little, indeed, is their king considered by them as an efficient part of the government, that the act in which he personally appears, and which of all others seems most especially his own, the speech which he makes, is considered and treated in their parliament, as the speech of his minister; and so is the fact. The British monarchy, if monarchy it must be called, is certainly a good government, well suited to that country. Whether it would suit America would be known only by experiment. Probably it would not, but certainly it could not now be established. If we inquire by what power it is sustained in England, we shall find it is the good sense and mild spirit of Englishmen, the same power by which it was established. A similar spirit, with a fair portion of common sense, induced the Americans to adopt that system under which they live, and it may reasonably be expected, that a continuance of the same mind and temper will preserve to them, for a long time, the blessings of order, liberty, and law.

As the *Answer to War in Disguise* shows, American arguments for the rights of neutral shipping under international law fell increasingly on deaf ears as the British tried to inflict economic damage on France. In fall 1806, Napoleon retaliated with the Berlin Decree, forbidding all commerce with Britain, whether in French, allied, or neutral ships. Caught between the interests of American trade and their sympathies for France, the Jeffersonians tried to use trade first as a bargaining tool with both sides, and then as a weapon, beginning with the Non-Importation Act of 1806.

The treaty under discussion here was negotiated in late 1806 by James Monroe and William Pinckney, and signed December 31, 1806. It was intended to replace the Jay Treaty of 1795; but Monroe also had specific instructions from Jefferson to resolve the issue of impressment of American sailors by the British navy. The British, however, refused to yield on impressment. When he received the treaty in March 1807, Jefferson refused to submit it to the Senate for ratification.

The authorship of the pamphlet is uncertain. The first edition was published in 1807, probably in Philadelphia. Many bibliographies attribute it to Charles Brockden Brown, although Brown scholars have questioned

The British Treaty (n.p., n.d. [probably Philadelphia, 1807]). American Antiquarian Society Early American Imprints, series II (Shaw-Shoemaker), no. 12217. From the copy in the pamphlet collection, L. A. Beeghly Library, Juniata College which, however, attributes the pamphlet to Rufus King. (This copy is the only one I have learned of that attributes the pamphlet to King.) The title page of the British edition of 1808 reads: "The British Treaty, by Governeur [sic] Morris, Esq. of New York, Ambassador to the French Republic During the Reign of Robespierre. With an appendix of state papers; which are now first published. And, by William Cobbett, esq., a refutation of the present political sentiments of himself. London: Printed for John Joseph Stockdale, 41, Pall-Mall, 1808." I thank the Boston Athenaeum for the opportunity to examine its copy of this edition.

the attribution.[1] The British edition of 1808, however, lists Morris as the author, and although the evidence is ambiguous, there is good reason to believe it is his. In general, the views expressed in the pamphlet are consistent with those Morris expressed both publicly and privately regarding the policies of the Jefferson administration. We know from other sources that Morris did not think highly of James Madison, and that while he got on well with Jefferson personally, he regarded him more highly as a scholar than as a statesman. Thus the comments on their characters, which claim to be based on personal knowledge, are consistent with both Morris's opinions and his opportunities for firsthand observation.

Other internal evidence of his authorship includes using "Maddison" and "Munro" for Madison and Monroe, both of which are habitual with Morris. The pamphlet also quotes from the letter Morris drafted for the Constitutional Convention, transmitting the finished document to Congress, and the account of the debate in the convention over whether to permit export taxes reflects the position he took at the time of the convention.

Against these pieces of evidence, the passage dissecting Madison's and Jefferson's morals is unusually personal for Morris. He normally does not come so close to discussing the private morality of public figures. Thus while it is likely the pamphlet is by Morris, there remains room for doubt.

---

1. David Lee Clark, *Charles Brockden Brown: Pioneer Voice of America* (Durham, N.C.: Duke University Press, 1952), 261: "the *British Treaty* . . . was almost certainly not Brown's." Clark adds that a copy of the pamphlet probably owned by Oliver Wolcott lists Morris as the author. I would like to thank Philip Barnard of the Charles Brockden Brown Electronic Archive and Scholarly Edition for his help with this issue.

TO
THOSE MEMBERS OF CONGRESS
WHO HAVE
THE SENSE TO PERCEIVE
AND THE
SPIRIT TO PURSUE
THE
TRUE INTERESTS OF THEIR COUNTRY,
THIS PAMPHLET IS DEDICATED

Preface.

The matter of the following sheets was long since prepared, but the publication was suspended from unwillingness to interfere in the measures of government; and from the apprehension that such interference, instead of doing good, might produce evil. A majority of our countrymen seems determined to approve whatever our rulers do; and even to give praise for what they leave undone. We believed, therefore, that, borne on a tide of popularity, they would disdain what we could say; and might pursue their course still more pertinaciously should we declare our opinion that it leads to ruin.

This, though an evil, was not the greatest which we apprehended. We have long seen the American people acting and thinking under an impression that the wisest and most virtuous among us have an interest distinct from their fellow citizens; that they wish to tyrannize and oppress; that they want to be lords and kings. And although it is acknowledged that nothing could be more absurd than a scheme to establish monarchy or aristocracy, it has been taken for granted, that men noted for their judgment are engaged in that ridiculous project. If this produced no other effect than to exclude them from the national councils, we should consider it as a misfortune. We should, however, console ourselves with the hope, that a quiet course of things would render the employment of their talents unnecessary; or that, if storms should cloud the political horizon, they would, as virtuous citizens, be ready at the call of their country. But we have seen a more serious consequence result from the false direction of public sentiment. The measures which such men recommend are considered as part of the system attributed to them. And when they exercise the common right and perform the common duty of freemen, to express their opinion of any measure of government which appears to them unwise or improper, it is attributed to a desire of making mischief between the people and their friends. Indeed, a singular advantage has been taken even of their talents, to render their exertions ineffectual. Such, it is said, is their power to persuade, that those who listen are lost; wherefore the people must turn a deaf ear to their arguments. And such, it is said, is their power to misrepresent, that the President and his friends dare not indulge themselves in explaining the principles of his conduct. But since the people know he is their sincere friend, the ablest and best man in America, they cannot act more prudently than to repose confidence in him; and adopt the maxims which emanate from his mind. Hence it has happened that, generally speaking, whatever those who administer the government have thought proper to say or do, has been received and adopted as perfectly wise; from which, at length, has resulted the very great evil, that where their opinion or conduct has been traced up to maxims dangerous and false, error has been adopted as an article of faith. Seeing all this, we could not but apprehend that it might be dangerous to publish the matter contained in the following pages. We feared that, from blind confidence on one side, and blind enmity on the other, false notions might prevail and be established respecting our exterior relations, of which foreigners would not fail to take advantage. But it is no easy matter to get loose from treaties with a great power. And although it is a misfortune to be bound by treaties unequal and injurious, that is not the only misfortune. The jealousy of rival powers is excited, and they take every convenient occasion to make us feel their resentment.

A late event has roused public indignation; and Americans, waking from their long dream, appear desirous of knowing their condition. We see with honest pride the spirit of our country. Neither submission to insult with the view to save money, nor the disgraceful expedient of purchasing delusive tranquillity, have yet unnerved the public mind.

It may be expected that we should say a few words on this event. We put aside what preceded the assault on the Chesapeake, because, even if our government had been in the wrong (a subject on which as yet we form no opinion), the attempt to search a public ship of war appears to us unjustifiable; and more especially so on our own coast.[2] We firmly believe the

2. On June 22, 1807, the British ship HMS *Leopard* attacked the USS *Chesapeake* off the coast of Norfolk, Virginia. The *Chesapeake* surrendered and allowed the British to board in search of deserters from the Royal Navy.

British will not attempt a justification; but will, for their own sakes, grant satisfaction. We do not mean to say that they can be bullied into submission. They are a high-spirited nation, and will not be bullied. If any thing prevents them from giving satisfaction, it will be a demand in terms so injurious as to put us in the wrong. Then, indeed, we may be answered in a tone to repel the insult of threatening language; which, as it is addressed to fear and not to justice, implies the opinion that we have to deal with scoundrels and cowards. When, therefore, we express an opinion that the British government will, for its own sake, give satisfaction, it is from the condition expressed by Admiral Berkeley, and which would at any rate have been implied, that they are willing in their turn to submit their ships of war to search. This we believe they never will submit to, and therefore presume Admiral Berkeley will loose his commission for making the offer.[3]

We may be mistaken in our view of the course of events. Things may be brought to the alternative of submitting to insult or going to war. In that case, not pretending to conceal the misfortunes which must attend hostility, we think every thing is to be done and suffered to vindicate the national honour. These are the constant sentiments of our hearts, unmoved by irritations of the moment. These also are the deliberate conclusions of our judgment. If any gentlemen suppose the war will be feeble and harmless, they are deceived. It must be severe and bloody. But it must be sustained manfully. And we have so good an opinion of England, that we think she will not like us the worse for fighting her on the point of honour. In the mean time it becomes us to sustain the dignity of our character by the language and deportment of self-respect. Let it be remembered that foul and abusive terms come with propriety from the mouths of none but prostitutes and cowards.

In the following sheets we have endeavoured to avoid reproach and crimination. In some instances indignation has burst forth. We might, it is confessed, now soften the terms. But really there are occasions on which wholly to restrain the warmth of expression implies a defect of honest sentiment. And there are subjects also, to treat which in the cool style of narration, is to betray the cause of virtue.

Aware that it may be said we are personally hostile to the administration, we think it proper to put the question at rest, by declaring candidly our opinion. We consider, then, Mr. Gallatin as an efficient man of real talents.

---

3. George Berkeley was recalled to England, but soon was sent back into service in support of Wellington's armies in the Peninsular Campaign.

We did not approve, neither do we now approve of his appointment; but we forbear to assign the reasons, because, as far as it has come to our knowledge, his conduct is not reprehensible. We believe, moreover, that he is not swayed by pecuniary motives. We are convinced that he touched nothing in the Louisiana concern, and have no reason to suppose he will pocket any part of the sum to be expended in purchasing the Floridas. We consider Mr. Maddison as a man of considerable genius, though somewhat slow, and of great industry. We approved of his appointment. We knew indeed that he was a man of feeble mind; and had seen with concern that he gave himself up to Mr. Jefferson, without reserving the use of his own judgment. When we first knew him, he was a youth of ingenuous temper, whose ignorance of the world exposed him to become the prey of any sharper (of either sex) by whom he might be assailed. From a defect of firmness in the texture of his mind, and perhaps also from a defect of education, he was not in the habit of recurring always to fixed principles for a decision on conduct and opinions. So long, however, as he hung on the arm of Washington, his course was steady, and gained him honour. But the instant he let go that hold, he fell into a ricketty condition, from which he never recovered; and is now in a deep decline of character, for which we fear there is no remedy. The first violent symptom was a panegyric on the French constitution: the more extraordinary, as that instrument, in all its prominent features, was opposite to the constitution he had assisted in making, and laboured earnestly and successfully in persuading us to adopt. It would be painful to mark the steps by which this gentleman has descended to his present condition; the mere instrument of Mr. Jefferson. We believe him still honest and well disposed. We think he would make an excellent first clerk in the Secretary of State's office, and sincerely regret the want of qualities and talents for the place he occupies. Mr. Jefferson is a man of pleasing, modest, unassuming manners. His conversation, generally amusing, is frequently instructive. Though not deep in any one science, he has that acquaintance with them all which becomes a scholar and adorns a gentleman. He has a considerable share of genius; and there is, in his deportment, an air of frankness and of deference to others, which are agreeable to all, and are sure of captivating the young and inexperienced. If there be blemishes in his private character, we have nothing to do with them. We consider him as a public man, and in this view he has great defects. Like others who have fallen into the idle habit of questioning established truth, his faculty of weighing evidence is impaired. Hence such an astonishing degree of credulity, that he could not only believe the French were free while suffering oppression the most cruel and bloody that ever poor wretches groaned under, but (finding it printed in a French book) he believed, and gravely told the Congress, there is a great mountain of salt in Louisiana. Mr. Jefferson has also the misfortune to be a schemer, perpetually occupied with some strange out-of-the-way project. If this were confined to speculation, it would be a harmless foible; but he tries to carry his projects into effect. Sometimes he prevails on the Congress to adopt them, and then poor sailors are sent a-ducking over the ocean in gun boats. At other times he is less successful, as when he proposed to stow away ships of the line upon shelves. He labours also under such defect of mental vision, that he seldom sees objects in their natural state and true position: just as when we look through a fog, many things near us are not perceived, and those we see appear larger and nearer than they really are.

We have said Mr. Jefferson is not deep in any science. He is more deficient in that of politics than in any other; and indeed it is impossible he should ever become a statesman; because a clear, distinct, and comprehensive view of objects, with a ready conception of their bearings on each other, is a needful prerequisite. A second prerequisite is so to weigh evidence, presumption and probability, as properly to give or withhold our faith: in short, to believe what we ought, and no more. A third is never to indulge notions which have not experience to recommend them: for though it be possible that after the many years which history numbers, and the many thousand events it records, something new in the science of ethics may be discovered, it is not likely; and if it were, the maxim of physicians should be adopted, to make experiments on bodies of little value, and not on the body politic. If any gentleman assume as a principle that mankind can be governed by reason; and insist, notwithstanding the evidence of all history, ancient and modern, sacred and profane, that we may prudently rely on reason for the defence of nations, we would advise him to commence a course of experiments with his own family, and see how far reason will go there. If successful, let him proceed to those with whom he transacts business. Let him reason them into the support of his pecuniary or political views, without any regard to their own interest. If again successful, let him go or send to such a man as Bonaparte, and tell him 'tis unreasonable that boys should be taken from their parents to fight and perish in the plains of Poland. That, instead of employing large armies, it would be cheaper and better to pick out a few able negociators, if any can be found among his own subjects; but if not, to borrow Messrs. Armstrong and Munro, and send them to persuade the Emperor of Russia and King of Prussia to surrender their dominions.[4] That a proposition so reasonable in itself, and supported by so much eloquence, could not be rejected. If Napoleon, being persuaded himself, should in this quiet, friendly way persuade his brother Alexander, the specific would indeed have the sanction of fair experiment, and might safely be adopted. It would surely be a great improvement. Happy condition! without fleets or armies, judges or constables, laws or executioners, to sit secure and happy under the broad shade of reason! But if it should prove, on trial, that neither in a family, a city, a national assembly, or with a leader of nations, the force of reason can be relied on; if it should again, for the ten thousandth time, be demonstrated, that what has been true since the world began, remains true at the present hour, and the gentleman still insist on his project, he could not be much respected as a politician. But though Mr. Jefferson is not, and, from the reasons just mentioned, can never become a statesman, he is a man of great address. Having a quick sense of danger, he has studied the means by which it may be avoided. Knowing the instability of popular opinion, he knew that to rely on it was unsafe. He determined, therefore, to avoid responsibility. This is the cardinal point by which the course of his administration has been directed, with undeviating attention. Consistently with this plan, he associated the house of representatives in the exercise of his functions. The leaders, to whom he applied, were charmed with the mark of confidence, and beyond all measure delighted with that republican spirit which, instead of seeking unlawful power, so freely and frankly discharged itself of the lawful power with which it had been invested. When, over and above that excessive condescension, the patronage of office was laid at their feet; when they were invited to select the proper subjects for appointment; and when they were told that they, the immediate representatives, were the organs through which he wished to learn that will of the people which it was his pleasure and pride to obey, how could they suspect the motive to be selfish? It was natural to believe the fountain pure when its waters were so refreshing. In this way, however, the house of representatives was brought to initiate executive business, and, taking responsibility from his shoulders, to invest him with unlimited power. Like a sly animal in the fable who likes roast chesnuts, but will not put his paws in the fire, he crept behind the curtain, and persuaded a friendly cat to undertake that part of the business;

4. John Armstrong was U.S. minister to France from 1804 to 1810, and later secretary of war in the Madison administration. James Monroe, as minister to Britain from 1803 to 1807, had negotiated the treaty under discussion here.

content, provided he gets the nuts, to leave with others all the honour of raking them out of the embers. By this course of conduct, Mr. Jefferson has not only injured the constitution, and established a system of corruption; but (extending the web of intrigue to influence elections over the whole country) he has composed a congress of such materials, that respect for the national government is much diminished. He has placed himself also in a state of dependance, whereby he is driven to do unrighteous things, and which disables him from becoming useful, should any course of events restore him to the love of honest fame.

Of the other members of our administration nothing need be said; neither shall we take notice of those who are occasionally charged with communicating the President's wishes to the Legislature: a sort of ministers whom Mr. Randolph has described in terms of no little acrimony.[5] Having mentioned this gentleman's name, we will add, that he appears to possess, in an eminent degree, some distinguishing traits of the Virginia character: A lively genius, a bold spirit, a high and haughty mind, with the habit of thinking for himself, and commanding others. Unfortunately for him, he took up false notions at an early period, and committed himself to such an extent, that he finds it difficult to eradicate the impressions from his mind, or free himself from the perplexities with which they entangle his conduct. The executive government, having studied his character, were glad to employ him. He was their sword and shield. But there were some views and plans which it was deemed unsafe to confide to a person of his temper. His indignation at the discovery was exprest in terms not easily mistaken. But though he flounces, he cannot break loose. He is not deficient in personal courage; but he dare not leave his party. Indeed, he is haunted by the panic fear, that the high and honourable sentiments he has expressed will lead the world to believe him a federalist. This apprehension, though whimsical, is not singular. It has, though with far less reason, laid hold on a kind of up and down man who writes letters to his constituents in Vermont.[6]

5. John Randolph of Roanoke (who would later become Morris's brother-in-law) broke with Jefferson and became a leader of the "Quids" faction in the Democratic-Republican party in 1806.

6. Although the practice of writing circular letters to constituents was common among Democratic-Republican congressmen in the South and West, it does not appear that Vermont Congressmen had adopted the practice. See Noble E. Cunningham Jr., *Circular Letters of Congressmen to their Constituents, 1789–1829* (Chapel Hill:

THE
BRITISH TREATY.

The gentlemen now in power used formerly to insist that republics should have no secrets. Times have changed, and they have changed with the times. We have secrets in abundance. Indeed, we have little else. The state of our affairs with foreign nations, and the conduct pursued towards them, are concealed with sedulous attention. But notwithstanding the care of our rulers, a corner of their curtain is sometimes lifted up. We have learnt a few state-secrets; and may, perhaps, in due time, bring them to light. For the present, however, curiosity must rest satisfied with the British treaty; suspended, as every one has heard, on doubts and apprehensions in the President's mind. We make this communication, because, among other reasons, stories have gone abroad which are not true. We are far from desiring that our rulers should, on all occasions, tell all they know. But we think they should on no occasion give currency to falsehood. The treaty is said to have been sent back because a note delivered by the British negotiators required us to make common cause against France. No such note was delivered. It has been reported also, that our non-importation law drove the minister of his Britannic Majesty into the required concessions. This also is among the things which are not. Without stopping to notice other aberrations from truth, we proceed to give the purport of that treaty, with a few observations.

The first article, like the first of that concluded on the 19th November, 1794, by Mr. Jay, is merely formal; and the second confirms the first ten articles of the old treaty. It is, therefore, proper to give a glance at them.

The first, as is already mentioned, is merely formal; and the second is executed.

The third gives to each party the right of passing through the territories of the other, in America, except within the limits of the Hudson's Bay Company. We find in it the following clause. "But it is understood, that this article does not extend to the admission of vessels of the United States into

---

University of North Carolina Press, 1978), 1:xxiv. Morris may be thinking of former Vermont representative Matthew Lyon, who represented Vermont 1797-1801, and then represented Kentucky 1803-1811. Lyon was jailed for violating the Sedition Act in 1798, and was reelected to Congress while in jail. He defended his conduct in a circular, *Colonel Lyon's address to his constituents. To the freemen of the western district of Vermont. Vergennes Gaol, January 10th, 1799* (n.p., 1799).

the sea-ports, harbours, bays or creeks of his Majesty's said territories, nor into such parts of the rivers in his Majesty's said territories as are between the mouth thereof and the highest port of entry from the sea, except in small vessels trading bona fide between Montreal and Quebec, under such regulations as shall be established to prevent the possibility of any frauds in this respect: Nor to the admission of British vessels from the sea into the rivers of the United States beyond the highest ports of entry for foreign vessels from the sea. The river Missisippi shall, however, according to the treaty of peace, be entirely open to both parties:[7] and it is further agreed, that all the ports and places on its eastern side, to whichsoever of the parties belonging, may freely be resorted to and used by both parties, in as ample a manner as any of the Atlantic ports or places of the United States, or any of the ports or places of his Majesty in Great-Britain."

The fourth article, after mentioning that "it is uncertain whether the Missisippi extends so far to the northward as to be intersected by a line to be drawn due west from the Lake of the Woods, in the manner mentioned in the treaty of peace," provides "for a joint survey of the northern part of that river"; and agrees, that, "if on the result of such survey it should appear that the said river would not be intersected by such a line," the parties will regulate the boundary in that quarter by amicable negotiation.

The fifth article, after mentioning that "doubts had arisen what river was truly intended under the name of the River St. Croix," provides for ascertaining that river, and the latitude and longitude of its mouth and source.[8]

The sixth, seventh and eighth articles have been executed.

The ninth provides for persons holding lands in the dominions of one of the parties who are subjects or citizens of the other; and the tenth is a stipulation in favour of moral honesty, viz. that neither party shall sequester or confiscate debts or property in the funds, &c.

The third article of the new treaty provides for and regulates commerce between the United States and the British East-Indies, in the same terms as the thirteenth article of the old treaty, except that the words, *and sailing direct from the ports of the said States* are inserted in the first clause, which now runs thus: "His Majesty consents that the vessels belonging to the citizens of the United States of America, and sailing direct from ports of the

7. The Treaty of Paris of 1783, ending the Revolutionary War.
8. The St. Croix River forms part of the boundary between Maine and New Brunswick.

said States, shall be admitted and hospitably received in all the sea-ports and harbours of the British territories in the East-Indies," &c.

The fourth article of the new treaty is the same as the fourteenth of the old one, and stipulates for a general liberty of trade between the United States and the British dominions in Europe.

The fifth article of the new treaty is the same as the fifteenth of the old one (regulating the duties on ships and merchandize), with two exceptions: The first reserves to the United States the right previously reserved to Great-Britain, of imposing a tonnage duty equal to what shall be imposed by the other party. The second is made by substituting a new clause for the reservation formerly made by Great-Britain, of "the right of imposing on American vessels entering into the British ports in Europe, such duty as may be adequate to countervail the difference of duty now payable on the importation of European and Asiatic goods when imported into the United States in British or in American vessels." Instead of this, the following words make part of the new article. "And in the trade of the two nations with each other, the same duties on exportation or importation of goods or merchandize shall be imposed, and the same drawbacks and bounties allowed in either country, whether the exportation or importation shall be in British or American vessels."

The sixth article of the new treaty states that the parties cannot agree about our trade to the British West-Indies; but that "while they will attempt an amicable agreement, both may exercise their existing rights."

The seventh of this, like the sixteenth of the other treaty, provides for the appointment of consuls, &c.

The eighth of this, like the seventeenth of the other, provides for speedy decision on the capture and detention of vessels suspected of carrying enemy's goods or contraband of war. There is added a promise on the part of Great-Britain, that hereafter indemnification shall be granted for unjust seizure, for detention and vexation.

The ninth article is the same as the eighteenth of the old treaty (respecting contraband), only that tar and pitch are excepted from the catalogue, unless when going to a place of naval equipment.

The tenth article is the same as the eighteenth of the old (respecting blockade), with the addition, that passengers not in the military service of an enemy shall not be taken and made prisoners.

By the eleventh article, citizens of the United States may carry European goods to the colonies of enemies of Great-Britain (from the ports of the United States), provided that both vessel and cargo be bona fide American property, that the goods shall have been unladen within the United States, and that (in addition to that part of the duty already reserved from the drawback on exportation) the further sum of one per cent. ad valorem on such goods shall be paid. They may also export from the United States to Europe, the produce of colonies of the enemies of Great-Britain, provided they, being neutral property, shall have been unladen as before, and that two per cent. ad valorem be paid on exportation in addition to what is reserved on the drawback. After the expiration of the treaty, all antecedent rights on these subjects are to revive.

The twelfth article extends to ships of Great-Britain, and of all nations who shall adopt the same regulation, the protection of our neutrality from a marine league to five miles from our shore.

The thirteenth article is substantially the same as the nineteenth of the old treaty, regulating privateers.

The fourteenth is the same as the twentieth of the old treaty, respecting pirates.

The fifteenth article of this treaty, like the twenty-first of the other, prohibits the subjects or citizens of one party to accept commissions from enemies of the other, and to commit acts of hostility.

The sixteenth, like the twenty-second of the other, forbids reprisals before a demand of satisfaction.

The seventeenth is the same as the twenty-third of the old treaty, which, after stipulating that "the ships of war of each of the contracting parties shall at all times be hospitably received in the ports of the other," provides that American vessels driven by "stress of weather, danger of enemies, or other misfortune," to seek shelter, shall be received in ports into which such vessels could not ordinarily claim to be admitted. This stipulation is now made reciprocal.

The eighteenth article, like the twenty-fourth of the old treaty, prohibits the armament of privateers belonging to the enemies of either, and the sale of their prizes in ports of the other party.

The nineteenth is the same as the twenty-fifth of the old treaty, permitting ships of war to bring in their prizes and take them away again without payment of duties, and prohibiting the entry of ships of the enemies of either party, which shall have made prize, unless driven by stress of weather; in which case they are to depart as soon as possible.

The twentieth is the same as the twenty-sixth of the old treaty, providing for merchants and others in one country when war breaks out with the other.

The twenty-first of this, like the twenty-seventh of the other, relates to giving up persons charged with murder or forgery.

The twenty-second is a new article respecting shipwrecks, and promising humane treatment.

The twenty-third secures to each the rights of the most favoured nation, and declares that "all treaties hereafter made by either with any nation, shall ipso facto be extended in all their favourable operations to the other."

The twenty-fourth engages to join in abolishing the slave trade.

The twenty-fifth contains the stipulation that this treaty is not to interfere with antecedent engagements. And,

The twenty-sixth limits the duration to ten years from the exchange of ratifications.

It is dated the 31st December, 1806; but previous to the signature two notes were given, by the British to the American commissioners. The first keeps open for future discussion a claim of Britain not to pay more on goods sent from Canada or New-Brunswick, into the territories of the United States, than is paid on the importation of such goods in American ships. The second note declares that the King of Great-Britain has directed his commissioners, before they sign the treaty, to deliver that note, in order that a fair understanding may be had by all parties of his Majesty's views, in consequence of the blockading decree, to which the attention of the American commissioners is invited.[9] The decree is so recent in point of time, and so novel and monstrous in substance, that his Majesty is at a loss to calculate on events: but supposing, however, that it will be formally abandoned or totally relinquished by Bonaparte, or in case he is mistaken in that supposition, he rests with confidence on the good sense of the government of the United States, that they will not submit to an innovation so destructive of the rights of neutral commerce. Should he, however, be mistaken in all these points, and the enemy should actually carry into execution his threats, and neutral nations acquiesce in such usurpation, he may probably, though reluctantly, be obliged to retaliate. The treaty secures to the United States so many privileges of neutral commerce, that at a time when his Majesty and all neutral nations are threatened with such extension of belligerent pretensions from his enemies, without any explanation from the United States what they will do in case Bonaparte attempts to force on them his decree, his Majesty must reserve to himself to act according to

9. Napoleon's Berlin Decree was issued November 21, 1806, while the negotiations for the treaty were taking place.

contingencies in that particular, the signing of the treaty notwithstanding. And as the distance of the American commissioners from their government renders a previous explanation impossible, his Majesty authorises his commissioners to finish the treaty. This is done under the fullest persuasion, that, before the treaty returns to Europe from America ratified, time will discover the formal abandonment or tacit relinquishment of the enemy of his pretensions; or in case that should not take place, that the government of the United States, by their conduct or assurances, will secure his Majesty that they will not submit to innovations so destructive of maritime rights. But in case Bonaparte enforces his decree according to its tenor, and if neither by the assurances nor conduct of America a disposition is shown to oppose it, his Majesty wishes it to be fairly and clearly understood, that he will not consider himself bound by the signature of his commissioners to ratify; or in case he ratifies, he will not and cannot be precluded from adopting such measures as may seem necessary for counteracting the designs of his enemy, whenever they shall occur, and be of such an extraordinary nature as to require extraordinary remedies.

Before we notice particular parts of this treaty, it seems proper to observe that the signature of ministers, confidential agents, under immediate control of the chief executive magistrate, imposes on him the duty to ratify what they have done. Cases may indeed be put in which this duty, resulting from principles of good faith, does not attach. Thus, when the agents employed have either foolishly or corruptly betrayed their trust, and violated their instructions, he from whom their authority was derived has in reason and conscience the right to disavow them: for it is well understood that the general power conferred by his commission, on a diplomatic agent, is specially limited by his instructions; so that if he promise what they do not authorize, his principal is not bound by the unauthorized engagement. Hence the prudential reserve, that treaties shall be ratified before they take effect. But in a case of this sort, it follows of course, that the agents be recalled as well as disavowed. Otherwise it is fairly to be inferred that they have not exceeded or varied from their instructions, but that their master breaks his faith to remedy the mischief resulting from his improvidence.

It cannot be forgotten how strenuously the gentlemen now in power used to insist that America, happily placed at so great a distance, should keep herself free from the negotiations and the wars of Europe. The phrase was "let us have nothing to do with them." A respectable federalist once replied. "Very well gentlemen. But how will you prevent them from having something to do with you?" Indeed this, like other maxims of the same origin, is not only questionable on the ground of policy, could we conform to it, but is utterly impracticable. It was used however with considerable advantage on certain occasions. If for instance it was said of any one whom these gentlemen did not like, he is well versed in the political concerns of Europe, it was promptly and pertly asked, What have we to do with Europe? And if it was observed that such men should be employed to negotiate our treaties, the complete answer was, We want no treaties. Sometimes it was added, with characteristic sagacity, let us take care of ourselves. But how? Without entering into broad questions of expedience, or examining how far we should connect ourselves with other nations, we shall only remark, in this place, that our administration after publishing those notions as sage maxims of state, year after year before they came into office, have been occupied in negotiation ever since. With what ability we presume not to say. With what success will hereafter appear.

A prudent man called on to transact business with which he is unacquainted, applies to skilful persons for assistance. But if in the common affairs of life, with which all are in some degree conversant, prudence dictates the propriety of employing agents of skill and experience, how much more are we called on to entrust such persons alone with the negotiation of national concerns; seeing that these can be but little known to the greater part of mankind. It would require a diplomatic treatise to show in how many ways, an ignorant negotiator may be deceived, to the injury of those whom he represents: a treatise which such negotiator would perhaps disdain to read, and which would therefore be useless, for able men do not want it, and the great mass of the community have sufficient employment in their own concerns. To give, however, some general idea on this subject, we will take one of the usual stipulations in a commercial treaty, *viz.* that which grants to both parties all the rights of the most favoured nation. This seems, at the first blush, fair and equal. Whether it be so in reality, must depend on what those rights are; and to acquire a knowledge of them, the treaties which each has formed with other nations must be carefully examined. That we may not, on this occasion, offend any particular sect of politicians, we shall seek an example in the farthest regions of Asia. The Emperor of China opens to foreigners only one port in his dominions, where he treats them all alike. All participate in the scanty permission to trade with an exclusive company of Chinese merchants; and all feel the contempt of that people and government for every stranger. Let us suppose a treaty made with the Emperor, by the United States, in which the above mentioned clause should be inserted; and let us also suppose, that by a treaty with some other power,

Prussia for instance, reciprocal liberty of trade had been given; each party paying in the ports of the other no greater or other duties than native citizens. The Emperor might in that case claim for his subjects a right to trade with every part of our country as freely as our own citizens, and yet confine us to a single port of his dominions, permit us to trade with none but particular merchants in that port, and oblige us to pay higher duties than his own subjects. True it is, we might object to his claim, and insist that he should pay for a free trade with us the same reciprocity with which it had been purchased by Prussia. We will not enter into the argument, because the main bearing of it is not now before us. We mean only to show, by a plain case, that he who negotiates a commercial treaty ought to know something of the situation in which the other contracting party stands. It would not be amiss, also, that he should know a little of commerce and of the law of nations.

We proceed now to make a few observations on the treaty above communicated; and, for the greater perspicuity, shall notice in their order the provisions it contains, and then something which it does not contain.

On the first and second articles of the old treaty there is nothing to be said; but the third merits a little attention. It is, however, to be premised, that, standing among those which were made perpetual, the British negotiators might have objected, had it been proposed on our part to expunge it; although by the course of events it had become void in some respects, and unreasonably burthensome in others. These events, however, entitled us to insist on certain modifications. It will be recollected that this article, after granting the reciprocal right of passing through the territories of each other in America, formally excepts the country lying within the limits of the Hudson's Bay Company, and (in consistence with the British colonial system) prohibits American ships from entering the ports or navigating the rivers of his Britannic Majesty; with this single exception in our favour, to pass between Quebec and Montreal in small vessels, subject to British regulations. We, on the other hand, give them a right to enter all our rivers, and to navigate freely to the highest ports of entry. But, with respect to the Missisippi, it was stipulated that it should remain (according to the treaty of peace) open to both parties, with a reciprocal right of resort to all the ports and places on its eastern side.

A person who cursorily views the subject may wonder at the last mentioned stipulation: and indeed the clause relating to the Missisippi in the treaty of peace itself, has, to some, been a matter of surprise. Information, therefore, may not be improper. It is well known, that, by the treaty of peace, the Missisippi, down to the thirty-first degree of north latitude, became our western boundary; and that by the provisional articles executed the 30th November, 1782, (long before the peace between England and the other belligerent powers) it was stipulated that they should be inserted in and constitute the treaty of peace. This, however, was not to be concluded until terms of peace should be agreed on between Britain and France. These were so long on the anvil, that our definitive treaty was not concluded until the 3d of September, 1783; near a year after signing the preliminary articles. The Floridas had (as every one knows) been ceded to England, in 1763, and taken by Spain in the course of our revolutionary war. It is an acknowledged principle of public law, that conquest of territory is not complete until a cession of it is made by the treaty of peace. Britain had, therefore, when our provisional articles were signed, a postliminary right to the Floridas; and she had the intention to enter again into possession, which intention was communicated to us. Consequently, when the British and American negotiators stipulated with each other for the free navigation of the Missisippi, each gave a real substantial right, and each received a real substantial compensation. That Great-Britain intended to reserve to herself the Floridas, appears from a secret article relating to them in the provisional articles; and her treaty with Spain was negotiated and agreed to conformably with that intention. It was stipulated that Spain should restore them, and receive an equivalent. But circumstances foreign to the present inquiry, having led his Britannic Majesty to decline granting the equivalent proposed, he at length consented to cede the Floridas in full right to Spain. According to our construction of the provisional articles, Spain received that country subject to the right of navigation which we had acquired. She, however, might well contest the point, because the grant was made to us by a power not in possession at the time, nor at any time after. The controversy with Spain respecting that navigation cannot be forgotten. We of course availed ourselves of every argument, and among others asserted the supposed right of those who dwell on the banks of navigable rivers to pass through the territory of their neighbours in their progress to the sea. This question, often agitated, has been decided differently, in fact, according to the different relations of power; but in principle and general practice it has been held that no such right exists. A strong case in point is that of Denmark, who exacts a duty from ships of all nations passing to and from the Baltic. The grant of Britain, therefore, being one ground of our claim, then unsettled with Spain, Mr. Jay prudently inserted a recognition of it in his treaty. The stipulation, in so far as it related to any right conferred on

Britain, was indeed a nullity; because the Missisippi, not extending so far north as had been supposed, she did not possess one inch of territory on its shores: neither had she any right, or even pretext to enter its mouth, then in peaceable possession of his Catholic Majesty.

Such was the state of things when the old treaty was made; but circumstances have materially changed. We have purchased not only that part of West-Florida which joins the Missisippi, but the island of New-Orleans also. It is true, that, from conduct which we shall not, on this occasion, develope, we have furnished to Spain a good pretext, perhaps a good reason, for withholding our share of West-Florida. But let those matters be settled as they may, it is unquestionable that we have acquired the right to exclude the British from the Missisippi. Should it be pretended that the stipulations in the old treaty give them a right to navigate that river, it may be answered, first, that those stipulations are made in reference to, and conformity with the treaty of peace; and, secondly, that our grant extended only to things which we possessed, and can by no fair construction embrace what we might afterwards acquire. This principle of common sense forms an acknowledged maxim of public law.

We conceive it evident, therefore, that British vessels have no more right to enter the Missisippi than American vessels have to enter British harbours in the West-Indies. Whether it would be wise to grant such right may be questionable; but certainly we ought not to grant it without an equivalent, much less in the very article, and, as it were, in the same breath by which we renounce our claim to enter and navigate the St. Lawrence. We have on the shores of this river, and of its tributary waters, a great extent of valuable land; yet, by the sweeping clause which confirms without modification the first ten articles of the old treaty, we should resign all claim to navigate the St. Lawrence from the sea, and afford to the British a pretence to navigate the Missisippi through its whole extent. Such would, we presume, be the construction of British commentators. If denied on our part, it might become the source of cavil, perhaps of quarrel. If admitted, we should discover that the concession of a great and valuable privilege had been unwittingly made, without the slightest equivalent. Should Great-Britain wish to trade with us on the Missisippi, she would certainly pay for it, by granting us a like permission on the St. Lawrence. This would do her no injury, nor even occasion any inconvenience. Nay, it might, under certain circumstances, be advantageous to her. To us it is of great and growing importance. Our territory on the waters of the St. Lawrence is worth much more than what we purchased from France, and have now to dispute with

Spain, under the name of Louisiana. Our citizens who inhabit that part of America, would be materially benefited if their produce could be sent, in American bottoms, free from war-freight and insurance, to seek the best markets. They are at present confined to the ports of Montreal and Quebec, where they must take the prices British merchants choose to give, or transport their goods one hundred and fifty miles to Albany.

The fourth article of the old treaty was framed to obviate difficulties in the second article of the treaty of peace, fixing as our northern boundary a line to be drawn due west from the Lake of the Woods to the Missisippi. And the fifth was framed to obviate difficulties respecting our eastern boundary.

Subsequently, however, to the year 1794, a survey of the interior of America, by British merchants established in Canada, under the name of the North-West Company, had proved that a line due west from the Lake of the Woods would run north of the Missisippi; so that no further measures were needful to ascertain that point. The River St. Croix, also, had been identified. Two points, however, remained to be settled; the line from the Lake of the Woods to the Missisippi, and the termination of that which was to run north from the source of the St. Croix, on which depends a large tract of country in the district of Maine. Connected, also, with our eastern boundary, is an object of little intrinsic value (Moose Island), but important to the trade of Massachusetts, and to the revenue of the United States. Another matter of considerable importance, particularly to the State of New-York, had remained unnoticed. This was the ascertaining those islands in Lake Erie, Lake Ontario, and the River St. Lawrence, which belong to the United States. Much time must elapse before the north-eastern corner of Maine, or the regions at the source of the Missisippi, can be cultivated or sold; but it was discovered in 1801, that depredations were committed on islands in the St. Lawrence, producing excellent white pine, and on islands near the mouth of Detroit, covered with valuable red cedar. It is moreover self-evident, that a tract of doubtful jurisdiction, extending upwards of one hundred and twenty miles along the northern frontier of New-York, from the village of St. Regis to the head of Grand Isle, must impede the regular course of justice, and encourage to the commission of crimes by the hope of impunity. In the first year of Mr. Jefferson's administration this matter was brought before Congress, and, after due investigation, appeared of such importance, that "a sum not exceeding ten thousand dollars was appropriated to defray the expense which should be incurred in negotiating with the government of Great-Britain, for ascertaining and establishing the boundary line between the United States and the British province of Upper Canada." This law was approved by Mr. Jefferson on the third day of April, 1802. The object of the Legislature could not be mistaken, for the appropriation of money shows they did not contemplate merely a convention between the American minister in London and the British cabinet, that would cost nothing. The amount of the sum granted proves also that it was the intention of Congress to have the business performed in a solid and durable manner. The President must therefore have known, even if the object had not been specially declared by those who brought it forward, that it was the desire of Congress to *ascertain* and *establish* the boundary line by commissioners, who should repair to the spot, designate the limits, and cause proper monuments to be erected.[10] Every one acquainted with our public proceedings knows that a grant of authority is considered as an injunction to perform the act specified. That gentle manner of expressing the public will was adopted from respect for the first magistrate. Moreover, if the two houses should require any thing which he deems improper or inexpedient, he will of course withhold his assent; wherefore his approbation implies a promise that he will comply with their wishes. Thus then the law just cited amounts to an order of Congress, and a promise of the President to *ascertain* and *establish* the boundary between the United States and Upper Canada. It remains to inquire whether that engagement has been complied with; and if not, what were the impediments.

Instructions were given to the American minister in London, which embrace all the matters above mentioned, excepting only those contemplated by the law. The minister accordingly treated with the British government; and such was their confidence in him, and their liberality towards us, that he was desired to frame a convention agreeably to his own wishes. He drew it in the very words of his instructions, and it was immediately executed. Every thing asked was granted, and there can be no doubt that if the object of the law had been brought forward, it would have been as readily and as satisfactorily adjusted. At present it remains as it was, the evils daily increasing.

The convention, however, made complete provision for the subject matter of the fourth and fifth articles of the old treaty. It fixed our eastern boundary, settled the course of a line from the Missisippi to the Lake of the Woods, and confirmed our title to Moose Island. It was duly sent over

10. The records of Congress's proceedings in those days are incomplete, but Morris was a senator at the time and was present for the deliberations on the bill.

to America; was received, and was mentioned by the President to the Congress as a satisfactory arrangement. So far all went on smoothly. But previous to a ratification, the Louisiana treaty came forward, and seems at once to have fascinated our administration. Instead of considering the conditions of this costly bargain, they considered only how they should secure the merit of making it to themselves. And instead of adopting prudent measures to possess the valuable tract east of the Missisippi, which was clearly within the grant, they set their fancies to work in stretching the boundary north and west, so as to reach the polar circle and Pacific Ocean. Careless of the centuries which must roll away before we can populate our old domain, the President, in his anxiety not to loose one acre of those prodigious deserts which extend from Lake Superior to Nootka Sound, refused to ratify the convention, lest it should be supposed that something was thereby surrendered of what we had purchased under the name of Louisiana. This may seem incredible, and we will not vouch for the truth. The true cause of his refusal may be one of those mysteries which it is convenient to hide from the people. But it is a fact that the convention was not ratified, and that the President assigned for the omission the reason just mentioned. Whether it will satisfy our fellow-citizens we cannot pretend to guess. Perhaps, like other things which pass our comprehension, it may be sanctioned by that confidence in his wisdom which numerous individuals and respectable bodies so eagerly announce to the world. We believe, and not without reason, that it gave great umbrage to the British court. They considered themselves as trifled with, and could not help considering those who administer our government as capricious and inattentive to the rules of good breeding and the principles of good faith. When we compare the tenour of the note above mentioned from his Britannic Majesty, with this deportment of our President, the advantage, we are sorry to say it, is all on the monarch's side. His commissioners had agreed to a treaty; but, at the moment of signing, a circumstance of extraordinary nature arose, leading to a belief, that, should the claim set up by his enemy be acted upon, and should we submit to threatened plunder, the great duty of a sovereign to protect his subjects might compel him to adopt measures of retaliation. Under circumstances of that sort, the injury we might sustain would be justly imputable to our own conduct. We could not, therefore, have complained: and no previous explanation on his part was necessary. Yet, so scrupulous was the King, so anxious that his reputation for good faith should be not only unsullied but unsuspected, that he provided against all possible imputation by a clear and pointed declaration. Our President, on the contrary, after ordering negotiation, after obtaining a convention in the very terms he had dictated, and after publicly declaring his satisfaction with it, all at once refuses to ratify. What excuse he may have made, or whether he made any, we pretend not to know; but we hope he did not assign the reason above mentioned; because it is not only insufficient, but dangerous. It is predicated on the false position, that covenants respecting territory we possess will be obligatory as to that which we afterwards acquire. Whence it would follow, that the purchase of Louisiana, and that which we are about to make of the Floridas, must enure to the benefit of England for every commercial privilege in the treaty of 1794.

Having taken this cursory view of the ten permanent articles in the old treaty, we proceed to those matters, the provisions relating to which had expired. It will be recollected that the gentlemen by whom, and under whose auspices the new compact was formed, had selected, from the whole of Washington's administration, the treaty with England as the object of their peculiar censure, and most pointed crimination. That treaty, though negotiated under circumstances of peculiar difficulty and disadvantage, was devoted to popular odium without examination. It was said to curtail our trade, drain our treasury, surrender our seamen, restrain our manufactures, discourage our agriculture, involve us in war, and degrade us to the state of British provinces. That treaty, concluded by a statesman of sound sense, consummate prudence, and incorruptible honesty; approved by a Senate of no mean talents, and ratified by the illustrious Washington; that treaty, for defending which men respected for their discernment, their judgment and fidelity, were exposed to the insult of an enraged and misguided populace; that treaty is no more. After fulfilling the hopes of good men, and falsifying the predictions of others; after procuring a surrender of the western posts, and thereby terminating Indian wars; after closing the wound our public faith had received, by laws contravening the treaty of peace; after obtaining, for injury done to our trade by British cruisers, a compensation greater than any thing which had ever been paid by one nation to another; and, above all, after securing us from an alliance with France, by which we could have gained nothing, but must, like her other allies, after the loss of our wealth, our commerce, our industry, and our morals, have sacrificed our independence on the altar of Gallic ambition; that misrepresented, decried, and vilified treaty has expired. It expired when its enemies had exclusive possession of the government; when, by the influence of party, they had unlimited power; and when a majority of the people, renouncing the use of reason, reposed in them unbounded confidence. It expired when England, whom they had pourtrayed, in 1794, as on the verge of bankruptcy, and in the last stage of decrepitude, was not only laden with a new and accumulated burthen of debt, but was engaged singly in a war against France, Spain and Holland. America, on the contrary, had increased in strength and wealth beyond all example, and possessed resources beyond all hope. In a word, we were released from our engagements with Britain, at the moment of all others, when those now in power, had their opposition been founded in reason or truth, were bound to perform what they said it was so easy for their predecessors to accomplish; and for the omission of which, they branded with foul imputation the ablest and best men in America; men who would do honour to any age or nation. In these circumstances it might be asked, if our rulers have remedied (in 1806) the evils which (in 1794) they imputed to their predecessors as criminal neglect. It might be asked whether England had ceased to impress seamen from American vessels, and permitted our ships to protect the goods of her enemy? Whether she had reduced the impost on our raw materials, or taken off the excess of duty on her own manufactures exported to America, beyond what they pay on going to other countries? Whether she has permitted us to enjoy a free trade with her colonies, or modified her navigation act in our favour? Whether she has discontinued the exercise of her right of search, or relinquished her system of blockade? To these questions no satisfactory answer can be given. We shall not, therefore, urge them. It is not our object to be severe; for if it were, we should say, Gentlemen, you complained of sacrifices made by the treaty of 1794; and not only opposed the ratification, but tried hard to excite opposition after it had been ratified, and thereby become the supreme law of the land. Now, then, point out distinctly those sacrifices, if you would exculpate yourselves from the charge of uttering falsehood to excite sedition. And having designated them, give good reason for bearing patiently now, when there is nothing to be gained, and nothing to be feared, what you insisted should not be submitted to then, for valuable consideration, and to avoid impending danger. In the alternative to which you have reduced yourselves, say! were the American people deceived then, or are they betrayed now? This would be the language of crimination. But we have no wish to criminate. We really believe these gentlemen complained so much because they knew so little.

We proceed, therefore, coolly and impartially to examine what they have done, and to compare it with what they denounced. If their work be better, let them, notwithstanding the more favourable circumstances, have praise and glory. If worse, let us pity and forgive. They insisted, that with respect to our India trade, the old treaty had worked material injury, by depriving us of privileges enjoyed before—That it took away the benefit of coasting between the different ports of Asia, and prevented us from supplying Europe with commodities direct from India—That it was a grievous hardship to be obliged to return home, and unlade the cargoes of the East before they could be vended abroad—That a little intelligence would have taught our negotiator the importance of the privileges he gave up, and a very little firmness have enabled him to secure them. To prove his incapacity, or infidelity, it was observed, that immediately after the treaty was made, an act of the British Parliament bestowed gratuitously on all the world, more than we had obtained by great sacrifices. It was vain to reply, that what one law had granted, another might resume—That to secure great objects, by surrendering small ones, was better than to leave both at the discretion of those who might take them away—That although the interest of Britain led her at that moment to permit, that we and others should enjoy more than she had granted to us by treaty; yet her interest might change, or new men might adopt new measures, from false or partial views, from pique or caprice. To this, and to every thing else, a deaf ear was turned. The object was not to reason, but to condemn, and therefore assertion was accepted for proof, and clamour for argument. Let us then compare the third article of this new treaty with the thirteenth of the old one, and see how our India trade will stand. Worse than before—much worse. Every old restriction remains, and a new one is added of most serious effect. Our vessels trading to India must now sail direct from ports of the United States. Formerly they could be fitted out and laden in Europe. They could proceed from Germany or Holland to France and Spain, take in brandy, wine and bullion; thence to Madeira, and so on. This cannot now be done; they must sail *direct* from the United States.

It has already been mentioned, that the fifth article of the new treaty contains regulations respecting the duties on ships and merchandize. To estimate their worth, we must compare them with provisions made on the same subject by the fifteenth article of the old treaty. This reserved a right to Britain of countervailing, by duties on our vessels entering her ports, the excess of duties paid on European and Asiatic goods in her vessels entering our ports: a difference which operated strongly in our favour, and made us almost the exclusive carriers of articles for our own consumption. Britain saw, with concern, the flourishing state of our navigation; and tried to restrain it by making regulations according to the right she had reserved. But the attempt was vain; for she could not lay a burthen on the articles carried

to her in our ships, without injuring her general system of trade and manufactures. Thus, although each enjoyed equal rights, our's could be, and
were, exercised with advantage; her's were useless. A difference of this sort
must exist, when nations, under circumstances materially different, make
reciprocal covenants of the same import. Of this the new article before us
presents an instance of no common magnitude. It declares that the same
duties, drawbacks, and bounties shall be allowed by both parties, in the
trade of the two nations, whether the exportation or importation shall be
in British or American vessels. By these few, but potent words, our relative
situations are completely reversed, and a few years of peace would nearly
annihilate our navigation. This apparently liberal provision was always a
favourite object of the late Mr. Fox, whose intuitive genius saw clearly its
effect. Indeed, rather than fail of obtaining it, he was willing to open, on
the same terms, their West-Indies to our shipping. It was a favourite also
with our President, because it has a sort of philosophic appearance: perhaps
also, because it seems to favour those who cultivate tobacco. That it would
injure them, as well as every other class of the community, is evident, both
from reason and experience. It is evident from reason, because that commodity must, like others, be reduced in price, when one nation has a monopoly of the trade; and that must happen when the navigation of the world
belongs to one nation. It is evident from experience, because the price of
tobacco has advanced as American navigation has increased. But without
spending time in seeking the reasons for particular opinions, let us examine the article. There was a time when ships could be built in the United
States cheaper than in Europe; and although they were navigated at greater
expense, yet the advantages of sailing derived from their construction, and
the superior activity of our seamen, enabled us to compete for freight with
the Dutch and English. But circumstances have greatly changed. Ships,
from the high wages given to our mechanics, and the high price to which
timber has risen, cost more than in Europe. Sails and rigging are out of all
proportion dearer, and so are seamen's wages. In time of peace, insurance
will also be cheaper on British than on American ships. Thus, then, we are
to contend for the carriage of our produce, and of the articles we consume,
with a nation possessing the advantage over us in equipping and navigating
ships as well as in the insurance. Perhaps it may be said that we can build as
cheap as the English; and it shall, for argument's sake, be admitted that we
might build even a little cheaper. But this circumstance would be of little
avail when opposed by others so much more powerful. Nay, were they all
equal, the superior capital of Britain, and the resulting lowness of interest,

would be decisive in her favour. It may be said that trade and money seek a level, which in time would be found. In other words, that the wages of ship-carpenters, black-smiths, rope-makers, sail-makers, and seamen would fall so low, from being out of employ, that notwithstanding the higher price of hemp, iron, copper, duck and cordage, our merchants might (at some future day) resume the contest with better chance of success. Rare consolation! Our merchants being ruined, and, in consequence, the dependent members of our country's commerce reduced to misery, these poor people, to obtain bread for their families, must work lower than men of the same description in Europe, so as thereby to compensate the higher price of materials: in which case a merchant may begin again, if he shall have been so prudent or fortunate as to save a little from the wreck of his affairs. On general principles this result might be admitted. But is it certain that our sailors would remain idle rather than embark in British bottoms? Is it certain that the numerous artificers now employed in building and equipping ships would quietly starve, instead of seeking other employment? Is it certain that young persons would continue to learn trades of such little hope? We acknowledge that different impressions are made on our minds. We believe that the blow given to our trade and navigation by this improvident concession, would throw them back to what they were twenty years ago. And we have no shadow of doubt, that by the prostration of our commerce, every order of our fellow citizens would be grievously afflicted.

But if the fifth article of the new treaty be of such portentous import in itself, what is it when connected with that which immediately precedes, and that which immediately follows; or rather, what is it not? We have seen that our ships trading to India must sail from and return to our own ports; and that, in the trade of the two nations, equal duties shall be imposed, be the ships British or American. When these conventions are ratified, nothing more will be needful for Britain, to perfect her system, than to modify the monopoly of her India Company, so far as to permit all her merchants to trade freely with Asia, provided they do not bring Chinese and India wares to Europe. A British ship could then sail from London, pick up in the way whatever might be needful to the assortment of her cargo, traffic along the coast of Malabar and Coromandel, proceed to China, and at length come full fraught with tea, coffee, sugar, spices, silks and cottons, to the United States. She could undersell our own adventures in our own ports, and return laden with our most valuable commodities, and our coin, to reward the industry of those who live under a wise government. If any one should imagine that we could trade to India under such disadvantages, we intreat him to apply for information to an intelligent merchant in whom he has confidence. We could show, by facts amounting to a demonstration, the truth of what we advance; but it would occupy too much space. We refer to merchants, without regard to their political sentiments. But the India trade requiring large capital, it is possible that small dealers may, under the influence of envy, be not unwilling that foreigners should run off with the benefit which has hitherto cheered and cherished our commercial enter-prize. Let such persons look at the next succeeding article, which states, that as the parties cannot agree about our trade to their West-Indies, they will attempt an amicable arrangement, and, in the mean time, both may exercise their existing rights. A more cutting irony was never perhaps in-serted in a national compact. What are the existing rights? That of the British is to exclude us from their islands; a right they will certainly exer-cise. If, in return, we prohibit them from bringing the colonial produce from the islands direct to us, we must go and fetch it from Europe; paying, of course, in addition to the prime cost in the islands, a freight across the Atlantic in their ships. But the mischief would not stop there. They would not give us the trouble of fetching it, but would themselves bring it out; for which we must also pay. They could underwork us, for the reasons al-ready assigned; besides, their ships, which must otherwise come in ballast to take a cargo of lumber to the West-Indies, or other bulky produce of the United States, would for a very light freight bring us rum and sugar. Nay, they would have a still greater advantage. Returning to Falmouth from the West-Indies, they would only go through the ceremony of entry and clear-ance, and, saving all charges and commissions, come directly over to the United States. To exercise our right, therefore, in this way, would only do us mischief. It may, perhaps, be supposed, by some, that we could supply our wants from the French or Spanish islands. But it is easy to see that every other nation would be as eager to secure to itself the whole advantage of its colonial trade as Great-Britain, and indeed we have found it so by ex-perience. Besides, it is a strange way of conducting business to make a very bad bargain with one, in the very uncertain hope of a better bargain with his neighbour. We have, however, another right which is not impaired by the treaty. It leaves us at liberty to make them pay roundly on the export of our produce to their islands; but this would be a bounty on the agricul-ture and arts of Canada and Nova-Scotia, than which nothing could be more agreeable to the British government. Such duty, however, cannot be laid, for although the right is not impaired by the treaty, the exercise of it is inhibited by the constitution. To say, therefore, with apparent equity and equality, that both may exercise their existing rights, is bitter mockery to men in our pinching condition.

It has often been remarked by observers of human nature, that the fond and foolish many (in the blindness of ignorant passion) run counter to their own wishes, and do precisely what they strive to avoid. If such inconsequence were chargeable only on those who, enrolling themselves under the banners of faction, have the prescriptive right to be absurd, it would be so much in the common order as not to deserve a moment's notice. But the bell-weathers of the flock are, generally speaking, as poor and simple cattle as the rest. It is supposed that they who direct our affairs, if they have any special sentiment beyond the desire to continue in office, are moved by a snarling, snappish humour towards England. Indeed, they have reason to be somewhat angry with the British government, because its measures have defeated their claim to the character of statesmen. It is certainly owing, in some degree, to the efforts of that government, that England has neither become bankrupt, nor been enslaved, nor starved, nor subdued by France; all which they have constantly predicted for the last fifteen or twenty years, with a zeal and perseverance the more laudable, as they derived no support from reason, truth or probability. Men who look only skin-deep for motives, and take words for the evidence of things, were led to suppose that they who coupled Washington and Britain together, for the sake of abusing both, were as much the enemies of one as the other; and that when in power, their measures would be marked by wrath against the lords of the ocean. But no opinion could be more unfounded: so far at least as action is concerned, the hostile temper, if it really exist, has produced only acts of friendship and good will. There has indeed been much complaint, much cross language, and not a little of idle, empty menace. But what evidence have our rulers given of a disposition to injure Britain, or even to secure our country against her power? Have they prepared a fleet to join other powers in vindicating the liberty of the sea? Have they fortified our ports against that aggression which we have to apprehend from Britain alone? Have their regulations at home or negotiations abroad assisted the spirit and enterprize which have raised us to be the second naval and commercial nation? Surely they have not. They have boasted, negotiated, been flattered, and duped. They have laid our commerce and navigation at the feet of Britain; so that a stranger who, deaf to the clamour, should attend only to the conduct of our rulers, might suspect that some of that British gold, so much talked of, had found its way into their pockets. We take this occasion, however, to declare that we harbour no such unworthy idea.

In the eighth article, after agreeing, as in the seventeenth of the old treaty, that all proper measures shall be taken to prevent delay in deciding the cases of ships and cargoes brought in for adjudication, on the suspicion of enemy's property or contraband of war, and in the payment or recovery of any indemnification adjudged or agreed to be paid to the master or owners; the British commissioners have added, on the part of their sovereign, a promise, that hereafter indemnification shall be granted for unjust seizure, and detention, and vexation. This gratuitous covenant is a master-piece. The tribunals were bound by the principles of public law to award, adjudge, and enforce prompt payment of indemnification for the injuries specified. What, then, is the effect of this promise? It neither imposes a new obligation on the admiralty courts, nor invests them with a new authority; but rather implies a doubt with respect to the law; because, if that be acknowledged, no auxiliary promise can be required, unless indeed the national justice be questioned; in which case no promise can be relied on. Thus, then, the law, which, founded on reason and equity, would be liberally construed, is reduced to a gratuitous engagement; which being penal, as regards delinquents, will be construed strictly. Wherefore the power of the court remaining as it was, the exercise of it is restrained; and our right is rendered less clear, and must become less productive. Such appears to us the necessary effect of any such provision, be the form what it may. But the British commissioners, by inserting the word *hereafter*, have taken from us the claim to compensation for injury already sustained. And our negotiators, by admitting that word, have given up thousands due to their fellow-citizens. American suitors, in the British courts of Admiralty, will now be told, that under the law of nations, as it stood before this treaty, violence would have been punished, and indemnification been granted for injuries sustained; but, the two nations having agreed to bury the past in oblivion, the hands of the judge are tied up by the act of his superiors. That he cannot grant, neither ought they to ask what the two governments have agreed to relinquish.

The dexterity of the British commissioners is again displayed in the eleventh article. The questions which gave rise to a pamphlet called War in Disguise, and to a book written by Mr. Maddison, are fresh in the recollection of all.[11] This book, indeed, as was shrewdly observed in the house of representatives, gave up the matter in dispute at the very outset. By

---

11. Madison's pamphlet was *An Examination of the British Doctrine, which subjects to capture a neutral trade, not open in time of peace* (Philadelphia, 1806). Morris had also replied; see *Answer to War in Disguise* (chapter 29, above).

quitting the ground of right, derived from, and the appendage of national sovereignty, to rely on a supposed general consent, which results from convenience and changes with circumstances, our Secretary of State unfortunately played his game into the hands of his adversary. We cannot admit, however, that a weak argument shall destroy a good cause. The case has been stated by others, whose reasons we will neither repeat nor refer to; because the question is recent, and because the general opinion (not only of America but of Europe) is well established. The right of a neutral to proceed from his own ports to those of a belligerent, with articles his own property, not contraband of war, is admitted; and the pretended right to examine how he came by the goods, is considered as an odious usurpation. It is, we say, a principle generally assented to, as resulting from the nature of sovereignty, that no person shall inquire into the means by which, or the place from which property has been brought within the territory of a neutral state, further than as it may serve to cast light on the question, whether it belong to a neutral or belligerent. This principle seems to be so intimately blended with the national sovereignty, that it cannot be surrendered. We have no view to the convenience or profit of merchants. On the proper occasion we shall pay those gentlemen the respect to which they are entitled; but we do not consider this as the proper occasion. We are now engaged in matter of a higher order than commercial interest; one which is not to be tested by considerations of profit and loss. We must, therefore, examine the article in its relations to a national right, which, in our opinion, it has surrendered.

It begins by permitting us to carry European goods to the colonies of enemies of Great-Britain, from the ports of the United States. Thus one point is given up; the right of trading freely from one port of a belligerent to another; a right acknowledged and asserted by all good writers on public law. It is not our object to please a party, but to establish truth. We anxiously wish that our country may take a firm stand on principle: and that her honour, dearer to us than the blood which warms our heart, may not be compromised in a contest of doubtful complexion. Wherefore, that we may be well understood, and that we may not be misunderstood, we promise and acknowledge, that, while the powers of Europe maintain their colonial system, and relax from it occasionally under the pressure of necessity, or from the prospect of advantage, there is a presumption that trade carried on by neutrals, between a belligerent country and her colonies, is merely a cloak and cover injurious to the other belligerent. He therefore can, rightfully, exact strong evidence that the property is neutral. And since melancholy experience proves that, on such occasions, perjury appears at the call of interest, to protect fraud, it ought not to be wondered at, that he should so far extend the force of presumption as to receive it in contradiction to testimony. When, under this aspect, the matter is discussed with the neutral government, both stand on fair ground. The neutral, whose right of sovereignty is not questioned, will, from a sense of justice, agree to regulations by which the property in goods shall be more clearly ascertained. And since, after all possible checks, fraud will be committed when the opportunities are inviting, he may, from the same sense of justice, be induced to admit, that the circumstances attending such a trade are sufficiently strong to justify the induction of the belligerent. And it would not be at all improper for him to agree on severe penalties, to be exacted from those who persist in covering the goods of one enemy from the pursuit of another. We venture to believe, that this fair and candid course would subserve the interest of the neutral himself. If, however, from an interested connivance in the fraud, or from partiality to the other belligerent, he will not enter into fair stipulations, the rights of the adverse party not only remain, but are strengthened; and he may justly extend the exercise of them: always understood, that the neutral who thinks himself aggrieved may resort to arms. In this fair course there is no assumption of superiority on one side, no submission to insult on the other. The independence of the neutral is not questioned; his sovereignty is not violated. The fiscal result would, indeed, be the same, whether it be assumed as sufficient proof of French property that goods on board an American ship were going from Bordeaux to Martinique, or declared that the trade not being permitted in time of peace, the property, though American, shall be confiscated; but the consequence, as it affects our honour, would be widely different. Besides, the former principle is of necessity bounded within narrow limits; but the maxim, that a neutral shall carry on only his usual and accustomed trade, may be extended so as to embrace whatever the belligerent may desire. Once agree to it as a principle, and attempts to limit the operation will be vain. Moreover, it must be always remembered, that a stipulation in one treaty is more fatal to the question of right, than the pillage of a dozen wars. The pillager may indeed cite, as precedent, his former violence on every new occasion. The argument that one injury will justify another, has been frequently urged, and as frequently refuted; but when, by solemn compact, one party acknowledges as a right the injurious claim of another, he is bound by his own act, and must submit to the consequence.

The article before us permits the carriage of European goods, from our ports, to the colonies of enemies of Great-Britain, under three conditions.

The first is, that vessel and cargo are *bona fide* American property. This condition is proper and consonant to public law. Had the subsequent restrictions been stated as conventional evidence of that fact, they would, in the present point of view, have been unexceptionable. But standing as they do, distinct additional conditions, they are the acknowledgment, on our part, that we have not the right to carry our own property from our own ports to the colonies of a belligerent; an acknowledgment which ought not to be made.

The second condition is, that the goods shall have been unladen in the United States. Here another unfounded claim of Britain is admitted; a claim which, with all the deference due by citizens of one country to the government of another, we presume to believe she was wrong to make, because she would hardly permit it to be exercised against her own merchants. We feel a strong persuasion, therefore, that if this point (which had been assumed by her courts) had been properly represented to her ministers, they would have abandoned it. But certainly, even if, from prudential motives, we should submit to such an exercise of power, we ought never to acknowledge that it is legitimate. The stipulation in this treaty is precisely what Britain must desire, and every way injurious to us. In relation to our claims for the past, her courts will say, you have deliberately assented to our principles. In future wars they will set it up anew, and insist, that as we submitted before from rational conviction, (and we shall hardly be disposed to stultify and brutify ourselves by alleging that we acted from folly and fear,) we ought again to submit. But, should it so happen that we, being at war, while Britain is at peace, should claim the privilege she takes, her government would resist; and we should find ourselves in the wrong. They would frankly admit, that, to promote the interests of the war in which they were engaged, they had found it necessary to make an extraordinary stretch of power. That we had, indeed, complained, and our government had, for the form sake, remonstrated; but, wishing well to their cause, and desirous of promoting their success, as far as it could without breaking with friends at home, or making enemies abroad, had thought it on the whole most adviseable to submit. They would go on, in support of this assertion, to observe, that when matters came to be adjusted, by treaty, an article was inserted confirmatory of the practice. But so far were the parties from admitting any general principle, or supposing that we should ever think of retaliating, that the article related solely to us, provided for a special case of the moment, and contained no reciprocal stipulation. We should then be politely told, that, to make the cases analogous, we must show that preponderance of force to which we had thought it reasonable and just to submit. This would be no easy matter. But, a matter much more difficult would be to bend the high spirit of England, and persuade her to brook national degradation. While on this part of the subject, it may not be improper to add, that the language which, under the circumstances supposed, it might be competent to Britain to hold hereafter, it is competent to France to hold now. Our assent to this unequal stipulation may be considered as evidence of partiality. Our government may, in proof of its love to France, quote its friendly professions; but, whether Napoleon and Benevento repose in the President's professions that confidence which many among us express in his talents, may admit of some doubt.[12]

The last condition under which we are permitted to exercise our right, is, that we shall lay an export duty of one per cent. on European goods sent from the United States to colonies of the enemies of Great-Britain. Hitherto the sacrifices made affect only commercial interest and national honour; objects for which much indifference has formerly been expressed by some great men of the day. They freely declared, that for neither they would risque the chance, nor bear the expense of war. They were, nevertheless, loud in expressions of love for the constitution. That constitution, once the theme of their execration, is now the idol of their affection. And with reason; for they have found out the secret of turning it to good account. But the constitution says, in express terms, "no tax or duty shall be laid on articles exported from any State." And the treaty exacts, as a condition on the carriage of goods from the United States to the islands, that in addition to the duty reserved on exportation from the drawback, the further sum of one per cent. ad valorem shall be paid. We are not among those who consider the restriction in our constitution as wise. We know it to be among those which, unreasonably insisted on by some members of the national convention, was submitted to by others, from "that deference and concession which the peculiarity of our political situation rendered indispensable."[13] The clause, however, is there. Legislative ingenuity will no

---

12. Charles Maurice de Talleyrand-Perigord (1754–1838) had been made Prince of Benevento by Napoleon in 1806, and was French foreign minister until 1807.

13. The quotation is from the letter, drafted by Morris, transmitting the finished Constitution to Congress (chapter 15, above). Morris opposed the prohibition on export taxes at the Constitutional Convention, in part because he viewed the clause as a support of slavery. *Records of the Federal Convention of 1787*, ed. Max Farrand, rev. ed. (New Haven: Yale University Press, 1911–87), 2:221–23, 306–7.

doubt be exerted, if needful, in reconciling it with the article of the treaty. Merchants will perhaps be told there is no compulsion. They may pay or let it alone. If they pay, the custom-house will give a certificate. If not, they may depart and take their chance. Perhaps, in greater tenderness for the constitution, it may be thought adviseable that the legislature be silent, leaving matters to be settled between the executive and the merchant. This would be an excellent contrivance; for it would enable the President, with two thirds of the Senate, who (as every body knows) have unlimited confidence in him, and were chosen for that very reason, to tax the good people of these United States; provided they can get the assistance of a stout maritime power. It might be asserted, on the part of Great-Britain, that the soldiers of Napoleon, who undergo hardships scarcely credible, and have entreated their enemies to terminate at once their misery and existence, would certainly revolt, if physical as well as moral means were not employed to secure their obedience — That the narcotic effects of tobacco, which they use in profusion, have astonishing influence in calming nervous irritation; whence it is evident that Napoleon's troops could not bear up under their calamities, without a pipe of tobacco. This argument has the merit of resembling that by which it has been demonstrated, that France carries on the present war with sugar and coffee received from this country. It would, therefore, equally justify the prohibiting our merchants to furnish the enemies of Great-Britain with tobacco, under the usual penalty of confiscation. After a few months more of able negotiation, a new clause might be tacked to the treaty, allowing tobacco to go free, provided an export duty were paid of ten per cent. This would enable the collectors, always, however, with the merchant's consent, to levy the ten per cent. Experience has proved, that, if no direct application be made by the tax-gatherer, this enlightened nation cares not what is collected, nor how it is applied. Some of them, indeed, suspect that possibly they may pay, in the price of necessaries they consume, a small part of the duty on imports. But this new contribution would come so completely out of the merchants, that it would be quite delightful. It might, moreover, be applied at the discretion of the President, and save the necessity of asking Congress for appropriations to objects undefined. This would be another prodigious advantage. For although such appropriations, once supposed to be unconstitutional and dangerous, are now found to be proper and very convenient; yet some friends of government feel a little squeamish, look a little awkward, and have somewhat of a qualm in voting for them. Wherefore, as it is troublesome to deal with men of timorous conscience, it would be no small improvement on our system, so to arrange matters as that business might go on smoothly without their assistance. It would, moreover, be of use to the poor men themselves, who find it rather difficult to satisfy certain troublesome creatures, called constituents, that the new congressional game of blind-man's-buff is altogether fair. Hitherto, indeed, they have got through tolerably well by the aid of that excellent word confidence; but since nothing human is immortal, so it begins to be suspected that confidence, even in the President, may at length expire. Some new expedient, therefore, ought to be adopted. And what so proper as to raise taxes by treaty?

The article having provided for our trade with the belligerent colonies, and prudently left the trade from them unnoticed, so that, for any thing which appears, Britain may seize colonial produce coming from her enemy's ports to the United States, goes on to regulate the export of such produce to Europe. It is permitted under conditions similar to those just noticed. The goods must be unladen, and they must pay an export duty of two per cent. ad valorem. Let it not, we pray, escape the reader's notice, that the conditions imposed by no means affect what is called the neutral carrying trade; that is to say, the unfair practice of covering, as neutral, the goods of a belligerent. They neither arise out of the right which one enemy has to attack and destroy the commerce of another, nor do they tend to check the abuses about which we have heard such loud complaint. If, indeed, enemy's goods were subjected to the charges of landing and relading, together with the duty on export, while bona fide neutral goods were exempted, it would doubtless discourage the illicit trade. But this was not the object. The whole scope and tenor of the article is to lay our trade under impositions and disadvantages, so as to favour and encourage the trade which the English (by connivance of their government) carry on with their enemies. We have before us a copy of royal instructions to the Lieutenant-Governor of Jamaica, dated at St. James's, the fifth day of July, 1804, in the forty-fourth year of his Majesty's reign. They run thus. "Whereas we have thought it expedient that permission should be given to vessels belonging to the subjects of his Catholic Majesty, having not more than one deck, to trade between the free ports established in the island of Jamaica and the Spanish colonies in America, according to the regulations of the several acts for establishing free ports in our West-India islands, notwithstanding any hostilities that may occur; and whereas we have thought it expedient, that, notwithstanding such hostilities, permission should likewise be given to British vessels, navigated according to the laws now in force, to trade between the said free ports in the island of Jamaica and the Spanish colonies in America, provided such British and Spanish vessels shall have a license from the Lieutenant-Governor or Commander in Chief of the island of Jamaica, and provided such British and Spanish vessels shall import into the free ports in the island of Jamaica, such goods only as are hereafter enumerated, viz. wool, cotton wool, indigo, cochineal, drugs of all sorts, cocoa, tobacco, logwood, fustick and all sorts of wood for dyer's use, hides, skins and tallow, beaver and all sorts of furs, tortoise shells, hard wood or mill timber, mahogany and all other woods for cabinet ware, horses, asses, mules and cattle being the growth and production of any of the colonies or plantations in America belonging to the crown of Spain, and all coin or bullion, diamonds or precious stones, coming from thence; and provided such British and Spanish vessels shall export from such free ports only the said goods and commodities, and also rum, the produce of any British island, and also all goods, wares, merchandizes and manufactures, which shall have been legally imported, except masts, yards and bowsprits, pitch, tar, turpentine, and all other naval stores and tobacco.

"We do hereby authorize you, our Lieutenant-Governor, or Commander in Chief for the time being, of the island of Jamaica, to grant licences accordingly. And do further require and enjoin you to give all necessary encouragement and protection to such Spanish vessels, and likewise to all British vessels trading between the free ports in the said island of Jamaica and the Spanish colonies in America, under the regulations herein before prescribed."

A perusal of these instructions will show the true value of what has been said in courts, and printed in pamphlets, about reducing the enemies of Britain by destroying the resources of their commerce, and about the injury done to her military and naval operations by the unjust and unlawful interference of those wicked neutrals. Go to the bottom of the business, and we find a mercantile struggle for money, in which the government assists by its power, its influence, and its negotiations. Mere counting-house politics. Not the most remote idea of injuring France or Spain, by inhibiting an intercourse with their colonies, but a scheme to engross that trade to themselves. Accordingly, when they negotiate with us, the single object is to burthen and trammel our trade with such charges and regulations as may give their merchants a preference. Our negotiators have kindly gone along with theirs, and, in the excess of their complaisance, have ceded, not only the interests of trade, but the attributes of independence.

That nothing might be wanting to complete the goodly work, this eleventh article closes with a declaration, that, after the expiration of the treaty, (viz. in ten years) all antecedent rights on these subjects are to re-vive. And thus we acknowledge as rights, provided the exercise be sus-pended for ten years, claims which should never be admitted under any pressure of necessity. We may, nay, we must, submit to superior power; un-less, as in our war for independence, it shall please the Almighty to smile on and reward our resistance of oppression by his holy favour. But there can be no necessity, use or advantage in acknowledging oppression to be jus-tice. If we dare not resist, let us quietly submit. But let us not kiss the rod, or, like prisoners of the inquisition, applaud its clemency while we writhe in torture.

The twelfth article, considering the love of peace which our rulers pro-fess, and the defenceless condition to which they have reduced us, passes all comprehension. It extends to Great-Britain, and to all other nations who will adopt the same regulation, the protection of our neutrality from a marine league to five miles from our shores. This being agreed on, if a Spanish cruizer should, at four miles distance, take a British ship, what are we to do? According to the treaty she must be restored. According to general practice she is a good prize: And if we may judge from experience, captors are more inclined to keep bad prizes than to surrender good ones. They would undoubtedly and justly refuse to give up the British ship. The British minister would as undoubtedly and as justly insist on the perfor-mance of our stipulation. What are we to do? Shall we go to war for the recovery of a British ship lawfully taken by a Spaniard, while we permit the same Spaniard, and every one else, unlawfully to take our own ships? More-over, if the President should determine to take and restore the prize, what are his means? His frigates are fast in the mud. He has no public force at command, and it has been the undeviating policy of his administration not to have any, lest he should be held accountable for the use of it; or rather, for suffering it to look idly on, while our fellow citizens are insulted, plun-dered, killed. What are we to do? The British insist. The Spanish refuse. Take which side we will we must be in the wrong. The President might indeed make excuses and apologies. He is said to be able in that line. But the English are not in the habit of receiving apologies instead of cash. We should be charged with perfidy. We should be threatened with reprisals. What are we to do? Nothing remains but the old expedient of paying for peace. Congress must then appropriate to that object some of the money collected from trade; for they have no other. And thus our merchants, after being pillaged by both parties, must pay them for plundering each other.

The clause in the twenty-third article which declares, "that all treaties hereafter made by either with any nation shall, *ipso facto*, be extended in all their favourable operations to the other," is very broad. By the second article of our treaty with France, "the King and the United States mutually engage not to grant any particular favour to other nations, in respect of commerce and navigation, which shall not immediately become common to the other party, who shall enjoy the same freely if the concession was freely made, or on allowing the same compensation if the concession was conditional." Our treaty with Sweden contains the same clause. The un- limited terms of this new stipulation, especially when compared with those more guarded of preceding compacts, will support a claim of Great-Britain to possess, without compensation, privileges we may grant to others for valuable consideration. To say the covenant is reciprocal is a falacy; for it is one thing to be reciprocal in form and words, but another to be reciprocal in fact and effect. If we mistake not, it is substantially the same as if we had stipulated solely and gratuitously, that Britain shall enjoy every privilege we may allow to any other nation. Indeed, our agreement with France and Sweden, though more fair, was not quite safe. Let it be remembered that old nations have long since formed their systems of finance, commerce and navigation; which, by the aid of experience, and in the lapse of time, have been made to accord with their extent, population, soil, climate, produc- tions and manufactures. There is, then, little probability that any change will be made, from which we can derive advantage. But the case with us is widely different. That our power and wealth must increase, if our union be preserved, and we are governed with tolerable discretion, can admit of no doubt. We shall probably both acquire and grant privileges in our diplo- matic transactions. We ought not, therefore, to tie up our hands, by pro- spective conditions with any nation, and least of all with Great-Britain; be- cause she has long since brought her commercial system to perfection. The covenant on her part must be sterile. We can derive nothing from it; but are bound by it to treat with the rest of the world under her pleasure, and for her benefit. We preclude ourselves from granting an exclusive privilege, whatever advantage might be gained or evil avoided. If the proposition be made, we must answer, it is not in our power; we are already bound to En- gland, and must ask her permission.

The twenty-fourth article presents to us a fair flower of philosophy. We agree to join in abolishing the slave trade. As a comment on this article, we take leave to introduce what we consider as a contemporaneous exposition. In the British House of Commons, on the twenty-third of February, not two months after the treaty was signed, Lord Howick (the British minister of foreign affairs), after stating that the slave trade was both unjust and impolitic, founded in robbery, kidnapping and murder, and afforded incentives to the worst passions and crimes, and therefore ought to be abolished, added, that there were some general points that had been adduced in its support to which he was desirous of adverting. Amongst these was the argument which had been urged with earnestness, that the principle of the abolition of the trade would lead to emancipation. To this objection the minister frankly replied, that at present the negroes were not in a condition to be immediately emancipated; but he had no doubt, and would not conceal his opinion, that the effect of abolishing the trade would be to abolish slavery itself. We are not the advocates of slavery. We do not consider ourselves authorized to hold our fellow creatures in bondage. But we do not arrogate the right of judging others; nor presume to make our conscience a rule for theirs. We are bound by compact to our brethren in the Southern States, and cannot in good faith attempt to wrest from them what they consider as property, and without which their other property would be good for nothing. Nay, if we had lawful authority to emancipate the slaves south of Pennsylvania, we should, with the example of St. Domingo before our eyes, proceed with caution, and tremble with the apprehension, that, in remedying an evil we should let loose a legion of crimes.[14] Europeans can speculate at their ease on events so distant as to appear more like history than action. It is otherwise with men on the spot, who see the rage of incarnate devils, and hear the shrieks of their victims. When statesmen of wisdom and experience speak the language of enthusiasm; when they who can resort to arms for a few seal-skins on the other side the globe, are thrown into spasms of sensibility for the sufferings of negroes, who are dancing all the while to the sound of their banjoes, there is reason to suspect something beside sentiment. If we take the trouble to examine facts, we shall find the British colonies full manned with Africans, while those of their rivals want hands. St. Domingo must, when subdued, be peopled anew. Moreover, if all these colonies were sunk in the sea, it would but enhance the value and increase the revenue of the British dominions in Asia. To abolish the slave trade, therefore, is good sound British policy. To bottom the measure in argument, on these efficient principles of interest, would not sound so well as to boast of philanthropy, and express the detestation of robbery and murder. But what motive have we to make the above-mentioned compact,

14. Slaves in the French colony of Saint-Domingue had rebelled in 1791 and achieved independence in 1804, renaming the country Haiti.

and what is to be its effect? Was each party, in the apprehension that his conscience would not keep him to his duty, desirous of bolstering up the moral sense with diplomatic engagements? Or was it intended to preclude debate in Parliament and in Congress? If domestic operation alone was intended, diplomatic engagements were neither necessary nor proper. The respective legislatures should have been left at liberty. If it was intended to form an alliance offensive and defensive against the slave trade, our ministers should have inquired a little into our means and situation. Are we, we the pacific, to commence a career of knight-errantry for black dulcineas? Are we, we who keep thousands in bondage, to declare that no one shall follow our example? Truly it would seem as if we were doomed to fight for every thing except our own interest, our own rights, and our own honour.

We pass over the rest of what this treaty contains, to consider what it does not contain; previous to which, however, we must observe that, notwithstanding our willingness to excuse the administration, by imputing its defects to the gentlemen negotiators, we are deterred by a belief that such imputation would be unjust. If, indeed, those gentlemen had been recalled, we should be convinced the fault was theirs. But they are continued in office. The administration, therefore, consider them as still deserving of confidence. They have then conformed to their instructions, and the treaty is such as they were directed to make. Hence we are driven, in spite of ourselves, to conclude that what has been said is true—That the treaty was sent back, not from any disapprobation of its contents, but because it does not contain a relinquishment, by the King, of his claim to take British seamen from the merchant vessels of America. If it be true that our government have taken their stand on this ground, and for the reasons just assigned, this seems to be unquestionable, we are brought to a point which demands our serious consideration. If reason be against the British claim, let it be resisted; but if otherwise, God forbid we should engage in war to establish injustice.

The question is two-fold; whether England can rightfully compel her native subjects to man her fleets, and (if so) whether she can lawfully exercise that right over such of them as are in the ships of another country. Let it be premised, that as they pretend no right to take a native American, that case is not within the scope of our inquiry. Let it also be premised, that when nations are agreed respecting matters of right, the way is open to expedients for mutual convenience. Matters of interest frequently interfere, and require appropriate arrangements by mutual concession, for mutual advantage. But matters of right are of different nature and sterner stuff.

They cannot interfere, unless where nations are at war; because it cannot be right for one to prevent what another has a right to perform: Wherefore the right being established, submission is implied. Were it otherwise, war must be the natural condition of man; because the right to do on one side, and the right to oppose on the other, constitute precisely the state of war.

It is a first principle of every government, that it can rightfully command the military service of its citizens and subjects. If this be not admitted in America, we are in a wretched condition. We have no fleet; we have not, and it is to be hoped we never shall have, a standing army. If, therefore, the militia cannot be compelled to defend their country, what is to become of us?

But it is said that, admitting the general principle, an exception is to be made in favour of those who leave one State and swear allegiance to another. The British government, however, insists, that no man can divest himself of the duties which he owes to his country. Other nations maintain the same principle; which, both by reason and by general consent, forms a maxim of public law. The usual stipulation in treaties, that the subjects or citizens of one of the contracting parties shall not engage in the military service of an enemy of the other, rests on this foundation, and would, without it, be an idle phrase. It is true that a different doctrine is maintained by some who pretend to instruct us in matters which concern our intellectual nature, our moral duties and political rights; matters which, having escaped the statesmen and sages of antiquity, have (as they say) been lately discovered. We, however, are not disposed to adopt novel doctrines, but presume that those who have gone before us, came into this world with as much sagacity as those lately born. And we know that many of them, with equal opportunities for reflection, had greater advantages of experience in national affairs. Putting aside, however, the objection of novelty, others present themselves to the most cursory observer, which it would be tedious to enumerate. Suppose that Arnold, after swearing allegiance to the King of Great-Britain, had returned to this country, and claimed the rights of a British subject.[15] Surely there would have been but one sentiment, but one voice. Light minds may amuse themselves in blowing up the bubbles of metaphysical wit, but sober men will not stifle those chaste and righteous sentiments which bind them to their country. They will not permit rash innovators, "cloathed in a little brief authority," to abolish maxims venerable

15. Benedict Arnold (1741–1801) accepted a commission in the British Army and settled in England after the war.

alike for their antiquity and wisdom.[16] In a word, they will not relinquish the undoubted right of America to the military service of her citizens. If, however, it should be deemed proper that each be at liberty to take advantage of the social compact while it suits his convenience, and to release himself from its obligations when called on to perform them, let it be so enacted. It will then be law for us; but it will not thereby become law for other nations.

It may be said that man has a natural right to change his country and his allegiance. But it will be difficult to adduce proof that will not equally prove each individual to be above the law, or what is tantamount, that each can, at his pleasure, release himself from its authority: whence it must follow, that the law, binding only those who choose to be bound, is a nullity; a thing which not only does not exist, but which cannot exist. And after all, even if we should adopt that extravagant theory, the difficulty must remain: other nations will not dispute with us the doctrinal points we assume to govern or to amuse ourselves; but they will not permit us, under cover of our doctrines, to invade their rights. It behoves us, therefore, before we carry such notions into practice, to inquire whether we are prepared to force them upon other nations; for we must either embark in that extreme project, or acknowledge the rights which they exercise over their own subjects. So little, indeed, are the advocates for the supposed right of expatriation in harmony with themselves, that they have, on a different but notable occasion, strongly insisted that no one nation has a right to interfere in the domestic arrangements of another. We do not admit this axiom, in its fullest extent, because we conceive that when it is a domestic arrangement of one nation to subjugate others, all have a right to interfere, on the common principle of self-preservation. But no man, we believe, ever claimed for England a right to determine what laws the French Republic should make or repeal respecting French citizens. Neither has it, as yet, been directly asserted that such power can be justly exercised over us by the French Republic. We conclude, therefore, it will not be pretended that we have such right over Britain. And if we have not, it must be admitted that an Englishman, coming to America, comes subject to the obligations imposed by the laws of his native country; which obligations are known, and of course excepted in the compact by which he becomes an American citizen. If this be admitted, and it can hardly be denied, the difficulty about certain papers

16. Shakespeare, *Measure for Measure*, act 2, scene 2, line 118; Shakespeare says "dressed" rather than "cloathed."

given to seamen, and called protections, must vanish. The protection cannot avail against the prior right of his native country. Indeed, the facility with which it is obtained, in many of our sea-ports, is a sufficient reason why it should not be respected. It is frequently granted to men just arrived from the British dominions, whose language betrays the fraud; and who, when afterwards questioned by a British officer about the alleged place of their nativity, cannot tell whether it is to be found in New-England or Virginia. Surely it cannot be expected that a powerful nation, whose existence is staked on the chance of war, will be the dupe of such clumsy contrivance.

It has been already observed that a British subject cannot, according to the laws of that country, disengage himself from the obligation to render military service; and that we cannot release him, because we cannot make or repeal the laws of England. To this it will be replied, that, having uncontrolable authority to legislate for ourselves, our act of naturalization, by conferring the right of citizenship, cancels anterior incompatible duties. And this being a case in which supreme authority has made contrariant provisions, the last must prevail. Certainly it must, if they who made it had a right to do what they are supposed to have done. Enough has already been said on the right. We shall only add here, that no question can arise while the party continues in America, because the British government cannot seize him within our territorial limits. Neither can a question arise if he should return home, because he would then be where we have no jurisdiction. But it may be asked, what will be the condition of an Englishman, naturalized here, who may have been brought by force within the power of his native country? Unquestionably it must be that which the law of England provides; for we cannot interfere, unless he was seized in our dominion.

Here, then, arises the second question, whether, admitting that England possesses the right she claims over her native subjects, it can properly be exercised in American ships. Those who hold the negative contend, that, taking a man from under the protection of our flag is a violation of our territory. It becomes proper, therefore, to inquire into the nature and extent of this protection. And here the first leading circumstance is the common right to navigate the ocean, whereby all are there at home. It is by virtue of this right, that powers at war take property of their enemies in a neutral ship. The ocean belonging as much to the one as to the other, if the neutral says the capture was made in my dominion, the belligerent replies, it was made in mine: and the arguments to support one assertion establish both or neither. Until lately, it was not attempted to take enemy's goods in the territory of a neutral power; and it is worthy of remark, that this has been done by the nation which, for half a century, has urged the establishment of a maxim, that neutral ships shall protect enemy's goods. The conduct of Napoleon on this occasion is rather an example to be avoided, than a precedent to be pursued, and cannot strengthen the right of search. But it does not weaken that right. Let it, however, be remembered, that although it is usual to stop and search merchant ships, a similar practice towards public vessels of war is inadmissible. These are national fortresses, and bear (in the proper sense) the national flag. To such vessels alone, the idea of protection by the flag is applicable. The distinction between them and merchant ships is material to the present subject. Nations justly claim respect to their vessels of war, and from that claim corresponding duties arise. When any thing wrong is done by them, the national honour is bound to make satisfaction: but the case with merchant vessels is widely different; and the condition of sovereigns would be wretched and base if every trick and fraud of a smuggler could implicate their honour. Yet, if we insist on the same respect to a private ship of trade as to a public ship of war, we must hold ourselves equally accountable for the conduct of both. Hence the universal consent, that merchant vessels may be examined, detained and confiscated, according to the nature of the case; and where they are injured, to compensate by money. For money being the object of trade, the national character is in no wise affected by what is done or suffered in the pursuit. Seeing, therefore, that a power at war has a right to take the ship and bring it into port, he must have a right to take his own subject out of the ship. It would be idle to suppose that a flag which cannot protect the ship itself, could protect the persons on board; or that it would be a violation of sovereignty to take part, when it is no violation to take the whole. But even if such distinction could be established, the matter would not be mended. If, for instance, Great-Britain should admit that one of our merchant vessels enjoys, while in the open sea, such an emanation of sovereignty, that, to take away one of the crew, would be tantamount to an invasion of our country; reserving, nevertheless, the established right by which the ship may, for adjudication of doubtful points, be sent into a British port: by exercising that right the ship could be brought within those limits where the exclusive territorial authority attaches. The suspected man would then, after examination, be regularly put on board a man of war, and nothing would, of course, be allowed for detaining the ship, and taking her out of her course.

Hence it is evident, that, by abandoning the known principles and usage of nations, we should involve ourselves in a labyrinth of difficulties for no good purpose and to considerable loss.

But it is said there is manifest absurdity in pretending that, because goods may be taken, and after due trial be confiscated, men may be taken and condemned without trial. It is monstrous to submit the dearest thing we have, our liberty, to the will of military men, who have an interest in taking it away. This argument is ingenious, but in our apprehension not solid. If British subjects only are impressed, it is none of our concern. Englishmen may do with each other what they please. If an American be impressed, it is probably from mistake, and he suffers a misfortune incident to his profession; being one of those evils, by reason whereof he is intitled to and receives extraordinary wages. We will not, however, elude the argument, but meet its full force. We say, then, that if the violence be intentional, and done by order of the sovereign, it is a legitimate cause of war, and ought so to be considered and treated. But if done by the officer, without the order of his government, it is one among the many wrongs, for redress of which resort must be had to the tribunals. The officer impressing does it at his peril, and the impressed seaman would, we believe, obtain ample compensation from a Westminster jury. We venture to add our opinion, that if a few clear cases of this sort had been prosecuted at the public expense, it would have done more to correct the practice, so far as real American citizens are concerned, than all the clamour of the last ten years. At any rate, nothing can fairly be imputed to the sovereign, until his courts refuse to do justice. If an officer in our navy should assault and imprison a British subject, and application were made to our Secretary of State by the British Minister, would he not be referred for redress to our courts of justice? Surely the President would not on a complaint, though supported by exparte affidavits, break an American officer without trial.

To this it may be replied, and with much weight of argument, that although the officer is personally accountable to the injured individual, the government he serves is also accountable for repeated injuries, though done without its order; because in arming officers with power, and cloathing them with authority, it is a duty to provide against and prevent abuse. This we admit, and deduce from it the consequence that Britain, in exacting the military service of her subjects, ought to respect the rights of our citizens. Here, however, we must, in fairness, consider those circumstances which are inseparably connected with the question. Speaking as we do, the same language; our manners and customs also being the same; there is real difficulty in distinguishing a British from an American seaman, even when the officer acts with pure and upright intentions. Moreover, the very mode adopted to mark out our citizens has increased, instead of diminishing the difficulty. Seamen carelessly loose, or wantonly destroy, or fraudently dispose of their protections; so that while many, whose countenance and pronunciation declare them to be (what they really are) native Americans, have no protections; their comrades from Scotland and Ireland, whose looks and language clearly designate their country, present their protections in proper form. On application, therefore, to the British government, and the consequent inquiries, facts frequently appear of such nature as might puzzle a discerning judge, much more a plain sea-officer.

Thus, by the peculiarity of its attending circumstances, the question is brought to a kind of dilemma; and, principles being acknowledged, it is contended, on our part, that Britain ought to forego a right which, from her own shewing, cannot be exercised without invading the rights of America — That she, being the actor, is bound to adopt regulations by which our citizens may be secured from violence. The case, considered in this aspect, is certainly strong. But to the proposition that she shall forego her right, she replies, that without supposing, much less asserting, that the United States contemplate the seduction of her seamen into their service, it is impossible not to see that such would be the result — That without regarding the loss of one country and gain of another from that event, a consequence far more important commands her attention — That she is at war with the most powerful monarch on earth, who threatens invasion and conquest — That she has but slender means of defence at land, and may (should the invasion take effect) be blotted from the list of nations — That, even if not subdued, she would be exposed to imminent peril and most grievous calamity — That her only defence, her fleet, can no longer be relied on if her present resources for manning it be destroyed. Wherefore, the exercise of her right cannot be relinquished without hazarding her existence — That without insisting, as she might, on the interest we ourselves have in her success, and on the certainty that, if she is crushed by the weight of Napoleon's arms, we also must become French provinces, she can safely appeal to our reason and justice, to decide whether it is fair and right to place the convenience of one party on a line of equality with the existence of another. She declares her willingness to enter into any equitable arrangements to secure the rights of our citizens. But if no expedient can be devised which will produce the desired effect, she must exercise the right of self-preservation; though from circumstances not of her making nor under her controul, we are subjected by it to inconvenience and even to injury. In fine, that if we insist on her relinquishing her only means of defence, she must, though reluctantly, join in an appeal to the God of battles.

We have already observed, that when parties are agreed as to matter of right, the way is open to arrangements for mutual convenience. We now add our sincere belief, that men of integrity and good sense, who would candidly seek, would certainly find expedients to reconcile the exercise of her rights with the security of our citizens. We see, however, with much concern, that instead of endeavouring to remove, pains are taken to increase and multiply obstructions in the way of a fair and honest arrangement; and that, instead of simplifying the question, it is endeavoured, by the use of general terms and severe invectives, to persuade the people of America that Great-Britain ought to relinquish a right on the exercise of which materially depends her national existence.

Hitherto we have discussed the question on principles of public law, and have not permitted any breath of interest to blow either way. Let it not, however, be forgotten, that our ships of war go freely into British ports, are hospitably received, and are suffered to depart without question, though manned in a great proportion by British subjects. Surely they have as good right to demand their seamen as we have to demand ours.

But it may be asked, if this be a true state of the question on the ground of right; and if it be doubtful on the ground of policy, whether we should strenuously insist on our right; whence came the clamour, and whence the cry of oppression? We do not conceive ourselves called on to account for so vain a thing as clamour. But, since the occasion is of portentous import, we will state the facts. We gain much, during the war, on trade which usually flows in other channels. Hence an extra demand for seamen, which America cannot supply; so that this lucrative commerce will be less extensive than our merchants desire, if they cannot procure seamen from other countries. Other neutrals are actuated by similar motives. We, however, speaking the same language, can have no want of British seamen, if, besides high wages and security from capture, we can protect them against impressment by British ships of war. Our merchants, therefore, have easily persuaded themselves to believe that a British seaman, with one of the protections above-mentioned in his pocket, ought not to be taken out of their ships. In this faith they clamoured. Some of them, whose moral and political notions are peculiarly agreeable to those who manage our affairs in the way they like best, have contrived to enlist the government in this scheme of traffic. But if, by contending on such bad ground, we are brought into war, our merchants will be the first to suffer. Such of them as have property must tremble at the consequence. The cry, however, will be kept up by those whose deranged affairs find an interest in confusion, and by the fiery spirits, who readily sacrifice their country to their ambition. But what will be our condition, if we walk on in this crooked path? We have advanced a claim, which, however the agents of those who wish to embroil us may pretend to approve, will be scouted by all the world: for the position we take is not only untenable in itself, but opposed to the interest of other nations. Nevertheless, to establish this claim, though without any chance of success, we shall perhaps be committed to a dangerous course of events. If Britain, struggling for life, be driven to desperation, she must strike. At the first blow our commerce is gone. She would be enriched with millions of our spoil, and we should, in a few months, acknowledge the rights which our rulers seem disposed to resist by the last extremities; for it is absurd to suppose the American people will bear the privations and hardships of war, to support a scheme of injustice.

One good consequence has, however, resulted from the notion assumed by our rulers. There is too much reason to believe, that, if the usual course had been pursued with regard to the treaty, a constitutional majority of the Senate (from the confidence which they were chosen to exhibit in the President) would have given their ready approbation. That onerous contract would then have been fastened about our necks for ten years, and some of its evil consequences for ever. That we are not at this moment the commercial vassals of England is, therefore, in no small degree, to be attributed to the extravagant notion, that America is bound to protect every vagabond against the lawful authority of his own country. If, in the exercise of the British claim, or in any thing else, our sovereignty and independence are invaded, let no thought of consequences prevent us from asserting our honour. To preserve that is our first duty, our highest concern. With it we shall enjoy liberty, peace and commerce. Without it we shall enjoy nothing long; for a nation which looses her honour cannot preserve her independence. But we forbear to urge what we conceive to be unnecessary, when speaking to a high-minded people.

We entreat our fellow citizens to consider seriously the situation in which they stand—to suspend the rage of party strife—to examine facts—to reason for themselves. We put in no claim of merit. We solicit not their favour, much less their suffrage. Let them honour those whom it pleaseth them to honour. But let them not forego the use of their understanding. They may perhaps be told that we are enemies to the people. Be it so.

Wise men consider those as their friends who give them useful information. But, admitting us to be enemies, reason and truth, even in the mouth of an enemy, are still reason and truth. The people may believe of us what they please, and call us by whatever odious name their favourites may select or invent. All we ask of them is to show their friendship to themselves, by attending to what concerns themselves; instead of sitting still, their eyes closed, their ears shut, while they are bought and sold like miserable slaves.

The Beaumarchais[1] case was one of the most contentious episodes of the Revolutionary War. As Morris explains in these letters, not only were the claims themselves potentially embarrassing to both France and the United States, but they also gave rise to a factional fight in Congress over the conduct of American agents Arthur Lee and Silas Deane that briefly paralyzed the government. Thomas Paine, as the secretary to Congress's committee on Foreign Affairs, tried to help the Lee faction by leaking Beaumarchais's claims to the press in January 1779, impairing relations with America's only ally by revealing the secret help of the French government before independence was declared.[2] As these letters indicate, the case continued to reverberate in American politics.

The occasion of these two letters was the presentation of Beaumarchais's claim, yet again, by the French minister to the United States in 1807, and the subsequent report of Attorney General Cesar Rodney endorsing the claims. Rodney's opinion was delivered in a December 7, 1807, letter to Secretary of State James Madison; that report, together with a commentary that does not appear to be by Morris, appeared in the *Evening Post* of January 7, 1808. Morris had responded briefly to the French minister's assertion of the claim in 1807; on January 11, 1808, Morris gave a fuller reply to Rodney's endorsement.

The New-York Evening Post, February 24, 1807, p. 2; January 11, 1808, p. 2. Courtesy American Antiquarian Society.

1. Pierre-Augustin Caron de Beaumarchais (1732–99) is best remembered as the author of *The Barber of Seville* and *The Marriage of Figaro*, but he was also a secret agent for the French government. In 1776, with the secret financing of the French and Spanish governments, he set up Roderigue Hortalez and Company to provide supplies to the American revolutionaries.

2. Mintz, *American Revolution*, 117–21, has a good account of the episode and of Morris's role in it. For the subsequent history of the claim, see Brian N. Morton and Donald C. Spinelli, *Beaumarchais and the American Revolution* (Lanham, Md.: Lexington Books, 2003), 317ff.

Ten years later, after Morris's death, the subject of the Beaumarchais claim was raised yet again in Congress. The *Evening Post* reprinted the essay with the following introductory note:

> *The Beaumarchais claim.* In answer to numerous applications from gentlemen in congress, I re-publish the following article; and shall follow it with a still more satisfactory elucidation of facts, from the same source;[3] in the hope, that it will be now put at rest forever.
>
> The information contained in the following article was written by the late Gouverneur Morris, and furnished for publication in 1807, when the claim of Beaumarchais was first presented to congress. No man then living was probably so conversant with the facts detailed.[4]

February 24, 1807

Beaumarchais. In the revolution war, America received supplies of Cloathing and Military Stores from Mr. de Beaumarchais. It was notorious that this gentleman was incapable of furnishing them from his own resources—it was believed therefore, that he derived his means from the Royal Treasury. Afterwards, when Mr. Franklin, the American Minister, settled our accounts with Monsieur de Vergennes, the United States were charged under three distinct heads, viz: Loans, Subsidies, and Free Gift. The payments under each of these heads was distinctly pointed out, except that of one million given in 1776; and when Mr. Franklin desired to know what had become of that money, he was told that being a gift, no explanation was necessary. Mr. Franklin was, or appeared to be satisfied. Before that settlement, however, Mr. Beaumarchais, who had an agent in America, pressed for payment of supplies, furnished and obtained from Congress Bills for two million four hundred thousand livres on their Ministers in Europe, who, by the bye, had no means of payment. Mr. Gerard, the French Minister at Philadelphia, (brother to Mr. Rayneval, a Secretary in the Count de Vergennes Office) patronized Mr. de Beaumarchais' demand, which however was represented by some of the public servants in Europe, as wholly

3. That is, the article of January 11, 1808, reprinted below.
4. *New-York Evening Post*, February 5, 1818, p. 2.

unfounded, and a mere scheme to put money in the pockets of individuals. There was much opposition therefore in Congress. The resolution was carried, on the principle, that America, having received the supplies, ought to pay for them: That, to say the Court furnished funds, was an assertion without proof; and the claim being made with the privity and countenance of the French Minister, it was to be presumed agreeable to his superiors: Finally, that as the American minister in Paris, would hardly accept the bills before he was assured of means to pay them, the Court could, if they pleased, set matters right there.

These Bills made afterwards a serious deduction from a subsidy of six millions, granted by the King for carrying on the war. When Monsieur de la Luzerne, the successor of Monsieur Gerard, learnt that the subsidy had been anticipated in that manner, he expressed dissatisfaction in strong terms, and desired, that if Mr. de Beaumarchais made any more claims, he might be referred for payment to the French Court.

The claim slept for a long time, and as it seemed pretty clear that the million unaccounted for had been fingered by Mr. de Beaumarchais, it was natural to press for a disclosure, in order that it might be charged to him here, in the settlement of his accounts; but Mr. Franklin, conceiving perhaps that the circumstance was not important, made the settlement above mentioned. Perhaps he could obtain no other—perhaps he did not feel himself in a condition to insist that the alledged gift should not appear in the account, till the application of it was disclosed. Perhaps the old gentleman thought it most prudent to let the article stand open for such elucidation as time might afford.

Two reasons may be assigned for secrecy. The one, of a public nature, certainly had weight. France had affected a strict neutrality previous to the treaty by which our Independence was acknowledged, and had occasionally given assurances to that effect; and even at Lord Stormont's instigation, had seized goods and embargoed vessels destined[5] to this country. On these occasions, Beaumarchais made strong representations, claiming his rights as a citizen, and complaining of the injury to his property. These, which were calculated for Lord Stormont's inspection, proved a little too much. Persons who understood the French government, knew that such remonstrances would not have been hazarded by any one, not previously sure of protection. If however, after so many assurances, it had been acknowledged that this very Mr. Beaumarchais was employed by the Ministry to send out

5. In 1808, "distined"; corrected to "destined" in 1818 reprint.

these very goods at the King's expence, it would have furnished the British government with the proof they wanted.

The second was perhaps the efficient reason, though of a private nature. Perhaps the French Minister, good naturedly, wished that America, in prosperity, should refund to the King's subjects, what had been granted by his Majesty's bounty in our adverse condition, and he might not be unwilling that Mr. Rayneval, an old and able servant, should share a handsome sum with Mr. Beaumarchais.

After the King was dethroned, the American Minister in France was so fortunate as to obtain a copy of Mr. Beaumarchais' receipt.[6] Now as the French government formerly alledged the free gift of a million, and as the receipt of Mr. Beaumarchais has been since given to shew how that million was disposed of, it seems no more than reasonable at this time, when they demand payment for Mr. Beaumarchais, that they should prove the million in question was applied to our use in some other way.

New-York Evening Post. Monday, January 11[, 1808]

Beaumarchais' Claim. We do not recur to the claim of Beaumarchais for the purpose of adding to the evidence and observations already before the public; which, if we mistake not, must have convinced all impartial men that this claim is unsupported in justice or law, the opinion of Mr. Cesar A. Rodney, Attorney General of the United States, to the contrary, notwithstanding.

Our object in again adverting to this subject is to demonstrate by incontestable evidence, which we have just been so fortunate as to discover, that, admitting even the million of livres paid Beaumarchais, were *not* paid on account of the U. States, as is asserted by Mr. Attorney, and of course cannot enure to our benefit, yet, that we are not, and never were under any obligation to pay it—and further, that possessing as our government do possess, the documents now to be laid before the public, they cannot be ignorant that the demand of Beaumarchais' heirs is unfounded and fraudulent.

A brief recapitulation of certain facts may not be amiss.

The war of Independence commenced in 1775. Early in the following spring Silas Deane, then a Member of Congress, was sent by them to France

6. The minister, of course, was Morris himself.

to solicit aid from the King; he arrived at Paris in the month of June 1776, some months before which, Beaumarchais had been sent by the French Government to London, for the purpose of communicating through some secure channel, to Congress the disposition of the French Cabinet to assist America in her struggle with England.

Beaumarchais, who appeared in London as Roderigue Hortalez, found out, and formed an acquaintance with Arthur Lee, of Virginia, then residing in London—Beaumarchais opened his business to Lee, engaged him to make his communication to Congress, and arranged with him the mode in which France should send to America supplies, of the value of two hundred thousand pounds sterling—this commission being executed, Beaumarchais returned to Paris, from whence he kept up a secret and enigmatical correspondence with Lee, concerning America; Beaumarchais retaining the name of Roderigue Hortalez, and Lee assuming that of Hannah Johnson, so as to avoid suspicion, under the appearance of a love intrigue.

Lee lost no time in communicating through Doctor Franklin to Congress, the important information he had received from Beaumarchais; and Congress on the faith of this communication, soon afterwards appointed Doctor Franklin, Silas Deane, and Arthur Lee to be their commissioners at Paris.

Doctor Franklin and Mr. Lee did not arrive in France until the close of 1776, or the beginning of 1777—Deane's previous arrival had enabled the French Government to concert with him the safest and most advantageous manner of sending out the supplies which had been promised through Beaumarchais. The business was performed by Deane and Beaumarchais, and three large ships, the Amphitrite, the Mercure, and the Seine, laden with military stores, chiefly taken out of the French Arsenals, were, in spite of the spies and remonstrances of the English Ambassador, dispatched before the arrival of Doctor Franklin and Mr. Lee.

In the following summer, circumstances occurred that induced, at least, one of the Commissioners to suspect that Beaumarchais, in connexion with others, would claim compensation for the supplies which had been gratuitously furnished by the French Government, & in the forwarding of which Beaumarchais had merely been employed as an agent. The Commissioners therefore wrote Letters to the Committee for Foreign Affairs, informing them that these supplies were a *free gift* of the King; and although they were shipped in the name of Roderigue Hortalez & Co. that this was a *mere device* to conceal the King's interference, and that *no compensation would ever be demanded or expected.*

These Letters, dated Sept. 6 and 7, 1777, were delivered, by the Commissioners, to Captain John Folger, of Nantucket, then at Paris, to be delivered by him to Congress.

Captain Folger did not arrive till January 1778, on the 11th of which month he delivered his dispatches to the President of Congress. But on being opened they were found to contain nothing but blank sheets of paper. The truth is, some clever *Falconi* had contrived, before they left Paris, to play at cup and balls with them; dexterously withdrawing them and substituting these blanks.[7]

Much agitation and disappointment were created by this singular occurrence. Folger was arrested, examined by a Committee of Congress, and thrown into close confinement. Governor Caswell, of North-Carolina, when Folger arrived, was desired to examine the persons who came over in the vessel with Folger, and inform Congress of every circumstance that might come to his knowledge respecting these dispatches; but all to no effect.

It has been stated that these Letters were dated the 6th and 7th of Sept. 1777; On the 10th of the same month Beaumarchais executed, before two Notaries of Paris, an instrument, constituting John Baptiste Lazarus Thevencan de Francey, to be the Attorney of Roderigue Hortalez & Co. and authorizing said Attorney to repair to America, and there liquidate, demand, and receive payment for the supplies shipped in the Amphitrite, Mercure and Seine.

Silas Deane, who cooperated with Beaumarchais in forwarding these supplies, certified the authenticity of this power of attorney; whose import, it would seem, he could not be ignorant of, and de Francey reached Philadelphia about the same time that Folger arrived there with the blank dispatches.

As Deane, on the 7th of September, signed with Franklin and Lee a dispatch, informing Congress that all the supplies that had been sent were the *free gift* of France, and three days afterwards authenticated Beaumarchais' power of attorney, authorizing de Francey to demand payment for these supplies, it can scarcely be doubted that Deane was privy to the views of Beaumarchais; on which supposition, there seems to be little difficulty in fixing upon those whose knowledge and opportunity enabled them to withdraw the dispatches sent by Folger, and to substitute in their stead similar envelopes covering nothing but blank paper.

7. Signior Falconi was an Italian magician who performed in the United States from 1787 on.

Had the dispatches instead of the blanks, arrived by Folger, the claim of Beaumarchais would have been instantly rejected; but the dispatches having met with the above misfortune, De Francey, who arrived with or soon after Folger, immediately presented the claim, authenticated under the signature of Deane, and obtained a resolve of Congress for its payment.

The duplicates of these unfortunate dispatches were at last received and the mystery discovered. Soon afterwards Simeon Deane, brother of Silas, arrived with the treaties concluded with France, and in a few weeks was followed by the French fleet under Count D'Estang, in which Mr. Gerard the first French minister, and Silas Deane were passengers—Deane had been suspected and recalled, and those whose memories embrace that period of our history, will still recollect with regret, the suspicions, the jealousy, and the feuds which then and for several years afterwards existed in our public Councils, concerning the management of our foreign affairs. Suffice it to remark that Congress, perhaps unavoidably, were led to approve of measures, which in happier circumstances, they would not have hesitated to condemn. It was not deemed expedient at the time to permit the import of these dispatches to transpire, nor even to allow them that influence upon the public measures to which they were fully entitled.

These prudential considerations no longer govern; times are changed, men are changed, and our relations with France are also changed; so that no sufficient reason now exists why these dispatches should any longer be regarded as state secrets.

Besides, their publication at this time, may save to the nation a large sum, which Congress are about to *grant* for supplies which both France and Beaumarchais, her agent, have confessed to have been a *free gift*—This is not the only motive; the publication of these documents *at the present juncture* may serve to awaken useful reflections on *other and still more important interests.*

The extracts which follow are faithful copies and may be relied upon as authentic.

DOCUMENT NO. I

Letter from Arthur Lee to the Committee of Foreign Affairs
PARIS, Oct. 6, 1777

Upon the subject of returns, I think it my duty to state some facts relative to Hortales. The gentleman who uses this name came to me about a year and a half ago, in London as an Agent from this Court, and wishing to communicate some things to Congress. At our first inter-

view he informed that the Court of France, wished to send an aid to
America of £200,000, in specie, arms and ammunition, and that all they
wanted to know, was this, through what island the remittance could be[8]
made. We settled the Cape as the place; and he urged me by no means to
omit giving the earliest intelligence of it, with information that it would
be remitted in the name of Hortales. At our next meeting he desired
me to request that a small quantity of tobacco, or some other production, might be sent to the Cape, to give it the air of a mercantile transaction, repeating over and over again that it was for a cover only, and
not for payment, *as the whole remittance was gratuitous.* Of all this I informed Dr. Franklin by sundry opportunities, at the same time I stated
to Mr. Hortales, that if his Court would dispatch eight or ten ships of
the line to our aid, it would enable us to destroy all the British fleet, and
decide the question at one stroke. I repeated this to him in a letter after
his return to Paris, to which the answer was, that there was not spirit
enough in his court for such an exertion, but that he was hastening the
promised succours.

Upon Mr. Dean's arrival the business went into his hands, and the aids
were at length embarked on board the Amphitrite, Mercury and Seine.

The original went by Captain Folger.

(Signed)   *ARTHUR LEE.*

DOCUMENT NO. II

*Letter from Dr. Franklin, Silas Dean, and Arthur Lee to the Committee of
Foreign Affairs*
PARIS, Sept. 7th, 1777

We have lately presented an earnest memorial to both Courts,
(France and Spain) stating the difficulties of our situation, and requesting that if they cannot immediately make a diversion in our favour, that
they would give a subsidy sufficient to continue the war without them,
or afford the states their advice and influence in making a good peace.
Our present demand to enable us to fulfil your orders, is for about
8,000,000 livres. Couriers, we understand are dispatched with this
memorial to Madrid, both by the Ambassador of Spain, and the Minister here, and we are desired to wait with patience, the answer, as the two
Courts must act together. In the mean time they give us fresh assurances
of their good will to our cause, and we have just received a fourth sum
of £50,000. But we are continuously charged to keep the aids that are

---

8. Corrected from "me" in the newspaper version.

or may be afforded to us as a dead secret, *even from Congress*, where they suppose England has some intelligence, and they wish she may have no certain proof to produce against them with the other powers of Europe.

The apparent necessity of your being informed of the true state of your affairs obliges us to dispense with this obligation. But we entreat that no part of it may transpire. Nor of the *assurance we have received that* NO REPAYMENT WILL EVER BE REQUIRED *from us of what has been already given us, either in money or military stores.*

(Signed)　　　*BENJAMIN FRANKLIN,*
SILAS DEANE,
ARTHUR LEE.

Thus we have, in the official letter of Arthur Lee, the confession of Beaumarchais himself, that it was not he, but "*the Courts of France and Spain*, who sent us the £200,000 in specie, arms, and ammunition." And that *the whole remittance was* GRATUITOUS. And we have in the official letter of the three commissioners, the assurance of both these Courts "who acted together," that "no repayment would ever be required of us for what had been given either in money or military stores." Lastly, we have Beaumarchais' own receipt to the Count of Vergennes, (introduced in our former remarks) admitting, that the money had been received from the minister, and promising to account to him for it, but for which he never has accounted, as appears by the receipt's being not taken up; which is perfectly reconcileable with our view of this transaction, and not with any other. To conclude:

What loop hole is now left for the learned advocate of this demand of half a million, though backed by the French ambassador,* to hang a doubt upon? if government, possessing as they do the very documents above quoted, have not put those documents into the hands of the learned advocate, who has reported in favour of the demand, what shall we think of them? If they have what shall we think of Mr. Attorney General? And should Congress decide in favour of the claim, what will the nation think of *them*?

The following letter on the same subject I received on Saturday evening. [Coleman's note.][9]

---

* General Turreau sent a note last winter to the administration, insolently saying "the French government *has raised its voice* in favour of the claim."

9. In 1818, edited to read: "The following letter on the same subject I received from a correspondent of the first respectability." Coleman several times introduces letters from Morris with similar language; but we may wonder why Morris would add the

To the Editor of the Evening Post:

Sir—Your very able and judicious remarks concerning the pretended claim of Beaumarchais's heir on the United States, induce me to trouble you with the following:

That vouchers expended for money in secret services, were not destroyed under the Sovereigns of the house of Bourbon, "The Memoirs of Dalrymple," show beyond contradiction.[10] Their contents were entirely transcribed from originals found in the French archives. They display in a satisfactory manner, the *honour* and *disinterestedness* of English Democrats; and relate, how a Russel plotted with a French Ambassador; and how a Sidney was pensioned by a French tyrant, the enemy of England.[11] The Memoirs of several Ambassadors of Louis XIV, and Louis XV, as those of a Barillon, of a D'Aveaux and others, also mention the worth and patriotism of Dutch as well as of British Democrats, purchased and employed by them, under their respective missions. They prove that most of those popular heroes, who were hailed as *virtuous patriots* by their countrymen, were in fact, traitors to their country, and dangerous instruments in the hands of its foes and rivals. These ambassadors all refer to vouchers deposited at the office of the Foreign Ministry.

If Talleyrand's revolutionary diplomacy differs from what was formerly practised; cogent reasons have no doubt occasioned an alteration, which conceals for posterity every voucher of this *honest* minister's labors. With regard to the claim in question on the light purse of our fellow-citizens, I heard, when I lately left France, that Mademoiselle Beaumarchais was only to have one twelfth of the money which could be deluded or extorted from the United States, and that the remaining sum was to be divided between A.B.C. in *America;* and X.Y.Z. at Paris. The latter personages you must remember, tried once before, ten years ago, to swindle *beaucoup d'argent*[12] from the American government, and their political honesty is therefore known; but as to the A.B.C. in America, since the fashion now is to destroy

material in the letter. The answer may be that Morris prepared his initial response before January 7, when the *Evening Post* published Rodney's opinion with a lengthy rebuttal that is apparently not by Morris. This letter may thus be an afterthought to the original essay.

10. Sir John Dalrymple, *Memoirs of Great Britain and Ireland; from the dissolution of the last Parliament of Charles II. till the capture of the French and Spanish fleets at Vigo* (London, 1790).

11. William Russell, Lord Russell (1639–83), and Algernon Sidney (1623–83).

12. "A lot of money."

all vouchers, their names will be an everlasting secret, should not the malice and hatred of a military despot drag them from oblivion as evidences of the integrity and patriotism of American Democrats.

Before I finish, it may be useful to inform Messrs. Jefferson, Madison, Rodney, &c. of a general report at Paris last October, that a fresh demand of the repayment, with *interest* of the three millions of livres given by Louis XVI to the United States, would soon follow the decision of our government in favor of the present claim.

I am, Sir,

AN AMERICAN TRAVELLER.
January 9, 1808.

33 ❦ To the People of the United States (1810)

American relations with England continued to deteriorate after Madison succeeded Jefferson as president in 1809. Morris had long thought that Madison's handling of foreign policy as secretary of state was incompetent. As this essay indicates, he was coming to believe that as president Madison had surpassed himself.

⌁

FELLOW CITIZENS,

It may not be improper for an old friend and servant to address you, and to wish, though he has little hope, that we may have a happy year. I will not scrutinize the President's late message, and the correspondence sent with it to Congress. There are speakers enough there, and writers enough elsewhere, to show, that if he was not out of his senses, he must have counted largely on your folly. Perhaps he has formed a just judgment, and will find you still willing to believe one who transmits an assertion with the evidence to contradict it under the same cover. Perhaps you are content to continue the laughing stock of the world, while you boast that no nation in it is so wise as yourselves. If this be so, even doze on till the whole edifice of your government comes tumbling about your ears. Such of you as are determined to believe not only without evidence, but against evidence; such of you as fondly clinging to falsehood, shut your eyes against truth, had better lay this paper on one side: it will not suit your taste. Go to your ordinary business, the Merchant to his Counting-House, the Lawyer to his Office, and the Farmer to his Barn. Wrap yourselves up in your cloak of confidence. A prick of the bayonet will make the dullest among you skip. Those who will not see now, will soon feel. There is not much time to spare, and none to lose.

Reprinted from *The American Citizen (New York)*, January 24 and 25, 1810. Courtesy American Antiquarian Society. The manuscript is in the Gouverneur Morris Papers, Rare Book and Manuscript Library, Columbia University, item 856. It was also published as a pamphlet (New York: n.p., 1810), American Antiquarian Society Early American Imprints, series II (Shaw-Shoemaker), no. 21500.

You were told long ago, that the persons you had chosen to rule over you were incompetent. An extreme reluctance to believe in bad motives, induces me still to cherish the opinion that our misfortunes spring from their imbecility. But the cause is not so important as the consequence. If the country is brought to ruin it will not be much matter whether that event shall have been the result of stupidity or corruption. It has been the leading maxim of our administration for at least eight years, that Great-Britain was on the verge of ruin, and it was their favourite topic of declamation before they came into power. But the fact is, that on the present first day of January, in the year of our Lord 1810, she is more powerful than at any preceding period. The tedious talk you have so often heard about the weight of her debt is flat nonsense, and the men who chatter thus, display their ignorance of what passes before their eyes and under their noses. But admit assumption, improbable as it is, that Britain shall become bankrupt: will she have a ship of the line or a frigate the less? Will she have a single soldier or a single musket the less? Or can we, in consequence of her bankruptcy, get the goods we want for nothing? Surely not. France made a bankruptcy after her revolution, and before she got back again under a single master; was her power thereby diminished? Surely not. What reason then have you to suppose that people who speak English will suffer more from such an event than those who speak French? If any such reason there be, how happened it that the United States were not ruined by becoming bankrupt during our revolutionary war? Our paper currency was then sold at a hundred for one, and we have not heard that the British bank notes were below par; but we have seen our merchants, during that embargo which was to ruin Britain, give eleven hard dollars for ten in those notes. Is this the bankruptcy you were taught to believe in? I tell you that if your rulers believed in it themselves they were arrant blockheads; and appeal to the fact. But if they did not believe in it, and meant only to deceive the people, it is fitter for you than for me to fix on the name by which they are to be distinguished.

Another thing on which they have equally relied, and about which you are equally deceived, is the power of France. The French Emperor is less powerful now than when he inveigled the Spanish Princes. It would take too much time to demonstrate that truth. I content myself, therefore, with making the assertion. Those who choose not to believe it are welcome to their own opinion. Time will either set them right or prove me to be wrong. The matter is not important to the subject which I have now in hand, for be the French power what it may, it must be a nullity to us should we engage in a war with Britain. Your wise ones may dream, if they please, of conquering Canada, but they may be roused from their slumber by five and twenty thousand British troops in the Chesapeake: on southern ground they may discuss a question of liberty and equality with men who watch the opportunity to make a practical comment on maxims they have learnt from the conversation of their masters.

You were told that the embargo would reduce Britain to implore your mercy. Nay, the stupid rant is still repeated, though you now find that more than a year ago James Madison, Robert Smith,[1] and Albert Gallatin implored (through the medium of a British minister) the mercy of the British monarch. Let them equivocate as they please, about the terms of their different conversations, they confessedly gave Mr. Erskine[2] to understand that they were willing to grant more than the British government had originally asked. This point is of such magnitude that it deserves your serious examination. All that Britain asked, when Bonaparte published his Berlin decree,[3] was that we should repel so manifest an attack on our independence with becoming indignation, instead of which your rulers bore it patiently and quietly near a year, in spite of fair warning given, that if (contrary to every honourable sentiment) we should submit to that insult, the British King would be obliged to retaliate. Nay, your late President made, of this very warning, his excuse for rejecting a treaty negociated by one of his bosom friends. We shall say nothing about the terms of that treaty, because bad as they were, your affairs have been so wretchedly mismanaged since it was made, that you will hardly get any so good now. The neglect to do what the dignity of America required, on occasion of the Berlin decree, drew at last from the British Council those orders of which you have heard so much, and of which it is sufficient to say, in this state, that they were milder than might (under all circumstances) have been expected. Our rulers, in consequence, as they say, of these orders (and we will let them tell their own story) laid their famous embargo. A measure which Mr. Canning[4] treated with sovereign, and I venture to tell you, with merited contempt. By the way, it is not worth your while to fume, and foam, and utter nonsensical

1. Robert Smith (1757–1842) had been secretary of the Navy in the Jefferson administration, and became secretary of state in 1809.

2. David Erskine (1776–1855), British minister to the United States from 1806 to 1809.

3. The Berlin Decree was issued by Napoleon on November 21, 1806, in response to British Orders in Council earlier that year.

4. George Canning (1770–1827), British foreign secretary.

threats when treated with merited contempt; for you do but increase the laugh at your own expense. Act honestly and wisely you will be respected; act knavishly and foolishly you will be despised. This usage of nations you may learn without consulting Puffendorf or Vattel; and believe me, it deserves consideration as much as any thing you will find in any body's book. But although Mr. Canning treated your embargo and your embargo makers with a sneer of profound contempt, Mr. Jefferson insinuated, in one of his messages, that he offered to remove all restraint on the commerce with England, and preserve it on the commerce with France, if Great-Britain would withdraw her orders in council. It is but fair to acknowledge that he sent, with that message, the proof that his insinuation was false; but had it been true (and it was so considered and treated by his friends) the natural inference would have been that he is one of those Calibans "whom stripes may move, not kindness:"[5] for after pretending to be offended at a gentle hint that such orders must result from submission to Bonaparte, after flouncing, and bouncing, and half ruining the country by his ridiculous project (for I am content to suppose that the embargo was not dictated by Bonaparte) at length, while smarting under the British lash, he offered to do, like a slave, what he might have done in the first instance like a gentleman. This I say would have been the case had he made the offer which he pretended to have made. His successor exhibits himself in a still more pitiful condition; for it is not denied that an offer was made through Mr. Erskine, substantially the same with that which Mr. Jefferson pretended to have made through Mr. Pinckney. How much more was offered is not easily ascertained. Mr. Pinckney was understood to offer a stipulation that British ships might execute our laws, but he says he was misunderstood. Mr. Erskine understood that we were ready to give up a trade with the colonies of belligerents; but it is said that he also misunderstood. Now, admitting both these misunderstandings, it is evident that something was offered on each of these points; and that something was more than Britain asked originally, or now asks: for so Mr. Jackson[6] has expressly said on behalf of his Sovereign. But however vague may have been the offers, and whether they were well or ill understood, Mr. Canning it seems understood the men he had to deal with. He neither believed in the talents of Mr. Erskine, nor in the candour of Messrs. Madison, Smith and Gallatin. He therefore, by letter

5. William Shakespeare, *The Tempest*, act 1, scene 2.
6. Francis Jackson succeeded Erskine as British minister to the United States in 1809.

to Mr. Erskine, recapitulated the offers made in three clear distinct propositions, and (giving permission to show the whole letter) bade him inform the American President that, if he would subscribe to those propositions, the British government would thereupon withdraw the orders in council as to America, and send out a minister to form a treaty. And here, by the bye, you have a proof of the value of your embargo. You see the British government continue to treat it with contempt while we were told that they were sinking under it, and while we feel ourselves distressed by it beyond all endurance; fail not to observe, also, that in the present moment your restrictive notions are treated with the same perfect indifference. In that issue to which your rulers have foolishly brought your affairs, the British government has wisely resolved to convince them that by imposing restraints on her commerce, we chiefly injure ourselves. And I feel it my duty to express on this occasion, my serious conviction, that if she should inhibit the export of her manufactures to the continent of Europe, they would be obliged (in spite of all the vain boastings and idle efforts of the French Emperor) to go in search of those goods to the spot which she might choose to enrich by making it the place of deposit. These are truths, fellow citizens, which it concerns you to know, and which your rulers ought to have known before they embarked our all upon a vast ocean of experiment. But to return, Mr. Erskine was obliged, first, to avow the communications made, taking to himself the blame of misconceiving or misrepresenting the conversations (if such had been the case); and, secondly, to exact the acknowledgment of that right which had been denied to Britain of retaliating the injurious conduct of her enemy. This was the effect of the first propositions, about which there is no dispute. I say, Mr. Erskine was obliged to make this avowal, because the permission to show his instructions was equivalent to a command; and in fact, he did make a full communication of them. Messrs. Madison, Smith, and Gallatin may deny this if they please; but no man of common sense will believe them, even were they all three to swear; because the thing speaks for itself. That they made offers of some sort or other they do not pretend to deny, and only equivocate about the terms. If it be asked why they did not make the bargain then which they made afterwards, they can give but one answer, viz. that Mr. Erskine had then no authority.

As to the idle pretence, now set up by Mr. Madison, that such an authority is included in general letters of credence, he must know better. If he don't, he is fitter for a school boy than for a President. But he does know better, as it would be easy to show from the very message in which he makes that ridiculous assertion; but this would be a waste of time. Now, therefore, Mr. Erskine having no authority, they knew they should be obliged to wait till he could get it; and as the embargo was pinching hard, they made splendid offers, as a lure, to get that authority vested (about the time when Mr. Madison should become President) in a weak young man whom they knew they could easily dupe. Mr. Canning's letter abovementioned is the only authority he ever got on that subject. I say the only authority, and will prove it presently; but am first to observe that it must have been communicated from beginning to end; not only because the power granted is so connected with the rest as not to be separated, but because Mr. Erskine being unable to produce any other authority, they must either stand up and tell you they made a treaty (or, as they please to call it, an arrangement) with a man unauthorized; and they might just as well have made such an arrangement with one of their negro coachmen; it would have been equally binding on the King of Great-Britain; or they must acknowledge that Mr. Erskine's authority, viz. this letter of Mr. Canning, was communicated to them. And so as to that ridiculous pretence, that Mr. Erskine might have had some other authority, some other instructions, &c. &c. let them, if they dare, come forward and say that any such were shown to them, and I shall immediately, in the name of the American people, demand a copy. If they hesitate to produce that copy, I denounce them for sacrificing the public interest, and prostituting the national honour, by making a solemn compact with an unauthorized British agent. I say unauthorized, for if they have no authentic power from the King of Great-Britain in their hands ready to be produced, none such exists, so far forth as the honour and interest of this country are concerned. They pretend to believe the British government perfidious. If this be their faith, they had an additional reason for pursuing the usual course of business; for demanding a communication of the authority before they would treat, much less conclude. I go therefore one step further. If they have not now ready to produce, and regularly deposited in the archives of the department of state, either an original of Mr. Canning's letter, or at least a certified copy, they deserve to be severely punished. They have been guilty of a manifest breach of public trust and confidence, they have compromised the interest and committed the honour of the American people by making a national compact with a British agent, without possessing the means to prove that he was authorized. Nor will it excuse them to say Mr. Canning has sent this letter to the House of Commons. It is not in the journals of a British House of Commons that we are to hunt for our state papers. They must be found in the office of our Secretary of State. When from that office these gentlemen shall have produced the letter, I will go one step further still, and denounce them for acting on the part of the United States without authority. I say the President assumed a power with which he was not vested. And I prove it thus. If this thing they call an arrangement is of the nature of a public treaty, and binding (as such) on the American people by force of the constitution, the previous assent of two thirds of the Senate was necessary. But there was no such assent. The Senate was not consulted, it was not even convened. The President had no right, therefore, as President acting under the constitution. And if Mr. Madison pretends to justify his conduct as a special agent, under a particular law, he must show a compliance with that law. This he cannot do. The law authorized him to perform a certain act after a certain event therein mentioned should have happened. But he took it on himself to do that act, not only without knowing or believing the event had happened, but knowing positively that it had not happened. He performed that act on the bare promise of an agent, not merely unauthorized, but acting to his certain knowledge in direct violation of his orders.

Thus then we see an American President and a British Minister, each of them knowing the other to be without authority, act a farce of negociation, then come forward to give the world this result of their diplomatic skill, this arrangement, and, finally, affect surprize that the King of Great-Britain will not sanction their children's play with his royal authority. So far, perhaps, the matter is merely laughable. But when this same President affects not only surprize, but indignation; when he ventures, as the august representative of the American people, to charge the British Monarch with perfidy, because he will not acknowledge himself to be bound by an act void from the very beginning; for this best of all possible reasons, that both the contracting parties acted without any shadow of right; when thus he drives us on to an unjust war, to dry up the fountains of our wealth, submit to sore taxation, and pour out the best of our blood on questions so frivolous, and for a purpose which (whatever suspicions may be abroad) I shall not presume to investigate, but leave him there to his conscience and his God; then I say the scene becomes too awful to admit of a light expression or a trivial thought. It then becomes every man to hold solemn communion with his own heart. If Mr. Madison is our sovereign imperial Lord, whose mandate we must obey, whose standard we must follow, then on him might we disburthen our souls of the crime. But if this nation is a republic; if we the people are free agents, then we are accountable agents. Accountable to him who is the Lord of all, and who will ask at our hands the blood which we shall shed, or which, when capable of preventing it, we may suffer to be shed on ridiculous questions of etiquette, in which (besides their intrinsic insignificance) our government is clearly and decidedly wrong. So far are they from having a right to complain of Great-Britain, that the right of complaint is on the other side: and a still greater right have we, the American people, to complain of the double perfidy. They could not justly have complained if the British Minister, in their late correspondence, had held the language which they have imputed to him, but which he did not hold. The charge of falsehood, which they suppose to have come from him, was the cry of their own conscience. I have just now demonstrated that they must grossly have neglected their duty if they have not in their possession the letter from Mr. Canning to Mr. Erskine, and if they did not positively know from Mr. Erskine that he had not any other authorization. They saw that in the natural course of things, their long train of deceit would be laid bare to the American people. Mr. Jackson tendered to them a commission under the broad seal of England, empowering him to treat. And, while he thus offered them his complete unquestionable authority, he told them distinctly that, so far from exacting conditions which they might deem offensive, he would not even propose any thing, but was ready to receive and discuss any offers which they might make. They had already tied up his tongue, and insisted that the negociation should be in writing. But when called on to make in writing their propositions, which, when so made, would leave no room for equivocation, they pretend that he had given them the lie. But ask them where and how, not a man of them can tell where, not a man of them dare tell how. By a fair and manly conduct he has given the lie to those false pretences, to those delusive insinuations by which they have deceived the American people. Let them, if they please, pretend that this is the language of a British tory. I despise that pitiful clamour. It cannot reach me. But admit it to be the language of the vilest wretch who ever broke a British goal,[7] is it the less true? Does a murderer become innocent because his accuser is a thief? Examine the facts, fellow citizens, and judge for yourselves.

But some men will cry out, what! shall we not support our own government? "Shall we become a divided people?" A certain Mr. Giles[8] has held a deal of this tory talk in the American Senate. And you will hear the same thing over and over again from that herd of miserable cattle, the office hunters, whose republicanism and patriotism consist in the desire to live at

---

7. Thus in all the sources; presumably an error on Morris's part for "gaol."
8. William Branch Giles (1762–1830), U.S. senator from Virginia 1804–15.

ease upon the public treasure. What care they for the liberty of the people if they can get so much property of the people as to pass their days in idleness! These fellows may call themselves republicans, democrats, federalists, or any thing else, according to the company they happen to fall in; they may run about coaxing, and wheedling, and squeezing, and cringing, and try to wriggle themselves into consequence; it is our duty to beware of them. For my own part, I had rather place in power the man whose opinions are most decidedly hostile to my own than one of these changelings. He who holds, avows, and acts up to his opinions honestly, even if in the wrong, merits respect; and there is some ground of hope that, being converted by reason and experience, he will go steadily right. But these chaps, who turn and turn and turn as suit their interest, may turn with equal ease to a foreign power, from the same motive. And this brings me back to the notion that we must support the government, or rather the President, through thick and thin. A doctrine more slavish, and, at the same time, more absurd, was never broached. Submission to an absolute monarch is not half so absurd; for he, having a deep interest in the welfare of his people, must be not only a scoundrel, but a fool, if he can be bribed to betray them. Will any man pretend that a President of the United States has the same deep interest in the welfare of the American people? History exhibits instances innumerable of republican leaders in foreign pay. We now know that the most flaming English patriots received French gold: yea, those men who for liberty's sake (as they said) drove off James and put William on the throne. Nay, we have seen that profligate Charles the Second acting his part, in the pay of France, to destroy the liberties of Europe: including, of course, those of his own country. Far be suspicion from my heart, but it is impossible not to be alarmed at the dangerous, the damnable doctrine that we must at all events support the President whether he be right or wrong. If that shall ever become the practical principle of our government, our liberties are gone. I mean not to insinuate that Mr. Madison has been, will be, or can be corrupted. I do not even advert to those circumstances which have excited, if not suspicions, at least unpleasant reflections in the minds of discreet and candid men. But I do not hesitate to say, that if we vest a power in the President to transfer us like sheep, it will not be long before some President will turn over those silly sheep to the butcher. Such is human nature. And is it possible to suppose that such power can have been contemplated by the constitution? If it be, let us not lose an instant in committing that constitution to the flames, and scattering the ashes to the winds of heaven. A curious thing, indeed, is a constitution full of checks and balances to preserve us from a king of our own native breed, but which enables a magistrate, elected for a short time, not by the people, but by a caucus, (for such is the practice) to sell us out and out to a foreign despot. I should be ashamed to say more on this head.

But a delicate question will be asked. What are we to do? What, indeed, can we do? Must we rebel? Must we destroy the constitution, that ark of our political safety? It does not become a solitary individual to obtrude opinions on a whole nation. When it was his duty to counsel, that duty was performed; and he performs now the duty of a citizen to caution. He has no right, and will not presume to advise. He neither holds nor desires to hold any office of profit, trust or confidence, and is willing to support, as far as in his power he can, as far as in conscience he may, the legitimate government of his country. He certainly does not mean to stand alone against a host, nor would he urge any other individual to do so unless in self defence. But experience has taught him that the people will find out for themselves the means of salvation. He may be, and hopes he is, mistaken, but he thinks he has long perceived symptoms of a design to enslave this country. He remembers when the doctrines of that same Mr. Giles were familiar in the mouths of those who would fain have persuaded America to submit to the British parliament. He remembers, for he is one of those who felt the indignant sentiment of freemen to whom slavery is proposed with rewards offered, and danger threatened. He remembers, for he shared in the generous councils which saved our country. Nevertheless, he will not presume to counsel you now. A bald head and grey beard are not alone sufficient sureties against rashness. But he fondly hopes that the representatives of the state of New-York, shortly to be convened at Albany, will, if needful, adopt measures suitable to the circumstances of our country. To that country, an early and long a faithful servant, he has ever gloried in the name of

AN AMERICAN.

This address was probably given to a group of New York voters sometime in April 1810, when Democratic-Republican Governor Daniel D. Tompkins was running for reelection against Jonas Platt. Party competition in New York was keen in this era, because it was a swing state and thus key to the national fortunes of the Democratic-Republican party. The current and previous vice presidents, George Clinton and Aaron Burr, had both been New Yorkers; Tompkins himself would serve as vice president under James Monroe.

Morris's address ignores New York politics, however, and instead develops further his criticism of the Madison administration's conduct of foreign policy.

Fellow Citizens

I conceive it proper to communicate to you my Sentiments on public Affairs previous to the ensuing Election of a Governor, which will, in all Probability, decide the Fate of our Country. Your present Governor has been careful to display his Subservience to the federal Administration. His Efforts, and those of his Patrons, to carry thro Measures hostile to the Interest of the American People and fatal to their Freedom are recorded Proofs that if you bestow your Confidence on them it will be abused.

I shall not imitate those who, on occasions like the present, pour forth a Torrent of unfounded Invective. I cannot avoid making serious Charges, but I shall adduce Facts to support them, and you shall judge. During the Course of those Events to which I am about to refer, the Eyes and Ears of

Gouverneur Morris Papers, Rare Book and Manuscript Library, Columbia University, item 855. The archivist has dated the manuscript as "prob. 1808," but until 1821 New York governors were elected for three-year terms; Daniel Tompkins was elected in 1807 and reelected April 26, 1810. Two incidents mentioned in the manuscript, the Degen, Purviance, & Co. bankruptcy and the letter from Champagny to Armstrong, occurred in summer 1809, making 1810 a more likely date for the speech.

many among us were closed by false Representations, so as neither to see Truth nor to hear Counsel. But this should not form a Subject of Reproach, for we are Men and cannot therefore be exempt from human Infirmity. It is the common Lot of our Nature to be, at Times, so blinded by Prejudice or transported by Passion as not to make just Observation of Characters Measures and Events. In that diseased Condition of Mind, we may assent to, and even applaud, Opinions and Actions which on cool Reflection we condemn and abhor.

As no one of us pretends to be perfect, we ought not to expect Perfection in those who rule over us; so that if the national Administration had committed those Faults only which Men of good Intentions may be led into by Negligence or Incapacity, however we might have felt Regret we should not have uttered Complaint. But they have assailed the Constitution, impoverished the Citizens, dried up the Revenue, squandered the Treasure, hazarded the Peace and surrendered the Independence of the united States. Each of these Points I mean to establish by Facts.

The first Message of Mr. Jefferson to the national Legislature was an Assault on the Judiciary, and therefore on the Constitution, of which it is an essential Part. His Followers, believing perhaps that he possest the Wisdom he wanted and the Virtue he pretended, gave (in Compliance with his Wishes) a deadly Blow to the Constitution, under the Pretext of saving public Money. They bade us look up to them as the faithful, and the only faithful, Guardians of our Treasure. They accused their Predecessors of Prodigality and Peculation. They promised to be saving and honest. The Falsity of the accusation has been long since demonstrated. As to the Promise, a List of Defaulters lately published proves that they their Agents and Friends have plundered the Treasury of more than enough to defray the Expense of the Judiciary to the present Day. More than $400,000 received by Collectors, South of this State, appear to be wholly lost. But the first was not the only Blow which has been aimed at the Independence of the Judiciary. In the persevering Malice which has pursued that Department, we trace the Spirit of the Administration. A Spirit equally hostile to Liberty and the Constitution. A Spirit which, to enforce the baneful System of Restrictions on Trade, subjected us (as far as Edicts which tho cloathed with the Forms, were opposed to the Principles of the Constitution could subject us) to the arbitrary Sway of Collectors holding their Power at the mere Will and Pleasure of the President. These dependent Officers were authorized (as far as such Edicts could give Authority) to send armed Men, on their bare Suspicion or Pretence of Suspicion, to violate the Asylums of domestic Tranquility. Neither Time nor Circumstances will permit now, to discuss the Powers delegated to the national Legislature. It is sufficient, for the present Purpose, to remind you that the same men and, as it were, in the same Breath contended that these despotic Edicts were constitutional and that the Constitution must be supported, as the Palladium of our national Security. Mark them Fellow Citizens, Mark the Sycophants well; for they have pretended, and will have the Audacity again to pretend, that they are the Friends of Freedom, the Friends of the People.

I say they have impoverished the Citizens of these united States. Need any other Proof be adduced than what we have experienced under the Embargo, and what we still experience from commercial Restrictions. I can safely appeal to the Knowlege of every intelligent Man in the State when I ask if Produce meets as ready a Sale at as good a Price or if Goods can be procured of equal Quality as cheap as when the Members of the national Administration came into Office. And if it should be objected that the Means of deciding on a Matter so extensive are not within the Compass of common Information, let any Man answer to himself this simple Question, does my Harvest supply my Family as amply and leave me as large a Ballance in Cash as it did Eight years ago. When that is done let him compare his present Condition with the Promises then made to obtain his Vote. If any Friend of the national administration shall say this is too strict a Measure, let him if he can name any one of their Promises or Professions which has not been contradicted by their Conduct save only their devoted adherence to France.

I say they have dried up the Revenue of this Nation. They came forward, at first, with a solemn Mockery of Patriotism. They affected a Desire to repeal oppressive Taxes. And they repealed Taxes on Luxury and Vice. But soon, under Pretext of a War with African Pirates, they encreased the Weight of Taxation on the Poor. That War ceased long since, but the Taxes continue. They continue too to boast of their Pity for the Poor. With an equal Contempt of Truth they boast of their Oeconomy; and yet, from their own Shewing, it appears that a large Loan is required to defray their ordinary Expences. When they came into Power the Treasury was not only full but overflowing. The public Arsenals were well supplied. There was some public Force. But now the Arsenals are empty, we have no public Force, nor can they shew one useful Object for which money has been expended. And yet the Treasury also is empty; & During the last Year, the Expenditures have exceeded the Receipts by more than a million.

I say they have squandered the public Treasure. Before they came into

Office they declared themselves the Reformers of every Abuse. They were not only to open every Source of Abundance but to shut every Drain of Extravagance. And what do we find? We find a nation impoverished, a Treasury exhausted, Abuses every where, Oeconomy no where. They began by selling, at considerable Loss, a Part of our Navy. Another Part was stuck in the Mud to rot. Stores laid up in the Arsenal for large Ships were wasted in fitting out small ones. And vast Sums were lavished in building useless Baubles called Gun Boats. Pertly deriding the Wisdom of Ages, they rashly adopted every new Project and fondly cherished every new Projector. Thus the public Purse has become a public Prey. Their General spends at his Pleasure, disdaining Limit and spurning at Control. Subordinate Officers vie with each other in licentious Extravagance. Among the public Defaulters we find Captains Lieutenants Contractors and Paymasters against whom Suits are instituted for large Sums: besides near Eighty thousand Dollars due by Degen Purviance and Company on a Transaction of such questionable Nature, and involving the Characters of men high in Office to such a Degree, that I forbear to mention the Circumstances, believing it most proper that they should be examined by the national Representatives.[1] These are a few Instances, the mere Outlines; but to fill up the Picture of Extravagance would require a distinct History of their Administration. A Task not only tedious and invidious but useless. For why soil our Fingers to probe the foul Corners of Corruption when an imminently impending Catastrophe proves the Virulence of the Poison? They acknowlege that we are on the Verge of national Bankruptcy, and (Bankrupt like) boasting of Credit, tell us they can borrow. This then is the Termination of their Sagacious Projects, their splendid Professions, and boasted Oeconomy. They took Charge of our Affairs in the Flood-Tide of Prosperity; while Money was pouring in with a Profusion which the most sanguine could not venture to expect or even to hope. Gorged with the Abundance pro-

---

1. Degen, Purviance, & Co. were agents for the U.S. Navy in the Mediterranean. When the firm went bankrupt in 1809, questions were raised about misuse of government funds, and about whether the secretary of the Navy had himself purchased some of the firm's bills of exchange. See the *Report of the secretary of the navy: made in obedience to the resolutions of the House of Representatives of the twenty fourth and twenty seventh ult.* [December 1810] *respecting several bills of exchange drawn on Degen, Purviance, & Company, navy agents of the United States, at Leghorn, in Italy: January 7, 1811. Read, and ordered to lie on the table. Printed by order of the House of Representatives* (Washington: A. and G. Way, printers, 1810 [1811]), 44 pages.

vided by their Predecessors, they called aloud for new Means of Expense. Not the Shoals of Gun Boats, nor Thousands applied to Palaces on the Potowmack, nor Millions to purchase Morasses on the Mississippi; Not all their Wantonness of Waste could drain our overflowing Coffers. Find out, said the Arch Deceiver, some Mode of applying the Surplus Revenue lest excessive Wealth should tempt us to war. But now, when compelled to rouse us from the golden Dream, we open our Eyes on national Bankruptcy. We must borrow to pay the Interest of what we owe. We want, says the Genevan,[2] a Loan of four Millions!!! Remember how loudly they complained of Loans when their Predecessors were compelled to borrow under the Pressure of Savage War on our Frontiers or to provide against foreign War which their Clamors have invited, or to quell Insurrections raised by their Intrigues. But now, when a public Debt must be incurred to pay their Salaries, the boasting Folly which plunged our Country into this sad Condition, plumes itself on being able to derive, from public Credit, new Means of Prodigality. But that Credit was founded on the Wisdom and Oeconomy of those whom they reviled. Can it be expected that Men will trust their Money to Ignorance and Extravagance? If indeed they beheld a large Revenue on one Side, and a sudden Demand for Money on the other, they would readily lend because they could reasonably expect Payment. But when they see our Revenue dwindle, in two short years, without any national Calamity, but by the mere Effect of Stupidity, from sixteen down to six and a half Millions, can they possibly trust the present Administration: especially when it is evident that a Persistence in the Course now pursued must soon reduce those six and a Half millions to Nothing? Nay! had Great Britain accept[ed] the Challenge they foolishly gave, even while I speak, at this very Moment, the whole Revenue would be gone. Dependent on Trade, it must perish with Trade; and Trade must perish when exposed to a thousand Ships of War. Yet such is the Navy of Britain. Before they can borrow, therefore, they must give Security to keep the Peace. And what Security can they give? Their Promise. Oh miserable Reliance! Will Foreigners believe those who are false to their own Country? Is their profligate Threat to sequester Property in the Funds and Banks to be the Proof of their Integrity; or is their joint Resolution to declare a palpable Falsehood the Voucher of their Veracity? Perhaps, indeed, some new Scheme of Deception may be played off in the Shape of a Contract to supply Money;

2. Albert Gallatin (1761–1849), secretary of the treasury 1801–14, was born in Geneva, Switzerland.

but unless different Measures be pursued, and to that End different Men be appointed, our Finances are ruined. The Revenue derived from Commerce must fail; and then, if large direct Taxes be not levied the Government must crumble to Dust.

I tell you they have hazarded our Peace. On the late outrageous Dismissal of a Minister of Peace it becomes honest Men to speak plainly. There are occasions where Self Respect imposes Silence on those who cannot applaud their Rulers: but there are Occasions, also, where Silence would be Treason. I have carefully examined the Evidence laid before the Public; and, on that Evidence, I hesitate not to say: First that frequent Efforts of Great Britain to make honorable Satisfaction for an Insult to our Flag in the Affair of the Chesapeak, have been eluded in frivolous Pretences and repelled with unjustifiable Haughtiness.[3] Secondly, that the Power of the british Minister, Mr. Erskine, to treat, respecting the orders in Council, appears to have been contained in a Letter of Instructions from the british Secretary of State; and combined with them. Thirdly that if, as is alledged, that Power was not communicated to the Members of the American Administration, they were unjustifiable in making a Compact with one who under such Circumstances, must be considered as an unauthorized Agent. Fourthly that if, on the contrary, they had a Knowlege of his Power, they were still more unjustifiable in making a Compact which, being wholly inconsistent with the known Instructions of the Minister, they could not but consider him not only as an unauthorized but also as an unfaithful agent. Fifthly that in either of the Cases supposed, the President assumed an Authority not delegated to him, either by the Laws or the Constitution, when he issued his Proclamation grounded on that Compact, because, not having been approved of by the Senate, it was not binding as a Treaty; and because, the Conditions specified in the Law not having been fulfilled, the Power granted on those Conditions did not vest in, and (of Course) could not rightfully be exercised by him. Sixthly that the peremptory Demand made on Mr. Jackson, the late british Minister, to assign the Reasons why his Sovereign did not ratify that unauthorized and unfaithful Compact was after the Explanation long before given by the british Secretary of State to the American Minister in London, unnecessary to any good Purpose.

3. On June 22, 1807, the British warship HMS *Leopard* attacked the USS *Chesapeake* off the Virginia coast. The *Chesapeake* surrendered after managing to fire just one shot; the British then boarded the ship, and removed four men they claimed were deserters from the Royal Navy.

Seventhly that the imperious and offensive Manner in which that Demand was made, by Men who could not be unconscious of the Impropriety of their own Conduct in that very Transaction, evinces a decided Spirit of Hostility. Eighthly that, altho the british Minister might justly have retorted the Charge of Perfidy, so indecently insinuated against his Sovereign, he confined himself to a calm Re-Statement of Facts (within their Knowlege) which fully justify the Rejection of a Treaty made without Authority and in Violation of Instructions. Ninthly that being disappointed in the Expectation to drive him, by their insulting Demeanor, into such Warmth of Expression as might color the contemplated Violence, they boldly accused him of insinuating Charges which, it is evident from what they themselves have published, he neither made nor insinuated; and, on the Ground of that unsupported Accusation they abruptly broke off all further Communication. Tenthly that this outrage irreconcileable with Common Sense on any other Terms, demonstrates their Predetermination not to accomodate the existing Differences with Great Britain, but on the contrary, to render the Dispute with that Nation irreconcileable. Eleventhly that an Attempt to plunge these States at the present Moment into a War with Great Britain, a War which must prove ruinous to the Commerce and (of Course) to the Revenue of our Country, which cannot but be oppressive to every Order of our Citizens, and which will (in all human Probability) prove fatal to American Freedom, can be accounted for only by Views irreconcileable with our Honor and Interest. And Twelfthly that the Conduct of the Administration towards France enables us to discover and ascertain those Views. But this leads me to the last Charge.

I say they have surrendered our Independence. It cannot be expected that I should, on this occasion, produce the Evidence which may hereafter convict them in a Court of Justice; for, while they continue in Office, it must be in their Possession or in that of their Accomplices. All that can be asked, therefore, is to shew such probable Grounds of Belief as are sufficient to direct the Conduct of reasonable Men in their important Concerns. I state then first, that while they have captiously seized and ostentatiously displayed every Incident which could excite a hostile Spirit against Britain, they have patiently borne and industriously concealed the Insults and Injuries of France. Thus, we hear loud Clamor when a british Seaman is impressed from an American Ship, but not a Whisper when hundreds of American Seamen are taken from American Ships and confined in french Dungeons. Thus, when british Orders retaliated french Decrees, our Minister in London was directed to make incessant Complaint, but the Decrees themselves excited no Murmur. Thus, if an American Ship is sent to a british Port for Adjudication a Cry is raised against that Nation as Plunderers and Pirates, but when France captures or destroys every American Ship she can catch at Sea and sequesters every Atom of American Property she can seize on Shore we hear only a Lisp of Regret that no Change has taken Place in our Relations with that Country. Whence that morbid Sensibility in one Case, and whence this ignominious Stupor in the other? Secondly I state that important Measures of our Administration appear to have been dictated by the french Emperor. Thus, when he prohibited Trade with England an Embargo was immediately laid in America. That Measure was indeed in appearance levelled alike at England and France, but when it is recollected that, the french Decree and british Orders having mutually forbidden a Commerce with the adverse Power, the former were from the Want of naval Force almost a dead Letter, while the british Navy carried the latter into full Effect so that our Commerce with France was already annihilated, it is evident that the Embargo could operate only as to England. The french Emperor viewed it in that Light. He gave it his approbation and exprest his Displeasure when it was discontinued. Thus, we have lately seen the Dismissal of the british Minister published in France at the Moment when it took Place in this Country. Such a Coincidence may be accidental but would, even if it stood alone, be suspicious; for we know that french Printers dare not make such Publications without the Emperors Permission. Coupled with attending Circumstances, such as the Refusal to receive a Minister from the Spanish Junta, the Attempt to send a Minister to the Spanish usurper, and the very questionable Mission to Russia, it acquires the Force of Evidence. We have seen it published also in France that these States are about to join in a northern League against Britain. If this Assertion be false it shews the Emperors Contempt for our Administration, and if true it proves that, while he treats our Country with wanton Outrage, they shew him every Mark of Confidence and Respect. Thirdly I consider it as strong presumptive Evidence that the Charge, tho frequently and publickly made, has never been clearly and substantially contradicted. More than a year ago the Influence of Napoleon on our Councils was openly alledged in the national House of Representatives, yet those Facts the Disclosure of which would establish or refute the Accusation are sedulously concealed. The Negotiation with Great Britain has been minutely displayed. We see with Amazement a Letter from the Secretary of State to the American Minister at the british Court, in all our Gazettes, published long before it could be received, and probably before it was sent. Why this odious Publicity on one Side and why on the other so much Secrecy and Disguise? No one will now dare pretend a Hope of adjusting our Differences with the french Emperor on any other Terms than by obediently joining him in the War against Britain. He has precluded all such Pretence, by publishing the Letter of his Minister Champagny (of the 23d of last August) to General Armstrong.[4] It is difficult to determine whether the Effrontery with which that Minister asserts the most palpable Falsehoods, the Audacity with which he prescribes our Line of Conduct, or the Contempt which he displays for the Administration and the People of America should most excite our Resentment Indignation or Abhorrence. The Publication of his Letter however, speaks a Language which cannot be misunderstood. It is the Close and Climax of french Negotiation. At first the Emperor tried to provoke us by Insult. That failing he concluded we had no Sense of Honor and gave us up to unlimited Plunder. His Pride, which requires national Submission, was not satisfied with the Obsequiousness of our Rulers while they concealed his Domination. By publishing, therefore, to all Europe Champagny's Letter he says distinctly to the American people "you shall no longer pretend Ignorance of my Contempt. Submit to my Sovereign Will or, if you dare, resist." Fellow Citizens, it becomes every man among us to ask himself whether a nation which, after hearing such Language, continues to expostulate and entreat can be considered as independent.

If you are content to lead a Life of Ignominy and become at length Slaves to some Minion of the Corsican Despot, vote for those Men who applaud

---

4. The letter of August 23, 1809, from Champagny to Armstrong, who was U.S. minister to France, was published in many American newspapers in late 1809 and early 1810 (in some papers it is dated August 22). The British, by an Order in Council (November 11, 1807), and the French, by the Milan Decree (December 17, 1807), had imposed blockades on each other, and each was claiming the right to seize neutral ships trading with the enemy. Armstrong had complained to Champagny about French seizures of American vessels. In the letter, Champagny invokes the Milan Decree, which calls upon neutral nations (such as the United States) to "force the English to respect their flags." Champagny argues that if the British revoke their Order in Council, the Milan decree will automatically be repealed, and concludes: "But it is for the United States, by their firmness, to bring on these happy results [Britain and France dropping their blockades]. Can a nation, that wishes to remain free and sovereign, ever balance between some temporary interests, and the great interests of its independence, and the maintenance of its honor, of its sovereignty, and of its dignity?" (*New-York Commercial Advertiser*, December 6, 1809, p. 3).

the national Administration. Vote for those Men who have monopolized the Offices of the State. Vote for those Men who haughtily boast that you dare not displace or even displease them. But if you wish to live free, if you wish to have a due Share in the public Councils, if you feel the honest Pride of Republicans, and if you dare shew what you feel, chuse Men to govern the State which the State need not blush to own. Chuse Men who have Dignity of Sentiment and Soul. Men who have Sense and Spirit to act their own Part not Puppets played by a Master. I therefore recommend to your notice and ask your suffrage for [evidently a list of candidates followed].

These are honest independent Americans attached to no foreign Nation. If they were taken from an obscure hiding Place, it might be needful to descant on their Qualities and Talents, but they are known tried and approved Servants of this Republic. I am perswaded they will do their Duty; and I feel a perfect Conviction that whenever the Power of the Union shall be confided to native honest and true Americans we shall regain our lost Reputation.

35 ✦ Letters to the *Evening Post* on Albert Gallatin's Plan for Enforcing the Non-Importation Act (1811)

Beginning in 1806, the Jefferson and Madison administrations enacted a series of measures restricting American commerce. They intended to use economic pressure to force Great Britain to end its practice of impressing American sailors, and to force the British and the French to respect the neutrality of American shipping. The Embargo Act of 1806 was succeeded by the Embargo Act of 1807 after the *Chesapeake* affair, then by the Non-Intercourse Act of 1809, and Macon's Bill No. 2 in 1810. These laws had little effect on the Europeans, but succeeded in devastating American commerce.[1] They also encouraged widespread smuggling.

In a report to Congress dated November 26, 1811, Treasury Secretary Albert Gallatin detailed the problems in enforcing the latest act and suggested some remedies.[2] The proposals were drastic ones, however, and indeed fell little short of Gallatin's earlier, private suggestion to Jefferson: "not a single vessel shall be permitted to move without the special permission of the Executive."[3] It does not appear that Gallatin's suggestions were ever put into effect.

When reports of Gallatin's suggestions appeared in the press, Morris was traveling from New York to Washington, where he and DeWitt Clinton were to lobby for federal support for the Erie Canal. He left New

---

1. Lance Banning gives a brief account of these measures in *The Jeffersonian Persuasion: Evolution of a Party Ideology* (Ithaca, N.Y.: Cornell University Press, 1978), 290–94.

2. The report is in the appendix to *The Debates and Proceedings in the Congress of the United States*, 12th Cong., 1st Sess. (Washington, D.C.: Printed and Published by Gales and Seaton, 1853), 2101–4, http://memory.loc.gov/cgi-bin/ampage?collId=llac &fileName=024/llaco24.db&recNum=460. Gallatin had recognized the need for harsh measures as early as 1808, urging Jefferson to provide collectors "with the general power of seizing property anywhere" (Leonard W. Levy, *Jefferson and Civil Liberties: The Darker Side* [Cambridge: Harvard University Press, 1963; repr., Chicago: Ivan R. Dee, 1989], 122).

3. Levy, *Jefferson and Civil Liberties*, 122.

York on December 4 and arrived in Washington on the 15th. We have no manuscripts of these letters, and so we cannot be completely sure that they are his. But they appear over his usual pseudonym, and their brevity is consistent with the fact that Morris was traveling and thus writing in haste. Further, in the fifth letter he mentions that he had not actually seen Gallatin's report until after some or all of the earlier essays were written, which may mean he did not see it until after his arrival in Washington.[4] Finally, the tone of the essays reflects his general opinion of the Madison administration and its policies and is consistent with views he expresses elsewhere.

[No. I. December 19, 1811]

TO THE EDITOR OF THE EVENING POST

SIR,

It is not the forlorn hope that any thing I can say will have the least effect in arousing the unwary and careless, or informing the ignorant, amongst my countrymen, that has given rise to this letter. If their utter blindness were not a judgment sent to punish national sins, the exertions of genius and learning would long ere this have restored the nation to its senses. I despair that any means merely human, can have this effect. But it may for a time arrest our progress to ruin, to examine with the utmost freedom, yet at the same time with candour and impartiality, the public acts of the

---

4. The newspapers may not have published the full report. It does not appear in the Washington, D.C., papers as far as I have been able to find. *Poulson's American Daily Advertiser,* in Philadelphia, has a brief account reprinted from the *Alexandria Gazette* on December 5: "Mr. Gallatin's letter to the committee of commerce and manufactures, yesterday read in the House of Representatives, holds out another comfortable prospect to the American people. In order more strictly to enforce the Non-Intercourse law, the Secretary recommends the appointment of Inspectors to overlook the custom house officers, the empowering of persons to search houses, &c. Where will all this folly end?"
New-York Evening Post, December 19, 1811, p. 2. Courtesy American Antiquarian Society.

government. This, at all times, is the duty of every good citizen, and particularly of those who have the management of the public journals: but it is more imperiously their duty when the nation, over whose political interests they are placed as centinels, is by any means whatever rendered supine, and totally regardless of their best interests. At such a season, the political harpies who are ever on the watch for prey stalk abroad: The liberty, the property of the citizen becomes insecure, and frequently falls in sacrifice to their ambition or avarice. No American who loves his country, and who has taken any pains to discover her true interests, can look back on the last four years of her history, without giving a sigh to the memory of her departed greatness, or *forward* to her destination, without an awful presentiment that it will serve as a warning instead of an example.

It is now almost three weeks since a report was presented to the American Congress, by the Secretary of the Treasury, recommending for their adoption, as the supreme law of the land, a set of measures, which the basest minion of the most powerful monarch in Europe, would, even in the present period of despotic tyranny, have recommended with hesitation and alarm—Yet in America, a land where civil and religious liberty were supposed to exist in a degree beyond the experience of any other people: In America, where our forefathers voluntarily undertook, and persevered in, a bloody & cruel war, for seven long years, striving against every discouragement, enduring every hardship, & suffering every privation, rather than submit to the smallest infringement of their personal liberty, *their* children have, without even a single public expression of disapprobation, received in their supreme legislature & published in every journal throughout the land, a report which, if adopted, lays the axe at the root of public and private liberty—a report which robs every dwelling of its sanctity, takes away the constitutional provision of a trial by jury, and removes every barrier which the laws have thrown around private property by declaring that *no testimony* shall be received in opposition to the *opinion* of its own officers. And who is the man, (fit instrument of the most gloomy despotism!) that has dared to propose so monstrous an invasion of private right? To the shame of the country which gave birth to a Rosseau, to the still greater disgrace and shame of the American nation, which he rules with a rod of iron, he is a Genevan.

Permit me here to close this letter—I feel unable to control the indignant feelings of my heart, and wish, in the discussion to which I may be lead, to avoid every intemperate expression.

AN AMERICAN.

TO THE EDITOR OF THE EVENING POST.

SIR,

The oppressive measures which, under various plausible pretexts, have lately been introduced into the country, are the offspring of that love of power, which proceed towards its object regardless of means or consequences. In the bosom of that man whose object is dominion, every other passion holds a subordinate station. The nearer he approaches towards its attainment, the more eager he grows in the pursuit, and the more open and daring in the means he employs. The same person who, at one time, from his ardent attachment to liberty and the rights of the citizen, boldly ventures to "*stop de veels of government*," and, to get rid of a trifling tax which he feels a little oppressive, exposes his neck to the halter, is transformed in the short period of twelve years, into a second Jehu; furiously riding over the necks of the people, and trampling upon their dearest rights.[5] Who could have believed that the man, who dared to charge our beloved Washington with the support of an act violating private rights, and intended to destroy public liberty, would himself so soon have proposed to take away the trial by jury, and throw open the sanctuary of the citizen to the rude and lawless inspection of a hungry banditti, governed by no better motive than self-aggrandizement! Those old and sagacious patriots, who had already passed in safety through one revolution, risking all that was dear to man, to accomplish their country's deliverance, who, when it was accomplished, regardless of popular clamour, steadily and firmly pursued the course de-

New-York Evening Post, December 21, 1811, p. 2. Courtesy American Antiquarian Society.

5. Three different issues are covered in this sentence. First, as a leader of Republicans in Congress in the 1790s, Gallatin used the House's power of the purse as a way of thwarting the Federalist administrations. Second, Gallatin's western Pennsylvania congressional district was a scene of the Whiskey Rebellion. Although he participated in some meetings, it is an exaggeration to suggest that he had been an active participant in the rebellion. (See Raymond Walters, *Albert Gallatin: Jeffersonian Financier and Diplomat* [New York: Macmillan, 1957], 65–86, for a more sympathetic treatment.) Third is the Biblical parallel. Jehu overthrew Joram, a successor of Jeroboam. The story is told in 2 Kings 9–10; the relevant verse seems to be 10:31: "But Jehu took no heed to walk in the law of the Lord God of Israel with all his heart: for he departed not from the sins of Jeroboam, which made Israel to sin."

manded by her honour, her interest and her safety, they did expect such conduct from such a man, and with a foresight which would have immortalized an ancient seer, they then proclaimed it to the nation with a confidence, which the event has fully justified. But they spoke to the wind. As easily can the raging of the sea be controlled and composed, when the tempest tears it up, as the popular mind, when passion and prejudice have driven reason from her seat. But I am approaching a subject which has been so often, without any effect, brought home to the very senses of the people, that to present it again, even under the form of a mathematical demonstration, would be an absurdity of which I shall not be guilty.

Mr. Gallatin's report to Congress on the subject of the non-importation act, is grounded on the presumption that all the American merchants are without principle, and the foreign agents of the government unworthy of any credit. If this were really the fact (and the charge comes with a very bad grace from a foreigner whose life a forfeit to the offended laws was spared by the mercy of the government),[6] the remedy proposed by Mr. Gallatin is far worse than the disease it would attempt to cure. And if this were really the fact, where are we to look for the cause of so rapid and so total a depreciation of honorable sentiment and conduct, in a body of men, to whose integrity and fair dealing, the experience of every mercantile nation bore ample testimony? What sir, must have been the policy of that government, what the inevitable tendency of its measures, which, in the short space of four years, completely have demoralized the great mass of its population? And what *ought* to be the feelings of the most injured and insulted country, when the very man, whose bad head and worse heart gave birth to those measures, who did all he could to produce such [one or two lines are obscured here], offers his alternatives as if unconscious that a choice is only proposed between disgrace and ruin—I ask, what *ought* to be their feelings? For alas, it is too evident that an indifference amounting almost to total apathy, pervades the public mind on this, and every other subject, unconnected with party politics.

But strong as have been the temptations to a general disregard of the commercial regulations of the government; insulted in his character and injured in his property, as the merchant in this country has been; although forced to suffer the abominable tyranny of the petty tyrant of the cus-

6. See the previous note. Morris implies that Gallatin was not prosecuted for his role in the Whiskey Rebellion thanks to the government's clemency; in fact, there was no evidence to support charges (Walters, *Albert Gallatin*, 83–85).

tom house, and to see that property which industry and enterprise had just brought within his reach, torn from him by the eager hand of the legalized robber, although forced to see and to suffer all this, yet he is not the wretch the right honourable Secretary would persuade us to believe him to be. It is true the loss of his property affects him—it is true, the very gorge of his soul rises in abhorrence against the man whom he regards as equally the scourge of his country, and his individual oppressor. And when he beholds his wife and children, through his instrumentality, deprived of their support, he cannot help raising his eyes in anguish to heaven, and asking, ah why was this foreigner ever suffered to land on our peaceable shores!

AN AMERICAN.

[No. III. December 23, 1811]

TO THE EDITOR OF THE EVENING POST.

SIR,

   The first measure proposed in Mr. Gallatin's official report, for the prevention of frauds on the part of the merchant, is the establishment of an inquisitorial tribunal, which is to be paramount to the constitution, the laws, and indeed to the whole jurisprudence of the country.[7] The Constitution of the United States has reserved to every citizen the inalienable right of a trial by his peers in every case affecting his life, his liberty, or his property. So very precious have the different states esteemed this valuable privilege, that even in the most trivial subjects of controversy, for the determination of which petty magistrates have generally been deemed sufficient, the right of demanding a jury of their country, has always been expressly reserved to either party. It may indeed be called the leading characteristic feature which marks the distinction between free and despotic governments; for as

New-York Evening Post, December 23, 1811, p. 2. Courtesy American Antiquarian Society.

   7. At issue here is the second part of the first proposal: "2. To direct a summary mode, by sworn examiners, to decide, at the time of arrival, on the origin of the article, which decision shall be admitted as conclusive evidence in case of trial." Morris objects on the ground that in American law, jury decisions were conclusive as to the facts in dispute—a right enshrined in the Seventh Amendment.

long as the judgment of twelve indifferent and impartial men, unbiassed by
the hope of gain or the dread of injury, must finally settle every subject of
controversy between men, so long will a reasonable security be continued
for life, for liberty, and property. Before such a tribunal every citizen can
appear with a confidence in exact proportion to the justice of his cause. On
the fairness and the strength of his testimony, he relies as the sole ground
on which a judgment will be given either for or against him. Here no tale-
bearer who catches from every breath the insinuations of malice or revenge, dare shew his face. The hearsays and opinions of friends or enemies,
are alike disregarded. The fact alone is to be determined, and that determination must be *according to evidence*. What Sir, is the proposition of Mr. Gallatin? That examiners shall be appointed in every district (by whom?) who
shall *inspect* the different articles of merchandize imported into this country, and declare in what place that merchandize was manufactured, or in
what part of the world it was produced, and their *opinion* shall be decisive
of the fact!!!

Let no obsequious office hunter or determined party man, presume to
offer as an apology for this daring blow at the liberties of the country, that
to these inspectors evidence of the fact may be submitted. What American in whose veins runs a single drop of that blood which achieved their
glorious revolution, would not spurn the base permission? But miserable as
would be the apology, our lordly Secretary has rejected it altogether. What
is the reason he gives for the establishment of this inquisition? And on
what ground is it to be defended? The frauds, the perjuries, the deceptions
practised by the Merchant in procuring and preparing this very evidence.
False invoices, false bills of lading, false certificates from their foreign correspondents, false clearances, false consular documents, are declared to be
the very ground work of these illegal and fraudulent practices. The officers of this inquisition are told in so many words, that their own *senses* are
to be the sole intention for their *judgment*, and that *their judgment* is to be
final. Well then citizens of *free* and *united* America, Mr. Gallatin will very
kindly relieve you from the trouble, expense, and delay of furnishing yourselves with any particulars of the property you may hereafter receive from
abroad. *They* are altogether false and fraudulent; and if you wish to preserve
your characters as fair and honorable men, you will wait the result of this
Treasury examination, before you enter your goods at the Custom House
according to your own knowledge and belief; lest you should unwarily incur the guilt, or at least become liable to all the pains and penalties, of
wilful and corrupt perjury. For if Mr. Gallatin or his agents have sagacity

enough to discover the particulars of growth, product and manufacture, by their own sight, taste, or smell: and upon this evidence alone can legally take away the property of a citizen, I see no reason under heaven why the same evidence shall not also deprive him of his liberty if a custom-house officer's *oath* be opposed to it. Permit me to congratulate you fellow citizens, on the exquisite gratification of having at the head of your Treasury a man of *infinite* penetration and who has the still more wonderful faculty of endowing either Mr. Schenck,[8] or Mr. anybody else, with equal intelligence at his pleasure.

AN AMERICAN.

[No. IV. December 24, 1811]

TO THE EDITOR OF THE EVENING POST.

SIR,

It is a most consoling reflection to a good man, that over the affairs of this world there is an all-wise Providence, who taketh the wise in his own craftiness, and causeth the folly and wickedness of man to praise him.[9] As applied to him, causes and effects are words of no meaning: for in his hand the meanest instrument is sufficient to bring about the greatest event. When in the course of his Providence, a solid foundation was to be laid for the liberties of Great-Britain, the insulting conduct of a petty officer to a peasant girl, was overruled for its accomplishment;* and when the time for

8. Peter A. Schenck was surveyor of the customs for the District of the City of New York from 1806 to 1814.
New-York Evening Post, December 24, 1811, p. 2. Courtesy American Antiquarian Society.
9. The first phrase is from Job 5:13; Paul quotes it in 1 Corinthians 3:19. The second may be Psalm 76:10 paraphrased or quoted from memory: "Surely the wrath of man shall praise thee: the remainder of wrath shalt thou restrain."

* During the reign of Richard II. an oppressive tax of three groats was laid upon every person who had attained a certain age; and this was exacted in a most unjust and arbitrary manner. One of those pests, vulgarly called tax gatherers, applied to a blacksmith for three groats for his daughter, who, the father declared, was under age. The tax man offered in a most indecent and insulting manner to prove she was of sufficient age, upon which the blacksmith struck him dead with his sledge. The

the independence of this country had arrived, a trifling duty, objectionable only on account of the principle it involved, gave rise to the contest in
which it eventuated. But altho' He can bring good out of evil, it is not less
the duty of every good man to prevent that evil as far as his individual exertions can do it, by detecting and exposing its authors. In this country we
appear to be almost left to ourselves, and to the consequences of our own
wilful folly. Public good has given place to private advantage; and to retain
the emolument of office, the peace, the liberty, and the honor of the nation
are hazarded without scruple. Is it then to be wondered at, that amidst this
universal scrambling, attempts should be made by ambitious individuals, to
obtain any unlawful degree of power and consequence? Is it to be wondered
at, that attempts should be made to steal away the liberties of the people?
It is not; nor is at all unreasonable to expect, that at a future day some adventurer, more daring than the common herd, in the confusion occasioned
by his own sly arts, will attempt to grasp an imperial sceptre—Already is
the commerce of the country annihilated. Already are measures recommended, far better suited to the meridian of the French capital, than of
these states. The property of the merchant is to be arrested from him at the
will of the custom house officer; the house of every citizen to be entered
and searched at his discretion. That scourge and pest of every country, the
informer, is let loose to prowl at large, confident of his prey—What has
he to fear? The law allows him to search in dwelling-houses for prohibited
merchandise—The mere opinion of his comrade can determine any thing
he may then fancy, to be prohibited. The examination is at an end, & the
property changes owners. I ask, where under *such a law* is the security for
any private right whatever? Life and liberty as well as property might, and
probably will, very frequently become the sacrifice. I will not say that these
measures are proposed to feel the pulse of the nation, that they are the anterior presages of a systematic attack upon public liberty—But I do say,
that if we had at the head of this nation, a subtle, ambitious bold intriguer;
or a quiet, easy, diffident man, with *one* of *such* qualities at his elbow, and
such measures were patiently endured, I should tremble for the liberty of
my country.

AN AMERICAN.

---

whole country immediately flew to arms, and finally obtained many very important
privileges, which could never have been obtained by negociation, and which in fact
the country was not fully prepared to enjoy. [*Hume's History.*]

Who knows what one of the Genevan domiciliary visits may yet effect?

TO THE EDITOR OF THE EVENING POST

SIR,

In one of the first amendments to the Constitution of the United States, an omission in that instrument (a casual one no doubt) was supplied, which appears to the common sense of a plain man like myself, to be *somewhat* in opposition to the second measure proposed by Mr. Gallatin. It is in these words — "The *right* of the people to be secure in their persons, *houses*, papers and effects, against *unreasonable searches and seizures* shall not be *violated:* and no warrants shall issue but upon *probable* cause, supported by *oath or affirmation*, and particularly describing the *place* to be searched, and the persons or *things* to be *seized*." The *right* thus reserved by the states in their compact with each other, is also expressly reserved by the people (I believe) in all the state constitutions. It is a right which they never did, and I trust they never will give up, but at the point of the bayonet; for the moment that, under the colour of law, (no matter what the pretext be) this right can be violated with impunity, that moment is the last of our liberty. The official report of the Secretary of the Treasury, solemnly and with due consideration made, to my comprehension recommends to Congress a direct and positive infringement of this article of the Constitution. I have not the report by me, but by the abstract made of it and published in all the papers, I understand a discretionary power is proposed to be lodged in the hands of the inspectors of the customs, to enter at their pleasure the dwelling-house of any citizen to search for prohibited articles;* no warrant is to be issued,

---

New-York Evening Post, December 26, 1811, pp. 2–3. Courtesy American Antiquarian Society.

* Since the above was written I have obtained a copy of the report itself. A remark of considerable importance which, on the very cursory perusal I was at first able to give it, entirely escaped notice, is here subjoined. It is the very artful manner in which this flagitious measure is wrapped up. It is contained in the fourth suggestion (we all have felt the force of Mr. Gallatin's suggestions!) which appears to relate solely to the prevention of smuggling from Canada. The whole paragraph consists of three sentences, of which the first and last are only applicable to the concerns of a particular district. Thus artfully smuggled, a superficial reader (out of that district) would run over it without the slightest idea that he had any personal concern in it;

no oath or affirmation of probable cause, no description whatever of the place to be searched, or the thing to be seized. Under such a law, the mere will of any one of Mr. Schenck's creatures, at any hour of *the night*, might burst open the doors of the most peaceful and unoffending citizen; search in every place of concealment; tear up the floors—nay, drag from under the terrified women and children the very beds on which they were slumbering! Will any man tell me that this picture is a fanciful extravagance; that it can never be realized; that no one would hazard the consequences with which the indignation of the *people* would overwhelm its authors? And, fellow citizens, are you prepared to place this enormous power in the hands of any man, under the ridiculous expectation that it will not be abused— When was ever such power entrusted to any human being and exercised with perfect propriety? But to what description of men are your most private retirements to be thus exposed? To your judges, your magistrates, the first and the best men of your city; to candid, impartial, honest and well-meaning citizens, who take no share of your spoil, and are more interested in your quiet than in your disturbance? No. Such characters could find under the provisions of the constitution and the existing laws, the means of enforcing obedience and restraining licentiousness. No. Such characters are not wanted, they must be kept in awe! It is to the inspectors of the custom-house, who like the pestilence, walk in darkness. It is to the very man, under whose oppressive exercise of an authority very far short of this, the city of N. York groans and dies: whose appetite for gold, insatiate as the grave, can never be appeased—it is to such men, fellow-citizens, that you are to be asked to throw open the doors of your habitations! It is to such men that whatever you possess of curious, or valuable, or convenient, is to be submitted for *their opinion*, of *its* growth, product, or manufacture.

I am sensible Sir, that to very many of my fellow citizens a subject of

---

separated from its arbitrary connexion, its awful extent and meaning becomes intelligible to every capacity.[10]

10. Gallatin's fourth suggestion reads: "It is believed that the prevention of smuggling from Canada depends more on the vigilance and activity of the collectors, and persons employed by them, than on any additional legal provision. It seems, however, necessary to extend generally to inspectors the power of searching houses, which, by the collection law, is given only to the collectors, or persons acting under a special appointment for each case. It has also been suggested that a permission to import salt from Canada would, in other respects, facilitate the execution of the law."

importance as this, will bring deep and solemn reflections. Accustomed as they have been to constant innovations on their constitutional rights, to repeated experiments upon the strength of their attachments to them, and at every new blow to retire without a struggle and almost without a murmur, they were not conscious of the sacrifice *now* demanded of them. Their misfortunes and their sufferings have left them but little time for examination. But I trust sir, a greater attention will hereafter be given to the acts, of the government and its officers, and that the editor of this, and other public journals, will not be found asleep at their posts when the enemy is so near.

AN AMERICAN.

[No. VI. December 27, 1811]

FOR THE NEW-YORK EVENING POST.

SIR,

A few remarks on the remaining heads of Mr. Gallatin's report will close these numbers. The indignant feelings which gave them birth, may have drawn from me expressions somewhat different from the soft and courtly strains to which his ears have been accustomed. But I trust that in no part of them is to be found a single perversion of the truth. The fifth article of the ninth section of the constitution contains the following provisions: first "that no tax or duties shall be laid on articles exported from any state"— second "that no preference shall be given, by any regulation of commerce or revenue, to the ports of one state over those of another"; and third "*that no vessels bound to, or from one state, shall be obliged to enter, clear or pay duties in another.*" Let us now turn to Mr. Gallatin. "In relation to coasting vessels it is proposed, first, that they *should be obliged to enter and clear,* though *ostensibly* bound to *another port* in the *same,* or an *adjacent state;* making only the proper exception in favor of Packets, or of vessels employed solely within the same."[11]

What words can convey more perfect contradiction? Sir, in the very face

---

New-York Evening Post, December 27, 1811, p. 3. Courtesy American Antiquarian Society.

11. This is Gallatin's second suggestion. Morris or the editor omits the last three words, "river or bay."

of his own solemn oath, Mr. Gallatin has recommended to the Congress of the American people, a *violation in terms* of that constitution which is the sole security for our liberties, and which they also have sworn to support; and that Congress have referred to the consideration of a committee, the expediency and propriety of giving their sanction to the deed!

To multiply words on this subject would be idle. If the simple knowledge of the fact, thus solemnly pressed on their consciences, lead not to its punishment, it is in vain to talk—The record of it will forever remain a foul blot upon the history of these states. Perhaps it may find our children groaning under the oppression of a tyrant, and will serve to shew them how their liberties were lost.

The appointment of Commissioners to overlook the different Collectors, to ensure their fidelity and vigilance, and report annually to the *Treasury*, is also to me a subject of alarm. I see in it an immense addition to the already *over-powering* influence of the *Treasury*, and anticipate from it no advantage to my country. There are about forty districts in the United States: Appoint in each of these, four men of the greatest political weight and influence; give to them a respectable salary, and let them be dependant for its continuance upon the will of a Secretary of the Treasury, and your country may not long have cause to thank you for the money you have saved her.

The servile imitation of French frippery, is another feature in this report, to which I would call the serious attention of my countrymen. It is not, however, on account of any mischievous effects immediately to be apprehended from it. The certificate of origin, connected with the new mode of trial recommended by Mr. Gallatin, is incapable of doing either good or harm. It is not intended to influence the *opinion* of the *examiners;* nor is it in any way calculated to afford security to the Merchants. It gives them no other promise than the liberty of an entry, and the difference is not very material whether their property be torn from them before or after that formality.

The introduction of licences is another hopeful plant from the same soil; a mere empty compliment to the Emperor of France and King of Italy "our good and great ally." I confess sir, when I consider the present state of our country, taking her last look at the fair fields of peace and happiness which she has so long considered as her home; about to enter upon a new and untried scene, a dreary waste covered with dark and gloomy clouds, with guides, weak and ignorant at best, perhaps treacherous, and a friend, strong and powerful, but deceitful, perfidious and wicked, my hopes are overborne by the weight of my apprehensions. But we have one certain resource still left us: that Almighty Being who rides in the whirlwind and directs the storm, in whose presence and before whose power all the nations of the earth are as the small dust of the balance, can accomplish her deliverance. He alone can do it. Let all his people join in imploring his merciful interposition and unite their exertions with those of every well disposed citizen to remove the causes which have brought his judgements upon the land.

AN AMERICAN.

As early as 1777, Morris advocated building canals to connect the Great
Lakes with the eastern seaboard. Morgan Lewis later recalled that on
a visit to General Schuyler's headquarters after the evacuation of Fort
Ticonderoga, "Mr. Morris, whose temperament admitted of no alliance
with despondency,"

> announced in language highly poetic, and to which I cannot do justice,
> that at no very distant day, the waters of the great western inland seas,
> would, by the aid of man, break through their barriers and mingle with
> those of the Hudson.[1]

Although eventually many came to share in Morris's grand vision, it was
not until 1810, when Thomas Eddy and State Senator Jonas Platt persuaded DeWitt Clinton of the merits of a canal, that any action took
place. That April, Platt introduced legislation creating a Commission on
Internal Navigation and naming seven members, including Clinton and
Morris. In June 1810 the Commission began an expedition across western New York, then largely wilderness, to survey possible canal routes.
Its first report, in March 1811, was written primarily by Morris, who had
been elected chairman by his fellow members. That report showed that a
canal was practicable; the next month, the legislature extended the com-

---

Report of the Commissioners Appointed by an Act of the Legislature of the State of New-York,
Entitled "An Act to provide for the Improvement of the Internal Navigation of the State,"
Passed April 8th, 1811. For the Consideration of all Matters Relating to the Said Inland
Navigation (Albany: Printed by S. Southwick, 1812). American Antiquarian Society
Early American Imprints, series II (Shaw-Shoemaker), no. 26285. Courtesy Ameri-
can Antiquarian Society. A draft of the report in Morris's hand is in the Gouverneur
Morris Papers, Rare Book and Manuscript Library, Columbia University, item 861.
Morris discusses the other commissioners' acceptance of his draft report in his diary
entries of March 8–11, 1812.

    1. Letter to Hermanus Bleeker, May 26, 1828. The letter is included in the appen-
dix of David Hosack, *Memoir of DeWitt Clinton* (New York: J. Seymour, 1829), 250.

mission's mandate and added Robert Fulton and Robert Livingston as members. Among its new tasks was to investigate sources for financing the project.

In December 1811, Morris and Clinton went to Washington to seek federal funding. They received a cool reception from President Madison and Treasury Secretary Albert Gallatin, and were rebuffed by Congress as well. This report, drafted by Morris in February and March of 1812, reflects the commissioners' determination to move forward with the canal, even though New York would have to finance the entire project itself.

⋅⟨⟩⋅⟨⟩⋅

The Commissioners appointed in and by an Act to provide for the Improvement of the Internal Navigation of the State, beg leave to
REPORT:

That, in obedience to the directions of the said act, they made application to Congress and to the Legislatures of the several states and territories, copies of which are annexed in the papers marked No. 1, and No. 2.[2] They conceived it proper also, to address the President of the United States, on the subject of their appointment, and annex a copy of their letter to him, No. 3.

Moreover, considering the magnitude of the object, they deemed it advisable to depute two of their members to the general government, with their letter to the President, and application to the Senate and House of Representatives. A copy of the report made by that deputation, on the 24th of last month, is also annexed, marked No. 4. It appears from this report that, although it be uncertain whether the national government will do any thing, it is certain they will do nothing from which immediate aid can be derived. The deputation found itself obliged, by prudential considerations, not only to blend the navigation between Lake Erie and Hudson's river, with objects, some of which are subservient to local interest, but to refrain from asking an advance or even an appropriation of money. The utmost they hoped to obtain was a grant of land. A grant so limited as not to take effect until after the canal should be completed, at the expense of New-York.

---

2. The appendices have been omitted.

It might have been expected that so moderate a request, (coupled with the offer that no toll should be taken) would have been immediately granted.

The motives which led to doubt and delay, are unknown to the commissioners; and their profound respect for those to whom is committed the conduct of our national affairs, forbids them to hazard a conjecture. But if the offer had been, or should be accepted, still the canal is to be made by the state. So that if the bounty of Congress had granted the entreated boon, it would have been merely the purchase, at less than its cost, of a most valuable object; by paying for it a tract of unsaleable land.

The commissioners, in their first report, took the liberty to express the opinion, that an offer of the canal should be made to the national government; and they saw with pleasure and with pride, that the Legislature (concurring in this opinion) adopted the most honorable measures for inducing the United States to acquire it. But, the offer made and not accepted, the state is at liberty to consult and pursue the maxims of policy. These seem imperatively to demand that the canal be made by her, and for her own account, as soon as circumstances will permit. It is believed that a revenue may be derived from it, far exceeding the interest of what it will cost; and it seems just that those of our citizens who have no immediate interest in the work, should find retribution for their share of the cost (if any) in a revenue which will lessen their future contributions. Whether this subject be considered with a view to commerce and finance, or on the more extensive scale of policy, there would be a want of wisdom, and almost of piety, not to employ for public advantage those means which divine providence has placed so completely within our power.

The commissioners have received some replies to the applications they made to the states and territories.

The Legislature of Tennesee, on the 16th of November, resolved that their Senators and Representatives should be requested to support any laudable attempts made to the Congress of the United States, soliciting the aid of the general government in relation to the canal navigation between Hudson's river and the great lakes.

On the 4th of November the Legislature of New-Jersey say,

> Although we feel a deep interest in promoting every attempt to open a communication, by means of canal navigation, between the great lakes and the navigable rivers running through the Atlantic states; and are fully sensible that such communication would tend to enrich, consolidate and strengthen the union; yet as we have not sufficient means for

completing the plans of public improvement within this state already projected, and deemed of the first importance to our immediate prosperity, it would not be advisable, at present, to lend assistance to improvements in other states. And although we anticipate with pleasure, judging from the enlightened policy hitherto pursued in extending public improvements by our national government, that the time is not far distant when, from the rapidly encreasing wealth of our country, the vast plans of extending canal navigation will be carried into effect, so as to form a chain of communications from the waters of the Hudson river to the great lakes, and from the lakes to the Missisippi: Yet, as that period has not arrived, we see nothing to warrant us in giving instructions to our representatives in Congress, as to the measures they shall pursue, when this subject shall come before them.

The Legislature of Connecticut, at a general assembly holden at New-Haven, on the second Thursday of October, resolved that it was inexpedient to take any measures on the application of the commissioners appointed by the state of New-York for opening a communication by means of a canal navigation between the great lakes and Hudson's river. The reasons assigned by the committee, on whose report the resolution was made, were, that the state could not supply money, and (having elected able men to assist in the councils of the nation) confided national interests to the unbiassed judgment of those whose duty it was to attend to them, and whose means of information are such as to enable them to perform that duty in the best manner.

The Legislature of Vermont, on the 30th and 31st October, expressed the opinion that the object was well worthy of consideration; but conceiving the period when they received the communication to be too late to decide on a subject of such importance, they postponed the further consideration to their next session.

On the 29th and 30th of January, the Legislature of Massachusetts, with the impartial and dignified wisdom of conscious greatness, resolved unanimously that the Senators of that commonwealth should be instructed, and their representatives requested, to use their influence for promoting, by all reasonable encouragement, (in such mode as Congress in their wisdom might direct) the opening of a communication, by means of a canal navigation, between the great lakes and Hudson's river: regard being had to the special benefit which would accrue to the state of New-York from the accomplishment of that project.

The Legislature of Ohio, also, have (as will be perceived by the message of his excellency the Governor) fully approved of the plan.

The commissioners have moreover received a paper signed Reuben Attwater, acting Governor of Michigan, A. B. Woodward, J. Witherell, and countersigned Jos: Watson, secretary, which is of the following purport: "Whereas the commissioners of internal navigation in the state of New-York have addressed to the Governor and Judges of the Territory of Michigan, certain communications relative to a canal in the state of New-York, which being considered, resolved unanimously, that in the opinion of the undersigned, the canal contemplated by the commissioners of internal navigation in the state of New-York, from Black Rock to Rome would not be so desirable as a canal round the cataract of Niagara, and another by the Falls of the Oswego. Passed the tenth day of January, one thousand eight hundred and twelve."

The commissioners have too much respect for these gentlemen to suppose they would have given this opinion without information and consideration. Wherefore, they must infer that the information received was not founded in fact; or that, not having habitually turned their attention to objects of this sort, they are not so well qualified to judge, as the consciousness of intelligence respecting matters more familiar to their minds may have led them to suppose. The commissioners, previous to their former report, viewed the country, caused surveys to be made, obtained all the information in their power, listened to the reasons on either side with impartial attention; and although they have not the vanity to oppose their judgment to that of professional men, persist in believing that the conclusions they drew were not unfounded. They feel so much the more confidence in their opinion, as it accords with that of Mr. Weston, whose abilities as an engineer (in this particular department) are unquestioned. To that gentleman their report was transmitted by one of his friends; and in reply (after treating of the means to obtain sufficient water at the summit level of Rome) he says "supposing your fears on this subject to be removed, you have no further obstacles to encounter, in your progress westward, until you arrive at Oswego falls. From thence to Oswego is the great work. I know not whether I ever declared that it was *impossible* to conduct a canal by this route, I should rather think it was the technical term *impracticable*, of course restricted in the sense mentioned in the report; and under those limitations, I still deem it so; and such I am pursuaded it will be declared by every *practical* professional man. But supposing your wishes accomplished, the question then occurs, would the trade of the lakes be directed into this channel, from its natural one down the St. Lawrence. On the superior facilities afforded by this river, for the transportation of produce, I perfectly agree with the commissioners, having traversed it twice between Kingston and Montreal, and each time viewed it very attentively. I can therefore assert with confidence, that I know of no existing navigation, of such extent, which can be rendered perfect at so small an expense. However, should your noble plan, of uniting Lake Erie with the Hudson, be carried into effect, you have to fear no rivalry. The commerce of the enormous extent of country bordering on the upper lakes, is yours forever; and to such an incalculable amount as would baffle all conjecture to conceive."

If the Michigan gentlemen were alone in their opinion, it might be useless to say any thing, seeing there is little probability that any contribution will be required from them. But there are, it is said, men of influential character who preach the same doctrine. To this effect they assume, what remains to be proved, not only that lock navigation by the falls of Oswego and cataract of Niagara is practicable, but that it is both cheaper and better than a canal direct from the Niagara to the Hudson river. On the practicability it would be superfluous to add a remark; for those who believe they can, from a cursory view or no view at all, judge better than such men as Mr. Weston, after critical examination of the ground, will hardly expect to obtain the confidence of others, however great their reliance on themselves. Nevertheless, these gentlemen are entreated seriously to consider whether it be prudent, or even honest, to hazard misleading those who think well of them, and thereby involving the state in great and fruitless expense. And this must be the consequence of undertaking the work they recommend. That the cost will be great is certified by all who possess competent judgment and information. That it will be fruitless may be proved by facts visible to every one, who chooses to open his eyes. In the gazettes of this city are advertised the rates at which goods will be carried from the ports of lake Ontario, to Ogdensburgh, and thence to Montreal. The first are lower than have heretofore prevailed between Lewis town and Oswego. The second are fifty-five cents in scows, and eighty-eight cents in boats, for a barrel of flour. But to ascend Oswego river by locks, and then, after crossing Oneida lake, to ascend Wood creek in boats, which, for great part of the way, must be rowed by men, would, it is believed, cost not less than fifty cents per barrel; because, if three men bring up thirty barrels in five days, at fifty cents per barrel, they would earn only one dollar per day each; allowing for toll nothing, for delay while waiting for freight nothing, for wear and tear of the boat nothing, and nothing for the return empty, if no freight should offer.

Thus it seems probable that produce could not be taken from Oswego to Rome, for less than from Ogdensburgh to Montreal; so that the communication which professional men, after due examination, consider as impracticable, unless at an enormous expense, wholly disproportionate to the object, but which some gentlemen assume, without examination, to be very simple, would, if completed, be of no avail. Instead of drawing to us the trade of our neighbors, it would turn much of our trade to them. Farmers who cannot send their produce by land, from beyond Geneva to Albany, must carry it to one of the few bad harbors on Lake Ontario, thence to wait the arrival of schooners from Ogdensburgh. But, it is certain, even if a commerce with those vast regions which surround the great lakes, be put out of the question, that the inhabitants of our western counties must be greatly benefitted by a navigable canal, dug at a distance from Lake Ontario. Let the mind be turned to a tract of country, fifty miles wide, and stretched out east and west on the south side of that lake. It cannot be denied that, if good harbours were abundant on its shores, and if the adjacent country offered good roads, the average distance of land carriage must be at least twenty-five miles. But, inasmuch as the harbours are few, it must be sixty or seventy from many parts of the tract. Under these circumstances, let it be supposed that a canal should be run east and west through the middle. As that would be accessible in every part, it is evident that the extreme distance of land carriage would be less than the mean distance at present. The conclusion is so clear, that to say more would not shew proper respect to the wisdom of the Legislature. There is another part of the subject, however, which stands in close connexion with what has just been advanced, and which, coming in support of Mr. Weston's opinion on the effect of the canal in securing to this state the commerce of the western world, it would be unjust to withhold.

The commissioners pray leave, then, to revert to and develope the basis of a calculation stated in their first report. Two horses can, in still water, draw a boat laden with fifty tons at the rate of two miles and a half in an hour, wherefore the progress in eight hours will be twenty miles. This, then, is the smallest distance which can reasonably be expected in one day. Now, as three men will be required to manage and steer a boat, the daily allowance of five dollars may be made for men and horses, being one dollar each; and that is surely enough. But a further allowance must be made for use of the boat, profit of the owner, and time unavoidably lost. It may be well to appropriate to these objects all the return freight, and charge the whole expense, to and fro, on what may be called the export cargo. This will, of course, double the amount, and bring it to ten dollars for twenty miles, or fifty cents per mile. Wherefore the extent of what it can cost to transport fifty tons one mile, on a canal, being fifty cents, the rate is one cent per ton per mile. To this, perhaps, it will be objected, that experience in this state does by no means justify so low an estimate. But there is no such experience, for there is no canal navigation in the state: and the commissioners have already, in their first report, stated the objections to following rivers, creeks, brooks and torrents, by the main strength of men, instead of drawing boats by horses along the tranquil surface of a canal.

Let it be supposed that the windings of a canal will so far exceed those of the present road, as that the length from lake Erie to Hudson's river shall be three hundred and fifty miles; consequently that the transportation of a ton will cost three hundred and fifty cents. To this let two hundred and fifty more be added, for toll, the amount will then be six hundred cents per ton; and taking ten barrels of flour to a ton, the transportation of each barrel will cost sixty cents. If to this twenty cents be added for freight to New-York, the total will be but eighty cents, from the port of discharge on Lake Erie, to the commercial emporium of New-York, and the risque of this route is so trifling as not to merit notice. By the advertisement already alluded to, it appears that the lowest price of freight (and for part of the way in hazardous craft) is ninety-three cents per barrel of flour, from Lewistown to Montreal. Instead of adding for insurance, let something be taken away, and let it be supposed that hereafter both freight and insurance shall cost but ninety cents, even then nine barrels of flour will be taken from above the falls of Niagara to New-York, for the same price that eight can be taken now from below those falls to Montreal. The expense of passing from Lake Erie to Lake Ontario must be added. And here, let it be asked, what kind of locks are those which gentlemen project round the cataract of Niagara. Every expense which may be needful to facilitate the navigation through the rapid at Black Rock must be encountered, in the one case as in the other. But when a large vessel, from Lake Erie, shall have brought her cargo to within a small distance of the cataract, it would be ridiculous to put it on board of small boats merely to descend by locks, to Lake Ontario, and then put it again on board of large vessels to cross that Lake. It would be equally ridiculous to attempt the transportation, on either Lake, in small boats. The locks, then to be of use, must be such as will take up and let down vessels which navigate the lakes. These then are the locks which the state is desired to make, in the expectation that after a vessel from the upper lakes shall have descended into Ontario, she will stop at the difficult and dangerous port of Oswego, instead of going on easily and safely to Ogdensburgh. The inventors and abettors of this project may have the best and most patriotic intentions, but their scheme, if carried into effect, would encrease (by the resources of New-York) the wealth of Canada and the power of Great-Britain. Before this subject be dismissed it may not be improper to compare the expense of transportation on a canal with that on a turnpike road. The cost of carriage from Albany to Utica, by land, is seventy-five cents per hundred, or fifteen dollars per ton. Were the distance one hundred miles, (which it is not) one fifth of it, or twenty miles, would cost three dollars, and forty miles would cost six. The proposed canal will, then, to every useful purpose, produce the same effect as if Lake Erie were brought within forty miles of Hudson's river. In other words, the great Lakes, those inland seas, admitting of a navigation with vessels of the largest burthen, and girt by shores exceeding two thousand miles, would be connected with the Atlantic by a portage of only forty miles. The country between Hudson's river and lake Erie, within twenty miles of the canal, a country whose natural advantages are not surpassed by any other of equal extent on the globe, would, thus, be virtually condensed within a space whose medium distance from the tidewaters of the ocean would be but thirty miles. Hence the most important consequences to the prosperity of our country would be produced. Among these, as an item worth millions, may be reckoned the saving of those articles which would otherwise not be produced, or would be suffered to perish from the impracticability of bringing them to market.

It is impossible to ascertain, and is difficult to imagine, how much toll would be collected. The amount of transportation might be estimated by subjecting probabilities to calculation. But, like our advance in numbers and wealth, calculation outruns fancy. Things which twenty years ago a man would have been laughed at for believing, we now see. At that time the most ardent mind, proceeding on established facts by the unerring rules of arithmetic, was obliged to drop the pen at results which imagination could not embrace. Under circumstances of this sort, there can be no doubt that those microcosmic minds which, habitually occupied in the consideration of what is little, are incapable of discerning what is great, and who already stigmatise the proposed canal as a romantic scheme; will, not unsparingly, distribute the epithets, absurd, ridiculous, chimerical, on the estimate of what it may produce. The commissioners must, nevertheless, have the hardihood to brave the sneers and sarcasms of men, who, with too much pride to study, and too much wit to think, undervalue what they do not understand, and condemn what they cannot comprehend.

Wise legislators will examine and reason upon facts. Viewing the extent and fertility of the country with which this canal is to open a communication, it is not extravagant to suppose that, when settled, its produce will equal the present export of the atlantic states; because it contains more land, and that land of a superior quality.

Those who contemplate the rapid encrease of population, especially in that quarter, must be convinced the period is not remote when those regions will be cultivated. Indeed they already embrace an extensive tract, which has been subdued by the arm of industry. The amount of articles transported on the canal which will be consumed at home, must, if circumstances should preserve, here, the proportions usual in similar cases, exceed that part of them which is sent abroad. Nevertheless, without extending our view to the commerce of other ports, it is sufficient to take the simple facts that upwards of 250,000 tons of shipping belong to this state, and that the value of domestic produce exported is upwards of ten million dollars. Now 250,000 tons of goods, at $40 per ton, make up that sum; and grain at $40 per ton will not average less than one dollar per bushel. Many of the exported articles are unquestionably more valuable, but some are less valuable than grain. Is it then an extravagance to suppose, that the present export of domestic produce is not far short of 250,000 tons; and that it will be doubled by means of the canal. But lest this assumption should be a ground of cavil, let every article of domestic consumption be added. Will it then appear improbable that, twenty years hence, the canal should annually bring down 250,000 tons? It has already been assumed that a toll of 250 cents per ton should be taken; which, on boats going and returning, will give five dollars per ton, and yield, therefore, one million two hundred and fifty thousand dollars.[3] If this sum be too great, let one fifth be struck off for expenses and diminution of toll on bulky articles of little value. A million remains. Is that million too much, take away four hundred thousand: still there will remain six hundred thousand dollars: the interest at six per cent. of ten million. Should the canal, therefore, cost even that large sum, it will soon pay the interest and very soon afterwards, by natural and necessary encrease, discharge the principal. Standing on such facts, is it extrava-

3. Peter L. Bernstein argues that these figures "would turn out to be too conservative by a wide margin" (*Wedding of the Waters: The Erie Canal and the Making of a Great Nation* [New York: Norton, 2005], 163).

gant to believe that New York may look forward to the receipt (at no distant period) of one million dollars net revenue from this canal. The life of an individual is short. The time is not distant when those who make this report will have passed away. But no term is fixed to the existence of a state; and the first wish of a patriot's heart is that his own may be immortal. But whatever limit may have been assigned to the duration of New-York, by those eternal decrees which established the heavens and the earth, it is hardly to be expected that she will be blotted from the list of political societies before the effects here stated, shall have been sensibly felt. And even when, by the flow of that perpetual stream which bears all human institutions away, our constitution shall be dissolved and our laws be lost, still the descendants of our children's children will remain. The same mountains will stand, the same rivers run. New moral combinations will be formed on the old physical foundations, and the extended line of remote prosperity,[4] after a lapse of two thousand years, and the ravage of repeated revolutions, when the records of history shall have been obliterated, and the tongue of tradition have converted (as in China) the shadowy remembrance of ancient events into childish tales of miracles, this national work shall remain. It shall bear testimony to the genius, the learning, the industry and intelligence of the present age.

The commissioners will not, as they might, dwell on the advantages which the commerce of the state must derive from opening a scene so vast to its incessant activity. Neither will they hint at the political influence which must result from holding a key to the commerce of our western world. This subject, too delicate for discussion, is appropriate to the high consideration of legislative intelligence, and should not, by subordinate agents, be approached but with prudential respect.

The commissioners beg leave to advert to a question which comes more properly within their sphere. What will this canal cost? An important question, but one to which they cannot give a satisfactory answer. They have taken pains to extend investigation, encreased the number of surveys, and accumulated the knowledge of facts. In proportion to the information acquired is their conviction, that the plan is practicable, and that the probable expense, compared with the advantage, is moderate, very moderate; for they persist in believing that it may be accomplished for five or six million of dollars. But they have neither the needful information on which to calculate, nor have they the professional ability. Mr. Weston, an engineer of

---

4. Presumably a mistake for "posterity."

great and acknowledged talents and experience, who has already been employed in that capacity, both in this state and in Pennsylvania, (in the letter, a part of which has already been cited) says,

> From the perspicuous topographical description, and neat plan and profile of the route of the contemplated canal, I entertain little doubt of the practicability of the measure. Perhaps this is the only question which the legislature should be particularly anxious to have resolved. The expense, be it what it may, is no object when compared with the incalculable benefit; though doubtless it will deserve attention that the money granted be wisely and economically expended. As the survey already made is only what is technically called a running level, much allowance ought to be made with respect to eligibility of the route, and amount of descent. Indeed, to determine the proper line of canal will require the utmost skill of the professional engineer. Its due performance is of vital importance. A small mistake therein, from whatever cause arising, may occasion the needless waste of thousands. Too much care cannot be taken, in the first instance, in exploring the country in every practicable direction, that the final decision may be founded on the result of a comparison of the different routes, as combining shortness of distance with cheapness of execution. The extraordinary regularity in the third or western division, induces me to concur, without hesitation, in the plan recommended by the commissioners, of cutting the canal with an uniform descent, in preference to the usual mode of carrying it on a level. It is true that the latter custom has, almost invariably, been adopted in Europe, but the inducements thereto have generally been the scanty supply of water on the respective summits, the shortness of the different levels, and the tolerably equal amount of tonnage conveyed in opposite directions. None of these circumstances occur in the instance before us, for the supply of water, as is justly observed, is pure and inexhaustible. The length of line from the mouth of the Tonewanto to Cayuga river, is upwards of one hundred and twenty miles; an extent of canal without lockage, unequalled by any now in existence; and the chief amount of tonnage will be always downwards. For these reasons I strongly recommend the adoption of the plan.

Without taking up those hypothetical suggestions which present themselves, on such an occasion, to one whose experience of difficulties, whose knowledge of means, and whose intellectual resources lead to the notice of things which escape common observation, it is evident that the commissioners would be unpardonably presumptuous should they pretend to accuracy of calculation, before sufficient materials are collected to decide the judgment of a professional man, such as Mr. Weston. In speaking of what they hazarded in their first report, he says, "the allowance of twelve and a half cents per yard, for common cutting, is ample, but the estimate of the average quantity of earth to be excavated, is underrated." He thinks, too, that the obstructions arising from trees and roots, are greater than was apprehended. The estimate of one thousand dollars per foot, for lockage, is, he says, sufficient, but two dollars per cubic yard, for such masonry as would be required for aqueducts, is too low; and he says, that the expense of double locks, though great, will not, as was supposed, be increased in a two-fold ratio. The commissioners perceived that an error had been made in their first report, respecting the cost of an embankment over the outlet of the Cayuga lake; but there is no need of correcting it; because, from the surveys of last season, it appears that the ground between that and the Seneca lake, is too low for so high a level. Unless, therefore, a more favorable route can be discovered, the course by an inclined plane cannot be pursued throughout, and it may become necessary to descend eighty or ninety feet, so as to cross the outlet of the Cayuga by an embankment of moderate height. In this case, the communication from lake Erie will consist—1st. Of an inclined plane to the Seneca outlet: 2d. Of a descent by locks to a lower line: 3d. Of a level canal as far east as the face of the country may indicate: 4th. Of an elevation, at the end of it, by locks, to the Rome summit: 5th. Of a level canal from thence to where descent may become needful: And 6th. Of an inclined plane from that place to a bason near the Hudson river. In the course of so vast a work, much must depend on the nature of the soil; and it may sometimes be cheaper to obtain that which is good, by extending the distance, than to cure natural defects on a more direct course. It may, in some cases, also be advisable to avoid deep cutting, by a circuit, and in others, to cut deep for a shorter line. It is evident that the commissioners cannot make a correct estimate. It is nevertheless their duty to present the best which their information and abilities will permit, taking care that their allowance be rather too high than too low. They assume, then, that the distance may, for the reasons assigned, be lengthened to three hundred and fifty, instead of three hundred miles; or that, to avoid the additional distance, an expense equivalent to it may be encountered. They moreover take the quantity to be excavated, at twice what was mentioned in their first report, viz. at thirty cubic yards, instead of fifteen, and, (to embrace the various contingencies which may occur,) assume the cost of digging, at near twenty cents per cubic yard, instead of twelve and an half, which Mr. Weston, (who founds his opinion on experience acquired by conducting such works, in this country,) considers as amply sufficient for common cutting. This will give ten thousand dollars for every mile; a smaller sum than has been expended by private companies in the United States on some turnpike roads; but fully sufficient, it is believed, to cover any expense which can attend that part of the business.

Thus the cutting of the canal would cost three millions and an half. A descent, by double locks, of eighty or ninety feet, and the consequent ascent to regain a proper level, may be put, in round numbers, at half a million more. Together, four millions. The embankment over the Cayuga outlet, with the needful culverts, may cost three or four hundred thousand, but say half a million, and set the excavation at the Tonewanta at three hundred thousand; the aqueduct over the Genesee, with many smaller aqueducts and culverts, at two hundred thousand; making another million: to which one more may be added, for works at Black Rock rapid, a bason near the Hudson; and those contingencies which necessarily attend an undertaking of such magnitude: in the whole, six million dollars. The Commissioners may be mistaken, but they have no reason to believe it will cost so much.[5]

They hasten to the examination of two other points. Has the state sufficient resources? Ought the business to be undertaken now, or postponed to a future day? On the resources of the state they would speak with caution, did the sum bear an important proportion to her wealth. But it is almost a contradiction in terms to suppose that an expenditure of five or six million, in ten or a dozen years, can be a serious consideration to a million men enjoying one of the richest soils and finest climates under heaven. When, in addition to these leading facts, it is considered that there is scarcely a spot on the globe which possesses such advantages for commerce, and that the number of inhabitants doubles in twenty years; the facility of encountering the object proposed by immediate taxation, is one of those evident propositions which argument may rather obscure than elucidate. If the facility of bearing such a trifling weight required it, proof the most full and complete might be found in every gazette. It will not be pretended that the national revenue (raised by indirect tax on the consumption of less than six million of souls) was oppressive, though it exceeded twelve million of dollars. No man has been galled by, none has felt that burthen, which amounts (never-

5. According to Bernstein, this is what the canal eventually did cost (*Wedding of the Waters*, 115).

theless) to two dollars a head. The share paid by this state, therefore, supposing our average consumption to be the same as that of our neighbours, is two million: four times what would be required to make, in ten or a dozen years, the projected canal. Or let the subject be examined in another point of view. The encrease of wealth, in this state, has been (and for evident reasons must be) much more rapid than the encrease of inhabitants. The value of property is at least quadrupled in the period during which population is doubled. The present amount of property has been estimated at five hundred million. Perhaps it is more. But should it be much less, time will soon bring it up to, and immediately push it beyond that sum; which may therefore be taken as the standard. Of consequence it follows, that an annual tax of half a million would be but one tenth per cent on the value of real and personal estate. Take the matter again in another point of view, and, admitting that the rich pay the portion of tax that would fall on the poor in a distribution by poll, which (let the tax be laid as it may) must happen, the average contribution will be that of a family in medium circumstances. Wherefore, as a population of one million embraces two hundred thousand families, the average contribution, to raise a revenue of five hundred thousand dollars, would be five dollars from two families. Half of that, or two hundred and fifty cents, is, then, the sum which the head of a family in easy circumstances would be called on to pay, if money were raised by direct tax to carry on the work. In that case, there can be no doubt that a wise Legislature would open sources from which adequate revenue could be drawn, not only without injury, but even with advantage to the community. But of this there is no necessity. The credit of the state is sufficient. And if a calculation were made on principles of compound interest, it would appear that the sum to be expended, with interest, until the canal shall yield sufficient revenue, will not exceed what that income would discharge in a reasonable time. If therefore the Legislature say, let it be done—it will be done.

But shall they say so now? Shall it be done now, or shall it be postponed to a future day? Those who wish to postpone are respectfully asked, whether they suppose time will render the matter easier? Will it alter the shape of the country? Will the land to be used for the canal cost less when it shall be planted as an orchard, tilled as a garden, or covered by a house, than in its present condition? Will timber and lime be cheaper when wood, now worth nothing, shall have grown dear? Is it certain that the state of public affairs will be as favourable then as now? Will not a fertile imagination invent as good reasons for postponement then as now? And to what day shall it be postponed? Must it be to the day when a Legislature shall have *that* patriotism which the idea of postponement presupposes the present Legislature to want? The commissioners reply with pain to arguments which imply insult. Who is there so base as not to repel the charge of selfishness? What man so cold as not to feel the dignified desire of immortalizing his name, by contributing to a monument of national magnificence, unequalled by any thing on earth?

A state, in its corporate capacity, is an invisible, intellectual existence. If that to which we belong could be reduced to personal identification, could it become an individual, or (that being impossible) could we suppose an individual to be owner of the state, what should we think of his understanding did he hesitate to double the value of his property, and increase his revenue threefold, without labour, without expense! Yet such is the present case, unless it can be called an expense to run in debt for an object which will pay both principal and interest before the debt falls due. Or suppose this individual to be an infant, would his guardians do their duty should they let slip the golden opportunity so to promote the interest of their ward? But the Legislature is guardian of the state.

The foregoing reflections lead to one of the duties enjoined on the commissioners. They were directed to apply to the proprietors of land through which the canal may be carried, for cessions to the people of this state. Such applications have been made, and they have no doubt that the proprietors will contribute in just measure. Some grants would have been already made, but for difficulties in the form originally proposed, and from a desire that they should be proportionate to the tracts the grantors respectively hold.

The commissioners have also in execution of the duties imposed by the act, endeavored to ascertain whether loans for the object of it can be obtained on the credit of this state. They find that, notwithstanding the scarcity of money consequent on the war which has so long raged in and ravaged Europe, a loan of five million dollars can be obtained, *there*, on the credit of the state, for a term of ten or fifteen years, at an annual interest of six per cent.

The commissioners have enquired the terms on which the western inland lock navigation company will surrender their rights. They ask one hundred and ninety thousand dollars for the shares held by them, exclusive of three hundred and fifty shares held by the state. This being thought too much, they were urged to confine their demand within such moderate bounds as might be acceptable. Copy of their reply, of the 13th February, is in the paper marked No. 5, hereunto annexed.

The commissioners have, in obedience to the directions of the act, sought for, and will employ a capable engineer as soon as a suitable character can be procured. None but a man of the first rate talents, tried integrity, and approved experience, can be relied on for that previous investigation which is indispensable. In the mean time, they have employed surveyors to continue their search of the best probable route.

It was not within the circle of their duty to ascertain the conveniences presented by nature for an internal navigation northward, wherefore, although there can be no doubt that an examination of the country, with that view, might be useful, they forbore the attempt. In that quarter lies a large and fertile territory peculiarly our own—moreover, it will be seen by the bill annexed to the report of the deputation sent to Washington, that a communication by means of a canal, between Lake Champlain and Hudson's river, is one of those things which are deemed of national importance. It would certainly tend to preserve brotherly affection in the great American family; and the reciprocal advantages which it would procure to New-York and Vermont, would strengthen the bands of our union with the eastern states, so conducive to our mutual prosperity.

All which is humbly submitted.

GOUV. MORRIS,
S. V. RENSSELAER,
DE WITT CLINTON,
SIMEON DE WITT,
W. NORTH,
THOMAS EDDY,
ROB. R. LIVINGSTON.
Albany, March, 1812.

37 ❧ An Address to the People of the State of New York on the Present State of Affairs (1812)

For Morris, the War of 1812 was more than simply the result of diplomatic ineptitude on the part of the Madison administration. The war was the end of a chain of measures, beginning with the Non-Importation Act in 1806, that had seriously damaged the commerce of the Northern states. It was almost as if the Southern states, having established control over the national government, were working systematically to complete a design Morris had predicted at the Constitutional Convention:

> The train of business & the late turn which it had taken, had led him he said, into deep meditation on it, and He wd. candidly state the result. A distinction had been set up & urged, between the Nn. & Southn. States. He had hitherto considered this doctrine as heretical. He still thought the distinction groundless. He sees however that it is persisted in; and that the Southn. Gentleman will not be satisfied unless they see the way open to their gaining a majority in the public Councils. The consequence of such a transfer of power from the maritime to the interior & landed interest will he foresees be such an oppression of commerce, that he shall be obliged to vote for ye. vicious principle of equality in the 2d. branch in order to provide some defence for the N. States agst. it. . . . There can be no end of demands for security if every particular interest is to be entitled to it.[1]

New York Herald, August 29, 1812, pp. 1–2; *New-York Evening Post*, August 26, 1812, pp. 2–3. Courtesy American Antiquarian Society. The manuscript is in the Gouverneur Morris Papers, Rare Book and Manuscript Library, Columbia University, item 867, but some of the pages are out of order and others are missing. Except where noted, spelling, punctuation, and capitalization are as they appear in the newspaper.

1. Speech in the Convention, July 13, 1787, in *Records of the Federal Convention of 1787*, ed. Max Farrand, rev. ed. (New Haven: Yale University Press, 1911–87), 1:604. The "particular interest" of the Southern states was slavery, and their security was the three-fifths clause, which gave them extra weight in Congress and in the Electoral College.

Two years later, Morris would quietly back the Hartford Convention and its abortive bid for a separation of North and South. This essay, which begins to prepare the ground for such a move, comes as close as he ever comes to a public advocacy of such a separation.

⊹⊱⊰⊹

Fellow-Citizens,

Having, formerly, attempted to point out those consequences of the course pursued in our public affairs which we now experience, and found a majority of you attached to our Rulers and to their Measures, I conceived it my duty to wait in respectful silence for events. I should not venture, therefore, to intrude on your patience, now, but that opinions are inculcated, which, according to my apprehension, tend not only to increase the evils of our condition, but to render them irremediable. Still, however, I doubt whether you be in the proper temper to listen: for, altho your sufferings have disposed you to *think*, a more bitter cup of misery must I fear be swallowed before you can digest the wholesome food of truth. In the mean time, pains are taken to inflame your minds, and drive you to a state so desperate, that one half the nation may be destroyed to save the other.

If on so important an occasion it were proper to think, much less to speak, of one's self he who addresses you would venture to believe that few men in the United States are more bound than he by sentiment and by interest to the preservation of our National Union. His solicitude may, perhaps, have given him a groundless alarm, but he seriously believes that the general current of events, for some years past, drives us rapidly towards a condition in which no human power can prevent these States from separating into two, or more sections, independent of each other. He is not so weak as to believe that the feelings or efforts of solitary individuals can resist or divert that impetuous current; but he thinks the danger should be made known to all who love their country. For as a cancer shoots deep before the skin is discolored, so there are diseases in the political body which become mortal before they are evident to cursory observation. He, therefore, who would save his country from the approaching catastrophe must point it out in season to his fellow citizens. It may be proper, in a monarchy, to let the people enjoy their ideal safety, and communicate their danger to none but the King or his Ministers; but in a Republic, the people, alone, can save themselves. To them, therefore, must be disclosed the state to which they have been brought. Let no offence be taken, for no blame is meant. Each of the contending parties has been sometimes wrong. In other words both are composed of men. Their aberrations from the rules of propriety have been proportionate to the degree of their hatred for each other; because, in that proportion has passion usurped the seat of judgment; in that proportion has prejudice clouded the understanding; and in that same proportion has a vengeful spirit driven the love of justice and of mercy from our Hearts. It is then of the first necessity to extinguish a flame of discord by which, if it be suffered to rage, our liberty must be consumed. To this effect, let every man preach to his Fellow Citizens by his example. To qualify himself for that healing ministry let him doubt, a little, of his own infallibility, and believe that his neighbor may have been as honest in differing from him as he is in differing from his neighbor. Let him then examine facts and arguments, without regard to party distinctions. For altho these be excellent contrivances to raise unqualified individuals to posts of trust and profit, they seldom do good to the people.

I repeat it, Fellow Citizens, the union is in danger. But let not that danger be encreased by senseless outcry against those who believe in the utility of a separation. Let us not enflame old factions under new names. This cannot prevent the mischief, but may render its attendant circumstances more distressing. It is better to examine the argument coolly, correct misstatements candidly, and relieve grievances (if any there be) honestly.

The advocates for a separation contend that inasmuch as the only legitimate object of Government is public good, any system by which one part of the community is sacrificed to the other must be unjust. That to resist oppression is a natural right, and appertains, therefore, as well to the weak as to the strong. That the expedience of exercising a right must always depend on circumstances, but that it is not extinguished, neither can it be considered as surrendered, by submission to power. They insist that these principles apply, substantially, to all political associations, but literally and distinctly to the Constitution under which we live. That our federative form of Government was not adopted for the general good alone, but to secure the special interest of each particular part. That when concessions were made by the States for the sake of union, it was not because union was the end of their association, but because they considered it as one of the rational means to preserve their liberty and promote their prosperity. Hence, it is argued that if, in the course of events, that union should prove injurious, and, far more, if it should be rendered destructive to the interest of one or more States, efforts made for its preservation, by those States, would involve the folly of sacrificing the end to the means instead of rendering the means subservient to the end.

They proceed to relate that, for the sake of union, one important concession was made by the northern States with extreme reluctance because they deemed it unjust; and the haughtiness with which the southern States insisted on it was offensive. Nothing, therefore, but a pressure of necessity would have induced them to submit to a regulation whose object and effect were to encrease the representation of those States, in proportion to the number of men whom they[2] should hold in bondage: So that the violation of natural right was rewarded by political prerogative, and they became masters of their brethren, by making the negroes their slaves.[3]

To this complaint, which is not without some appearance of reason, it is replied that the unequal representation now objected to was the legitimate offspring of fiscal calculation and political wisdom. It was admitted, say they, as a maxim, that representation should be proportioned to wealth and numbers combined. It was supposed that population and wealth, other circumstances being equal, bear such mutual relation that one might be taken as a measure of the other. That had this rule been pursued, the southern states would have had a representation proportioned to the whole number of their inhabitants; instead of which it was conceded by them, not to them, that slaves (as a standard of wealth) should be estimated in the proportion of three to five. And moreover, it was established, as the price of inequality, supposing it to exist, that direct taxes should be in proportion to the representation. Wherefore, the whole matter being candidly considered, it would appear that they were losers by the bargain; and had conferred, not received, a favor.

This reasoning, if not conclusive, is abundantly sufficient to confirm men in the faith which it is their interest to maintain. But as few arguments are unanswerable, so it is replied that the conclusion here, will not follow from the premises nor stand the test of arithmetic. That taking a number of free men in the northern states, ten thousand for instance, and adding an equal number for property, there will result as the unit of representation twenty thousand. That according to the constitution, seven thousand free men with five thousand slaves will produce the same unit of representation; whereas,

2. The manuscript reads "they"; the newspaper reads "this."

3. Morris alludes to the three-fifths clause, which he had opposed at the Constitutional Convention using some of the arguments he uses here. See his speeches in *Federal Convention of 1787*, 1:581–82, 588, 593, 604; 2:221–23.

according to the argument, adding to the seven thousand free men seven thousand for wealth we have fourteen thousand, and adding thereto three thousand for the wealth evidenced by five thousand slaves, the total is but seventeen thousand; wherefore, to make up the deficiency, the five thousand slaves must be counted over again as equal to three thousand citizens. Thus the fact remains, as originally stated, that five negro slaves to the south have a political weight equal to that of three white freemen to the north. It is insisted further, that the argument, such as it is, rests on a false foundation. That slaves, men reduced by the loss of Liberty to a level with beasts, are no better evidence of wealth than other cattle. That, in truth, the mass of wealth compared with the number of free citizens is less, much less, in the southern than in the northern states. And, as to the price stipulated for an additional representation, it has never been paid. That direct taxes were first eluded, then opposed, and, when at last apportioned, have not been collected in the southern states. So that they became, in effect, an alleviation of the south and an additional burden on the north. That they were used moreover, as the engine to subvert an administration favorable to commerce and establish, in its stead, an administration of slave holders, who, envying the prosperity of the northern states, endeavoured to dry up it's source by ruinous commercial restrictions and have now, actuated by the same spirit, exposed them to the desolation of a war alike unnecessary and unjust.

This language is too strong for conciliation. Let it be remembered that the bargain complained of was made, and having been submitted to the consideration of all concerned, was ratified. That if it has produced the mischief supposed, the northern states must blame themselves; because had they been united the vote of their brethren could not have prevailed against them. And that the national administration was supported in the course it has pursued, almost as much by representatives from the north as by those from the south. Candor, therefore, forbids the belief that a spirit hostile to this section of the union has dictated their measures. The more zealous advocates of the government go further and insist that no good purpose can be answered by looking back to a course which, whatever it may have been, is now concluded. That war has been declared by the competent authority. That whatever may have been the motives, and whatever may be the opinions about them, it is not the less certain that war exists, and, existing, must be prosecuted with spirit. This, say they, is required not only by the national compact, but by national honor; and he who will not cheerfully bear his part is no true citizen. He is a traitor and should be treated accordingly.

Now this language, setting aside the wrathful temper which it exhibits, does not (in my apprehension) contain sound argument. The assertions are predicated on propositions too broad, and which prove too much. It may verily, in one sense, be vain to look back: for the moments which are past cannot be recalled; neither can the acts done be undone. But that consideration ought not to crush enquiry into the conduct of those by whom bad acts may have been committed. When criminal servants are called to account for wicked measures, it would be a strange justification to say "You are too late. The business is done. You must not look back, but go forward and get through as well as you can." This, I say, would be a strange justification to an offended people. And it seems equally strange that a declaration of war should be adduced as a sufficient reason for itself and for every step which led to it. War is one of the greatest national calamities, and not unfrequently terminates in destruction. Shall a man then stand up and say to his indignant country "True it is that having done you much evil before, I have now brought you to ruin; but the sufficient proof that I did right is that you are ruined." For my part, fellow-citizens, I cannot perceive the force of such logic, neither can I admit that every man is bound to prosecute every war which the rulers of his country may think proper to declare. It becomes needful on this occasion, to ask whether the eulogies we have heard on American rights for the last twenty or thirty years are merely the jests in a political farce, or whether the people be indeed the sovereign of these United States. If, notwithstanding our boasted rights, a few gentlemen at Washington can tie us neck and heels and throw us into a den of wolves, and we may not lawfully cut the cords, there is an end of the question. In that case let us submit and suffer, but let us no longer boast. If, on the contrary, this be a free people it is entitled to form an opinion on public measures and act up to that opinion. If it be a sovereign people, it is accountable, like every other sovereign, to the everlasting and omnipotent God. Let the subjects of a monarchy fold their arms, if they please, in an unjust war, and lull remorse by laying all on their prince. The Father of Mercy may, perhaps, forgive them. But can we hope for, shall we dare ask for mercy, if we shed the blood of man in an unrighteous quarrel? Fellow Citizens! Pause. Think. Tell me—Are we reduced to the condition of those whom in our revolutionary war we beheld with contempt? Are we at market like Hessian mercenaries? Is it true that we must, at the bidding of our masters, march to the conquest of Canada? And when a subsidiary alliance shall have been formed with the French Emperor, shall thirty or forty thousand American farmers be shipt off like cattle to a butchery in the West-Indies? This, nevertheless, is an evident consequence, from principles advanced and maintained by many, who stile themselves friends of the administration, friends of the constitution. Nor is this all. The same principles, so evidently destructive to every spark of freedom, are fraught with danger in the ordinary current of affairs. They prompt rulers to pursue a desperate course, by laying down as a maxim that they have nothing to fear, however atrocious their proceedings, provided they draw over them the veil of war. But if any Members of Congress, or others, were so vain as to suppose that this nation would take fire at the sound of their drum and rush on to mischief like midnight drunkards, they will find themselves mistaken. Such unworthy ideas may be applicable to the vagabond wretches who compose a mob; and familiar to the scoundrels who excite a mob. But let them know that we, the people of America, are not their subjects: still less their slaves. We are not bound to fight for frantic notions or idle whims. We learnt from our fathers to know better both our rights and duties. Our fathers, Englishmen, whom it is the trick of some to speak of as slaves, taught us, by their example, not to prosecute an iniquitous war. When their King Charles IId was bribed by Bonaparte's predecessor, Lewis XIVth, to wage war, in name against Holland, but in truth against liberty, our fathers refused to bear a part. They withheld supply. They withheld service. They compelled their perfidious prince to make peace. And, but for their firmness then, we should not venture to pronounce the name of freedom now.

Surely, fellow-citizens, it will not be pretended that if members of Congress were bribed, by French gold, to take part with the emperor against England, we should be bound to carry on their corrupt war with the same zeal as if it were a war of our own; to support and defend, not to overturn and destroy the liberties of mankind. Far be it from me to say or insinuate that the Congress was bribed. I do not believe it. Nor will I descend to consider how far their measures may have been (what many believe they were) mere electioneering manoeuvres. But I take leave to say, with all proper respect for the Congress, that the motives which stimulated them to war will not alter its physical or moral Effects. Whether it proceed from corruption, from prejudice, from wrath, from fear or from folly, it equally tends to ruin. And supposing all those who voted for it, to have been as pure as some of them were petulant, our ships will not the less be lost, our seamen will not the less be taken, our commerce will not the less be destroyed, nor will our frontiers be the less exposed. If, in the course of this war, just or unjust, our city be laid in ashes or subjected to contribution; if our citizens be slaughtered; our farmers ruined; our merchants reduced to bankruptcy; can we, by proving the war to have been just, convert the ashes into houses, bring back the contributions to replenish exhausted banks, restore to our merchants their capital and credit, repair the ruined farms, refund the oppressive taxes, or raise to life the dead? Surely we cannot. And if, at last, exhausted by the contest, we give up, to get peace, the claims for which we went to war; will proof that the war was just prove it to have been wise also? Most assuredly not. And if, which is but too probable, we become bound by a treaty of alliance with the emperor of France to uphold his inordinate power, to enforce the claims of his unbounded ambition, to shed our blood in his pernicious quarrels, to behold our citizens seized under a system of military conscription, manacled & driven, like criminals condemned to the gallies, wherever his prefects may command, will it alleviate the inconceivable misery of such national degradation to be told that it is the consequence of fighting for national honor? Oh, no. No. The nauseous draught of ironical compliment cannot soothe the pangs of a wretch on the rack. Alas! Our wealth will then be turned into want, our pride will become meanness, our freedom slavery, and our honour shame. Should not those, then, who see our condition in this light, take every proper step to obtain the restoration of peace? All that can be saved of blood and treasure, in a contest big with ruin and void of hope, is a clear gain; and it must be an abuse of terms to call him a bad citizen (far less a traitor) who would prevent an useless effusion of the blood and treasure of his country.

No, say the few who urge a hot prosecution of the war, no: let us add the northern star to our constellation. Let us conquer Canada. But is Canada worth conquering? Time was that the British government would have given it, if asked for in a friendly way, because in truth it is a costly appendage. On what principle can it be accounted for, that the rulers of a country, great part of which is uninhabited; a country whose government, and almost every man in it, has land to sell; a country in which husbandry and the arts languish for want of men; that the rulers of such a country should endeavor to purchase land with the lives of its citizens? We want men and money, we don't want land; and yet we are about to squander men and money in the uncertain hope of adding millions of acres, covered with eternal snow, to the millions of fertile soil which we already possess: and which remain useless from the want of hands.

I will not examine, Fellow-Citizens, whether we have, what civilians term justifiable cause of war. It is a question which every one of you can consider for himself. A public investigation might lead to angry discussions which should be avoided by those who seek harmony and peace. Another irritating topic also shall be but slightly touched. Indeed I mention an opinion which has got abroad, that one object of the War was to check the growth of this State, merely to declare my belief that it is unfounded. Yet I must acknowledge that if a desire to arrest the rapid progress of our prosperity had existed, no better mode of gratifying it could have been devised than a war with England. It exposes on the north an undefended frontier of many hundred miles to predatory incursion; and on the south, the greatest commercial City of the Union to bombardment. Moreover, a War ruinous to Commerce must be most injurious to the most commercial State. These considerations favor so much the insinuation that a special view to our injury influenced the late events, as to lessen the surprize that it should be admitted by candid, well meaning men. Persons of plain, good sense, when they see an act highly imprudent committed by one, of whose understanding they entertain a favorable opinion, naturally cast about for his inducements to it, and are apt to admit of any, having a semblance of common sense, rather than resolve his conduct into folly or madness. But I trust that such irritating notions will be cast aside. They are uncharitable. They imply a guilt too great to be admitted without proof. Indeed, a charge so heinous, should not be insinuated on mere presumption. But altho' we cannot suppose the ruin or depression of New-York to have been an object of, or inducement, to the War, we cannot shut our eyes to the evil consequences which must result from it to her citizens. Neither can it be denied, that being more exposed than others, it becomes their especial duty to obtain, if possible, a speedy Peace.

But what shall be done to remedy the mischief? *Remove the Cause.* Our differences have brought us to our present condition. Let us then unite. If we go on jangling till we are bound in Gallic chains, it will afford no relief to reproach each other with having been the cause of our common misery. Let party-zealots begin at early morn and rail till late at night, they will be neither richer, freer, nor happier; they will acquire neither wisdom, virtue nor glory. Permit me, then, to address each party in the same terms. Let me say to both: "Gentlemen I acknowledge you to be right. Being so in your own opinion you must be so in mine, because you have the perfect right to judge for yourselves. I acknowledge too that your adversaries are wrong: for that must be admitted, if you are right. But have, I pray, the charity to believe that although they judge ill, they mean well. Above all, consider that their strength is equal to yours, and that a state divided against itself cannot stand. Make then a virtue of necessity, if other virtue be wanting, and unite with them to save us all."

But how, it may be asked, is the desirable union, if produced, to be rendered efficient. To answer that question might be presumptuous. It does not become an unauthorized individual to mark out the course for a great community. Permit me, therefore, Fellow-Citizens, to confine myself within those bounds which befit the respect I feel for you. Let me recommend an examination of our history. A nation will generally find more convenient rules and examples at home than abroad, and things known by experience are more fully understood than such as are only heard of or seen at a distance. In days of yore, when Americans were oppressed, they found in their anterior institutions the needful forms; and evoking,[4] by the magic of patriot sentiment, the souls of their Sires from the grave, they found the invigorating spirit for those antient forms. Men, assembling from regions, which, though remote, were not more separated by distance than by prejudice, interest and habits of rivalship, were at once united: for they bore the public sentiment in their bosoms, the public voice on their lips. Doubt not that common feeling, in a common cause, will unite the efforts of good men for the common safety.

But it may be objected that former examples do not apply, that there is no need of recurring to them, that we may safely trust the Congress, that constitutional organ of the public will. But how, if that organ be not in unison with the public mind? We are told by persons of sound understanding, tho somewhat of a jealous disposition, that when the congress meet there are offices to give, contracts to make, public money to handle. I persuade myself that the national legislature is pure, but there are many who cannot be persuaded, surmises are abroad, strange things are said. And what wonder that men should say strange things when they speak of such strange conduct? But setting unworthy suspicions aside, it is evident that our national Legislature cannot entertain some of the many important questions now agitated because they involve a decision on the propriety of its own conduct. Is the war just, is it wise, is it necessary? A majority of the congress have already answered these questions in the affirmative. Before their seats can be filled by successors, not yet chosen, more war loans may be opened, more paper money may be issued, dangerous treaties may be concluded, foreign troops may be introduced, and then our national union is gone forever. Listen to what is said, look at what is doing among our neighbors; and rely on it, that by no contrivance of political machinery can the wealth and strength of this nation be kept in subjection to its poverty and weakness.

4. The manuscript reads "evoking"; the newspaper, "working."

I know it may be said that all confidence should be reposed in the national Government, because the whole community have but one interest, as respects foreign affairs, and that we may safely trust to the interest of our rulers even tho we doubt their integrity. But there is no mistake more common than to decide on what men will do from what we suppose they ought to do, or what we believe them called on to do by their own interest. The fabric of this argument is raised on three distinct propositions, not one of which can safely be relied on. First it is taken for granted that we know what it is their interest to do. But, to this effect, we must be able to place ourselves precisely in their situation, and be apprized of facts many of which perhaps we never shall know nor even hear of. Secondly, it is presumed that men know their own interest. But this presupposes a degree of information respecting public affairs, which, humanly speaking, it is impossible for the mass of mankind to arrive at; and a measure of intelligence which it has pleased divine Providence to impart to very few among the sons of Adam. Thirdly, it is, tho generally, too hastily admitted that those who know the interest of the community to which they belong will steadily and faithfully pursue it. We ought to consider that they may have, or, which comes to the same thing, may believe they have a private interest different from that of the public. Many are they who have made themselves rich and great by reducing their country to misery and ruin. If men were always virtuous and wise, politics would cease to be an intricate science. But history is much less the splendid picture of wisdom and virtue, than the faithful record of folly and vice. Leaving however, the wide and instructive field of historic truth, let us examine familiar and recent domestic facts. And, first, a mere inspection of the map, and slight knowledge of those who inhabit the shores wash'd by the waters of the Chesapeak, would lead one to conclude that a fleet, alone, can defend their plantations from plunder, and their dwellings from destruction. And thence again it would be fair to conclude that they would strongly and perseveringly contend for Naval Armament. But the reverse of this induction is the fact. Not only the general mass, whose ignorance and presumption, there as elsewhere, lead to false notions of their own power and importance, but men of superior mind, men of considerable information and respectable talents, maintain the same doctrine with the multitude. Hence then it is evident that either they or we must be mistaken on what so materially concerns them. Again: If we cast an eye on our interior Country, consider the feebleness of its infant establishments, the paucity of its resources, the importance of opening roads and improving interior navigations, the utility of manufacturing institutions, the necessity of Peace for those purposes, of commerce to accumulate capital and of population to open every source of their prosperity, viewing, I say, and considering these things, we should suppose that they, of all people in the world, would be the last to plunge their country into War: more especially as they must thereby expose themselves to taxes, which they have neither the will nor the power to pay. And yet from that very quarter have we heard the loudest yell of war. Again: It is said that a Representative from the eastward, not deficient in understanding, whose constituents are much opposed to, because they are sorely aggrieved by the War, gave it nevertheless his constant voice and steady support. And to prove that he did not act ignorantly or foolishly, it is said that some half dozen of his sons receive comfortable stipends from the public chest.

How fallacious, then, is the trust that the Government of the United States, will make peace because, (in our opinion) it is their interest to be at peace. If this argument were worth a rush, it might be proper to ask why that Government broke the peace. Surely the reasoning is more correct that the same motives, be they what they may, which induced them to declare the war will induce them to persist in it now that it is declared. The less that precipitate measure can be reconciled to the principles of prudence, the greater cause we have to fear that it is the result of principles not under the control of political wisdom. We cannot from the very nature of the case, know what those principles are; and from our ignorance arises our apprehension. The field of conjecture being open to all, some may hit on notions to satisfy themselves; and in ordinary cases it might be well to indulge such consolatory notions. They tend to our quiet if not to our safety. But the present is no ordinary case. A few months, a few weeks, a few days may fasten on our necks a French alliance. Foreign troops may arrive to reinforce foreign mobs. We may then see at New York the scenes of Baltimore.[5] If any man pretend that we may rely on the government for protection, that the government would interpose its authority to prevent outrage, we are compelled to ask why were not the riots in Baltimore suppressed? Why were they permitted to rage for weeks? Why suffered, and by the want of opposition encouraged to proceed from pillage to murder? Militia have been called for unconstitutionally to wage a foreign war, why were they not called constitutionally to preserve domestic peace? Why not

5. On July 27, 1812, a pro-war Baltimore mob stormed the jail where several Federalist newspaper editors were in protective custody, took them away, and beat them. One, James Lingan, later died from his injuries.

to enforce obedience to the laws of the Union which were set at defiance, and that for the purpose of violating neutral rights under the very nose of the government, and in the very instant that they made of us a belligerent? Evidently there was a want of power or a want of will, and in either case it is impossible to repose confidence in such a government. Confide then, fellow citizens, in yourselves. Unite! unite! and save yourselves.

AN AMERICAN.[6]

6. The editor of the *Evening Post* adds this note: "*An American.* In the production under this signature, the reader will probably recognize the superior endowments of a writer who, some years since, more than once adorned our columns, with original essays which arrested notice throughout the United States. Dull indeed must be the apprehension, and great the want of sagacity, of him who does not soon find that he is engaged with one of the master spirits of the nation. It cannot, I feel confident, fail of awakening that deep and universal attention which its extraordinary merits imperiously demand."

38 ❧ Discourse Before the New-York Historical Society (1812)

Although the War of 1812 had made Morris pessimistic about the future of the American union, it did not diminish his faith in the great potential of New York state. In this discourse he sets forth his evidence for that faith. Appropriately for this audience, and consistently with his long-held views, Morris argues here that the past is the key to the future.

Mr. President and Gentlemen
of the Historical Society,

It was my purpose, in obeying your orders, to make a sketch of our history from the year 1763 to the year 1783, and compare our condition at the close of two victorious wars, in both of which this state was distinguished among her brethren as the principal theatre and greatest sufferer. This important period, of twenty years, marked by one of those events on which history delights to dwell, will, I trust, be related with philosophic impartiality by some future Hume, to amuse and instruct posterity, when their ancestors shall have mouldered to dust. But reflection told me the time was not yet arrived. Moreover, the bounds of a discourse like this are too narrow to embrace the more prominent incidents and characters. Another circumstance contributed to deter me. However rapid and concise the narrative, egotism could not wholly have been avoided. This circumstance not only forbade the attempt first contemplated, but raised difficulties, which I feared to encounter, in selecting some anterior term. Connected, by the ties of consanguinity, with persons deeply engaged in those feuds by which, at an early day, the colony was agitated, I trembled lest duty and affection

Discourse Delivered before the New-York Historical Society, at Their Anniversary Meeting, 6th December, 1812. By the Honourable Gouverneur Morris, First Vice-President of the Society (New-York: Published By James Eastburn, 86 Broadway, Opposite Trinity Church, 1813). American Antiquarian Society Early American Imprints, series II (Shaw-Shoemaker), no. 29221.

should wrong the memory of their foes: lest some incautious word of praise or blame should obscure the lustre of truth. I must therefore entreat your pardon that, shunning what may be deemed the more proper course, I venture to present some reflections on prominent historical facts and geographical circumstances which distinguish our state.

On a cursory glance at the map of North America, our eye is caught by that deep indent, where Long-Island (whose eastern point lies between thirty and forty leagues west of the south end of Nantucket Shoal) after stretching thirty leagues, on a course but fifteen degrees to the southward of west, is separated by a deep bay from the main land, whose general direction, from Sandy-Hook to Cape Hatteras, is but seventeen degrees to the westward of south. The upper end of that bay, divided from the lower by Staten Island, is nearest to the valley which embosoms the great lakes, the St. Lawrence and the Mississippi, of any sea-port on the Atlantic; and the hills which intervene are neither so numerous, so lofty, nor so steep, as those by which other routes are obstructed. The city of New-York, at the head of this bay, from causes which will probably endure as long as the earth itself, is generally accessible; and the navigation to it is frequently open when that of more southern situations is barred by frost. The channel on the west end of Long-Island, though broad and deep, may be so obstructed as to frustrate hostile attempts. The other channel, whose mouth is two degrees to the eastward, and therefore of easier and safer access in dark bad weather, presents a secure and pleasant passage till within eight miles of this city. There a rapid whirlpool and projecting rocks (our Scylla and Charybdis) render it so narrow and difficult that, although perfectly safe at a proper time and with a good pilot, it may easily be rendered too hazardous for an enemy. By the first of these channels, vessels outward bound, within a few hours after casting off from their moorings, gain the open sea. By the second, those which arrive can, with common prudence, reach safe anchorage without a pilot: and the distance from the mouth of the one to that of the other is such that both cannot easily be blockaded by the same squadron. These circumstances alone point out New-York as a commercial emporium.

But there are others which contribute largely to the same effect. Besides many small streams, the great Connecticut river pours its waters into the eastern channel; and the western shore of Manhattan island is washed by the Hudson, navigable fifty leagues by large vessels: and what is peculiar to this noble canal, ships take with them a favoring tide beyond all the ranges of mountain east of that great valley already mentioned, which stretches upwards of fourteen hundred miles in a southwestern direction from the island of Orleans, in the St. Lawrence, to the city of Orleans, on the Mississippi. To this valley an inland navigation from the Hudson can easily be extended northward to the St. Lawrence, and westward to the great lakes, whose depth, whose extent, whose pellucid water, and whose fertile shores, are unparalleled. It is probable that if our western hemisphere had been known to antiquity, those immortal bards who crowned their thundering Jove on the peak of Olympus, would have reared to commerce a golden throne on the granite rock of Manhattan. They might have pictured her, as receiving in a vast range of magazines, from Harlaem village round to Haerlem cove (a distance of twenty miles) the willing tribute of mankind: as fostering industry in the remotest regions, scattering on barren shores that plenty which nature had denied, dispensing to millions the multiplied means of enjoyment, and pouring the flood-tide of wealth on this her favored land. Not indeed that wealth, which the plunder of war and the wages of vice, exalts a rapacious head over a servile croud: but that honest wealth which, accompanied by freedom and justice, comforts the needy, raises the abject, instructs the ignorant, and fosters the arts. Such are the outlines of a picture which, adorned by classic coloring, might, with the Iliad, have been recommended to his royal pupil by that sage whose mind, acute and profound, was equally skilled in moral, physical, and political science.[1]

The first settlement of this state coincided with its natural advantages. While Englishmen came to America, either flying from ecclesiastical intolerance, or pursuing the treasure its savages were supposed to possess; Dutchmen, inspired with the spirit of trade, instead of sitting down on the skirts of the new world, boldly penetrated to the head navigation of the Hudson. They built there a fort, in the year 1614, and gave it the name of that august family, whose talents and labors, in the cabinet and the field, secured the liberty of England, as well as of Holland, and established the independence of Europe.[2]

The Dutch exhibited a new and interesting spectacle. Near half a century had elapsed since, confederated with the other ten provinces of the low countries, they took up arms to oppose the establishment of the inquisition. After a struggle of thirteen years, abandoned by their associ-

---

1. Aristotle, the teacher of Alexander the Great.

2. The first Dutch settlement at what is now Albany was known as Fort Nassau, in honor of the House of Orange-Nassau; it was replaced by Fort Orange in 1624.

ates, they had to contend for civil as well as for religious liberty, not only against their bigoted and bloody foe, but against their former friends also; then submitted to his power. They had, for many preceding ages, been free. The supreme authority belonged to the states; who met on their own adjournment, and without whose consent neither laws could be passed, nor taxes raised, nor war declared.[3] These privileges, which every sovereign had sworn to defend, were respected by Charles V; but formed no obstacle to the ambition of his unfeeling son. Thus the revolutions (if without the violation of language that term can be so applied) of Holland, of England, and of America, bear a striking resemblance to each other. Each was a contest to maintain the liberty already enjoyed, and defend it against usurpation. In England, a powerful nation, surrounded by the sea, dismissed their prince and placed on his throne the husband of his daughter. This work was easy and effectual. In America, the inhabitants of a great continent, separated from the invader by the Atlantic ocean, favored at first by the wishes and at last by the arms of other nations, were successful after a short though severe struggle. But in the case of Holland, seven poor provinces, whose surface (about eight and a half million of acres) does not exceed one of our senatorial districts,[4] whose population, a century after establishing their independence and when they had reached to the highest point of prosperity, was but two million; about double our present number. These poor provinces sustained a conflict of thirty years with the most powerful nation in Europe. They opposed the ablest generals, at the head of the best troops, of that most warlike age. An awful scene! interrupted, not closed, in April, 1609, by a truce of twelve years. When that expired, another contest ensued of seven and twenty years. At length (on the 24th October, 1648) almost a century (eighty-two years) from the time they first took up arms, their independence was acknowledged by the treaty of Westphalia.

It is natural here to ask, by what miracle did these feeble provinces resist that mighty empire? The sufficient, and only sufficient, answer is, by the will of him who holds in his hand the destinies of mankind. He bade their gloomy climate produce a persevering people, whose industry no toil could

3. Grotius de Anti. Repub. Bal. cap. 5. [Morris's footnote. Hugo Grotius, *De antiquitate reipublicae Batavicae* (Leiden, 1610).]

4. Busching's Geography, Introd. to the Netherlands, sec. 3 and 5. The Germans divide the degree into 15 geographical miles, which gives in round numbers about 13,600 acres to the square geographical mile; of which he gives to the Netherlands 625. [Morris's footnote.]

abate, whose fortitude no danger could dismay. He gave them leaders sagacious, intrepid, active, unwearied, incorruptible. He, as of old, from the
eater brought forth meat, and from the strong sweetness. He gave them
food from a tempestuous ocean, and treasure from the jaws of devouring
despotism. But if, with reverence, we seek those causes to which reason may
trace events, we shall find the miracle we admire to have been the work of
commerce. From the sea they gathered means to defend the land against
hostile armies on one side, and against the sea itself on the other: for the
singularity of their situation exposed them, alike, to be inundated and to
be subdued. The sea, which threatened and still threatens to overwhelm
them, gave access to the riches of both the Indias. They pursued, along that
perilous road, the persecutors of mankind, and wrested from their grasp
the unrighteous plunder of Mexico and Peru. Thus, surrounded by danger,
impelled by want, inured to toil, animated by exertion, strengthened by
faith, stimulated by hope and exalted by religion, a few miserable fishermen, scattered on a sterile coast, were converted into a race of heroes. They
acquired power in the struggle for existence, and wealth under the weight
of taxation.

Such, gentlemen, were our Dutch ancestors, who immediately after concluding the twelve years truce, came hither and brought with them their
skill, their integrity, their liberty, and their courage. From a sense of justice, that animating soul of commerce, without which it is a dead, and must
soon become a corrupt and stinking carcase, they entered into treaty with
the natives; in whom they found patience, fortitude, and a love of liberty
like their own. While the seven united provinces, by their steady perseverance, astonished the nations of the east; our six confederate tribes, by
their military prowess, subdued those of the west. The first treaty formed
between the Dutch and the Maquaas, or Mohawks, has been frequently
renewed; and few treaties have been better observed. The excellent discourse[5] delivered to you last year, leaves me nothing to say of those tribes.
Permit me, however, to express the astonishment, in which you will doubtless participate, that men, reputed to be wise and learned, should suppose
the people of this state, born, brought up, and situated as they are, can be
restrained from commercial pursuits.

Half a century after fort Orange was built, Charles II. of England, within
three years from his restoration, granted this state to his brother the Duke
of York; and in that year (1664) it was conquered by the British arms. En-

---

5. By the Hon. De Witt Clinton. Ed. [Footnote in original.]

gland, which Elizabeth (after reigning near five and forty years) had left in the possession of peace, wealth, and glory, passed two and twenty more under a conceited pedant, powerful in words and poor in act. He had neither the courage to establish nor the magnanimity to abandon prerogatives, which, inconsistent with the spirit of his age and country, became every day more and more intolerable. Thus the scholastic imbecility of a projector prepared the tragic scene, in which his son was doomed to act and to perish. A hideous scene, where the spectators beheld, with horror and dismay, justice violated, honor polluted, religion degraded, and freedom destroyed. But great crimes were palliated, as they were perpetrated, by great talents. The infamy of murder and usurpation was ennobled by the sword of victory. And the multitude dazzled by the splendor of success, that adoration which is due to virtue alone was blindly and basely offered at the shrine of power. In seventeen years after Charles ascended his father's throne, he was engaged in civil war. At the close of another seventeen years he was led to the scaffold.[6] During nine years the British sceptre was in the iron grasp of Cromwell. He made the nations tremble. But in less than three years from his decease, the son of Charles was restored. Fortunately for our freedom, this witty sensualist who, if we are to believe one of his profligate companions, "never said a foolish thing and never did a wise one,"[7] although he had the sense to perceive, had not the steadiness to pursue nor the address to secure the advantages of his situation. He might have put himself in possession of absolute power over a nation inured to war and naturally brave. He might have held in his hand the fate of Europe. He might have been the rival of Louis the fourteenth: perhaps his superior. Instead of this, he basely became his pensioner, and in that mean condition waged war with the United Netherlands. But a majority of his parliament, too wise to be deceived, too brave to be intimidated, too honest to be seduced, obliged him to make peace, by withholding the means to make war. The first of these

6. Morris takes some license with the chronology here. Charles I came to the throne in 1625 and the Civil War began in 1642, but he was executed seven years later, in 1649.

7. Epitaph of Charles II by John Wilmot, Earl of Rochester; in full:
> Here lies a great and mighty king
> Whose promise none relies on
> Who never said a foolish thing
> Nor ever did a wise one.

Charles II is said to have replied: "'Tis very true: for my words are my own, and my actions are my ministers'."

wars was terminated in three years by the treaty of Breda, which gave New-York to the British crown, the 26th of January, 1667.

After a licentious reign of near two and twenty years, the throne of inglorious Charles was mounted by his bigoted brother James; who, crowned in 1684, fled to France in 1688. Half a century had elapsed, from the time when Charles the first made his rash levy of ship money, to the accession of his son James.[8] In the former half of this period the English character was degraded by hypocrisy and crime, in the latter by impiety and vice. During the first five and twenty years, we had no connexion with them. On the contrary, for two years, from 1652 to 1654, there was war between Oliver Cromwell and the States General. During the last five and twenty, we were secured against the contagion of their immorality, by distance, by poverty, and by the simple manners and habits which characterized our Dutch ancestors. Six years after New-York was ceded to Charles the second, it was retaken by the Dutch, but restored to England the 9th February of the next year (1674) by the treaty of Westminster. In little more than fifteen years from that period, an insurrection under Leisler took this city for king William; whose war with France (terminated by the treaty of Ryswick in 1697) lasted eight years. After a short breathing of four years, however, it was renewed, in the beginning of the last century, and lasted thirteen years more: till, at length, the treaty of Utrecht, on the eleventh of April, 1714, followed by the death of queen Anne in August of the same year, and of Louis XIV. on the first of September in the next year, gave to our country a more durable repose. For though it might have been imagined that our distance and our insignificance would have secured us, a lowly bush, from tempests which tore the tops of lofty trees; yet, bordering as we do on Canada, so long as France continued in possession of that province, every war in which she was engaged with England, laid waste our frontiers and, calling forth every effort for their defence, exhausted our resources. From this rapid sketch, gentlemen, it appears that, children of commerce, we were rocked in the cradle of war, and sucked the principles of liberty with our mother's milk. Accordingly we find that, long before that controversy which rent the British empire asunder, in disputes with royal governors attempting to stretch authority beyond its just bounds, there was a steady appeal, by our fathers, to the principles on which the Belgic and British patriots relied in their opposition to tyranny.

8. The first levy of "ship money" by Charles I, as an expedient to replace taxes enacted by Parliament, was in 1634.

The revocation of the edict of Nantz, in the year 1685, drove many French protestants to seek an asylum on our shores, and governor Hunter, in the year 1710, brought with him a number of palatines. Thus our ancestry may be traced to four nations, the Dutch, the British, the French, and the German. It would have been strange had a people, so formed, been tainted with national prejudice. Far from it. We are, if I may be allowed to say so, born cosmopolite; and possess, without effort, what others can with difficulty acquire by much travel and great expence. But as no earthly good is pure, so this equal respect and regard for strangers diminishes the preference to natives, on occasions where natives ought to be preferred; and impairs the activity, if not the strength, while it removes the blindness of patriotic sentiment. In like manner, it may be numbered among the advantages of commerce, that a liberality which extends to foreign correspondents the gentle appellation of friend, encourages the growth of general benevolence. It is at the same time to be lamented, that with this amiable sentiment is connected a fondness for the fashions and productions of foreign countries which is injurious to the simplicity of ancient manners. But, from the combined operation of these causes, the emigrant from every nation finds himself, here, at home. Natives of the Alps, the Pyrenees, the Appenines, the highlands of Scotland, and the mountains of Wales, as well as those who inhabit the banks of the Shannon, the Thames, the Seine, the Rhine, and the Danube, (meeting here) see in each other the faces of fellow-countrymen. It results, from our mixed population, that he who wishes to become acquainted with the various languages and manners of mankind, need not ramble into distant regions. He also who would trace up society to its origin, can here behold it in the rudest condition. He can safely shut the volumes of philosophic dreaming, and look into the book of nature which lies open before him. Ethical reasoning may, here, be raised on the foundation of fact. If it be admitted, as a principle in the natural history of animals, that the state in which a particular species of them is most powerful and abundant, is the best suited to its nature, and therefore its natural state; it may be concluded that the natural state of man is that in which they are most numerous, and in which they have the most activity, strength and beauty. If this conclusion be just, we need but open our eyes on our savage brethren to be convinced, by a comparison of them with civilized man, that in so far as regards our own species, the state of nature and of society are one and the same. The half-naked Indian, who now sits shivering on the banks of Niagara, while he views that stupendous cataract, may view also the ships, the houses, the clothing and arms of his civilized fellow-creatures, and hear the thunders of their cannon roar louder than the torrent. If he compares his feeble means and wretched condition with their power and wealth, he cannot but be sensible of his great inferiority. And much more will civilized man who, daring death at the call of duty, not only spares an unresisting foe, but soothes his distress, relieves his wants, and heals his wounds, much more will he feel superiority over the savage hunter of men, whose rule of war is general slaughter, whose trophies are torn bleeding from the skulls of women and children, and who gluts his ferocity by the torture of helpless prisoners. The civilized man will perceive also, if history has occupied his attention, by comparing the laws of ancient and modern war, the influence, and, in that influence, the truth of our holy religion. If it be true that one great end of history is to communicate a knowledge of mankind, and, by making man acquainted with his species, facilitate the acquisition of that most important science, the knowledge of himself; we may be permitted to believe that a faithful narrative of deeds done by our fathers will eminently merit a studious regard. The comparison which will, obtrusively, present itself between the aboriginal tribes, the various colonists, the emigrants from Europe, and the troops of different nations, will display a more perfect picture of our species than can easily be delineated on any other historical canvass. Neither will the strong lineaments of character be wanting. Those arduous circumstances which marked our origin and impeded our growth; those ravages to which we were exposed, not only until the treaty of Utrecht, but in the war from 1744 to 1748, terminated by the treaty of Aix la Chapelle, in that which began in 1755 and ended in 1760 by the conquest of Canada, and in our war with Great-Britain, from April, 1775, to November, 1783; above all, the persevering efforts to defend our country, in that long period of near one hundred and seventy years from the first settlement by the Dutch in 1614, to the time when this city was evacuated by the British in the close of 1783, during which there was little repose (except in a space of thirty years which elapsed between the peace of Utrecht and the war of 1744) brought forth men worthy of respectful imitation, and formed the mass of our citizens to the hardihood of military life; notwithstanding a soil and climate which, teeming with abundance, tempt to the enjoyment of ease and luxury.

May we not be permitted also to believe that they are by nature brave? Pardon, gentlemen, a digression which, though it should conclude nothing, may furnish amusement; perhaps reflection. He who visits the nations which Tacitus and Caesar have described, will be struck with a resemblance between those who now inhabit particular districts, and those who dwelt there so many centuries ago. Notwithstanding the wars and conquests which have laid waste, depopulated and repeopled Europe; notwithstanding the changes of government and those which have been wrought by the decline and by the advance of society and the arts; notwithstanding the differences of religion, and the difference of manners resulting from all other circumstances; still the same distinctive traits of character appear. Similar bodies are animated by similar souls. We find, also, extending our view a little further east and taking in a larger surface of the globe, that peculiarities in civil establishment and political organization, corresponding with the peculiarities of national character, have, from the earliest ages, distinguished those regions. We find that the attempt of tyrants to establish despotism, in some countries, was frequently baffled; while the endeavor of patriots to secure freedom, in others, was equally fruitless. He who considers the changes wrought by the tide of time on the face of our globe, this solid earth itself alternately raised above the ocean or plunged beneath its waves, and perceives those peculiarities of form and mind, which remain unchanged through such a long succession of generations, must be struck with the idea of the simple Indian who, pressed to sell the possession of his tribe, replied, "We grew out of this ground. In its bosom our fathers repose. What! Shall we call upon their bones? Shall we bid them arise and go with us to a strange land?"

We, gentlemen, grew out of this same ground with our Indian predecessors. Have we not some traits to mark our common origin? This question will be answered with more precision when, after the lapse of centuries, the blood of our progenitors, operating with less force, the changes produced, not only in man but in other animals, by that unknown cause which exhibits a peculiar race in each particular country, shall be more fully displayed. Let us, however, collect the facts which now present themselves. Among the curiosities of newly discovered America was the Indian canoe. Its slender and elegant form, its rapid movement, its capacity to bear burdens and resist the rage of billows and torrents, excited no small degree of admiration for the skill by which it was constructed. After the lapse of two centuries, the ships of America were equally admired in the ports of great naval powers, for their lightness, their beauty, the velocity with which they sail, the facility with which they are managed. Nautical architecture may be considered as one of the most important branches of mechanic knowledge. The higher order of mathematic science has been called into act for its advancement. And certainly a line of battle ship is one of the most powerful engines that was ever framed. In comparison with it, the ancient inventions for defence or destruction dwindle, almost, to insignificance. And yet our untutored ship-builders have, by the mere force of genius, excelled their European brethren in this difficult, complex art. So great is the difference, that children distinguish, at first sight, the American ship ascending the Elbe to Hamburgh: a city of considerable trade long before Columbus was born. Again—We find among our savage tribes, the commemoration of events by painting: rude, indeed, but more distinct than in other barbarous nations. May I not remark that an American is at the head of that art in England, and that many others, who excel in it, drew their first breath on our shores. Again—Let me recall, gentlemen, to your recollection, that bloody field in which Herkemer fell.[9] There was found the Indian and the white man, born on the banks of the Mohawk, their left hand clenched in each other's hair, the right grasping, in a gripe of death, the knife plunged in each other's bosom. Thus they lay frowning. Africa presents a number of nations, like those of America, uncivilized. But how different! I will not say inferior, for they also have excellence peculiar to themselves. They are not, indeed, either painters or builders; but no where, not even in Italy, is the taste for music more universal.

If we believe, with Frederick the Great, that reason and experience are the crutches on which men halt along in the pursuit of truth, it may not be amiss to ask the aid of what is known about the Indian character and history, in order to draw the horoscope of our country. What is the statesman's business? If futurity were known, the simplest which can be imagined. For, as in reading Virgil we find the verse so smooth that every scholar thinks he could easily make as good; so, in glancing his eye along the page of history, an indolent reader figures to himself that he too could be a prince of Orange, a Walsingham, a Richelieu. And so indeed he might, by the aid of self-command, common prudence and common sense, could he see into futurity and penetrate the thoughts of those with whom he is to act. But there lies the difficulty.

Let us see then whether some other characteristic of the aborigines may not open to us a view of ourselves, and the perspective of our country. It has already been noticed that the Dutch, on their arrival, found the Indian tribes free. They were subject neither to princes nor to nobles. The Mohawks had not, like the Romans, naturalized those whom they subdued. It

9. Nicholas Herkimer (1728–77) was fatally wounded at the Battle of Oriskany, while leading the attempt to relieve Fort Schuyler. Indian auxiliaries fought on both sides in the engagement.

was a federal nation, a federal government, a people as free as the air they breathed; acute, dexterous, eloquent, subtle, brave. They had more of the Grecian than of the Roman character. The most strongly marked, perhaps, of their moral features, was a high sense of personal independence. Is it not likely that this may be the character of our children's children? May we not hope that the liberty to which we were bred, will be enjoyed and preserved by them? It must, indeed, be acknowledged that an extent so vast as that of the United States is less favorable to freedom than a more confined domain, and gives reason to apprehend the establishment of monarchy. Moreover, the anxious patriot may well tremble at the prevalence of faction, at the attempts to prostrate law, and at those absurd principles of mob power, as wildly preached by some as they are wickedly practised by others. Still there is ground of hope. Still it is permitted to believe that those who pursue despotic power, along the beaten path of democracy, and expect to establish their dominion over the people, by flattering the populace, will be sorely disappointed. The soul of this nation cannot be subdued. Neither will those who tread the soil in which the Mohawks are entombed submit to be slaves.

I shall not be surprised that ideas of this sort are treated as visionary speculations. When the great Chatham, in January, 1775, having moved an address for recalling the British troops from Boston said, in a speech which will ever do honor both to his eloquence and discernment, "America, insulted with an armed force, irritated with a hostile army before her eyes, her concessions, if you *could* force them, would be suspicious and insecure. But it is more than evident that you cannot force them to your unworthy terms of submission. It is impossible. We ourselves shall be forced ultimately to retract. Let us retract while we can; not when we must. I repeat it, my lords, we shall one day be forced to undo these violent oppressive acts. They must be repealed. You will repeal them. I pledge myself for it that you will in the end repeal them. I stake my reputation on it. I will consent to be taken for an idiot if they are not repealed." When the venerable statesman thus poured forth prophetic eloquence, the wise ones of that day, exulting in *"a little brief authority,"* shrugged up their shoulders and said, with a sneer of affected commisseration, poor old peer![10] He has outlived his understanding. In fancy to be sure he is young and wild, but reason is gone; he dotes. So, too, in the height of Gallic phrenzy, there was a cry raised to hunt down those who, reasoning and reflecting, foresaw and foretold a military despotism as the natural, the necessary result of such unexampled atroci-

10. The quotation is from Shakespeare's *Measure for Measure*, act 2, scene 2.

ties. It became a fashion to speak of those who warned their country against the contaminating touch, the infectious breath of licentious pollution, as enemies of liberty, as mad with aristocratic notions, as whimsical and fantastic. But now the predictions of Chatham and of Burke are verified. And it may now be asked, where are the men who called those eloquent sages fools? They are precisely where Chatham, who knew mankind, would have predicted. They are in authority and enjoy the blind confidence of disciples who, when their masters shall have blundered on ninety and nine times more, will most faithfully adhere to them in their hundredth blunder.

Returning from this digression, I take leave to observe that our state will support a population of four millions. Already it exceeds nine hundred thousand white inhabitants, although twenty years ago it was but little more than three hundred thousand. When, therefore, the salubrity of our climate, the fertility of our soil, the convenient situations for manufacturing establishments, and our advantageous position for trade are considered, there is reason to believe the period not distant when we shall count four million inhabitants: and certainly our wealth, if we are blest by a good government, must keep pace with our population. New-York, connected with her eastern brethren and New-Jersey, had in 1810 more than two million and a half of white inhabitants; wherefore we may reasonably conclude that in half a century they will contain eight millions; for in 1790 their number was short of one million and a half, and in 1800 was near two: having encreased about one third in each term of ten years, but more than three fourths in the whole term of twenty years, viz. from 1,476,631 to 2,597,634. Though not yet distinguished as a manufacturing people, yet, judging by those fruits which the inventive genius of our fellow-citizens has produced, we may reasonably foster, even in that respect, exulting expectations. Numerous at land, we are not strangers at sea. Our country abounds in iron, and the use of it is not unknown to her children.

If, then, monarchy and aristocracy establish themselves in other portions of America; if the variously colored population of states, in which domestic slavery prevails, should be condemned to civil and political slavery; if they should be subjected to haughty caciques; let us hope that here we may be led by the council of our sachems. Let it not, however, be supposed, that a breach of the federal compact is intended: for, setting aside all attachment to national union, so essential to public tranquillity, if a separation of the states were contemplated, the Delaware would not be chosen as their boundary. But when the great extent of our country, when the violence of rash men, when the dangerous inequality of civil condition, when the contempt which some express for others, alarm those whose lives have been devoted to liberty, it is natural to look about and enquire, if there be no asylum to which freedom may fly when driven from her present abode. In such moments of anxious solicitude, it is no small consolation to believe that here, whatever may be her fate elsewhere, here, gentlemen, her temple will stand on a foundation immoveable. Here we have, at this moment, more free citizens than the whole union could boast of in 1775. And here I fondly hope, here I firmly believe, the spirit of 1775 still glows in the bosoms of the brave.

It is among the circumstances which ought not to be overlooked, in this general view of our history, that the practice of law has been strictly modelled on that which prevails, in what we formerly called our mother country. That land of good nature and good sense from which we learned the most useful lessons of our lives: our liberty, our laws and our religion. Wits may scoff at the pedantry of special pleading, the barbarous phraseology of lawyers, and stern severity of judges who, trampling on the flowers of eloquence, check babbling and confine the bar within the bounds of strict logic: but those who think will perceive that, inasmuch as things are expressed by words, precise expression can only be effected by words of established signification; and since the rule of conduct cannot be applied until the fact be established, it is a pre-requisite that such precise assertion be made by the one party, and such precise negation by the other, as distinctly to state the facts to be ascertained. The judges of fact can then accurately determine on its existence, and, that done, the judges of law can apply the rule. Every case, so adjudged, will serve as a rule for cases which may afterwards arise; and thus the general principles of natural justice, the maxims of ancient usage, and the positive injunctions or inhibitions of legislative providence, are extended to the infinite variety of human actions and relations: so that liberty and property are secured. Nor is it, as many have hastily supposed, an evil, that law is expensive to suitors: for, as far as the suitor himself is concerned, by deterring him from litigation, it strengthens (if his cause be good) the sentiment of benevolence, and enforces (if bad) the duty of justice. By lessening the number of suits, it diminishes the causes of discord. Trifling injuries which, if unnoticed, would soon be forgotten, may, by a vindictive spirit, be made the subject of controversy and separate families for more than one generation. Moreover, this great expence of law is a great public economy; for when cheap lawyers, multiplying trivial causes, croud tribunals with a host of jurors, parties, witnesses, and their needful attendants, many fields lie uncultivated, many work-shops are neglected, and habits of idleness and dissipation are acquired, to the manifest injury and impoverishment of the republic.

Is it a suggestion of fancy, or am I warranted in supposing that rigid practice of law may give somewhat of precision to general modes of thinking; that it may even render conversation less diffusive, and therefore more instructive; that the accuracy of forensic argument may communicate vigor to parliamentary debate; that the deep sense and grave deportment of the bench and bar may have imparted to our character more of solidity than it would otherwise have possessed? This city was long the headquarters of a British army, and familiar intercourse with officers, many of whom were men of family and fashion, while it gave (perhaps) a little of that lustre and polish which distinguish the higher ranks of society, could not but dispose young people to levity and mirth, more than is suited to the condition of those who must earn their living by their industry. Man is an imitative animal. Not only his deportment, his language and his manners, but even his morals depend, in a great degree, on his companions. Let us suppose two individuals, of twin resemblance as to intellectual disposition and power, one of them frequently attending on courts of strict practice, the other on those, where lengthened declamation wears out tedious days on questions of trifling import. Would not the latter slide into a loose mode both of thinking and speaking; might he not conceive that to talk long is to talk well; might he not attend too much to the melody of periods, too little to the precision of thought; might he not, at length, be exposed (from indulging the habit of loose thinking) to the danger of loose acting? It requires accuracy of investigation and clearness of perception to distinguish right from wrong when, in doubtful circumstances, self-interest is concerned. A man, therefore, may easily be induced to do wrong, in compliance with what he feels to be his interest, when he thinks it *may* be right: especially when he thinks that those who are to judge *may* be prevailed on to decide in his favor. Is there not, on the other hand, reason to suppose that he, whose course of life has led him to scenes of sharp enquiry, who has listened to arguments of precise logic, who has participated in decisions of legal strictness, is there not reason to believe that this man will use a diction more concise, possess a judgment more acute, and observe a more correct line of conduct?

These probable, or at least possible, effects of forensic accuracy, may be encreased, or diminished, or destroyed, by the ever varying circumstances of our civil and social condition. Nay, their very existence may be questioned, or attributed to other causes. Talents and habits of observation

must be exercised to make the due investigation. But there is one important consequence which cannot easily be overlooked or assigned to any
other cause. I allude to the value of property in this state, and merely mention it, because detailed observations would be tedious, perhaps invidious.
Permit me, however, to notice the more prominent reasons why it must
produce that effect, in the political associations of mankind. It is evident,
at the first blush, that a purchaser of land will give more for a good than
for a doubtful title, and it is equally evident that titles must be less secure
where scope is given to declamation, than where strict practice and close
logic are required. If we look a little nearer, we shall perceive a more extensive consequence. The creditor who is certain of getting speedily what
is due to him, provided the debtor possess sufficient property, will be more
liberal of credit than where the recovery of debts is tedious and uncertain.
But credit is equivalent to money, and, like money, not only enhances the
price of property, but, obviating the want of money, becomes, to the nation
in which it prevails, a substitute for that intrinsic value, part of their capital stock, which would, otherwise, be sent abroad to procure the precious
metals.

Indulge me, gentlemen, while on this subject, in another observation.
The more strict and regular is the practice of law, the greater is our certainty that the guilty will be punished; and, of necessary consequence, that
the innocent will be protected. The law, when it is a terror to evil doers, is
the safeguard not only of property but of life, and of that which wise and
virtuous citizens value more than life. It is the protector of liberty. Where
the law is supreme, every one may do what it permits, without fear; and
from this happy condition arises that habit of order which secures the public peace. But when any man, or association of men, can exercise discretionary power over others, there is an end of that liberty which our fathers
enjoyed and for which their sons bled. Whenever such an association, assuming to be the people, undertake to govern according to their will and
pleasure, the republic which submits—nay, the republic which does not immediately subdue and destroy them, is in the steep downhill road to despotism. I cannot here, gentlemen, help congratulating you on the high standing of our city, during late events, and adding my feeble approbation to the
full applause so justly bestowed on its magistrates. To say more might look
like adulation. To say less would be a want of gratitude.

Among the singularities of our history, is the slow progress of population, previous to the year 1783, compared with that of other states. James-
town in Virginia, was founded in 1607, Quebec in 1608, New-York in 1615,

New Plimouth in 1620. Thus in the short space of fourteen years, these different plantations of mankind were made. The settlement of Pensilvania was undertaken full sixty years later: and yet at the commencement of the war for defence of our rights, one hundred and fifty five years after the first settlement of New-Plimouth, and only ninety four years after the first settlement of Pensilvania, the population (according to the congressional estimate) was of

The eastern states, exclusive of Vermont, nearly as 70
That of New-York, Vermont and New-Jersey, ... 33
That of Pensilvania and Delaware, ... 33
And that of Maryland and Virginia, ... 64

Together, 200

Moreover, according to that estimate, the proportion of the states of Virginia, Pensilvania and New-York was
Virginia, ... 44
Pensilvania, ... 33
New-York, including Vermont, ... 22

Together, 99

But Virginia had been planted 168 years, New-York 160, and Pensilvania only 94, which gives a proportion to
Virginia, of, ... 39
Pensilvania, ... 22
And New-York, ... 38

99

So that the population of Virginia had advanced, compared with the term of settlement, 5, and Pensilvania 11, while New-York was deficient 16. The citizens of Pensilvania, warmed with that attachment to their country so honorable to man, attributed their superior prosperity to natural and moral advantages which they believed themselves to possess. They supposed their climate more mild than ours, more salubrious than that of Virginia, their soil more fertile than either, and they contrasted the simplicity of manners among those called quakers, and their equality of civil condition, with what they supposed to be the luxury and aristocracy of men to whom manors had been granted, and who were the masters of slaves. The citizens of New-York, however, believed that the comparative prosperity of Pensilvania might more naturally be attributed to circumstances more evident, and of less doubtful operation. Without acknowledging either a moral or civil superiority, they believed that nature had given them as good a climate, a better soil, and a more favorable situation; but their country had been from the beginning, a theatre of war, and stood in the fore front of the battle. New-York was, like Joseph, a victim of parental kindness. Not, indeed, that her brethren, like his, were disposed to sell or kill the favorite child; but that their enemy endeavoured to subdue her, as the means more effectually to annoy them. The only accurate solution of such questions is made by time. For as experience is the groundwork, so is time the test of political reasoning. At the end of seven years from the period when the estimate mentioned was made, by the first congress, another severe hurricane of war had blown over our state and laid it in ruins. Our frontier settlements had been broken up, and a part of our capital reduced to ashes. Our citizens were banished or beggared, and our commerce annihilated. Whatever doubts, therefore, may have been entertained as to the accuracy of proportions taken in 1775, there was no doubt left in 1783 but that we were below the ratio assumed when the war began. In less than eight and twenty years, from that time, the census was taken on which the representation in congress is apportioned. And according to the ratio thereby established,

The eastern states, exclusive of Vermont, are as 53
New-York, Vermont, and New-Jersey, ... 60
Pensilvania and Delaware, ... 38
And Maryland and Virginia, ... 49
——
Total   200

Or allowing for the black population, which is not fully represented, the number would be,

In the eastern states, exclusive of Vermont, as 51
New-York, Vermont and New-Jersey, ... 58
Pensilvania and Delaware, ... 36
And Maryland and Virginia, ... 55
——
Total   200

If this be compared with the first proportion, viz. that made by estimate in 1775, we shall find that the eastern states have decreased 19, Virginia and Maryland 9, while this state with Vermont and New-Jersey, have increased 25, Pensilvania and Delaware 3. Or taking the relation between Virginia, Pensilvania and New-York which was

Then, Virginia, ... 44	Now, ... 35
Pensilvania, ... 33	 29
New-York, with Vermont, .. 22	Without Vermont, ... 35
99	99

It appears that Virginia has decreased 9, and Pensilvania 4, making the 13 which New-York has gained. In respect to Virginia, however, the variation may arise from those colonies which have left the antient dominion to people southern and western states. It may be well, therefore, to confine our view to a comparison of this state with her sister Pensilvania. In July 1775 the congress estimated the population of Pensilvania and that of New-York, then including Vermont, in a proportion of three to two, which gives to

Pensilvania, ... 30
New-York, ... 20

50

but by the late apportionment of Representatives,

Pensilvania has 23
New-York, ... 27

Together, 50

So that in the space of twenty-eight years of peace, from 1783 to 1811, Pensilvania has lost seven in thirty, and New-York has gained seven in twenty, on their relative proportion: and this too without including Vermont. Finally, the matter may be examined in a still more simple point of view, and, speaking in round numbers, if the estimate of 1775 be considered as tolerably accurate, Massachusetts has encreased one half, Pensilvania has doubled, and New-York quadrupled since it was made.

Excuse me, gentlemen, for dwelling so much on a calculation which may appear to some as mere amusement. It shows by conclusions, which, founded on arithmetic, cannot be questioned, that the growth of this state was impeded only by the wars in which it has been so often, so deeply, and so disastrously engaged. From 1614, when Fort Orange, now Albany, was built, to 1810, when the last census was taken, there are seven terms of 28 years. During the first six terms, which ended in 1782, we had not attained to more than one fourth of our present condition. It has already been observed that the settlement of Pensilvania began in 1681, but as it may be contended that antecedent settlements in Delaware and New-Jersey facilitated the undertaking of Mr. Penn, we may go back a few years and suppose it to have commenced in 1670, from which time to that in which the last census was taken, there are five terms of 28 years. In the first four Pensilvania attained to one half of her present condition, and had acquired more by one half than we had in six. But in the last term they have little more than doubled while we have quadrupled. But it may be said that no reliance ought to be placed on the estimate made by congress in 1775, and that comparisons drawn from proportions then assumed, are not convincing. It may be well, therefore, to test the question by a standard whose accuracy cannot be denied. The census of 1790 gave to Pensilvania 424,099 white inhabitants. The encrease in ten years was 38 per cent, in the next ten years 34 per cent, (or in the whole twenty years 85 per cent) so as to amount in 1810 to 786,804. The census of 1790 gave to New-York only 314,142 white inhabitants: being to Pensilvania *even then*, only in the proportion of near 3 to 4. The encrease in ten years was 77 per cent, in the next ten years 65 per cent, (or in the whole twenty years 192 per cent) so as to amount in 1810 to 918,699: being to Pensilvania, in the proportion of 7 to 6. And now let a glance be cast at the position of those lands which have been settled, in those two states, within the last twenty years. They are separated from each other by the River Delaware, for more than fifty miles, and then only by a mathematical line, for more than two hundred miles. It may be asserted, without danger of contradiction, that along this extensive frontier, New-York is more thickly settled than Pensilvania. Without contending, therefore, as to civil or moral advantage, it can hardly be denied that a soil and climate which have attracted such great population in the last term of 28 years, would have thickly settled the state long ago, had it not been for a political cause, which, while it retarded the population of New-York, and because it retarded the population of New-York, promoted and accelerated the population of Pensilvania. That great political cause, unhappily for us, again brought into operation, was war with the possessor of Canada. It has already been noticed, that in the last ten years our number has increased 65 per cent. This city has in that period, (nearly keeping pace with the aggregate) encreased 60 per cent. But the western district has encreased at the rate of 175 per cent. If we add the counties of Montgomery, Essex, Clinton, and Franklin, so as to embrace the whole northern frontier, the rate of encrease is 163 per cent: the amount upwards of 261,000, whereas, that district, those counties and this city excepted, the ratio for the rest of the state was only 20 per cent; and the amount little more than 75,000. In effect near 262,000 out of not quite 373,000, our total increment, belong to our northern and western country; so that seven tenths of that growth, which we beheld with astonishment and exultation, was the produce of a country now exposed to the chance and disasters of war. Nearly one other tenth was in the capital. This, gentlemen, is neither the place nor the occasion to enquire into the policy, much less the justice of those measures, by which we are distressed. Bowing with deference to the national government; I am willing to suppose that, in so far as regards the United States, the war may have been begun and is now carried on justly, wisely, happily; but for us, most unhappily. Every member of this society is, undoubtedly, disposed by every proper exertion and every possible sacrifice, to support the honor and independence of our country. But he must be void of discernment who does not perceive that war, with the greatest naval power, is no happy condition for a commercial people. Whether America will eventually rejoice in trophies gained, territory acquired, and privileges torne, from an enemy subdued; or whether she shall weep for defeats sustained, dominion lost, and rights surrendered, must depend, under God, on the manner in which this war shall be conducted, and the wisdom and integrity of the negotiations by which it shall be concluded. But, whatever may be the feelings of our sister states; whether they, as events may indicate, shall clothe themselves in scarlet or in sack-cloth; our house will, in all probability, be a house of mourning.

It is by the lights of history and geography that we discern the interests of a country, and the means by which they can best be pursued and secured. Am I mistaken in concluding, from the foregoing details, which may, I fear, have been tedious to you, that we should encourage husbandry, commerce, and useful arts as the great columns which are to support the fabric of our wealth and power. That we should promote order, industry, science, and religion, not only as the guardians of social happiness, but as the outworks to the citadel of our liberty. And finally that we should, as the best means of effecting those objects, so arrange our concerns as that the management of public affairs be entrusted to men of wisdom, firmness, and integrity. I will venture to add the idea that, in any political change which circumstances may induce, we should respect the example of our predecessors, the Six Nations, and not be persuaded to ask for a king that he may go out before us, like the other nations, nor submit to the sway of hereditary nobles.[11] It

---

11. 1 Samuel 8:19–20: "But the people refused to listen to the voice of Samuel; and they said, 'No! but we will have a king over us, that we also may be like all the nations, and that our king may govern us and go out before us and fight our battles.'" This is also quoted by John Locke, *Second Treatise*, section 109.

would be a fatal delusion if, for the military vigor of one institution, or the political cunning of the other, we should surrender that freedom which ennobles man. Nor would it be less fatal that, with a view to simplicity and unity, we should permit the consolidation of too great a mass: for history teaches that republican spirit is liable to ferment, when in a large vessel, and be changed to the corroding acid of despotism.

39 ❧ Oration Before the Washington Benevolent Society (1813)

The Washington Benevolent Society was founded in New York in 1808 as a Federalist counterweight to the Democratic-Republican Tammany Society. Within a few years there were many such societies across the New England states, New Jersey, and Pennsylvania. Like the Tammany Society, its membership met in secret, but it also held public meetings.[1] Morris does not appear to have had a hand in organizing the society. As this address makes clear, however, despite his reservations about such mass political groups, he sympathized with this one.

ORATION, &C.

Fellow Citizens,

A society which bears the name of WASHINGTON is assembled to celebrate the Birth of our empire. When *that* name is pronounced in connexion with *this* festival, what tumultuous recollections rush on the heart! The value of freedom—the duty to defend it—unsullied virtue—immortal fame. But let us endeavour to reduce our ideas to order.

Seven and thirty years have been borne on the current of time since our Independence was declared. Of the actors in that scene but few remain.

An Oration, Delivered July 5th, 1813, Before The Washington Benevolent Society, Of The City Of New-York, In Commemoration Of American Independence. By The Hon. Gouverneur Morris (New-York: Published by the Society, and sold by A. T. Goodrich & Co. No. 124 Broadway; J. Seymour, printer, 1813). American Antiquarian Society Early American Imprints, series II (Shaw-Shoemaker), no. 29222. Courtesy American Antiquarian Society. An account of the oration appears in the *New-York Evening Post* of July 17, 1813. I have silently corrected typographical errors in the pamphlet.

1. Dixon Ryan Fox, *The Decline of Aristocracy in the Politics of New York*, Studies in History, Economics, and Public Law, vol. 56, no. 198 (New York: Columbia University, 1919), 89–100.

The greater number of those who now perform a part on the stage of life, were then in their nurses arms, their mothers' wombs, or only to be numbered among possible existences. It may not be improper, then, for one who was a witness, to delineate the sentiments which prevailed. His feeble testimony may assist in cleansing the American character from representations by which it has been sullied; for it has become a fashion, with some, to celebrate this anniversary by invective; and, mingling low abuse with vain applause, portray the men who stood forward to defend their country as slaves of vulgar resentment, or baubles of childish passion. There were then, indeed, as there are now, and as there ever will be, a herd who proved their patriotism only by their noise. Many of these, in the hour of trial, sought safety under the British flag; but when the American standard waved triumphant, they crawled from their hiding places, and found security in contempt. Afterwards, by degrees, they wriggled themselves into the confidence of a heedless people, and became again vociferous: founding a claim to exclusive patriotism on clamour against British influence. These are the men who stigmatized Washington as a tory, and those who shared his confidence and fought by his side, as a gang of conspirators.

Let it not be forgotten, that our contest with Britain was in defence of liberty. Those who engaged in it did not wait the galling of oppression, but opposed oppressive claims. In their minds a love of liberty was mingled with a sense of honour. They might perhaps have suffered themselves to be despoiled, but they could not bear to be disgraced. They were not blind to probable consequences. They had property, families, reputation; and, according to the calculations of human prudence, might anticipate an ignominious death. Imagination could not fail to present to their view helpless orphans, driven from the paternal mansion to beggary and wretchedness. They derived no consolation from comparing the force of the opposed parties. The alternative, therefore, which reason presented, was basely to submit or bravely to perish. Under such impressions, men of calm temper, fair characters, and religious sentiments, after solemn communion with their own hearts, determined to hazard their all. Their trust was in the Almighty. They knew that the God of battles is the God of righteousness; and they felt their cause to be just.

Weighty arguments were not wanting to dissuade them. It was urged, that the supremacy of Parliament was a characteristic trait in the British constitution; that it was the pride and boast of British subjects; that it was the palladium of that liberty which they and we adored; that the union of the British empire was the base of its power and glory; that we shared in the lofty pre-eminence which British subjects enjoyed; that a separation from the mother country would expose both her and ourselves; that union was essential to the common security; that, should we succeed in breaking the arch of Empire, we should be crushed in its ruins. A strong appeal, also, was made to national antipathies; to resentments against France; for we were yet smarting with wounds received in the seven years' war. The savage yell, mingled with the shout of *vive le roi*, yet tingled in our ears. We were told by friends who adhered to Britain, and such there were whose conduct, though different from ours, was equally dictated by a sense of duty, that we should become the prey of Gallic ambition; that, seduced by the wiles of a crafty court, we should exchange the privileges of England for the fetters of France.

These arguments were dispassionately weighed, and the result was a conviction that no earthly good is so valuable as Liberty: That it was our duty to deliver to our children, unimpaired, the rights we had received from our fathers: That, in the performance of duty, it is not permitted to deliberate; but, accountable to God for our actions, we are bound to submit the result to his sovereign will. These, indeed, were not the sentiments of fiery zealots, whose standard of patriotism was persecution. But these *were* the sentiments of that phalanx which marched with firm steps through the horrors of civil war. As they were not deterred by danger, so they were not seduced by hope, nor deluded by insidious propositions. When it was suggested that an American representation in the British Parliament would justify submission to its authority, they perceived that this expedient, (which in the moment of unsuspecting confidence might have been thankfully adopted) would only give to wrong a colouring of right. Reflection showed, that between the parent state and the colonies, there was such diversity of interest that, if subjected to the same legislative authority, one must be sacrificed to the other. For it is a serious truth, that where, from permanent causes and geographical situation, a line of difference is drawn between members of the same community, no political contrivance can render a free form of government safe to the minority. The majority, feeling it a duty to keep possession of power, will consider more the end than the means. Far from being controlled by the presence of a minority, they will act *as* absolutely as if they were alone, and with *more* severity. For, to the pride of power, opposition having the air of insult, both pity and justice will be consumed by wrath. It was under the influence of these considerations, that every offer of conciliation was not merely rejected but repelled. Standing alone, with no prospect of foreign aid, the acknowledgment of Independence was insisted on as a preliminary to negociation. These, fellow-citizens, were the counsels of moderate men, acting from a sense of duty, not instigated by revenge, but believing that their opponents (though mistaken) might be honest as themselves. This was the conduct of Washington. His heart was too pure to admit malice as a guest; his mind too lofty for illiberal reflections. As he fought with the gallantry of a soldier, and felt with the enthusiasm of a patriot, so he thought with the dignity of a statesman. At the close of the conflict, our gallant army, like their venerable chief, buried their enmity when they sheathed their swords.

Under his conduct they defended our liberty against a foreign foe, and, but for him, we might have been taught, by woful experience, that those who defend can also destroy the freedom of their country. There are, in all armies, men of turbulent temper and inordinate ambition. Among the officers who served under Washington, were some who hated him; but they were not numerous. There were many of discerning minds, devoted to liberty, who had seen with concern that the articles of confederation were but a rope of sand; that these states, being kept together only by external pressure, peace would dissolve their union. They saw, or thought they saw, in that suspicious jealousy which withheld authority from the national government, a source of no distant despotism. They saw, or thought they saw, that we were doomed to pass through the medium of anarchy to the condition of slaves. Their hearts were wrung with those torturing apprehensions, and they wept over their wounds. Nevertheless, with the characteristic energy of great minds, they gathered hope from circumstances big with despair. They thought, by keeping the army together until provision should be made for discharging its arrears, they could create a necessity for new-modelling the general government, and investing it with sufficient power; they believed that, from an army led by Washington, nothing was to be apprehended; and they flattered themselves that he, from this consideration, might be prevailed on to continue in the command.[2] They were mistaken; they had not considered that sentiments which would restrain him from *abusing*, would prevent him from *accepting* unlawful power. There were, moreover, circumstances which would have rendered success doubtful, even if he had engaged in the enterprise. That army was, chiefly, composed of the yeomanry of New-England, desirous of returning to the

---

2. Morris is referring to the Newbergh Conspiracy of March 1783. What he does not say is that he was one of "them," although his exact role in the episode has never become fully clear.

bosom of civil and social life. There had been no previous exacerbations of party spirit, to marshal different members of the community against each other in hostile array. Moreover, that army had not been enlisted to achieve conquest or gratify ambition. They were patriot soldiers, engaged to defend their rights against foreign aggression. They were, in truth, the army of liberty. Nevertheless, it was believed, by men of sound mind, that even *they* might be brought to act against their country, should it refuse to redress their grievances.

Thus a great lesson was taught to those who were in a situation to know what was passing. They knew that the country, fatigued, exhausted, and worn out by war, sickened for repose: That the prospect of a new contest would shake the firmest temper: That, to oppose this veteran army, numerous levies must be raised and maintained: That the funds needful for that purpose would be sufficient to discharge what was due to our defenders: That the authority which could raise taxes for one purpose, might equally raise them for another: But that, so long as authority was withheld from the government, opposition to the army would be impossible. In the mean time, the troops would subsist by contributions; and there were not wanting considerate men, in civil life, who, knowing the defects of our confederation, would have seen, with no evil eye, the efforts to produce an efficient government, not reflecting that laws imposed by power are seldom marked by mildness.

Heedless, indeed, must they have been who could pass through such scenes without wholesome reflection. We had been often told, that standing armies are dangerous to republics; and now we could read the same thing in the great book of the world. We had been taught, by experience, that no people, however brave, can prudently rely for defence on militia alone. These, setting aside the insupportable expense, being unaccustomed to a camp, perish by disease. Not being habituated to actual service, they are incapable of that unshaken order, that prompt obedience, and those steady efforts, without which opposition to veteran troops is almost impossible. Such considerations, combined with our geographical situation, render the maxims of our policy clear and distinct. It was evidently proper to keep up, as guards and garrisons for forts, arsenals, and posts on the frontiers, the skeleton of an army, so large that experienced officers might not be wanting in a case of emergency. But, above all, it was proper, as soon as the national resources would permit, to build, equip, and keep in service a reputable naval force. To this effect, it was necessary to indulge the national disposition for trade, and encourage the fisheries. The same navy which protected our country would protect her commerce; and commerce, so protected, would support the navy. This was, and this is the scheme of Washington's policy—How simple—how safe—how easy—how efficient! This policy contemplated the preservation of peace, as long as it could be done without sacrificing national honour. Not the fantastic honour of a captious duelist, nor the nice punctilios of regal pride; but that broad principle of right on which the dignity and independence of nations repose. These United States, possessing all that reasonable creatures can ask; a domain fertile, extensive, too extensive perhaps; a climate favourable to every useful production; a rational religion, just laws, free government— what have we to gain by war? and what have we not to lose? Oh folly! Oh madness! to stake a fortune against a feather, in a game whose every turn is stained with human blood!

But we are engaged in war; it becomes us, therefore, as free men, to inquire into its cause and object; moreover, it is our duty, as accountable beings, to examine the ground of quarrel, and give aid or opposition, according to our moral sense. Let no man persuade himself that the guilt of unjust war will be imputed, only, to the government under which he lives. No; were that government absolute as the grand Signior, still there is a power supreme, to whom our paramount obedience is due. Let no man hug the hope of success, however flattering the appearance, where the cause is unholy. Momentary flashes of victory may dazzle the world's eye; battle may be gained after battle, and province after province be subdued: but the hour of retribution will come; the trumpet of vengeance will sound—the cups of conquest shall be dashed from the vain-glorious lip; and armies, swept away, shall vanish like a morning dew. Look into the volume of sacred science. Do you not believe? Examine the annals of human history. Do you still doubt? Open your eyes. Behold what is now passing in the world.

And, even if the rest of the world should suppose that the eye of Omniscience could be closed in sleep, we, at least, should remember that we owed our deliverance to an Almighty arm. This day should admonish us that we, more than all others, should endeavour, by a conduct scrupulously just, to secure the Divine assistance. It is not needful, on the present occasion, to look back at past transactions. These may subserve the purposes of satire or panegyric; they may serve also as a clue to future labyrinths of political intrigue; but we have nothing now to do with satire, panegyric, or intrigue; there is now no ground for sophistry, no room for evasion. We are at war, avowedly, to protect British seamen against their own country. Is such war just? Is it wise? There are, who pretend that the cause avowed is not the real cause; there are who, styling themselves friends of the administration, claim for them, as incident to their calling of politicians, the privilege to deceive, to withhold the truth, and communicate such matter, (true or false,) as will make an impression favourable to their designs. These advocates, having read perhaps in satirical writings, that great statesmen are great knaves, seem to think that great knaves must be great statesmen; and decorate their idols by the attribution of perfidy and falsehood, as with precious gems. They ought to consider that, taken at their words, they preclude their favourites from claiming trust, faith, or confidence, at home or abroad. Far be it from us to disgrace ourselves by such imputations on our rulers. Let us, standing on the ground of reason, history, and experience, insist that falsehood is the resource of feeble minds: of that mean cunning which, entangled in the meshes of its own duplicity, creeps out by a lie. Wisdom foresees, and, foreseeing, provides against events. A noble candour marks its conduct. Cautious not to hazard an assertion; scrupulous not to violate an engagement; true to itself, honourable to its enemies, impartially just to all, it finds, under the pressure of misfortune, a neverfailing resource in public confidence. Far be it, then, from us to suppose that our government has any object but that which they profess: and let us examine that object.

Until lately, it never entered into the heads of well-informed men, to question the right of a nation to the military service of its own citizens. The practice on this subject has been constant and invariable. It would seem, therefore, that, even if the reason were doubtful, such universal consent would prevent the most powerful prince from opposing a current of opinion which has flowed steadily, in the same channel, from the earliest age. Much more might modesty prevent an inferior power from raising the standard of a new doctrine; and, above all, from requiring the assent of others on no better ground than its own will. There is in such course something so offensive, that, even were the principle reasonable and just, it could not fail to shock the sense of national dignity, and make disagreeable impressions on a dispassionate observer.

The great mass of mankind, precluded by their special vocations from making matters of this sort their study, must rely, in legal questions, on the authority of others; and it might suffice to refer to all reputable writers on public and municipal law, as well as to the solemn decisions of our own tribunals; challenging those who entertain a different opinion to support it by a single authority. But, as the occasion is of deep concern, we will, instead of hiding ourselves behind the rampart of authority, venture out into the field of reason. A distinction has, it is said, been lately made, respecting this object, between rights under public and under municipal law; and, on that ground, it is pretended that the right of a nation to its own citizens, does not depend on, nor form part of, the law of nations. But surely the law of nations requires that each respect the rights of others, whatever they may be, or however derived. To violate those rights, therefore, is contrary to that law. Moreover, what idea can we form of the law of nations, if that be no part of it which is the law of every nation? Questions respecting property, are, and must be, decided by municipal law. Does it follow that, according to the law of nations, one may take property belonging to the other? Or can it be lawful to take men, and unlawful to take goods? Moreover, on the broad question of justice, what matters it whether the wrong-doer violate public or municipal law?

Shall I trespass on your patience, fellow-citizens, to prove the duty of defending our country? God forbid. I will not insult your understanding, nor wound your feelings. What! prove to Americans—who glory in the name of Washington—and that, too, on the fourth of July, that it is their duty to defend their country! As well attempt to prove that they see the sun, or breathe the air, or feel the pulsation of their own honest hearts. That great Being who fashioned his creatures from the clay, formed and fitted them for society. To man, society is not only advantageous, but indispensable: for years must pass away before children can exist without the care of their fellow-creatures. Citizens, therefore, contract in earliest youth indissoluble obligations. But it would have been an insufficient resource to have left the care of children and defence of states to the reason of parents and soldiers. The Almighty has filled the bosom of parents with love for their children; and every parent has, in his own sentiments a standard by which to measure the duty of other parents. The same Almighty wisdom has impressed on every human heart the love of its native country. He who shivers on the shores of the frozen sea, or pants beneath the burning sun of Africa; those who groan under the yoke of despotism, as well as those who bask in the rays of freedom, all love their country. In the dictates of that love they find the duties of other men; if men there be who have no such affection. To such men—to men who, driven from their native soil by vices or crimes, would stifle the dictates of nature in the embrace of a selfish philosophy, it may be well to exhibit the consequence of their tenets. If the supposed right of expatriation exists, it must exist at one time and place as well as at another. If it belong to one, it must belong to many. If we have a right to abandon our native country and become subjects of another, we must have the right to abandon her without assuming a new allegiance. But if all this be so, any number of citizens, in the northern and western parts of our states, may lawfully cast off their allegiance, and either join Great Britain, or declare themselves neutral. In like manner, any gang of sailors may lawfully change their condition, declare themselves independent, and exercise hostility against the rest of mankind. According to this principle, there can be no piracy—no treason. True it is, that communities may be separated, and the political union between different parts of a nation be dissolved. Imperious circumstances may render this not only lawful, but laudable; not only justifiable, but indispensable. Of this truth, the day we celebrate is a splendid example. But to assert that individuals have the same right, and may exercise it on no better ground than their own caprice, is pregnant with such absurdity, that I feel ashamed to have dwelt so long on the subject before intelligent men.

But, it will be said, this war is not waged to compel a relinquishment of British rights to British sailors, but to prevent that abuse of it by which they impress Americans; and here we meet with a list of more than six thousand—I cannot say names, for it appears that to swell that exaggerated list, the same names are repeated: I cannot say native Americans, for it is not pretended that they are natives; neither can I say naturalized British seamen—for here is no evidence of naturalization; but I can say that, if native Americans be meant, it is probable, from investigations made by the state of Massachusetts, that they do not amount to one hundredth part of that number. Admitting, however, the complaint to be founded in its utmost extent, let us pause and examine the claim, on the part of America, which has been advanced with so much confidence and so much clamour. I venture to say it rests on a principle destructive to liberty. This assertion may surprise. Bear with me, then, a few minutes, and lend your patient attention. The cry raised against Britain has been very loud. That government, it is said, should prevent the abuse. But how? a ready answer is given—by punishing officers who do the wrong. But how? The British are a free people; their rulers cannot imprison nor amerce them without trial; neither will British spirit submit to the cashiering of officers unheard. Let us make the case our own: Suppose some foreign government should charge an American with having injured its subjects; what course shall be taken by the President of the United States? shall he punish the person charged, without evidence, without trial, without giving him a chance to defend himself? Are American citizens to be thus condemned unheard? Is this the new law of nations which is to prevail over the old? I hope not. The old course, on such occasions, is to refer the complaint to a court of law, assuring the complainant that his cause shall be impartially examined by the proper tribunals, and justice done according to their decision. Can we, rightfully, ask more from another nation than we, in our turn, will perform? In what law shall we find this prerogative? Certainly not in the law of justice. Is it then in the law of force? Where are our fleets? and where our armies? and where the treasure to support fleets and armies? We stand committed, and have gone to war against a principle held sacred by all, and against a practice which, if restrained otherwise than by applying to civil tribunals, is to be so restrained by the stipulations of treaty. But such stipulations must be reciprocal. Those, therefore, which we are willing to submit to, we may equitably propose; and to those which we *exact*, we must *submit*. In treating with England, there is little to apprehend; because British ministers dare not accede to a treaty which would infringe the rights of Englishmen; and even if they had that temerity, the law of England would not bend its stubborn neck to the yoke of such a treaty. But different indeed may be the case when, on this or any similar subject, an American President, less honest and more ambitious than he who now directs our affairs, shall treat with an absolute prince, then it may be agreed, as a proof of friendly respect for a faithful friend, an honourable ally, that when charges are regularly made against the subjects or citizens of one country, by the government of the other, trial shall be considered as unnecessary, and execution issue. If, at that time, a citizen shall be found, of sterling worth, strong in virtue, and high in the confidence of his country, who dares oppose approaching despotism, he may quickly be disposed of under these reciprocal stipulations. Are you, fellow-citizens, prepared for such treaties? Are you willing to surrender your liberty, and the liberty of your children, into the hands of a President or an Emperor? If you are, assemble no more to celebrate this anniversary: let the name of Washington dwell no longer on your lips; let his remembrance be obliterated from your hearts. But you are not so base. You will not tear to pieces the charter of your rights. And for whom are you called on to make the sacrifice; and what is the boon to be obtained? Every thing is at hazard to protect men who abandon their country in the hour of her distress. Fellow-citizens! Do you feel the sacred love of country? I know that you do. Are you capable of abandoning your country in the day of danger? Oh no! If you were, you would not assume the name of Washington. That name would crimson your cheeks with the blush of guilt. Can you then approve of, can you otherwise than detest, the men who abandon their country? Surely it is not possible to be at once virtuous and the friend of vice. Surely they have not a proper sense of duty to their country, who would seduce others from the performance of that duty, or protect them in the violation of its dictates. Do you believe in the justice of him who receives stolen goods? Do you believe in the chastity of a bawd?

But it is said that our government has taken new ground; that we are to fight here and to negociate elsewhere for the liberty of the seas. In other words, to establish, as a principle, that neutral ships shall not be searched. The right to search such ships is a necessary incident to the right of capture in war; and, as such, has been exercised by the United States from the day of the declaration we now celebrate. Our tribunals, like those of other countries, have invariably condemned the property of enemies taken in the ships of a friend, and liberated the property of friends taken in the ships of an enemy. Can we then ask Great Britain to surrender a right generally acknowledged, and which we ourselves have constantly exercised? Admitting it would be convenient to us that she should relinquish it in our favour, (we reciprocally giving it up to her,) surely we cannot insist on the surrender of her *right* for our *convenience*. We may, properly make it the subject of friendly convention, and endeavour to procure the object of our wish by the offer of compensation; but surely it is unjust to make war on a nation because the sovereign will not surrender his rights. It follows, therefore, that whether the object of our government be to protect British seamen against impressment, or American merchantmen against search, it is equally an unjust war.

And it is not less unwise than unjust: for if the contemplated regulations were established, it would be our interest to have them revoked. Separated, as we are, by a vast ocean from every power which can injure us, our defence must be on that ocean. Our complete, our cheap, and *safe* defence, is a navy. After a war of forty years, we should have nothing to fear from a victorious fleet. During the course of it, our expense would not be half so great as the maintenance of military force to defend us against an invading army: not to mention that the invader might, by laying contributions, oblige us to bear his expense as well as our own. But what is expense, compared to the waste of lives, by opposing militia to mercenary troops! And what is life, compared to liberty; which must be endangered, if not lost, when a victorious general, at the head of a disciplined army, devoted to his person and flushed with human slaughter, shall turn their swords on the bosom of his country? If, then, as we sincerely believe, a naval force be our best and only safe defence, how deeply does it concern us to provide that, during peace, none but native Americans shall navigate our merchant ships; so that, in war, we may rely on the bravery and fidelity of native sea-men: and also to provide that, if there be among them any so lost to honour and virtue as to desert their country, they may find no protection, against her arm, under a foreign flag? Neither is it our defence alone that is to be made at sea. At sea, and there only, can we carry on operations of offensive war, with any prospect of success, against the greater number of those with whom we may have to contend. If we turn our face to the Atlantic ocean, we have on our right the treasures of the world. These must pass before us, on their way to Europe, and reward our maritime skill and enterprise, when at war with nations to whom they belong. The whole will be our prey, un-less the transportation be in fleets under strong convoy; and a considerable part, however convoyed, must fall to our share. The very necessity of pro-viding such convoy is, in itself, an inconvenience which will be seriously felt. So that a war with the United States, when possessed of a respectable navy, would not be sought by any European power. And when, from the combination of those chances which no human eye can foresee, such war shall take place, the greatest power will soon accede to reasonable terms of conciliation. But let it be once established, that a few breadths of bunting, tied to the mast of a merchant ship, shall cover the property against cap-ture, and, from that moment, our best means of offence are annihilated. Thus, then, it is evident that the right of a nation to take her own seamen from neutral merchant ships and the right of searching those ships to de-tect contraband of war and make prize of enemy's property, are among our most important rights, the loss of which we should never cease to lament. And yet, we now wage war to destroy those very rights. We waste our trea-sure to disarm our country, and shed our best blood to protect the worst of our enemy's subjects. Can this be wise?

I will not, fellow-citizens, trace the ills we suffer up to their source. That is an object of legislative wisdom. If attempted here, we might be charged with hostility to the union. For, strange as it must seem, it is nevertheless true, that those who inculcate principles inconsistent with all social union, charge the opponents of their disorganizing principles with an intention to separate the Eastern from the Southern States. That the course pursued, for some time past, will, if persisted in, occasion that separation, there can be little doubt; but he who spent the flower of youth and the strength of manhood in labouring to promote and confirm the American union, can never, but in the last necessity, recommend its dissolution. Federalists are too proud of the name they bear, to view, unmoved, the danger to which our federal compact is exposed. The followers of Washington cannot wish to pluck a star from the constellation of his glory. This day, which calls to fond remembrance our brotherhood in the war for freedom, our fellowship in its sufferings, and that union of heart which preceded, and produced our political union, this is not the day to tear asunder the bands of affection, and strangle the charities of our political existence. But although we deprecate the impending separation, yet we conceive that, under existing circumstances, prudent men should prepare for events, and fortify their hearts for such struggles as the cause of justice and their country may require. Under the pressure of these circumstances, I attest the revered name of Washington; I attest the cause which has marked this day of glory, while I remind you, that liberty is the greatest earthly good, and to defend it the first human duty. I call on you, therefore, by all you hold most dear, never to desert, under any pretence, or for any consideration, the sacred cause of freedom. Be just to others—be just to yourselves.

These essays cover a range of fiscal and foreign policy topics. Their common theme is a critical appraisal of the Republicans' stewardship of the nation since 1801.

TO THE EDITOR OF THE EXAMINER
APRIL 9, 1814

Sir,

You have doubtless remarked, in reading history, that before those refinements of taste, which display atrocious deeds in velvet words, it was customary to denominate princes, and other great men, by their qualities, vices and defects. Thus one was called the wise, one the cruel, another the bald, a fourth long-shanks, and so on. We are grown too fastidious for this simple language, which, like the ox-eyed Juno of Homer, has a brutality of sound to modish ears. I incline, nevertheless, to believe, that when a republican historian, should the republic last long enough to produce a historian, examines our annals he will distinguish the administration of the *last twelve* years, from those which preceded, and, I humbly hope, from those which are to follow, as the *perfidious.* Now seeing that this idea may seem harsh, I will offer a few of the reasons on which it is founded, waving three several grounds, on each of which I would undertake to establish the charge, before an intelligent, impartial judge.

I shall, in the first place, say nothing of transactions with foreign powers; and be equally silent, in the second place, about promises made to us that

The Examiner: Containing Political Essays on the Most Important Events of the Time 1, no. 21 (April 9, 1814): 345–55. The essay was reprinted in the *New-York Evening Post* on April 13 and 14, 1814. The manuscript is in the Gouverneur Morris Papers, Rare Book and Manuscript Library, Columbia University, item 869. Reprinted here from the copy in Firestone Library, Princeton University.

we should be relieved from taxes, economy be introduced into the management of public affairs, liberty be more effectually guarded, peace be preserved, and at any rate, that our country should not be subjected to the expense, nor stained with the guilt, of offensive war. I shall, in like manner, thirdly, abstain from noticing the numerous violations of our constitution, from the repeal of the judiciary, to that grinding act of oppression, the embargo. These three themes are left untouched, not only because men's minds are too much heated, to relish truth, but because I mean not simply to *prove*, but to *demonstrate*, the charge: wherefore, avoiding logical inference, I shall adhere to mathematical conclusion. I ask no other favour, than the admission of what none will, I presume, deny, that two and two make four; with its converse, equally self evident, that if two be taken from four, there will remain but two.

The only subject susceptible of this demonstration, is, as you have doubtless anticipated, the finances. Before I proceed, I beg it may be distinctly understood, that no deduction shall be drawn from acts, for which a specious apology may be devised, although it would not be admitted according to the usual mode of treating this subject. I even go further, and allow that cases may be supposed, and perhaps occur, in which it would be justifiable, not to redeem the pledge of public faith, usually given by nations, who make loans: cases, in which the lenders would have no demand on the justice of government. Thus, for instance, we may suppose the creation, by government, of a dozen million of debt, and the division of it among themselves, without paying a cent into the treasury; or giving twenty million of stock, when only five or ten million of cash were received; or giving ten to fifteen million of stock to the Emperor of Monomatapa (to be distributed by him among their friends) for a desart in the centre of Africa.[1] Every man must feel that a representative, who should apply the bread of his constituents to satisfy such claims, under the general principle of preserving public faith, would have more of delicacy than discretion. Snatching at the shadow, he would lose the substance of justice; and performing the doubtful duty to creditors, violate an unquestionable and most sacred duty to his constituents. No inference, therefore, shall be drawn from neglect, if such there be, to redeem a general pledge which, like the fashionable phrase, pledging men's lives, their fortunes, and their sacred honour, have become rather a flower of rhetoric than a serious engagement. Men of experience

1. Monomotapa was a medieval African empire centered in what is now Zimbabwe and Mozambique.

place no reliance on these fiery declarations: a vapour which, hot from the still-head, soon melts into air. An hour's sober reflection, after a night's sound sleep, dissipates the fumes of zeal, which promoted these proffers, and displays antecedent obligations not to be violated. Men owe care, food and protection to their wives and children. Their very flocks and herds have just demands on their attention; and before they abandon their farms, in quest of adventures, memory will run over every field: till, at length, the proceedings of the yesterday's meeting seem like a troubled dream.

I can, moreover, suppose a representative to be convinced that debts, having been properly incurred, ought to be paid, and yet withhold his assent from the proposed taxes, either because they infringe rights, secured by compact, because they are injurious to the community at large, or oppressive to some particular description of people, or because they bear unequally on his immediate constituents. These and other reasons may so weigh with a majority, as to prevent them from adopting the specific provisions proposed although desirous of taking up their just share of the burden. In such cases, it would be hard to charge them with perfidy. I shall, therefore take no notice, either of general pledges and professions, or of the omission to comply with them. My object is *demonstration;* and I hope my readers, turning a deaf ear to probability, will require *certainty*, founded on the known established *rules of arithmetic.*

I address myself more particularly to gentlemen, who lent their *names,* last year, to the administration for large sums. I say their *names:* because, though many of them disbursed *money*, in the hope of *profit*, by selling their stock afterwards, at an advanced price, yet in many cases it was partly, if not wholly, a loan of *names.* These names, words of great power to produce such great effect, being written on pieces of paper, called negotiable notes, and deposited in banks, together with other pieces of paper, called certificates of six per cent stock, these gentlemen prevailed on those banks to let them have, at an interest of six per cent. other pieces of paper, called bank notes, with which they paid for the stock aforesaid; that stock bearing also an interest of six per cent. but which they had purchased of government (if I remember right) sixteen per cent. under par. So that by borrowing five million, which bore an interest of three hundred thousand, they bought six millions, bearing an interest of three hundred and *sixty thousand;* and thus they gained, by writing their names, an income of *sixty thousand dollars.* Add to this the prospect, should the stock rise to par, of pocketting a million. This, no doubt, is handsome. It is turning those letters of the alphabet, which enter into the composition of a name, to good account. But there are, as usual, two sides to the medal. One represents plenty showering abundance; the other displays certain little doubts, involving certain little difficulties, which may impair, if not destroy, the cabalistic power of those potent names. The government have already spent, or (as some will have it) squandered, those pieces of paper, called bank notes; by reason whereof, as also by the multiplicity of banks, and the destruction of commerce, those same notes are looked at with a suspicious eye, by folks who persuade themselves to believe that a *hard dollar* is quite as good, if not a little better, than a *soft one*. Hence it happens, that timid people begin to pray the banks to be so good, as to give, according to their contracts, hard dollars for soft ones. Under these circumstances, the banks find it convenient to send the aforesaid pieces of paper, called negotiable notes, to the subscribers, and endorsers of them; those will find it convenient to pay, if they can only sell those other pieces of paper, called certificates of stock, at the cost, or a little more. But should it happen, and, as the devil, that father of all mischief, has contrived things, it is highly probable, that no purchasers offer, they must sell those pieces of paper for a little, and perhaps a great deal, less than the cost. There are indeed, some in the world, so mischievous, as to say they cannot be sold at any price; being good for nothing. This I take to be a slander. Soft paper, tolerably clean, is always good for something. I am nevertheless inclined to believe, that these pieces of paper, for which gentlemen were so kind as to lend their names, in the hope of pocketing an advance of twenty per cent. on what they advanced to the government will hardly fetch the stipulated cost; because a great deal more such paper is about to be thrown on the market, and, as is said, a great deal of other paper, by no means agreeable to the amateurs. The splendid hopes of those gentlemen were, it is said, excited by positive assurances from Monsieur Gallatin, that his mission to Petersburgh would infallibly produce peace: for that the mediation was merely a contrivance to save the honour of administration.[2] Mark that! *The honour of administration!* That the president would give up the point in controversy, by *decision of the mediator.* And, here, I pray the gentlemen of the potent names will excuse a small digression. It is wonderful that they should have been such gudgeons, as to swallow Monsieur Gallatin's hook, when he offered *twelve* million of *stock*, for *ten* mil-

---

2. In 1813, President Madison sent Treasury Secretary Albert Gallatin to Russia, which had offered to mediate in the War of 1812. That mission was not successful, although Gallatin stayed in Europe as U.S. representative for the negotiations that led to the Treaty of Ghent in 1814.

lion of *bank notes*, telling them there would be peace, which would enable them to take two million from the people, of whose property he was, at the same time, the official and *sworn guardian*. When he told them this sacrifice of millions was made to save the *honour of government*, how happens it that they did not suspect *him* of a little *honesty?* Was it not charitable to believe that he was making the best bargain in his power, though bad indeed was the best, regardless of what might betide men, to whom he owed no duty, and for whom, considering how much the transaction smells of the synagogue, he could feel but little respect? Or, again, how happens it that, believing he was so much of a *rogue*, as to throw away *two million* dollars of the people's money, to soothe Mr. Madison's vanity, he should, nevertheless, have so much *honesty* and *truth*, as to merit *their* trust and confidence? Returning from this digression, and presuming that nothing hitherto said is intended to support the charge of perfidy, I repeat my particular request to these gentlemen, lenders, subscribers, stock holders, or by whatever other name or description they incline to distinguish themselves, that they will examine, critically, what I am about to say; and to refute, if they can, the smallest fractional part of the charge. It is highly important to them; for, if they can establish a belief in the honesty of our rulers, it may help them to the fleeces of some fine *Boston sheep*, who have not yet been shorne.

And now, without further preface, I proceed to the subject. It will be recollected that on the third day of March, in the year of our Lord one thousand seven hundred and ninety one, George Washington, then president of the United States, approved of and signed a law, laying duties on spirits distilled within the United States; the proceeds of which were SOLEMNLY PLEDGED FOR THE PAYMENT OF THE PUBLIC DEBT. This tax, it is well known, was imposed for a three fold reason; one, that there was a want of more revenue; another, that the duties on imports were already so high, as to excite apprehensions of smuggling; and a third, that dependence on commerce, *alone,* for revenue, placed us too much at the mercy of a great maritime power. It will further be recollected that, in the year 1802, and under Mr. Jefferson's administration, the law, laying and appropriating these duties, WAS REPEALED! I have now laying before me a sketch of the debate, which took place, on this occasion, in the senate; and think I cannot better establish my charge, than by quoting the close of a long and, to most readers, a tedious speech of Mr. Morris, in opposition to the proposed repeal. That gentleman, having endeavoured to establish his opinion that the revenue from commerce (between seven and eight millions) would rather diminish than increase; that it bore hard on the most indigent class of the community, and would injure the manufactures, which sundry parts of it were intended to promote, proceeds thus:

I have heard it said that, however improper it may be to repeal these taxes, it is now too late to object; for that, after the recommendation of our first magistrate, they are considered by the people, as no longer to be paid. I will not question the veracity of those, who make this assertion; but I must beg leave to withhold my assent. The people of this country know, that to their representatives, alone, is delegated the right of taxation. This is no part of the executive power. I will not say, that the recommendation was unconstitutional; I will not say, that it was unjustifiable; but I will say that it was imprudent. And if it does indeed, involve the consequence which has been stated, I must add that it is injurious. It would have been more proper to have left the unbiassed consideration of this great subject to the two houses of congress. But, sir, though I cannot approve, I will not condemn the conduct of our chief magistrate. He, I presume acted from what he conceived to be his duty. Let us then imitate his example and perform what, on due advisement, shall appear to us, to be our duty. Let me say, sir, there is too much of precipitancy, too much of rashness, in this repeal. It would be wiser to wait until we possess a knowledge of those facts, on which a sound system must be founded. Our experience of the past gives no sufficient light for the future. There is, moreover, during the present, and there will be, for some succeeding years, an unusual pressure of our public debt, arising from heavy installments of foreign loans. This, therefore, is not the moment to make a change. I have, indeed, heard the advocates of the repeal say they are desirous of paying the public debt, not only according to the terms to which we stand pledged, but at an earlier day. If this be so, how can they think of taking off taxes; or by what new and strange innovation or device, do they expect *to pay debts*, by *diminishing income?* I should have supposed that the best way to effect that object would be to increase the revenue, lessen our expenses, and apply our whole means to the payment of what we owe, *steadily and faithfully.*

Mr. President, one word more. Hitherto I have considered this question on the broad ground of policy, of expediency, and of public economy. I have endeavoured to show that duties are the most expensive species of tax. That, from a change in the political affairs of the world, and in our own particular situation, there is reason to suppose our revenue will suffer considerable diminution; that it is more than probable duties so high, as those under which our commerce now labours, will be evaded; and thence I have endeavoured to draw the natural conclusion that, instead of repealing the internal taxes, we should lessen the duties, and raise that part of which is taken off in the seaports, by direct tax in the country. *All this was under the idea, that you have a right to repeal these taxes.* But by recurring to the first volume of your laws, in the 335th page, I find, that the sixtieth section of an act laying duties upon spirits distilled the United States runs thus. (*Mr. Morris read that section and the sixty second section.*)

Now then I ask, can we rightly take off this tax, without laying on an equivalent, before our debts are paid? I will not say, it is unconstitutional, though, while we yet had a constitution, I should have opposed it on that ground. I will not say, you have not the power to do it; because, under the new doctrine of your legislative omnipotence, I see not the bounds of your power. But I remember well, and let me now call back to the recollection of this senate, what past on a late important occasion [*the repeal of the judiciary.*] It was asked, when we have made a grant, can we resume it? when we have contracted a debt, can we refuse to pay it? when we have made a promise, can we violate it? To these questions it was answered, no. Here is a vested right in third persons. The government is bound. *In the case of a debt, it has received a consideration, and the engagements taken with the public creditor cannot be broken.* I ask, then, what words, in our language, or in any language, can be more full, more solemn, or form a contract more sacred, than those I have just read? The net amount of the duties is *pledged* to our creditors, and *appropriated* to the payment of our debts; and to the end that it may be *inviolably* applied in conformity to that appropriation, and may *never* be converted to any other purpose, a *separate account* is to be kept, and it is again declared, *that the duties shall continue to be collected and paid, till the debts for which they are pledged shall be fully discharged and satisfied.* If these terms be not binding on the legislature, let us hear the form, if any can be found, of a contract more obligatory. I ask those who mean to vote for this repeal, what they meant by the declaration that *vested rights could not be resumed, and that engagements taken with public creditors could not be broken?* If, by a wild exertion of licentious force we tear asunder these bonds, can we again ask of mankind any share of confidence? *Can we expect to enjoy credit when we show ourselves regardless of our plighted faith?*

Sir, I consider the repeal as inconsistent with the true interest of the great body of our people. It appears to me dangerous both to our revenue and to our commerce. But above all, I consider it as a *flagrant viola-tion of public faith.*

The law was, nevertheless, repealed, and the revenue already amount-ing to $650,000 and which, rapidly increasing, would soon have exceeded a million, was wrested from the public creditors. It will be noted more-over that, by returns from the treasury, it appeared that the revenue from the sale of lands was about four hundred thousand dollars, and from the duties on imports and tonnage, not quite *eight* million, whereas, it required *nine* million, and a half to meet the public expenditure, without any allow-ance for contingencies. But whether the revenue from commerce was, or was not, equal to the public expenditure; whether it would, or would not, increase or diminish, is immaterial. It must be admitted, unless it be con-tended, that two and two do not make four, that this revenue from internal taxes, whether a whole or, only half a million, was just so much taken away of what had been solemnly pledged for the payment of the public debt.

Shortly afterwards, a bill was proposed, couched in equivocal, and, as the minority contended, unintelligible terms, under the seductive title of "An act, making provision for the redemption of the whole of the public debt." They attributed the obscurity to a conviction, that the revenue, re-duced in the manner above mentioned, being inadequate to the professed appropriation of 7,300,000 dollars, new loans were necessary to discharge instalments, shortly falling due. But these loans, however they might re-lieve the pressure for payment of debts, could in no wise be considered as an appropriation *from the revenue,* unless they were taken as *part of the reve-nue.* This idea, expressed in plain terms, was not only ridiculous, in itself, but went to contradict assertions made only a few days before, when the internal taxes were repealed; it was endeavoured, therefore, so to word the law, as to produce, without declaring, that effect. The phraseology may be seen by turning to the law: it is immaterial to our object. But it is not im-material to glance at the state of things, when this *nominal* provision was made. Among the items of revenue, that from the post-office had been ex-empted from appropriation, under the idea that it should be applied, first, in extending communications; secondly, in accelerating the transportation of letters; and, thirdly, in reducing the rate of postage. The other articles of revenue, taken in the aggregate, were appropriated, primarily, to the cur-rent expense, and the whole of what should remain, to the sinking fund. Whatever, also, might remain unexpended, of the first appropriation, was appropriated to the sinking fund, for paying the interest, and discharging the principal, of the public debt. These provisions, taken together, amount in short to this, that whatever was not actually spent for the current service, should be employed in paying our debts. It is evident, therefore, that, in as much as every cent of revenue, was ALREADY appropriated to the *redemption of the whole of the public debt*, the bill, bearing that title, was a mere trick. A harmless trick, had it been possible that the amount of unexpended revenue should, every year, be precisely the same, with the pretended appropriation of 7,300,000 dollars: which would then have been a mere nullity. But in one of two contingencies, naturally to be expected: that the balance unexpended should exceed that sum; the new appropriation (being comprehended in the old) would still be a nullity; unless to give it effect, it should be construed into a limitation, and consequently a violation of public faith. In the other contingency, viz. that the balance of revenue, after deducting the current expense, should fall short of the stipulated sum, it was a promise of what could not, in the nature of things, be performed. It was a new pledge, to produce a new breach of public faith, without colour of necessity, or shadow of reason. This law, then, was, on the face of it, either a nullity or a perfidy. But how, it may be asked, could men of sense (and certainly there were some such in the majority) agree to an act so flagitiously absurd? The answer is plain: They could not but know, that this repeal of the internal taxes was a flagrant outrageous act of perfidy, and would be considered as such. Fearing it might injure their popularity, they conceived it necessary to furnish their partisans with a pretext, for asserting their desire to preserve public faith. But it may, again, be asked, could they believe the people would be such fools, as not to detect the trick? Strange as it may seem, they relied on the public prejudice, credulity, or simplicity; and, stranger still, experience has proved the correctness of their opinion. Ever since the act was passed, they have claimed credit for making provision, to pay the whole of the public debt; and a majority of the people have sanctioned the claim, by repeated grants of their confidence. But, to return, it so happened, that there was, at this moment, three million of dollars in the treasury, which, according to the explanation just given, was appropriated to, and formed part of, the sinking fund. Monsieur Gallatin, however, and, perhaps, his predecessors, considered this sum, as a reserve to meet certain claims, under treaties with France and England; and in his report, on which the proceedings, now in contemplation, were founded, taking a distinction between debts and claims, stated these three millions as being (in a manner) appropriated to claims. But his distinction, could it have been established, destroyed his *quasi* appropriation to claims: because all the unexpended money was, by law, appropriated to debts. And, what is more extraordinary, while he showed his skill in splitting hairs, for the sake of a distinction, fatal to his doctrine, he was no less earnest in blending ideas the most distinct, *debt* and *revenue*. By considering the money which might be procured on loan, as *revenue*, and that in the treasury, though appropriated to the payment of debts, yet, (being held to answer claims,) as disposable for current expenses, the revenue was sure to hold out, let it be ever so small, because it would be increased by *loans*. I had not forgotten, but omitted to mention, in its place, because it is too ludicrous for serious consideration, an argument, much relied on, when the internal revenue was destroyed. Congress, in the appropriation of 1791, had reserved a right, "to substitute other *duties and taxes*, of equal value, to all or any of the *duties and imposts*." The repealing gentlemen, having voted for what they *said* (although they *knew* better) would make a *saving*, equal in amount to the net revenue from *taxes* to be repealed, insisted that this supposed *saving* was the same thing, as to lay new taxes. According to their vocabulary, a *vote* of economy was synonimous with an *excise* on whiskey; and therefore, although it was evident that, notwithstanding all possible saving of expense, and all probable increase of revenue, there would be a considerable deficiency in the sum they were about to appropriate, for the splendid purpose of redeeming the whole of the public debt, they persisted in the fallacious semblance of appropriation; and, authorizing new loans to discharge old ones, called the money, to be borrowed, a part of the revenue. Thus were provided for, two, of three cases, one of which must happen, under this specious appropriation, viz. a *possible* case, that the balance of receipts, beyond the expenditures, should be precisely 7,300,000 dollars; and the *probable* case, that it would fall short of that sum. The third, and, to public creditors, important case, that it might exceed 7,300,000 dollars, remained a flat violation of faith solemnly pledged in 1791. It was in consequence of this wanton perfidy, that cash accumulated in the treasury (at least it was said so) to such an amount, that Mr. Jefferson invited the congress to help him to spend it; lest, by growing too rich, they should be tempted to commit the sin of war. Before we proceed, it is proper to notice, that the prediction of the minority was verified. The revenue fell short; and, to eke it out, the government increased duties, under the name of the Mediteranean Fund, which was to last no longer than our war with the Barbary States. Nevertheless the fund was continued, though the war was finished.

Let us pause, here, to ascertain what *was* meant and *is* to be understood by an appropriation of taxes to pay debts. It may seem strange to suppose, that an idea, so simple, as to be almost self-evident, should require explanation; but we must keep on clear ground, if we would arrive at demonstration. By an *appropriation of taxes to pay debts*, we understand, that the whole sum, arising from such taxes, after deducting the expense of collection, should be laid out, first, in defraying the interest of the debt; secondly, in discharging so much of the principal as may fall due; and thirdly, in paying such creditors, as consent to receive; or, what amounts to the same thing, in purchasing stock. But two questions may be raised, as to what is the *public debt?* Is it the sum *already* due, alone? Or does it comprise what may, hereafter, *become* due? If only the former, and it should hereafter appear that something is due under a now existing contract, is that a part of the debt; or if, the means to discharge an installment being deficient, the creditor agrees to prolong the term, does the sum, for which such agreement is made, continue to be part of the debt? There can be, it is believed, no doubt that both these cases are within the general meaning of what is already due. A third case then presents itself; suppose that, to pay such instalment, a new loan be made, is that also to be considered a part of what is already due? This question also, ought, it is conceived, to be answered in the affirmative. It is then asked, whether a loan for any other purpose, be not equally within the appropriation to pay debts? But here we are bound to make a negative reply, because any other decision would be to make an appropriation to pay debts, a mere mockery. Thus, for instance, to appropriate a tax, producing, net, one million, to discharge a debt of fifteen million, bearing six per cent. interest, would secure the payment within a period, which, though long, can be measured with precision. It gives, of course, solid ground, on which to value the stock. But if it be understood, that such appropriation shall extend to an additional debt of fifteen or even five million, it evidently forms little or no security, seeing that the revenue would no longer be sufficient to pay the interest, much less the principal. Presuming that no man of sound mind, will maintain a different opinion, there remains only one more preliminary question. I hope no one will laugh at the prudery of all this preparation. The question is, on an appropriation like that now under consideration, is the interest of debt redeemed this year, to be taken from the sum applied the next; so as to lessen the appropriation annually, by amount of interest on the principal paid? This question will perhaps be answered by asking me, how that can be called the appropriation of a whole revenue, only part of which is to be employed, after the first year? And, lest I should be so dull as not to comprehend this socratic argument, I may be desired to recur to arithmetic; and, assuming as certain, that which may be made certain, to fix the supposed net revenue, at a sum, (say ten million,) and state the question numerically, as thus: the law having appropriated ten million annually to redeem the public debt, after a certain time, so much of the principal is discharged as to reduce the interest one million, does the appropriation require an employment next year of ten million, or only nine? I must acknowledge that, according to the original postulatum, that if two be taken from four, there will remain only two, it cannot be denied, that one being taken from ten, there will remain but nine. Nevertheless, nine not being ten, the employment of nine will not satisfy the appropriation of ten. Wherefore, the whole ten must be employed. And therefore, in the original case, of which this last is merely an elucidation, the whole net revenue must be applied. And let it be further noted, in this place, that by statutes, passed in 1792 and 1795, express provision was made, to apply the interest of debts paid to the discharge of debts still due, so as to leave no doubt respecting the sinking fund, provided in that era of honest legislation.

Now, then, having had time to take breath, we are ready to proceed on our journey; and we go but a little way beyond perfidy the second, before we come to perfidy the third. We find an addition to the debt, of no less than fifteen million, for land, bought, not indeed of the emperor of Monomotapa, nor in the heart of Africa, but of the emperor of France, in the heart of America. Land, moreover, which did not belong to either of those emperors, but to the king of Spain; according to European notions; and to our red brethren the Indians, according to the principles of public law; provided always that right does not depend on complexion. Let any honest man, put himself in the place of one who lent his money to the American government, or purchased their stock, during the term which intervened between the solemn pledge of all our revenue in 1791, and the repeal of taxes in 1802. What will he think of that repeal, of the subsequent limitation of the sinking fund, should the revenue exceed a definite sum, and finally of this thumping addition to the debt without imposing new taxes? In the year 1796, the funds of Saxony, bearing three per cent. interest, were above par; the funds of Holland, bearing two and a half per cent. interest, were (before the war) at par. Had we preserved peace, and good faith, it is probable that our three per cents would have risen to par. Where are they now?

It would be tedious to proceed, step by step, through the various meanderings of our financial legislation. Every one who is so inclined, may do it himself; keeping in view the principles established, and which shall now be applied to recent events. Let us then, according to the last arrangement, take the annual appropriation of eight million to a sinking fund, and, supposing matters to have been conducted with fairness, down to the end of the year 1811, cast an eye at the accounts laid before congress, by the commissioners of the sinking fund, on the seventh day of February, 1814. We find, that on the first of January, 1812, there remained, of the last year's appropriation, unapplied, $502,513 85

That there had been, during the year 1812, a gain
on remittances to Europe, of   91,532 88
That there had been a gain on the purchase of stock,
(being the capital of stock carried to account of stock
purchased, and which cost less,)   3,102 81

To which ought to be added, the interest of stock previously purchased. This is not stated in the account, but we get at it by taking, what is stated for the next year, viz. 1813, under that head, 1,932,107 92; and deducting interest at six per cent. on stock purchased, and paid in 1812, viz. principal 2,259,681 82, is 135,580 90,

                                                                  1,796,527 02
Finally the annual appropriation of   8,000,000
                                                                 _____
                                                                 10,393,676 56
Deduct for so much employed in 1812,   −4,710,954 39
                                                                 _____
There ought, therefore, to have been in the
hands of the commissioners, on the first day of
the year 1813, an unexpended balance, of   5,682,722 17

To this must be added, an interest of at least six
in the hundred, seeing that to raise cash, six was
paid this year, on less than a hundred.   340,963 33

Add the interest on stock purchased and paid,
as per account,   1,932,107 92
Add also the profit on remittances in 1813,   98,452 06
Add the annual appropriation of   8,000,000
                                                                 _____
We have a total of   16,034,245 48
From which is to be deducted, drawn for on account
of the debt, 11,110,117 73, and so much which is stated
in the account as corresponded, 442,254 11,   11, 482,871 84
                                                                 _____
                                                                 $4,541,373 64
                                                                 _____

Thus, there appears to be four and a half million of the annual appropriation, diverted from the legitimate object. Those who held the old six per cent, three per cent. and deferred, stock, had a right to this sum, at least, supposing the application of what was actually employed, to have been proper; a subject we shall presently examine. It was the bounden duty of the administration, to have employed this sum, in paying or purchasing that debt, then below par, and thereby sustaining its price. On this, they who became the holders of it, had a right to rely, and are literally cheated out of what they are obliged to sell for, under what they could have obtained, had all the money appropriated, been fairly employed.

But it remains to inquire how the sum actually disposed of was applied. To this end, from materials furnished by the commissioners, are made the two following accounts marked A. B.

A. Employed in payment of the public debt in 1812.

1. Principal of the domestic debt,	2,259,681 82		
Interest on do.	1,688,290 38		
		$3,947,972 20	
2. Interest on the foreign debt.		10,634 15	
		3,958,606 35	
3. Interest on Louisiana stock domesticated	105,237		
do. do. Payable in Europe	614,787		
Commission charges and loss on exchange	32,324 04		
		752,348 04	
		$4,710,954 39	

B. Drawn for, to be employed in 1813.

1. Principal and interest of domestic debt suppose as in 1812.		$3,947,972 20	
2. To discharge interest on Louisiana stock in Europe	679,673 74		
Estimated amount of do. domesticated	139,332		
		819,005 74	
3. To pay interest and principal of domestic debt	4,713,421 61		

Deduct article 1 3,947,972 20 } 4,087,304 20
and 2d item of article 2 139,332 }

    Remains for principal and
    interest of other domestic debt   626,117 41
4. A small article of debt not explained   29 48
5. Interest and part principal of temporary loans   1,477,067 10
6. Do treasury notes   4,839,925 20
    Amount of account rendered (a wrong cast
    in that account of 40 cents corrected) $11,110,117 73

Now it appears, that the first and second articles in account A, and the first in account B, are those to which, alone, the old appropriation of 1791 applies; and, as the revenue greatly exceeded the expenses of government, or all the boastings on the subject were downright lies, this original appropriation must have been violated to an enormous amount. In neither of these years has there been expended, on the object of it, four million. Of course not one half even of the annual eight million has been applied to its legitimate object. Moreover, we have seen before, that the interest, on stock purchased, amounting to nearly two million, ought to have been added, so that, in fact near ten million should have been employed each year, leaving, therefore, an annual deficiency of six million. To make this more intelligible, it is to be noted that in Mr. Secretary Jones's[3] report to the commissioners, which makes part of their report to congress, the interest on stock paid and purchased, to an amount little short of two million, is distinctly stated, as one of the funds from which he made up so much of the annual appropriation of eight million, as was placed at the disposal of the commissioners; that from the revenue of the United States, viz. from the sale of land and the duty on imports and tonnage, little more than five million and a half were taken, and that (the interest aforesaid included) little more was paid than seven million and a half. In one sense, therefore, though God knows in a sense very different from that in which it was used by the honest men of 1791, and understood by public creditors, this is a sinking fund. It is a decreasing fund, not to sink, but to be sunken by, the public debt. It was diminished, as we have seen, $650,000 by repealing the taxes in 1802, and immediately after it was, if not sunk, prevented from rising, by limitation to a specific sum; so that if the revenue had quadrupled, the excess, beyond that sum, must have accumulated, a dead mass in the treasury, instead of drawing, or (what is equivalent) saving interest,

3. William Jones, secretary of the navy, was acting secretary of the treasury while Gallatin was on his diplomatic mission in Europe.

by paying creditors which would not only have invigorated credit but, by pouring so much treasure into the market, have lowered interest, and facilitated to enterprising active citizens, the means of extending their industry; and thereby promoted the public prosperity. Not only was the sinking fund sunken by defalcation and limitation, but it appears to have been annually diminished by the amount of stock paid or purchased the preceding year. To show the different effect of a sinking fund according to its true intent, and a fund so sinking every year, let a nation be supposed to owe one hundred million, bearing six per cent. interest, and (to discharge it) make the annual appropriation of eight million. This appropriation, regularly applied, will pay the debt within twenty-four years; whereas by payment of the interest and two per cent. of principal annually, the same effect will not be produced in less than half a century. It is evident that in this latter case, the eight million, will be lessened every year by $120,000; so that the last year's payment will be only $2,120,000. The same *practical* result will be produced by *nominal* payment of $8,000,000, charging the whole interest 6,000,000 *as paid* and carrying the interest on $98,000,000, already liquidated viz. $5,880,000 to the *debit of the appropriation*. According to this arrangement, the sum last mentioned (though carried to both sides of the commissioners' account) would lie quietly in the treasury: Mr. Secretary counting it, with great gravity and solemnity, out of his right hand into his left.

The second article in account B, and third in account A, is the payment made on stock given to the French emperor. This comprises, according to account H, in the commissioners' report, a sum paid for principal of this stock $147,200 of which, according to account L of the same report, cost in the end of 1812 and beginning of 1813 $146,370. It appears, also, that during the same period $266,127 were paid for $267,200 borrowed in 1812. Now as every one knows that six per cent. stock was given, nearly at the same time, much below its nominal value, to raise money, we may judge of the economy which presides over the management of our pecuniary concerns. There has been paid, of our honest old debt, a little more than thirty-three million. Whether what remains will ever be paid I shall not inquire, but proceed to observe that the third, fifth and sixth articles of account B, apply to the payment of sums borrowed for, and expended on, the present war. They amount to no less than $6,343,110 to which must be added $324,200 borrowed in 1812 and $326,500 of Louisiana stock making a total of near seven million. Now the whole of the honest old six per cent. and deferred debt hitherto discharged is but $11,105,108 to which, if $698,355 of the honest old three per cent be added we have a total which is short of twelve million. Compare these items. The appropriations made to discharge our debts, in the days of our integrity, have been whittled away almost to the shadow of what they ought to be. They have been cut down by repeal, confined by limitation, reduced by defalcation, and crushed by embargoes, non-importations and other oppressive artificial contrivances. After all this, we find near seven million of what remains applied (in one year) to objects not contemplated, nor even thought of, much less comprised in that original appropriation. Nay the sixth article of account B will inform us that more than four million has been applied to payment of notes issued from the treasury for the current expenses. For instance, suppose a million, in notes, given to a commissary or contractor in January (instead of cash) to feed the army. These notes sold (at discount) for cash are paid in December (at par) and charged by the commissioners of the sinking fund as so much expended to *discharge the public debt*, under a legislative appropriation made many years before. Is it possible to imagine a more barefaced perfidy?

Should the commissioners pretend, that the law for issuing treasury notes, authorized the receipt of them in payment of taxes, and that being so received, they reduced, by so much, the sum which could be applied towards the appropriation, I ask what the deficiency of revenue has to do with their office? It is their duty, to apply the money they receive in payment of the debt to which that money is appropriated. Surely they should have refused to meddle with the notes; and, acknowledging the receipt of such cash alone as they did receive, have shown how it was employed. If the treasury received in taxes, and paid over to them part of the debt, which it was their duty to discharge, they should (on one side of their account) have charged themselves specifically with the amount, and discharged themselves (on the other) in correlative terms. This, Mr. Vice President, (who was bred a merchant,) must know, notwithstanding the confusion of intellect for which he is proverbial.[4] But I ask any man of common sense, I care not what may be his politics or religion; whether they might not, with equal propriety, have carried to this account, a million of hard money, put in the paymaster's hands, for the object of his department?

And now let us view this business in mass. The total of accounts A and B, is 15,821,072 dollars and 12 cents; add the balance of what ought to have been

4. Elbridge Gerry was vice president from March 4, 1813, until his death in office on November 23, 1814.

applied, during the years 1811 and 1812, to wit, $4,501,873 64, and we have $20,322,945 76 taking from this the amount of the first and second articles in account A, and the first article in account B, together $7,906,578 55, and there remain $12,416,367 21: upwards of twelve million of which ought to have been, and which was not applied, during the last two years, in paying the honest old debt of the United States.

I will not attempt to rouse public indignation; I should as soon drive my spurs, up to the rowels, in a dead horse. Those who have borne the embargo, will bear any thing. Perhaps when carrion now stretched on the common, shall be roused into action by the beaks of knavish crows, the American people may show something like sensibility. Then, perhaps, though their wrists and ancles be callous to the galling, their ears may be annoyed by the clanking, of their chains. But you, gentlemen contractors, to furnish funds for this unholy war, one word more, with you. When this nation shall again be governed by honest men, if that event should ever happen, you will perhaps (doling out a piteous tale of patriotic zeal) invoke the sanctity of public faith. But remember you trusted men, who in the very moment, and by the very act, which pledged their faith to you, *violated* the faith, ALREADY PLEDGED, by better men, to men as good as you. When they pledged, or (to speak correctly) affected to pledge, the public faith, for money, raised at USURIOUS interest, to be squandered in actual, if not formal, alliance with him, who spread ruin over the European continent, to destroy every vestige of freedom, they BROKE THE FAITH, pledged for payment of that SACRED DEBT, which had been contracted to *defend* and establish the LIBERTY of this western world! They pledged nothing to YOU, but what had been bound to OTHERS, by a precedent pledge, in terms as strong as language can express. On what ground, then, are you to ask payment from honest men? Will you attest the holiness of public faith? You, who participated in the perfidy by which it was violated? Will you ask of justice, the payment of what you lent to injustice? Will you ask this nation to give you their BREAD, because you conspired to spill their BLOOD? You, who, fed by the hand of abundance, far from feeling, or pretending the urgence of necessity, complained of no want, but the want of profitable employment for your wealth! On what religious, moral, or political principle will *you* rely? Be assured, that you have but one chance. Follow the physician's advice—*accipe dum dolet.*[5] Insist, before you advance another cent, that sufficient permanent revenue be provided, and *appropriated.* The integrity of succeeding legis-

---

5. Get your fee while the patient is suffering.

lators will, it is hoped, restrain them from breaking such an engagement. But should they walk in the PERFIDIOUS paths, through which this debased, disgraced nation, has wandered for a dozen years, although you may not be pitied for your misfortune, and even if you should be blamed for your misconduct, you will not, justly, be laughed at for YOUR FOLLY.

AN OBSERVER.

FOR THE EXAMINER, MAY 14, 1814

I have read the debates in congress, on questions respecting the war, with special attention; and conceive the course of argument followed by the friends of peace to be satisfactory in its general scope and direction, although there is an objection, not so completely obviated, as many well meaning men may wish. The whole matter may be comprest within a small compass. The administration asked supplies. The opposition refused to support a war which they consider as unwise, if not unjust. But they were told that the questions of wisdom and justice were out of season. "The war exists, and the government must be supported." It was justly replied, "if this be admitted as a rule, it will induce weak or wicked administrations, to involve the country in war, by way of getting support." "No, (said the war men), turn out the administration, if you can, when the term comes round; but do not, in the mean time, leave the country defenceless." The opposition replied, with great truth, "we cannot help leaving our country in that condition, for the administration avow the design of employing whatever means they can obtain, to acquire the enemy's possessions, instead of defending our own. If you will join us, in prohibiting offensive operations, we will join you, in measures of defence." The war men object to any such prohibition, as being unconstitutional, or at any rate unwise. "If (say they) the hands of government be thus tied up, and the enemy be (as he must be) apprized of it, he will apply, to annoying us, the means now employed in his own defence; and will, moreover, have no inducement to

Examiner: Containing Political Essays on the Most Important Events of the Time 2, no. 1 (May 14, 1814): 13-15, from the copy in Firestone Library, Princeton University. The manuscript is in the Gouverneur Morris Papers, Rare Book and Manuscript Library, Columbia University, item 870.

make peace. In short, if you will not enable the administration to act in the mode they deem most advisable, you leave them, us, and yourselves, at the mercy of an enemy the most"—and then follow a number of coarse epithets, which it is neither honourable to use, nor reputable to repeat. The answers made to this objection do not entirely relieve the anxieties of every candid mind. The most sufficient, according to my apprehension, was this. "Try the enemy's temper by proposing fair terms. If he will not accede to them, we will join in vigorous prosecution of the war, *provided the conduct of it be entrusted to men whose talents and integrity give a chance for success.*" The war men will doubtless represent this proposal, as unfair. They will say, that their opponents offer to grant money, on the sole condition that it be expended by themselves; and will put in their mouths this language—"We federalists, finding we cannot turn you out, engage, provided you will put us in, to vote with you for granting money to ourselves." This was neither the intent nor the import of the proposition; neither can it be so construed, unless by the previous admission *that no men of talents and integrity to conduct the war to a successful issue, can be found in what they are pleased to call the republican party.* Nevertheless it will be so represented. I take the liberty, therefore, to suggest, with that diffidence which the splendid display of talents and information by the friends of peace could not fail to inspire, that the negociation for peace presents no difficulty, as to the ostensible point in dispute. The right of a belligerent to take his seamen from neutral merchant ships, cannot be denied, and the question turns only on modifications, in the exercise of it, to suit those singular circumstances, in which Britain and America happen to stand relatively to each other. This being the case, by what argument shall it be proved that we risque any thing in leaving the matter to Britain herself? The article, on that as on other subjects, must be reciprocal; so that what she exacts from us, when belligerent, she must concede to us, when neutral. How, then, can those who complain of her haughtiness, apprehend that she will dictate terms inconsistent with national dignity, seeing that she must, in her turn, submit to those very terms. This observation is too simple to have escaped men of acute mind; and therefore I am induced to suppose there is more in the matter than I am aware of; but I have always held, and never (I believe) shall change the opinion, that no success, however brilliant, on either side, will operate a particle of change in the treaty, so far as relates to impressment. Whether we conquer Canada, or lay down our arms, Britain, when at war, will take her seamen from our merchant ships; and we, when at war, will take our seamen from her merchant ships. The contest, therefore, according to my comprehension, is without an object, as it relates to that point. If there be (as many, and not without reason, supposed) latent motives or designs, I have nothing to do with them, but to declare, not only as a friend of mankind, but as a creature endued with common sense, that not one dollar should be granted to support a war for latent objects.

But there will be, I fear, another and a most serious difficulty in making peace, which ought to have been foreseen by those who made war. Perhaps it was foreseen and disregarded. During our revolutionary struggle, when Spain was about to offer her mediation, it became necessary for congress to state their ultimatum. It was suggested by the French minister, who communicated the intended offer of Spain, that the more moderate our demands, the more likely was it, that we should obtain her support. The debates on this momentous occasion were long and warm. The eastern states held fast to a right of fishing on the banks of Newfoundland. Virginia and her adherents were disposed to run westward across the continent, but would hear of nothing short of the Mississippi. Many delegates from the middle states were disposed to limit our empire, on the west, by the Alleghany; and urge our claim to the fisheries as a matter not to be relinquished, but in the last necessity. The debate was drawn out to such length, that before it was closed, the news of war between Spain and England was received. Thus it lay over to a subsequent occasion, when a French minister of more address cajoled congress into a resolution to leave the conditions of peace to his most christian majesty. Our ministers in Europe received instructions, in conformity, which they disregarded. Perceiving the game, which had been played to secure the country beyond the Alleghany for France, by agreeing that the fisheries should be inhibited to America, they struck up at once a bargain with the British ministers. These, as soon as the great measure of acknowledging our independence was resolved on, determined to purchase our good will, and take us, if possible, out of the hands of their enemy. To this determination we owe, perhaps, our extent to the Mississippi, which some then thought, and many now think, we had been better without; and certainly we owe to it the right of fishing on the banks of Newfoundland. France could not, had she been so disposed, have forced this concession from her enemy; and France was not so disposed. She wished, by excluding us and by other diplomatic manoeuvers, to secure for her own subjects the supply of fish to Spain and Italy.

We are now again at war with the mistress of the ocean. A war which, whatever we may think of it, she considers as unjust and most unkind. We appear to her, as one who stabs his friend, in the very act of performing a friendly office; as the most base of Bonaparte's vassals, being the only one for whom no excuse can be made. Britain has the power to exclude us from the fisheries. Is there not reason to fear that she may have the will also? And is there any solid ground to expect, or even to hope, that those who declared war with so much improvidence, who have waged it with so much imbecility, and persist in it with so much obstinacy, will have the will (much less the power) to obtain, for the eastern states, a participation in the fisheries? During the course of this portentous summer, Britain may, if she pleases, gain a firm footing in the southern states. Should this be the case, there is, in my mind, no shadow of doubt that our administration would, to regain their adherents in the south, abandon the fisheries. Those great nurseries of seamen, without which we can have but little chance to become a maritime power, will, I fear, be closed against us. This will, to be sure, be a magnificent finale to a war for seamen's rights. Let those look to it whom it chiefly concerns.

AN OBSERVER.

FOR THE EXAMINER, JUNE 25, 1814

The fate of Europe is decided. France, subjected to her ancient Kings and reduced to her ancient limits, will no longer exhaust herself to subdue her neighbours. Cultivating the arts of peace, she will become a blessing to the world, after having been so long its scourge and curse. The more or less of territory which may be parcelled out to sovereigns, east of the Atlantic, will determine their relative weight in the balance of power, which directly concerns them, and indirectly concerns us.

Great Britain, in restoring the Bourbons, has committed a political sin; but on this, as other occasions, the wisdom of man may be foolishness with God. The late King of France was persuaded, against the feelings of his heart, to espouse the cause of America.[6] When, afterwards, his subjects rose against him, he lamented the example which he had set. But, humanly

The Examiner: Containing Political Essays on the Most Important Events of the Time 2, no. 6 (June 25, 1814): 81–85, from the copy in Firestone Library, Princeton University. No manuscript for this essay has been found.
     6. Louis XVI.

speaking, it was the interest of Britain to keep on the French throne an usurper, whose enmity with Spain would have rendered her alliance with that power as constant and firm as it was with Portugal. The consequence of this step, which the ministers may not have been able to avoid, being urged, perhaps, by their allies, and certainly by the sympathies of Englishmen, may appear some five and twenty, or thirty years hence. At present a gush of gratitude in the French monarch, and the necessity of peace, to heal the wounds inflicted on his kingdom by the late ambitious tyrant, will prevent opposition to the British cabinet.

To us it is important that there be, in the house of Bourbon collectively, a balance to the naval power of Britain; although the good we are to derive from it is remote. At present we must expect that Spain, as well from attachment to Britain for friendly support as from resentment of the injuries and insults heaped on her by our government, in the hour of her affliction, will see with complacency whatever we may suffer from a vigorous exercise of British power.

Sundry speculations are abroad respecting the conduct which Great Britain may pursue towards us, and that which federalists will adopt, under certain contingencies. Perhaps it may be well for men to make up their minds on these subjects: In considering the probable course of events, it is material to ascertain the opinions and sentiments of those who are likely to be the principal actors. Those are kings, kings too of ancient families, against whom the ruling party in this country have incessantly poured forth abuse for upwards of twenty years. This may not offend, but it cannot conciliate. Reflecting men, among their ministers, will not fail to observe that our government repelled the loyal Spaniards and insulted the British monarch, but flattered and caressed a criminal who had usurped the throne of France. They will couple this with the seduction of subjects from their allegiance, and the attempt to protect traitors against the laws of their country. They may conclude that we are instigated by a spirit incompatible with public order.

I am not one of those who believe the conduct of nations, princes, or individuals, to be wholly selfish. Those who hold a faith so little honourable to our nature, will do well to contemplate the sublime scenes lately displayed at Paris. It may give them a better opinion of their species. G. Britain may perhaps continue to exhibit that magnanimity which base minded jacobins attributed to fear. But there are discreet men, who believe she owes it to herself to make us feel her power. That her dignity requires the adoption of a Roman rule, finely expressed by the poet, "parcere subjectis et debellare superbos."[7] We boast the privilege of governing ourselves. How well qualified for that office, it is fitter for others to feel than for me to express. Confessedly it is an essential point in the management of foreign affairs, to form a just estimate of ones own strength and of theirs whom we are to deal with, so as not to embark in dangerous enterprises for objects of trifling value. The Roman senators made themselves masters of this subject; comparing their power with that of others, took care not to make war with those who could beat them, but prudently pocketted affronts till a convenient opportunity presented itself for resenting them with effect. Thus they became, by degrees, the masters of their neighbours, till having subdued and amalgamated with themselves all Italy, they were irresistible. It is idle to suppose that every man in the community can find leisure to study the state and condition of foreign powers, or even their own. What does the sovereign people of New-York know about the sovereign people of Kentucky? Just as much as the sovereign people of Kentucky know about the sovereign people of New-York. And yet these high and mighty sovereigns, with sundry others of equal worth and wisdom, undertake to weigh all the states of Europe in the scale of their own intelligence. We see, and shall I fear severely feel, the consequence in a war begun without sufficient reason, prosecuted for no valuable object, maintained at a prodigious expence, pregnant with great danger, and leading to utter ruin. These high and mighty sovereigns may perhaps receive a corrective lesson from the hand of experience, and as long as the remembrance of it shall last, may govern themselves with a little more discretion.

But setting aside the selfishness and the magnanimity of our foe, it behoves us to recollect that we have not a patent right for the exclusive exercise of anger and resentment. Others have passions as well as ourselves. Those of the British are roused and must be indulged, whatever may be the wish or will of their ministers. The Prince Regent, and those about him, may view Messrs. Madison and Co. with contemptuous pity, but a spirit of resentment prevails through the nation, and it is the interest of many to keep it up and stimulate it to action. If, therefore, a peace be concluded before we taste the bitterness of that potion which we mingled for them, let it be remembered among the other miraculous events of this wonderful year. Believing, as I do, the conduct of the American government to have been unjust, I believe the Almighty will visit the sin not only on their heads, but on the heads of those who, by supporting them, adopted it and made

---

7. "Be sparing with the conquered and bring down the proud." Virgil, *Aeneid* 6:853.

it their own. I can readily suppose that the menace of an intention to exclude us from the fisheries and trade to the East and West Indies is a mere newspaper paragraph; but I can also suppose that influential characters in Great Britain, are interested in the exclusion, and am inclined to believe that we may be, if not shut out from, much restrained in the West Indies. France will recover St. Domingo, and Spain hold her American dominion. We know it was their policy to secure the trade of their own colonies to themselves. And although the conduct of Britain was more liberal, we have too much reason to apprehend that those three nations will now come to an understanding with each other, in which neither our opinion will be asked, nor our interest consulted. Some commercial intercourse with the British East Indies may perhaps be obtained; but we shall, I apprehend, meet with more difficulty in that respect now than heretofore. The fisheries, important to us all, are a vital interest to our eastern brethren. I wish, sincerely, we may not be deprived of them, and am not without hope, when I consider the firm and honest opposition made in the eastern states to this execrable war. Our former privilege may, perhaps be renewed, in favour to them; for as to force, it is out of the question: and the pretence is ridiculous. Should our independence be assailed, America, united, is invincible. But foreign conquest is a different affair. And of all conquests, none are so unlikely as those which are to be effected by naval expeditions, under the direction of our southern lords. Those who declaim, in high style, on what we can do, and what we will do, reckon, I fear, without their host; and when called on for their share of the bill, may lower somewhat of their lofty demeanour.

This leads to the consideration of what federalists will do, under certain contingencies. But before we glance at it, let us steadily view our hold on the fisheries. I doubt whether our administration will endeavour to obtain them. If I do them wrong I am sorry for it, but in my conscience, I believe they have such enmity to commerce, as gladly to see the commercial states stripped of that valuable right. I acknowledge that Mr. Madison was, in the national convention, an advocate for the power rooted in congress to favour American navigation in preference to that of foreign powers. But we all know that until lately, the idea of naval force was contumeliously scouted by those under whose influence Mr. Madison was chosen, and by whose aid he carried on his vibratory measures. We may perhaps be told, on the same authority which assured us Bonaparte was invincible, and his Berlin decrees repealed, that our rulers are disposed to recover the right which they rashly committed to the chance of war. But who will be security for the truth of their assertions. After the disgusting scenes of duplicity and falsehood which we have witnessed, the most solemn assurances, from the highest authority, have no weight with honourable men. Their confidence is gone. I say, then, it behooves true hearted Americans to consider, seeing in what hands the power is lodged to make peace, whether we have any chance to obtain a share in the Newfoundland fisheries; except from the grace and favour of our enemy.

And now, then, as to the conduct which federalists may pursue. I shall not pretend to say what they will do, for many a federal coat covers a jacobin heart. Every now and then some of these gentlemen strip themselves to be measured for a coat of office, which may keep them warm though it do not fit, and if not gracefully, is at least audaciously worn. Those who, still calling themselves federalists, pant and pine for power may take this occasion to join our rulers. Whatever may be the result, they may console themselves with the reflection that their conduct is not unprecedented; and sing, out of their political hornbook, "in Adam's fall we sinned all." But some true hearted federalists will continue to oppose a faction which combined itself with the Corsican usurper to hunt freedom out of the world. We read in some federal papers, that if Great Britain shall not agree to moderate terms, she will find herself engaged in a different war from what she has hitherto waged, and, in particular, that if she does not yield the fisheries, we shall fight; Gods how we shall fight! But let this be scanned. Let it be supposed that Britain should refuse not only to make peace, but even to hold a treaty with Mr. Madison, because of his duplicity and devotion to the fallen despot. That language which Alexander, in the name of the allied sovereigns, used to the prophet himself, England may well hold to his disciples.[8] But it would be a sore insult. Those, therefore, who are arming cap-a-pie,[9] for a windmill conflict might sally out on such an occasion, with no slender chance of adventures. But will federalists embark their lives and fortunes, in deadly contest, on such ground. Before they engage to support a war, which many of them consider as unjust, and which all of them consider as unwise, it behooves them to ask not only for whom, and for what they are to fight, but whether they are like to get that for which they expend their treasure and shed their blood. In taking Mr. Madison for their Dulcinea, and calling on the world to acknowledge his good faith and impartiality,

8. Relations between Tsar Alexander I and Napoleon changed several times in the course of their reigns, but soured permanently after Napoleon invaded Russia in 1812. Afterward Alexander formed a new alliance that ultimately defeated Napoleon.
9. Head to foot.

under the pain and peril of mortal combat, though they may excite laughter, they cannot command respect. But for whom are they to fight? They are to fight for men who hold them in bondage, who have proscribed them, who have, under the forms of law, plundered and threatened to kill them. It is a handsome maxim in theory, that oppressive laws will not be passed in a republican government, because those by whom they are enacted must be equally subjected to them with their fellow citizens. But this consolatory phrase is false. The same faction which enacts oppressive laws, appoints wicked agents to execute them exclusively on their opponents. Our experience under the embargo, and its concomitant edicts tests the value of that and other stale sayings by which honest men have been cheated, from generation to generation, down to the present month of June, in the year of our Lord 1814. Will federalists, then, fight for their present rulers? If they do, they will (successful or unsuccessful) be fairly entitled to the benefit of such rulers! But no, say those who blow the trumpet, it is not to establish, but to get rid of those rulers, that we fight, so as that we and our friends may get in their places. An admirable project! But consider, gentlemen, that you will be victorious or defeated. If beaten you are but where you were, and where you would have been had you remained quietly at home. Will the sovereign people, which clings closer and closer to Messrs. Madison and Co. at every successive defeat, and whose tender love converts their very extravagance into virtue, like them less, and you more for being beaten and banged in each others company. Will they not, as heretofore, laugh at your folly or despise your meanness? But you are not to be beaten: you are to be victorious. Be it so. And what then? Will the people discard in success those whom they cherish in disgrace? He who believes this will not forfeit political salvation by the want of faith. But on what is the hope of success founded. Is there specific virtue in a federal dollar to breathe from the national chest, a spirit of wisdom and economy? Will our chieftains in snuffing up the dog-day effluvia from federal volunteers, inhale heroic ardour and military skill? If nothing like this can be expected; if the war is to be carried on as it has been, one mountainous blunder gigantically piled on another, what chance is there for success? But it is not for the rulers, it is for the government we are to fight. Wait then till the government is attacked; and even then inquire, before you turn out, what it is and where it is. To the first question we shall doubtless be answered, it is the constitution. And what, pray, is the constitution? I know what it was, as well perhaps as my neighbours. I know also, that it is not what it was, but has been grossly perverted to the worst purposes. I shall not attempt, here, to anatomize bodies politic and disclose the scene of their operations; but, adhering to the good old book which tells me, in that language of simple wisdom, which all can easily comprehend, *a tree is known by its fruit.* I say it must be a bad tree which produces such fruit as the embargo. And *where* is this government? It is in the southern swamps, and western wilds. If Britons go there to invade, will federalists go there to defend it? If so, much good may it do them.

But it is not the administration, neither is it exactly the government, it is the American union, and above all American liberty which is to be defended. When American liberty is invaded let the virtuous and the brave pour out again their hearts blood in its defence. But is it certain that the union and liberty are inseparable. Is it certain that they are connected? Is it certain that they are compatible? It is certain that the union was formed to secure liberty, and it is certain that the northern states made large concessions to compass the union. While the fascinating word equality was repeated from mouth to mouth, and re-echoed from the hills to the waves, they assented, for the sake of union, to an unequal compact. They purchased and they paid for the union, flattering themselves that it placed liberty beyond the reach of danger. But how stands the fact? Let the best informed in the ranks of jacobinism step forward and point out, if he can, a statute, an edict, an ukase, an any thing during the last century in all Europe (not excepting France under Bonaparte) which made so audacious an attack on the liberty of man as the late embargo. By it, that incommunicable right of legislation which the people had entrusted to the congress, they transferred to the president. Not only was his will declared to be law; but refining on the wicked ingenuity of that ancient tyrant, whose edicts written in small character were placed on the top of a lofty column, the president's will, expressed in secret instructions to the instruments of his power, was to have the force and effect of law. His custom house officers could stop citizens on the high road, take their property, and if resisted, take their lives. If a plundered or maimed citizen appealed to the courts of justice for redress, it was sufficient for the president's agent to assert, in general terms, that the charge was false, and on trial, the facts being established, to draw forth the secret instruction and be justified. Let Tripoli or Algiers produce any thing equal to this. The Deys and Bashaws of Africa and the East, commit acts of detestable tyranny: but these are mere abuses of power. The tyrants of Tunis, Tripoli and Algiers do not enact such laws. And let it not be forgotten, but deeply engraven on every honest heart, that this nefarious system was prepared exclusively for the eastern states, and screwed on their necks. I say, exclusively, for it is notorious that New-York, and the ports south of it, were strictly blockaded by the enemy. On them, therefore, the embargo could not operate. To them it was a dead letter. Is it then to support a union and a government fruitful in such oppression that federalists are to fight? But no, it is for their country.

> Beloved country! name forever dear,
> Still breath'd in sighs, still uttered with a tear.[10]

Perish the wretch that will not defend thee. But have federalists a country? In this they are proscribed. Let the best among them, those who during the contest for independence were most eminent in council or the field, solicit the humblest office: let the veteran soldier bare a bosom scarred with honourable wounds, and pointing to children who pine in want, ask the place of a deputy's deputy to procure them bread; the single word federalist shall close his lips, shall justify the sleek upstart's denial, and send the supplicant away to starve. At the same moment let a wretch, whose crimes have driven him from his native land, come forward, his head close cropt, the countenance of a savage, with the manners of a blackguard, and the doors of office fly open. He marches away in triumph, to collect the people's money and abscond. Or let a shameful sycophant commence some idle tale which he calls a discovery, by saying, *I was a spy, I am a scoundrel,* the treasury chest is unlocked, and the fifty thousand dollars which rewarded his villainy proclaim the folly of his dupes. This country belongs to jacobins. Those who levy armies, make loans, impose taxes, share among them the public treasure, declare war, mock at our misery, shut their ears to our groans, and leave us exposed to an enemy whose wrath they have studied and laboured to inflame, while they prosecute with unheard of extravagance, romantic expeditions which expose us alike to ridicule and to ruin, those are the men who should fight to defend the power they meanly acquired and basely abuse. If federalists like such rulers they ought also to fight. Perhaps their masters, if successful, may be so kind as to grant what Lazarus prayed for, the crumbs which fall from their table. Perhaps too, the enemy, if victorious, may take pity on them. Much, very much indeed, will they deserve to be pitied.

I shall not pretend to guess what federalists will do, much less to decide on what they ought to do. I am neither a seer nor a pedagogue, but merely

AN OBSERVER.

---

10. Morris's adaptation of lines from Alexander Pope's *Eloisa*, lines 30–31: "Oh, name for ever sad! for ever dear! / Still breath'd in sighs, still usher'd with a tear."

TO THE EDITOR OF THE EXAMINER.
Sir,
The able editor of the Evening Post has had the goodness to notice, last Saturday, some hints from me, which you published a week before.[11] I take leave to acknowledge the honour; and if I do not reply either so fully or so gravely as he may wish, he must do me the justice to believe it is from no want of respect.

I am bound to thank him for the information that Niagara will return to us by the law of postliminium; which I am the more rejoiced at, because, according to the present appearances, there is little likelihood of recovering it in any other way.[12]

He informs me also, that a right to fish on the great bank belongs to us, by the laws of nature and nations, in common with Great Britain and the rest of the world. I am much obliged by this information, because I never knew it before, and even now, much as I respect his authority, I hope he will look into the matter a little further; for if he should be commissioned to negotiate about it, and stranger things have happened, he may find that the British have more to say for themselves than he is aware of.

I am sorry not to have hit his taste, by a *grave* discussion of the nation's rights. He will, I hope, feel a little disposed to excuse me when I assure him, I did not mean then, neither do I now mean, to enter into any such discussion. I do not choose to appear the advocate of our enemy's rights, claims or pretensions. At the same time, I do not mean to retract any opinion I have advanced. It was my wish that our friends should avoid rash declarations. We are already engaged in a war, on a question of right, about which those who set up the claim, must soon find themselves in the wrong; if they have not already been so fortunate as to make that discovery. I cannot think it advisable to multiply such questions. It is easy to infuse into men's minds an exaggerated idea of their rights. But, when led into error, it is not so easy to

---

The Examiner: Containing Political Essays on the Most Important Events of the Time 2, no. 10 (July 23, 1814): 145–48, from the copy in Firestone Library, Princeton University. No manuscript for this essay has been found.

11. The unsigned reply is in the *New-York Evening Post*, July 2, 1814, pp. 2–3.

12. The doctrine holds that property taken by an enemy in wartime is restored to its former legal status after hostilities cease. Morris discusses the principle further below.

undeceive them. It is my wish that the fishery should be restored: whether held by right or permission. The subject is too delicate to say many things which pertain to it. I fear that, instead of securing, we may jeopardize it, by our over zeal, or over security.

But though I do not choose to say all which I think, I do not venture even to suppose that any person can be justly chargeable with indiscretion for discussing what he supposes to be the nation's right, as gravely as he pleases. I am content, also, that he contrast my phrases to embellish his argument: and, if it be done with effect, will join in applauding the wit. I pray him, nevertheless, to consider that, as neither country is bound by what we say, he will not have gained much by making me appear to contradict myself.

Thus, if it were admitted that every thing of *vital interest* to part of a country, is a *perfect right* of the whole, those who contend for the British doctrine might simply observe, that I had improperly used the epithet *vital*. I am not ashamed to acknowledge, if that epithet converts *interest* into *right*, that I have sinned against the laws of language. I hope, however, to be pardoned by those, who, in discovering the crime, will recollect that the expression was used in a light newspaper essay, not in a grave diplomatic discussion. At any rate, before sentence is passed, they will be pleased to consider, in mitigation, that although food is of vital importance to a hungry man, it is not quite certain that he could justify taking a loaf from a baker's basket, a steak from a butcher's stall, or a cod from a fisherman's car. I still believe the fisheries of vital importance to the eastern states, and hold the same opinion respecting commerce; not meaning, nevertheless, to say that without commerce and the fisheries, every man woman and child must perish. I have seen both commerce and fisheries destroyed by the embargo, and repeat, that it behooves all true hearted Americans to consider, seeing in what hands the power is lodged, to make peace, whether we have any chance to obtain a share in the Newfoundland fisheries except from the *grace and favour of our enemy.* And I shall be glad to know how we are to get hold of them, if given up by our negotiators.

The able editor seems displeased with the merchants of St. John's. But when he considers that they are our enemies, and interested in the question, he may perhaps be disposed to make some allowance for their portion of human frailty. From what he has quoted of this memorial, it seems *to me* they believe the existence of Britain, "as a great and independent nation, depends upon her dominion on the ocean." And, so believing, they "wish to exclude foreigners from sharing again in the advantages of a fishery from which a large portion of their national defence will be derived." These notions are not, I believe, confined to those merchants. But I perhaps, not understanding English, am mistaken; and their object may be, "to shut us out from fishing on the ocean, by virtue of their dominion on the same." This, which is the construction of the able editor, he considers as "an unreasonable, unjust and *preposterous* claim, to which we as a nation can never yield." I believe England never pretended to prevent nations from fishing on the ocean, and would probably agree that the claim, if extended so far, is unfounded. But let not the memorialists of St. John's, be condemned for what they do not say. If the claim be confined to the banks, I would pray leave to recommend a little serious consideration.

As I said before, I shall not enter deeply into this question. He has quoted the 3d article of our treaty with Great Britain, and observes that, "although the words purporting to be an agreement that we should *continue to enjoy the right*, are not words of grant nor necessary, yet it was thought prudent to insert them, *ex abundanti cautela*."[13] If the profound lawyer and statesman, who penned that article should see this comment, he would smile. Let us suppose that in like manner *ex abundanti cautela*, it had been stipulated that we should continue to enjoy the right of navigating the ocean and killing whales. I must be permitted to doubt whether "our commissioners would have been highly commended for it by the nation."[14]

The able editor, however, "putting it in (what he calls) the most favourable light for Great Britain, and allowing that we *acquired the right* to fish by treaty, feels very confident in asserting, that we thereby *acquired such a title* to it, that whenever another treaty shall be made between the parties, we shall be *perfectly entitled* to the restoration of it, by the law of postliminium," which means, if I understand English (of which, nevertheless, I must not be over confident) that, according to the law of nations, he who by treaty acquires *a right*, acquires thereby such *a title* to that right, that after engaging in war he is *perfectly entitled* to the restoration of it (the right) when peace is made, by the postliminary right. Had this been known in old times, it would have saved the trouble, in making new treaties, of renewing old ones. No less than seventeen of these are recapitulated and confirmed in the treaty of 1763, between Great Britain, France, Spain, and Portugal. My notion has hitherto been, that if our treaty with England be (as it probably will be) renewed and confirmed in the treaty of peace, and no alterations or exceptions be made, things will return to the condition they were in be-

13. Out of an abundance of caution.
14. Morris is actually paraphrasing here.

fore the war: So that if the enemy shall have made any disposition of real property during his *possessory right*, such property will return to its former owner by the *postliminary right*.

I find, Mr. Examiner, that I have not the happy art of expressing myself clearly. If I had, the intelligent editor of the Evening Post would not so wholly have mistaken my meaning, as to suppose, that it was "in pursuit of the declared purpose to scan the justice and expedience of a war carried on, rather than yield our claim to the fisheries," that I put the case of a refusal on the part of Great Britain even to treat with our present rulers.

Not believing (as I am now bound to believe on the authority of the Evening Post) that a right to fish on the banks of Newfoundland belongs to us, and to all others, as a necessary incident to national independence; being moreover desirous to waive the examination of that question; but intending to inspire doubt as to the propriety of pledging ourselves gratuitously on the contingency of future events, I selected a case less questionable, according to my notion, than the fisheries. If the editor will have the goodness to read what I have written, in this view, he will acquit me of the absurdity with which I stand charged; doubtless from the loose and inaccurate manner in which I was so unfortunate as to convey my ideas.

And now, Mr. Examiner, having made the *amende honourable*, let me, before I am turned over to the executioner, be permitted to cite, for the amusement of your readers, I do not pretend to instruct, a few articles of treaties among the powers of this world. They will see with astonishment, the mistaken notions entertained by European statesmen, about these same fisheries.

On the 10th of February, 1763, a definitive treaty of peace was made between Great Britain, France and Spain, since called the treaty of Paris. The fifth and thirteenth articles run thus: [15]

> ART. 5. The subjects of France shall have liberty to fish and dry fish on a part of the coast of Newfoundland, such as is specified in the 13th article of the treaty of Utrecht, which article is renewed and confirmed by the present treaty, (excepting, &c.) and his Britannic majesty consents to leave to the subjects of the most christian king the liberty of fishing in the gulph of St. Lawrence, on condition that the subjects of France

---

15. In the treaty, the King of France is "His Most Christian Majesty," while the King of Spain is "His Most Catholic Majesty." Morris actually quotes Article 18 of the treaty, not Article 13.

shall use the said fishery only at a distance of three leagues from all the coasts belonging to Great Britain, as well those of the continent as those of the islands situate in the said gulph of St. Lawrence. And as to what concerns the liberty of fishing on the coasts of the island of Cape Breton, out of the said gulph, it shall be permitted to the subjects of the most christian king to use the said fishery only at the distance of fifteen leagues from the coasts of the said island of Cape Breton, &c.

ART. 13. His catholic majesty, for himself and his successors, desists from all pretence which he may have formed, in favour of the *Guipuscoans*, and others his subjects, to the right of fishing in the environs of the island of Newfoundland.[16]

On the 6th February, 1778, a treaty of amity and commerce was concluded between France and the United States. The ninth article runs thus:

The inhabitants, merchants, commanders of ships, masters and seafaring men of the states, provinces, and domains of the two parties shall reciprocally abstain from and avoid fishing in all the places possessed or which shall be possessed by the other party. The subjects of his most christian majesty shall not fish in the harbours, bays, creeks, roads, coasts and places which the United States possess, or shall hereafter possess. And, in like manner, the subjects, people and inhabitants of the said United States shall not fish in the harbours, bays, creeks, roads, coasts and places which his most christian majesty now possesses or shall hereafter possess. And if any ship or vessel be surprised fishing, in violation of the present treaty, the said ship or vessel and her cargo shall be confiscated after the proof thereof shall have been made: it being well understood, that the exclusion stipulated in the present article shall have place only as much and as long as the king and the United States shall not have granted in that respect an exception to some other nation.

The tenth article runs thus:

The United States, their citizens and inhabitants shall never disturb the subjects of the most christian king, in the enjoyment and exercise of the right of fishery on the banks of Newfoundland, any more than in the indefinite and exclusive enjoyment which belongs to them on that part of the coasts of that island, designated in the treaty of Utrecht, nor

16. Fishermen from the Basque province of Guipuscoa (Guipúzcoa) had traditionally fished in the waters off Newfoundland.

in the right relative to all and each of the islands which belong to his most christian majesty. The whole conformably to the true sense of the treaties of Utrecht and of Paris.

On the 3d of September, 1783, a definitive treaty of peace and friendship was concluded at Versailles between Great Britain and France. The second article runs thus:

> The treaties of Westphalia of 1648, the treaties of peace of Nimiguen of 1678 and 1679, of Ryswick of 1697, those of peace and commerce of Utrecht in 1713, that of Baden of 1714, that of the triple alliance of the Hague of 1717, that of the quadruple alliance of London of 1718, the treaty of peace of Vienna of 1738, the definitive treaty of Aix la Chapelle of 1748, and that of Paris of 1763, serve as the base and foundation to the peace and to the present treaty: and, to that effect, they are all renewed and confirmed in the best form, as well as all the treaties in general which existed between the high contracting parties before the war, and as if they were here inserted word for word, so that they ought exactly to be observed in future in their whole tenor, and religiously executed on both sides in all the points from which it is not derogated by the present treaty of peace.

The fourth, fifth and sixth articles are as follows:

> ART. 4. His majesty the king of Great Britain is maintained in the property of the island of Newfoundland and the adjacent islands, as the whole was secured to him by the thirteenth article of the treaty of Utrecht excepting the islands of St. Pierre and Miquelon, which are ceded in full property, by the present treaty, to his most christian majesty.
>
> ART. 5. His most christian majesty, to prevent the quarrels which have taken place heretofore between the English and French, consents to renounce the right of fishing which belongs to him in virtue of the thirteenth article of the above mentioned treaty of Utrecht, from Cape Bonavista to Cape St. John, situate on the eastern coast of Newfoundland in the fiftieth degree of north latitude. And his majesty, the king of Great Britain, consents, on his part, that the fishery assigned to the subjects of his most christian majesty, beginning at the said Cape St. John, passing by the north and descending on the west coast of Newfoundland, shall extend to the place called Cape Raye, in the latitude of forty-seven degrees and fifty minutes. The French fishermen shall enjoy

the fishery assigned to them by the present article as they could of right enjoy that which is assigned to them by the treaty of Utrecht.

ART. 6. As to the fishery in the gulph of St. Lawrence, the French may continue to carry it on conformably to the 5th article of the treaty of Paris.

AN OBSERVER.

41 ✿ Oration on Europe's Deliverance from Despotism (1814)

In the essay for the *Examiner* published four days before this speech, Morris had described the British move to restore the Bourbon dynasty as "a political sin." This is probably a reference to the fact that the British had acted without consulting, and indeed against the wishes of, the other allied powers. As this address makes clear, however, Morris regards the restoration as a good thing for France and for Europe in general.

—❈—

'Tis done. The long agony is over. The Bourbons are restored. France reposes in the arms of her legitimate prince. We may now express our attachment to *her*, consistently with the respect we owe to *ourselves*. We recall to remembrance that interesting period, when, in the fellowship of arms, our souls were mingled at the convivial feast, and our blood on the field of glory. We look, exulting, at the plain of York. There French and American troops contended, in generous strife, who first should reach the goal of victory. There, the contest for independence was closed. There, was sealed our title to be numbered among the nations.

Thank God, we can, at length, avow the sentiments of gratitude to that august family, under whose sway the fleets and armies of France and Spain were arrayed in defence[1] of American liberty. We then hailed Louis the Sixteenth PROTECTOR OF THE RIGHTS OF MANKIND. We loved him.

An Oration, Delivered On Wednesday, June 29, 1814, At The Request Of A Number Of Citizens Of New-York, In Celebration Of The Recent Deliverance Of Europe From The Yoke Of Military Despotism. By the Honourable Gouverneur Morris, Esq. Published at the request of the *Committee of Arrangements* (Salem, [Mass.]: Sold by Cushing and Appleton, 1814). From the copy in the pamphlet collection, L. A. Beeghly Library, Juniata College. The pamphlet was also published in New York (New-York: Printed and Published by Van Winkle and Wiley, Corner of Wall and New-streets, 1814). In the American Antiquarian Society Early American Imprints, series II (Shaw-Shoemaker), the New York printing is no. 32171 and the Salem printing is no. 32172.

1. In the New York version, "defence"; in the Salem version, "defenee."

We deplored his fate. We are unsullied by the embrace of his assassins. Our wishes, our prayers, have accompanied the loyal Spaniards in their struggle; and we blush that Americans were permitted to offer only wishes and prayers.

How interesting, how instructive, the history of the last five-and-twenty years! In the spring of 1789 the states general of France were convened to ward off impending bankruptcy. The derangement of their finances was occasioned by the common artifice of cheating people into a belief that debts may be safely incurred without imposing taxes. Large loans had been made, but no funds provided. At the opening of that august assembly, the minister of finance declared it would have been easy to cover the deficit, without calling them together, but the king wished their aid to correct abuses.

This hazardous experiment terminated, as was foreseen by intelligent observers, in the overthrow of ancient establishments. The States General usurped, under the name of National Assembly, unlimited power, and used it with an equal want of wisdom and justice. They destroyed the rights of property; issued paper money; framed an impracticable system of government, and released their king from a prison to place him on a throne, whose foundation they had undermined. Their successors overturned it in less than a year, and again threw the king into prison, whence, in less than six months, he was led to the scaffold.

This virtuous monarch, our friend in the hour of danger, was the victim of his own goodness. Ardently desirous to ameliorate the condition of subjects, for whom he felt the fondness of a father, he thought no sacrifice of power too great if it could promote their felicity. He had been persuaded that his prerogative, useless to him, was oppressive to them. Dangerous error! He had been told, and believed, that in their loyalty he had a perfect defence against the intrigues of turbulent demagogues. Fatal delusion! This just, this merciful prince, was led to execution amid the insulting shouts of a ferocious mob. He was guarded by militia, who felt horror at the office. The Royal Victim, collected in himself, was occupied, during the long procession, in beseeching the divine majesty to pardon his rebellious subjects. But the stroke which severed from the body his innocent head, cut them off from forgiveness, until they should have expiated the crime by lengthened years of misery.

O! it was a crime against nature and against heaven—a murder most foul and cruel—a deed at which fiends might have wept. I was in Paris. I saw the gush of sorrow. I heard the general groan. Every bosom anticipated the sentence of an avenging God. It was like a second fall of man. An awful scene of affliction, guilt, and horror. All were humbled to the dust, save only those who exulted, in screams of diabolic rapture, at their success in driving an assembly, over which they tyrannized, to this nefarious act.

Mark here the guilt to which faction leads. That assembly, in general, consisted of two parties; those called Girondistes, at their head the representatives from Bordeaux, who wished for a federal republic; and the Jacobins, who concealed, under the loud cry for a republic one and indivisible, a design to restore monarchy. Both of them treated with the imprisoned King. He trusted himself to the party of the Gironde. It seemed less criminal than the other, and was more numerous. From that moment the jacobins doomed him to destruction, that they might destroy their opponents. Those who assaulted the palace, to tear off that semblance of monarchy which the constituent assembly had left, were now called forth to overawe the faction of the Gironde. The assembly surrounded by armed men, a majority was frightened into a sentence of death against their innocent captive—a sentence which the intelligent foresaw would involve their own.

And so it did. The inexorable Danton dragged them before his revolutionary tribunal, and poured their blood on the scaffold wet with that of their murdered monarch. Thus, every circumstance of guilt and shame was combined, in their last moments, to embitter the bitterness of death.

On the same scaffold, condemned by the same judges, perished Danton himself. He perished, conspiring to place the imprisoned son on the throne of a father whom he had laboured to destroy. He believed that Louis XVI had been too much disgraced to reign over a proud nation. Combining, therefore, the courage of a hero with the energy of a conspirator, and unrestrained by religion or mercy, he determined to strike off the head which he thought unfit for a crown. In the rapid march of fate, his own soon fell. Insulted with the semblance of trial, convicted without proof, condemned unheard, he roared, in a voice of thunder, "I have been told, and now believe, that the punishment of man is the fruit of his crime. Wretches! I gave you the power of dooming innocence to death, and I, by your doom, must die. The same justice shall overtake those who sent me here and you also."—The voice of the savage was prophetic.

Those who slaughtered their prince and made havoc of each other; those who endeavoured to dethrone the King of Heaven, and establish the worship of human reason—who placed, as representative of the Goddess of Reason, a prostitute on the altar which piety had dedicated to the holy virgin, and fell down and paid to her their adoration, were at length, compelled to see and to feel, and in agony to own that there is a GOD. I cannot

proceed—My heart sickens at the recollection of those horrors which deso-
lated France. That charming country, on which the bounty of heaven has
lavished blessings, was the prey of monsters. To tell the crimes, everywhere
and every hour perpetrated, would wound the soul of humanity, and shock
the ear of modesty. But where, my country, oh! where shall I hide the blush,
that these monsters were taken to *your* bosom?

I retract the charge—Nations of the earth! believe not the imputation.
The virtuous sons of America were not guilty of ingratitude. Much as they
love liberty, the name of liberty did not drive from their hearts the great
friend of liberty, THE PROTECTOR OF THE RIGHTS OF MANKIND. No,
holy martyr! their grateful bosoms re-echoed thy dying groan. In humble
submission they viewed events whose mystery they could not comprehend, and waited the development of eternal wisdom. They beheld licentious crime, under the name of liberty, roaming over the broad surface of
France, seeking virtue for its prey, defiling innocence, despoiling poverty,
and laying the very face of nature waste. They saw it voracious at home, victorious abroad, every where triumphant. Europe was appalled. Her princes
trembled. The new-hatched, unfledged, French republic soared, as on eagle
pinions, beyond the clouds. Dazzled by the lustre of her victories, the
moral eye could scarcely perceive the guilt of those profligate leaders who
dictated law to a prostrate world. Drunk with success, slaughtering their
countrymen, pillaging their neighbours, seducing subjects from their allegiance, and preceding the storm of conquest by the poison of corruption,
they reviled whatever antiquity and custom had rendered respectable, made
sport of religion, treated public law as romantic nonsense, and trampled on
the decencies of private life. Yet they found admirers every where. What
wonder that they should have found adherents here! This country is not
without bankrupts, both in fortune and in fame; nor fiery spirits prompted
by ambition. There are among us some who, wishing to be great, disdain
to be good; who, in pursuit of riches and power, indifferent to right and
wrong, take the nearest way. Many, too, there are, who ignorantly swallow
every idle tale; many who, puffed up with conceit, will no longer listen to
truth when she offers instruction. A mind bloated by vanity loves to feed
on falsehood, and drink the flattery by which its dropsied understanding
is drowned. But in that moment, when crowned heads in Europe crouched
to the French directory, an insult aimed at the honour of America was instantly resented. This dignified conduct of the new world astonished the
old—Our character was raised to the highest pitch—raised, alas! only to be
precipitated, by the impetus of its fall, more deeply in shame.

This occasion does not require, neither will it admit of a history, or even the rapid recapitulation, of important events. We have seen the tumults of democracy terminate, in France, as they have everywhere terminated, in despotism. What had been foreseen, and foretold, arrived. The power of usurpation was directed and maintained by great talents. Gigantic schemes of conquest, prepared with deep and dark intrigue; vast masses of force, conducted with consummate skill; a cold indifference to the miseries of mankind; a profound contempt for moral ties; a marblehearted atheism, to which religion was only a political instrument, and the stern persevering will to bend every thing to his purpose, were the means of Napoleon to make himself the terror, the wonder, and the scourge of nations. The galling of his iron yoke taught Frenchmen feelingly to know how much they had lost in breaking the bands of their allegiance. They had, indeed, to amuse them, the pomp of triumph, the shout of victory, and the consciousness of force which made the neighbouring nations groan. But the fruits of their labour were wrested from them to gratify the extravagance of vanity, or supply the waste of war. Their children were torn from their bosoms, and marched off in chains to the altar of impious, insatiable ambition. Aged parents, who, with trembling step, had followed to bid the last of many sons a final, fond adieu, in returning to their cottage, once the scene of humble happiness, but now stript by remorseless collectors of every thing which could be sold, looking round in vain for the little objects to which use and need had given value, and seeing only the remnant of that loaf from which they had taken their last meal, moistened with bitter tears, turn their eyes to heaven, then, throwing themselves into each other's arms, exclaim, My child! my child! Such, France, were thy sufferings. Thus was the innocent blood of thy sovereign visited upon thee. Frenchmen! by these woes were you taught to feel the present, the avenging God. It was this deep agony which led you to declare to your sovereign's brother, in the language of nature and truth, "Sir, we bring you our hearts; the tyrant has left us nothing else to give."

In the month of September, 1812, the son of an obscure family, in a small island of the Mediterranean, was at the head of a greater force than was ever yet commanded by one man, during the long period to which history extends. His brows encircled with an imperial diadem, his sword red with the blood of conquered nations, his eye glaring on the fields he had devoted to plunder, his feet trampling on the neck of kings, his mind glowing with wrath, his heart swoln with the consciousness of power unknown before, he moved, he seemed, he believed himself a god. While at one extremity of Europe his ruthless legions drenched, with loyal blood, the arid soil of Spain, he marched, with gigantic stride, at the other extremity, to round his vast dominion in the widest circle of the civilized world. Already he had pierced the Russian line of defence. Already his hungry eagles were pouncing on his prey—Pause—View steadily this statue of colossal power. The arms are of iron; the breast is of brass; but the feet are of clay. The moment of destruction impends. Hark! The blow is given—it totters—it falls—it crumbles to dust. This mighty man, this king of kings, this demi-god, is discomfited. He flies—He is pursued—He hides. Stripped of royal robes, distracted with apprehension, flapping the wings of fear, he scuds in disguise across the wide plain of Poland, not daring to look behind. He takes a moment's breath, and slakes the feverish thirst of his fatigue in the waters of the Elbe. A second flight brings him to the Rhine. After a third effort, he is within the walls of Paris.

Here again he reigns. Here the crafty statesman contrives, and the gloomy tyrant collects, the renewed means of warfare. Again, unhappy France, must thy garners and thy veins be opened. Again, and under the doubled weight of oppression, must thou groan. Vain are expostulations; vain the tumultuous cry for peace; vain the shrieks of despair.

Alexander, the great, the good, advances. He moves, at the head of his hardy Russians, from the ashes of Moscow, toward the banks of the Elbe. At his approach, the plundered, insulted subjects of Prussia rise to vindicate their honour. The Germans burn to avenge their wrongs. But Napoleon has anticipated his enemy. He is, in force, on the Elbe. His vigour and activity are successful. Again he quaffs the luscious draught of victory. Drunk again with hope, he shuts his ear to the counsel of prudence. But, true to his principles, he calls fraud to the aid of force; and, accepting the mediation of Austria, displays the insidious craft of a perverse policy. For what? To elude a peace which, conceding vast territory, and restoring his captive legions, would have placed him again in a condition to menace, insult, and oppress the world. But no. A confidence in his talents, a confidence in his fortune, have made him blind. He confides in fortune, the god of atheism, which, analyzed, is nothing more than the combination of events we cannot discover; in which, nevertheless, though unknown, there is no more of chance than there was in a comet's orbit ere Newton was born. But the adoration of that which derives its essence from ignorance, accords with *their* wisdom who deny the existence of that Being by whom ponderous planets, hurled through the infinite void, are compelled to move in their prescribed course, till time shall be no more. Bonaparte, elate with rash confidence, eluded negotiation. At length the father of his wife found himself constrained, by duty and honour, to join the allies. At this connexion, which could not have been unexpected, Napoleon was not dismayed. Calculating on the hollow faith of coalitions, in which a diversity of interest often keeps asunder the hearts whose hands are united; forgetting, or not knowing, that his tyranny had formed a league against him stronger than the union of states; a league, of which all mankind were members, and general sentiment the soul; he still flattered himself, that by the weight of his arms, and the edge of his craft, he could sever the bands of this new alliance. To this end, the bravery of his soldiers, the skill of his officers, the dexterity of his ministers, and all the resources of his genius, were exercised and exhausted, during the last summer. The plains of Saxony were wasted with inexorable severity. Pestilence and famine marched in the train of war, to thin the ranks of mankind—to extend the scene of human misery—and prepare a wide theatre for the display of British benevolence.

At length, after many battles, the well planned movements of the allies obliged Napoleon to abandon Dresden. From that moment his position on the Elbe was insecure. But pride had fixed him there: perhaps, too, the same blind confidence in fortune. His force was collected at Leipsic. Leipsic, in the war of thirty years, had seen the great Gustavus fall in the arms of victory. Leipsic again witnessed a battle, on whose issue hung the independence, not of Germany alone, but of every state on the continent of Europe. Hard, long, and obstinate, was the conflict. On both sides were displayed an union of the rarest skill, discipline, and courage. As the flood-tide waves of ocean, in approaching the shore, rush, foam, thunder, break, retire, return—so broke, retired, and returned the allied battalions, impetuously propelled by the pressure of their brethren in arms. And as the whelming flood, a passage forced through the breach, rends, tears, scatters, dissipates, and bears away its unnumbered sands, so was the tyrant's host overwhelmed, scattered, and borne away.

And now behold a scene sublime! Three mighty monarchs lay down their crowns and swords; they fall on their knees; they raise their eyes and hands to Heaven; they pour out thanksgiving to the God of battles—to him, the King of kings, sole, self-existent, in whom alone is might, majesty and dominion. With one voice they cry, "*The Lord is with us! Brother, the Lord is with us! Glory be to the Lord!*" Contrast this spectacle with that which had been exhibited thirteen months before on the plains of Russia.

The anxious hour is past. We respire. The air is embalmed with blossoms of liberty. Humanity rears her head from the dust, smooths her disheveled locks, and wipes away the tear. She greets you, victors! princes! heroes! christians! She bids you follow the path to immortal glory, pointed out by the finger of heaven. March. Lo! already the opposed armies are separated only by the Rhine. Here again the olive branch is tendered to the fierce Napoleon. Perhaps experience may have made him wise. Perhaps he has learnt in the school of adversity to moderate his desires. Perhaps, confiding in fortune no more, he may begin to believe there is a God who governs the world. No. The mysterious plan of Providence is yet incomplete. Napoleon's pride is yet untamed. He confides in wintry storms, which bid the weary soldier rest. He confides in the lofty barrier of the Pyrenees. He confides in the fortresses along his frontiers. He confides in the neutrality of Switzerland, and the reverence of his enemies for public law. The violation of that law was, with him, an ordinary measure of war. The plunder of neutrals was, with him, an ordinary fiscal resource. And yet he believes that his foes will be restrained by principles he never regarded. He is not deceived. He relies, too, on assurances wrung from the subjugated Swiss; supposing the sentiments of men to be stifled in the bosom of his slaves. He is mistaken. The allied armies, insensible to frost and fatigue, defying alike the rage of elements and the rage of man, throw themselves over the Rhine. They march through the cantons of Switzerland, not merely authorized by their permission, but furthered by their assistance; masking strong places by corps of observation, they penetrate the interior of France, on the east and the north, while Wellington pours in, on the south, his Britons, Spaniards, and Portuguese. Mark! The representatives of Bordeaux were first to proclaim a French republic. Bordeaux is first to unfurl the royal standard. Napoleon, surrounded, beaten, on the verge of ruin, remains unmoved. The allies, anxious to spare the effusion of blood, and terminate the misery of Europe, again tender peace, with the possession of undivided, undiminished, France. They are actuated by motives of humanity, and governed by dictates of human policy. But he and they, mighty though they be, are only instruments in a mightier hand. The heart of this modern Pharaoh is hardened. He will not release those whom he holds in bondage. His demands, far from being suited to this[2] condition, would have been unreasonable even had he been victorious. His severity had silenced truth. His violence obliged all who approached, to feed his vain glory with pleasing falsehood.

Ignorant, therefore, of his peril, he believes the French attached to his person. Yes; strange as it may seem, he, who led them so long through every

2. In the Salem printing, "this"; in the New York printing, "his."

stage and degree of suffering, believes himself to be the object of their tender affection. But why wonder at his self delusion? Has not the same strange thing been asserted by men among us, reputed wise! Nay, has it not been believed by hundreds and thousands of their followers; men who shut their eyes to reason and their ears to truth, from the fear of perceiving their own delusion? In the great scheme of Providence, as far as man may, without impiety, attempt to raise the veil, miraculous events appear to be wrought by human intervention. Thus we discover, in the preceding tyranny of Napoleon, the cause of that self deception and false information which prompted his extravagant conduct. Spectators, amazed that an adventurer, followed by a few exhausted dispirited soldiers, remnant of reiterated defeats, in the midst of a great nation which holds him in abhorrence, should persist in refusing the throne of France unless other thrones were added, cannot resist the conviction that he is blinded by the direction of the Almighty will. And yet we can trace back the present madness to preceding crimes. Thus punishment springs from offence. That determined, inflexible will, which had beaten down so many thrones, now recoils on himself, and drives him to ruin.

Again the cannon roar. The long arches of the Louvre tremble. The battle rages. The heights of Montmartre are assailed—they are carried. The Allies look down, victorious, on the lofty domes and spires of Paris. Lo! the capital of that nation, which dictated ignominious terms of peace in Vienna and Berlin; the capital of that nation, which wrapt in flames the capital of the Czars, is in the power of its foes. Their troops are in full march. The flushed soldier may soon satiate his lust, and glut his vengeance. See before you, princes, the school of that wildering philosophy, which undermined your thrones. In those sumptuous palaces dwell voluptuaries, who, professing philanthropy, love only themselves. There recline, on couches of down, those polished friends of man, who, reveling in the bosom of delight, see with indifference a beggar perish, and calmly issue orders for the conflagration of cities, and the pillage of kingdoms. Listen to the voice of retributive justice. Throw loose the reins of discipline. Cry havoc! avenge! avenge! No—Yonder is the white flag, emblem of peace. It approaches. They supplicate mercy. Halt!

Citizens of America, what, on such an occasion, would Napoleon have done? Interrogate his conduct during fifteen years of triumph. See this paragon of philosophers spread ruin around him—his iron heart insensible to pity—his ears deaf to the voice of religion and mercy. And now see two christian monarchs, after granting pardon and protection, descend from the heights of Montmartre, and march through the streets of that great city in peaceful triumph. See, following them, half a million of men, women and children, who hail, with shouts of gratitude, Alexander the deliverer. They literally kiss his feet; and, like those of old, who approached the Saviour of the world, they touch, in transport the hem of his garment, and feel sanctified. He enters the temple of the living God. In humble imitation of his divine master, he proclaims pardon and peace. Those lips, which, victorious in the plain of Leipsic, cried out Glory to God! now, again victorious, complete the anthem of benediction. "Glory be to God in the highest, and on earth peace! Good will toward men!" Let all nature join in the triumphant song, Glory! Glory! to God; and on earth peace!

Ye, who are promoters and supporters of war! Ye whose envenomed tongues have slavered out invective on all who wear legitimate crowns! Ye who represent sovereigns as wild beasts, for whose destruction all means are lawful! Approach; behold. Come ye, also, who, wrapping yourselves up in self conceit, look with affected pity on such as believe in a Saviour; ye who dwell, with cynic satisfaction, on crimes committed by fanatics! Look there. Those kings are christians. And thou, too, Democracy! savage and wild; thou, who wouldst bring down the virtuous and wise to thy level of folly and guilt! thou child of squinting envy and self tormenting spleen! thou persecutor of the great and good! see, though it blast thine eyeballs, see the objects of thy deadly hate. See lawful princes surrounded by loyal subjects. See them victorious over the legions of usurpation. See, they are hailed, followed, almost adored, by the nation they conquered, pardoned and liberated. See that nation seize the first moment of freedom to adopt a constitution like that of England—the land of our great and glorious forefathers—the land you abhor—the land at which your madmen, if heaven indulged them with power, would hurl the bolts of vengeance, and merge millions of their fellow men in the billows of the surrounding sea. Yes, Democracy, these are the objects of thy hate. Let those, who would know the idol of thy devotion, seek him in the Island of Elba.

He abdicates. He shows thee, Democracy, his kindred blood. He takes money for his crown. Look at him—him whom you hailed as invincible, omnipotent. He goes guarded to protect him from being murdered by those lately his subjects. He goes, assassin of d'Enghein, a pensioner of the house of Bourbon.[3]

---

3. Louis-Antoine-Henri de Bourbon-Conde, duc d'Enghien (1772–1804), was executed after being abducted and tried by a military court at Napoleon's behest.

That royal house now reigns. The Bourbons are restored. Rejoice, France! Spain! Portugal! You are governed by your legitimate kings, Europe! rejoice. The Bourbons are restored. The family of nations is completed. Peace the dove descending from heaven, spreads over you her downy pinions. Nations of Europe, ye are her brethren once more. Embrace. Rejoice. And thou, too, my much-wronged country! My dear, abused, self-murdered country, bleeding as thou art, rejoice. The Bourbons are restored. Thy friends now reign. The long agony is over. THE BOUR-BONS ARE RESTORED.

Morris had expressed reservations about the justice and efficacy of the federal government raising revenue through direct taxes as early as 1789 (see chapter 16). As it happened, however, Congress used this power only once before the War of 1812, in 1798. The costs of the war, however, led Congress to impose direct taxes again, in 1813 and 1815.[1] In 1815 it also added a duty on household furniture and gold and silver watches.[2]

Both of the direct tax laws offered states a discount for "assuming" the state's quota of the tax; that is, for paying the tax directly to the treasury, rather than having citizens pay the federal collectors. New York's legislature voted to assume the 1815 tax on March 24, 1815.[3] The tax on furniture and watches, however, could not be assumed. Morris's argument here, that these are also direct taxes, had been addressed by the U.S. Supreme Court in *Hylton* v. *U.S.*, 3 U.S. 171 (1796). In that case the Court held that a tax on carriages was an excise, and thus did not need to be apportioned as a direct tax.

⟊⟊⟊⟊⟊

Sir,

I pray Leave, thro the Medium of your Paper, to address a few Words to the Legislators of our State. Having assumed the direct Tax, laid by Congress, they have relieved us from one oppressive Consequence of the late War. Let those who have Leizure and Inclination examine this Measure in

Gouverneur Morris Papers, Rare Book and Manuscript Library, Columbia University, item 871. Sparks's note on the manuscript reads, "To the Legislators of New York printed"; however, a published version has not been located.

1. Acts of July 22 and August 2, 1813, 3 Stat. 22 and 3 Stat. 53; and Act of January 9, 1815, 3 Stat. 164. The *Statutes at Large* may be found online at http://memory.loc.gov/ammem/amlaw/lwsllink.html.

2. Act of January 18, 1815, 3 Stat. 186.

3. *Albany Argus*, April 4, 1815, p. 2.

it's Relation to Party Politics. I believe it, viewing the Circumstances in which many of our Fellow Citizens find themselves, to be humane and just: for the direct Tax is, to my Mind, unjust and cruel. Let me not be told that I should be silent, on that Subject, because Federalists set the Example. I am yet to learn that Wrong can, by the Countenance of a Party, become Right. I believe Black would still be black tho every Angel in Heaven should call it White. I do not believe the Ingenuity of Man can devise a just Land-Tax for America, or one that will not be, in many Instances, oppressive even tho it's Amount be small compared with our Means. This is not the Time, nor the Place, neither is it my Object to assign the Reasons of this opinion. The Tax having been imposed by proper Authority, acting within constitutional Limits, we were in Duty bound to pay it, if the Legislature had not taken the Load from our Shoulders. Permit me nevertheless, to say that Persons in the more cultivated Counties and more wealthy Classes of our State are not, generally, in Condition to judge how such Taxes operate along our Frontiers. To one who purchased a Farm on Credit, has to build some Shelter for his Wife and Children, clear and plant a Field to provide for their Sustenance, and is obliged, under these Exigencies, to run in Debt for Necessaries, every Dollar, nay every Cent, is precious. Strugling with Want and the Rigor of inclement Skies, he is unable to comply with the Conditions of Sale, and depends on the Mercy of the Person from whom he purchased. That this is the general State of Setlers, on wild Land, is notorious. It is notorious, too, that Landholders are in the Habit of indulging them with Time, and facilitating the Means of Payment by accepting, as Money, their Labor on Roads and other Objects mutually beneficial. I ask of those who feel the Touch of humane Sentiment whether it be not barbarous to tax these poor People who, unless they borrow, cannot pay. I entreat those also, who are gratified by the severe Taxation of great Landholders to consider the Consequence if they, pressed by fiscal Agents, are reduced to the Choice of seeing their Property sacrificed at Vendue, or pressing, in Self-Defence, on their poor Debtors. The Misery which must ensue need not be pourtrayed to Men of intelligent Minds or humane Hearts. But this is not my Object.

I wish some of those Gentlemen who, in their zeal to revive public Credit and support the War, laid heavy Impositions on their unoffending Brethren, would have the Goodness to say whether a Tax on Land, Houses, Furniture, Slaves, and Cattle, be or be not a direct Tax. There are so many novel notions floating along the Surface of this World's Judgement that I dare not pronounce, positively, on Propositions clear to my Intellect, lest the vigorous Arm of some choice Party Spirit should scourge my Presumption with the Lash of his Satire. Have Pity, I beseech you, Sir on "a poor infirm weak and despis'd old Man" who learnt his Mother Tongue before you was deposited in your Mother's Womb.[4] Attribute his Ignorance of English to the Misfortune of having spoken it while he was an English Subject. The Declaration of Independence has freed us, to judge from the Sayings Writings and Doings of him who penned it, not only from the Law and Equity but from the Grammar and Dictionary of England. In Consequence of the Privilege thus acquired, Words are applied in a Sense wholly different from that which prevailed when I was a Boy. Thus the Peace lately made is called glorious, which Idea would have been expressed, forty years ago by the Term ignominious.

I hope I shall be pardoned for declaring my Belief that a Tax on Houses Lands Slaves Cattle or Furniture is a direct Tax; and for inferring that it ought to be apportioned among the States in the Ratio pointed out by the national Compact.[5] I have paid Taxes, for many Years, on my House Land Furniture and Cattle; and such of my Neighbors as own Slaves paid a Tax on them also. It may be presumed, therefore, that when our State Legislature shall apportion the direct Tax, lately assumed, we shall have to pay, as usual, on real and personal Property. Our Household Furniture will, thus, be double taxed: with what Propriety let Common Sense decide. It will perhaps be a sufficient Justification to say it will fall principally on the Rich: a Sort of Creatures which are considered, by some, as lawful Game to be hunted like Deer or destroyed like Wolves. Be it so: but before a Price is put on their Heads let it be considered that Wealth is no Proof of Wisdom or Virtue and should not, therefore, be denounced as aristocratical, that if the Rich be driven away their Foes, having no longer a common Object of Enmity, may fall out among themselves; that Patriotism, the Trade of

---

4. The quotation is from Shakespeare's *King Lear*, act 3, scene 2.

5. Article I, section 3 of the Constitution provides that "Representatives and direct Taxes shall be apportioned among the several States . . . according to their respective Numbers," and includes the three-fifths clause for counting slaves. The Supreme Court had addressed this contention with respect to a tax on carriages in *Hylton* v. *United States*, 3 U.S. 171 (1796). Alexander Hamilton argued that the tax was an excise that need not be apportioned, and the Supreme Court agreed with his position. The meaning of "direct taxes" was never clarified at the Constitutional Convention; Madison recorded in his notes that on August 20, "Mr. King asked what was the precise meaning of *direct* taxation? No one answd." *Records of the Federal Convention of 1787*, ed. Max Farrand, rev. ed. (New Haven: Yale University Press, 1911–87), 2:350.

such as want to be rich and will not work, may perish; and finally that such a Measure may prove fatal to Democracy itself, seeing that, if Wealth be banished, no one, however generous, can distribute Gin. It may, moreover, be worthy of Consideration, in our Zeal to punish the Sin of Riches, that a Tax on Furniture, instead of doing the Work, will have an opposite Effect. A Tax more on Vanity than on Wealth, it will, as far as it goes, add to the Miser's Preference of well secured Bonds and well shaved Notes. He who happens to have nine thousand disposable Dollars and a Wife disposed to purchase splendid Furniture will, by indulging her Taste, enable a Number of industrious Workmen to supply their Families with Comforts which Habit has rendered necessary and, in so doing, to pay their full Share of Revenue derived from Duties and other Imposts on Consumption. But, as Matters now stand, he might, by yielding to her Wishes, subject himself to an annual Tribute of one hundred Dollars. If, instead of this Oblation to Taste, he sacrifice on the Altar of Plutus, one of his infernal Majesty's high Priests, known on Earth by the Name of Broker, would bring him Pieces of Paper denominated Six per Cent Stock, purporting to be worth fifteen thousand Dollars, and promising the annual Interest, payable half yearly, of nine hundred. He stands then between the Broker who offers nine hundred Income and the Wife who tempts to one hundred Tribute. Difference one thousand which is, I humbly conceive, giving too great odds to the God of Usury. There is another fearful odds to the Community. If, tempted by the Broker, he fall from the Faith in his Wife, those Tradesmen who would have been fed by her Expence must, instead of sharing the nine thousand Dollars, pay annually nine hundred for the Interest on his Stock. The Amount of their Tax will not, it is true, be encreased but, by his Preference of Stock to Furniture, their Means of paying must be diminished if not destroyed.

The Tax, however, is laid and we poor Sheep must part with our Fleeces "let Consequence be what it will" happy to save our Skins: for whether the People are ruined or how they are ruined is of little Moment provided they become gentle Hewers of Wood and submissive Drawers of Water to those who speculated on their Misery and the Folly of their Rulers.[6] Far be it from me to diminish the Enjoyment of free Citizens while performing such important public Duties. I only wish to suggest, before the Word Justice shall have been wholly revolutionized, that our State, in settling Accounts with Congress for the direct Tax, might insist that the Amount

6. The quotation may be from the ribald poem "A True Tale of a Country Squire" (1731).

of this Imposition on Furniture shall be apportioned according to the constitutional Rule, and that we the People shall have Credit for the amount overpaid. It can require no Argument to prove that those who dwell North of the Potowmack and East of the Alleghany must pay more, of this Tax, in Proportion to Numbers, than those on the South and West of that Limit. If a similar Tax had been laid on Slaves, our Southern Brethren would have thought themselves entitled to Credit for the Proceeds in Diminution of their Share of the direct Tax. If a Tax of four Dollars a Head had been laid on a Planter, owning twenty five prime Slaves, in Carolina worth, at three hundred and sixty Dollars each, nine thousand Dollars, it would have been a fair Set-off, to the Amount of one hundred Dollars, against the direct Tax on his real and personal Estate. Or if a Tax of one third of a Dollar a Head had been laid on a Village in Rockland County owning three hundred Cows worth, at thirty Dollars each, nine thousand Dollars, it would have been a fair Set-off, to the Amount of one hundred Dollars, against the direct Tax on their real and personal Estate. Cows yield, it is said, about thirty Dollars each, per annum, gross amount in Butter Calves and the Food of Pigs, from which twenty to twenty five must be deducted for Labor and Provender. Negroes yield, it is said, about one hundred and forty Dollars, gross amount, from which forty to sixty must be deducted for Cloaths Food Physic and overseeing. So that the net Profit of nine thousand Dollars worth of Carolina Negroes and Rockland Cows will be about the same; to wit, the horn-headed Cattle fifteen hundred to three thousand and the wool-headed Cattle two thousand to five and twenty hundred, being in each Case an average of about twenty two hundred and fifty Dollars. If, in both Cases, ten per Cent on the Capital be deducted for Interest and Risque there will remain thirteen hundred & fifty; being a Profit of fifteen per Cent. Note, here, that, if these Estimates are just, one prime Negro is worth a dozen prime Cows; wherefore a dozen prime Cows are worth one prime Negro; and therefore the Citizens of Rockland ought to have as much Representation in Congress for twelve hundred horn-headed Cattle as the Citizens of Rice-Land for one hundred wool-headed Cattle. With this Difference nevertheless, in Favor of Rockland, that an old Cow, fat, will sell for nearly as much as a young Cow, lean, whereas an old Negro, whether fat or lean, is good for nothing or worse; being, like Negro Children, a mere Expence. But, to return from this Digression, the Slave Holders of Rice-land and the Cow Holders of Rockland might justly represent that the proposed Duty is nearly eight per Cent on the net Income derived from their live Stock, and ought, therefore, to be considered in the other direct Tax on Property, including the same live Stock. How much more justly may the Citizen of Philadelphia claim Credit for a Tax on his Chairs Tables Plates and Dishes which yield no Revenue and are merely the Means used in consuming Revenue? This Reasoning may be incorrect in itself or improperly expressed, but it is fairly meant; and I put myself on the Charity of my Country for Pardon if I have misunderstood or misapplied the Words direct and indirect, just and unjust, glorious and ignominious.

I am Sir
your humble Servant

An American

Morris became the second president of the New-York Historical Society in 1816. In this inaugural discourse, he reflects on the lessons of history. This theme had been on his mind at least since the beginning of the French Revolution. In France, Morris had seen at first hand how the same political principles might take very different forms in the context of different national histories. He concludes, however, with a look ahead, and an optimistic preview of America's future.

⊹≻═──═≺⊹

GENTLEMEN,

The place your partial kindness has called me to occupy seems to require, and I hope, therefore, will excuse an attempt to point out some benefits which may be derived from this Institution. Something more to repay the munificence of our State Legislature than the grateful sentiment which it has inspired.

Let me, however, before I enter on the subject, express our thanks to the honourable Corporation of New-York for the convenience we derive from their goodness. The intelligent liberality which devoted a spacious building to Science and the Arts, not only reflects honour on them, but sheds lustre on this great commercial emporium of the United States. Let the sordid collect and the riotous squander hoards of useless or pernicious treasure; be it yours, municipal fathers, to expend the fruit of honest industry on objects which embellish your city, and spread the influence of learning, genius, and taste over the hearts and minds of its numerous inhabitants. Your conduct has proved your conviction, that, in order to promote virtue

An Inaugural Discourse, Delivered before the New-York Historical Society, by the Honourable Gouverneur Morris. (President,) 4th September, 1816. The 206th Anniversary of the Discovery of New-York, by Hudson (New-York: Printed and Published by T. & W. Mercein, 1816). American Antiquarian Society Early American Imprints, series II (Shaw-Shoemaker), no. 38292. Excerpts from this address were published in the *New-York Evening Post* and the *New-York Herald* on September 25, 1816.

and multiply the sources of social bliss, wise magistrates will direct the people to laudable pursuits, and impressing on them a just contempt for sensual gratification, raise and adorn the moral dignity of man.

We live in a period so enlightened, that to display the use of History would be superfluous labour. It would be the mere repetition of what has already been expressed, by eminent authors, on various occasions. They have told us that History is the science of human nature; philosophy teaching by example; the school of princes.

Dazzled by the splendour of such brilliant eulogy, the mind's eye is bereft of distinct vision. But reason, pausing and collecting her powers, raises a great preliminary question: What is History? Is it the eloquence of Livy, the shrewdness of Tacitus, or the profound sense of Polybius?

Not only those who have participated in the conduct of national affairs, but those also, whose attention has been engrossed by personal concerns, cannot have failed to observe, that facts, as well as motives, are frequently misrepresented. That events are attributed to causes which never existed, while the real causes remain concealed. Presumptuous writers affecting knowledge they do not possess, undertake to instruct mankind by specious stories founded on idle rumour and vague conjecture. Those who are well informed smile at the folly. Great minds disdain to tell their own good deeds: it seems, moreover, to those who have managed public business, almost impossible that the tittle tattle of ignorance should meet with belief. Nevertheless, such writings, though sheltered by contempt, from contemporaneous contradiction, are raked out, in a succeeding age, from the ashes of oblivion, and relied on as authority. History, compiled from such materials, can hardly teach us the science of human nature. It is, at best, an entertaining novel with the ornament of real names. Philosophy, indeed, at a later day, may bring her balance of probability, put the evidence of opposed facts in different scales, and deduce fair-seeming conclusions from an assumed principle that man is a rational creature. But is that assumption just? or, rather, does not History show, and experience prove, that he is swayed from the course which reason indicates, by passion, by indolence, and even by caprice? When the foundation is false, the superstructure must fall. Such writings, therefore, however illumined by the rays of genius, or adorned by the charms of style, instead of showing man a just image of what he is, will frequently exhibit the delusive semblance of what he is not.

When we consider History, in the second point of view, as teaching morality by example, it seems evident that examples, if not drawn from real life, instead of informing, may mislead the mind, and instead of purifying, corrupt the heart. Neither is it certain that wholesome nourishment will always be extracted even from truth. Like other food, it may be so mixed and manipulated as to nauseate, or so seasoned as to give false appetite, stimulate morbid sensibility, and excite spasmodic action. A facetious writer who, in a rapid view of centuries, ridicules the misery of injured virtue, displays the glory of successful vice, laughs at the restraint of moral principle, and chuckles at the commission of crimes, may (if he please) call his work philosophy teaching by example; but example so selected and genius so employed, are more likely to accomplish a scoundrel than to form an useful member of society.

Again, if History be taken as the school in which statesmen are to be taught, there can be little hope that politics — that sublime science to make a nation great and happy — will be acquired by reading the relation of mutilated events, attributed to false causes. Such compilations tend to inculcate erroneous notions; and these, where the fate of millions is concerned, can never be indifferent. If measures pregnant with misery are considered as sources of prosperity, the best intentions may produce the worst effects.

Mature reflection, therefore, will diminish our surprise that many, skilled in History, are ignorant of the world. Long is the list of learned men who know not how to manage the common concerns of life, and not a few are rendered, by the violence of untamed passion, incapable of controlling themselves, much less of governing their fellow-creatures. Perhaps it is not rash to suppose that more accurate, more extensive, more useful knowledge of our nature may be derived from the intuitive perception and personificating power of Shakespeare, than from the laborious research and acute discussion of Hume.

Many important events are on record, and however dark and doubtful the testimony of ancient chronicles, there exists a great number of authenticated facts. These, when collected, may be called the Skeleton of History. But how much must depend on judgment and skill in putting the scattered materials together: and, again, the solid bones duly placed and connected, those muscles must be added which give symmetry, strength, and grace. At last the goodly form, complete in all its fair proportion, when language spreads a finish over the promoethian frame, how must its appearance be affected by the colouring it receives? The same event, treated by different historians, comes white from one hand, tinged with a rosy blush from another, and from another black.

The reflection and experience of many years have led me to consider the holy writings, not only as most authentic and instructive in themselves, but as the clue to all other history. They tell us what man is, and they, alone, tell us why he is what he is: a contradictory creature that, seeing and approving what is good, pursues and performs what is evil. All of private and of public life is there displayed. Effects are traced, with unerring accuracy, each to the real cause. We see, in the beautiful story of Joseph, how envy, destroying the peace of families, leads to cruelty and to crime. How a dignified condition is degraded by lust. How the wrath of despised wantonness stimulates a woman to deadly revenge. How the heart-burnings in a shepherd's family drove a minister of state to the foot of Pharaoh's throne. And how, for purposes still more important, a shepherd-boy was enabled to govern a mighty kingdom.

From the same pure Fountain of Wisdom we learn that vice destroys freedom; that arbitrary power is founded on public immorality, and that misconduct in those who rule a republic, necessary consequence of general licentiousness, so disgusts and degrades the nation, that, dead to generous sentiment, they become willing slaves. We read that, in the latter days of Samuel, the judges *"turned aside after lucre, and took bribes, and perverted judgment."*[1] A more miserable state of society can hardly be conceived. Then laws to protect the weak against the strong, the innocent against the wicked, become instruments of oppression and torture. Then order is lost, confusion rules, and, to borrow expressions from the favourite bard of nature,

> Wrong becomes right, or rather, right and wrong,
> Between whose endless jar justice resides,
> Have lost their names; and so has justice too.[2]

Reduced to this forlorn condition, the more sedate and respectable members of the community, seeing no security for property or for life, seek shelter under the wings of absolute power. *"The elders said make us a king to judge us like all the nations."*[3] Samuel, his aged bosom still warm with patriotic sentiment, endeavoured to preserve the old form of equal right. To this

---

1. 1 Samuel 8:3.

2. Shakespeare, *Troilus and Cressida*, act 1, scene 3, lines 116–18. As usual, Morris is quoting from memory. The speaker is Ulysses:
> Force should be right, or rather right and wrong,
> Between whose endless jar justice resides,
> Should lose their names, and so should justice too.

3. 1 Samuel 8:19–20.

end, he assembled the people, and displayed a highly wrought, but faithful, picture of evils which would grow out of despotism. In vain. Men sore with present suffering have not temper to reflect on remote consequence. In the maddening moment, they are deaf even to the voice of a prophet. *"The people said, we will have a king over us, that we may be like all the nations, that he may judge us, and go out before us, and fight our battles."*[4] Here is a profound lesson of political wisdom, given long before Aristotle's Ethics, very long before Machiavel's Discourses on the first Decade of Livy, and still longer before Montesquieu's Spirit of Laws. When the last of these authors, in sprightly repetition of his predecessors, tells us that virtue is the principle of republics, he offers human testimony to confirm divine authority. That form of government which God himself had established, that code of laws which God himself had promulgated, those institutions which infinite wisdom had provided, in special relation to the climate, soil, and situation of the country, to the genius, temper, and character of the people, became intolerable from the prevalence of vice and impiety. It is a trite maxim, that man is governed by hope and fear. The desire of pleasure, wealth, and power, the apprehension of poverty, pain, and death, prompt generous reward, speedy severe punishment, are the human means to invigorate duty, stimulate zeal, correct perversity, and restrain guilt. But experience teaches that profligates may gain all the enticements of life, and criminals escape punishment, by the perpetration of new and more atrocious crimes. Something more, then, is required to encourage virtue, suppress vice, preserve public peace, and secure national independence. There must be something more to hope than pleasure, wealth, and power. Something more to fear than poverty and pain. Something after death more terrible than death. There must be religion. When that ligament is torn, society is disjointed, and its members perish. The nation is exposed to foreign violence and domestic convulsion. Vicious rulers, chosen by a vicious people, turn back the current of corruption to its source. Placed in a situation where they can exercise authority for their own emolument, they betray their trust. They take bribes. They sell statutes and decrees. They sell honour and office. They sell their conscience. They sell their country. By this vile traffic, they become odious and contemptible. The people, compelled to gulp down the poison they had mingled, feel their vitals twinge, and in anguish exclaim, *Away with these pretended patriots. Begone, hypocrites. Begone. Let a single man be invested with executive and judicial authority.* Master

4. Ibid.

and owner of the state, he will, for his own sake, protect it against foreign foes, and provide for an impartial administration of justice; that his subjects, secured and enriched, may multiply and thus increase his wealth and power. In the simple language of Holy Writ they say, *"He will judge us, and go out before us, and fight our battles."* Two centuries have not yet passed away since Europe saw a similar effect from a similar cause. The Danes, writhing under oppressions of their nobility, conferred absolute power on their king, by general suffrage.

We find in Sacred History another important political lesson: that the possession of sovereign power corrupts the best heart. The second Jewish king, a man peculiarly favoured by the King of kings, after leading an exemplary private life, no sooner ascends a throne, than, a prey to unbridled desire, he becomes first vicious, then criminal.[5] If, as the advocates of infidelity have gratuitously supposed, that book had been written by bigoted priests, they would have concealed the guilt of their pious protector. They would have held him out, an impeccant example, for admiration and imitation. They would have covered, with bright varnish, the hideous traits of adultery and assassination. But truth, telling what he was, gives a lesson awfully instructive. It teaches the frailty of our nature, and the danger of trusting too much power even to the purest hands.

Another sublime lesson follows, in the succeeding reign. The widest scope of genius, the completest acquirement of science, the maturest strength of intellect, are combined in one man; and that man wears a crown. By his wisdom he accumulates the world's wealth in one of its narrowest districts. He rears a stupendous monument of pious magnificence. It is consecrated to the living God. And, then, the royal architect commits follies that would almost disgrace an idiot. In the prostration of manly strength, he seeks pleasures that elude his grasp; leaving, in a bosom chilled by age, the dulness of satiety, and the loathings of disgust. Happy had the wise man's weakness been restrained, even in that excess. But, alas! his bright intellect is so obscured, by the apathy of exhausted desire, that he worships sticks and stones, in pitiful condescension to the consorts of his lust.[6] If this part of the story were tested, by fashionable rules of evidence, we should perhaps be told that, as superlative wisdom cannot be combined with excessive weakness, the tale of his debauchery must be an interpolation, by some foe

5. The story of King David is mainly told in 1 and 2 Samuel.
6. King Solomon's story is told in 1 Kings; the story of his foreign wives turning him to the worship of their gods is in 1 Kings 11.

to his fame, or the account of his talents, an invention to gratify national pride. Thus Solomon's character might come, from the philosophic crucible, all gold or all dross. But experience avouches the historic truth. We have known, in English annals, a man whose capacious mind embraced all science. With a rare power of intuition, he not only pointed out the means by which knowledge might be enlarged, but seems to have perceived the remote bound to which it could extend. And yet that wonderful man sullied his soul, by accepting a bribe. The character a great English poet gave to Chancellor Bacon, is not wholly inapplicable to the Jewish king: "The greatest, wisest, meanest of mankind."[7]

But the most important of all lessons is, the denunciation of ruin to every state that rejects the precepts of religion. Those nations are doomed to death who bury, in the corruption of criminal desire, the awful sense of an existing God, cast off the consoling hope of immortality, and seek refuge from despair in the dreariness of annihilation. Terrible, irrevocable doom! loudly pronounced, frequently repeated, strongly exemplified in the sacred writings, and fully confirmed by the long record of time. It is the clue which leads through the intricacies of universal history. It is the principle of all sound political science.

The lapse of ages, and the change of manners, of religion, of government, of customs, and of character, frequently render examples of one age and country inapplicable to the circumstances of other countries and of other times. The ferocity of barbarians, and the perfidy of courtiers, become, indeed, more striking by satiric contrast; but rude hospitality cannot be made a model for polite conviviality; neither can the charms of refined conversation correct, by example, the coarseness of rustic mirth. As little can the stern severity of Roman virtue, though it swell the youthful bosom with enthusiastic admiration, teach the conduct which befits a Christian people. Hearts chastened by the religion of love would recoil from the Brutus who beheads his son, and the Brutus who plants a dagger in the breast of his friend, but for the lavish encomium of orators, poets, and historians. Those celebrated names are embalmed by the incense of eighteen centuries, and our sight grows dizzy as we snuff the deleterious fragrance of flowers strewed on their tombs by lengthened generations. But when the gloomy Philip consigns Don Carlos to an early grave; when the amorous

---

7. Alexander Pope, *An Essay on Man*, epistle 4, line 282:
   If Parts allure thee, think how Bacon Shin'd
   The wisest, brightest, meanest of mankind.

Henry sends Biron to the scaffold, we cannot but pity such interesting victims, though their lives may have been justly forfeited to the law.[8] Whence this difference of sentiment? It may, perhaps, be found in that difference of manners which makes us view with horror the Roman practice of sending their superannuated slaves to perish on an island on the Tiber, and fills us with astonishment that the African Scipio should be celebrated for chastity, because he did not violate a distinguished female prisoner.[9] The laws and manners of every nation, taken in the mass, have, generally speaking, a due relation and proportion. They so influence and correct each other, that the business of life goes smoothly on. The social harmony is full. There is no jar. And, though some features may be too salient, there is no deformity. Yet particular institutions may be selected, which, submitted to foreign judgment, will be pronounced monstrous or ridiculous. Travellers, who view what they see through the medium of preconceived notions, measure what they meet with by the standard of early education, and weighing the conduct of others in the scale of their own opinion, find that, wherever they go, there is much to blame and much to reform. But when strangers, blinded by prejudice, are raised to power, they multiply proofs, already too numerous, that regulations uncongenial to national feeling are inconvenient, if not injurious, and that rash reformation leads to ruin. From the same cause it happens that institutions which have been fruitful of good, in one age or nation, may be as fruitful of evil in another nation, or another age.

Every man, therefore, will find the history of his own country the most interesting and the most instructive. Moreover, as the state of society is changed, by time and chance, the laws, too, must change. New disorders require new corrections, and when the reason of ancient ordinances no longer exists, they fall into oblivion. History and law, therefore, are sister sciences. They support and enlighten each other. But the history of one country can have little connection with the laws of another, and still less can the native code be modified by exotic manners.

Permit me then, gentlemen, to offer my cordial congratulations to you, and, through you, to our fellow-citizens, that this Institution is rapidly collecting and accumulating materials for a history of our own country.

---

8. The conflict between Don Carlos and his father, Philip II of Spain, later became the subject of Verdi's opera *Don Carlos;* Charles de Gontaut, duc de Biron, was executed for treason by Henri IV in 1602.

9. This story about Scipio the Elder is in Livy, *Ab Urbe Condita,* 26:49–50.

Materials which, establishing facts by indisputable authority, will enable the future historian accurately to deduce effects from the true cause, correctly to portray characters taken from real life, and justly assign to each his actual agency. Let us, humble as we are, and humble we ought to be comparing ourselves with the Eastern hemisphere, let us proudly aver, that if, in modern history, the period, when barbarous hordes broke the vast orb of Roman empire, be one great epoch, the discovery which immortalized Columbus, presents another not less worthy of attention. If that era, when Europe poured her crusading population on the southern shores of the Mediterranean Sea, mark the lowest depression of human character, its greatest elevation will be found in the present age. Our struggle, to defend and secure the rights of our fathers, tore away that veil which had long concealed the mysteries of government. Here, on this far western coast of the broad Atlantic Ocean; here, by the feeble hand of infant unconnected colonies, was raised a beacon to rouse and to alarm a slumbering world. It awoke, and was convulsed. What tremendous scenes it has exhibited! The history of our day is, indeed, a school for princes; and, therefore, the proper school for American citizens. Exercising, by their delegates, the sovereign power, it is meet they know how to assert and how to preserve their freedom. Let them learn the mischief that follows in the train of folly. Let them learn the misery that results from immorality. Let them learn the crush of impiety. Let them learn, also, for such we trust will be the final event, that when the altars of idolatrous lust had been overturned, and those of JEHO-VAH restored; when nations severely scourged had sincerely repented, they were favoured with as much civil liberty, and as much social enjoyment, as consist with their absolute and relative condition. Permit me, also, to cherish a belief that the partial distress and general inconvenience produced among us, by late events, will have a salutary influence on public manners. War, fruitful as it is of misery and wo, is nevertheless medicinal to a nation infected by the breath of foreign pollution, engrossed by the pursuit of illicit gain, immersed in the filth of immoral traffic, or unnerved by the excess of selfish enjoyment. It draws more close the bond of national sentiment, corrects degrading propensities, and invigorates the nobler feelings of our nature.

I add, gentlemen, with the pleasure and the pride which swell your bosoms, that America has shown examples of heroic ardour not excelled by Rome, in her brightest day of glory, and blended with milder virtue than Romans ever knew. These examples will be handed down, by your care, for the instruction and imitation of our children's children; make them acquainted with their fathers; and grant, Oh God! that a long and late posterity, enjoying freedom in the bosom of peace, may look, with grateful exultation, at the day-dawn of our empire.

—+>———<+—

GENTLEMEN,

By the occasion which called us together, we are reminded that Hudson discovered, in 1609, the river which bears his name. Imagine his amazement, had some prophetic spirit revealed that this island would, in two centuries from the first European settlement, embrace a population of twice fifty thousand souls.

Europe witnessed, in eight years, four events which had great influence on the condition of mankind. The race of English monarchs expired with Elizabeth in 1603. Henry the Fourth of France was assassinated in 1610. In the same year the Moors were expelled from Spain. And, in the next, Gustavus Adolphus became king of Sweden. These events excited, as they ought, much attention. But the discovery of Hudson's River, within the same period, was of such trivial estimation as to occupy no space in public annals.

Oh man! how short thy sight. To pierce the cloud which overhangs futurity, how feeble. But why be surprised that European statesmen, two centuries ago, were indifferent to what passed on the savage coast of America; when, at the same time, the existence of Russia was unnoticed and almost unknown.

Little more than a century has elapsed since the decisive victory of Pultowa introduced the empire of the Czars to the society of European nations; an empire which stretched out from Germany to Kamschatska, from the Black Sea to the Frozen Ocean, contains a greater extent than was ever traversed by the Roman eagle in his boldest flight.[10] That vast empire, so lately known, and so little understood, resisted, unshaken, the shock of embattled Europe, poured the rapid current of conquest back from the ruins of Moscow to the walls of Paris, and stands a proud arbiter of human destiny.

A mission of no common sort was lately about to proceed from the New World to the Old. From that which in 1600 was a dreary wilderness, to that

10. Peter the Great of Russia defeated Charles XII of Sweden at Poltava on June 27 (O.S.; July 8, N.S.), 1709, marking Russia's emergence as a major power.

which in 1700 was a cold morass. It was contemplated that a vessel of novel invention, leaving this harbour, should display American genius and hardihood in the port of St. Petersburgh. If this expedition be suspended or laid aside, it is not from any doubt as to its practicability.[11]

There are persons of some eminence, in Europe, who look contemptuously at our country, in the persuasion that all creatures, not excepting man, degenerate here. They triumphantly call on us to exhibit a list of our scholars, poets, heroes, and statesmen. Be this the care of posterity. But admitting we had no proud names to show, is it reasonable to make such heavy demand, on so recent a people. Could the culture of science be expected from those who, in cultivating the earth, were obliged, while they held a plough in one hand, to grasp a sword in the other? Let those who depreciate their brethren of the West, remember that our forests, though widely spread, gave no academic shade.

In the century succeeding Hudson's voyage, the great poets of England flourished, while we were compelled to earn our daily bread by our daily labour. The ground, therefore, was occupied before we had leisure to make our approach. The various chords of our mother tongue have, long since, been touched to all their tones by minstrels, beneath whose master-hand it has resounded every sound, from the roar of thunder, rolling along the Vault of Heaven, to the "lascivious pleasings of a lute."[12] British genius and taste have, already, given to all "the ideal forms that imagination can body forth," a "local habitation and a name."[13] Nothing then remains, for the present age, but to repeat their just thoughts in their pure style. Those who, on either side of the Atlantic, are too proud to perform this plagiary task, must convey false thoughts, in the old classic diction, or clothe in frippery phrase the correct conceptions of their predecessors. Poetry is the splendid effect of genius moulding into language a barbarous dialect. When the great bards have written, the language is formed; and by those who succeed

11. Robert Fulton planned for steam navigation across the Atlantic. Fulton's *Savannah* sailed to Europe and back three years later, in 1819.

12. Shakespeare, *Richard III*, act 1, scene 1, line 13.

13. Cf. Shakespeare, *A Midsummer Night's Dream*, act 5, scene 1, lines 12–17:

> The poet's eye, in a fine frenzy rolling,
> Doth glance from heaven to earth, from earth to heaven;
> And as imagination bodies forth
> The forms of things unknown, the poet's pen
> Turns them to shapes, and gives to airy nothing
> A local habitation and a name.

it is disfigured. The reason is evident. New authors would write something new, when there is nothing new. All which they can do, therefore, is to fill new moulds with old metal, and exhibit novelty of expressions, since they cannot produce novelty of thought. But these novel expressions must vary from that elegance and force in which the power and harmony of language have been already displayed.

Let us not, then, attempt to marshal, against each other, infernal and celestial spirits, to describe the various seasons, to condense divine and moral truth in mellifluent verse, or to imitate, in our native speech, the melody of ancient song. Other paths remain to be trodden, other fields to be cultivated, other regions to be explored. The fertile earth is not yet wholly peopled. The raging ocean is not yet quite subdued. If the learned leisure of European wealth can gain applause or emolument for meting out, by syllables reluctantly drawn together, unharmonious hexameters, far be it from us to rival the manufacture. Be it ours to boast that the first vessel successfully propelled by steam was launched on the bosom of Hudson's River. It was here that American genius seizing the arm of European science, bent to the purpose of our favourite parent art the wildest and most devouring element.

The patron—the inventor are no more. But the names of Livingston and of Fulton, dear to fame, shall be engraven on a monument sacred to the benefactors of mankind. There generations yet unborn shall read,

> Godfrey taught seamen to interrogate,
> With steady gaze, tho' tempest-tost, the sun,
> And from his beam true oracle obtain.
> Franklin, dread thunder-bolts, with daring hand,
> Seized, and averted their destructive stroke
> From the protected dwellings of mankind.
> Fulton by flame compell'd the angry sea,
> To vapour rarified, his bark to drive
> In triumph proud thro' the loud sounding surge,[14]

This invention is spreading fast in the civilized world; and though excluded as yet from Russia, will, ere long, be extended to that vast empire. A bird hatched on the Hudson will soon people the floods of the Wolga, and

---

14. Probably Morris's own composition. Thomas Godfrey (1704–49) was the inventor of the octant and a sometime companion of Benjamin Franklin, who discusses Godfrey in his *Autobiography*.

cygnets descended from an American swan glide along the surface of the Caspian Sea. Then the hoary genius of Asia, high throned on the peaks of Caucasus, his moist eye glistening while it glances over the ruins of Babylon, Persepolis, Jerusalem, and Palmyra, shall bow with grateful reverence to the inventive spirit of this western world.

Hail Columbia! child of science, parent of useful arts; dear country, hail! Be thine to meliorate the condition of man. Too many thrones have been reared by arms, cemented by blood, and reduced again to dust by the sanguinary conflict of arms. Let mankind enjoy at last the consolatory spectacle of thy throne, built by industry on the basis of peace and sheltered under the wings of justice. May it be secured by a pious obedience to that divine will, which prescribes the moral orbit of empire with the same precision that his wisdom and power have displayed, in whirling millions of planets round millions of suns through the vastness of infinite space.

FINIS.

The War of 1812 brought back to the fore an issue that Morris had first treated almost a half century earlier, that of paper money. In 1769 he had argued against an issue of bills of credit by the then New York colony. In this letter, he urges the banks of New York to reconsider a reported plan to start reducing the amount of circulating paper. He urges them to think about the probable effects of the new National Bank (chartered in 1816 and due to begin operations early the next year), as well as those of the outbreak of peace in Europe, on the future of American finance.

GENTLEMEN,

It is said that men of influence among you, deriving benefit from the distress of the times, urge you to call for payments, which cannot be effected without great sacrifice of property. If I believed these aspersions, I would not trouble you with this address. But in the persuasion that you would rather promote the interest of institutions over which you preside, than subserve usurious projects, I take the liberty of suggesting some hints to your consideration.

The subject of Paper Money is too copious for the narrow compass of this paper. But the substance of a long treatise may be comprised in a few words. When paper and specie are nearly on a level, it can do no good to diminish the circulating medium. I say *nearly* on a level, because as you well know, circumstances distinct from depreciation affect the price of bullion. There can be no doubt that when paper depreciates, a resulting want of confidence will accelerate depreciation, and that the same want will

---

New-York Courier, October 15, 1816. The letter was also published, with some corrections, in the *New-York Columbian* on October 17. The manuscript is in the Gouverneur Morris Papers, Rare Book and Manuscript Library, Columbia University, item 872. The manuscript has a note in Morris's handwriting, "published 15 Octr 1816," and below it Sparks has written "Bank."

lessen the effect of efforts to raise its value. But when such efforts shall have brought it nearly to par, a slight circumstance may restore the equilibrium.

Permit me to place this matter in a simple point of view. Not knowing facts, I merely suppose the condition of your several institutions to be a little variant; so that, without questioning solidity, some may be more at ease than others. I have, indeed, heard that, by agreement among you, an interest of 7 per cent is charged on the paper which each holds of others, and that the resulting balances have created a designation of debtor and creditor Banks. Now let it be supposed that one or two of the best conditioned, or creditor Banks, should enable Brokers to pay up at par, with specie, the paper of that Bank which is the greatest debtor. No one I believe, will doubt that such paper would, immediately be considered as of equal value with the precious metals. And it is moreover evident that the purchasers, receiving 7 per cent on the notes bought, would gain more than by discounting at 6 per cent. This however, is merely for elucidation.

It is, I understand, a fact, that Bank Notes and Specie are nearly on a level in this city. If so, it is evident that commerce is not burthened with an excess of paper. It seems therefore, Gentlemen, worthy of your consideration, that a large sum of specie is locked up, partly in the chest of the new National Bank, partly in other chests, awaiting the time when future instalments are payable to that institution. This circumstance must have injured your notes, because it lessened the amount of coin which they represent. Hence it follows that the efforts which restored them to their specified value must have exceeded what would have been needful, had the mass of American specie been subject to your operations. Is it not then possible that, when the chest of the new Bank shall be opened and hoarded bullion thrown into circulation, you may discover that you have gone a little too far? Your Notes will doubtless be at par; but will you find safe and profitable employment for your funds?

Let this matter be examined. Considering the pressure for payment that has been so long continued, your present debtors must, generally speaking, be unable to discharge their engagements, without great loss. Many may be ruined. This may be deemed of trivial importance by master spirits who, taking things upon the great scale, tell us that, A gaining what B loses, the mass of the national wealth continues the same. But it is far from being a matter of indifference to you, whatever it may be to the nation at large. If those measures which throw such men as B out of the commercial circle, make men like A very rich, they will divide among them the little trade which is left to our country; and they will not need your assistance. They will find it more convenient to deposit their cash in the Mammoth Bank from which, by reason of their capital and credit, they can get Mammoth discounts to make Mammoth speculations. It will, I believe, soon appear that the money capital of our country is more than her commerce requires. If so, many of your substantial customers who may, by making sacrifices, have discharged their engagements, will no longer want your assistance. A burnt child dreads the fire; and prudent men will be afraid of insuring obligations which, by a sudden change of circumstances, may become burthensome or ruinous.

There is a consideration connected with this subject which may not have struck every mind with equal force. The penury of European governments, consequent on their late convulsive efforts, must shortly be relieved. A diminution of expense and the increase of revenue, naturally arising from peace and plenty, will bring their affairs into order. This will, as by magic, increase the money of the world to an amount not readily conjectured. It may be worth while therefore, to show the course and consequence of such events. The British debt is between seven and eight hundred million sterling. Take the aggregate debt of France, Holland, Russia, Prussia, Austria, &c. to be five or six hundred million and you have a mass of not less than six thousand million of dollars.[1] Let us suppose this debt to be now in the stock market, at two thirds of its nominal amount, or four thousand million. It follows that there must exist, in Europe, individuals whose funded property amounts to that enormous sum, and that when, from any cause or combination of causes, this debt shall rise to par, there will be individuals of the same description who possess two thousand million more than the present amount. Let us suppose the rise to be gradual, and not to hazard unreasonable conjecture, that it may be completed in ten years, by a regular progress. If so, Europe, taken in mass,[2] will have an average annual increase of pecuniary wealth equal to two hundred million dollars. In the beginning this sum will find domestic employment. Those who continue to hold their share of stock, will possess an increased capital without an increase of revenue; and those who sell will be replaced by those who buy. The rise therefore being slow, would not produce a great or sudden change if the indebted nations made no effort to redeem their stock, and if each stockholder spent his whole income. But neither of these postulates is cor-

1. The phrase "and you have a mass of not less than six thousand million" is in the manuscript and in the *Columbian* but is omitted from the *Courier.*

2. In the *Columbian* and manuscript, "in mass"; in the *Courier,* "en masse."

rect. Many stockholders spend but a small portion of what they receive and employ the rest in new loans. Now if we calculate the low interest of three per cent on six thousand million, it amounts to one hundred and eighty million per annum, or fifteen million dollars monthly. Let two thirds be taken off, for the stockholders expense, there will remain five million per month to be disposed of in loans or otherwise. This, when the channels of commerce are full, is no trifle. But this is not all. Leaving on one side the measures of other nations to redeem their debt, the sinking fund of Great-Britain exceeds the annual sum of twelve million sterling. That is to say, the commissioners of the sinking fund apply five million dollars every month in buying up the national debt. If then five be added to the other five, we have no less than ten million dollars monthly in addition to the disposable money of Europe. We must not forget that this great engine has already been in operation for more than a year. We, indeed, have not yet felt its influence. Neither could it be expected; for the back water, if I may be allowed the expression, must run off before a machine can go with full power. But it begins to touch our funds which, under circumstances of discredit at home, have risen, nominally, in the British market; and even if they had not risen, *nominally*, the rise in value of British Bank Notes makes an *actual* advance of ten per cent. Now, let it be considered, that when their three per cents are at seventy-five per cent, stockholders get but four per cent on their capital. If then, American six per cents be well secured, by effective revenue, the British stockholder who sells his three per cent at seventy-five, and purchases our six per cent at par, will add one half to his income.

To return from a digression which may appear tedious, you will be pleased to consider, Gentlemen, whether it is not for the interest of your institutions, putting aside every consideration of private convenience and public advantage, rather to increase than diminish your discounts. Suppose the creditor Banks should so far extend their aid as that debtors to the debtor Banks might pay them enough to bring you all on a level, and then, each drawing in a little where there is reason to apprehend, letting out a little where credit is unquestionable, and leaving private capital to relieve those to whom you cannot, at present, extend your aid, all quietly wait that moment when the national reservoir shall be opened. Would not this promote your permanent advantage? On the whole, Gentlemen, may not it be well to ask yourselves this simple question; which is most wise, to secure for ourselves the good customers we now have, or drive them to deal with the National Bank; leaving us to pick up the crumbs which fall from that table?

The Directors of the National Bank cannot make dividends unless they lend their cash, and they cannot lend unless they can find borrowers. But, although the necessities of those who borrowed increase, their number diminishes. Some pay; others become bankrupts. Moreover, it is but too evident that much of our little commerce will be carried on by foreigners and, therefore, by foreign capital. It is, therefore, beyond all question that the demand for money next spring must be less than it is now. Can then the capital of the National Bank, in addition to that of the pre-existing Banks find employment? Should no new war arise to shake again the moral foundations of the world, there can be little doubt but that, in two years, the rate of interest must fall. In that period there will be added to the mass of pecuniary capital two hundred and fifty million dollars over and above four hundred million for the increased value of stocks and the general accumulation of wealth from agriculture, commerce and manufactures throughout the civilized world. Moreover, as capital increases in our country, money will be lent, to men of estate, on bond and mortgage. When this happens, much of the business you have done, on what are called accommodation notes, will cease; a business which though it does not consist with European ideas of banking, is the most secure of any; when the Drawers and Endorsers possess competent real property.

But it will perhaps be said, the pressure has not produced its full effect. Let it be continued till our notes are at par. But, Gentlemen, have the goodness to ask yourselves two questions. First how much more paper must be brought in. To make the answer do not, as the saying is, starve the business. Set down one, two, or if you please, three million dollars. Then ask the second question, how much capital of the National Bank will seek employment in this city. To make this answer, reverse the last course and limit the sum within the narrowest bounds. You can hardly bring it below five millions.[3] But reduce it, if you please, to three. From these two answers you cannot fail to conclude that, if your pressure be suspended, till the great Bank goes to work, your customers can easily get the goods you want from that manufacture. You cannot fail, also, to draw this further conclusion, that you can then proportion your call to the precise sum needful. Moreover, the knowledge you possess will enable you to make your call in such manner as to keep your safest and best customers. And now gentlemen, pardon me for asking whether, all circumstances duly considered, you think it wise to lose the interest of one, two or three million of dollars, the

3. This sentence is omitted in the *Courier.*

sum above supposed, without any correspondent benefit; and not only with a probability approaching almost to certainty, that you will do yourselves harm, but with the absolute certainty that you will distress and may ruin some worthy citizens. With sincere regard I am

Gentlemen, your obedient servant,

AN AMERICAN.

This was evidently a draft for an address, but the audience and the occasion are not recorded. The classical references suggest that it was to be given to an educated audience, and the absence of topical commentary implies a nonpolitical occasion. Morris had become thoroughly discouraged in his later years about the direction of American politics. He was convinced that the Democratic-Republican party, and especially the Southern slave-holding faction that dominated it, would ruin the country if not checked. He was also convinced that they would begin by ruining the Northern commercial states. Even so, Morris's "temperament admitted of no alliance with despondency," and he was convinced that even with all of its problems America had the makings of a great nation.[1]

⁘

Had it been permitted to consult my Wishes on this Day I should have selected a Theme more suited to my Talents or rather have shrouded their Weakness in the Veil of Silence. For I feel but too well that in venturing to discuss the Subject of national Greatness I must fall short of the Ideas in your Minds and disappoint your Expectations. Instead of irradiating with the Light of Genius I must take the more humble Course of Investigation and begin by Enquiring what is national Greatness. Does it consist in numbers wealth or Extent of Territory? Certainly not. Swoln with the Pride inspired by such Circumstances the Persians Addressed their Master as the Great King but Darius felt in repeated Discomfiture the Superiority of a great Nation led by Alexander. We see in our Day a Prince who may

Gouverneur Morris Papers, Rare Book and Manuscript Library, Columbia University, item 873. On the manuscript Sparks has a note, "An address. date and occasion?" This document, edited by Willi Paul Adams, was also previously published in *Amerikastudien* 21 (1976): 332–34.

1. Morgan Lewis, letter to Hermanus Bleeker, May 26, 1828. The letter is included in the appendix to David Hosack, *Memoir of DeWitt Clinton* (New York: J. Seymour, 1829), 250.

boast that the Sun never sets on his Domaine yet his Authority superseded in his Ports and insulted in his Capital. It would seem as if his Territory were extended around the Globe only to Display before all the World his ignominious Condition. Such is the State of that proud Monarchy which once menaced the Liberties of Europe. But who trembles now at the name of Spain? There is none so abject. Nay should there exist a Government in which Fear is the incurable Disease no Paroxism would be excited by the Menace of Spain. To the Wise a Word is sufficient and therefore it will be needless before this Audience to prove that a Nation small like Greece may rise to the Heighths of national Greatness while Littleness shall mark every public Act of a numerous People. And equally needless must it be to express what you cannot but feel that in Proportion to the high Esteem Respect & Admiration with which we view the Splendor of Greece in the Day of her Glory is our profound Contempt for those who presiding over a powerful People shall tamely submit to the multiplied Repetition of Indignities. These are Feelings so natural that to disguise them would be vain to suppress them impossible. I could indeed were I to indulge a licentious Imagination suppose a number of Men who without national Spirit or Sentiment shall presume to call themselves a Nation. I can suppose a Herd of piddling huckstering Individuals base and insensible except to Blows who in the Stroke of a Cudgel estimate only the Smart and comparing it with the Labor and expence of Resistance submit Resentment to the Rules of Calculation. I can suppose such Wretches stretched over a wide Surface which they call their Country but which they hold as Tenants at Will to the first Invader. Nay I can suppose them to be governed by Wretches still more vile who derive their Power from the meanest Propensities who sacrificing on the Altar of Avarice to get the means of indulging their Malice and render a beggarly Account of the Saving of Doits while national Honor national Dignity and national Glory are wholly forgotten. All this I say may be figured by a Fancy which disdains the Confine of Reason and Truth. But from such a Picture the ingenuous mind must turn loathing away with Contempt and Detestation. We feel that if the Disgusting Image could be realized a Horde so selfish would soon be swept away or reduced to their proper Condition of Slaves. We are consoled therefore by the Reflection that whenever Providence may permit the Existence of such a political Monster it will be only that its speedy and compleat Ruin may deter other nations from a Conduct so mean so base so vile.

Let us pause. Perhaps there never was a Society of Men so compleatly void of virtue. But between them and the brave Band at Thermopylae the

Gradations are infinite. Perhaps it may be asked if Genius & Excellence in the Arts constitute national Greatness. To this Question the Answer must be given with Caution and not without some Modification. The Ages of Pericles of Augustus & of Louis the fourteenth were indeed ages of Splendor. They were unquestionably the Evidence but I must venture to believe they were the Result not the Cause of national Greatness. A Nation truly great cannot but excel in Arts as well as in Arms. And as a Great Mind stamps with its own Impression the most common Arts so national Greatness will shew itself alike in the Councils of Policy in the Works of Genius in Monuments of Magnificence and the Deeds of Glory all these are the Fruits but they are not the Tree. Here I anticipate the general and the Generous Question. Does it not consist in Liberty? That Liberty is a kind and fostering Nurse of Greatness will be chearfully and cordially admitted but as we have seen national Greatness where there was no Freedom so we have seen free Nations where Baseness rather than Greatness constituted the national Character. The Intrepidity of the Swiss Troops is generally known and acknowledged. In a Contest for Freedom with the Duke of Burgundy the Nation was great and covered itself with Glory but alas how chang'd how fallen when distributing stipendiary aid thro hostile Hosts their Valor was arrayed against itself. Brothers fell by the Swords of Brothers they became at length the proverbial Examples of a mercenary Disposition. And then neither Liberty nor Discipline nor Courage could rescue helvetian Fame from the Charge of Baseness.

Thus then We have seen that a People may be numerous powerful Wealthy free brave & inured to War without being Great. And by reflecting on the Reason why a Combination of those Qualities and Circumstances will not alone suffice we are led to the true Source and Principle of national Greatness. It is in the national Spirit. It is in that high haughty generous and noble Spirit which prizes Glory more than Wealth and holds Honor dearer than Life. It is that Spirit the inspiring Soul of Heroes which raises Men above the Level of Humanity. It is present with us when we read the Story of antient Rome. It wells over Bosoms at the View of her gigantic Deeds and makes us feel that it must ever be irresistible while human Nature shall remain unchanged. I have called it a high haughty generous and noble Spirit. It is high—Elevated above all low and vulgar Considerations. It is haughty—Despising whatever is little and mean whether in Character Council or Conduct. It is generous—granting freely to the weak and to the Indigent Protection and Support. It is noble—Dreading Shame and Dishonor as the greatest Evil esteeming Fame and Glory beyond all

Things human. When this Spirit prevails the Government, whatever its Form, will be wise and energetic because such Government alone will be borne by such Men. And such a Government seeking the true Interest of those over whom they preside will find it in the Establishment of a national Character becoming the Spirit by which the nation is inspired. Foreign Powers will then know that to withhold a due Respect and Deference is dangerous. That Wrongs may be forgiven but that Insults will be avenged. As a necessary Result every Member of the Society bears with him every where full Protection & when he appears his firm and manly Port mark him of a superior Order in the Race of Man. The Dignity of Sentiment which he has inhaled with his native Air gives to his manner an Ease superior to the Politeness of Courts and a Grace unrivalled by the Majesty of Kings. These are Blessings which march in the Train of national Greatness and Come on the Pinions of Youthful Hope. I anticipate the Day when to command Respect in the remotest Regions it will be sufficient to say I am an American. Our Flag shall then wave in Glory over the Ocean and our Commerce feel no Restraint but what our own Government may impose. Happy thrice happy Day. To reach this envied State we need only to Will. Yes my Countrymen our Destiny depends on our Will. But if we would stand high on the Record of Time that will must be inflexible.

Index

Janson is the name given to an old-style serif typeface named for Dutch punch-cutter and printer Anton Janson. Research in the 1970s and early 1980s concluded that the typeface was the work of a Hungarian punch-cutter named Miklos (Nicholas) Kis. In 1685, while apprenticing in Amsterdam under Dirk Voskens, Kis cut several typefaces, including a roman text face upon which present-day Janson is based. Kis also cut Greek and Hebrew typefaces for use in printing polyglot bibles. Janson shows a strong influence of the Dutch Baroque typefaces. A revival of the face was designed in 1937 by Chauncey H. Griffith of the Linotype foundry.

Janson Text replaced Caslon as the face of choice for fine bookmaking. Its strong design and clear stroke contrast combine to create text that is both elegant and easy to read. In this font version, Tseng Information Systems has lengthened descenders and modified stroke weights to render the type more like its earlier appearance when printed letterpress.

This book is printed on paper that is acid-free and meets the requirements of the American National Standard for Permanence of Paper for Printed Library Materials, z39.48-1992. ⊚

Book design by Barbara E. Williams
BW&A Books, Inc., Durham, North Carolina

Typography by Tseng Information Systems, Inc.
Durham, North Carolina

Printed and bound by Victor Graphics, Baltimore, Maryland